TEST YOUR KNOWLEDGE OF METAPHORS

1. WHO WAS THE ORIGINAL "REAL McCOY"?

An American boxer who became world welterweight champion in 1890.

■

2. WHAT IS THE DIFFERENCE BETWEEN "A DARK HORSE" AND "A TROJAN HORSE"?

A dark horse is a person with unsuspected talents; a Trojan horse is a trick (it refers to the large gift horse full of soldiers used to bring about the fall of Troy).

■

3. WHY IS "A WHITE ELEPHANT" SOMETHING TO AVOID?

These gifts of sacred pachyderms from the King of Siam often ruined their recipients with the expense of their upkeep.

■

4. WHAT DOES IT MEAN "TO PLAY DUCKS AND DRAKES"?

To not take a matter seriously.

■

5. WHERE WAS "THE CAT LET OUT OF THE BAG"?

At public fairs, where cats wrapped in sacks were passed off as piglets.

■

6. WHAT IS "A MILCH COW"? (HINT: THIS BOOK IS ONE!)

An easy and plentiful source of some desired benefit.

AND EXPAND YOUR COMMAND AND UNDERSTANDING OF ENGLISH WITH...

METAPHORICALLY SPEAKING

The book that "leaves no stone unturned"!

METAPHORICALLY SPEAKING

A DICTIONARY OF 3,800 PICTURESQUE IDIOMATIC EXPRESSIONS

N. E. RENTON

A Time Warner Company

This book was first published in Australia by Schwartz and Wilkinson, Melbourne.

Warner Books Edition

Warner Books, Inc., 1271 Avenue of the Americas, New York, NY 10020
A Time Warner Company

Printed in the United States of America
First Warner Books Printing: August 1992
10 9 8 7 6 5 4 3 2 1

Library of Congress Cataloging in Publication Data
Renton, N. E.
Metaphorically speaking : a dictionary of 3,800 picturesque idiomatic expressions / N.E. Renton.
p. cm.
"First published in Australia by Schwartz and Wilkinson, Melbourne"—T.p. verso.
Includes bibliographical references.
ISBN 0-446-39353-3
1. English language—Idioms—Dictionaries. 2. English language—Terms and phrases. 3. Figures of speech—Dictionaries. 4. Picturesque, The—Dictionaries. 5. Metaphor—Dictionaries.
I. Title.
PE1689.R46 1992
423'.1—dc20 92-363
CIP

Book design by Giorgetta Bell McRee
Cover illustration by Peter de Sève
Cover design by Don Puckey

To all the people who think that they never use any metaphors

Foreword

In a time when the visual image is such a powerful influence on our attitude and thoughts, it is well to be reminded of the miracle of language. How and when was it invented? How do we explain its richness and variety? By what extraordinary transformation did words which have quite literal and specific meanings take on metaphysical significance? Which expression conveys the most vivid meaning, ''the top dog,'' or its definition, ''the person in the most powerful position?''

The metaphor wins every time.

For metaphor is the spice of language. It also activates the reader's or listener's inner eye to produce images which are just as vivid as visual ones. Without its color, wit and concreteness would disappear.

Here is a dictionary and thesaurus of metaphors which is both a practical guide to meaning and a stimulus to enquiry. Only a person in love with words could have compiled it; and there are surprises in it for even the most knowledgeable student of language. Mr. Renton achieves the aim that Sir Philip Sidney saw as the central principle of poetry—to teach by delighting.

Leonie Kramer

Every Man And His Dog Use Metaphors

Metaphors which have the community's seal of approval roll off the tongue so readily that by any yardstick they are invariably thick on the ground. A person in the pink who plays his cards right and who takes up the cudgels for the cause will without going overboard or changing tack find an avalanche of metaphors under his very nose. Unless he puts a foot wrong or goes off half-cocked he will regard them all as useful tools and as grist to his mill. He will already be in the picture and will not need to engage in a witch-hunt or rely on the grapevine in order to put his finger on them.

Without matters getting out of hand or losing any momentum it stands out a mile that metaphors are in the blood of every Tom, Dick and Harry worth his salt and willing to show the flag. Many expressions have been gathering dust for donkey's years and are so much a hallmark of our society that their down to earth use at the drop of a hat does not ring a bell or cause any eyebrows to be raised.

Contents

PART I *1*

1: INTRODUCTION

Background *3*
Objectives *4*
Coverage *5*
Arrangement *6*
Borderline Cases *8*
Common Keywords *8*

2: SOURCES OF METAPHORS

Metaphors from Literature *10*
Metaphors from Politics *11*
Metaphors from Religious Sources *12*
Metaphors from Heraldry *13*
The Role of Foreign Languages *14*

3: THE METAPHOR IN DAILY USE

The Prevalence of Metaphors *15*
The Graphic Nature of Longer Metaphors *15*
Mixed Metaphors *16*
Metaphors in Transition *17*

4: METAPHORS IN VARIOUS CATEGORIES

The Thematic Section *20*
Sport *20*
The Human Body *21*
Animals *21*
The World of Sail *21*
Music *22*
Commerce *22*

Amusements Generally 23
Statistics of Usage 23

5: METAPHORS EXPRESSING IDEAS IN CERTAIN SUBJECT AREAS

The Thesaurus 24
"Difficulty" as a Concept 25
Money Matters 26
Metaphors Used Euphemistically 27

6: SELECTED CASE STUDIES

The Living English Language 29
Duplications 30
Plays on Words 30
Emphasis 31
The Need for Precision 31
Overlap 32
Negative Expressions 33
Nonsense Expressions 34
Colloquialisms 34
Sexist Language 35
Double Metaphors 35
Popular Misconceptions 35
Words are Fun! 37

7: SOME GRAMMATICAL ASPECTS

Grammatical Form of the Metaphor 38
Principles Used in the Listings 39
Metaphors Involving a Change to the Part of Speech 39
Verbs Requiring Special Subjects 40
The Use of Quotation Marks 40
Idioms 41
Synecdoche 41
Personification 41
Hyperbole 41
Irony 42

PART II: 43

8: DICTIONARY
Metaphors Arranged Alphabetically by Keyword 45

9: THEMATIC SECTION

Metaphors in Various Categories
Animals ... *292*
Art ... *305*
Aviation ... *306*
Buildings ... *306*
Cards ... *312*
Chess ... *313*
Circuses ... *313*
Clothes ... *314*
Colors ... *318*
Commerce ... *321*
Crime ... *323*
Death ... *324*
Education ... *325*
Farming ... *326*
Food and Drink ... *327*
Furniture ... *333*
Gambling ... *335*
Geography ... *336*
Government ... *341*
Heraldry ... *342*
History ... *342*
Human Body ... *344*
Law ... *375*
Manufacture ... *376*
Meteorology ... *378*
Mining and Oil ... *381*
Music ... *382*
Mythology ... *384*
Nautical ... *386*
Plants ... *389*
Religion and Biblical ... *393*
Science and Medicine ... *396*
Sex ... *399*
Sport ... *400*
Theater ... *405*
Transport ... *407*
War and Military ... *410*

10: THESAURUS

Metaphors Expressing Ideas in Certain Subject Areas
Abuse ... *416*
Achievement ... *416*

Activity *418*
Advantage *421*
Agreement *423*
Aim *423*
Alternative *424*
Anger *425*
Annoyance *425*
Approval *426*
Argument *426*
Behavior *428*
Belief *429*
Benefit *429*
Bigness *431*
Care *432*
Chance *432*
Change *433*
Confusion *434*
Correctness *435*
Courage *435*
Criticism *436*
Danger *437*
Decision *437*
Development *438*
Difficulty *439*
Disappointment *442*
Displeasure *442*
Ease *443*
Employment *444*
End *445*
Enthusiasm *448*
Equality *450*
Excess *450*
Expectation *451*
Expense *452*
Experience *453*
Expertise *454*
Fact *454*
Factor *455*
Failure *456*
Falsity *458*
Frankness *458*
Fright *459*
Future *459*
Happiness and Enjoyment *460*
Harm *460*

Hope *461*
Idea *461*
Inference *463*
Interest *463*
Interference *464*
Involvement *465*
Judgment *466*
Knowledge *466*
Leadership *468*
Likelihood *468*
Membership *469*
Misleading *470*
Mistake *470*
Money *471*
Monitoring *472*
Naivete *473*
Nonsense *473*
Opinion *473*
Opportunity *474*
Past *476*
Pleasure *476*
Possibility *477*
Power *478*
Practicability *479*
Praise *479*
Pretense *479*
Prevention *480*
Price and Value *480*
Pride and Humility *481*
Problem *482*
Punishment *483*
Readiness *483*
Refusal and Rejection *484*
Reputation *485*
Responsibility *485*
Result *487*
Retirement *489*
Revenge *489*
Reversal *489*
Risk *490*
Sadness *491*
Sameness *491*
Satisfaction *492*
Secrecy *492*
Situation *493*

Skill *495*
Slowness *496*
Smallness *496*
Speech *498*
Speed *500*
Standard *500*
Start *501*
Strategy *502*
Stupidity *502*
Success *503*
Surprise *506*
Truth *506*
Unexpected Happenings *507*
Unrealistic Ideas *508*
Unwelcome *508*
Waiting *509*
Wealth *509*
Welcome *510*
Work and Effort *510*
Worry *512*

Appendix 1: Keywords Occurring Most Frequently *513*
Appendix 2: Statistical Summary of the Categories *515*
Appendix 3: Material for Party Games *519*
Appendix 4: Metaphors Derived From the Bible *521*
Appendix 5: "Yes, Prime Minister" *528*

PART I

1

INTRODUCTION

It is one of the maxims of the civil law that definitions are hazardous
Samuel Johnson *(The Rambler)*

I am a Bear of Very Little Brain and long words bother me
A.A. Milne *(Winnie-the-Pooh)*

BACKGROUND

A cynic once defined a metaphor as "a simile with the words of comparison left out." Less frivolously, the *Concise Oxford Dictionary* puts it as the "application of name or descriptive term to an object to which it is not literally applicable." The word is derived from two Greek roots—*meta* with and *phero* bear—which in combination denote "transfer" (of meaning).

The modern English language—as employed in ordinary conversation, as used on radio and television, as seen in newspaper and magazine articles and headlines, and as found in more serious literature—is remarkably full of metaphors. Some of these have been in currency for a hundred years or more, giving rise to the description "fossil poetry."

Many metaphors involve colorful analogies. Every day one talks of "missing the bus," of "being in the same boat" as someone else, of "getting down to brass tacks" or of "not having a crystal ball." People are always "getting a feather in their cap," "earning brownie points," "building bridges," "grasping at straws," "muddying the waters," "cutting the Gordian Knot" and "missing something by a whisker."

For the most part such *figures of speech* involve combinations of words sounding very familiar to their audience and their use is quite subconscious. In practice very few metaphors are written inside quotation marks. Such a tell-tale sign is generally absent, thus clearly indicating that the writers were not focusing on the aspect that their words did not represent the literal truth. Fowler in *Modern English Usage* characterizes such phrases as "dead metaphors."

A metaphor is often used because it can convey a particular shade of meaning much more succinctly than other words. This work demonstrates that metaphors serve to enrich both speech and writing, although at the price of making communication in English much more difficult both for foreigners and for computers used on translation tasks.

OBJECTIVES

This book includes, as self-contained listings, a dictionary, a thematic section and a thesaurus. It is intended as a handy reference tool for both general readers and educational institutions in all English-speaking countries.

The book is designed to serve a number of assorted purposes, including the following:

1. To set out in an easily-read and popular style the meanings of the various metaphors
2. To help persons for whom English is a second language
3. To assist writers and public speakers to become more articulate
4. To provide resource material for teachers of English wishing to design imaginative courses
5. To give an overall perspective of the subject
6. To show students and lovers of words the richness and diversity of the living English language
7. To refresh memories of half-remembered phrases
8. To provide some amusement from the patterns presented by the different categorizations
9. To illustrate that some particular words and concepts are especially prevalent in figurative use
10. To provide raw material for party games, advertising copy, church sermons, crossword puzzles and other specialist applications.

The book takes into account the fact that English can rightly be described as "the language of buried metaphors" and that this feature, while no doubt fascinating to word-buffs, must be very frustrating to non-native speakers. Even secondary students for whom English is their first language tend to see things very literally.

Each metaphor has been given a separate entry, thus avoiding the practice in many dictionaries of jumbling up related material, which saves space but causes inconvenience to users. The form of presentation in this book also allows similar-sounding figurative formations to be compared and contrasted with each other very easily.

While from the nature of the subject matter this work inevitably involves some overlap with other books on idioms or picturesque expressions, it is original in terms of the selection of the phrases included, of their presentation and analysis, and of the simplicity of the definitions given.

COVERAGE

This short word-book, despite its specialized nature, makes no pretense as to completeness—that would be an impossible task, particularly as people with an eye out for resemblances are free to coin their own metaphorical expressions at will. However, the book contains some 14,000 dictionary-style alphabetical entries listing over 3,800 different metaphors commonly found in current usage, selected from the wide range available on the basis of the criteria described above. Many of these could be described as "classical" expressions, but the book also includes some other metaphors of special interest because of their origins in fields such as history, mythology, religion, commerce, science or classical literature or because they are illustrative of typical modern innovations.

Minor instances of figurative phrases based on local customs and circulating only in some communities can be found. However, most of the tabulated metaphors will be readily understood throughout the entire English-speaking world. This is, no doubt, due to the common origins of the language in the case of metaphors of long standing and to their use in films and television in the case of the more recent formations.

There is some overlap between metaphors, cliches, idioms, colloquialisms and even pithy sayings and proverbs. No attempt has been made to draw very fine distinctions, although similes, jargon and euphemisms have for the most part been deliberately excluded. Many outright slang terms have also been ignored, although a few borderline cases have been admitted. Some common picturesque expressions which may not strictly speaking be metaphors have been included where it seemed likely that this would be of convenience to users of this book.

Phrases such as "the chair upheld the point of order," "he has a good pen" or "the land belonged to the crown" are examples of the figure of speech known as *metonymy* and are also outside the scope of this book. In the same vein, expressions such as "I want a *word* with you" (in reference to a desired lengthy discussion), a subdivision of the figure of speech called *synecdoche* (see Chapter 7), have been disregarded.

Prepositions used metaphorically have also been excluded: "to be *in* difficulties," "to be *within* one's rights," "to be *beyond* help," and so on.

The main criterion for listing an expression was that in normal contexts its words are not used in their true or literal sense. However, in each case the user's intention would have been to convey a message which was meant to be readily understood by his particular public and which expressed a specific idea in a picturesque or emphatic way.

To enable the book to remain at a reasonable length, obscure phrases occasionally found in textbooks but which are not actually in current circulation have for the most part been excluded.

The richness of the English language can be demonstrated and put in perspective by comparing the number of metaphors mentioned above as included in this book even on this limited basis—namely, over 3,800—with the number of words in "Basic English"—a mere 850.

ARRANGEMENT

The bulk of this book is in three separate parts. First of all there is a main list in Part I which sets out each metaphor dealt with and which gives a deliberately brief yet concise explanation of its import. Occasionally where appropriate some further background information is added. This is followed in Part II by subsidiary lists showing the relevant metaphors occurring in each of a number of readily identifiable categories. Part III is a special section, not normally found in dictionaries. It is designed more for writers than for readers, although it is hoped that the latter will still find it of interest. It contains lists showing metaphors classified according to the broad subject areas in which they express ideas or concepts. These lists will also be of particular relevance to public speakers when preparing their material.

In addition, some general comments relating to metaphors at large and dealing with historical and other interesting aspects of the subject are made in Chapter 2 and the succeeding chapters. Some of these comments are based on a computer analysis made while researching this project. In particular, the categories relevant to Part II are discussed further in Chapter 4. They have regard to the *literal* or original meaning of the words—not to their *figurative* or borrowed usage. The basis of the thesaurus in Part III is explained in Chapter 5. A number of miscellaneous case studies are presented in Chapter 6. Some aspects of grammar and punctuation are dealt with in Chapter 7.

Of course, short definitions—while no doubt convenient to most users—do suffer from one disadvantage, in that they cannot readily cover exhaustively all the various shades of meaning being attributed to some phrases in actual practice.

The main list is in alphabetical order of the "keyword" of the phrase, usually the noun or the verb but on occasions where appropriate an adjective or an adverb. Simple verbs occurring frequently—*be, get, give, have, let, put, take,* etc.—have, however, been ignored. For the convenience of readers many metaphors and their explanations have been set out in the alphabetical sequence under more than one keyword. This eliminates the need for a separate index or extensive cross references. This presentation thus overcomes a weakness and an annoying feature of the few other books in this area. (Nouns are shown in the singular, except where only the plural form is relevant. Similarly, adjectives and adverbs are normally shown in the positive degree and verbs in the active voice and in the infinitive. Transitive verbs are shown with an appropriate object, such as "someone" or "something.") With minor exceptions—for special reasons—pronouns, prepositions, conjunctions and interjections are not listed.

It should be recognized that because English is a living language most metaphors can occur in numerous variations depending on the taste or the mood of the writer or speaker. For instance, words of qualification or alternatively of emphasis can be added or omitted. Many subjects can also be approached from more than one angle—for example, the expressions "something *coming* to light" and "someone *bringing* something to light" were both regarded as involving the same figurative concept and only the latter version was included in the list. Similarly, "to *run* for cover" and "to *duck* for cover" were treated as really being the one metaphor despite the use of a different verb in the two versions.

In some instances a pair of opposite metaphors exists—for example:

"to run off the rails" and "to be back on the rails"
"to give a thumbs up" and "to give a thumbs down"
"to be on the right track" and "to be on the wrong track"
"cold-hearted" and "warm-hearted"
"to be the first cab off the rank" and "to be the last" (or "latest") "cab off the rank"
"to give someone the green light" and "to give someone the red light"

and so on.

In other instances two related words exist—for example, "crusade" and "crusader," or the same word is used as two different parts of speech—for example, "to snowball" and "the snowball effect."

For space reasons some editorial selection has had to be made in many such cases. Thus if a phrase is not found at the first attempt a different keyword should be tried (such as a synonym or an antonym, a derivative or related term, or a word from a different part of the phrase). (In a few selected cases two alternative versions of a particular keyword or a particular phrase have been included for ease of reference.)

Hyphenated and unhyphenated compound words which are not tabulated as such will be found shown under their components. In practice the words "one," "someone," etc., used for convenience in the listings can be replaced by other appropriate words—nouns or pronouns, etc.

The subsidiary lists in the thematic section (Part II) are each in alphabetical order of the keyword relevant to the category concerned. This approach should assist readers wishing to locate metaphors momentarily forgotten. Where appropriate, a phrase is included in more than one category or even more than once in the same category. The lists themselves are in alphabetical order of category.

The subsidiary lists in the thesaurus (Part III) are each in alphabetical order of the full metaphor in the form in which it appears in Part I. The lists themselves are in alphabetical order of subject area.

This book is essentially a practical work, more concerned with examples of metaphors actually encountered in daily use than with the obscure theories of metaphor devised by some academic commentators. Writers, whether using existing metaphors or coining new ones, and whether setting out to do so deliberately or acting subconsciously, are not really assisted by theoretical considerations. Nor is such theory of much interest to readers coming across metaphors, whether or not they understand the underlying message.

BORDERLINE CASES

A number of phrases such as "to jump at the opportunity," "to swallow one's pride," "to sift the evidence" and "to have a sweet tooth" contain some words used literally as well as other words employed figuratively. Other examples are "to be bankrupt of ideas," "to shoulder the blame," "to sing someone's praises," "not to mince words" and "a passport to success." In such cases only the figurative components have usually been treated as giving rise to tabulated keywords, although for ease of reference some exceptions to this principle were made.

One of the difficulties faced by compilers of dictionaries such as this one is how to draw a clear-cut and unambiguous dividing line between words having more than one literal meaning and words used figuratively. For example, while the verb "to stand" has a primary literal meaning of "to have or take up an upright position" it also has over 20 secondary meanings, found in expressions such as "to stand on one's dignity," "to stand up for one's rights," "to stand a case over," "to stand firm," "to stand for tax reform," "to stand on ceremony," "to stand one's ground" and so on. Most expressions of this type have been regarded as being literal, in contradistinction to expressions which can convey a mental picture of an erect person, such as "to stand up and be counted," "to stand out from the crowd" and "to stand on one's own two feet."

COMMON KEYWORDS

Appendix 1 shows—purely as a curiosity—the tabulated keywords occurring most often, set out in order of their frequency. (For this purpose a compound word listed as such has been treated as being a different word from its components.)

Words representing important parts of the human body score particularly well—"head," "hand," "eye," "heart," etc. Some of these words are, of course, also used in other contexts—for example, "head" in "head of steam," "head of the pack," the "head of a nail," "heads and tails" on coins, heads of animals, etc. The word "hand" is also used in three different senses—a part of the body; an employee or worker; and the cards dealt to a player in a game of cards.

The most common noun among the tabulated metaphors which is not related to the human body is "water" and the animal referred to most often is the dog.

Phrases containing these very common keywords may in some cases be found more easily if the search is based on one of the secondary keywords.

2

SOURCES OF METAPHORS

The greatest thing by far is to have a command of metaphors
Aristotle *(The Poetics)*

Much matter decocted into a few words
Thomas Fuller (definition of a proverb in *The Worthies of England)*

METAPHORS FROM LITERATURE

Metaphors abound in poetry, but such a specialized usage is dealt with by many other analysts and is outside the scope of this book.

Somewhat surprisingly, comparatively few metaphors in contemporary use by the general public have their origins in the major literary works.

William Shakespeare was responsible, inter alia, for ''something is rotten in the State of Denmark'' (in *Hamlet*), ''the devil can cite scripture for his purpose'' and ''to want one's pound of flesh'' (both in *The Merchant of Venice*).

Of course, other Shakespearean passages, such as ''all the world's a stage,'' are sometimes quoted by people, but these have not really passed into the modern language as living metaphors.

Cervantes contributed ''to tilt at windmills'' and ''neither fish, flesh nor good red herring'' (both from *Don Quixote*).

Hans Christian Andersen wrote a story entitled ''the Ugly Duckling,'' while the expression ''curate's egg'' dates back to a *Punch* cartoon first published last century which featured a curate's response to his bishop, a response to the effect the parts of his breakfast egg were excellent!

Sir Walter Scott wrote ''O, what a tangled web we weave'' (in a line continuing ''When first we practice to deceive!'')

''To do a Jekyll and Hyde'' refers to a book by Robert Louis Stevenson.

Catch 22 and *The Last of the Mohicans* are the titles of novels by

Joseph Heller and James Fenimore Cooper, respectively. *Box and Cox* is the name of a play.

The concept of somebody being a real Scrooge refers to a character in Charles Dickens' *A Christmas Carol.*

Virgil, who died in 19 B.C. probably originated the modern expressions involving the Trojan horse and the Greeks bearing gifts.

Many well-known quotations are, of course, literally true and thus do not rank as metaphors—for example, John Donne's famous "no man is an island."

The works of Shakespeare also lend themselves to the coming of brand new expressions. For instance, a writer recently mentioned the "Macbeth Principle," in reference to the view that if something unpleasant needed to be done, then it should be done without delay (or, as the immortal bard himself put it, "if it were done when 'tis done, then 'twere well it were done quickly").

METAPHORS FROM POLITICS

While politicians no doubt invent numerous metaphors in the course of their daily speech making, few of these seem to survive.

Oliver Cromwell's famous direction to Sir Peter Lely to paint his portrait "warts and all" has, however, become a contemporary idiom.

Benjamin Disraeli once told a conference that he was "on the side of the angels."

Sir Winston Churchill invented the term "the iron curtain," but the Churchillian ring to some of his other sayings has probably militated against their use in ordinary situations.

Churchill is also credited with describing his successor, Clement Attlee, as a "sheep in sheep's clothing."

In America at the turn of the century President Theodore Roosevelt coined the oft-quoted expression "speak softly and carry a big stick."

Two phrases attributed to another United States president—this time Harry S. Truman—are "if one can't stand the heat one should stay out of the kitchen" and "the buck stops here." The latter expression built up on a much earlier metaphor, "to pass the buck," which in turn referred to the buckhorn knife passed around the table during certain card games in order to indicate who the dealer was.

A well-chosen political metaphor can be remarkably powerful in its psychological effect—consider, for example, the expression "the cold war."

Clever politicians can also use existing classical metaphors to good advantage—for instance, British prime minister Harold Macmillan once said of an opponent: "If Harold Wilson ever went to school without any boots, it was merely because he was too big for them."

METAPHORS FROM RELIGIOUS SOURCES

The ancient non-Christian European religions gave rise to a number of current expression, such as "to be in the lap of the gods" and "Delphic."

Primitive tribes in Africa originated the term "mumbo jumbo," while Australian Aboriginal culture was the source of the expression "to point the bone at someone."

Both the Old and the New Testaments of the Bible contribute a number of phrases which are used by both believers and non-believers in circumstances far removed from those of their origin. Some of these phrases sound distinctly biblical, but many others do not.

For example, the Old Testament uses the oft-quoted "to hold out an olive branch," "the writing is on the wall," "to cast one's bread upon the waters" and "an eye for an eye, a tooth for a tooth." Somewhat surprisingly, the very modern term "to be in an ivory tower" also comes from this source.

Other Old Testament passages which give rise to currently-used expressions involve forbidden fruit, David and Goliath, the walls of Jericho, a fly in the ointment, the tower of Babel, the road to Damascus, the mark of Cain, feet of clay, manna from Heaven, the flesh pots of Egypt and the wisdom of Solomon. "To sell one's birthright for a mess of pottage" (in other words, for a mere portion of soup) is another contemporary expression, although one which admittedly sounds rather quaint because of its archaic language.

The famous test word *shibboleth* has also passed into the language as the term for an out-dated political principle. (It is actually a Hebrew word meaning "stream in flood." Its significance in biblical times was that the way in which it was pronounced made it possible to tell an Ephraimite from a member of another tribe, because of his inability to pronounce the initial "sh" sound in some words correctly.)

The New Testament uses the popular "by their fruits ye shall know them" and refers to a wolf in sheep's clothing, the salt of the earth, putting one's hand to the plow, turning the other cheek, killing the fatted calf, being a doubting Thomas, separating the sheep from the goats, being a good Samaritan and seeing the mote in another person's eye.

For metaphors which are derived from the Bible the chapter and verse citations pertaining to them are set out following the definitions given in this book. Such metaphors are also shown in Appendix 4, arranged for ease of reference in alphabetical order of both the keyword and the relevant book of the Bible.

A special classification called "Religion and Biblical" is included in

Part II. However, this approaches the subject from a completely different perspective from that just presented, focusing more on words such as *angel, devil, saint, soul, heaven* and *hell,* rather than on actual religious origins.

Actually the use of such terms raises an interesting philosophical point which is best illustrated by an example. Consider the expression ''to send someone to Coventry.'' This can clearly be used literally in relation to the English city of that name, and those employing the expression would obviously believe that such a place existed. However, the same expression can also be used figuratively in the sense of ''to ostentatiously and collectively ignore a person by way of punishment.'' In contrast, whether heaven and hell really exist is a question of faith rather than a matter of fact. In these circumstances, can phrases such as ''manna from heaven'' (unexpected benefits) or ''on a cold day in hell'' (never) be truly regarded as metaphors by those who do not in the first instance ascribe any literal meaning to the words ''heaven'' or ''hell''?

METAPHORS FROM HERALDRY

Metaphors derived from heraldry are comparatively rare and those which exist are not without their controversy.

For instance, the phrase ''blue ribbon'' (of superb quality) probably refers to the insignia of the Order of the Garter, the highest of the ancient British Orders of Chivalry. However, many heraldry experts feel that the expression really refers to the ribbons used in agricultural shows or at race meetings rather than to the blue ribbons worn by knights on ceremonial occasions.

The ''blot on the escutcheon'' (a blemish on a person's character, in reference to one of nine possible marks of disgrace placed on a shield in earlier days) is better known in heraldry as an ''abatement of honor.'' The expression actually refers to the charges (that is, to the designs, figures or symbols) placed on coats of arms in order to show that the bearer has been guilty of some unknightly conduct or dishonorable action. Few examples were encountered in practice, because, understandably enough, men would rather not display arms at all than show their disgrace to the world. Blots were in any case regarded as only temporary, as they could be erased by some compensating deed of honor.

The term ''bar sinister'' in reference to illegitimacy has not been regarded as a true metaphor, but in any case the expression is heraldic nonsense, as bars (horizontal stripes on a coat of arms) can from their very nature be neither ''dexter'' nor ''sinister.'' Furthermore, the various symbols used for denoting bastardy in heraldry include the bend, the baton and the border, but never the bar.

THE ROLE OF FOREIGN LANGUAGES

Although not widely realized, some ordinary English words originate from the metaphorical use of certain Latin terms—"companions," from *cum panis,* people who eat bread together; "colleagues," from *cum* and *legere,* persons who are chosen with each other; "to conspire," from *cum* and *spirare,* to breathe together; and so on.

In a few instances, English has actually borrowed current metaphors from a foreign language. The following eleven French phrases are examples of this:

"*danse macabre*"
"*bete noire*"
"*creme de la creme*"
"*volte face*"
"*tour de force*"
"*faux pas*"
"*coup de grace*"
"*enfant terrible*"
"*esprit de corps*"
"*touche*" and
"*carte blanche,*"

as is the Italian "*prima donna.*"

In a slightly different class is the Swedish word "*smorgasbord,*" which is used both literally of food and figuratively of other things.

Similar remarks also apply to the Latin phrase "*postmortem,*" which is used both literally as a medical term and figuratively in other contexts.

3

THE METAPHOR IN DAILY USE

The sole aim of the metaphor is to call up a visual image
Aristotle

The intolerable wrestle with words and meanings
T.S. Eliot *("Burnt Norton")*

THE PREVALENCE OF METAPHORS

Metaphors are so prevalent that if one were to specifically look out for them it would completely spoil one's reading and listening and thus detract from the author's purpose.

There are only a few areas of writing in which metaphors are deliberately carefully avoided. Two examples would be material prepared specifically for non-native speakers and material intended for translation into foreign languages.

Another example would be legislation and legal documents generally, where precision is essential and where beauty of expression is an unaffordable luxury. Even the modern trend toward "Plain English" drafting would not make metaphors acceptable in such contexts.

Metaphors are, of course, less likely to be used in technical material such as car or computer manuals than in, say, either ordinary conversation or literary works, whether prose or poetry.

Figurative expressions have on occasion had their opponents—in 1670 one Samuel Parker went so far as to seriously advocate an Act of Parliament actually forbidding the use of "fulsome and luscious" metaphors in England!

THE GRAPHIC NATURE OF LONGER METAPHORS

The standard metaphors listed in this book range from single words to longer phrases and on rare occasions even to complete sentences (see also Chapter 7).

Many idiomatic expressions depend for their effect on the ideas represented by the *combination* of words rather than by the words individually—consider, for example, the metaphors "to pour oil on troubled waters," "a storm in a teacup" and "to shut the stable door after the horse has bolted."

Writers can, of course, create graphic messages by incorporating metaphorical ideas into longer passages. For example, the plain "a chink of light" can be built up into "a welcome ray of light piercing the gloom." Again, one can draw attention to the ravages of inflation by sentences such as: "Money saved for a rainy day now buys a much smaller umbrella than it used to."

Similarly, ever-increasing government regulation with its many anomalies can be criticized by pointing out that the "level playing field is getting more bumpy all the time."

A lawyer discussing the nature of certain evidence once made his point to the court very neatly in the following terms:

If there is a large elephant on your front doorstep, then it is not a bad idea to take notice of it, even if you cannot weigh it exactly.

Taking particular care can be described as "checking whether every *i* has been dotted and making sure that every *t* is crossed."

Original metaphors drawing on contemporary practices can also be very effective. For example, something particularly large or unusual can be described as "justifying an entry in the *Guinness Book of Records*."

MIXED METAPHORS

An anonymous author once wrote "never mix your drinks or your metaphors" and this accords with the traditional advice on this subject given to young writers. However, mixed metaphors frequently arise in practice without any intention on the part of their creators and without their absurdity necessarily distracting readers.

For example, a government official investigating a fraud case was recently reported as saying:

When the music stops the house of cards collapses and the emperor is found to be wearing no clothes.

Again, a politician has criticized his opponents for "orchestrating the emasculation" of a particular law.

The most frequently quoted mixed metaphor comes from a speech by Sir Boyle Roche to the Irish Parliament some 200 years ago:

Mr Speaker, I smell a rat; I see him forming in the air and darkening the sky; but I'll nip him in the bud.

One further example: "While the iron is hot, stay on your toes, keep the ball rolling and don't throw a spanner in the works."

Of course, even a single metaphor can sound absurd—for example, a reference to the Yiddish Art Theater as a "Mecca for Jewish theater-goers."

It is also possible to create amusing results by twisting and parodying commonly-used metaphors, as in "Mr. Smith is all *tip* and no *iceberg*. He always has his head buried under the desk."

The lists in this book will provide raw material for party games—see Appendix 3—and also for script-writers seeking to achieve comic effects by stringing together chains of unrelated or inconsistent metaphors, as in the following two illustrative passages:

Keep your back to the wall, your shoulder to the wheel, your ear to the ground, your nose to the grindstone, your eye out for trouble, your chin up, your head down and your feet firmly on the ground.

Our staff get exercise by jumping to conclusions, flying off the handle, carrying things too far, dodging responsibility and pushing their luck.

METAPHORS IN TRANSITION

Sometimes expressions which originally started off in figurative usage later on make a complete transition and over time virtually become "regular" words—for instance:

"to be petrified"
"to unmask" someone
"to be in the limelight"
"to have overtones"
"to set up a smokescreen"
"to be in the pipeline"
"a watchdog role"
"a snowball effect"

as well as both components in "a pastor and his flock."
Possible further examples of this trend would include the nouns:

"a backlash"
"a catalyst"
"a pipedream"
"a whitewash"
"a framework"
"an avalanche"
"a loop-hole"
"a crusade"
"a sounding board"
"a nightmare"

"a yardstick"
"a stalemate"
"a blueprint"
"a bottleneck"
"a watershed"
"a scenario"
"a stumbling block"
"a footing"
"a scapegoat"
"a breadwinner"
"a windfall"
"a nosedive"
"a deadline"
"a figurehead"
"heresy"
"fanfare"
"pecking order"
"chicken feed"
"spectrum" and
"imprimatur;"

the adjectives:

"pedestrian"
"fruitless"
"apocryphal"
"half-baked" and
"short-sighted;"

and the verbs:

"to encapsulate"
"to backfire"
"to crystallize"
"to polarize"
"to choreograph"
"to highlight"
"to undermine a person"
"to ferret something out"
"to hand pick"
"to paralyze a city"
"to pontificate"
"to backpedal"
"to crucify a person" and
"to pre-empt something."

Other such verbs are mentioned later in the section headed "Metaphors involving a Change to the Part of Speech" in Chapter 7.

It seems likely that many of the other terms in this book, particularly those lacking short synonyms, are heading in the same direction and will become "regular" words in due course.

4

METAPHORS IN VARIOUS CATEGORIES

Words are, of course, the most powerful drug used by mankind
Rudyard Kipling

That's nothing to what I could say if I chose
Lewis Carroll (the Duchess in *Alice in Wonderland*)

THE THEMATIC SECTION

The 37 different sets of tabulations in the Thematic Section (Part II) reflect the attempt at classification referred to in Chapter 1. They are included mainly as a matter of general interest, but also because in some cases the category gives a shorthand indication as to the origin of the metaphor concerned.

Of necessity the categorization process involved the making of a number of arbitrary decisions. There is, for example, some overlap between certain animals and plants viewed as such or alternatively regarded as food or alternatively again as a product of farming. Some words were accordingly allocated to the *nearest* available category. However, despite this roughness the counts go some way toward demonstrating the unevenness of the literal subject matter which gives rise to the phrases listed.

The comments below will serve as a brief general introduction to this aspect, but the detailed listings really speak for themselves.

SPORT

Understandably, analogies based on sport are fairly common: "to be given riding instructions," "to be slow off the mark," "to be right behind the eight ball," "to play by the book," "to throw in the towel," "to give a blow by blow description," "to hit someone below the belt," "to jump the gun", "saved by the bell," "hook, line and sinker," "a master stroke" and "track record"—to name just a few.

Cricket terms are particularly prevalent in the countries favoring that game: "it's not cricket," "to have the runs on the board," "to have had a good inning," "to be on a sticky wicket," "until stumps are drawn," and so on.

THE HUMAN BODY

However, the most frequent references involve parts of the human body: "to scratch one's head," "to twist someone's arm," "to burn one's fingers," "to have broad shoulders," "to have one's ear to the ground," "to step on someone's toes," and so on. Some people get "itchy feet" while others merely get "cold feet."

Nearly a quarter of all entries relate to just this one important category.

ANIMALS

The next most popular category is the one based on animals: "to let sleeping dogs lie," "to throw a cat among the pigeons," "to take the bull by the horns," "to be an ostrich," "to stir up a hornets' nest" and "to buy a pig in a poke"—not to mention "black sheep," "red herrings," "dark horses," "underdogs," "sacred cows," "guinea pigs," "sacrificial lambs," "flies in the ointment," "can of worms" and the well-known "dog in the manger."

The range of animals found in metaphors is quite uneven—some less common species, such as giraffes, platypuses and zebras, are not represented at all.

The term "animal" has been used in its correct sense, including birds, fish, insects and so on, and not merely mammals.

In some cases it is not clear whether a particular expression refers to human beings or to animals. For example, the analogy in "to put flesh and bone on something" could have either in mind.

THE WORLD OF SAIL

The era of sailing ships has left its legacy in phrases such as "to learn the ropes," "to trim one's sails," "to change tack," "to be plain sailing," "to nail one's colors to the mast," "to sail close to the wind," "to take the wind out of someone's sails," "I like the cut of his jib" and "the calm before the storm." There is also the pair of opposites, "to sail under false colors" and "to show one's true colors."

One of the expressions mentioned above, "to be plain sailing" (to be quite straight forward and very easy), is actually a corruption of "plane sailing," in reference to navigation by means of a "plane chart" on which meridians and parallels of latitude are represented by equidistant straight lines, an approximate method which ignores the curvature of the earth and which is therefore simpler for short distances.

Sailing expressions are shown in the "Nautical" category.

MUSIC

Music is another rich source. Examples include "to change one's tune," "to sing for one's supper," "to hit a sour note," "to have another string to one's bow," "to softpedal," "to be a one-man band" and "to face the music." There are also the rather similar in meaning "to beat one's drum" and "to blow one's own trumpet"—presumably in contrast to the position of the person who "plays second fiddle" to somebody else.

The listings include three similar examples based on the verb "to strike" and the adjective "right," namely, "to strike the right chord" (to appeal successfully to someone's emotions), "to strike the right key" (to find the appropriate solution) and "to strike the right note" (to make a good impression). While these definitions have been given to demonstrate the shades of meaning which are possible, the phrases may well be being used more or less interchangeably in practice.

Other variations to this theme are "to strike a responsive chord" (to get a favorable reaction to a proposal) and the plain "to strike a chord" (to sound familiar or to recall something to mind). The last-mentioned idea can also be rendered as "to ring a bell."

COMMERCE

Expressions such as "A1 at Lloyd's," "to give someone a blank check," "the other side of the coin," "to show dividends" and "to be below par," together with the concept of something "not adding up," have all come into wider usage from the world of commerce.

The terms "to burn one's fingers" and "to fly a kite"—the latter in the sense of issuing uncovered checks in the hope of covering them before clearance—have moved in the reverse direction, although this particular phrase is also used in a different way in politics (the testing of public reaction to contemplated legislation by leaking broad details of it to the media).

AMUSEMENTS GENERALLY

Apart from sport and music, as discussed above, many other forms of popular amusement are understandably enough also noteworthy sources of metaphors—for instance, art, theater, circuses, gambling and various indoor games such as cards and chess.

The origins of some of the expressions relating to cards which are in popular use today may not be obvious on the surface. For example, a "showdown" occurs in poker games when the players put their cards down on the table face up in order to show the strength of their hands, while "level pegging" refers to the marking of the score with pegs in cribbage.

Two other cards phrases, "passing the buck" and "the buck stops here," have already been mentioned in Chapter 2.

STATISTICS OF USAGE

Appendix 2 summarizes the main categories adopted. It also shows their relative frequencies and the number of items in each. Apart from anything else, the statistics provide an interesting sociological commentary on the activities which most readily spring to mind when writers and speakers wish to make a point by using an analogy. In most cases the association will be readily understood by readers and listeners with a twentieth-century English-speaking cultural background.

About 13 per cent of the listed metaphors did not conveniently fit into any of these categories, while some of the defined categories such as "Sex" and "Heraldry" produced astonishingly low scores.

5

METAPHORS EXPRESSING IDEAS IN CERTAIN SUBJECT AREAS

Let thy speech be short, comprehending much in few words

Ecclesiasticus 32:8

Be not the slave of words

Thomas Carlyle (*Sartor Resartus*)

THE THESAURUS

The Thesaurus (Part III) is to some extent the reverse of the Dictionary (Part I). Instead of starting with metaphors and then presenting their meanings, it starts with base words summarizing the meanings and then sets out the various metaphors relevant to the broad subject area concerned. (Sometimes for convenience several different subject areas are shown together, where the base word has more than one meaning.)

To illustrate, "taking a risk" is an area in which many metaphorical expressions abound, although they all have slightly different connotations:

"to go out on a limb"
"to stick one's neck out"
"to rush in where angels fear to tread"
"to take the plunge"
"to play with dynamite"
"to go through fire and water"
"to chance one's arm"
"to jump in feet first"
"to play Russian roulette"
"to take a punt"
"to be sitting on a volcano."

The opposite of this concept is "to play it safe." These and various other such phrases are shown under "Risk" in Part III.

Of course, the main alphabetical list in Part I also contains some entries which deal with subject concepts—for instance, phrases relating to "newness" can be obtained by looking up "new" and "old" in Part I, while some phrases implying completeness will be found under "all" and "every."

In some cases, the listings contain both positive and negative usages—thus entries actually relating to "Lack of Enthusiasm" will be found under the general heading "Enthusiasm," and so on.

The subject areas chosen for tabulation are set out alphabetically in the table of contents. As there is some overlap between them, users interested in a particular subject area may need to consult more than one list, depending on the shade of meaning desired—for example, it might be appropriate to look at the two lists headed "Risk" and "Danger"; or alternatively at the two lists headed "Risk" and "Chance."

Once again, the unevenness of metaphorical usage causes some surprise—for instance, why should there be three times as many expressions for the *end* of various activities (namely, 110) than for the *start* of something (namely, 39)?

"DIFFICULTY" AS A CONCEPT

To take a further example, the concept of "difficulty" gives rise to a great many figurative expressions. On the first encounter with a difficulty one "runs into a roadblock," "strikes a snag" or "runs into heavy weather." In fact, one "has a job in front of one" and may need "to put one's thinking cap on" in order to solve the problem.

If the difficulty is shared with other people then they are all "in the same boat." As one prepares to overcome the difficulty, one decides that "the show must go on" and alternatively "sharpens one's ax" or "battens down the hatches."

The actual attempt to overcome the difficulty involves "grasping the nettle," "taking the bull by the horns," "grabbing the devil by the tail" or "biting the bullet." After that one "jumps the hurdle," "irons out" the problem or "makes a good fist" at trying to fix it. If one fails, one "sinks deeper into the mire" (or "into the mud"). If one succeeds, one has "fallen on one's feet." One is then "out of the woods" and can "heave a sigh of relief."

To take unfair advantage of someone already in difficulty is "to kick a man when he is down." To desert a person who is in difficulty is "to leave him in the lurch." A period fraught with difficulties is "a sticky patch." Something very difficult is said to be "sheer murder."

There are well over a dozen different expressions for actually "being in difficulty." Some involve shades of additional meaning—

from (a): just being agitated because one is in a slight muddle,
through (b): being stuck in a delicate situation or experiencing bad luck,
to (c): facing near despair because some task is beyond one's capabilities.

In rough order of severity (least to most) these expressions are as follows:

"to be in a pickle"
"to be in a stew"
"to be in a jam"
"to be in a hole"
"to be out of one's depth"
"to have a hard row to hoe"
"to be pushing uphill" (or "fighting an uphill battle")
"to be on a sticky wicket"
"to have the cards" (or "the odds") "stacked against one"
"to be in a quagmire"
"to be in deep water" (or "in hot water") and
"to be in the soup."

A difficult query is a "sixty-four thousand dollar question." If, on the other hand, one encounters no difficulties at all, then one is said to be having a "dream run."

The above 42 illustrations do not, of course, exhaust all the possibilities.

MONEY MATTERS

Financial journals use ordinary metaphors all the time—for example, share prices either "skyrocket" or "go into a tailspin," takeovers are made "with much fanfare" and new chief executives "take the helm." Special metaphors with technical meanings also exist—for example, securities held by investors can be said to be "above the water" (above cost price).

Political allusions to spending taxpayers' funds occur in expressions such as "to pork barrel" and "to engage in pump priming." For a humorous effect, large sums of money can be referred to as "telephone numbers."

The actual word "money" used in its literal sense is found in the partly-figurative phrases "money for jam," "to see the color of someone's money," "to have money burning a hole in one's pocket," "putting one's money where one's mouth is," "money down the drain" and "the money is rolling in."

When a purely figurative expression for "money" is desired, words such as "pocket," "purse" or "penny" are often used, as in:

"to have deep pockets"
"to line one's pocket"
"to button up one's purse" and
"to cost a pretty penny."

However, not all terms fall into this pattern. People can be "in the black." They can also "feather their nest" or they may "burn their fingers."

Strange things happen when a country's sterling currency is decimalized. Phrases such as "in for a penny, in for a pound," "the penny dropped," "a ha'p'orth of tar," "penny-pinching" and the ungrammatical "he doesn't have two pennies to rub together" remain unchanged. On the other hand, "to throw in one's six pennies' worth" (sometimes rendered as "... one's two bobs' worth") becomes "to throw in one's two cents' worth," while "to have two bob each way" is converted to the version "to have fifty cents each way"—hardly close decimal equivalents.

Similarly, expressions involving imperial distances or weights do not always get metricated—for example, "to drain every ounce out of something," "to go the extra mile," "a yardstick," "a milestone," "not to give an inch," "to stand out a mile," "to get mileage out of some matter" and "to inch forward."

Of course, everyone with even 28.3 grams of common sense realizes that *exact* conversions would not be appropriate in all circumstances.

METAPHORS USED EUPHEMISTICALLY

Metaphors can be used as a device for being tactful or to soften a harsh message. For example, instead of saying to a person "you are an unmitigated liar" one can put it more gently—but just as effectively—in the form of "that is just a cock and bull story."

Similarly one can say "a cobbler should stick to his last," rather than "you are a fool for trying this"; "your friend is a slippery customer," rather than "your friend tried to cheat me"; and "it was under your very nose," rather than "you are an idiot for not spotting the obvious."

Again, in a business context a short reference to a "new broom" can sound more positive than a formal utterance about "changed management practices."

Whether this tactic really works and the words sound less hard may, of course, depend on other factors, such as accompanying the message by suitable body language, by a smile or by a twinkle in the eye of the speaker.

Other euphemisms will be found in Part III under headings such as:

"Mistake"—"to put the cart before the horse," etc.
"Naivete"—"to be babes in the wood," etc.
"Slowness"—"to drag one's heels," etc.
"Stupidity"—"to put forward a cock-eyed proposal," etc. and
"Unrealistic Ideas"—"to have one's head in the clouds," etc.

6

SELECTED CASE STUDIES

Proper words in proper places make the true definition of style
Jonathan Swift (''Letter to a Young Clergyman'')

''When I use a word,'' Humpty Dumpty said in rather a scornful tone, ''it means just what I choose it to mean—neither more nor less.''
Lewis Carroll *(Through the Looking Glass)*

THE LIVING ENGLISH LANGUAGE

The origins of most of the figurative expressions currently in circulation are lost in antiquity and their authors are unknown.

However, the heterogeneous nature of English metaphors and the power which they add to the language can best be demonstrated by examining some actual cases. The following illustrations are taken more or less at random from the vast collection used to compile this book.

It is, for example, intriguing to note that often words which when taken literally are quite inoffensive acquire not only color but also pejorative overtones when engaged as figures of speech—for example, ''to split hairs.''

On another tack (!), interesting effects can also be obtained by deliberately misquoting well-known expressions, producing renditions such as ''every silver cloud has a dark lining.''

The word ''metaphor'' itself can be used in a non-literal way. For example, a film on ''home entertainments and theater'' was given the subtitle ''metaphors of decadence and blurred reality,'' while one writer coined the phrase ''metaphors of evil'' in connection with ''contemporary German literature and the shadow of Nazism.''

It will be interesting to see whether the new computer technology inspires any additional metaphors for the wider community. As regards the reverse situation, many computer terms—such as ''bit,'' ''memory,'' ''hardware,'' ''window'' and ''word''—are ordinary English words given special meanings, rather than figures of speech. The word ''software'' (meaning a computer program) is an artificially-coined term, based on the long-established word "hardware" (meaning building materials, tools, etc., in ordinary usage—but also adopted by the computer industry to mean the physical components of a computer, as distinct from the programs). Perhaps the term "garbage" is a true metaphor—"garbage in, garbage out" (if there are errors in the input data then there will inevitably be errors in the output data).

DUPLICATIONS

On occasions a whole series of commonly-used metaphors is evolved in order to express just one simple idea—such as "to be within a bull's roar of something," "to be within a hair's breadth of something" and "to be within an ace of something"—or when speakers refer to only a postage stamp (or alternatively a cigarette paper or alternatively again a wafer or a tissue) separating either two objects or two close contestants in a race.

Again, wishful thinking has inspired several different phrases—those referring to the impossibility of turning the clock back, of unscrambling an omelette, or of putting the genie back in the bottle.

Some further examples of this pattern are "to miss the boat," "to miss the bus" and "to miss the train"—three transport phrases which all mean much the same thing—and "to hold a winning hand," "to hold all the aces" and "to hold the trump cards"—three phrases from the world of cards which once again have an identical meaning.

One can also be in something "up to one's shoulder," "up to one's neck," "up to one's elbow," "up to one's freckles" or even "up to one's eyeballs."

There are also many pairs of duplicates. To name just a few:

"to give a hand" and "to lend a hand"
"to escape by the skin of one's teeth" and "to escape by the skin of one's nose"
"to bore someone to tears" and "to bore someone to death"
"a thorn in one's side" and "a thorn in one's flesh"
"a drop in the ocean" and "a drop in the bucket."

"To be on the wrong tack" (another sailing term) parallels "to be on the wrong track" and "to be on the wrong tram" (from onshore activities).

PLAYS ON WORDS

Although similes in general are outside the scope of this book, special mention should be made of those which amount to a play on words rather than a true comparison—for example, "to charge like a wounded bull" (to impose excessive prices) and "to be flat out like a lizard" (to be hard at work).

EMPHASIS

Particular attention is drawn to a series of phrases which contain some words used quite literally in combination with figurative fancy expressions and elaborations inserted purely for the purpose of greater emphasis. Some examples of this pattern are as follows:

"to vanish into thin air"
"at a break-neck pace"
"crystal clear"
"every man and his dog"
"to be the end of the road"
"to get away with murder"
"to confront something head on"
"to refuse point blank"
"to save a bundle"
"a long time between drinks"
"why in the world?"
"No way!"
"in every nook and cranny"
"short and sweet"
"enough to sink a battleship"
"alive and kicking"
"the last of the Mohicans"
"to go post haste" and
"to cost an arm and a leg."

Again, it is sometimes said that prices are "going through the roof" or that some innovation is "the hottest thing since sliced bread."

In a slightly different class is the picturesque insult in which a person is described as being "lower than a snake's belly!"

Some metaphors used by way of elaboration really add little of substance—for example, "for my sins."

THE NEED FOR PRECISION

In many metaphors the precise words do not matter and synonyms or other variations according to the speaker's preferences can readily be used. In other cases, however, the exact word is essential. For example, the two words "street" and "road" are not interchangeable in either direction in:

"to be streets ahead"
"not to be in the same street as someone"
"to be on the right road"
"to be at the crossroads."

Similarly, something can be "up one's street" or more commonly "up one's alley," but never "up one's road."

Again, a person can "pull himself up" either "by his bootstraps" or "by his own shoelaces." But a person is "British to his bootstraps" without such an alternative.

OVERLAP

Is a "shot in the dark" really different from a "stab in the dark?" There are, no doubt, differences in the shades of meaning which may make one term or the other better in some particular circumstances. In the listings the former has been defined as an "intelligent or lucky guess" and the latter as a "sheer guess." However, in the context of a living language spoken by millions of people it should not be assumed that such clear-cut distinctions are made every time people use these expressions. These remarks apply not only to the specific illustration just given but also in the general case.

Again, some rather similar combinations of words occur in two or more really quite distinct metaphors. Thus, "that is a fine kettle of fish" (that is a terrible muddle) can be distinguished from "that is a very different kettle of fish" (that is something very dissimilar).

Again, "to undermine a person" (to injure his reputation) has only a small overlap with "to undermine a proposal" (to sabotage it).

"That is all water under the bridge" (that no longer matters) is not quite the same as "a lot of water has passed under the bridge since he came" (much has happened since he came).

"To give someone a hand" (to assist a person) is significantly different from "to give someone a free hand" (to authorize a person to act as he sees fit).

"To rekindle an old flame" (to inspire the reinstatement of a former loving relationship) might even refer to "an old flame" (a former lover).

"An activity on the horizon" (one expected, but not immediately) differs both from "a cloud on the horizon" (a faint indication of possible future trouble) and from the worse still "black clouds on the horizon" (anticipated bad news).

A person can either "see the light" (understand the real situation) or ''see the light at the end of the tunnel'' (be close to finalizing a long exercise), while a document can ''see the light of day'' (be made public). Again, a matter can be ''brought to light'' (drawn to general attention) so that those responsible can ''shed light on it'' (give explanations about it).

A person can ''keep his own eyes open for something'' (be on the lookout for useful information) or he can ''open someone else's eyes to something'' (alert another person to the truth of some matter). He can also receive a real ''eye opener'' (surprise) or he can go into something ''with his eyes wide open'' (fully conscious of the ramifications).

The expression ''to put one's feet up'' (to relax) can be contrasted with the expression ''to put one's foot down'' (to exert one's authority and insist on something).

In the area of near slang, ''to have a shot at someone'' (to tease a person) is very different from ''to have a shot at something'' (to make an attempt at achieving some goal).

NEGATIVE EXPRESSIONS

A great number of rather colloquial expressions seem to work only in the negative—for instance:

''it is not the end of the world''
''don't hold your breath for the outcome''
''he is not Robinson Crusoe''
''you're not here to win prizes''
''don't let the grass grow under your feet''
''that is not cricket''
''don't bust your boiler''
''it does not matter a row of beans''
''she didn't give an inch''
''that is not my cup of tea''
''I would not touch that with a ten-foot pole''
''that cuts no ice with me''
''he didn't miss a beat''
''he held a gun with no bullets''
''he is not the only pebble on the beach''
''it's not over till the fat lady sings''
''he did not turn a hair''
''nothing is sacred''
''she did not bat an eyelash''
''don't lose any sleep over this''
''I would not know him from Adam''
''not for love or money''
''he didn't have a dog's chance''

"it was no picnic"
"he did not put a foot wrong"
"she didn't pull any punches"
"I cannot for the life of me . . ."
"to make no bones about it . . ." and
"you haven't a leg to stand on."

The corresponding affirmative phrases would just not be idiomatic.
On a slightly different tack, the expression "he is no angel" is not at all the opposite of "he is an angel."

NONSENSE EXPRESSIONS

Then there are also some "nonsense" metaphors, such as:

"since the year dot"
"to increase exponentially"
"to the nth degree" and
"to move at a rate of knots."

These are all expressions which when taken literally are actually quite meaningless.
"To fly in the face of my specific orders" contains not one but rather two quite absurd terms.
There is also the expression "with 20/20 hindsight," which sounds more impressive and plausible than is really justified.

COLLOQUIALISMS

Some phrases can be used orally although they would be regarded as unacceptable in literary pieces—for instance:

"stiff cheese"
"fair crack of the whip"
"shoot!" (in the sense of "speak")
"buzz off"
"I'll nail him"
"I have to fly"
"he can get lost"
"if I've told you once I've told you a thousand times"
"between you and me and the gatepost"
"you can go and jump in the lake"
"you can eat your heart out"

''that is on your head''
''that is your funeral''
''keep your shirt on!'' and
''more power to your elbow.''

Another ''negative only'' expression, ''no dice,'' is also in the same category.

A rather different example is ''if he were alive today he would turn in his grave.''

SEXIST LANGUAGE

Many metaphors involve sexist language, having been coined long before attention was paid to such matters. Examples include ''the man in the street,'' ''a mansize job,'' ''soul brother,'' ''to separate the men from the boys,'' ''as every schoolboy knows'' and ''he is your man.''

Of course, not every reference to males paints that sex in a good light—consider, for example, the expression ''a man of straw.'' However, the relatively few references in metaphors to females tend to be unflattering—for instance, ''witchhunt'' and ''it's not over till the fat lady sings.''

DOUBLE METAPHORS

The expression ''a backseat driver'' is a rare example of a *double metaphor.* Clearly, the word ''driver'' is not being used literally even when the phrase is employed in the context of monitoring. When it is used with the figurative meaning of ''a person seeking to exercise control'' then the whole phrase becomes yet a further metaphor.

A more modern example is the radio term ''feedback.'' Originally it referred to the interaction between amplifiers and speakers, which must have suggested to its early users some analogy to food. The secondary concept in turn gave rise to the contemporary meaning of the phrase (a response from a target audience to those trying to influence it), an analogy based on an analogy.

POPULAR MISCONCEPTIONS

Some metaphors in colloquial use are based on a misunderstanding as to the correct meaning of the literal words. Six examples of this are as follows:

''A leading question'' (a very pertinent question): This involves the misuse of a legal term used in relation to cross-examinations—a term which actually means a question so framed as to suggest the answer.

"Opening gambit" (the first in a series of strategic moves): This is a tautological expression, which also involves a misunderstanding of a technical chess term concerned with the making of a sacrifice.

"To decimate" (to greatly reduce in size): This expression is often used in the sense of "to reduce *to* one tenth," although its original meaning was "to reduce *by* one tenth," in reference to executing every tenth soldier as punishment for mutiny or cowardice.

"To create a Frankenstein" (to create something wicked and out of control): This is a reference to the fictional *creator* of "Frankenstein's monster" in a story by Mary Shelley, in mistake for a reference to the monster itself.

"At the eleventh hour" (at the last moment): As a day has 24 hours and half a day has 12 hours, this phrase is doubly wrong; "at the twenty-fourth hour" would be much more logical. (The phrase actually refers to the twelve hours between sunrise and sunset, the "day" in biblical times.)

"To compound the felony" (having already acted improperly to make matters worse): This also involves the misuse of a legal term. Compounding a felony is the crime of agreeing for money not to prosecute a person for felony. In reality it is therefore an offense by a different person—not a second and worse offense by the original culprit.

As indicated under the heading "Hyperbole" in Chapter 7, the expression "light years" is often used incorrectly to mean "a long time." It is actually a term used in astronomy. A "light year" is the *distance* travelled by light in a 12-month period.

Another common practice is to use the phrase "to come full circle" —which obviously implies returning to one's original starting point—in mistake for another metaphor, "to turn around 180 degrees"—which means reversing one's previous stance and now going in the opposite direction.

Again, the mathematical term "lowest common denominator" is often used when speaking of the *highest* level of taste, etc., found among all the members of some target audience.

Some metaphors periodically get misquoted—for example, "to have a hard *row* to hoe" is sometimes rendered as the meaningless "to have a hard *road* to hoe."

Sometimes the popular meaning of a phrase acquires a different emphasis from that intended by the classical author. For example, "to be an albatross around someone's neck," from Samuel Taylor Coleridge's *Rime of the Ancient Mariner,* now usually means "to be a great burden from which one cannot easily escape.'' The original overtones of doom and the earlier meaning of the phrase, ''a source of bad luck,'' rarely apply nowadays.

WORDS ARE FUN!

Technically speaking, the phrase ''a rose by any other name would smell as sweet''—actually, another quotation from Shakespeare, this time from *Romeo and Juliet*—is not a metaphor. Clearly, the statement is literally true. However, speakers using it would not be referring to roses, or to smelling, or to sweetness. The phrase taken as a whole is clearly much more powerful than its separate components might suggest.

Finally, another curiosity. Sometimes an interesting reversal of the normal pattern occurs. A humorous effect can be achieved by actually employing a commonly-used figurative expression in its literal sense, as in the caption to an amusing press photograph published recently. This showed two policemen exchanging their official headgear with two pretty female party-goers wearing Mickey Mouse hats. The imaginative caption was ''If the cap fits . . .''

Words are fascinating and their study can be fun. Metaphors can almost be regarded as an art form. Readers who may never have become aware of the multitude of metaphorical usages even in their own speech will find, it is hoped, the analysis and examples in this book both entertaining and instructive.

7

SOME GRAMMATICAL ASPECTS

Terminological inexactitude

Winston Churchill

And torture one poor word ten thousand ways

John Dryden *(Mac Flicknoe)*

GRAMMATICAL FORM OF THE METAPHOR

Metaphors can take a great variety of different grammatical forms, including nouns by themselves—for example, "a figurehead," "a honeymoon"; nouns qualified by adjectives—"a round robin," "a lame dog"; adjectives by themselves—"apocryphal," "ham-fisted"; and adjectival phrases—"off the cuff," "for the long haul."

Nouns qualified by adjectival phrases with or without other adjectives are relatively common—"an ocean full of fish," "the other side of the coin," "a knight in shining armor," "a share of the cake," "a trap for young players," and so on.

A few metaphors are adverbial phrases—"with a heavy heart," "with a flourish of trumpets"; or adverbial clauses—"when the chips are down," "when it comes to the crunch," "when one's ship comes in."

Some metaphors are mini-sentences—"his name is mud," "there is no such animal"; exclamations—"chalk it up!," "tell it to the marines!"; or even questions—"just what is his game?," "were your ears burning?"

Some sentences start with the indefinite pronoun "it"—"it takes two to tango," "it will all come out in the wash."

A number of metaphors are direct conditional statements—"if the cap fits, then wear it," "if the mountain will not go to Mahomet, then Mahomet will go to the mountain." Others merely imply conditions—"first in, best dressed," "love me, love my dog."

About 70 per cent of all the expressions listed commence with a verb, although it can be argued in some cases that only the words following the infinitive comprise the real metaphor. Metaphors can involve a verb by itself—"to ruminate," "to pan out"; a verb with a noun or an adjective as a complement—"to be a tonic," "to be kosher"; a verb with an object—"to throw a long shadow," "to trump a person," "to beard the lion in his den"; a verb modified by an adverb or an adverbial phrase—"to ebb away," "to be in hand"; and so on.

Sometimes only the passive voice gives an idiomatic expression—for example, "to be cheesed off."

The phrase "to give the devil his due" is different again. It exists only in the infinitive and can be used only in parenthesis, as in: "To give the devil his due, John was always loyal."

There are really no limits to the grammatical forms which a metaphor can take. Furthermore, no logical rules govern this aspect.

PRINCIPLES USED IN THE LISTINGS

Where the infinitive is shown in the listings, all forms of the verb concerned are normally usable except where specifically stated otherwise—for example, "to rest on one's laurels" extends to "he rested on his laurels," "are you just going to rest on your laurels?," and so on. On occasions, however, an expression involving a verb exists in a more restricted way, such as "I could eat a horse," which is used mainly in the first person, or the near slang "join the club!," which is found only in the imperative mood. In such cases the listings show the commonly-used form of the metaphor.

Nouns shown with either the definite or the indefinite article in the listings are usually encountered only in that form.

No attempt has been made to correct the language of ungrammatical or inelegant expressions in popular use—for example, "fast and furious" (when used as an adverb) or "this is nothing to write home about."

METAPHORS INVOLVING A CHANGE TO THE PART OF SPEECH

Some expressions are based on nouns when used literally but on verbs when used figuratively, as in "a white ant" and "to white ant someone" respectively.

Other examples of this phenomenon include the following:

"to snowball"
"to pinpoint"
"to cave in"

"to earmark"
"to rubber stamp"
"to grandstand"
"to mushroom"
"to spearhead" and
"to mothball."

Some examples of phrases which moved in the reverse direction, namely, verbs when used literally and nouns when used figuratively, are as follows:

"a breakthrough"
"a standstill" and
"a walkover."

VERBS REQUIRING SPECIAL SUBJECTS

Some verbs used as metaphors can be combined with only a narrow range of nouns as their subjects in their figurative applications. For example:

only a *price* or a *value* can "skyrocket"
only a *telephone* or some similar piece of equipment can "run hot"
only *alleged facts* can be "taken at face value"
only an *unpleasant incident* can "come back to haunt a person"
only a *joke* or a *funny story* can "fall flat"
only an *argument* can be "shot to ribbons" and
only *information* can be brought "out into the open."

Again, only the participants in some contest such as an election can be said to be "running neck and neck."

THE USE OF QUOTATION MARKS

The metaphors listed in this book can, generally speaking, be regarded as perfectly respectable. As mentioned in Chapter 1, they are therefore not usually written inside quotation marks. Such punctuation would not really be appropriate, as it would indicate to readers either that the author felt guilty and apologetic about the use of the expression (in the case of slang) or that he was feeling particularly proud of himself for having invented something brilliant and wanted to draw special attention to it.

IDIOMS

Outside the scope of this book are a large number of colorful idioms which represent the literal truth—picturesque expressions such as "this is not the end of the world" (you will get over this setback), "he does not wear horns" (he is much more like you than you expect), "you should practice what you preach" (you should do yourself what you tell others to do) and "you got it in one" (your first hypothesis, as just enunciated, is correct).

SYNECDOCHE

In some metaphors the abstract is treated as though it were the concrete, as when a proposal is "thrown out of the window" or "swept under the carpet" or "taken with a grain of salt." Again, one can "pour cold water" on an idea or "knock it on the head."

A person can "come to grips" with a problem, "bare" his soul, "unveil" a plan, "eat" his words or know something "inside out."

Such phrases are further examples of the figure of speech called *synecdoche*.

PERSONIFICATION

Other metaphors involve *personification,* for instance, "to break the back" of a task, a "glaring error" and "the kiss of death."

Again, the solution to a problem can "stare someone in the face."

HYPERBOLE

The expression "light years" is both a metaphor and a *hyperbole*. It can legitimately be used to mean "a great distance." However, it is also frequently used—quite incorrectly, as it happens—in the sense of "a long time."

On the other hand, "breathing space," despite appearances, does refer to an interval of time.

The expression "if I've told you once I've told you a thousand times" also involves a hyperbole.

Some metaphors comprise deliberate oversimplifications or understatements, as "to dot the *i*'s and cross the *t*'s" and "to turn an honest penny."

IRONY

Some metaphors involve elements of *irony*—for example, ''deafening silence'' and ''people stayed away in droves.''

It is also possible to invent metaphors in order to be ironical. For instance, a copper coin tendered in mistake for a silver coin can be described as being ''rather sunburnt.''

PART II

8

DICTIONARY

A

A *from a to z*
from start to finish

A1 *to be A1 at Lloyd's*
to be in perfect order (refers to the classification of ships in Lloyd's register in London)

ABANDON *to abandon ship*
to abrogate one's responsibilities or to abandon a project

ABOUT *to do an about-face*
to reverse a previously enunciated policy

ABYSS *to be close to the abyss*
to face imminent total destruction

ACE *to be within an ace of something*
to be extremely close to something

ACE *to have an ace up one's sleeve*
to hold an impressive counter-argument in reserve

ACE *to hold all the aces*
to be in an unbeatable position to defeat others

ACHE *heartache*
sadness

ACHILLES *to be someone's Achilles' heel*
to represent a weakness in an otherwise strong position (refers to the Greek warrior who was the hero of Homer's ILIAD)

ACID *to be the acid test*
to establish something beyond doubt

ACID *to put the acid on someone*
to make demands on a person

ACORN *tall oaks from little acorns grow*
even major enterprises have to have small beginnings (from "Lines written for a School Declamation" by David Everett)

ACT *to act out a charade*
ostentatiously to pretend to be doing something in an ethical fashion

ACT *to be a hard act to follow*
to be an impressive performance, not easily matched by the next person

ACT *to clean up one's act*
to fix up the deficiencies in one's affairs

ACT *to get in on the act*
to participate in some activity started by others

ACT *to get one's act together*
to organize one's activities so as to make them efficient

ACT *to read the Riot Act*
to reprimand persons who are excessively noisy (refers to the police reading out to a rowdy crowd extracts from a law requiring its dispersement)

ACTION *to have a piece of the action*
to be one of several parties to a project

ADAM *not to know someone from Adam*
to be unable to recognize a person

ADAM *since Adam was a boy*
for a very long time

ADD *it adds up*
it makes sense

ADD *that takes on added color*
there are now further facts which alter the appearance of a matter

ADD *to add apples to oranges*
to quite illogically lump unconnected things together

ADD *to add fuel to the fire*
to make a bad situation worse

ADRIFT *to come adrift*
(of a plan) not to work out as intended

ADVOCATE *to act as a devil's advocate*
to put a point of view which one does not hold in order to draw out the best arguments regarding a proposition (refers to a church official vetting a candidate for sainthood)

AFLOAT *to stay afloat*
to remain solvent

AGAINST *to swim against the tide*
to take up a minority position

AHEAD *full bore ahead!*
proceed forward!

AHEAD *full steam ahead!*
get going as fast as possible!

AHEAD *to be ahead of the field*
to be better than one's competitors

AID *a band aid*
help which is superficial or ephemeral rather than substantial or permanent

AIR *a castle in the air*
an impracticable proposition

AIR *a feeling in the air*
a premonition held by many people

AIR *to be a breath of fresh air*
to be a pleasant change from the past

AIR *to be full of hot air*
to have an exaggerated opinion of one's own importance and to boast about it

AIR *to clear the air*
to remove any possible misunderstandings

AIR *to have too many balls in the air*
to attempt to do more than can be coped with

AIR *to leave something up in the air*
to continue with an unresolved problem

AIR *to pluck figures out of the air*
to just make figures up arbitrarily

AIR *to produce something out of thin air*
to get hold of something in circumstances where this seemed impossible

AIR *to put on airs and graces*
to act in an affected manner

AIR *to throw one's cap into the air*
to celebrate some achievement

AIR *to throw one's hat into the air*
to express joy

AIR *to vanish into thin air*
unexpectedly to disappear

AIR *to walk on air*
to be joyful

AISLE *to have an audience rolling in the aisles*
to amuse an audience

ALADDIN *an Aladdin's cave*
a place full of unexpected treasure

ALARM *the alarm bells are ringing*
It is unwise to proceed

ALARM *to sound alarm bells*
to give warning

ALBATROSS *to be an albatross around someone's neck*
to be a great burden (popularized by Coleridge's ANCIENT MARINER)

ALEC *to be a smart Alec*
to give witty but cheeky responses to one's superiors or customers

ALIVE *to be alive and kicking*
to be in good form

ALIVE *to eat someone alive*
to soundly defeat a person

ALL *I would not do so-and-so for all the tea in China*
I will never do so-and-so

ALL *a Jack of all trades*
an amateur who can turn his hand to anything

ALL *all hands on deck*
everybody is requested to help out

ALL *all hands to the pumps*
everybody is requested to help out

ALL *all hell broke loose*
great confusion erupted

ALL *all his Christmases came at once*
he was overjoyed

ALL *all roads lead to Rome*
all alternatives will have the same outcome

ALL *all that glitters is not gold*
things are not always what they seem

ALL *all the dogs are barking*
this news is being widely disseminated

ALL *it is all grist to the mill*
this is useful but unexciting additional material

ALL *it will all come out in the wash*
the facts will emerge as work proceeds

ALL *not to be all beer and skittles*
not to be all pleasant and easy

ALL *not to put all one's eggs in one basket*
to spread one's risks

ALL *someone's fingers are all thumbs*
a person is clumsy with his hands

ALL *to all sing from the same hymnal*
to act consistently with each other

ALL *to be all ears*
to be very attentive

ALL *to be all eyes*
to observe very closely

ALL *to be all over but the shouting*
to be virtually finished

ALL *to be all systems "go"*
to go ahead as fast as possible

ALL *to be all that it is cracked up to be*
to be as good as the claims made for something

ALL *to be all washed out*
to feel feeble

ALL *to compete on all fours with someone*
to strive on equal terms

ALL *to get the worst of all worlds*
to get a series of disadvantages without achieving any corresponding advantages

ALL *to hold all the aces*
to be in an unbeatable position to defeat others

ALL *to hold all the cards*
to be assured of victory

ALL *to laugh all the way to the bank*
to appreciate one's good fortune

ALL *to let it all hang out*
to unburden oneself

ALL *to pull out all stops*
to make maximum effort

ALL *to spark on all cylinders*
to work extremely well

ALL *to walk all over someone*
to act in a way which completely disregards another person's sensibility

ALL *to want to jump all one's fences at once*
to be unrealistic

ALL *warts and all*
with the unfavorable features as well as the favorable ones (Oliver Cromwell's direction to an artist painting his portrait)

ALLEY *to be up one's alley*
to be right within a person's expertise or area of interest

ALLEY *to rush into a blind alley*
to make a precipitate move which does not lead one anywhere

ALLIANCE *an unholy alliance*
a working relationship for a nefarious purpose between unlikely partners

ALPHA *from alpha to omega*
from start to finish (refers to the first and last letters of the Greek alphabet)

ALTAR *to sacrifice something on the altar of some belief*
to give up some benefit as a matter of principle

AMENDMENT *to plead the Fifth Amendment*
to refuse to answer an unwelcome question (refers to the Fifth Amendment of the United States Constitution, which provides protection against self-incrimination)

AMMUNITION *ammunition*
arguments helpful to a case

ANCHOR *the sheet anchor*
the source of one's confidence

ANCHOR *to anchor*
to fix firmly

ANCHOR *to weigh anchor*
to move to another address

AND *neck and neck*
(of contestants) with little between them

ANGEL *a fallen angel*
a previously trusted person who has transgressed

ANGEL *fools rush in where angels fear to tread*
unsophisticated persons take unwise risks in circumstances where more knowledgeable persons would exercise caution

ANGEL *someone's guardian angel*
someone's friend, watching over him and advancing his interests

ANGEL *to be an angel*
to be very helpful

ANGEL *to be no angel*
to have a great many serious faults

ANGEL *to be on the side of the angels*
to be on the side of righteousness (from a speech by Benjamin Disraeli)

ANIMAL *there is no such animal*
that does not exist

ANIMAL *to be a political animal*
to want to be in politics

ANOINT *the anointed one*
the desired successor

ANSWER *the answer to a maiden's prayer*
an unexpected but very welcome happening

ANT *to white ant someone*
to surreptitiously seek to destroy a person

ANTEDILUVIAN *antediluvian*
very outmoded (lit., "before the Flood")

APART *to be miles apart*
to have great philosophical differences

APART *to be poles apart*
to have ideas which are very different

APART *to drift apart*
to lose contact or to change feelings once held in common

APART *to tear someone apart*
to ruthlessly destroy another person's case

APOCRYPHAL *apocryphal*
fictitious but resembling truth and illustrating a point (refers to certain Old Testament books included in only some versions of the Bible)

APOLOGY *to be an apology for something*
to be a poor substitute for something

APPETITE *to whet one's appetite*
to arouse one's curiosity or interest

APPLE *a rotten apple*
an isolated dishonest person in an otherwise honest group

APPLE *in apple pie order*
in perfect order and condition

APPLE *to add apples to oranges*
to quite illogically lump unconnected things together

APPLE *to be the apple of someone's eye*
to be a person of whom another person is proud

APPLECART *to upset the applecart*
to engage in conduct disturbing a peaceful state of affairs and thereby cause discomfort

APPLY *to apply the blowtorch to something*
to totally destroy something

APRON *to be tied to someone's apron strings*
to be excessively influenced by a female

ARCHITECT *to be the architect of something*
to be the person devising something innovative

AREA *to be a gray area*
to be in an undefined position straddling two or more possibilities

ARM *I would give my right arm for something*
I am very keen to acquire something

ARM *a shot in the arm*
something to revive a person's enthusiasm

ARM *at arm's length*
between parties who are strangers bearing no special duty to each other and who have no financial or other relationship with each other (a legal term)

ARM *to be armed to the teeth*
to carry many weapons

ARM *to chance one's arm*
to take a great risk (refers to the stripes on the uniforms of non-commissioned officers)

ARM *to cost an arm and a leg*
to be excessively expensive

ARM *to have a long arm*
to have far-reaching power

ARM *to lose one's right arm*
to lose some highly-valued assistance

ARM *to twist someone's arm*
to coerce another person to do something against his will or better judgement

ARM *with open arms*
enthusiastically

ARMCHAIR *to get an armchair ride*
to be given a particularly easy time

ARMOR *a chink in someone's armor*
an opportunity to take advantage of a weakness

ARMOR *a knight in shining armor*
a very helpful person, who is also gallant and idealized

ARMPIT *to be in something up to one's armpits*
to be very deeply involved in something

ARMS *to be up in arms against something*
to express violent opposition to a proposal

AROUND *to get around some difficulty*
to use an approach which overcomes some difficulty

AROUND *to get around someone*
to induce a person to do as one wishes

ARROW *another arrow in one's quiver*
an additional reason

ART *to raise something to a fine art form*
to become very clever at doing something

ARTHUR *I don't know whether I'm Arthur or Martha*
I haven't time to think

ARTICLE *an article of faith*
a fundamental belief on which certain behavior is based

ASCERTAIN *to ascertain the lay of the land*
to establish the pertinent facts and opinions

ASHES *to rise from the ashes like a Phoenix*
to be the replacement for something destroyed in some disaster (refers to a mythical bird which was supposed to rise from the ashes of its funeral pyre with renewed youth)

ASHES *to wear sackcloth and ashes*
humbly to demonstrate repentance

ASK *someone asked for it*
a person deserves his fate

ASS *to make an ass of oneself*
to act stupidly in public

ATMOSPHERE *atmosphere*
psychological environment

ATMOSPHERE *in a rarefied atmosphere*
in ignorance of the real world

ATTACH *to have strings attached*
to be subject to conditions

AUNT *an Aunt Sally*
a person who can readily be singled out and criticized as the proxy for a group

AVALANCHE *avalanche*
a great volume manifesting itself in a short time

AVENUE *avenue*
method of approach

AWASH *to be awash with something*
to have plenty of something

AWAY *to be carried away*
to be excited by something imaginative

AWAY *to be unable to keep people away with a big stick*
to be faced with a large crowd or much demand

AWAY *when the cat is away the mice will play*
in the absence of supervision discipline will be lax

AX *an old battle-ax*
a formidable, quarrelsome and hostile woman

AX *the ax has fallen*
it is now too late

AX *to ax*
to cancel

AX *to have an ax to grind*
to have a vested interest; to bear a resentment or a grudge

AX *to sharpen one's ax*
to get ready for a difficult task

AX *where the ax falls*
who gets terminated

B

BABE *out of the mouths of babes*
(as indiscreetly revealed) the truth

BABE *to be babes in the wood*
to be excessively naive and inexperienced and thus ripe for exploitation

BABEL *a tower of Babel*
a noisy and confused assembly (Genesis 11)

BABY *to be left holding the baby*
to be tricked into accepting responsibility for someone else's problems

BABY *to be one's baby*
to be one's area of responsibility

BABY *to throw out the baby with the bathwater*
to discard a major benefit in the course of obtaining a comparatively minor advantage

BACK *a backseat driver*
a person seeking to exercise control

BACK *a thought in the back of one's mind*
an undeveloped idea

BACK *as soon as someone's back was turned*
at the moment it became possible to do something without a person's knowledge

BACK *back-breaking*
overburdening

BACK *behind someone's back*
in a way which deliberately conceals an activity from a person

BACK *feedback*
response from a target audience to those seeking to influence it

BACK *it fell off the back of a truck*
(of goods) they were stolen; (of a politically sensitive document) it was leaked to me

BACK *on the back of something*
by virtue of something

BACK *put your back into it!*
work energetically!

BACK *so-and-so would give one the shirt off his back*
so-and-so is very generous

BACK *something is on the back burner*
consideration is postponed pending further research

BACK *the straw which broke the camel's back*
the latest step, which, when added to a large number of seemingly harmless previous steps, sets off a disaster resulting from the cumulative effect

BACK *through the back door*
unofficially or surreptitiously

BACK *to backpedal*
to reverse to some extent previously applied policies

BACK *to back someone into a corner*
to drive a person into a position from which escape is difficult

BACK *to back the wrong horse*
to have faith in, give support to and/or invest in a project which proves to be unsuccessful

BACK *to be able to do something with one hand behind one's back*
to be able to do something very easily

BACK *to be back on deck*
to have returned after an absence

BACK *to be back to scratch*
to have to start all over again

BACK *to be fed up to the back teeth*
to be disgusted

BACK *to be like water off a duck's back*
(of advice or criticism) to be completely rejected

BACK *to break the back of a task*
to complete the bulk of the work

BACK *to bring someone back to the pack*
to make a person conform

BACK *to cover one's back*
to take precautions

BACK *to engage in back biting*
to criticize in an unfriendly manner

BACK *to get back on one's feet*
to recover from an illness or some other setback

BACK *to get off someone's back*
to leave a person alone to carry on without constant criticism

BACK *to get one's own back on someone*
to extract revenge

BACK *to get someone's back up*
to annoy or antagonize a person

BACK *to go back to square one*
to start all over again

BACK *to have eyes at the back of one's head*
to know more of what is going on than is generally realized

BACK *to have one's back to the wall*
to be hard-pressed by creditors or opponents

BACK *to make a rod for one's own back*
to act in disregard of likely disadvantages for oneself

BACK *to need to watch one's back*
to find it necessary to take care in case others act against one's interests

BACK *to pat oneself on the back*
immodestly to congratulate oneself

BACK *to pat someone on the back*
to congratulate a person or to reassure a person

BACK *to put one's back into something*
to work hard at achieving some goal

BACK *to put someone back in his box*
to make it clear to a person that his views are not welcome

BACK *to put someone back in his place*
to make it clear to a person that he should not continue to act as though he had greater seniority than he really has

BACK *to put someone on the back foot*
to cause a person to adopt a lower profile

BACK *to put something back on its feet*
to repair something

BACK *to ride on the back of someone*
without effort to benefit from the prior efforts of others

BACK *to scratch one another's backs*
to help each other

BACK *to see the back of someone*
to know that a person is no longer involved in something

BACK *to stab someone in the back*
to deliberately and surreptitiously harm a person who regarded one as a friend

BACK *to take a backseat*
not to actively involve oneself

BACK *to tie someone's hands behind his back*
to make it impossible for a person to act at all

BACK *to turn back the clock*
to have another opportunity to do something which should have been done already or to undo something which cannot be undone

BACK *to turn one's back on someone*
to decline to further assist or deal with a person

BACKBONE *backbone*
chief strength or character

BACKFIRE *to backfire*
to be counterproductive

BACKGROUND *background information*
supplementary information relating to some matter which enables the main information to be seen in context and understood better

BACKGROUND *one's background*
the environment in which one grew up

BACKHANDED *a backhanded compliment*
a polite expression seemingly of praise but really intended as an insult

BACKLASH *a backlash*
adverse reaction to some move

BACKROOM *a backroom boy*
an expert unable to communicate effectively with the lay public

BACKWARD *to bend over backward to do something*
to go to great trouble to accommodate another person's wishes

BACKWARD *to take a step backward*
to move farther away from one's goal

BACKWASH *backwash*
consequence

BACKWATER *a backwater*
a place of little activity

BACKYARD *in one's own backyard*
in one's own domain

BACON *to bring home the bacon*
to be successful

BACON *to save one's bacon*
to escape harm

BAD *to give a dog a bad name*
to malign a person

BAD *to make bad blood between two parties*
to cause ill feeling between two parties

BAD *to throw good money after bad*
to waste further money in a vain attempt to recover money already lost

BAG *a mixed bag*
some advantages and some disadvantages

BAG *a whole bag of tricks*
a series of articles or a series of artificial devices

BAG *it is in the bag*
the enterprise has succeeded

BAG *to let the cat out of the bag*
to reveal an embarrassing secret (refers to the exposure of cheats at fairs, attempting to pass a cat wrapped in a sack off as a piglet)

BAG *to pack one's bags*
to signal one's intention to depart

BAG *yes sir—yes sir—three bags full!*
(in servile response to some request) yes, very willingly!

BAIL *to bail someone out*
to render assistance to someone unable to help himself

BAIL *to bail out of something*
to abandon an enterprise in anticipation of disaster

BAILIWICK *to be in someone's bailiwick*
to be some other person's responsibility

BAIT *to swallow the bait*
to succumb to a temptation deliberately put in one's way

BAKE *half-baked*
not well thought out

BALANCE *to balance the books*
to get one's own back

BALANCE *to balance the picture*
to put the other side of the story or to quote facts in contradiction

BALANCE *to tip the balance*
to provide further information or argument which results in an issue, which could have been decided either way, being determined in a particular way

BALANCE *to weigh two alternative propositions in the balance*
to assess the relative significance of two alternative propositions

BALL *a crystal ball*
accurate knowledge of the future

BALL *the ball is in someone's court*
it is some other person's responsibility

BALL *to be a new ball game*
to be subject to completely revised rules or very different conditions

BALL *to be in the right ballpark*
to be approximately correct

BALL *to be line ball*
to be equal

BALL *to be on the ball*
to be fully informed

BALL *to be right behind the eight ball*
to be in a position of extreme disadvantage

BALL *to blackball someone*
to reject a person as unsuitable

BALL *to have a ball*
to have an enjoyable time

BALL *to have the ball at one's feet*
to have unlimited opportunity

BALL *to have too many balls in the air*
to attempt to do more than can be coped with

BALL *to keep an eye on the ball*
to monitor a fast-changing situation

BALL *to keep the ball rolling*
to take advantage of the existing momentum or to participate actively

BALL *to keep up with the ball*
to stay on top of the situation

BALL *to pass the ball along*
to cooperate with others

BALL *to play ball*
to cooperate

BALL *to run with the ball*
to make the most of the opportunity

BALL *to start the ball rolling*
to commence and enthusiastically advance an activity involving people

BALL *to take one's bat and ball home*
as a gesture of spite to remove an essential ingredient which one has contributed to a joint enterprise

BALLOON *to go down like a lead balloon*
to receive a very cool reception

BALLOON *when the balloon goes up*
when the adverse facts come to light

BANANA *a banana republic*
a country with a poor economy

BAND *a band aid*
help which is superficial or ephemeral rather than substantial or permanent

BAND *a one-man band*
a person performing many different roles single-handedly

BANDWAGON *to hop onto the bandwagon*
to join the majority (the antonym of "bandwagon effect" is "underdog effect")

BANDY *to bandy something about*
to discuss something in a light-hearted manner

BANG *a big bang*
a sudden major change in the environment

BANG *to bang one's head up against a brick wall*
to fight an unwinnable case

BANG *to finish with a bang*
to conclude something in grand style

BANK *to laugh all the way to the bank*
to appreciate one's good fortune

BANKRUPT *to be bankrupt of ideas*
to be bereft of ideas

BAPTISM *a baptism of fire*
the commencement of an operation which presented great difficulty

BAR *no holds barred*
without any limitation

BAR *not to have a bar of something*
to be totally opposed to something

BARE *the bare bones*
(of a story) nothing but the essential elements

BARE *the cupboard is bare*
the wished-for resources are just not available

BARE *to bare one's soul*
talkatively to give a revealing insight into oneself

BARE *to bare one's teeth*
to imply threats

BAREFACED *barefaced*
shameless

BARGAIN *bargaining chips*
benefits which can be conceded in negotiations in order to obtain some advantage

BARGAIN *to be more than one bargained for*
to be more than one expected

BARK *all the dogs are barking*
this news is being widely disseminated

BARK *someone's bark is worse than his bite*
the harsh words belie the reality of mild action

BARK *to bark up the wrong tree*
to reach an incorrect conclusion

BARK *why keep a dog and bark oneself?*
it is silly to pay for assistance and then do things personally

BARN *to barnstorm*
to visit accompanied by a show of force

BARREL *a barrelful of something*
many of something

BARREL *lock, stock and barrel*
entirely

BARREL *to have someone over a barrel*
to take advantage of someone's weakened position in relation to oneself

BARREL *to look down the barrel of a gun*
to be given little choice in a matter

BARREL *to pork barrel*
to spend taxpayers' money in one area in order to attract political support

BARREL *to really scrape the bottom of the barrel*
to lower one's standards because one is short of important or relevant issues

BARREL *with both barrels blazing*
with great intensity

BARRICADE *to go to the barricades for something*
to very strongly believe in something

BARRIER *to break down the barriers*
to do away with the prejudice preventing something

BARROW *to push a barrow*
to promote a particular cause

BASE *to get to first base*
to succeed in getting others to start comprehending a problem

BASH *a bible basher*
a person who makes unwelcome attempts to force his religious beliefs on others

BASKET *a basket case*
a poorly-performing enterprise

BASKET *not to put all one's eggs in one basket*
to spread one's risks

BASKET *to put something into the "too hard" basket*
to defer consideration of a difficult issue

BASTARD *a bastard*
an unpleasant person

BASTION *the last bastion*
the only remaining defensive measure

BAT *not to bat an eyelid*
to fail to express any surprise

BAT *off one's own bat*
on a person's own initiative and without outside help

BAT *to go to bat for someone*
to carry out a task on another person's behalf

BAT *to have bats in the belfry*
to be mad

BAT *to maintain a straight bat*
to be efficient

BAT *to open the batting*
to be the first in a series of persons speaking or doing something

BAT *to take one's bat and ball home*
as a gesture of spite to remove an essential ingredient which one has contributed to a joint enterprise

BATED *to wait with bated breath*
to be excited in anticipation of some event

BATH *a bloodbath*
catastrophic losses

BATH *to give someone a bath*
to dramatically defeat a person

BATHWATER *to throw out the baby with the bathwater*
to discard a major benefit in the course of obtaining a comparatively minor advantage

BATON *to have a field marshal's baton in one's kit*
to be ambitious

BATTEN *to batten down the hatches*
to get ready for expected difficulties

BATTERY *to recharge one's batteries*
to have a recuperative break

BATTLE *a battle royal*
a fight or argument with many simultaneous participants

BATTLE *an old battle-ax*
a formidable, quarrelsome and hostile woman

BATTLE *to fight an uphill battle*
to face difficulties or to have formidable opposition

BATTLESHIP *enough to sink a battleship*
more than sufficient

BAY *to hold someone at bay*
to successfully resist an attacker

BAY *to keep the jackals at bay*
to pay one's creditors just sufficient to avoid repercussions

BAY *to set the hounds baying*
to excite the gossips by providing material which they can use

BE *to be kosher*
to fulfill all requirements (refers to food complying with all aspects of Jewish religious law)

BEACH *not to be the only pebble on the beach*
not to be the only available person

BEADLEDOM *beadledom*
stupid officiousness

BEADY *to have one's beady eyes on something*
to await the chance to acquire something to which one is not properly entitled

BEAK *to be a sticky beak*
to show excessive curiosity into matters not of one's concern

BEAM *to be off beam*
to be mistaken

BEAN *not to have a bean*
to have no money

BEAN *not to matter a row of beans*
to be utterly unimportant

BEAN *to be full of beans*
to be very cheerful

BEAN *to know how many beans make five*
to have common sense

BEAN *to spill the beans*
to indiscreetly reveal sensitive information

BEAR *I fear the Greeks even when they bear gifts*
I am suspicious of generous behavior from traditional opponents (from Virgil's AENEID, in reference to the Trojan horse)

BEAR *not to have been born yesterday*
not to be naive

BEAR *to be a cross which one has to bear*
to be a difficulty which one has to endure

BEAR *to be born on the wrong side of the blanket*
to be illegitimate

BEAR *to be born with a silver spoon in one's mouth*
to be brought up by wealthy parents

BEAR *to bear fruit*
to result in success

BEAR *to grin and bear it*
to suffer adversity cheerfully

BEARD *to beard the lion in his den*
to visit someone important at his headquarters

BEARER *a standard bearer*
a highly visible activist for a cause

BEAST *the nature of the beast*
the reality of the situation

BEAT *any stick to beat a dog*
any excuse will do if it serves one's purpose

BEAT *not to miss a beat*
to carry on without the slightest interruption

BEAT *one can't beat City Hall*
the ordinary citizen is powerless against bureaucracy

BEAT *to beat a drum for someone*
to propagate another person's cause

BEAT *to beat a retreat*
to abandon some project

BEAT *to beat about the bush*
to hide the unpleasant truth

BEAT *to beat by a long shot*
to defeat very convincingly

BEAT *to beat each other over the head*
to be always fighting

BEAT *to beat one's breast*
to express sorrow

BEAT *to beat one's drum*
to immodestly publicize one's own attributes

BEAT *to beat someone at his own game*
to outwit a person in his own specialization

BEAT *to beat someone to the punch*
to get to some objective ahead of some keen rival

BEAT *to beat the odds*
to do better than could reasonably have been expected

BEATEN *to be off the beaten track*
to do unconventional things

BEAUTY *beauty is in the eye of the beholder*
some things are matters for subjective judgments

BEAVER *an eager beaver*
a person with great drive and enthusiasm even if this causes annoyance to others

BEAVER *to beaver away*
to work diligently at some task

BED *a hotbed of crime*
a place where crime flourishes

BED *one has made one's bed and one will now have to lie on it*
one has to bear the consequences of one's actions

BED *to be no bed of roses*
to be difficult or uncomfortable

BED *to be on one's death bed*
(of an organization or a piece of equipment) to be about to cease functioning

BED *to bed something down*
to find a taker for something

BED *to get out of bed on the wrong side*
to be grumpy

BED *to jump into bed with someone*
to enter into a joint enterprise with another person

BED *to put something to bed*
to finally dispose of

BEDDING *feather bedding*
(in industrial relations) creating unnecessary jobs solely to increase employment; (in economics) assisting an inefficient industry by government grants or excessive tariff protection

BEDLAM *bedlam*
a scene of uproar (refers to the Hospital of St. Mary of Bethlehem, which was used as a lunatic asylum from 1547 onward)

BEDROCK *bedrock price*
lowest possible price

BEE *to be a busy bee*
to work with great diligence

BEE *to have a bee in one's bonnet*
to have an obsession

BEELINE *to make a beeline for something*
to go straight to something with great enthusiasm or to head for some goal by the most direct route

BEER *not to be all beer and skittles*
not to be all pleasant and easy

BEER *to be small beer*
to be quite unimportant

BEER *to cry in one's beer*
to show remorse

BEG *to beg on bended knees*
to request in great earnestness

BEGIN *charity begins at home*
a person's first responsibility should be to his family

BEHIND *behind someone's back*
in a way which deliberately conceals an activity from a person

BEHIND *to start from behind scratch*
to be faced with a handicap

BEHOLDER *beauty is in the eye of the beholder*
some things are matters for subjective judgments

BELFRY *to have bats in the belfry*
to be mad

BELL *bell-wether*
first indication

BELL *bells and whistles*
imaginative variations

BELL *right on the bell*
at the last possible moment

BELL *saved by the bell*
rescued before disaster strikes

BELL *the alarm bells are ringing*
it is unwise to proceed

BELL *to be a warning bell*
to be a warning

BELL *to bell the cat*
to do some dangerous but highly useful mission (refers to a fable in which none of the mice was willing to put a warning bell on a cat)

BELL *to ring a bell*
to sound familiar or recall something to mind

BELL *to sound alarm bells*
to give warning

BELLY *I've had a belly full*
I have had enough of this

BELLY *a fire in someone's belly*
great enthusiasm

BELOW *below the salt*
in a subordinate position (refers to the seating order at ancient Roman dining tables)

BELOW *to be below par*
to be less than the desired standard

BELT *to belt someone over the head*
to override someone's views or arguments

BELT *to get something under one's belt*
to achieve something

BELT *to hit someone below the belt*
to act unfairly toward another person

BELT *to tighten one's belt*
to lower one's rate of spending

BENCHMARK *a benchmark*
a standard by which something is measured

BEND *to be hell bent on something*
to be very determined to achieve something, regardless of the adverse consequences

BEND *to be round the bend*
to be crazy

BEND *to beg on bended knees*
to request in great earnestness

BEND *to bend over backward to do something*
to go to great trouble to accommodate another person's wishes

BEND *to bend the rules*
to overlook minor infractions of the rules

BERTH *to give someone a wide berth*
to go out of one's way to avoid contact with a person

BESIDE *to be beside oneself*
to be very agitated

BEST *first in best dressed*
persons acting early will do better than latecomers

BEST *to claim that something is the best thing since sliced bread*
to have an exaggerated opinion of the importance or novelty of an invention or practice

BEST *to put one's best foot forward*
to make a special effort

BEST *to want the best of both worlds*
to unreasonably desire to get some advantage without incurring a corresponding disadvantage

BET *a good bet*
a good proposition

BET *to hedge one's bets*
to take action involving a cost but which is designed to reduce the possible adverse consequences of some activity

BET *you bet!*
definitely!

BET *you can bet your life on something*
something is certain to happen

BETE *to be someone's bete noire*
to be a person whose ideas and actions cause upset and loathing in another person (French, "black beast")

BETTER *to be better than a poke in the eye with a burnt stick*
to be particularly welcome

BIBLE *a bible basher*
a person who makes unwelcome attempts to force his religious beliefs on others

BIBLE *to be the bible*
to be the authority

BIG *a big bang*
a sudden major change in the environment

BIG *a big wheel*
an important person

BIG *someone's eyes are bigger than his stomach*
a person is unrealistic

BIG *speak softly and carry a big stick*
be polite to your potential enemies but maintain an active and visible defense capability (from a speech by Theodore Roosevelt in 1901)

BIG *the big smoke*
the big city

BIG *to be a big fish in a little pond*
to be a person holding an important office but in an unimportant organization

BIG *to be too big for one's boots*
to have an unwarranted belief as to one's capabilities or status

BIG *to be too big for one's breeches*
to have an exaggerated idea of one's own importance

BIG *to be unable to keep people away with a big stick*
to be faced with a large crowd or much demand

BIG *to stand over someone with a big stick*
to intimidate a person in order to get him to act in a particular way

BIG *to wield a big stick*
to exert power

BILL *to fit the bill*
to meet all the requirements

BILL *to get a clean bill of health*
after proper investigation to be found not wanting

BIND *spellbinding*
fascinating to an audience

BIND *to bind someone hand and foot*
to completely limit a person's freedom to act

BIND *to catch someone in a bind*
to find a person in a difficulty from which he cannot readily extricate himself

BIRD *a bird in the hand is worth two in the bush*
a benefit currently available is more valuable than a seemingly much larger benefit which may or may not be achieved in the future

BIRD *a bird's-eye view*
a general overview or summary of a subject, emphasizing the major features

BIRD *a little bird told me*
I heard from an unnamable informant (Ecclesiastes 10:20)

BIRD *birds of a feather flock together*
persons of like interests gather in the same place

BIRD *that is strictly for the birds*
that is blatant and naive nonsense

BIRD *the bird has flown*
the person sought is no longer about

BIRD *the early bird gets the worm*
a person who acts ahead of others gets an advantage over them

BIRD *to be a rare bird*
to be an unusual type of individual

BIRD *to have a bird brain*
to be stupid

BIRD *to kill two birds with one stone*
to achieve a second objective in the course of achieving the first objective

BIRTH *to give birth to something*
to create or invent something

BIRTHRIGHT *to sell one's birthright for a mess of pottage*
through foolishness to exchange something of substance for something of little value (Genesis 25)

BIT *to champ at the bit*
to be impatient

BIT *to take the bit between one's teeth*
to face up to a problem

BITE *I could have bitten my tongue off*
I wish that I had not made such a hurtful remark

BITE *hard-bitten*
toughened by experience

BITE *someone's bark is worse than his bite*
the harsh words belie the reality of mild action

BITE *to be bitten*
to be swindled

BITE *to be bitten with something*
to become very enthusiastic over something

BITE *to bite*
to respond predictively to a remark designed to provoke

BITE *to bite off more than one can chew*
to be overly ambitious and thus unrealistic as to one's capabilities

BITE *to bite one's fingernails*
to anxiously await a decision

BITE *to bite one's lip*
to control one's anger

BITE *to bite someone's head off*
to rudely express displeasure at some person

BITE *to bite someone's nose off*
to speak to a person aggressively

BITE *to bite the bullet*
to face up to the difficulties of a situation

BITE *to bite the dust*
to die

BITE *to bite the hand that feeds one*
to show ingratitude

BITE *to engage in back biting*
to criticize in an unfriendly manner

BITE *to get only one bite at the cherry*
to receive no further opportunity

BITE *to have a hair of the dog that bit one*
to drink more in an attempt to overcome the effects of alcohol already consumed

BITE *to start to bite*
to start to be effective

BITTER *to be a bitter pill to swallow*
to be a great humiliation and disappointment which have to be endured

BLACK *a black hole*
an intermediate range of values producing anomalous results or a particularly obnoxious prison cell

BLACK *a black sheep*
a disreputable member of an otherwise reputable group

BLACK *in black and white*
in writing, spelling out all the details

BLACK *the pot calling the kettle black*
a person criticizing another person without realizing his own even greater shortcomings

BLACK *there are black clouds on the horizon*
bad news is expected

BLACK *things look black*
there is little hope of success or prosperity or a favorable outcome

BLACK *to be a black and white issue*
to involve very clear distinctions

BLACK *to be in someone's black books*
to be out of favor with a person

BLACK *to be in the black*
to have money

BLACK *to blackball someone*
to reject a person as unsuitable

BLACK *to give someone a black look*
to indicate one's displeasure with a person

BLACK *to have a black mark against one's name*
to have a tarnished reputation

BLACK *to paint a black picture*
to state a set of unfavorable factors

BLACK *to paint someone black*
to ruin a person's reputation

BLANCHE *carte blanche*
freedom to use one's discretion on behalf of another person (French, ''white card'')

BLANK *to draw a blank*
to be unsuccessful

BLANK *to give someone a blank check*
to give another person unlimited delegated authority

BLANK *to have a blank canvas*
to be bereft of ideas

BLANK *to refuse point blank*
to refuse outright

BLANK *to start with a blank sheet of paper*
to commence an exercise without being bound by any established practices

BLANKET *to be a wet blanket*
to be a spoilsport

BLANKET *to be born on the wrong side of the blanket*
to be illegitimate

BLANKET *to throw a blanket over a proposal*
to refuse to proceed with a proposal

BLAZE *to blaze a trail*
to be the first person to do something

BLAZE *with both barrels blazing*
with great intensity

BLEED *one's heart bleeds for someone*
one feels truly sad for a person's fate

BLEED *to slowly bleed to death*
to be heading in gradual steps toward total ruin

BLEEDING *to stem the hemorrhage*
to put a stop to the financial losses of a project

BLESSING *a blessing in disguise*
an unwelcome but salutary experience

BLESSING *to be a mixed blessing*
to be an outcome with some desirable and some undesirable features

BLESSING *to give one's blessing to something*
to indicate one's approval of something

BLIND *a nod is the same as a wink to a blind horse*
fine distinctions are not appropriate here

BLIND *blind Freddy could see that something is such-and-such*
it is very obvious that something is such-and-such

BLIND *the blind leading the blind*
persons without the necessary skills for a task purporting to impart those skills to others

BLIND *to be blind to something*
to be unaware of some matter and its significance

BLIND *to have a blind spot about something*
to fail to recognize the adverse aspects of something

BLIND *to rush into a blind alley*
to make a precipitate move which does not lead one anywhere

BLIND *to turn a blind eye to something*
to pretend something obvious does not exist (refers to action by Nelson when disregarding Admiralty signals)

BLINDER *to take one's blinders off*
to face reality

BLINDLY *to follow someone blindly*
to follow a person unquestioningly

BLOCK *roadblocks*
difficulties

BLOCK *someone's head is on the block*
a person is in danger of having his appointment terminated

BLOCK *stumbling block*
an impediment or difficulty preventing the easy completion of some project or a dilemma involving a moral issue

BLOCK *the cheering could be heard a block away*
there was great rejoicing

BLOCK *to be a chip off the old block*
to resemble one's father

BLOCK *to block someone's path*
to interfere with a person's opportunity to advance himself

BLOCK *to put one's head on the block*
to have the courage of one's convictions

BLOOD *a blueblood*
a person of high birth (refers to the appearance of veins on the skin of members of some royal families)

BLOOD *bad blood*
animosity

BLOOD *blood, sweat and tears*
hard work and much effort

BLOOD *bloodshed*
retribution

BLOOD *fresh blood*
newly joined members of some organization

BLOOD *full-blooded*
vigorous

BLOOD *hot-blooded*
very passionate

BLOOD *one's own flesh and blood*
one's offspring

BLOOD *the lifeblood*
the main or essential ingredient; or the person or factor instilling enthusiasm

BLOOD *there is blood in the streets*
much damage has been done to a cause

BLOOD *there is blood in the water*
something is likely to cause a person to go into a frenzy

BLOOD *there is blood on the floor*
this has caused great anguish

BLOOD *to be after someone's blood*
to be keen to make a person the victim of an angry confrontation

BLOOD *to be in someone's blood*
to be something about which a person is very knowledgeable or keen

BLOOD *to curdle one's blood*
to be horrific

BLOOD *to do something in cold blood*
to be cruel without feeling any emotion about it

BLOOD *to draw blood from a stone*
to do the impossible

BLOOD *to draw first blood*
to get an advantage

BLOOD *to give something a blood transfusion*
to give something new enthusiasm

BLOOD *to have blood on one's hands*
to be the person responsible for someone else's predicament

BLOOD *to introduce new blood*
to recruit new members to some organization

BLOOD *to let blood*
to allow some harm as the price for achieving some greater benefit

BLOOD *to make bad blood between two parties*
to cause ill feeling between two parties

BLOOD *to make someone's blood boil*
to make a person very angry

BLOOD *to see blood*
to be very angry

BLOOD *to smell blood*
to divine imminent victory

BLOOD *to thirst for blood*
to be eager for revenge

BLOODBATH *a bloodbath*
catastrophic losses

BLOODLETTING *bloodletting*
planned reductions

BLOODY *to get a bloody nose*
to suffer an undignified rebuff

BLOSSOM *to blossom*
(of a person's attributes) to develop

BLOT *to be a blot on someone's escutcheon*
to be a blemish on a person's character

BLOT *to blot one's copybook*
to spoil one's previously good reputation or record

BLOW *a blow-by-blow description*
a description overburdened by unimportant or irrelevant detail

BLOW *a body blow*
a very damaging event

BLOW *death blow*
incident which results in the destruction of something

BLOW *the affair blew up*
certain unwelcome facts have become publicly available

BLOW *to be a severe blow*
to be a great disappointment

BLOW *to blow hot and cold*
to vacillate

BLOW *to blow one's own trumpet*
to immodestly publicize one's own attributes

BLOW *to blow one's top*
to show anger (refers to a volcano)

BLOW *to blow something*
unintentionally to destroy some opportunity

BLOW *to blow something out of the water*
to destroy something

BLOW *to blow the cobwebs away*
to revive an old issue

BLOW *to blow the lid off something*
to expose something no matter how embarrassing this might be

BLOW *to blow the whistle on someone*
to report a person's improper behavior to the authorities or to publicize it

BLOW *to blow up*
(of a person) to express rage

BLOW *to blow up in someone's face*
to rebound on a person

BLOW *to get one's head blown off*
to be very soundly abused

BLOW *to see which way the wind is blowing*
to establish the factors relevant to a situation

BLOW *to soften the blow*
to take action to reduce the trauma of bad news

BLOW *to strike a blow*
to resume work

BLOW *to strike a blow for some principle*
to work toward the attainment of some principle

BLOWTORCH *to apply the blowtorch to something*
to totally destroy something

BLUE *a blueblood*
a person of high birth (refers to the appearance of veins on the skin of members of some royal families)

BLUE *between the devil and the deep blue sea*
to be faced with two equally unpalatable alternatives which cannot both be avoided

BLUE *blue ribbon*
of superb quality (refers to the insignia of the Order of the Garter)

BLUE *blue sky*
supremely optimistic

BLUE *blue-eyed boy*
person shown unjustified favoritism

BLUE *once in a blue moon*
very rarely (refers to the volcanic eruption at Krakatoa in 1883 when volcanic dust caused the moon to appear blue)

BLUE *to be a blue-chip stock*
to be of excellent quality

BLUE *to be a bolt from the blue*
to be a totally unexpected event

BLUE *to be in a blue funk*
to be terrified

BLUE *to come out of the blue*
to be totally unexpected

BLUE *to feel blue*
to feel depressed

BLUE *to go on till one is blue in the face*
to argue for a long time

BLUE *to have a blue fit*
to be very agitated

BLUE *to scream blue murder*
to make serious allegations

BLUE *true blue*
superbly loyal

BLUEPRINT *blueprint*
a master plan for some activity or a model which others can copy

BLUSH *at first blush*
prima facie

BOARD *a springboard*
a situation from which one intends to make a rapid advance

BOARD *across the board*
over the whole range of activity

BOARD *back to the drawing board*
the details need to be reconsidered

BOARD *to act as a sounding board*
to give, on request, constructive criticisms of ideas tentatively held

BOARD *to be above board*
to be quite legitimate

BOARD *to be on the drawing board*
to be in the process of being planned in detail

BOARD *to go overboard*
to act foolishly and in an excessive way

BOARD *to have the runs on the board*
to have a demonstratable record of achievement

BOARD *to pipe someone on board*
to welcome a person

BOARD *to take something on board*
to offer to give further consideration to a matter

BOARDER *to repel boarders*
to keep out unwanted persons

BOAT *to be in the same boat*
to share a common set of difficulties

BOAT *to get off the boat*
to disassociate oneself from some project

BOAT *to miss the boat*
to fail to exploit an opportunity

BOAT *to rock the boat*
to disturb the comfortable status quo

BOB *Bob's your uncle*
that solves the problem

BOB *to have two bob each way*
to equivocate

BODY *a body blow*
a very damaging event

BODY *over my dead body*
never

BODY *to keep body and soul together*
to keep alive

BOGGLE *the mind boggles*
this is astonishing

BOIL *hard-boiled*
toughened by experience

BOIL *it boils down to this*
the essential features are as follows

BOIL *to bring something to the boil*
to bring something to a climax

BOIL *to come off the boil*
to no longer require urgent attention

BOIL *to keep the pot boiling*
to ensure that an issue stays current

BOIL *to make someone's blood boil*
to make a person very angry

BOIL *to reach boiling point*
to reach a climax

BOILER *not to bust one's boiler*
not to exert oneself unduly

BOLT *nuts and bolts*
basic ingredients

BOLT *to be a bolt from the blue*
to be a totally unexpected event

BOLT *to shoot one's bolt*
to lose one's temper

BOLT *to shut the stable door after the horse has bolted*
to take preventive action only after the relevant event

BOMB *a bombshell*
an unpleasant surprise

BOMB *a time bomb*
a source of serious problems which are certain to surface later on

BOMB *to be a bomb*
to be grossly defective

BOMB *to put a bomb under someone*
to induce a person to take some action

BOMBARD *to bombard someone with something*
to overwhelm a person with material or to persistently assail a person with words of argument or abuse

BONE *a bone of contention*
the subject matter of violent disagreement

BONE *backbone*
chief strength or character

BONE *the bare bones*
(of a story) nothing but the essential elements

BONE *to cut costs to the bone*
to economize

BONE *to feel something in one's bones*
to suspect something without having any real evidence for it

BONE *to get close to the bone*
to cause discomfort by being accurate

BONE *to gnaw one's fingers to the bone*
to fret

BONE *to have a bone to pick*
to have a grievance which requires discussion

BONE *to make no bones about it*
to be brutally frank

BONE *to point the bone at someone*
to accuse a person (actually, an Australian Aboriginal method of applying a curse)

BONE *to put flesh and bone on something*
to supply details of a proposal previously revealed only in outline

BONE *to throw someone a bone*
to fob a person off with a symbolic but unimportant gesture

BONE *to work one's fingers to the bone*
to work very hard

BONEHEADED *boneheaded*
stupid

BONNET *to have a bee in one's bonnet*
to have an obsession

BOO *to be too frightened to say "boo" to a goose*
to be excessively shy

BOOBY *to win the booby prize*
to do worse than all others

BOOK *to balance the books*
to get one's own back

BOOK *to be a closed book*
to be a secret

BOOK *to be a turn up for the books*
to be a surprising development

BOOK *to be in someone's black books*
to be out of favor with a person

BOOK *to be in someone's good books*
to be well regarded by another person

BOOK *to close the book on something*
to terminate an activity

BOOK *to cook the books*
fraudulently to maintain false records of financial transactions

BOOK *to judge a book by its cover*
foolishly to go only by superficial appearances

BOOK *to play by the book*
to apply the rules strictly

BOOK *to take a leaf out of someone's book*
to model oneself on another person

BOOK *to talk one's book*
to present arguments which, while plausible, are really designed to foster one's vested interest

BOOK *to throw the book at someone*
to prosecute a person with all the vigor allowed by law

BOOK *to use every trick in the book*
to try very hard and use every conceivable argument

BOOKWORM *a bookworm*
a person who likes reading and study

BOOM *to lower the boom*
to terminate an activity

BOOT *the boot is on the other foot*
the real facts are the other way round

BOOT *to be too big for one's boots*
to have an unwarranted belief as to one's capabilities or status

BOOT *to give someone the boot*
to terminate a person's appointment

BOOT *to go in boots and all*
to do something very roughly

BOOT *to hang up one's boots*
to retire

BOOT *to have one's heart in one's boots*
to be terrified

BOOT *to lick someone's boots*
to show humility

BOOT *to put the boot in*
to reprimand a person

BOOT *to quake in one's boots*
to be afraid

BOOTSTRAP *to be British to one's bootstraps*
to be very demonstrative about one's Britishness

BOOTSTRAP *to pull oneself up by one's bootstraps*
to make a praiseworthy effort to better oneself unaided

BORE *full bore ahead!*
proceed forward!

BORE *to bore someone to death*
to greatly weary a person by dull and uninteresting conversation or by lack of action

BORE *to bore someone to tears*
to greatly weary a person by dull and uninteresting conversation or by lack of action

BORE *to bore the pants off someone*
to weary a person by dull and uninteresting conversation

BORN *not to have been born yesterday*
not to be naive

BORN *to be born on the wrong side of the blanket*
to be illegitimate

BORN *to be born with a silver spoon in one's mouth*
to be brought up by wealthy parents

BORROW *to live on borrowed time*
to live longer than expected

BOTTLE *a bottleneck*
a factor obstructing an even flow

BOTTLE *to be a full bottle on something*
to be very knowledgeable

BOTTLE *to bottle up some feeling*
to keep some feeling entirely to oneself

BOTTLE *to let the genie out of the bottle*
to cause something irreversible to take place

BOTTLE *to put the genie back in the bottle*
to undo something which cannot be undone

BOTTOM *from the bottom of one's heart*
very sincerely

BOTTOM *rock bottom*
very low

BOTTOM *the bottom line*
the conclusion which matters or the net effect of a series of developments

BOTTOM *to be at the bottom of the ladder*
to be in the most junior position in some hierarchy

BOTTOM *to be at the bottom of the totem pole*
to be in the most junior position in some hierarchy

BOTTOM *to really scrape the bottom of the barrel*
to lower one's standards because one is short of important or relevant issues

BOUNCE *to bounce back*
to resume a cheerful existence after some setback

BOUND *by leaps and bounds*
with surprisingly fast progress

BOW *shots across the bow*
warnings

BOW *to bow down*
to succumb to pressure

BOW *to bow out*
to retire from some activity

BOW *to draw a long bow*
to state a conclusion which while possible is unlikely on the known facts

BOW *to have a second string to one's bow*
to have an additional qualification appropriate to the task

BOW *to take a bow*
to receive recognition

BOWL *to be in a goldfish bowl*
to be very open to view

BOX *Box and Cox*
two persons who are never around at the same time (from the name of a play)

BOX *the whole box and dice*
all relevant components

BOX *to be in the box seat*
to be in a very powerful position to control activity

BOX *to be on one's soap box*
to hold forth on an issue about which one feels keenly

BOX *to be one out of the box*
to be unexpectedly superb

BOX *to open up a Pandora's box*
to do something which produces all sorts of undesired and unexpected side-effects (refers to the woman in Greek mythology who brought misery to mankind; the box contained human ills)

BOX *to put someone back in his box*
to make it clear to a person that his views are not welcome

BOX *to shadow box*
to go through the motions without achieving or intending to achieve anything

BOY *a backroom boy*
an expert unable to communicate effectively with the lay public

BOY *a whipping boy*
a person made to suffer for the faults of others

BOY *as every schoolboy knows*
as is recognized by everyone

BOY *blue-eyed boy*
person shown unjustified favoritism

BOY *since Adam was a boy*
for a very long time

BOY *to be a good boy*
to be cooperative

BOY *to separate the men from the boys*
to distinguish between those with and without certain skills

BRACE *to splice the main brace*
to serve an extra ration of rum

BRAIN *anyone with even half a brain*
everyone

BRAIN *hare-brained*
wildly stupid

BRAIN *someone's brain needs washing*
a person is very silly

BRAIN *to have a bird brain*
to be stupid

BRAIN *to have something on one's brain*
to be obsessed with some notion

BRAIN *to pick someone's brain*
to get the benefit of another person's knowledge and experience

BRAINCHILD *brainchild*
inspired original idea

BRAINSTORM *to brainstorm*
to pool thoughts in the course of a session designed to generate fresh ideas and especially to build upon the ideas of others

BRAINWAVE *a brainwave*
a suddenly occurring bright idea

BRAKE *to put the brake on someone*
to stop a person

BRANCH *to hold out an olive branch*
to make peace overtures (Genesis 8:11)

BRASS *not to have a brass razoo*
to be very poor

BRASS *to get down to brass tacks*
to discuss the aspects which really matter

BRAVE *to brave the water*
to enter a venture with courage and determination

BRAVE *to put a brave face on it*
to face adversity cheerfully

BREACH *once more unto the breach*
let us get on with the task (from Shakespeare's "Henry V")

BREACH *to stand in the breach*
to bear the brunt of criticisms

BREAD *a bread and butter issue*
a basic issue which is of importance to many people

BREAD *a breadwinner*
a person earning by personal exertion the income of a household

BREAD *to be someone's bread and butter*
to be a person's livelihood or to be a person's everyday experience

BREAD *to cast one's bread upon the waters*
not to expect gratitude or recognition for one's good works (Ecclesiastes 11:1)

BREAD *to claim that something is the best thing since sliced bread*
to have an exaggerated opinion of the importance or novelty of an invention or practice

BREAD *to know on which side one's bread is buttered*
to be aware of the important considerations

BREAD *to put jam on someone's bread*
to make a good situation even better

BREADTH *to be within a hair's breadth of something*
to be extremely close to something

BREAK *all hell broke loose*
great confusion erupted

BREAK *at a break-neck pace*
very fast

BREAK *back-breaking*
overburdening

BREAK *heartbreak*
despair

BREAK *not to break someone's door down*
to be quite unenthusiastic about someone's goods or services

BREAK *one cannot make an omelette without breaking eggs*
the desired end dictates the means even if they cause harm to others

BREAK *the straw which broke the camel's back*
the latest step, which, when added to a large number of seemingly harmless previous steps, sets off a disaster resulting from the cumulative effect

BREAK *to be a broken reed*
to be a weak and unreliable person

BREAK *to break a drought*
to resume supplies after an interval

BREAK *to break down the barriers*
to do away with the prejudice preventing something

BREAK *to break new ground*
to do something for which there is no precedent

BREAK *to break one's duck*
to end a spell without results

BREAK *to break one's neck to do something*
to be particularly keen

BREAK *to break ranks*
to identify oneself as having separate interests or views from the rest of a group

BREAK *to break the back of a task*
to complete the bulk of the work

BREAK *to break the ice*
to take the initiative in starting discussions

BREAK *to break the spell*
to spoil the effect

BREAK *to make or break someone*
to be a factor leading either to a person's success or to his failure, with no intermediate position

BREAKFAST *to be a dog's breakfast*
to be a very messy arrangement

BREAKFAST *to be able to eat someone for breakfast*
to be able to outwit a person very easily

BREAKTHROUGH *a breakthrough*
success in overcoming resistance to a proposal

BREAST *to beat one's breast*
to express sorrow or anger

BREAST *to make a clean breast of something*
to confess

BREATH *not to hold one's breath for something*
to give up all expectation

BREATH *to be a breath of fresh air*
to be a pleasant change from the past

BREATH *to draw a deep breath*
to get ready for exertion or for emotional news

BREATH *to take one's breath away*
to greatly surprise or astonish

BREATH *to wait with bated breath*
to be excited in anticipation of some event

BREATH *to waste one's breath*
to talk or request something without achieving anything

BREATHE *to breathe down someone's neck*
to cause annoyance to another person by remaining in his vicinity or by supervising him too closely; or to be narrowly behind another person in some competitive situation

BREATHE *to breathe easy*
(following some crisis) to relax

BREATHE *to breathe life into a corpse*
to revive something moribund

BREATHE *to get some breathing space*
to get more time in which to accomplish something

BREECHES *to be too big for one's breeches*
to have an exaggerated idea of one's own importance

BREEZE *it's a breeze*
it is easy

BRICK *it is London to a brick*
it is virtually certain

BRICK *one can't make bricks without straw*
one cannot achieve results in the absence of adequate resources

BRICK *to bang one's head up against a brick wall*
to fight an unwinnable case

BRICK *to be up against a brick wall*
to be unable to achieve anything because of intractable opposition or apathy

BRICK *to drop a brick*
to make a sudden shattering and unexpected announcement

BRICKBATS *to throw brickbats at someone*
to express displeasure with a person

BRIDGE *a lot of water has flowed under the bridge since then*
much has happened since then

BRIDGE *to be water under the bridge*
to matter no longer

BRIDGE *to bridge a gap*
to fill a need or make up a shortfall

BRIDGE *to bridge a gulf*
to overcome a wide divergence in views

BRIDGE *to build bridges*
to work at improving relationships

BRIDGE *to burn one's bridges*
to do something irreversible

BRIDGE *to cross a bridge only when one comes to it*
to await the crystallization of a situation before sorting it out

BRIDGEHEAD *a bridgehead*
an advance post set up to facilitate further access to some new market, etc.

BRIGHT *bright-eyed and bushy-tailed*
naive but enthusiastic

BRIGHT *the bright side*
the favorable aspects

BRIGHT *the one bright spot on the horizon*
the only hopeful aspect

BRING *to bring a plate*
to take food to a party

BRING *to bring someone down to earth*
to disillusion a person

BRING *to bring someone to heel*
to make a person conform

BRING *to bring something to the boil*
to bring something to a climax

BRING *to bring the house down*
to greatly amuse an audience

BRINK *to push someone over the brink*
by a small action to cause the absolute ruin (financially or emotionally) of someone already in peril

BRITISH *the very best of British luck*
you will have a hard time of it, but you carry my best wishes

BRITISH *to be British to one's bootstraps*
to be very demonstrative about one's Britishness

BROAD *a broad brush approach*
rough justice

BROAD *it is as broad as it is long*
it does not really matter

BROAD *to have broad shoulders*
to be able to cope well with responsibility

BROADEN *to broaden someone's mind*
to expose a person to a greater variety of experiences and interests than he had previously

BROADSIDE *a broadside*
a short verbal attack

BRONZE *to be cast in bronze*
to be virtually unalterable

BROOM *a new broom*
a changed regime which is likely to alter the status quo

BROTH *too many cooks spoil the broth*
one leader is all that is required

BROTHER *a soul brother*
a person of similar ideals

BROW *highbrow*
intellectual or cultural

BROW *to knit one's brows*
to indicate one's displeasure

BROWN *to be browned off*
to be fed-up

BROWNIE *to get brownie points*
to do a person a favor with the likely result that the recipient will do a favor in return in due course

BRUISE *to nurse one's bruises*
to face up to the consequences of defeat

BRUSH *a broad brush approach*
rough justice

BRUSH *to be tarred with the same brush*
to be damned merely because of one's association with another person

BRUSH *to brush someone aside*
to pass over and ostentatiously ignore a person

BRUSH *to give someone the brush-off*
to make it clear that one does not want dealings or conversation with a person

BRUSH *to have a touch of the tarbrush*
to be not quite a full-blood Caucasian

BUBBLE *a South Sea bubble*
an unrealistic financial venture which is bound to result in total loss

BUBBLE *the bubble has burst*
the inevitable has occurred or the scheme has come to ruination

BUCK *the buck stops here*
I accept full responsibility (sign on the desk of Harry S. Truman when president of the United States)

BUCK *to pass the buck*
in an uncooperative spirit to decline responsibility for a matter on the grounds that someone else more properly has responsibility for it

BUCKET *to be only a drop in the bucket*
to be quite insignificant in the total scene

BUCKET *to kick the bucket*
to die

BUCKET *to tip a bucket on someone*
to point out in a humiliating way another person's faults

BUD *to nip something in the bud*
to stop some activity in its early stages when stopping it is still relatively easy

BUGGY *the horse and buggy days*
long ago

BUILD *to build bridges*
to work at improving relationships

BUILD *to engage in empire building*
to set out to expand the size of the business or bureaucratic unit for which one is responsible, especially as a means of increasing one's own importance

BULL *a bull in a china shop*
a careless person likely to cause great damage

BULL *a cock and bull story*
an explanation which is completely unbelievable and unacceptable

BULL *to be a red rag to a bull*
to be something which makes a person very angry and very excited (refers to the erroneous belief that the color red, rather than the motion of waving, excites a bull)

BULL *to be within a bull's roar of something*
to be very close to something

BULL *to charge like a wounded bull*
to impose excessive prices (a play on words; not a simile)

BULL *to hit the bull's eye*
to make the correct decision

BULL *to take the bull by the horns*
to come to grips with the realities of a difficult problem

BULLDOZE *to bulldoze some proposal through*
to ensure the passage of some measure in complete disregard of criticism or opposition

BULLET *a gun with no bullets*
something incomplete and therefore useless for the desired purpose

BULLET *a magic bullet*
a guaranteed remedy

BULLET *to bite the bullet*
to face up to the difficulties of a situation

BULLET *to have a bullet which can be fired*
to have available an effective response which can be used at will

BUMP *to bump into someone*
to meet a person accidentally

BUN *a bunfight*
a minor and relatively friendly skirmish

BUNDLE *to drop one's bundle*
to become despondent

BUNDLE *to save a bundle*
to save much money

BURDEN *to put a burden on someone's shoulders*
to impose responsibilities on a person

BURN *burning question*
a much discussed question

BURN *heartburn*
regret at some non-achievement

BURN *to be better than a poke in the eye with a burnt stick*
to be particularly welcome

BURN *to burn one's bridges*
to do something irreversible

BURN *to burn one's fingers*
to lose money through foolishness

BURN *to burn oneself out*
to overexert oneself

BURN *to burn the candle at both ends*
to work excessively long hours

BURN *to burn the midnight oil*
to work late into the night

BURN *to fiddle while Rome burns*
to neglect important considerations while concentrating on trivial side-issues

BURN *to have money burning a hole in one's pocket*
to be impatient to spend or invest available funds

BURN *to keep the home fires burning*
to maintain normal domestic activity during the temporary absence of the breadwinner

BURN *were your ears burning?*
we were discussing you

BURNER *something is on the back burner*
consideration is postponed pending further research

BURST *the bubble has burst*
the inevitable has occurred or the scheme has come to ruination

BURST *the dam burst*
the cumulative effect of many things caused a disaster

BURST *to be bursting at the seams*
to be very crowded

BURY *dead and buried*
(of some issue) definitely concluded, especially so long ago as to be nearly forgotten

BURY *to bury one's head in the sand*
to refuse to face up to an unpleasant truth (refers to the reputed habit of ostriches in danger)

BURY *to bury the hatchet*
to abandon hostilities

BUS *the wheels are back under the bus*
normal activity has been resumed

BUS *to jump on the bus*
to join an activity already well under way

BUS *to miss the bus*
to fail to exploit an opportunity

BUSH *a bird in the hand is worth two in the bush*
a benefit currently available is more valuable than a seemingly much larger benefit which may or may not be achieved in the future

BUSH *to beat about the bush*
to hide the unpleasant truth

BUSHEL *to hide one's light under a bushel*
to keep others in ignorance of one's skills and experience

BUSHFIRE *to fight bushfires*
to deal with crises as they arise rather than take preventive action

BUSHY *bright-eyed and bushy-tailed*
naive but enthusiastic

BUSINESS *monkey business*
mischievous or underhand activity

BUSINESS *to mean business*
to demonstrate a serious intent to do something

BUSMAN *a busman's holiday*
leisure time spent in a way not significantly different from one's normal business activities

BUST *not to bust one's boiler*
not to exert oneself unduly

BUTT *to butt in*
to involve oneself uninvited in someone else's conversation

BUTT *to get up off one's butt*
to cease being apathetic

BUTTER *a bread and butter issue*
a basic issue which is of importance to many people

BUTTER *a butter fingers*
a person unable to catch and/or hold on to an object

BUTTER *someone looks as if butter would not melt in his mouth*
a person looks sweet and innocent

BUTTER *to be someone's bread and butter*
to be a person's livelihood or to be a person's everyday experience

BUTTER *to know on which side one's bread is buttered*
to be aware of the important considerations

BUTTERFLY *to have a butterfly mind*
not to concentrate on the matter on hand

BUTTERFLY *to have butterflies in one's stomach*
a feeling of anxiety

BUTTON *to button up one's purse*
to refuse to spend money

BUTTON *to hit the panic button*
to act hastily and irrationally

BUTTON *to press a button*
to make something happen

BUY *I buy that*
I accept that idea

BUY *to buy a pig in a poke*
to buy goods of unknown quality

BUY *to buy into some argument*
to seek to participate in some discussion

BUY *to buy something for a song*
to buy something very cheaply

BUY *to buy straw hats in winter*
to buy in a depressed market when most other people are sellers

BUZZ *to buzz off*
to go away

C

CAB *to be the first cab off the rank*
to start ahead of all others

CABBAGE *to be on someone's cabbage patch*
to engage in a competitive activity in a territory regarded by someone already there as rightfully belonging exclusively to him

CAIN *the mark of Cain*
disgrace (Genesis 4:15)

CAIN *to raise Cain*
to create a disturbance (Genesis 4:5)

CAKE *a share of the cake*
a portion of the total available for distribution

CAKE *that takes the cake*
that is quite absurd or outrageous or excessively cheeky

CAKE *to be a piece of cake*
to be very easy or greatly to one's liking

CAKE *to be icing on top of the cake*
to be an additional benefit in an already satisfactory scenario

CAKE *to want to have one's cake and eat it too*
to want two mutually exclusive alternatives

CALF *to kill the fatted calf*
to demonstrate welcome and forgiveness on a person's return (Luke 15:23)

CALL *he who pays the piper calls the tune*
a person contributing money or resources to a project is entitled to a say in its control

CALL *the pot calling the kettle black*
a person criticizing another person without realizing his own even greater shortcomings

CALL *to call a spade a spade*
not to mince words

CALL *to call it a day*
to cease involvement with some activity

CALL *to call off the dogs*
to abandon an audit or other inquiry

CALL *to call the shots*
to have the direction over a project

CALL *the calm before the storm*
the quiet period before an expected or inevitable crisis

CAMEL *the straw which broke the camel's back*
the latest step, which, when added to a large number of seemingly harmless previous steps, sets off a disaster resulting from the cumulative effect

CAMP *in our camp*
in the group representing our vested interest

CAMP *to have one's feet in both camps*
to have good relations with two opponents

CAN *a can of worms*
a heterogeneous collection of unexpected problems

CAN *to carry the can for someone*
to accept the blame for another person's actions or inactions

CANCER *a cancer*
an evil which is likely to spread

CANDLE *not fit to hold a candle to someone*
greatly inferior to another person

CANDLE *not to be worth the candle*
to be too expensive in relation to the true value

CANDLE *to burn the candle at both ends*
to work excessively long hours

CANE *to take a caning*
to suffer the adverse consequences of one's acts or omissions

CANNON *a loose cannon on the deck*
a mistake likely to cause trouble

CANOE *to paddle one's own canoe*
to do something unaided and in one's own way

CANTER *to win the prize in a canter*
to win very easily

CANVAS *to get off the canvas*
to recover after near defeat

CANVAS *to have a blank canvas*
to be bereft of ideas

CAP *a feather in one's cap*
a meritorious personal achievement

CAP *cap*
upper permitted limit

CAP *if the cap fits then wear it*
if your circumstances correspond with those described then you must endure the consequences

CAP *to cap a story*
to tell an even funnier story than the one just told

CAP *to earn a dunce's cap*
to do something stupid

CAP *to go cap in hand*
to show humility while soliciting a favor

CAP *to put one's thinking cap on*
to concentrate on finding a solution to a difficult problem

CAP *to set one's cap at someone*
(of females) to try to attract a person as a marriage partner

CAP *to throw one's cap into the air*
to celebrate some achievement

CARAVAN *the caravan will roll on*
the activity will continue

CARD *a house of cards*
an organization which gives a misleading impression of solidity

CARD *a three card trick*
a ruse used by a dishonest person in order to induce his victims to hand over some of their assets

CARD *a wild card*
an unexpected development

CARD *drawcard*
feature expected to attract a crowd

CARD *let the cards fall where they may*
irrespective of what happens

CARD *to be on the cards*
to be likely

CARD *to have a card up one's sleeve*
to secretly have information relevant to a transaction

CARD *to have the cards stacked against one*
to be faced with many difficulties frustrating a project

CARD *to hold all the cards*
to be assured of victory

CARD *to hold one's cards close to one's chest*
to keep one's plans and strategies secret

CARD *to hold the trump card*
to be in an unbeatable position to defeat others

CARD *to lay one's cards on the table*
to be utterly frank and open or to honestly disclose one's position

CARD *to play every card in the pack*
to try very hard and use every conceivable argument

CARD *to play one's cards right*
to approach a matter sensibly

CARD *to play the cards as they fall*
to deal with problems as they arise

CARD *to play the last card in the pack*
to lower one's standards in a final desperate effort

CARD *to play the trump card*
to make a final move, thereby defeating one's opponents

CARD *without any cards to play*
without the means to achieve something

CARE *a devil-may-care attitude*
a reckless attitude

CARE *not to care a pin for something*
not to have the slightest interest in something

CARPET *the red-carpet treatment*
courtesies extended to a person to make him feel important and welcome

CARPET *to be on the carpet*
to be lectured in regard to one's alleged misdeeds

CARPET *to get a magic carpet ride to something*
to be very fortunate in achieving some objective

CARPET *to sweep something under the carpet*
to pretend that some blemish does not exist

CARROT *sticks and carrots*
disincentives and incentives in combination (refers to the handling of donkeys)

CARRY *speak softly and carry a big stick*
be polite to your potential enemies but maintain an active and visible defense capability (from a speech by Theodore Roosevelt in 1901)

CARRY *to be carried away*
to be excited by something imaginative

CARRY *to carry a spare tire*
to be fat

CARRY *to carry a torch for someone*
to act as an enthusiastic advocate of another person's cause

CARRY *to carry coals to Newcastle*
to do something ridiculously unnecessary

CARRY *to carry the can for someone*
to accept the blame for another person's actions or inactions

CARRY *to carry the world on one's shoulders*
to resent being left to perform a huge task single-handedly (refers to Atlas, who was condemned to bear the heavens on his shoulders for leading the Titans against the gods)

CARRY *to carry weight*
to be influential

CART *to put the cart before the horse*
to do things in the wrong order

CART *to upset the applecart*
to engage in conduct disturbing a peaceful state of affairs and thereby cause discomfort

CARTE *carte blanche*
freedom to use one's discretion on behalf of another person (French, "white card")

CARVE *to be carved in marble*
to be virtually unalterable

CARVE *to carve out a niche for oneself*
to deliberately create an opportunity to use one's talents effectively

CASE *a basket case*
a poorly-performing enterprise

CASE *to be an open and shut case*
to be an unarguable proposition (a phrase popular in detective novels and probably a play on the two meanings of the word "case")

CASE *to have a cast-iron case*
to be absolutely assured of victory in legal proceedings

CASE *to make a Federal case out of something*
to attach far too much significance to a trivial issue

CAST *the die is cast*
the course of action in train is irreversible

CAST *to be cast in bronze*
to be virtually unalterable

CAST *to be cast in someone's mold*
to take after another person

CAST *to cast a chill over something*
to be a depressing influence over something

CAST *to cast a cloud over something*
to spoil the pleasure of an occasion

CAST *to cast a shadow over something*
to introduce a note of warning or sadness in regard to some matter

CAST *to cast an eye over something*
to look at something critically

CAST *to cast one's bread upon the waters*
not to expect gratitude or recognition for one's good works (Ecclesiastes 11:1)

CAST *to cast prudence to the winds*
to cease being prudent

CAST *to cast sheep's eyes at someone*
to look at a person amorously

CAST *to give a cast-iron guarantee*
to give a very secure undertaking to do something

CAST *to have a cast-iron case*
to be absolutely assured of victory in legal proceedings

CASTLE *a castle in Spain*
an impracticable proposition

CASTLE *a castle in the air*
an impracticable proposition

CAT *a cat and dog existence*
a life full of frequent squabbles

CAT *a cat may look at a king*
don't give yourself airs!

CAT *a copycat*
a person who imitates another person's ideas

CAT *a game of cat and mouse*
negotiations between two parties of unequal bargaining power during which the stronger makes some temporary concessions to the weaker without, however, affecting the latter's eventual total defeat

CAT *there is more than one way to skin a cat*
this can be achieved in a variety of acceptable ways

CAT *there is no room to swing a cat*
this place is very small (actually refers to a cat-o'-nine-tails)

CAT *to be a cat's paw*
to be a person who is being used as a tool by others

CAT *to be the cat's pajamas*
to have an exaggerated idea of one's own importance

CAT *to bell the cat*
to do some dangerous but highly useful mission (refers to a fable in which none of the mice was willing to put a warning bell on a cat)

CAT *to kick the cat*
to take out one's anger on some innocent party

CAT *to let the cat out of the bag*
to reveal an embarrassing secret (refers to the exposure of cheats at fairs, attempting to pass a cat wrapped in a sack off as a piglet)

CAT *to rain cats and dogs*
to rain heavily

CAT *to see which way the cat jumps*
to await developments

CAT *to throw a cat among the pigeons*
to cause consternation by revealing an unpleasant and unexpected fact

CAT *when the cat is away the mice will play*
in the absence of supervision, discipline will be lax

CAT *wildcat*
(of a strike) unofficial; (of an oil well) drilled as a pure prospect; (of a financial scheme) very hazardous

CATALYST *a catalyst*
a factor causing something to happen

CATAPULT *to catapult*
(of sales, etc.) to increase rapidly

CATAPULT *to catapult to fame*
to achieve fame unexpectedly quickly

CATCH *I wouldn't be caught dead without some object*
I regard some object as very important

CATCH *catch-22*
a situation made impossible because it requires as a prior fulfillment something which does not exist until that condition is satisfied (title of a novel by Joseph Heller)

CATCH *first catch your hare*
do things in logical order and after proper preparation (advice on how to cook a hare in Mrs. Beeton's celebrated COOK BOOK)

CATCH *to be caught by the tide*
to be dealt with by something inevitable

CATCH *to catch someone flat-footed*
to embarrass a person in the course of his making mistakes or being unprepared

CATCH *to catch someone in a bind*
to find a person in a difficulty from which he cannot readily extricate himself

CATCH *to catch someone in the net*
to unexpectedly involve a particular person in the course of activity designed to involve many others

CATCH *to catch someone off guard*
to surprise a person (a fencing term)

CATCH *to catch someone on the hop*
to take a person by surprise

CATCH *to catch someone red-handed*
to apprehend a person in the course of committing a crime

CATCH *to catch someone with his pants down*
to act when another person least expects it

CATCH *to catch someone with his trousers down*
to act when another person least expects it

CATCH *to catch someone's eye*
to attract the attention of another person or to seek permission to address that person

CATCH *to throw a sprat to catch a mackerel*
to risk a little in the hope of gaining much

CAVE *an Aladdin's cave*
a place full of unexpected treasure

CAVE *to cave in*
to yield to pressure

CEILING *ceiling*
upper permitted limit

CEMENT *to cement a relationship*
to do something in an endeavor to make a relationship permanent

CENT *to have fifty cents each way*
to equivocate

CENT *to throw in one's two cents' worth*
to modestly supply one's own facts or views

CENTER *the center of gravity*
the place most convenient to the greatest number

CENTER *to be center stage*
to have everyone's attention

CENTER *to be the center of the spider's web*
to control an operation which involves numerous and/or complex ingredients

CENTERPIECE *the centerpiece*
(of a proposal) the highlight or the main ingredient

CHAFF *to separate the wheat from the chaff*
to distinguish between important and unimportant ingredients

CHAIN *the weakest link in the chain*
the least efficient component in a project the overall efficiency of which is governed by the efficiency of the least efficient component

CHAIN *to drag the chain*
to perform unduly slowly

CHAIR *to get an arm-chair ride*
to be given a particularly easy time

CHAIR *to play musical chairs*
to be a part of a general reshuffling of duties or functions which is not necessarily to everyone's liking

CHALK *chalk it up!*
the success was unexpected

CHALK *to win by a long chalk*
to win very conclusively

CHAMELEON *a chameleon*
a person without character who changes his stance all the time to reflect the current circumstances

CHAMP *to champ at the bit*
to be impatient

CHANCE *a fat chance*
little hope

CHANCE *not a dog's chance*
no hope at all

CHANCE *not the ghost of a chance*
no hope at all

CHANCE *to chance one's arm*
to take a great risk (refers to the stripes on the uniforms of non-commissioned officers)

CHANCE *to have a snowflake's chance in hell*
to have no hope or possibility at all

CHANGE *a leopard cannot change his spots*
each person is born with certain unalterable characteristics

CHANGE *the cold wind of change*
the unpleasant realities of new circumstances

CHANGE *to be shortchanged*
to be given less than is due to one

CHANGE *to change one's mind*
to alter the views which one had previously formed

CHANGE *to change one's tune*
to alter one's publicly-expressed views

CHANGE *to change the whole picture*
to alter the major assumptions on which some assessment was based

CHANGE *to have a change of heart*
to form a new view in place of a strongly-held previous view

CHANGE *to ring the changes*
to exhaust the number of different ways of doing something (refers to the permutations used for ringing peals of church bells)

CHANGE *to swap horses in midstream*
to change direction during the course of a project

CHAPTER *to quote chapter and verse*
to authenticate the information

CHARADE *to act out a charade*
ostentatiously to pretend to be doing something in an ethical fashion

CHARGE *to charge like a wounded bull*
to impose excessive prices (a play on words; not a simile)

CHARGE *to recharge one's batteries*
to have a recuperative break

CHARITY *charity begins at home*
a person's first responsibility should be to his family

CHARLIE *tailend Charlie*
a person who habitually comes last

CHARM *to charm the pants off someone*
to delight a person

CHARYBDIS *to be between Scylla and Charybdis*
to be faced with two equally unpalatable alternatives which cannot both be avoided (refers to the voyage of Ulysses)

CHASE *a wild goose chase*
a foolish search for something which does not exist

CHASE *to chase a corpse*
to harp on something long ago resolved or a lost cause

CHASE *to chase every hare*
to be easily sidetracked

CHASE *to chase rainbows*
to be quite unrealistic

CHECK *to give someone a blank check*
to give another person unlimited delegated authority

CHECKMATE *checkmate*
defeat

CHEEK *cheek by jowl*
close to each other

CHEEK *to turn the other cheek*
to show that one has not been intimidated (Matthew 5:39)

CHEEK *tongue in cheek*
full of irony

CHEER *the cheering could be heard a block away*
there was great rejoicing

CHEESE *cheese paring*
stingy

CHEESE *stiff cheese!*
circumstances which may be unwelcome but which will not be altered and in respect of which no great sympathy is felt

CHEESE *to be cheesed off*
to be disgusted

CHEMISTRY *good chemistry*
a good ability to work closely together

CHERRY *to get only one bite at the cherry*
to receive no further opportunity

CHESS *to be a chess game*
to be a complex exercise, requiring great skill

CHESSMASTER *a chessmaster*
a clever strategist

CHEST *to get something off one's chest*
to confess

CHEST *to hold one's cards close to one's chest*
to keep one's plans and strategies secret

CHEST *to lock something up in the old oak chest*
to put in a safe place and out of mind

CHESTNUT *to pull someone's chestnuts out of the fire*
to retrieve a situation

CHEW *to bite off more than one can chew*
to be overly ambitious and thus unrealistic as to one's capabilities

CHEW *to chew fat*
to eat and talk together

CHEW *to chew someone's ear*
to force one's conversation on an unwilling listener

CHEW *to chew the cud*
to reflect on something

CHEW *to have something to chew on*
to have firm facts on which to base a decision

CHICKEN *chicken and egg*
two factors each of which results in the other

CHICKEN *chicken-hearted*
showing little courage

CHICKEN *the chickens are coming home to roost*
the consequences of past actions are becoming obvious

CHICKEN *to be chicken feed*
to be small and unimportant

CHICKEN *to count one's chickens before they are hatched*
to treat as fact the expected results of a future proposal

CHIEF *more chiefs than Indians*
a disproportionately large number of supervisors

CHILD *a problem child*
a source of unnecessary difficulty

CHILD *brainchild*
inspired original idea

CHILD *to be child's play*
to be easy or to require only elementary skills and knowledge

CHILD *to take food out of the mouths of children*
cruelly to deprive the needy

CHILDHOOD *second childhood*
dotage

CHILL *to cast a chill over something*
to be a depressing influence over something

CHILL *to send a chill down someone's spine*
to be worrying news

CHIN *to keep one's chin up*
to maintain one's morale

CHIN *to lead with one's chin*
by one's brash behavior to virtually invite one's opponents to take action against one

CHIN *to rub one's chin*
to muse

CHIN *to take it on the chin*
to cheerfully accept a misfortune

CHINA *I would not do so-and-so for all the tea in China*
I will never do so-and-so

CHINA *a bull in a china shop*
a careless person likely to cause great damage

CHINESE *a Chinese puzzle*
a perplexing enigma

CHINESE *Chinese walls*
a system to ensure that different parts of some organization do not gain access to each other's confidential information

CHINK *a chink in someone's armor*
an opportunity to do something which otherwise could not be done

CHINK *a chink in the wall*
an opportunity to do something which otherwise could not be done

CHINK *a chink of light*
a small hope of a solution or breakthrough

CHIP *bargaining chips*
benefits which can be conceded in negotiations in order to obtain some advantage

CHIP *that is the way the chips fall*
that is the actual situation

CHIP *to be a blue chip stock*
to be of excellent quality

CHIP *to be a chip off the old block*
to resemble one's father

CHIP *to chip in*
to contribute financially

CHIP *to have a chip on one's shoulder*
to unreasonably resent something

CHIP *to have had one's chips*
to have received all that is going to be forthcoming

CHIP *to turn one's chips in*
to convert one's assets or entitlements into cash

CHIP *when the chips are down*
when all facts are known and taken into consideration

CHISEL *to chisel away at something*
to reduce the size of something in a series of small stages

CHOICE *Hobson's choice*
no right at all to select (refers to Thomas Hobson, a horsekeeper in Cambridge, England, who offered customers seeking a change of horses a single beast on a "take it or leave it" basis)

CHOP *to chop someone off at the socks*
to stop someone's proposals prematurely

CHOP *to lick one's chops*
to look forward to something with pleasurable anticipation

CHORD *to strike a chord*
to sound familiar or recall something to mind

CHORD *to strike a responsive chord*
to get a favorable reaction to a proposal

CHORD *to strike the right chord*
to appeal successfully to someone's emotions

CHOREOGRAPH *to choreograph something*
to organize the detail of who does what and when in a project

CHRISTMAS *all his Christmases came at once*
he was overjoyed

CHUM *a green chum*
an inexperienced person

CIGARETTE *only a cigarette paper between them*
virtually equal or close together

CIRCLE *the wheel has turned the complete circle*
things are now back to where they were before

CIRCLE *to do a full circle*
to be back to where one was before or (in error) to go in the opposite direction

CIRCLE *to run around in circles*
to engage in excited but useless activity

CIRCLE *to try to square the circle*
to attempt the impossible (refers to a classical problem in geometry, namely, to construct with a compass a square of the same area as a given circle)

CIRCUIT *to short-circuit something*
to do something, eliminating various intermediate steps

CIRCUS *to be a real circus*
to be a highly disorganized affair

CITE *the devil can cite scripture for his purpose*
a person can quote a respectable or hostile authority while advocating a disreputable cause of his own (from Shakespeare's MERCHANT OF VENICE)

CITIZEN *a second-class citizen*
a person not treated as an equal

CITY *one can't beat City Hall*
the ordinary citizen is powerless against bureaucracy

CIVIL *to keep a civil tongue in one's head*
to be polite, especially under provocation

CLAIM *to stake a claim*
to indicate one's desire to obtain something

CLANGER *to drop a clanger*
to do something indiscreet or which offends social conventions

CLAP *to clap eyes on something*
to catch sight of something

CLASP *to clasp at straws*
to have a hopeless case but show unjustified optimism on noting minor positive features

CLASS *a second-class citizen*
a person not treated as an equal

CLASS *to be first class*
to be very satisfactory

CLAY *to have feet of clay*
to be vulnerable (Daniel 2:33)

CLEAN *a Herculean cleaning of the stables*
a thorough revision of operating procedure (refers to Hercules, a mythical Greek hero who cleaned the stables of Augeas)

CLEAN *a clean sweep*
the complete removal in an election of all sitting members

CLEAN *a cleanskin*
a person without a criminal record

CLEAN *a spring cleaning*
a thorough review occurring a long time after the previous one

CLEAN *to clean up a mess*
to sort out mistakes or neglect

CLEAN *to clean up one's act*
to fix up the deficiencies in one's affairs

CLEAN *to come clean*
to confess

CLEAN *to get a clean bill of health*
after proper investigation to be found not wanting

CLEAN *to have clean hands*
to be innocent or to act ethically

CLEAN *to keep one's nose clean*
to act with circumspection and honesty despite temptation to do otherwise

CLEAN *to make a clean breast of something*
to confess

CLEAN *to wipe the slate clean*
to forgive past indiscretions

CLEANER *to take someone to the cleaners*
to cheat a person financially

CLEAR *clear cut*
not borderline

CLEAR *the coast is clear*
there are no observers to one's activity around

CLEAR *to be crystal clear*
to have a very obvious meaning

CLEAR *to be in the clear*
to be exonerated or free from suspicion

CLEAR *to clear the air*
to remove any possible misunderstandings

CLEAR *to clear the decks*
to get ready for action

CLEAR *to clear the ground*
to dispose of the preliminaries

CLEAR *to come through loud and clear*
to be well understood

CLEAR *to have a clear picture of something*
to have a good understanding of something

CLEAR *to jump a hurdle*
to overcome a problem or difficulty

CLEAR *when the smoke clears*
when sufficient time has passed

CLEFT *to be in a cleft stick*
to be in a dilemma

CLIFF *to be a cliff-hanger*
to be very exciting

CLIMATE *climate*
commercial environment

CLING *to cling on by one's fingertips*
to have only a slender hold

CLIP *to clip someone's wings*
to reduce another person's freedom to act as he thinks fit

CLOAK *cloak and dagger activity*
secret activity

CLOAK *to cloak something*
to disguise the true nature of something

CLOCK *to turn back the clock*
to have another opportunity to do something which should have been done already or to undo something which cannot be undone

CLOSE *to be a close shave*
to be a narrow escape

CLOSE *to be a closed book*
to be a secret

CLOSE *to be close to one's heart*
to be a project on which one is very keen

CLOSE *to be close to the abyss*
to face imminent total destruction

CLOSE *to be too close to home*
to be too near the truth to be welcome

CLOSE *to close ranks*
to sink minor differences in order to present a unified front to a common enemy

CLOSE *to close the book on something*
to terminate an activity

CLOSE *to close the gate*
to deny an opportunity which was previously available

CLOSE *to draw the nets closer*
to intensify one's efforts

CLOSE *to get close to the bone*
to cause discomfort by being accurate

CLOSE *to sail close to the wind*
to act in a very dangerous manner

CLOSET *to come out of the closet*
to publicly admit one's homosexuality

CLOTH *to cut one's coat according to the cloth*
to accommodate oneself to limitations beyond one's control and to do the best in the circumstances

CLOTHES *to steal someone's clothes*
to plagiarize another person's ideas

CLOTHING *to be a wolf in sheep's clothing*
to be a hypocrite or to be dangerous although masquerading as something harmless (Matthew 7:15)

CLOUD *every cloud has a silver lining*
there are benefits even in seemingly adverse situations

CLOUD *there are black clouds on the horizon*
bad news is expected

CLOUD *to be in cloud cuckoo land*
to be mad or to have unrealistic expectations

CLOUD *to be on cloud nine*
to be very happy

CLOUD *to be under a cloud*
to be under suspicion or to be out of favor

CLOUD *to cast a cloud over something*
to spoil the pleasure of an occasion

CLOUD *to cloud one's mind*
to allow irrelevant or extraneous factors to affect one's impartiality or judgment

CLOUD *to have a cloud hanging over one's head*
there is doubt as to one's future

CLOUD *to have one's head in the clouds*
to be unrealistic

CLOVER *to be in clover*
to enjoy a life of ease and luxury

CLUB *join the club!*
you are only one of many people with similar problems

COACH *an opening wide enough to drive a coach and four through*
an excellent opportunity

COACH *to drive a coach and horses through something*
to demonstrate major errors in something

COAL *to be at the coal face*
to be in the place where the real work is done

COAL *to carry coals to Newcastle*
to do something ridiculously unnecessary

COAL *to haul someone over the coals*
to reprimand a person

COAST *the coast is clear*
there are no observers to one's activity around

COASTER *a roller coaster ride*
a series of successes followed by failures

COAT *to cut one's coat according to the cloth*
to accommodate oneself to limitations beyond one's control and to do the best in the circumstances

COAT *to hang onto someone's coat-tails*
to excessively rely on another person's initiatives

COAT *to trail one's coat-tails*
to invite a quarrel

COBBLER *a cobbler should stick to his last*
every person should confine himself to activities for which he has been trained

COBWEB *to blow the cobwebs away*
to revive an old issue

COCK *a cock and bull story*
an explanation which is completely unbelievable and unacceptable

COCK *cock-eyed*
stupid

COCK *to cock one's eye at someone*
to glance knowingly at a person

COCK *to go off half-cocked*
to act without adequate thought or preparation (refers to a gun at the half-ready)

COCKED *to knock something into a cocked hat*
to twist something so that its original form is hardly recognizable

COCKLE *to warm the cockles of someone's heart*
to delight a person

COCOON *in a cocoon*
in a safe and isolated environment

COFFIN *to be another nail in someone's coffin*
to represent a further step toward someone's downfall

COG *to be a small cog in a large wheel*
to be a relatively unimportant person in a large organization

COIN *the other side of the coin*
the arguments for the opposite point of view

COIN *to pay someone back in his own coin*
to retaliate in kind

COLD *a cold day in hell*
never

COLD *cold-hearted*
cruel or mean or unmoved

COLD *cold turkey*
the sudden cessation of drugs to an addict

COLD *in the cold light of day*
in an unemotional atmosphere at a later stage

COLD *that is cold comfort*
that appears on the surface to be reassurance and consolation but really it is not

COLD *the cold war*
the unfriendly relations between the communist nations and the rest of the world

COLD *the cold wind of change*
the unpleasant realities of new circumstances

COLD *to be a cold fish*
to be an unemotional person

COLD *to be in a cold sweat*
to be afraid

COLD *to blow hot and cold*
to vacillate

COLD *to come in out of the cold*
to be welcomed into a group

COLD *to do something in cold blood*
to be cruel without feeling any emotion about it

COLD *to get cold feet*
to become scared

COLD *to give someone the cold shoulder*
to ostentatiously ignore a person

COLD *to leave someone cold*
to fail to impress a person

COLD *to leave someone out in the cold*
to deny a desired objective to a person

COLD *to pour cold water on some idea*
to be unenthusiastic about some proposal or scornful of its apparent weaknesses

COLD *to put something into cold storage*
to put something aside for dealing with at some indeterminate future time

COLD *to send a cold shiver down someone's spine*
to horrify a person

COLLAR *to be hot under the collar*
to be very agitated

COLLISION *to be on a collision course*
to be headed for a clash with an opponent

COLOR *that is a horse of a very different color*
that is a much more acceptable proposition

COLOR *that takes on added color*
there are now further facts which alter the appearance of a matter

COLOR *to nail one's colors to the mast*
to publicly declare one's position and to maintain it in the face of criticism

COLOR *to pass with flying colors*
to be very successful

COLOR *to sail under false colors*
to pretend that one's real character or beliefs are different from what they really are

COLOR *to see the color of someone's eyes*
to see how a person matches expectations or requirements

COLOR *to see the color of someone's money*
to get evidence of the sincerity of a person's proposal

COLOR *to show one's true colors*
to disclose one's real character or beliefs

COLUMNIST *a fifth columnist*
a person using his position of trust to work for a rival cause

COMB *to go through something with a fine-tooth comb*
to conduct an extremely thorough investigation

COME *all his Christmases came at once*
he was overjoyed

COME *the chickens are coming home to roost*
the consequences of past actions are becoming obvious

COME *to argue till the cows come home*
to argue for ever

COME *to come adrift*
(of a plan) not to work out as intended

COME *to come apart at the seams*
(of an arrangement) to break down

COME *to come back to haunt someone*
(of an unpleasant incident) to be a constant reminder to a person

COME *to come down with a thud*
to be suddenly disillusioned

COME *to come in out of the cold*
to be welcomed into a group

COME *to come in thick and fast*
to arrive quickly and in great volume

COME *to come out into the open*
to start being frank

COME *to come out of one's ears*
to be plentiful

COME *to come out of the blue*
to be totally unexpected

COME *to come out of the closet*
to publicly admit one's homosexuality

COME *to come through loud and clear*
to be well understood

COME *to come to a full stop*
to completely cease activity

COME *to come to a head*
to reach culmination

COME *to come to grips with some problem*
to be on the way to solving a problem

COME *to come to someone's ears*
to come to someone's attention

COME *to come to the party*
to agree to someone's terms

COME *to come up smelling like a rose*
not to have a stain on one's character

COME *to cross a bridge only when one comes to it*
to await the crystallization of a situation before sorting it out

COME *to jump that hurdle when one comes to it*
to deal with a particular problem only when it becomes necessary to do so

COME *when one's ship comes in*
when one's business venture is successfully completed or when luck arrives

COME *when the crunch comes*
when the inevitable conclusion is reached

COMEDY *a comedy of errors*
a series of separate mistakes in relation to some matter (name of a Shakespeare play)

COMFORT *that is cold comfort*
that appears on the surface to be reassurance and consolation but really it is not

COMMAND *to be in a commanding position*
to have a strategic advantage

COMMAND *to be in command*
to be on top of a situation

COMMANDMENT *eleventh commandment*
unwritten rule

COMPANY *to have shares in a paper company*
to institute unnecessary clerical procedures

COMPARE *to compare notes*
to exchange information about some subject of mutual interest

COMPETE *to compete on all fours with someone*
to strive on equal terms

COMPLETE *the wheel has turned the complete circle*
things are now back to where they were before

COMPLETE *to turn a complete somersault*
to reverse one's established policy

COMPLIMENT *a left-handed compliment*
a thinly-disguised insult

COMPLIMENT *to return the compliment*
to reciprocate or to extract revenge

COMPOUND *to compound the felony*
having already acted improperly to make matters worse (the misuse of a legal term: compounding a felony is the crime of agreeing for money not to prosecute a person for felony; in reality it is therefore an offense by a different person—not a second and worse offense by the original culprit)

CONCERT *to be up to concert pitch*
to be ready

CONCRETE *to set something in concrete*
to make something virtually unalterable

CONFRONT *to confront someone head on*
to confront a person

CONJURE *to conjure up a picture*
to use words to convey a vivid impression

CONJURE *to conjure up something*
to produce something in circumstances where this seemed impossible

CONTEMPLATE *to contemplate one's navel*
to be introspective

CONVERT *to preach to the converted*
to say something to those who already believe in it

COOK *a Cook's tour*
a guided tour of inspection (refers to Thomas Cook, the travel company)

COOK *there are many ways to cook eggs*
there are many ways to achieve an objective

COOK *to be cooking with gas*
to be fully operational

COOK *to cook one's goose*
to do something which backfires on one

COOK *to cook the books*
fraudulently to maintain false records of financial transactions

COOK *too many cooks spoil the broth*
one leader is all that is required

COOKIE *that is the way the cookie crumbles*
that is the actual situation

COOL *cool it!*
calm down!

COOL *to cool one's heels*
to be kept waiting

COOL *to keep a cool head*
to stay calm and rational in a crisis

COOL *to play it cool*
to take a low-key and rational approach

COOP *to fly the coop*
to grow up and become independent

COP *to cop it in the neck*
to suffer a severe disaster

COPYBOOK *to blot one's copybook*
to spoil one's previously good reputation or record

COPYCAT *a copycat*
a person who imitates another person's ideas

CORD *to cut the cord*
to severe a connection (refers to the umbilical cord)

CORE *rotten to the core*
completely corrupt

CORE *to be the hard core*
to be the central and most difficult problem

CORN *to tread on someone's corns*
to upset another person by interfering in his area of responsibility

CORNER *cornerstone*
key ingredient

CORNER *from the four corners of the globe*
from everywhere

CORNER *to back someone into a corner*
to drive a person into a position from which escape is difficult

CORNER *to be around the corner*
to be imminent

CORNER *to be in a tight corner*
to experience a crisis

CORNER *to cut corners*
to lower one's standards in order to complete something more quickly

CORNER *to paint oneself into a corner*
to foolishly put oneself into a position from which escape is impossible

CORNER *to see something out of the corner of one's eye*
to only just see something

CORNER *to turn the corner*
to commence being successful after initial failures

CORPS *esprit de corps*
a feeling of camaraderie and concern for the good name of some organization of which one is a member (French, ''vital breath of a body'')

CORPSE *to breathe life into a corpse*
to revive something moribund

CORPSE *to chase a corpse*
to harp on something long ago resolved or a lost cause

COTTON *to be out of one's cotton-picking mind*
to act irrationally

COTTON *to keep one's cotton-picking fingers off something*
not to interfere in something

COTTON *to wrap someone in cotton wool*
to be overprotective toward a person

COUNT *the final countdown*
the last stages of something (refers to the launch of space vehicles)

COUNT *to count one's chickens before they are hatched*
to treat as fact the expected results of a future proposal

COUNT *to stand up and be counted*
to publicly announce one's position on some issue

COUNTRY *one looks for elephants in elephant country*
one needs to search in the right place

COUP *to receive the coup de grace*
to be finished off by an opponent (French, ''mercy stroke'')

COURSE *in the course of a day's march*
while carrying out one's normal activities

COURSE *it is horses for courses*
some combinations work particularly well

COURSE *to be on a collision course*
to be headed for a clash with an opponent

COURSE *to be on course*
to be progressing satisfactorily toward one's goal

COURSE *to be par for the course*
to be normal

COURSE *to plot a safe course through troubled waters*
to make a plan which overcomes certain difficulties

COURSE *to run its course*
to come to a natural end

COURT *the ball is in someone's court*
it is some other person's responsibility

COURT *to have a friend at court*
a person with influence who is willing to use it on one's behalf

COURT *to laugh something out of court*
to ridicule a proposition as having no basis whatsoever

COURT *to put oneself out of court*
to disqualify oneself from being considered for something

CONVENTRY *to send someone to Coventry*
to ostentatiously and collectively ignore a person by way of punishment

COVER *to cover one's back*
to take precautions

COVER *to cover one's hide*
to provide excuses or take other evasive action in an attempt to avoid the adverse consequences of one's actions

COVER *to cover one's tracks*
to hide the evidence of one's involvement

COVER *to cover oneself*
to create evidence so that if one is criticized or accused later on one can clear one's name

COVER *to cover the field*
to be comprehensive

COVER *to duck for cover*
to seek to avoid blame

COVER *to judge a book by its cover*
foolishly to go only by superficial appearances

COW *a cash cow*
a source of ready money

COW *a milch cow*
an easy and plentiful source of some desired benefit

COW *a sacred cow*
an institution so well established that it is virtually unalterable

COW *to argue till the cows come home*
to argue forever

COX *Box and Cox*
two persons who are never around at the same time (from the name of a play)

CRACK *someone is a hard nut to crack*
it is very difficult to persuade a person to do something

CRACK *the crack of dawn*
at the exact moment of sunrise

CRACK *to be a crack in the wall*
to represent a small unintended opportunity which can be exploited

CRACK *to be a fair crack of the whip*
to be just

CRACK *to be all that it is cracked up to be*
to be as good as the claims made for something

CRACK *to crack*
to have a mental break-down

CRACK *to crack down on something*
to seek to eradicate something

CRACK *to crack the whip*
to exert one's authority

CRACK *to have a crack at something*
to attempt something

CRACK *to paper over the cracks*
to institute extremely superficial and basically ineffective remedies

CRACK *to use a sledgehammer to crack a nut*
to devote vastly more resources to a project than is warranted by all the circumstances

CRADLE *to be the cradle of something*
to be the place where some idea was first nurtured

CRANNY *in every nook and cranny*
everywhere

CRASH *to gatecrash a gathering*
to attend a gathering without any right to be there

CRAWL *to crawl out of the woodwork*
to turn up unexpectedly and in large numbers

CREAM *to be cream on top of the milk*
to be an additional benefit in an already satisfactory scenario

CREATE *to create a Frankenstein*
to create something wicked and out of control (a reference to the fictional creator of a monster, in mistake for a reference to the monster itself)

CREATE *to create a storm*
to kick up a fuss

CREEK *to be up the creek*
to be completely mistaken; to be in trouble

CREEP *to make someone's flesh creep*
to frighten a person with something horrific

CREME *creme de la creme*
something quite superlative (French, "the cream of the cream")

CREST *to be on the crest of a wave*
to enjoy success which may not last

CRESTFALLEN *crestfallen*
dejected

CRICKET *a cricket team*
eleven people

CRICKET *not to be cricket*
to be unfair

CROCODILE *to shed crocodile tears*
to be a hypocrite

CROOK *by hook or by crook*
by fair means or foul

CROSS *to be a cross which one has to bear*
to be a difficulty which one has to endure

CROSS *to be at the crossroads*
to need to choose between several mutually exclusive alternatives

CROSS *to cross a bridge only when one comes to it*
to await the crystallization of a situation before sorting it out

CROSS *to cross one's mind*
to occur to one

CROSS *to cross someone's path*
to meet another person by chance

CROSS *to cross swords with someone*
to have a disagreement with another person

CROSS *to cross the Rubicon*
to make an irreversible decision in regard to some commitment

CROSS *to dot the i's and cross the t's*
to be meticulous in completing the documentation for a transaction

CROSS *to have one's wires crossed*
to be mistaken about key facts

CROSS *to keep one's fingers crossed*
to hope for a good outcome

CROW *as the crow flies*
by the shortest distance

CROW *to eat crow*
to accept a humiliating defeat

CROWD *to stand out from the crowd*
to be noticeably better than one's competitors

CROWN *the crowning point*
the height of a person's achievement

CROWN *the jewel in someone's crown*
the most significant component

CROWN *to wear one's crown of thorns*
to have one's own difficulties (John 19:5)

CROWN *uneasy lies the head that wears a crown*
responsibility involves some risks and some burdens (from Shakespeare's HENRY IV)

CRUCIFY *to crucify someone*
to unfairly do severe damage to a person's reputation or credibility

CRUEL *to cruel someone's pitch*
to spoil a person's chances

CRUMB *to throw someone a few crumbs*
to fob a person off with a few symbolic but unimportant concessions

CRUMBLE *that is the way the cookie crumbles*
that is the actual situation

CRUNCH *when it comes to the crunch*
when the matter comes up for decision

CRUNCH *when the crunch comes*
when the inevitable conclusion is reached

CRUSADE *a crusade*
an aggressive campaign to achieve some political or social objective

CRUSOE *not to be Robinson Crusoe*
to be one of a large number of people with a common problem (from Daniel Defoe's ROBINSON CRUSOE)

CRUTCH *a crutch*
an artificial non-permanent support

CRY *a cry for help*
a subconscious or indirect indication that a person is in need of psychological counselling

CRY *a shoulder to cry on*
sympathy

CRY *it is no use crying over spilt milk*
lamenting over a disaster achieves nothing

CRY *to be a far cry from something*
to be a long way from something

CRY *to cry "wolf"*
to repeatedly raise an unjustified concern with the result that one will be ignored when the circumstances change

CRY *to cry in one's beer*
to show remorse

CRY *to cry one's eyes out*
to express great sadness at a situation

CRY *to laugh all the way to the bank*
to appreciate one's good fortune

CRYSTAL *a crystal ball*
accurate knowledge of the future

CRYSTAL *to be crystal clear*
to have a very obvious meaning

CRYSTALLIZE *to crystallize*
to emerge in its final form

CUCKOO *to be a cuckoo in the nest*
to purport to be a member of a group of people although having no such right

CUCKOO *to be in cloud cuckoo land*
to be mad or to have unrealistic expectations

CUD *to chew the cud*
to reflect on something

CUDGEL *to take up the cudgels for someone*
to defend a person

CUFF *off the cuff*
impromptu

CUP *a storm in a teacup*
a controversy about a minor matter but one which looms large in the minds of the parties

CUP *not to be someone's cup of tea*
to be outside a person's expertise or area of interest

CUPBOARD *a skeleton in the cupboard*
an unpleasant truth the knowledge of which has been deliberately suppressed

CUPBOARD *the cupboard is bare*
the wished-for resources are just not available

CURATE *to be a curate's egg*
to be good only in parts (refers to an 1895 cartoon in PUNCH)

CURDLE *to curdle one's blood*
to be horrific

CURE *the cure is worse than the disease*
the remedy involves more disadvantages than if it were not applied

CURL *to make someone's hair curl*
(of news) to give someone a shock

CURLY *to get someone by the short and curly hairs*
to have domination over a person

CURRENT *an undercurrent*
a barely noticeable feeling of dissent in the community which is not being vocalized

CURSE *not worth a tinker's curse*
worthless

CURTAIN *curtain raiser*
introduction

CURTAIN *it's curtains!*
this is the end!

CURTAIN *the curtain rises on something*
something is about to start

CURTAIN *the iron curtain*
the border between the communist nations and the rest of the world (from a speech by Sir Winston Churchill in 1946)

CURTAIN *to ring down the curtain on something*
to treat something as concluded

CUSTOMER *a slippery customer*
a shifty person

CUT *clear cut*
not borderline

CUT *cut it out!*
stop doing that!

CUT *cut-throat*
highly competitive

CUT *one could have cut the atmosphere with a knife*
those present were very tense

CUT *the cut of someone's jib*
someone's personal appearance

CUT *to be a cut above the rest*
to be plainly superior

CUT *to be at the cutting edge of something*
to be in a position where important decisions need to be made

CUT *to be cut and dried*
to be well settled or long established

CUT *to be cut off at the knees*
to have a pet project aborted

CUT *to be cut to pieces*
to be very upset

CUT *to be cut up*
to be distressed

CUT *to cut both ways*
to involve both advantages and disadvantages of similar significance

CUT *to cut corners*
to lower one's standards in order to complete something more quickly

CUT *to cut no ice with someone*
to have little effect on a person

CUT *to cut one's coat according to the cloth*
to accommodate oneself to limitations beyond one's control and to do the best in the circumstances

CUT *to cut one's nose off to spite one's face*
to act in pique in a way which harms only oneself

CUT *to cut one's own throat*
to act in a way which damages one's own interests

CUT *to cut one's teeth on something*
to get one's first experience by doing something

CUT *to cut someone dead*
to snub a person

CUT *to cut tall poppies down to size*
to humiliate haughty persons

CUT *to cut the Gordian knot*
to solve, especially by force, a virtually insoluble problem (refers to a complicated knot tied by Gordius and eventually cut by Alexander the Great)

CUT *to cut the cord*
to sever a connection (refers to the umbilical cord)

CUT *to cut the ground from under someone's feet*
to unexpectedly withdraw support and in the process cause embarrassment or to demolish a person's case

CUT *to cut the painter*
to become separated

CUT *to have one's work cut out to do something*
it will be difficult to achieve something

CUT *to take shortcuts*
to do something by a faster but less thorough method

CYLINDER *to spark on all cylinders*
to work extremely well

D

DADDY *the daddy of them all*
the progenitor

DAGGER *cloak and dagger activity*
secret activity

DAGGER *to look daggers at someone*
to look at a person in a way which indicates great animosity

DAM *the dam burst*
the cumulative effect of many things caused a disaster

DAMASCUS *to be on the road to Damascus*
to see the error of one's ways (Acts 9:3)

DAMOCLES *to have a sword of Damocles hanging over one*
to be in imminent danger despite normal activity going on all around one

DAMP *a damp squib*
disappointingly ineffective action (refers to fireworks which fail to go off)

DANCE *nothing to make a song or dance about*
unexciting or unimportant

DANCE *to lead someone a merry dance*
to mislead a person

DANCE *to make a song and dance about something*
to create a fuss

DANSE *danse macabre*
gruesome final step (French, ''ghastly dance'')

DARK *a dark horse*
a person with unsuspected talents

DARK *a leap into the dark*
a rash move

DARK *a shot in the dark*
an intelligent or lucky guess

DARK *a stab in the dark*
a sheer guess

DARK *to be in the dark*
to be uninformed

DARK *to keep someone in the dark*
to deliberately keep a person uninformed

DARK *to keep something dark*
to keep something secret

DARK *to look on the dark side*
to be pessimistic

DARK *to whistle in the dark*
to feign greater confidence than one really has

DARKEN *never darken my door again*
do not ever return

DAWN *a false dawn*
an incident giving rise to unjustified hope

DAWN *light dawns*
the point is grasped

DAWN *the crack of dawn*
at the exact moment of sunrise

DAWN *to be the dawn of a new day*
to be the start of a different regime

DAY *a cold day in hell*
never

DAY *a field day*
a very enjoyable and successful occasion

DAY *a nine-day wonder*
an exciting event, but one which will cease to arouse interest when the novelty has worn off

DAY *a red-letter day*
an important occasion (refers to the color used to print saints' days on some calendars)

DAY *at the end of the day*
in due course or at the conclusion of a project

DAY *every dog has his day*
good luck comes sooner or later

DAY *he would not give one the time of day*
he is unwilling to help anybody

DAY *in Halcyon days*
in past happier times (refers to the 14 days about the winter solstice when winds were calm and to the mythical bird said to breed in a floating nest at that time)

DAY *in the cold light of day*
in an unemotional atmosphere at a later stage

DAY *in the course of a day's march*
while carrying out one's normal activities

DAY *late in the day*
only when a project is well advanced

DAY *one's days are numbered*
one is about to be abolished

DAY *the order of the day*
the customary behavior

DAY *to be the dawn of a new day*
to be the start of a different regime

DAY *to call it a day*
to cease involvement with some activity

DAY *to keep something for a rainy day*
to keep something in reserve

DAY *to see the light of day*
to be made public

DAYLIGHT *daylight robbery*
the charging of grossly excessive prices

DAYLIGHT *to see daylight*
to get the right answer

DEAD *I wouldn't be caught dead without some object*
I regard some object as very important

DEAD *a dead-end position*
a job with no prospects of advancement

DEAD *a dead letter*
a rule still in existence but no longer observed in practice

DEAD *dead and buried*
(of some issue) definitely concluded, especially so long ago as to be nearly forgotten

DEAD *drop dead!*
go away, I want no dealings with you

DEAD *over my dead body*
never

DEAD *to be a dead duck*
to have failed

DEAD *to cut someone dead*
to snub a person

DEAD *to get rid of the dead wood*
to terminate the services of unsatisfactory personnel

DEAD *to kill some proposal stone dead*
to abandon some proposal completely

DEAD *to leave others for dead*
to be vastly superior

DEAD *to make noise enough to wake the dead*
to be excessively noisy

DEAD *to run into a dead end*
to get nowhere in an investigation

DEADLINE *deadline*
time by which something must be completed

DEAF *to fall on deaf ears*
to be totally disregarded

DEAFENING *deafening silence*
great apathy and lack of enthusiasm

DEAL *a raw deal*
unfair treatment

DEAL *a sweetheart deal*
an agreement negotiated in private without full regard to the interests of those affected

DEAL *to deal the final hand*
to take steps which conclude a matter

DEAL *to wheel and deal*
to energetically enter into commercial transactions of dubious propriety

DEALER *sharp dealer*
person engaging in barely honest or mildly unethical practices

DEATH *a death wish*
the contemplation of action so foolish that it is likely to lead to utter disaster

DEATH *death blow*
incident which results in the destruction of something

DEATH *sudden death*
instantaneously or without phasing in

DEATH *to be in at the death*
to be present at the conclusion of something

DEATH *to be on one's death bed*
(of an organization or a piece of equipment) to be about to cease functioning

DEATH *to be the kiss of death*
to be something intended to be helpful but resulting in total destruction

DEATH *to bore someone to death*
to greatly weary a person by dull and uninteresting conversation or by lack of action

DEATH *to die a natural death*
by virtue of changed circumstances or the effluxion of time to be no longer relevant

DEATH *to sign one's own death warrant*
to foolishly do something which is inevitably bound to lead to utter disaster

DEATH *to slowly bleed to death*
to be heading in gradual steps toward total ruin

DEATH *to sound the death knell of something*
to indicate the impending end of something

DEATHKNOCK *on the deathknock*
at the last possible moment

DECIMATE *to decimate*
to greatly reduce in size (often used in the sense of "to reduce to one tenth," although the original meaning was "to reduce by one tenth")

DECIPHER *to decipher something*
to understand the significance of something

DECK *a loose cannon on the deck*
a mistake likely to cause trouble

DECK *all hands on deck*
everybody is requested to help out

DECK *to be back on deck*
to have returned after an absence

DECK *to clear the decks*
to get ready for action

DECKCHAIR *to rearrange the deckchairs on the Titanic*
to take some initiative which is quite useless because it does not take much greater change into account

DEEP *deep-rooted*
strongly felt

DEEP *still waters run deep*
a person with a quiet manner may have a surprisingly great knowledge of a subject

DEEP *to be in deep water*
to be in great difficulty

DEEP *to go off the deep end*
to lose one's temper

DEEP *to have deep pockets*
to have large financial resources

DEEP *to jump straight in at the deep end*
to do something without a proper lead-in

DEEP *to play a deep game*
to show cunning

DEEP *to sink deeper into the mire*
to get into further difficulties

DEEP *to sink deeper into the mud*
to get into even greater difficulty

DEFLOWER *to deflower*
to deprive of virginity

DEFY *to defy gravity*
to go up when the expectation is to go down

DEGREE *to give someone the third degree*
to apply pressure while questioning closely a person under suspicion

DEGREE *to the nth degree*
with great precision

DEGREE *to turn around 180 degrees*
to completely reverse a stance

DELIVER *to deliver the goods*
to achieve the objective

DELPHIC *Delphic*
deliberately obscure (refers to the oracle at Delphi)

DEN *to beard the lion in his den*
to visit someone important at his headquarters

DENMARK *something is rotten in the state of Denmark*
the situation is not correct (from Shakespeare's HAMLET)

DENOMINATOR *the lowest common denominator*
the highest level of taste found among all the members of some target audience

DEPTH *to be out of one's depth*
to find that some issue is too complicated or too difficult

DERAIL *to derail some strategy*
to cause a strategy to fail

DESPOND *a slough of despond*
a feeling of hopelessness

DESTROY *soul-destroying*
extremely boring and demotivating

DEVASTATE *to be devastated*
to be extremely disappointed

DEVELOP *to develop a head of steam*
to gain momentum

DEVIL *a devil-may-care attitude*
a reckless attitude

DEVIL *be a devil!*
take a chance!

DEVIL *between the devil and the deep blue sea*
to be faced with two equally unpalatable alternatives which cannot both be avoided

DEVIL *he must have a long spoon that sups with the devil*
great care is needed when negotiating deals with disreputable parties

DEVIL *poor devil*
person to be pitied

DEVIL *talk of the devil*
here is the person we were just discussing

DEVIL *the devil can cite scripture for his purpose*
a person can quote a respectable or hostile authority while advocating a disreputable cause of his own (from Shakespeare's MERCHANT OF VENICE)

DEVIL *the devil one knows is better than the devil one does not know*
the status quo is more comfortable than change

DEVIL *to act as a devil's advocate*
to put a point of view which one does not hold in order to draw out the best arguments regarding a proposition (refers to a church official vetting a candidate for sainthood)

DEVIL *to give the devil his due*
to be fair (a phrase used in parenthesis, and only in the infinitive)

DEVIL *to grab the devil by the tail*
to face up to difficulties

DIAMOND *to be a rough diamond*
to have many attributes but a gruff manner

DICK *every Tom, Dick and Harry*
just about everybody

DICTIONARY *someone has swallowed a dictionary*
a person uses excessively long words

DIE *no dice*
the proposal is totally unacceptable

DIE *the die is cast*
the course of action in train is irreversible

DIE *the whole box and dice*
all relevant components

DIE *to be dying to do something*
to be extremely keen to do something

DIE *to be the throw of a loaded die*
to be an act of deceit

DIE *to die a natural death*
by virtue of changed circumstances or the effluxion of time to be no longer relevant

DIE *to die hard*
not to give up easily

DIFFERENT *that is a horse of a very different color*
that is a much more acceptable proposition

DIFFERENT *to march to a different drum*
to show an independent approach

DIG *to dig one's heels in*
to become even more stubborn than at first

DIG *to dig one's own grave*
to take action which results in an unintended disaster for oneself

DIG *to dig one's toes in*
to become even more stubborn than at first

DIM *to take a dim view of something*
not to regard something favorably

DINNER *to be done like a dinner*
to be defeated and humiliated

DINOSAUR *a dinosaur*
a person with incredibly outmoded ideas

DIP *to dip one's toes in the water*
to gently explore an opportunity

DIRE *in dire straits*
in great need

DIRECTION *a step in the right direction*
the first in a series of measures designed to correct some problem

DIRECTION *it is pointing in the right direction*
success looks likely

DIRECTION *to head someone in the right direction*
to assist a person to achieve something

DIRT *to strike pay dirt*
to become successful

DIRTY *dirty*
unfair

DIRTY *to do someone's dirty work*
to do something unethical on behalf of another person

DIRTY *to get one's hands dirty*
to do the necessary but unpleasant or menial parts of a task

DIRTY *to wash one's dirty linen in public*
to expose one's domestic differences to the world at large

DISASTER *a pit of disaster*
great and unexpected misfortune

DISCLOSE *to disclose one's hand*
to give away information regarding one's intention

DISEASE *the cure is worse than the disease*
the remedy involves more disadvantages than if it were not applied

DISGUISE *a blessing in disguise*
an unwelcome but salutary experience

DISPATCH *to be mentioned in dispatches*
to be favorably mentioned (refers to military recognition for bravery)

DISSEMINATE *to disseminate ideas*
to spread ideas to a wide audience (lit., ''to scatter seeds in various places'')

DISTANCE *to keep one's distance*
to avoid familiarity

DISTANT *distant fields look greener*
activities of which one has no experience seem much easier than is really the case

DITCH *to make a last-ditch stand*
to make a brave effort to stave off final defeat

DIVE *to take a nosedive*
to suddenly and unexpectedly fall steeply

DIVIDENDS *to show dividends*
to be successful

DO *the left hand does not know what the right hand is doing*
one section of a large bureaucracy does not realize that another section is simultaneously doing something inconsistent

DOCK *to be in the dock*
to need to defend one's stance

DOCTOR *just what the doctor ordered*
exactly right

DOG *a cat and dog existence*
a life full of frequent squabbles

DOG *a dogfight*
a small side-skirmish, especially between airplanes

DOG *a lame dog*
a person under some disadvantage needing attention and assistance

DOG *a shaggy-dog story*
an amusing anecdote with an unexpected ending, often involving talking animals given certain human skills

DOG *a sly dog*
a person who is discreet about his weaknesses

DOG *a watchdog*
a person or organization monitoring behavior

DOG *all the dogs are barking*
this news is being widely disseminated

DOG *any stick to beat a dog*
any excuse will do if it serves one's purpose

DOG *dog-eared*
(of pages) well-thumbed

DOG *dog-tired*
tired out

DOG *every dog has his day*
good luck comes sooner or later

DOG *every man and his dog*
everybody

DOG *love me—love my dog*
if you accept me then you must also accept my associates

DOG *not a dog's chance*
no hope at all

DOG *one cannot teach an old dog new tricks*
people get irreversibly set in their ways

DOG *the tail wagging the dog*
a minor aspect with disproportionate effect on a major aspect

DOG *the top dog*
the person in the most powerful position

DOG *to be a dog in the manger*
to spitefully deny something to others, notwithstanding its uselessness to oneself

DOG *to be a dog's breakfast*
to be a very messy arrangement

DOG *to be a gay dog*
to lead an idle life while flaunting the symbols of wealth

DOG *to be in the doghouse*
to be in disgrace

DOG *to call off the dogs*
to abandon an audit or other inquiry

DOG *to give a dog a bad name*
to malign a person

DOG *to go to the dogs*
to be ruined

DOG *to have a hair of the dog that bit one*
to drink more in an attempt to overcome the effects of alcohol already consumed

DOG *to lead a dog's life*
to be ill-treated

DOG *to let sleeping dogs lie*
to refrain from raising an issue which is not obviously requiring attention

DOG *to rain cats and dogs*
to rain heavily

DOG *to throw something to the dogs*
to sacrifice something

DOG *two men and a dog*
very few people

DOG *underdog*
object of sympathy (the antonym of ''underdog effect'' is ''bandwagon effect'')

DOG *why keep a dog and bark oneself?*
it is silly to pay for assistance and then do things personally

DOLDRUMS *to be in the doldrums*
to be depressed or to show no activity (refers to a region of little wind near the equator, becalming sailing ships)

DOLLAR *a sixty-four thousand dollar question*
a pertinent but very difficult question (refers to a television quiz show in which an initial prize doubles with the successful answering of progressively more difficult questions)

DOMINO *a domino effect*
a series of disasters each of which after the first is precipitated by the one before

DONKEY *donkey work*
necessary but uninspiring routine work

DONKEY *for donkey's years*
for a long time

DONKEY *to talk the hind leg off a donkey*
to talk excessively

DONNA *a prima donna*
a person with an exaggerated opinion of his own importance which makes relations with others needlessly difficult (Italian, "first lady")

DOOR *a foot in the door*
the opportunity to do business

DOOR *never darken my door again*
do not ever return

DOOR *not to break someone's door down*
to be quite unenthusiastic about someone's goods or services

DOOR *one's door is always open*
people can take their problems to one at any time

DOOR *through the back door*
unofficially or surreptitiously

DOOR *to be out the door*
to have one's position terminated

DOOR *to beat a path to someone's door*
to seek a person out in great numbers

DOOR *to keep the wolf from the door*
to avoid imminent trouble

DOOR *to knock on doors*
to seek out opportunities to do business

DOOR *to leave the door open*
to issue a standing invitation for the resumption of some negotiations

DOOR *to open up doors*
to create opportunities

DOOR *to put something at someone's door*
to blame a person

DOOR *to show someone the door*
to ask a person to leave

DOOR *to shut the door on someone*
to deny another person a desired opportunity

DOOR *to shut the stable door after the horse has bolted*
to take preventive action only after the relevant event

DOOR *to slam the door in someone's face*
ostentatiously to refuse to have any dealings with a person

DOORSTEP *on one's own doorstep*
in one's own domain

DOT *from the year dot*
from time immemorial

DOT *to arrive on the dot*
to turn up at the exact scheduled time

DOT *to dot the i's and cross the t's*
to be meticulous in completing the documentation for a transaction

DOT *to sign on the dotted line*
to confirm one's agreement

DOUBT *a doubting Thomas*
a person who refuses to believe claims in the absence of proof (John 20:25)

DOUGHNUT *watch the doughnut—not the hole*
look for the positive aspects

DOWN *a down-to-earth solution*
a realistic solution

DOWN *low-down*
confidential information relevant to something

DOWN *that is money down the drain*
money has been wastefully lost on a failed project

DOWN *to be down in the mouth*
to be depressed

DOWN *to be down the track*
to be making progress

DOWN *to be further down the line*
to have a low priority

DOWN *to be on the downgrade*
to be of deteriorating quality

DOWN *to catch someone with his trousers down*
to act when another person least expects it

DOWN *to keep one's head down*
to work very diligently

DOWN *to kick a man when he is down*
to take unfair advantage of a person already in difficulty

DOWN *to put one's foot down*
to exert one's authority and insist on something

DOWNFALL *downfall*
ruination

DOWNHILL *to go downhill*
to deteriorate

DOZEN *it is six of one and half a dozen of the other*
it does not matter

DOZEN *to talk nineteen to the dozen*
to engage in much idle chatter

DRAFT *to feel the draft*
to experience unfavorable conditions

DRAG *to drag one's feet*
to perform unduly slowly

DRAG *to drag one's heels*
to perform unduly slowly

DRAG *to drag someone by the head and ears*
to force a person to reveal the true facts

DRAG *to drag the chain*
to perform unduly slowly

DRAIN *that is money down the drain*
money has been wastefully lost on a failed project

DRAIN *to drain every ounce out of something*
to get the maximum use or pleasure out of something

DRAKE *to play ducks and drakes*
not to treat the matter seriously

DRAW *back to the drawing board*
the details need to be reconsidered

DRAW *to be on the drawing board*
to be being planned in detail

DRAW *to be quick on the draw*
to act precipitately

DRAW *to be the luck of the draw*
to be a chance result

DRAW *to draw a blank*
to be unsuccessful

DRAW *to draw a deep breath*
to get ready for exertion or for emotional news

DRAW *to draw a long bow*
to state a conclusion which while possible is unlikely on the known facts

DRAW *to draw a veil over something*
pointedly to avoid discussing something

DRAW *to draw blood from a stone*
to do the impossible

DRAW *to draw fire*
to encounter criticism

DRAW *to draw first blood*
to get an advantage

DRAW *to draw the line at that*
to refuse to go any further

DRAW *to draw the nets closer*
to intensify one's efforts

DRAW *to draw the short straw*
to be the one appointed to do something

DRAW *until stumps are drawn*
until the project ends (refers to cricket)

DRAWBRIDGE *to pull up the drawbridge*
to refuse to cooperate

DRAWCARD *drawcard*
feature expected to attract a crowd

DRAWER *to tuck something away in a drawer*
to put something aside for the time being

DRAWER *top drawer*
first class

DREAM *a pipedream*
a fanciful notion, wished for but unlikely

DREAM *to be successful beyond one's wildest dreams*
to be far more successful than one could have expected

DREAM *to dream up some story*
to concoct a false story naively or maliciously

DREAM *to have a dream run*
to encounter no difficulties

DRESS *dress rehearsal*
preliminary skirmish

DRESS *first in best dressed*
persons acting early will do better than latecomers

DRESS *to be dressed up to the nines*
to be attired in excessively elaborate garments

DRESS *to dress someone down*
to scold a person

DRESS *to engage in window dressing*
to present figures in an artificially favorable light

DRIFT *to drift apart*
to lose contact or to change feelings once held in common

DRINK *it is a long time between drinks*
activity is occurring only very spasmodically

DRINK *to be meat and drink*
to be very pleasurable

DRIVE *an opening wide enough to drive a coach and four through*
an excellent opportunity

DRIVE *to almost drive someone to tears*
to present information designed to make another person express sympathy not warranted by the facts

DRIVE *to drive a coach and horses through something*
to demonstrate major errors in something

DRIVE *to drive a wedge between two persons*
to set out to cause two persons to confront each other

DRIVE *to drive someone from pillar to post*
to send a person to a series of places in a vain attempt to achieve something

DRIVE *to drive someone out of his mind*
to cause great worry to a person

DRIVE *to drive someone to the wall*
to ruin a person

DRIVE *to drive someone up the wall*
to annoy another person by one's actions

DRIVE *to drive the lesson home*
to take certain action which is unpleasant but which has the effect of registering a message

DRIVER *a backseat driver*
a person seeking to exercise control

DRIVER *to be in the driver's seat*
to be in charge

DRONE *a drone*
an idle person

DROP *at the drop of a hat*
very readily

DROP *drop dead!*
go away, I want no dealings with you

DROP *someone's jaw dropped*
someone registered obvious disappointment, incredulity or shock

DROP *the penny dropped*
a person has just realized a fact which should have been obvious (refers to old-fashioned pay toilets)

DROP *to be only a drop in the bucket*
to be quite insignificant in the total scene

DROP *to be only a drop in the ocean*
to be quite insignificant in the total scene

DROP *to drop a brick*
to make a sudden shattering and unexpected announcement

DROP *to drop a clanger*
to do something indiscreet or which offends social conventions

DROP *to drop into one's lap*
to turn up fortuitously

DROP *to drop names*
to slip names of celebrities allegedly known to the speaker into a conversation in an attempt to impress

DROP *to drop one's bundle*
to become despondent

DROP *to squeeze the last drop out of something*
to get the maximum advantage out of some favorable situation

DROP *to wait for the other shoe to drop*
to await the seemingly imminent and inevitable (refers to a man undressing, disturbing a neighbor by dropping one shoe, then frustrating his expectation by putting the other shoe down gently)

DROUGHT *to break a drought*
to resume supplies after an interval

DROVE *people stayed away in droves*
few people came

DROWN *to drown one's sorrows*
to drink by way of solace and in an attempt to forget some misfortune

DRUG *to be a drug on the market*
to be in overplentiful supply

DRUM *to beat a drum for someone*
to propagate another person's cause

DRUM *to beat one's drum*
to immodestly publicize one's own attributes

DRUM *to drum someone out of some organization*
to terminate in ignominy a person's employment or membership (refers to the ceremonial cashiering in the army to the beating of parade drums)

DRUM *to drum up support*
to actively seek out support

DRUM *to march to a different drum*
to show an independent approach

DRUNK *to be punch drunk*
to be stupefied by some news

DRY *a dry hole*
an exercise which after much effort proves fruitless

DRY *a dry run*
a trial exercise

DRY *the ink is hardly dry*
something intended to last a long time is to be changed shortly after its establishment

DRY *to be cut and dried*
to be well settled or long established

DRY *to dry up*
to cease

DRY *to keep one's powder dry*
to retain key arguments or resources in reserve for use later

DRY *to leave someone high and dry*
to withdraw all support from a person or to isolate a person from a desired involvement

DRY *to suck the lemon dry*
to get the maximum advantage out of some favorable situation

DUCK *a lame duck*
a person unable to fend for himself (a lame duck president - a president still in office but without influence because the commencement of his successor's term is imminent)

DUCK *in two shakes of a duck's tail*
in an instant

DUCK *to be a dead duck*
to have failed

DUCK *to be a sitting duck*
to be readily exploited

DUCK *to be like water off a duck's back*
(of advice or criticism) to be completely rejected

DUCK *to break one's duck*
to end a spell without results (refers to cricket)

DUCK *to duck for cover*
to seek to avoid blame

DUCK *to play ducks and drakes*
not to treat the matter seriously

DUCKLING *an ugly duckling*
a person initially thought unintelligent who develops and becomes brilliant (refers to a cygnet in a brood of ducks in a children's story of that name by Hans Christian Andersen)

DUE *to give the devil his due*
to be fair (a phrase used in parenthesis, and only in the infinitive)

DUMP *to be in the dumps*
to feel depressed

DUMP *to dump something in someone's lap*
to impose some responsibility on another person

DUNCE *to earn a dunce's cap*
to do something stupid

DUST *to bite the dust*
to die

DUST *to dust some idea off*
to revive some proposal

DUST *to gather dust*
not to be acted upon without being formally rejected

DUST *to throw dust into someone's eyes*
to deceive a person by presenting inaccurate or misleading information

DUST *when the dust settles*
when sufficient time has passed

DYED *dyed in the wool*
very loyal and partisan

DYNAMITE *to be dynamite*
to cause outrage

DYNAMITE *to play with dynamite*
to invite trouble by virtue of one's risky conduct

E

EAGER *an eager beaver*
a person with great drive and enthusiasm even if this causes annoyance to others

EAGLE *to have an eagle eye*
to be able to notice small mistakes very readily

EAR *a word in someone's ear*
a confidential discussion

EAR *dog-eared*
(of pages) well-thumbed

EAR *little pitchers have long ears*
children have a tendency to overhear things

EAR *one can't make a silk purse out of a sow's ear*
it is impossible to manufacture something of a high standard without appropriate raw materials

EAR *to be all ears*
to be very attentive

EAR *to be music to one's ears*
to be comments which one is very pleased to hear

EAR *to be out on one's ear*
to have one's services abruptly terminated

EAR *to be up to one's ears in something*
to be very deeply involved in something

EAR *to be wet behind the ears*
to be excessively naive and inexperienced

EAR *to chew someone's ear*
to force one's conversation on an unwilling listener

EAR *to come out of one's ears*
to be plentiful

EAR *to come to someone's ears*
to come to someone's attention

EAR *to drag someone by the head and ears*
to force a person to reveal the true facts

EAR *to fall around one's ears*
to collapse utterly

EAR *to fall on deaf ears*
to be totally disregarded

EAR *to get the wrong sow by the ear*
to reach an incorrect conclusion

EAR *to go in one ear and out the other*
to leave no impression

EAR *to have money flowing out of one's ears*
to be very rich

EAR *to have someone's ear*
to have a person's attention

EAR *to keep an ear to the ground*
to be well informed as to current developments

EAR *to keep one's ears open*
to be on the lookout for useful information

EAR *to lend someone an ear*
to pay attention to a person

EAR *to play it by ear*
to develop one's strategy to always fit in with circumstances as they change from time to time

EAR *to prick up one's ears*
to suddenly start paying attention to a conversation in progress as a result of a half-heard phrase

EAR *to send someone away with a flea in his ear*
to give a person frank but unwelcome facts (refers to fleas trapped in the armor of ancient knights)

EAR *to turn something on its ear*
to reverse something

EAR *walls have ears*
someone may be overhearing (words on wartime posters, reminding people of the existence of spies; may also refer to certain rooms in the Louvre, constructed so that conversations could be heard in other rooms)

EAR *were your ears burning?*
we were discussing you

EAR *with one's ears pinned back*
chastened

EARLY *the early bird gets the worm*
a person who acts ahead of others gets an advantage over them

EARMARK *to earmark*
to allocate to a specific purpose

EARN *to earn a dunce's cap*
to do something stupid

EARN *to earn one's stripes*
to deserve promotion

EARN *to earn peanuts*
to get a reward which is far too small in relation to the value of the services rendered

EARTH *a down-to-earth solution*
a realistic solution

EARTH *earth-shattering*
very significant

EARTH *how on earth?*
just how?

EARTH *to be the salt of the earth*
to be a person whose ordinary efforts benefit the community (Matthew 5:13)

EARTH *to bring someone down to earth*
to disillusion a person

EARTH *to charge the earth*
to impose very high prices

EARTH *to move heaven and earth*
to do everything possible

EARTH *to promise the earth*
to give extravagant assurances

EARTH *to run someone to earth*
to locate a person

EASY *to be easy meat*
to be an opponent who is readily outwitted

EASY *to be easy on the eye*
to be visually attractive

EASY *to breathe easy*
(following some crisis) to relax

EAT *I'll eat my hat if so-and-so happens*
I do not believe that so-and-so will happen

EAT *moth-eaten*
(of ideas, etc.) antiquated

EAT *the proof of the pudding is in the eating*
the success of a venture will be measured by its results

EAT *to be able to eat someone for breakfast*
to be able to outwit a person very easily

EAT *to eat crow*
to accept a humiliating defeat

EAT *to eat humble pie*
to apologize

EAT *to eat one's heart out*
to suffer bitterly

EAT *to eat one's words*
to retract

EAT *to eat out of someone's hands*
to be unduly compliant

EAT *to eat someone alive*
to soundly defeat a person

EAT *to eat someone out of house and home*
to ruin a person by eating all he has

EAT *to want to have one's cake and eat it too*
to want two mutually exclusive alternatives

EAT *you can eat your heart out*
you are entitled to feel sad or jealous

EAVESDROP *to eavesdrop*
to deliberately listen to conversations to which one is not a party

EBB *ebb and flow*
fluctuations

EBB *to ebb away*
to decline gradually

ECHO *to echo someone's words*
to repeat another person's views as though they were one's own

ECLIPSE *to eclipse someone*
to outshine a person

EDGE *gilt-edged*
very safe

EDGE *to be a two-edged sword*
to involve both advantages and disadvantages of similar significance

EDGE *to be at the cutting edge of something*
to be in a position where important decisions need to be made

EDGE *to be on a knife edge*
to be in danger

EDGE *to be on edge*
to be nervous

EDGE *to be on the edge of one's seat*
to be very excited at what is currently happening

EDGE *to be on the razor's edge*
to be in great danger

EDGE *to become frayed at the edges*
no longer to be quite appropriate

EDGE *to fiddle at the edges*
to do some relatively minor things which do not deal with the substance of a problem

EDGE *to give someone the edge*
to give a person an advantage over others

EDGE *to have a leading edge*
to have an advantage

EDGE *to push someone over the brink*
by a small action to cause the absolute ruin (financially or emotionally) of someone already in peril

EDGE *to set someone's teeth on edge*
to cause a person to feel unhappy at a situation

EDGE *to take the edge off something*
to weaken the force or impact of something

EDGE *to tinker at the edges*
to make minor or cosmetic changes without affecting the substance

EDGE *to tip someone over the edge*
to cause a person to become mentally ill

EDGEWAYS *to get words in edgeways*
to manage to interrupt a conversation in order to put a separate point of view

EGG *a nest egg*
life savings

EGG *as sure as eggs are eggs*
with great certainty

EGG *chicken and egg*
two factors each of which results in the other

EGG *not to put all one's eggs in one basket*
to spread one's risks

EGG *one cannot make an omelette without breaking eggs*
the desired end dictates the means even if they cause harm to others

EGG *there are many ways to cook eggs*
there are many ways to achieve an objective

EGG *to be a bad egg*
to engage in dishonest behavior

EGG *to be a curate's egg*
to be good only in parts (refers to an 1895 cartoon in PUNCH)

EGG *to have egg on one's face*
to be embarrassed by the results of one's own stupidity

EGG *to kill the goose that lays the golden eggs*
through excessive greed to destroy a very profitable enterprise

EGG *to teach one's grandmother how to suck eggs*
to try to tell a much more experienced person something very obvious to him

EIGHT *to be right behind the eight ball*
to be in a position of extreme disadvantage

ELBOW *elbow grease*
hard manual work

ELBOW *more power to your elbow*
may your praiseworthy efforts lead to success

ELBOW *to be up to one's elbow in something*
to be deeply involved in something

ELBOW *to elbow someone out*
to force a person out of some office and oneself into it

ELEMENT *to be in one's element*
to be very comfortable in familiar surroundings or in an environment in which one can cope very readily

ELEPHANT *a rogue elephant*
a person of vicious temper who acts in an undisciplined way

ELEPHANT *a white elephant*
an expensive and useless luxury (refers to gifts of sacred elephants by the King of Siam to persons then ruined by the expense of their upkeep)

ELEPHANT *one looks for elephants in elephant country*
one needs to search in the right place

ELEVEN *at the eleventh hour*
at the last moment (actually "at the twenty-fourth hour" would be more logical) (Matthew 20:9)

ELEVEN *the second eleven*
persons performing an important function but one which is less important than that performed by others (refers to cricket)

ELEVENTH *eleventh commandment*
unwritten rule

EMASCULATE *to emasculate something*
to delete the essential features of something

EMOLLIENT *to be an emollient*
to be a measure designed to make people more favorably disposed to one's wishes

EMPIRE *to engage in empire building*
to set out to expand the size of the business or bureaucratic unit for which one is responsible, especially as a means of increasing one's own importance

ENCAPSULATE *to encapsulate some idea*
to reduce the essential points of a complicated proposal to a small number of words

END *a dead-end position*
a job with no prospects of advancement

END *at the end of the day*
in due course or at the conclusion of a project

END *the tail end of something*
the very end of something

END *this is the end of the road for someone*
a person will have no further opportunity to do something

END *to be at the end of one's tether*
to be frustrated by a lack of knowledge, authority or patience

END *to be on the losing end of the stick*
to be worse off while the other party to a transaction becomes correspondingly better off

END *to be the thin end of the wedge*
by conceding a small point to create an undesirable precedent for much larger issues

END *to burn the candle at both ends*
to work excessively long hours

END *to go off the deep end*
to lose one's temper

END *to have hold of the wrong end of the pineapple*
to be utterly mistaken

END *to hold the wrong end of the stick*
to be completely mistaken about something

END *to jump straight in at the deep end*
to do something without a proper lead-in

END *to make ends meet*
to live within one's income

END *to run into a dead end*
to get nowhere in an investigation

END *to see the light at the end of the tunnel*
to be close to finalizing a long exercise

END *to seek the pot of gold at the end of the rainbow*
to have naive expectations

END *to tie up the loose ends*
to complete the minor outstanding items of some substantially finished project

ENFANT *an enfant terrible*
a person who raises pertinent but unpalatable issues (French, "terrible child," "a little terror")

ENOUGH *enough to sink a battleship*
more than sufficient

ENSHRINE *to enshrine*
to incorporate as an important part of something

ENTER *to enter the home stretch*
to commence the last stage

ESCAPE *to escape by the skin of one's nose*
to only just avoid some disaster

ESCAPE *to escape by the skin of one's teeth*
to only just avoid some disaster

ESCUTCHEON *to be a blot on someone's escutcheon*
to be a blemish on a person's character

ESPIRIT *esprit de corps*
a feeling of camaraderie and concern for the good name of some organization of which one is a member (French, "vital breath of a body")

ESTATE *the fourth estate*
the press

EVE *to be on the eve of something*
to occur just before some event

EVEN *to even the score*
to get one's own back for some past action

EVEN *to keep something on an even keel*
to ensure that something is not harmed

EVERY *as every schoolboy knows*
as is recognized by everyone

EVERY *every Pancake Tuesday*
only on rare occasions (refers to Shrove Tuesday, when pancakes are traditionally eaten)

EVERY *every Tom, Dick and Harry*
just about everybody

EVERY *every cloud has a silver lining*
there are benefits even in seemingly adverse situations

EVERY *every dog has his day*
good luck comes sooner or later

EVERY *every man and his dog*
everybody

EVERY *in every nook and cranny*
everywhere

EVERY *to chase every hare*
to be easily sidetracked

EVERY *to drain every ounce out of something*
to get the maximum use or pleasure out of something

EVERY *to play every card in the pack*
to try very hard and use every conceivable argument

EVERY *to resist something every inch of the way*
to utterly resist something

EVERY *to use every trick in the book*
to try very hard and use every conceivable argument

EVERYTHING *everything but the kitchen sink*
a lot of things

EVERYTHING *everything under the sun*
everything

EVERYTHING *to do everything by halves*
to do everything imperfectly or incompletely

EXHAUST *to exhaust the field*
to use up all the possibilities

EXHIBITION *to make an exhibition of oneself*
to behave in a way which invites ridicule

EXISTENCE *a cat and dog existence*
a life full of frequent squabbles

EXPEDITION *a fishing expedition*
an exercise designed to get information to which one is not strictly entitled

EXPLODE *to explode*
(of a person) to express rage

EXPOSE *to expose one's flank*
to allow others to take advantage of one

EXTRA *to go the extra mile*
to work beyond the call of duty

EYE *a bird's-eye view*
a general overview or summary of a subject, emphasizing the major features

EYE *a mote in someone's eye*
a fault in another person which is trifling in comparison to an unrecognizable major fault in oneself (Matthew 7:3)

EYE *a smack in the eye*
a rebuff

EYE *all eyes are on something*
everyone's attention is focused on something

EYE *an eye for an eye*
retaliation (Exodus 21:24)

EYE *beauty is in the eye of the beholder*
some things are matters for subjective judgments

EYE *blue-eyed boy*
person shown unjustified favoritism

EYE *bright-eyed and bushy-tailed*
naive but enthusiastic

EYE *cock-eyed*
stupid

EYE *in one's mind's eye*
using a vivid imagination

EYE *in someone's eyes*
in a person's judgment

EYE *lynx-eyed*
having acute vision

EYE *one would give one's eye teeth for something*
a person would very much like to achieve some objective

EYE *one-eyed*
biased

EYE *someone's eyes are bigger than his stomach*
a person is unrealistic

EYE *someone's eyes popped*
a person expressed great surprise

EYE *to be a sight for sore eyes*
to be something welcome

EYE *to be all eyes*
to observe very closely

EYE *to be an eye opener*
to be a surprise

EYE *to be better than a poke in the eye with a burnt stick*
to be particularly welcome

EYE *to be easy on the eye*
to be visually attractive

EYE *to be eye wash*
to be nonsense

EYE *to be in the eye of the storm*
to be at the center of a controversy

EYE *to be in the public eye*
to have one's every action subject to scrutiny by the community

EYE *to be one in the eye for someone* to represent an unexpected and unwelcome defeat

EYE *to be only a gleam in someone's eyes* to be a long way from final achievement

EYE *to be the apple of someone's eye* to be a person of whom another person is proud

EYE *to cast an eye over something* to look at something critically

EYE *to cast sheep's eyes at someone* to look at a person amorously

EYE *to catch someone's eye* to attract the attention of another person or to seek permission to address that person

EYE *to clap eyes on something* to catch sight of something

EYE *to cock one's eye at someone* to glance knowingly at a person

EYE *to cry one's eyes out* to express great sadness at a situation

EYE *to do someone in the eye* to cheat a person

EYE *to have an eagle eye* to be able to notice small mistakes very readily

EYE *to have an eye for something* to appreciate the appearance of something

EYE *to have eyes at the back of one's head* to know more of what is going on than is generally realized

EYE *to have one's beady eyes on something* to await the chance to acquire something to which one is not properly entitled

EYE *to have one's eyes glued to something* to concentrate on looking at something to the exclusion of other competing calls for attention

EYE *to have stars in one's eyes* (for emotional rather than rational reasons) to be ecstatic

EYE *to hit someone right between the eyes* to be brutally frank

EYE *to hit the bull's eye* to make the correct decision

EYE *to keep a weather eye out for something* to look out with particular care

EYE *to keep an eye on the ball* to monitor a fast-changing situation

EYE *to keep one's eye on someone* to supervise a person or to monitor a person's activities and behavior

EYE *to keep one's eye on something* to monitor a situation

EYE *to keep one's eyes open* to be on the lookout for useful information

EYE *to keep one's eyes open for something* to be on the lookout for an opportunity to do something

EYE *to keep one's eyes peeled for something* to be on the constant lookout for something

EYE *to make eyes at someone* to look at a person amorously

EYE *to open someone's eyes to something* to alert another person to the truth of something

EYE *to pick the eyes out of something* to choose the most valuable items from among a large number

EYE *to pull the wool over someone's eyes*
to deceive or deliberately mislead another person

EYE *to rub one's eyes*
to express astonishment

EYE *to see eye to eye with someone*
to agree

EYE *to see something with half an eye*
to sum up a matter instantly

EYE *to see the color of someone's eyes*
to see how a person matches expectations or requirements

EYE *to shut one's eyes to something*
to deliberately take no notice of something, especially in dereliction of one's duty

EYE *to throw dust into someone's eyes*
to deceive a person by presenting inaccurate or misleading information

EYE *to turn a blind eye to something*
to pretend something obvious does not exist (refers to action by Nelson when disregarding Admiralty signals)

EYE *with an eye toward doing something*
with the intention that something particular be done

EYE *with one's eyes wide open*
fully conscious of the ramifications

EYEBALL *eyeball to eyeball*
confronting each other and taking account of each other's reactions

EYEBALL *to be up to the eyeballs in something*
to be very deeply involved in something

EYEBROW *to raise one's eyebrows*
to express one's utter astonishment

EYEFUL *to get an eyeful of something*
to see something impressive

EYELASH *not to bat an eyelash*
to fail to express any surprise

EYELID *to hang on by the eyelids*
to have only a slender hold

EYESORE *eyesore*
extremely ugly object

F

FACE *a poker face*
a facial expression which does not reveal one's thoughts during negotiations

FACE *a slap in the face*
a calculated insult or action amounting to a rebuke

FACE *a straight face*
a facial expression which does not reveal one's thoughts in a humorous situation

FACE *someone's face fell*
someone registered obvious disappointment

FACE *to be at the coal face*
to be in the place where the real work is done

FACE *to be left red-faced*
to be embarrassed

FACE *to blow up in someone's face*
to rebound on a person

FACE *to cut one's nose off to spite one's face*
to act in pique in a way which harms only oneself

FACE *to do an about-face*
to reverse a previously enunciated policy

FACE *to face a rocky road ahead*
to be likely to encounter difficulties

FACE *to face the music*
to accept responsibility when confronted by one's critics

FACE *to fall flat on one's face*
to make a bad error of judgment

FACE *to fly in the face of some rule*
to blatantly disregard some rule

FACE *to go on till one is blue in the face*
to argue for a long time

FACE *to have a long face*
to look miserable

FACE *to have egg on one's face*
to be embarrassed by the results of one's own stupidity

FACE *to hurl something in someone's face*
to reproach a person in regard to something

FACE *to lose face*
to endure embarrassment by virtue of being defeated or having one's errors found out

FACE *to present a happy face to the world*
bravely to gloss over one's problems

FACE *to put a brave face on it*
to face adversity cheerfully

FACE *to put a new face on something*
to alter the way something should be regarded

FACE *to put one's best face on something*
to focus on the positive features surrounding a basically disastrous situation

FACE *to save face*
to be allowed to keep one's dignity despite having suffered a defeat or made an error

FACE *to set one's face against something*
to oppose some matter

FACE *to show one's face*
to put in an appearance

FACE *to slam the door in someone's face*
ostentatiously to refuse to have any dealings with a person

FACE *to stare someone in the face*
(of a solution, etc.) to become obvious

FACE *to take something at face value*
(of alleged facts) to accept something without question or challenge

FACE *to wipe the smile off someone's face*
to destroy a person's complacency

FACE *two-faced*
insincere

FACE *volte face*
a reversal of previously-held beliefs (French, "a turning around")

FACE *wipe that smile off your face!*
treat this matter more seriously!

FACE *you will laugh on the other side of your face*
you will regret this

FAILURE *heart failure*
a shock

FAIR *a fair-weather friend*
a person purporting to be a friend who offers no support in difficult times

FAIR *to be a fair crack of the whip*
to be just

FAIR *to be fair game*
to be someone who can legitimately be attacked

FAIRY *a fairy godmother*
a person showing great kindness

FAIRY *to believe in the tooth fairy*
to be particularly gullible

FAITH *an article of faith*
a fundamental belief on which certain behavior is based

FAITHFUL *the old faithful*
a greatly loved article

FALL *a fallen angel*
a previously trusted person who has transgressed

FALL *crestfallen*
dejected

FALL *downfall*
ruination

FALL *it fell off the back of a truck*
(of goods) they were stolen; (of a politically sensitive document) it was leaked to me

FALL *let the cards fall where they may*
irrespective of what happens

FALL *someone's face fell*
someone registered obvious disappointment

FALL *that is the way the chips fall*
that is the actual situation

FALL *the ax has fallen*
it is now too late

FALL *the roof has fallen in*
an enterprise has collapsed

FALL *the sky fell in*
a very serious problem arose

FALL *the wheels fell off*
the plan failed

FALL *they fell over themselves to do something*
they showed great keenness while doing something

FALL *to be riding for a fall*
to act in a reckless manner

FALL *to fall around one's ears*
to collapse utterly

FALL *to fall between two stools*
not to fit neatly into either of two available alternatives and waver between them

FALL *to fall by the wayside*
to abandon and not complete what one set out to do

FALL *to fall flat*
(of a joke) to be unappreciated by the audience

FALL *to fall flat on one's face*
to make a bad error of judgment

FALL *to fall head over heels in love*
to fall very much in love

FALL *to fall in a heap*
(of a proposal) to collapse utterly

FALL *to fall into line*
to conform with others

FALL *to fall on deaf ears*
to be totally disregarded

FALL *to fall on one's feet*
surprisingly to succeed despite difficulties

FALL *to fall over one's own feet*
to be very clumsy

FALL *to fall through*
not to eventuate as expected

FALL *to fall to pieces*
(of a plan) to collapse

FALL *to fall to the ground*
to fail

FALL *to play the cards as they fall*
to deal with problems as they arise

FALL *where the ax falls*
who gets terminated

FALL *windfall*
unexpected good fortune

FALSE *a false dawn*
an incident giving rise to unjustified hope

FALSE *to sail under false colors*
to pretend that one's real character or beliefs are different from what they really are

FAMILY *to sell off the family silver*
to sell off one's prized possessions

FAMINE *to be either feast or famine*
to go from one extreme to the other

FAN *to fan the flames*
to increase unrest

FANCYFREE *footloose and fancyfree*
unmarried and without any romantic attachments

FANFARE *with much fanfare*
with great enthusiasm and public acclaim

FAR *to be a far cry from something*
to be a long way from something

FAST *fast and furious*
in an exciting way, in quick succession

FAST *life in the fast lane*
existence full of exciting but worthless activity

FAST *to come in thick and fast*
to arrive quickly and in great volume

FAST *to play fast and loose*
to disregard one's obligations

FAST *to pull a fast one*
to engage in a dirty trick

FAT *a fat chance*
little hope

FAT *it's not over till the fat lady sings*
it is not finished yet

FAT *the fat is in the fire*
action with certain unstoppable consequences has now been initiated

FAT *to chew fat*
to eat and talk together

FAT *to trim the fat*
to increase efficiency by reducing outlays

FATAL *to be fatal*
to be sufficient to destroy some proposal

FATE *to seal someone's fate*
to cause a certain outcome adversely affecting a person

FATHER *father knows best*
as an expert I know better than you do just what is most suitable for you

FATTEN *to kill the fatted calf*
to demonstrate welcome and forgiveness on a person's return (Luke 15:23)

FAUX *faux pas*
something indiscreet or offending social conventions (French, "false step")

FAVORITE *favorite son*
person preferred by many people for some office

FEAR *I fear the Greeks even when they bear gifts*
I am suspicious of generous behavior from traditional opponents (from Virgil's AENEID, in reference to the Trojan horse)

FEAR *fools rush in where angels fear to tread*
unsophisticated persons take unwise risks in circumstances where more knowledgeable persons would exercise caution

FEAR *in fear and trembling*
in a state of apprehension

FEAST *a movable feast*
an event not customarily held on a set date

FEAST *to be either feast or famine*
to go from one extreme to the other

FEATHER *a feather in one's cap*
a meritorious personal achievement

FEATHER *birds of a feather flock together*
persons of like interests gather in the same place

FEATHER *feather bedding*
(in industrial relations) creating unnecessary jobs solely to increase employment; (in economics) assisting an inefficient industry by government grants or excessive tariff protection

FEATHER *to feather one's own nest*
to improperly arrange a transaction on behalf of others to one's own financial advantage

FEATHER *to make feathers fly*
to cause trouble to those misbehaving

FEATHER *to ruffle someone's feathers*
to engage in behavior which irritates another person

FEATHER *to show the white feather*
to indicate cowardice (refers to cross-bred birds, not regarded as useful in cock fighting)

FEATHER *to thrash with a feather*
to award only a minor punishment for a very serious offense

FEDERAL *to make a Federal case out of something*
to attach far too much significance to a trivial issue

FEED *to be chicken feed*
to be small and unimportant

FEED *to be fed up to the back teeth*
to be disgusted

FEED *to bite the hand that feeds one*
to show ingratitude

FEED *to feed the fire*
to exacerbate a situation

FEEDBACK *feedback*
response from a target audience to those seeking to influence it

FEEL *a gut feeling*
a belief based purely on intuition and unsupported by facts or evidence

FEEL *to feel one's oats*
to display self-importance

FEEL *to feel the draft*
to experience unfavorable conditions

FEEL *to feel the pinch*
to be adversely affected by financial stringency

FEEL *to feel the rough side of someone's tongue*
to be verbally abused by a person

FELL *in one fell swoop*
all at the same time

FELONY *to compound the felony*
having already acted improperly to make matters worse (the misuse of a legal term: compounding a felony is the crime of agreeing for money not to prosecute a person for felony; in reality it is therefore an offense by a different person—not a second and worse offense by the original culprit)

FENCE *on our side of the fence*
in the group representing our vested interest

FENCE *to be on the other side of the fence*
to have an opposing point of view or position

FENCE *to be over the fence*
to be unreasonable

FENCE *to mend fences*
to achieve a reconciliation

FENCE *to rush one's fences*
to act precipitately

FENCE *to sit on the fence*
to refuse to choose between two alternatives

FENCE *to want to jump all one's fences at once*
to be unrealistic

FERRET *to ferret something out*
by diligent research to discover some secret

FESTER *to open up a festering sore*
to upset a person by drawing attention to a long-standing grievance

FETTER *to fetter someone*
to stop a person acting on his own initiative

FEVER *to be at fever pitch*
to be in a state of excited activity

FIDDLE *to fiddle at the edges*
to do some relatively minor things which do not deal with the substance of a problem

FIDDLE *to fiddle while Rome burns*
to neglect important considerations while concentrating on trivial side-issues

FIDDLE *to play second fiddle*
to fulfill a subordinate role

FIELD *a field day*
a very enjoyable and successful occasion

FIELD *a level playing field*
competition on equal terms

FIELD *distant fields look greener*
activities of which one has no experience seem much easier than is really the case

FIELD *to be ahead of the field*
to be better than one's competitors

FIELD *to cover the field*
to be comprehensive

FIELD *to exhaust the field*
to use up all the possibilities

FIELD *to have a field marshal's baton in one's kit*
to be ambitious

FIFTH *a fifth columnist*
a person using his position of trust to work for a rival cause

FIFTH *to be a fifth wheel*
to be superfluous

FIFTH *to plead the Fifth Amendment*
to refuse to answer an unwelcome question (refers to the Fifth Amendment of the United States Constitution, which provides protection against self-incrimination)

FIFTY *to have fifty cents each way*
to equivocate

FIG *one would not give a fig for something*
one regards something as worthless

FIGHT *a bunfight*
a minor and relatively friendly skirmish

FIGHT *a dogfight*
a small side-skirmish, especially between airplanes

FIGHT *to fight an uphill battle*
to face difficulties or to have formidable opposition

FIGHT *to fight bushfires*
to deal with crises as they arise rather than take preventive action

FIGHT *to fight fire with fire*
to counter a dangerous situation by making an equally dangerous move

FIGHT *to fight tooth and nail*
to strive very hard to win

FIGHT *to have a fight on one's hands*
to encounter resistance or opposition to a proposal

FIGUREHEAD *a figurehead*
the ceremonial chief officer of some organization without any real power (refers to the carving at the front of a ship)

FILL *to fill a vacuum*
to take advantage of an opportunity not acted on by others

FILL *to fill in the fine print*
to provide the precise details in respect of something presently existing in broad outline only

FILL *to fill someone's shoes*
to be a good successor

FILTER *to filter through to someone*
(of information) to eventually reach a person

FINAL *the final straw*
the latest step, which, when added to a large number of seemingly harmless previous steps, sets off a disaster resulting from the cumulative effect

FINAL *to deal the final hand*
to take steps which conclude a matter

FIND *the river found its mark*
equilibrium between two pressures has been achieved

FIND *to find one's feet*
to develop one's skills

FIND *to find out the state of play*
to ascertain the current position of some project

FIND *water will find its own level*
people will reach an appropriate position relative to others

FINE *not to put too fine a point on it*
speaking bluntly

FINE *to fill in the fine print*
to provide the precise details in respect of something presently existing in broad outline only

FINE *to fine-tune something*
to adjust something in order to bring it to perfection or to make it fit the circumstances in a much more appropriate fashion

FINE *to go through something with a fine-tooth comb*
to conduct an extremely thorough investigation

FINE *to raise something to a fine art form*
to become very clever at doing something

FINE *to tread a fine line*
cautiously to take action in circumstances where either too much or too little will cause difficulties

FINGER *light-fingered*
good at stealing

FINGER *not to lay a finger on someone*
to refrain from hurting a person

FINGER *not to lift a finger to help someone*
to refuse to assist

FINGER *someone's fingers are all thumbs*
a person is clumsy with his hands

FINGER *to burn one's fingers*
to lose money through foolishness

FINGER *to gnaw one's fingers to the bone*
to fret

FINGER *to have a finger in something*
to be involved in something

FINGER *to have a finger in the pie*
to have an interest in a project

FINGER *to have green fingers*
to be good at gardening

FINGER *to have itchy fingers*
to be impatient

FINGER *to have one's fingers in many different pies*
to be engaged in a variety of separate activities

FINGER *to have one's fingers in the till*
to steal from one's employer

FINGER *to have one's fingers on the pulse*
to know what is going on

FINGER *to have sticky fingers*
to be dishonest

FINGER *to keep one's cotton-picking fingers off something*
not to interfere in something

FINGER *to keep one's fingers crossed*
to hope for a good outcome

FINGER *to let something slip through one's fingers*
to allow something to escape from one's ownership or control

FINGER *to point the finger at someone*
to accuse a person or allege some indiscretion on his part

FINGER *to pull one's fingers out*
to get on with a job with alacrity

FINGER *to put one's finger on something*
to identify the essential features of something

FINGER *to stir a finger*
to make some minimum effort

FINGER *to twist someone around one's little finger*
by charm to get one's way

FINGER *to wave a finger at someone*
to indicate mild displeasure at another person's actions

FINGER *to work one's fingers to the bone*
to work very hard

FINGERNAIL *to bite one's fingernails*
to anxiously await a decision

FINGERNAIL *to hang on by one's fingernails*
to have only a slender hold

FINGERTIP *to cling on by one's fingertips*
to have only a slender hold

FINGERTIP *to have some subject at one's fingertips*
to be very familiar with a subject

FINISH *a photo finish*
a close result in a contest

FIRE *a baptism of fire*
the commencement of an operation which presented great difficulty

FIRE *a fire in someone's belly*
great enthusiasm

FIRE *fire sale*
a forced sale, realizing bargain prices

FIRE *out of the frying pan into the fire*
from one bad situation to an even worse one

FIRE *sure-fire*
guaranteed

FIRE *the fat is in the fire*
action with certain unstoppable consequences has now been initiated

FIRE *to add fuel to the fire*
to make a bad situation worse

FIRE *to be in the firing line*
to be among the first to be under attack

FIRE *to draw fire*
to encounter criticism

FIRE *to feed the fire*
to exacerbate a situation

FIRE *to fight fire with fire*
to counter a dangerous situation by making an equally dangerous move

FIRE *to fire a parting shot*
to make a defiant gesture on leaving

FIRE *to fire a salvo at someone*
to present a series of criticisms to a person

FIRE *to fire a volley at someone*
to send a series of angry messages to someone

FIRE *to go through fire and water*
to undertake all attendant risks

FIRE *to hang fire*
to take no immediate action

FIRE *to have a bullet which can be fired*
to have available an effective response which can be used at will

FIRE *to have other irons in the fire*
to have the opportunity to do something else as an alternative

FIRE *to hold fire*
to defer criticizing

FIRE *to hold one's fire*
to delay proposed action

FIRE *to keep the home fires burning*
to maintain normal domestic activity during the temporary absence of the breadwinner

FIRE *to play with fire*
to invite trouble through one's foolish conduct

FIRE *to pull someone's chestnuts out of the fire*
to retrieve a situation

FIRE *to pull something out of the fire*
to salvage something in a seemingly hopeless situation

FIRE *to set the Thames on fire*
to do something noteworthy

FIRE *to set the world on fire*
to do something particularly brilliant

FIRE *to stoke the fires*
to provoke a violent reaction

FIRE *where there is smoke there is fire*
if there is a hint of trouble, then it is highly likely that there really is trouble

FIREMAN *a visiting fireman*
an important person calling on business to whom certain courtesies need to be paid

FIRESTORM *to run into a firestorm*
to be faced with many protests

FIREWORKS *fireworks*
aggressive behavior because of anger

FIRST *at first blush*
prima facie

FIRST *at first hand*
personally

FIRST *first catch your hare*
do things in logical order and after proper preparation (advice on how to cook a hare in Mrs. Beeton's celebrated COOK BOOK)

FIRST *first in best dressed*
persons acting early will do better than latecomers

FIRST *head first*
precipitately

FIRST *to be first class*
to be very satisfactory

FIRST *to be first off the mark*
to start ahead of all others

FIRST *to be the first cab off the rank*
to start ahead of all others

FIRST *to draw first blood*
to get an advantage

FIRST *to get to first base*
to succeed in getting others to start comprehending a problem

FIRST *to jump in feet first*
to take a calculated risk

FISH *a fishing expedition*
an exercise designed to get information to which one is not strictly entitled

FISH *a queer fish*
an unusual type of person

FISH *an ocean full of fish*
plenty of opportunity

FISH *neither fish, flesh nor good red herring*
unclassifiable by virtue of being neither one thing nor another (from Cervantes' *Don Quixote*)

FISH *that has nothing to do with the price of fish*
that is quite irrelevant

FISH *to be a big fish in a little pond*
to be a person holding an important office but in an unimportant organization

FISH *to be a cold fish*
to be an unemotional person

FISH *to be a different kettle of fish*
to be something very dissimilar

FISH *to be a fine kettle of fish*
to be a terrible muddle

FISH *to be a fish out of water*
to be in difficulty by virtue of being in a strange environment

FISH *to be in a goldfish bowl*
to be very open to view

FISH *to fish for compliments*
to drop hints in the hope that one will receive praise or recognition

FISH *to fish in troubled waters*
to profit from a disturbed situation

FISH *to have more important fish to fry*
to have more important things to do

FISHY *to be fishy*
to be suspicious

FIST *ham-fisted*
undiplomatic and clumsy

FIST *hand over fist*
rapidly overtaking each other during progress toward a common goal

FIST *hard-fisted*
stingy

FIST *tight-fisted*
stingy

FIST *to lose money hand over fist*
to lose money very fast and convincingly

FIST *to make a good fist of something*
to be successful in a difficult task

FIST *to rule with an iron fist*
to keep strict discipline

FISTFUL *to hold out a fistful of dollars*
to offer by way of inducement

FIT *if the cap fits then wear it*
if your circumstances correspond with those described then you must endure the consequences

FIT *not fit to hold a candle to someone*
greatly inferior to another person

FIT *not to get along with someone in a fit*
not to get along with a person

FIT *to fit the bill*
to meet all the requirements

FIT *to have a blue fit*
to be very agitated

FIT *to have a fit*
to be in a state of great agitation

FIT *to have a fit of the vapors*
to be horrified

FIVE *to know how many beans make five*
to have common sense

FLAG *to rally to the flag*
to show support for a cause

FLAG *to show the flag*
to visit a place in order to boost morale there

FLAG *to wave a flag for someone*
to promote a person's cause

FLAGSHIP *flagship*
most important member of a group of related entities

FLAK *to attract flak*
to attract criticism

FLAME *an old flame*
a former lover

FLAME *keepers of the flame*
persons keen to maintain old traditions

FLAME *to fan the flames*
to increase unrest

FLAME *to inflame a situation*
to aggravate a situation

FLAME *to pour gasoline on the flames*
to make a bad situation worse

FLAME *to rekindle an old flame*
to inspire the reinstatement of a former loving relationship

FLAME *to shoot someone down in flames*
to utterly destroy another person's arguments

FLANK *to expose one's flank*
to allow others to take advantage of one

FLASH *a flash in the pan*
something which begins promisingly but does not last (refers to the priming of old guns)

FLASH *in a flash*
in an instant

FLASH *to see red lights flashing*
to be conscious of the danger

FLAT *flat out like a lizard*
to be hard at work (a play on words, not a simile)

FLAT *to be in a flat spin*
to be in a state of high excitement

FLAT *to catch someone flat-footed*
to embarrass a person in the course of his making mistakes or being unprepared

FLAT *to fall flat*
(of a joke) to be unappreciated by the audience

FLAT *to fall flat on one's face*
to make a bad error of judgment

FLAVOR *to be the flavor of the month*
to be a commodity temporarily popular without a logical reason

FLEA *to send someone away with a flea in his ear*
to give a person frank but unwelcome facts (refers to fleas trapped in the armor of ancient knights)

FLEECE *to fleece someone*
to cheat a person out of some asset

FLESH *neither fish flesh nor good red herring*
unclassifiable by virtue of being neither one thing not another (from Cervantes' DON QUIXOTE)

FLESH *one's own flesh and blood*
one's offspring

FLESH *one's pound of flesh*
that which is due to one (from Shakespeare's MERCHANT OF VENICE)

FLESH *the spirit is willing but the flesh is weak*
the body is not up to the demands made on it

FLESH *to be a thorn in someone's flesh*
to be a person whose persistent presence and righteous views annoy

FLESH *to be more than flesh can stand*
to be more than a person can reasonably be expected to endure

FLESH *to flesh out the skeleton*
to supply the missing pertinent details

FLESH *to go the way of all flesh*
to die

FLESH *to make someone's flesh creep*
to frighten a person with something horrific

FLESH *to put flesh and bone on something*
to supply details of a proposal previously revealed only in outline

FLESH *to see someone in the flesh*
to see someone in person

FLESHPOT *fleshpots*
sumptuous living (Exodus 16:3)

FLEX *to flex one's muscles*
to exert one's personality or powers

FLOCK *birds of a feather flock together*
persons of like interests gather in the same place

FLOCK *flock*
congregation in the charge of a religious official

FLOG *to flog a dead horse*
to misguidedly do something patently useless

FLOODGATE *to open up the floodgates*
to take action which will have massive consequences

FLOOR *there is blood on the floor*
this has caused great anguish

FLOOR *to get in on the ground floor*
to invest on very favorable terms

FLOOR *to hold the floor*
to dominate a conversation

FLOOR *to wipe the floor with someone*
to inflict a humiliating defeat on a person

FLOTSAM *flotsam and jetsam*
derelict persons, without a fixed abode or stable life (refers to goods found floating and to goods thrown overboard deliberately, respectively)

FLOURISH *with a flourish of trumpets*
triumphantly

FLOW *a lot of water has flowed under the bridge since then*
much has happened since then

FLOW *ebb and flow*
fluctuations

FLOW *to have money flowing out of one's ears*
to be very rich

FLUSH *to flush out the facts*
to ascertain, after some effort, the truth of some matter

FLUX *to be in a state of flux*
to be subject to continuous change

FLY *I would love to be a fly on the wall*
I would love to hear what goes on

FLY *a fly in the ointment*
a flaw (refers to dead flies turning perfumes rancid) (Ecclesiastes 10:1)

FLY *a fly-by-night operator*
a confidence trickster

FLY *a highflyer*
an ambitious and/or successful person

FLY *as the crow flies*
by the shortest distance

FLY *someone can't hurt a fly*
someone is very gentle and kindhearted

FLY *the bird has flown*
the person sought is no longer about

FLY *there are no flies on someone*
a person is alert

FLY *time flies*
time passes very quickly, but if wasted can never be recovered (from Virgil's GEORGICS)

FLY *to fly a kite*
to issue uncovered checks in the hope that they will be covered before clearance or to test public reaction to legislation in contemplation by leaking broad details of it to the media

FLY *to fly by the seat of one's pants*
to act unprofessionally

FLY *to fly high*
to be ambitious

FLY *to fly in the face of some rule*
to blatantly disregard some rule

FLY *to fly off the handle*
to show irrational anger

FLY *to fly out the window*
to be lost

FLY *to fly the coop*
to grow up and become independent

FLY *to have to fly*
to need to leave in order to reach the next destination quickly

FLY *to let fly at someone*
to attack a person with strong words

FLY *to make feathers fly*
to cause trouble to those misbehaving

FLY *to make sparks fly*
to cause rapid activity to take place

FLY *to make the fur fly*
to create a disturbance

FLY *to achieve a flying start*
to get operational very quickly

FLYING *to pass with flying colors*
to be very successful

FOAM *to foam at the mouth*
to show anger

FOCUS *to bring something into focus*
to put some matter into its proper content and explain its true significance

FOCUS *to focus on something*
to concentrate attention on something

FOG *to be in a fog*
to be in a state of confusion

FOGGY *not to have the foggiest notion*
to know nothing at all about the subject

FOLD *the fold*
the body of believers (refers to an enclosure for sheep)

FOLD *to quietly fold up one's tent*
to surreptitiously abandon a previously-cherished stance

FOLLOW *to be a hard act to follow*
to be an impressive performance, not easily matched by the next person

FOLLOW *to follow in someone's footsteps*
to do as another person did

FOLLOW *to follow one's nose*
to act intuitively

FOLLOW *to follow the herd*
to do what most other people are doing

FOOD *food for thought*
material for examinatin in one's mind

FOOD *to take food out of the mouths of children*
cruelly to deprive the needy

FOOL *fools rush in where angels fear to tread*
unsophisticated persons take unwise risks in circumstances where more knowledgeable persons would exercise caution

FOOL *to live in a fool's paradise*
to delude oneself

FOOT *a foot in the door*
the opportunity to do business

FOOT *itchy feet*
a desire to travel

FOOT *nimble-footed*
quick to change the direction of one's activities when circumstances warrant

FOOT *not to let grass grow under one's feet*
not to let inertia or delay spoil something

FOOT *not to put a foot wrong*
to behave impeccably

FOOT *the boot is on the other foot*
the real facts are the other way round

FOOT *to be at one's feet*
to be in the immediate vicinity

FOOT *to be quick on one's feet*
to cleverly take advantage of a situation

FOOT *to be rushed off one's feet*
to be rushed

FOOT *to be six feet under*
to be dead

FOOT *to bind someone hand and foot*
to completely limit a person's freedom to act

FOOT *to catch someone flat-footed*
to embarrass a person in the course of his making mistakes or being unprepared

FOOT *to cut the ground from under someone's feet*
to unexpectedly withdraw support and in the process cause embarrassment or to demolish a person's case

FOOT *to drag one's feet*
to perform unduly slowly

FOOT *to fall on one's feet*
surprisingly to succeed despite difficulties

FOOT *to fall over one's feet*
to be very clumsy

FOOT *to find one's feet*
to develop one's skills

FOOT *to get back on one's feet*
to recover from an illness or some other setback

FOOT *to get cold feet*
to become scared

FOOT *to get off on the wrong foot with someone*
to make an unfavorable initial impression on a person

FOOT *to get one's feet wet*
to do the necessary but unpleasant or menial parts of a task

FOOT *to go hot foot*
to do something fast

FOOT *to have feet of clay*
to be vulnerable (Daniel 2:33)

FOOT *to have one foot in the grave*
to be dying

FOOT *to have one's feet firmly on the ground*
to know what one is doing

FOOT *to have one's feet in both camps*
to have good relations with two opponents

FOOT *to have one's foot on something*
to be about to acquire something or to be able to acquire something

FOOT *to have the ball at one's feet*
to have unlimited opportunity

FOOT *to have two left feet*
to be clumsy

FOOT *to jump in feet first*
to take a calculated risk

FOOT *to put one's best foot forward*
to make a special effort

FOOT *to put one's feet up*
to relax

FOOT *to put one's foot down*
to exert one's authority and insist on something

FOOT *to put one's foot in it*
to make a foolish mistake

FOOT *to put one's foot in one's mouth*
to say something foolish

FOOT *to put someone on the back foot*
to cause a person to adopt a lower profile

FOOT *to put something back on its feet*
to repair something

FOOT *to run someone off his feet*
to keep a person very busy on some physical task

FOOT *to shoot oneself in the foot*
to act in a foolish way and thus harm one's own cause

FOOT *to stand on one's own two feet*
not to require the help of others

FOOT *to start off on the right foot*
to commence an operation with great care to do it correctly

FOOT *to sweep someone off her feet*
to cause a person to lose all discernment

FOOT *to tread someone under foot*
to oppress a person

FOOT *to vote with one's feet*
to show one's displeasure by terminating an association

FOOT *to wait hand and foot on someone*
to accommodate a person's every real or imagined whim

FOOTBALL *a political football*
a political issue which is not being debated on its merits

FOOTHOLD *to gain a foothold*
to achieve a position from which further advances can readily be made

FOOTLOOSE *footloose and fancyfree*
unmarried and without any romantic attachments

FOOTNOTE *a footnote*
a passing comment by way of elaboration

FOOTPRINT *without leaving any footprints*
without making any impression

FOOTSTEP *to follow in someone's footsteps*
to do as another person did

FOR *a tooth for a tooth*
retaliation (Exodus 21:24)

FOR *an eye for an eye*
retaliation (Exodus 21:24)

FORBID *forbidden fruit*
something particularly desired just because it is not allowed (Genesis 2:17)

FORCE *to force someone onto his knees*
to inflict a humiliating defeat on a person

FORCE *to force someone's hand*
to take action causing another person to react

FORCE *to join forces*
to cooperate with one another in order to achieve a common objective

FORCE *tour de force*
feat of skill or strength (French, "feat of strength")

FORGIVE *anyone could be forgiven for believing that*
it is understandable that people would believe that

FORK *fork in the road*
turning point for decisions

FORKED *to speak with forked tongues*
to utter half-truths with the intention of misleading the listener

FORM *not to do something in any way, shape or form*
not to do something

FORM *to raise something to a fine art form*
to become very clever at doing something

FORT *to hold the fort*
to be in charge during the temporary absence of a superior

FORWARD *to give something a nudge forward*
to give modest encouragement to something

FORWARD *to inch forward*
to make slow but steady progress

FORWARD *to put one's best foot forward*
to make a special effort

FORWARD *to take a giant step forward*
to make a significant advance

FOUL *foul play*
treachery or murder

FOUL *to foul one's own nest*
to disparage one's home or workplace

FOUNDER *to founder on the shoals of something*
to come to grief because of unexpected dangers

FOUNTAINHEAD *fountainhead*
source of all wisdom

FOUR *an opening wide enough to drive a coach and four through*
an excellent opportunity

FOUR *four square*
honest and reliable

FOUR *from the four corners of the globe*
from everywhere

FOUR *to compete on all fours with someone*
to strive on equal terms

FOURTH *the fourth estate*
the press

FOX *a fox hole*
space which is really too small for a person's needs or comfort

FRAMEWORK *framework*
outline of a proposal, on which further details can be developed

FRANKENSTEIN *to create a Frankenstein*
to create something wicked and out of control (a reference to the fictional creator of a monster, in mistake for a reference to the monster itself)

FRAY *to become frayed at the edges*
no longer to be quite appropriate

FREDDY *blind Freddy could see that something is such-and-such*
it is very obvious that something is such-and-such

FREE *to get off scot free*
to go unpunished (refers to an exemption from tax)

FREE *to give someone a free hand*
to authorize a person to act as he sees fit

FREE *to give someone free rein*
to confer complete direction on another person

FREEZE *to freeze someone out*
to deliberately exclude a person

FRESH *fresh blood*
newly joined members of some organization

FRESH *to be a breath of fresh air*
to be a pleasant change from the past

FRIEND *to have a friend at court*
a person with influence who is willing to use it on one's behalf

FRIGHTEN *to frighten hell out of someone*
to alarm a person

FRIGHTEN *to frighten the horses*
to scare people off by one's ill-considered tactics

FROG *to have a frog in one's throat*
to be hoarse

FROG *to leap frog something*
to overtake something, with the likelihood of in turn being overtaken (refers to a game in which participants jump over each other in turn)

FRONT *to have a job in front of one*
to face difficulties

FROWN *to frown on something*
to disapprove of some matter

FRUIT *by their fruits ye shall know them*
their reputation will be based on their results (Matthew 7:20)

FRUIT *forbidden fruit*
something particularly desired just because it is not allowed (Genesis 2:17)

FRUIT *to bear fruit*
to result in success

FRUITLESS *fruitless*
yielding no benefit

FRY *out of the frying pan into the fire*
from one bad situation to an even worse one

FRY *to have more important fish to fry*
to have more important things to do

FUEL *to add fuel to the fire*
to make a bad situation worse

FULL *I've had a belly full*
I have had enough of this

FULL *an ocean full of fish*
plenty of opportunity

FULL *full-blooded*
vigorous

FULL *full bore ahead!*
proceed forward!

FULL *full steam ahead!*
get going as fast as possible!

FULL *to be a full bottle on something*
to be very knowledgeable

FULL *to be full of beans*
to be very cheerful

FULL *to be full of hot air*
to have an exaggerated opinion of one's own importance and to boast about it

FULL *to be in full swing*
to be very active

FULL *to come to a full stop*
to completely cease activity

FULL *to get full marks for something*
to deserve praise for something

FULL *to have one's hands full*
to be fully occupied

FULL *yes sir—yes sir—three bags full!*
(in servile response to some request) yes, very willingly!

FUN *fun and games*
amusement derived in the course of a serious activity

FUN *to be no fun*
to be difficult

FUNERAL *that is your funeral!*
that is the fate which you will have to suffer

FUNK *to be in a blue funk*
to be terrified

FUR *to make the fur fly*
to create a disturbance

FURIOUS *fast and furious*
in an exciting way, in quick succession

FURNITURE *to be part of the furniture*
to be so familiar that one's presence goes completely unnoticed

FURTHER *to be further down the line*
to have a low priority

FUSE *to have a short fuse*
to lose one's temper very readily

FUSE *to light a fuse*
to cause serious reactions

G

GAIN *to gain a foothold*
to achieve a position from which further advances can readily be made

GAIN *to gain ground*
to advance one's position relative to others

GAIN *to gain the upper hand*
to attain, after some effort, an advantage over another person

GAIN *what one loses on the swings one gains on the roundabouts*
there are advantages and disadvantages which offset each other

GALL *gall*
impudence

GALLERY *to play to the gallery*
to do something which appeals to the general public rather than something which is right

GALVANIZE *to galvanize someone into action*
to enthuse a person into doing something

GAMBIT *a gambit*
an opening move in a competitive situation which involves short-term losses in the expectation of long-term gains

GAMBIT *opening gambit*
the first in a series of strategic moves (a tautological expression which also involves a misunderstanding of a technical chess term)

GAME *I'll soon stop his little game*
his activities are not tolerated and I will ensure that they cease

GAME *a game of cat and mouse*
negotiations between two parties of unequal bargaining power during which the stronger makes some temporary concessions to the weaker without, however, affecting the latter's eventual total defeat

GAME *a game of poker*
negotiations in which the parties try to bluff each other

GAME *a game of snakes and ladders*
a series of ups and downs

GAME *a mug's game*
activity which wise persons would eschew

GAME *don't play games with me!*
do not insult my intelligence by that line of conduct

GAME *fun and games*
amusement derived in the course of a serious activity

GAME *game, set and match*
completion

GAME *it is just a game to someone*
it is an exercise which a person does not take seriously

GAME *so-and-so is the name of the game*
so-and-so is the essential element of the exercise

GAME *the game is up*
escape is now impossible

GAME *the only game in town*
the only event worthy of attention

GAME *to be a chess game*
to be a complex exercise, requiring great skill

GAME *to be a new ball game*
to be subject to completely revised rules or very different conditions

GAME *to be fair game*
to be someone who can legitimately be attacked

GAME *to beat someone at his own game*
to outwit a person in his own specialization

GAME *to give the game away*
to cease involvement with some activity

GAME *to lift one's game*
to raise the standard of one's performance

GAME *to play a deep game*
to show cunning

GAME *to play the game*
to observe the letter and the spirit of the rules or to act honorably

GAME *to stick to one's game*
to confine oneself to activities in areas in which one has knowledge and expertise

GAME *two can play at that game*
it is possible to retaliate

GAME *what is his game?*
what is the significance of his actions?

GAMUT *the whole gamut*
the whole range of some activity

GANDER *what is sauce for the goose is sauce for the gander*
arguments which apply in one case also apply in another

GAP *to bridge a gap*
to fill a need or make up a shortfall

GARAGE *garage sale*
sale of miscellaneous assets at cheap prices

GARDEN *everything in the garden is lovely*
everything is fine

GARDEN *to lead someone up the garden path*
to mislead a person by deliberately fallacious arguments

GARTER *I will have his guts for garters*
I am extremely angry and dissatisfied with him

GAS *to be cooking with gas*
to be fully operational

GASOLINE *to pour gasoline on the flames*
to make a bad situation worse

GASOLINE *to put a match to gasoline*
to make a bad situation worse

GATE *to close the gate*
to deny an opportunity which was previously available

GATE *to gatecrash a gathering*
to attend a gathering without any right to be there

GATEPOST *between you and me and the gatepost*
confidentially

GATEWAY *gateway to something*
method of achieving something

GATHER *to gather dust*
not to be acted upon without being formally rejected

GAUNTLET *to run the gauntlet*
to be subjected to criticism (from the Spanish word for "passage," in reference to punishment inflicted on delinquents made to run between two files of soldiers)

GAUNTLET *to throw down the gauntlet*
to issue a challenge (refers to the glove worn by a knight)

GAY *to be a gay dog*
to lead an idle life while flaunting the symbols of wealth

GEAR *to be geared up to do something*
to have equipment, labor and know-how in place adequate for some task

GEAR *to be in top gear*
to be making excellent progress

GEL *to gel*
to make sense

GENIE *to let the genie out of the bottle*
to cause something irreversible to take place

GENIE *to put the genie back in the bottle*
to undo something which cannot be undone

GET *it is getting to me*
it is affecting me psychologically

GHOST *not the ghost of a chance*
no hope at all

GHOST *to give up the ghost*
to die

GIANT *a giant*
a person whose ability and achievements exceed that of most other people

GIANT *to take a giant step forward*
to make a significant advance

GIDDY *to play the giddy goat*
to act the fool

GIFT *I fear the Greeks even when they bear gifts*
I am suspicious of generous behavior from traditional opponents (from Virgil's AENEID, in reference to the Trojan horse)

GIFT *to look a gift horse in the mouth*
to be suspicious about a benefit which has been volunteered

GILD *to gild the lily*
(actually: to gild refined gold, to paint the lily) to do something patently unnecessary

GILT *gilt-edged*
very safe

GIRD *to gird up one's loins*
to get ready for action

GLARE *glaring error*
patently obvious mistake

GLASS *people in glass houses should not throw stones*
those who are less than perfect are foolish to criticize others

GLASSES *to see something through rose-colored spectacles*
to appreciate only the advantages and to completely disregard the disadvantages

GLEAM *to be only a gleam in someone's eyes*
to be a long way from final achievement

GLEE *to rub one's hands with glee*
to express great satisfaction

GLITTER *all that glitters is not gold*
things are not always what they seem

GLOBE *from the four corners of the globe*
from everywhere

GLOVE *the gloves are off*
the challenge has been accepted

GLOVE *to take off the gloves*
to fight mercilessly or to debate with great ferocity

GLOVE *to treat someone with kid gloves*
to handle a person with great discretion

GLOVE *to work hand in glove with someone*
to work in close cooperation with a person or to be in collusion with a person to the detriment of others

GLOVE *with an iron hand in a velvet glove*
with a hard attitude made to seem soft

GLOW *a warm inner glow*
satisfaction at some achievement

GLUE *to have one's eyes glued to something*
to concentrate on looking at something to the exclusion of other competing calls for attention

GLUTTON *to be a glutton for punishment*
to act irresponsibly in the face of inevitable retribution

GNASH *to gnash one's teeth*
to express frustration

GNAT *to strain at a gnat*
to be scrupulous about trifles

GNAW *to gnaw one's fingers to the bone*
to fret

GO *from go to whoa*
from start to finish (refers to the command given to horses)

GO *from the word "go"*
from the beginning

GO *it was touch and go*
there were considerable risks—the objective was achieved, but only just

GO *to be all systems "go"*
to go ahead as fast as possible

GOAL *to score a goal*
to achieve an objective

GOAL *to score an own goal*
to blow oneself up

GOAT *a scapegoat*
a person unfairly blamed for something not his fault

GOAT *to play the giddy goat*
to act the fool

GOAT *to separate the sheep from the goats*
to distinguish between those with and without certain attributes (Matthew 25:32)

GOD *a little tin god*
a petty tyrant

GOD *the mills of God grind slowly*
retribution may be delayed but is inevitable

GOD *to be in the lap of the gods*
to be a matter of pure chance (refers to wax tablets inscribed with requests and placed on the knees of statues of Greek gods)

GODFORSAKEN *godforsaken*
dismal and without any redeeming feature

GODMOTHER *a fairy godmother*
a person showing great kindness

GOLD *a golden handshake*
a large payment in connection with or as an inducement to retirement

GOLD *a golden opportunity*
an unparalleled opportunity

GOLD *a pot of gold*
wealth

GOLD *all that glitters is not gold*
things are not always what they seem

GOLD *golden parachute*
generous provisions in a remuneration package which come into play in certain circumstances

GOLD *golden shackles*
financial arrangements designed to discourage employees changing employers

GOLD *silence is golden*
it is better not to incriminate anyone

GOLD *to be a river of gold*
to be a source of ongoing great profitability

GOLD *to be worth one's weight in gold*
to be very desirable

GOLD *to go for the gold*
to aim for victory (refers to Olympic medals)

GOLD *to have a heart of gold*
to have a generous disposition

GOLD *to kill the goose that lays the golden eggs*
through excessive greed to destroy a very profitable enterprise

GOLD *to seek the pot of gold at the end of the rainbow*
to have naive expectations

GOLD *to strike gold*
to have one's efforts suddenly rewarded by great success

GOLDFISH *to be in a goldfish bowl*
to be very open to view

GOLDFISH *what is this—a bunch of grapes or a bowl of goldfish?*
surely you know what this is!

GOLDMINE *a goldmine*
a source of much wealth or of many facts

GOLIATH *a Goliath*
a giant or a person whose ability and achievements exceed those of most other people (1 Samuel 17)

GOMORRAH *a Sodom and Gomorrah*
a place of vice (Genesis 18:20)

GOOD *this does my heart good*
I rejoice at this

GOOD *to be a good boy*
to be cooperative

GOOD *to be in good heart*
to be cheerful, especially in adversity

GOOD *to be in someone's good books*
to be well regarded by another person

GOOD *to be of good heart*
to be brave in adversity

GOOD *to have a good nose for business*
to be able to identify profitable business situations

GOOD *to see someone in a good light*
to regard a person favorably

GOOD *to throw good money after bad*
to waste further money in a vain attempt to recover money already lost

GOODS *to deliver the goods*
to achieve the objective

GOOSE *a wild goose chase*
a foolish search for something which does not exist

GOOSE *to be too frightened to say "boo" to a goose*
to be excessively shy

GOOSE *to cook one's goose*
to do something which backfires on one

GOOSE *to kill the goose that lays the golden eggs*
through excessive greed to destroy a very profitable enterprise

GOOSE *what is sauce for the goose is sauce for the gander*
arguments which apply in one case also apply in another

GOOSEBERRY *to play gooseberry*
to act as an unwelcome chaperon

GORDIAN *to cut the Gordian knot*
to solve, especially by force, a virtually insoluble problem (refers to a complicated knot tied by Gordius and eventually cut by Alexander the Great)

GOSPEL *to take something as gospel*
to believe that something is true

GRAB *to be up for grabs*
to be available virtually for the asking

GRAB *to grab the devil by the tail*
to face up to difficulties

GRACE *to put on airs and graces*
to act in an affected manner

GRADE *to be on the downgrade*
to be of deteriorating quality

GRADE *to make the grade*
to succeed

GRAIL *search for the Holy Grail*
work toward a difficult goal (refers to a vessel supposedly used by Christ at the last supper and featuring in the Arthurian legends)

GRAIN *something goes against the grain*
something is completely and frustratingly against a people's inclination

GRANDMOTHER *to teach one's grandmother how to suck eggs*
to try to tell a much more experienced person something very obvious to him

GRANDSTAND *to grandstand*
to boost oneself

GRANITE *to be carved in marble*
to be virtually unalterable

GRAPE *that is just sour grapes*
those are disparaging remarks made only because he is peeved and resentful at someone else's better fortune

GRAPE *to hear on the grapevine*
to learn unofficially

GRAPE *what is this—a bunch of grapes or a bowl of goldfish?*
surely you know what this is!

GRASP *to grasp at straws*
to have a hopeless case but show unjustified optimism on noting minor positive features

GRASP *to grasp the nettle*
to deal with a neglected difficulty

GRASS *a snake in the grass*
a person of low character

GRASS *grass roots*
at the lowest level

GRASS *not to let grass grow under one's feet*
not to let inertia or delay spoil something

GRASSHOPPER *since he was knee high to a grasshopper*
since he was a very young child

GRAVE *he would turn in his grave*
he would have been very surprised or displeased if he had known while still alive

GRAVE *to dig one's own grave*
to take action which results in an unintended disaster for oneself

GRAVE *to have one foot in the grave*
to be dying

GRAVITY *the center of gravity*
the place most convenient to the greatest number

GRAVITY *to defy gravity*
to go up when the expectation is to go down

GRAVY *to get on a gravy train*
to take steps to become a recipient of benefits which are available but undeserved

GRAY *to be a gray area*
to be in an undefined position straddling two or more possibilities

GREASE *elbow grease*
hard manual work

GREASE *to grease someone's palms*
to bribe a person

GREAT *to be going great guns*
to be making very successful progress

GREAT *to be great guns at something*
to be very skilled at something

GREEK *I fear the Greeks even when they bear gifts*
I am suspicious of generous behavior from traditional opponents (from Virgil's AENEID, in reference to the Trojan horse)

GREEK *something is all Greek to someone*
something is incomprehensible to a person

GREEN *a green chum*
an inexperienced person

GREEN *distant fields look greener*
activities of which one has no experience seem much easier than is really the case

GREEN *to be green*
to be naive

GREEN *to give the green light*
to grant permission

GREEN *to have a green thumb*
to be good at gardening

GREEN *to move on to greener pastures*
to commence a new, better career

GREEN *to turn green*
to become very envious

GREYHOUND *move over and let the greyhound see the rabbit*
move over

GRIN *to grin and bear it*
to suffer adversity cheerfully

GRIND *the mills of God grind slowly*
retribution may be delayed but is inevitable

GRIND *to grind to a halt*
to cease some activity despite expectations that it would continue

GRIND *to have an ax to grind*
to have a vested interest

GRINDSTONE *to keep one's nose to the grindstone*
to work with particular diligence

GRIP *to come to grips with some problem*
to be on the way to solving a problem

GRIP *to have something in an iron grip*
to hold something very securely

GRIST *it is all grist to the mill*
this is useful but unexciting additional material

GRIT *to grit one's teeth*
to get ready to suffer pain

GROAN *the table groaned*
the food was plentiful

GROUND *ground rules*
basic principles

GROUND *to be on shaky ground*
not to have strong arguments

GROUND *to be thin on the ground*
to be scarce

GROUND *to break new ground*
to do something for which there is no precedent

GROUND *to clear the ground*
to dispose of the preliminaries

GROUND *to cut the ground from under someone's feet*
to unexpectedly withdraw support and in the process cause embarrassment or to demolish a person's case

GROUND *to fall to the ground*
to fail

GROUND *to gain ground*
to advance one's position relative to others

GROUND *to get in on the ground floor*
to invest on very favorable terms

GROUND *to get something off the ground*
to take a project beyond its initial stages and make it operational

GROUND *to give ground*
to make some concessions or to retreat or to concede some arguments

GROUND *to go to ground*
to become unavailable to those seeking a person

GROUND *to have one's feet firmly on the ground*
to know what one is doing

GROUND *to have the high ground*
to have an advantage in moral terms

GROUND *to keep an ear to the ground*
to be well informed as to current developments

GROUND *to kiss the ground*
to suffer a loss

GROUND *to plow new ground*
to laboriously engage in an untried activity

GROUND *to prepare one's ground*
to get ready for a confrontation

GROUND *to run someone to the ground*
to discover the whereabouts of a person

GROUND *to stand one's ground*
to maintain a stance in the face of opposition

GROW *growing pains*
problems encountered by virtue of expansion

GROW *not to let grass grow under one's feet*
not to let inertia or delay spoil something

GROW *something grows on one*
one becomes gradually more favorably impressed with something

GUARANTEE *to give a cast-iron guarantee*
to give a very secure undertaking to do something

GUARD *new guard*
changed regime

GUARD *to catch someone off guard*
to surprise a person (a fencing term)

GUARD *to slip under one's guard*
to cause a mistake to be made despite care being taken to prevent this

GUARDIAN *someone's guardian angel*
someone's friend, watching over him and advancing his interests

GUIDE *guiding light*
yardstick for ethical behavior

GUINEA *a guinea pig*
a person on whom some new practice is tried out

GULF *to bridge a gulf*
to overcome a wide divergence in views

GUM *to be up a gum tree*
to be in difficulty or at the end of one's resources

GUM *to gum up the works*
to cause an activity to be halted

GUN *a gun with no bullets*
something incomplete and therefore useless for the desired purpose

GUN *a scattergun approach*
an effort going here, there and everywhere, instead of being properly targeted

GUN *a shotgun wedding*
a wedding held to ensure that an impending birth will be legitimate (refers to threats by the bride's father to kill the bridegroom)

GUN *to be a gun for hire*
to be a person willing to undertake assignments for a fee

GUN *to be going great guns*
to be making very successful progress

GUN *to be great guns at something*
to be very skilled at something

GUN *to bring out one's biggest guns*
to use the most impressive persons or arguments

GUN *to hold a gun at someone's head*
to put pressure on a person to make a particular decision regardless of his desires in the matter

GUN *to jump the gun*
to start before one is meant to

GUN *to look down the barrel of a gun*
to be given little choice in a matter

GUN *to outgun someone*
to outmaneuver a person

GUN *to spike someone's guns*
to cause something to become useless

GUN *to stick to one's guns*
to continue to hold certain beliefs notwithstanding opposition by others

GUN *to turn one's guns on someone*
to criticize a person

GURGLER *to go down the gurgler*
to be ruined

GUT *a gut feeling*
a belief based purely on intuition and unsupported by facts or evidence

GUT *gutless wonder*
coward

GUTFUL *to have had a gutful*
to be disgusted

GUTS *I will have his guts for garters*
I am extremely angry and dissatisfied with him

GUTS *to kick someone in the guts*
to take action needlessly hurtful to another person

GUTS *something has no guts in it*
something has no real value to it

H

HA'P'ORTH *to spoil the ship for a ha'p'orth of tar*
to engage in a false economy (the current word "ship" is actually a mistake for the original word "sheep" and the tar refers to the treatment of wounds)

HACKLE *to raise someone's hackles*
to make a person angry

HAIR *hair-raising*
scary

HAIR *not to touch a hair on someone's head*
not to harm a person

HAIR *not to turn a hair*
to remain composed

HAIR *to a hair*
exactly

HAIR *to be within a hair's breadth of something*
to be extremely close to something

HAIR *to get someone by the short and curly hairs*
to have domination over a person

HAIR *to have a hair of the dog that bit one*
to drink more in an attempt to overcome the effects of alcohol already consumed

HAIR *to keep one's hair on*
to remain calm in a crisis

HAIR *to keep out of someone's hair*
to let another person get on with his work in his own way

HAIR *to let one's hair down*
to relax

HAIR *to make someone's hair curl*
(of news) to give someone a shock

HAIR *to make someone's hair stand on end*
to give a person shocking news

HAIR *to split hairs*
to draw absurdly fine distinctions

HAIR *to tear one's hair out*
to be agitated

HAIR *to wear a hair shirt*
to practice self-discipline

HALCYON *in Halcyon days*
in past happier times (refers to the 14 days about the winter solstice when winds were calm and to the mythical bird said to breed in a floating nest at that time)

HALF *it is six of one and half a dozen of the other*
it does not matter

HALF *not to do anything by halves*
to do everything extremely well

HALF *to do everything by halves*
to do everything imperfectly or incompletely

HALF *to have half a mind to do something*
to be tempted or mildly inclined to do something

HALF-BAKED *half-baked*
not well thought out

HALF-COCKED *to go off half-cocked*
to act without adequate thought or preparation (refers to a gun at the half-ready)

HALF-HEARTED *half-hearted*
unenthusiastic

HALF-WAY *a half-way house*
an intermediate position

HALL *liberty hall*
a place where one is free to do as one wishes

HALL *one can't beat City Hall*
the ordinary citizen is powerless against bureaucracy

HALLMARK *a hallmark*
a standard (refers to the official assay mark on gold and silver, originally put on at the Goldsmiths' Hall)

HALT *to grind to a halt*
to cease some activity despite expectations that it would continue

HAM *ham-fisted*
undiplomatic and clumsy

HAM *to be the ham in the sandwich*
to be caught in the middle of a dispute between other parties

HAMMER *to go hammer and tongs*
to do something with great energy

HAMMER *to use a sledgehammer to crack a nut*
to devote vastly more resources to a project than is warranted by all the circumstances

HAMSTRING *to be hamstrung*
to have limited freedom to act as one would wish

HAND *a backhanded compliment*
a polite expression seemingly of praise but really intended as an insult

HAND *a bird in the hand is worth two in the bush*
a benefit currently available is more valuable than a seemingly much larger benefit which may or may not be achieved in the future

HAND *a left-handed compliment*
a thinly-disguised insult

HAND *all hands on deck*
everybody is requested to help out

HAND *all hands to the pumps*
everybody is requested to help out

HAND *at first hand*
personally

HAND *hand over fist*
rapidly overtaking each other during progress toward a common goal

HAND *high-handed*
overbearing

HAND *on the one hand*
putting one side of the proposition

HAND *one's right-hand man*
one's chief aide

HAND *single-handedly*
without help from other persons

HAND *sleight of hand*
deceit by trickery

HAND *the hand of fate*
chance

HAND *the left hand does not know what the right hand is doing*
one section of a large bureaucracy does not realize that another section is simultaneously doing something inconsistent

HAND *to accept something with both hands*
to accept something eagerly

HAND *to be able to do something with one hand behind one's back*
to be able to do something very easily

HAND *to be able to lay one's hands on something*
to be able to locate something

HAND *to be at hand*
to be in the vicinity, ready to help

HAND *to be in hand*
to be under control

HAND *to be in someone's hands*
to be being dealt with by someone with the necessary authority

HAND *to be out of someone's hands*
to be up for decision by a different person

HAND *to be putty in someone's hands*
to be far too easily influenced by another person

HAND *to bind someone hand and foot*
to completely limit a person's freedom to act

HAND *to bite the hand that feeds one*
to show ingratitude

HAND *to catch someone red-handed*
to apprehend a person in the course of committing a crime

HAND *to deal the final hand*
to take steps which conclude a matter

HAND *to disclose one's hand*
to give away information regarding one's intention

HAND *to eat out of someone's hands*
to be unduly compliant

HAND *to force someone's hand*
to take action causing another person to react

HAND *to gain the upper hand*
to attain, after some effort, an advantage over another person

HAND *to get one's hands dirty*
to do the necessary but unpleasant or menial parts of a task

HAND *to get out of hand*
to get out of control

HAND *to give someone a free hand*
to authorize a person to act as he sees fit

HAND *to give someone a hand*
to assist a person

HAND *to go cap in hand*
to show humility while soliciting a favor

HAND *to go down on one's hands and knees to someone*
with great humility to ask a favor of a person

HAND *to grab some opportunity with both hands*
to seize some opportunity with great enthusiasm

HAND *to hand on the torch*
to pass on accumulated knowledge

HAND *to hand over something on a silver platter*
to provide a valuable benefit for virtually nothing

HAND *to handpick someone*
to carefully choose a person for his individual attributes

HAND *to have a fight on one's hands*
to encounter resistance or opposition to a proposal

HAND *to have a hand in something*
to be one of the participants in some project

HAND *to have blood on one's hands*
to be the person responsible for someone else's predicament

HAND *to have clean hands*
to be innocent or to act ethically

HAND *to have one's hands full*
to be fully occupied

HAND *to have the whip hand*
to be in control of a situation

HAND *to hold a winning hand*
to be in an unbeatable position to defeat others

HAND *to hold someone's hand*
to give detailed on-the-job training and supervision

HAND *to hold the power to do something in the hollow of one's hand*
to have the right to make crucial decisions

HAND *to join hands with someone*
to cooperate with a person

HAND *to keep one's hands in*
to engage in activities which reinforce skills which one has previously acquired

HAND *to lay one's hands on something*
to acquire something

HAND *to lend a hand*
to assist

HAND *to live from hand to mouth*
being in poor financial circumstances to survive with little by way of safety margin

HAND *to lose money hand over fist*
to lose money very fast and convincingly

HAND *to play right into someone's hands*
to act so as to give a person an unintended advantage

HAND *to put one's hand to the plow*
voluntarily to undertake some task (Luke 9:62)

HAND *to put one's hand up*
to identify oneself

HAND *to put one's hands in one's pockets*
to spend

HAND *to rub one's hands with glee*
to express great satisfaction

HAND *to rule with an iron hand*
to keep strict discipline

HAND *to sit on one's hands*
deliberately to do nothing

HAND *to stir a hand*
to volunteer assistance

HAND *to strengthen someone's hand*
to give a person additional authority or greater moral support or more facts to support his case

HAND *to take something in hand*
to assume control over something

HAND *to throw in one's hand*
to give in or to give up

HAND *to throw up one's hands*
to express disgust

HAND *to tie someone's hands*
to prevent a person from acting as he sees fit

HAND *to tie someone's hands behind his back*
to make it impossible for a person to act at all

HAND *to tip one's hand*
to disclose details of one's position

HAND *to try one's hand at something*
to attempt a new activity, especially by way of experiment

HAND *to turn one's hand to something*
to tackle some project

HAND *to wait hand and foot on someone*
to accommodate a person's every real or imagined whim

HAND *to wash one's hands of something*
to emphatically decline future responsibility

HAND *to win hands down*
to win very convincingly

HAND *to work hand in glove with someone*
to work in close cooperation with a person or to be in collusion with a person to the detriment of others

HAND *to wring one's hands*
to express despair

HAND *with a heavy hand*
in an oppressive fashion

HAND *with a high hand*
arrogantly (Exodus 14:8)

HAND *with an iron hand in a velvet glove*
with a hard attitude made to seem soft

HAND *with an open hand*
generously

HANDFUL *a handful*
a small number

HANDFUL *to be a handful*
to be difficult to manage

HANDLE *to fly off the handle*
to show irrational anger

HANDLE *to get a handle on something*
to acquire understanding of something

HANDSHAKE *a golden handshake*
a large payment in connection with or as an inducement to retirement

HANDSTAND *to turn handstands*
to express great joy

HANG *a peg to hang a hat on*
something which provides a convenient or plausible excuse for some particular action

HANG *not to be a hanging matter*
to be only a minor mistake

HANG *one might as well be hanged for a sheep as for a lamb*
further action will not increase the adverse consequences already in train (refers to the stealing of both sheep and lambs being capital crimes under old English law)

HANG *there is a big question mark hanging over someone's head*
there are considerable doubts about a person's competence, integrity or suitability

HANG *to be a cliff-hanger*
to be very exciting

HANG *to get the hang of something*
to learn how to do something

HANG *to give someone enough rope to hang himself*
to give a person the opportunity to do something which is likely to get him into severe trouble

HANG *to hang by a slender thread*
to only just survive

HANG *to hang fire*
to take no immediate action

HANG *to hang on by one's fingernails*
to have only a slender hold

HANG *to hang on by one's nails*
to have only a slender hold

HANG *to hang on by the eyelids*
to have only a slender hold

HANG *to hang on by the skin of one's teeth*
to only just survive

HANG *to hang one's head*
to be ashamed of oneself

HANG *to hang onto someone's coat-tails*
to excessively rely on another person's initiatives

HANG *to hang up one's boots*
to retire

HANG *to hang up one's shingle*
to go into business offering expert personal services

HANG *to have a cloud hanging over one's head*
there is doubt as to one's future

HANG *to have a sword of Damocles hanging over one*
to be in imminent danger despite normal activity going on all around one

HANG *to have a threat hanging over one's head*
to fear some intimated unpleasant action

HANG *to let it all hang out*
to unburden oneself

HAPPY *to be trigger-happy*
to be impetuous

HAPPY *to present a happy face to the world*
bravely to gloss over one's problems

HARD *that is hard to take*
it is difficult to face up to the reality of this

HARD *to be a hard act to follow*
to be an impressive performance, not easily matched by the next person

HARD *to be between a rock and a hard place*
to be faced with two equally difficult and uncomfortable choices

HARD *to be hard to swallow*
not to be readily acceptable

HARD *to be hard on the heels of something*
to closely follow something

HARD *to be the hard core*
to be the central and most difficult problem

HARD *to die hard*
not to give up easily

HARD *to have a hard row to hoe*
to be a difficult assignment

HARD *to hit someone hard*
to greatly affect a person emotionally or to cost a person a lot of money

HARD *to put something into the "too hard" basket*
to defer consideration of a difficult issue

HARD *to take a hard line*
to be uncompromising

HARD-BITTEN *hard-bitten*
toughened by experience

HARD-BOILED *hard-boiled*
toughened by experience

HARD-FISTED *hard-fisted*
mean

HARD-HEADED *hard-headed*
realistic

HARD-HEARTED *hard-hearted*
unsympathetic

HARD-MOUTHED *hard-mouthed*
uncontrollable

HARD-NOSED *hard-nosed*
tough in negotiations

HARE *first catch your hare*
do things in logical order and after proper preparation (advice on how to cook a hare in Mrs. Beeton's celebrated COOK BOOK)

HARE *hare-brained*
wildly stupid

HARE *to chase every hare*
to be easily sidetracked

HARE *to run with the hare and hunt with the hounds*
to keep in with two opposing sides

HARE *to set a hare running*
in order to achieve some desired effect to initiate some related activity

HARMONIZE *to harmonize several things*
to make several things conform with each other

HARMONY *to be in harmony with someone*
to act in the same way as another person

HARNESS *in harness*
before retirement

HARRY *every Tom, Dick and Harry*
just about everybody

HARVEST *harvest*
end result of labor

HASTE *to go post haste*
to go very fast

HAT *I'll eat my hat if so-and-so happens*
I do not believe that so-and-so will happen

HAT *a peg to hang a hat on*
something which provides a convenient or plausible excuse for some particular action

HAT *at the drop of a hat*
very readily

HAT *not to just pick something out of a hat*
to choose carefully, after weighing all the considerations

HAT *to be old hat*
to be a very widely-known fact

HAT *to buy straw hats in winter*
to buy in a depressed market when most other people are sellers

HAT *to keep something under one's hat*
to maintain a confidence

HAT *to knock something into a cocked hat*
to twist something so that its original form is hardly recognizable

HAT *to pull a rabbit out of the hat*
to produce an unexpected and seemingly miraculous but highly desirable solution

HAT *to score a hat trick*
to have three successive favorable outcomes

HAT *to take one's hat off to someone*
to be full of admiration for a person

HAT *to talk through one's hat*
to say things which demonstrate the speaker's ignorance of the subject

HAT *to throw one's hat into the air*
to express joy

HAT *to throw one's hat into the ring*
to publicly announce one's interest in some position

HAT *to wear a particular hat*
to act in a particular capacity or for a particular vested interest

HATCH *to batten down the hatches*
to get ready for expected difficulties

HATCH *to count one's chickens before they are hatched*
to treat as fact the expected results of a future proposal

HATCHET *to bury the hatchet*
to abandon hostilities

HATCHET *to do a hatchet job*
to destroy some existing activity or to ruin a person's credibility

HAUL *for the long haul*
as a long-term proposition

HAUL *to haul someone over the coals*
to reprimand a person

HAUNT *to come back to haunt someone*
(of an unpleasant incident) to be a constant reminder to a person

HAY *to hit the hay*
to go to sleep

HAY *to look for a needle in a haystack*
to attempt something with a very small chance of success

HAY *to make hay while the sun shines*
to utilize an opportunity before it disappears

HAYSTACK *to find a needle in a haystack*
to find something when the probability of finding it is very small

HAYWIRE *to go haywire*
to refuse to function properly

HEAD *a hothead*
an impetuous person

HEAD *a hydra-headed monster*
an evil which is not readily destroyable

HEAD *a swelled head*
an exaggerated idea of one's abilities or status

HEAD *an old head on young shoulders*
experience, knowledge and maturity in a young person

HEAD *hard-headed*
realistic

HEAD *head first*
precipitately

HEAD *head over heels*
topsy-turvy

HEAD *heads I win—tails you lose*
whichever way this matter goes I will benefit at your expense

HEAD *heads will roll*
transgressors will be punished

HEAD *level-headed*
rational

HEAD *not to touch a hair on someone's head*
not to harm a person

HEAD *off the top of one's head*
based on experience but without detailed consideration

HEAD *pigheaded*
unduly obstinate

HEAD *pull your head in!*
do not interfere in this!

HEAD *someone's head is on the block*
a person is in danger of having his appointment terminated

HEAD *that is on your head*
you will have to accept responsibility for that

HEAD *there is a big question mark hanging over someone's head*
there are considerable doubts about a person's competence, integrity or suitability

HEAD *to bang one's head up against a brick wall*
to fight an unwinnable case

HEAD *to be able to do something standing on one's head*
to be able to do something very easily

HEAD *to be at the head of the pack*
to be the best of many or the de facto leader

HEAD *to be head and shoulders above the rest*
to be significantly more capable than others

HEAD *to be off one's head*
to be crazy

HEAD *to be over someone's head*
to be beyond a person's ability to understand

HEAD *to be unable to make head or tail of something*
to be unable to understand how something functions or what something means

HEAD *to beat each other over the head*
to be always fighting

HEAD *to belt someone over the head*
to override someone's views or arguments

HEAD *to bite someone's head off*
to rudely express displeasure at some person

HEAD *to bury one's head in the sand*
to refuse to face up to an unpleasant truth (refers to the reputed habit of ostriches in danger)

HEAD *to come to a head*
to reach culmination

HEAD *to confront someone head on*
to confront a person

HEAD *to develop a head of steam*
to gain momentum

HEAD *to drag someone by the head and ears*
to force a person to reveal the true facts

HEAD *to eat one's head off*
to eat excessively

HEAD *to fall head over heels in love*
to fall very much in love

HEAD *to get one's head blown off*
to be very soundly abused

HEAD *to give someone his head*
to let a person do as he wants to

HEAD *to go off one's head*
to lose one's temper

HEAD *to go over someone's head*
to bypass lower levels of authority and approach someone more senior instead

HEAD *to go to someone's head*
to cause a person to get an exaggerated idea of his abilities or status

HEAD *to hang one's head*
to be ashamed of oneself

HEAD *to have a cloud hanging over one's head*
there is doubt as to one's future

HEAD *to have a head start*
to have an advantage over others

HEAD *to have a threat hanging over one's head*
to fear some intimated unpleasant action

HEAD *to have eyes at the back of one's head*
to know more of what is going on than is generally realized

HEAD *to have one's head in the clouds*
to be unrealistic

HEAD *to have one's head screwed on straight*
to be shrewd

HEAD *to have rocks in the head*
to be mentally unbalanced

HEAD *to head someone in the right direction*
to assist a person to achieve something

HEAD *to hit the nail right on the head*
to astutely come to the correct conclusion

HEAD *to hold a gun at someone's head*
to put pressure on a person to make a particular decision regardless of his desires in the matter

HEAD *to hold one's head high*
to stay unruffled and to maintain one's dignity despite attempts by others to embarrass

HEAD *to just hold one's head above water*
to cope with problems but with little margin to spare or to stay solvent

HEAD *to keep a civil tongue in one's head*
to be polite, especially under provocation

HEAD *to keep a cool head*
to stay calm and rational in a crisis

HEAD *to keep a level head*
to stay calm and rational in a crisis

HEAD *to keep one's head*
to remain calm in a crisis or to unexpectedly retain an elected or appointed position

HEAD *to keep one's head down*
to work very diligently

HEAD *to kick heads in*
to demonstrate annoyance at or dislike of certain persons

HEAD *to knock an idea on the head*
to utterly reject a proposal

HEAD *to knock two heads together*
to make two persons come to their senses and deal with each other

HEAD *to laugh one's head off*
to greatly enjoy something

HEAD *to let one's head go*
to do as one wants to

HEAD *to let one's heart rule one's head*
to act on emotion rather than on reason

HEAD *to lose one's head*
to become confused

HEAD *to need something like a hole in the head*
to be landed with a completely undesired problem

HEAD *to need to have one's head examined*
to be foolish

HEAD *to promote someone over the heads of others*
to promote a person to a position more senior than that held by some persons previously outranking him

HEAD *to pull one's head in*
to retreat from a previously held stance

HEAD *to put one's head in the noose*
to recklessly and unnecessarily expose oneself to great danger

HEAD *to put one's head into the lion's mouth*
to recklessly expose oneself to great danger

HEAD *to put one's head on the block*
to have the courage of one's convictions

HEAD *to put our heads together*
to confer and pool ideas

HEAD *to rear its ugly head*
to make an unwelcome appearance

HEAD *to scratch one's head*
to be amazed or puzzled

HEAD *to scream one's head off*
to scream very loudly

HEAD *to shake one's head*
to indicate disbelief or wonder or disapproval

HEAD *to snap someone's head off*
to speak to a person aggressively

HEAD *to tackle someone head-on*
to confront a person

HEAD *to turn someone's head*
to cause a person to get an exaggerated idea of his abilities or status

HEAD *to turn something on its head*
to reverse something

HEAD *uneasy lies the head that wears a crown*
responsibility involves some risks and some burdens (from Shakespeare's HENRY IV)

HEAD *woolly-headed*
slightly muddled

HEAD *you want your head read*
you should reconsider this matter

HEADACHE *a headache*
a cause for worry

HEADWAY *to make headway*
to make progress

HEAL *to heal wounds*
to affect a reconciliation

HEALTH *to get a clean bill of health*
after proper investigation to be found not wanting

HEAP *to be at the bottom of the heap*
to be in the lowest position in a hierarchy

HEAP *to be destined for the scrap-heap*
to face a future in which one will have no meaningful role

HEAP *to fall in a heap*
(of a proposal) to collapse utterly

HEAR *the cheering could be heard a block away*
there was great rejoicing

HEAR *to hear a whisper*
to learn a rumored hypothesis

HEART *chicken-hearted*
showing little courage

HEART *cold-hearted*
cruel or mean or unmoved

HEART *from the bottom of one's heart*
very sincerely

HEART *half-hearted*
unenthusiastic

HEART *hard-hearted*
unsympathetic

HEART *heart and soul*
with great energy

HEART *heart failure*
a shock

HEART *heart-stopping*
exciting

HEART *one's heart bleeds for someone*
one feels truly sad for a person's fate

HEART *one's heart is not in some cause*
one has little enthusiasm for some cause

HEART *one's heart sank*
one realized the extent of some disaster

HEART *open-hearted*
cordial

HEART *this does my heart good*
I rejoice at this

HEART *to be close to one's heart*
to be a project on which one is very keen

HEART *to be in good heart*
to be brave in adversity

HEART *to be of good heart*
to be brave in adversity

HEART *to be someone after one's own heart*
to be a person who shares one's beliefs

HEART *to break someone's heart*
to act in a way causing great upset to another person

HEART *to eat one's heart out*
to suffer bitterly

HEART *to give someone heart*
to cause a person to cheer up

HEART *to have a change of heart*
to form a new view in place of a strongly-held previous view

HEART *to have a heart*
to have compassion

HEART *to have a heart of gold*
to have a generous disposition

HEART *to have a heart of oak*
to be brave

HEART *to have a heart of stone*
to be unfeeling

HEART *to have a heart-to-heart talk*
to have a confidential discussion on a highly personal matter

HEART *to have one's heart in one's boots*
to be terrified

HEART *to have one's heart in one's mouth*
to be startled

HEART *to have one's heart in something*
to be enthusiastic about and committed to a cause

HEART *to have one's heart in the right place*
to have a well-developed social conscience

HEART *to have one's heart set on something*
to be very keen to achieve something

HEART *to know something in one's heart of hearts*
to know something while reluctant to admit it, even to oneself

HEART *to let one's heart rule one's head*
to act on emotion rather than on reason

HEART *to lose heart*
to cease being enthusiastic

HEART *to pour one's heart out to someone*
to inflict one's woes on another person

HEART *to pull at one's heart strings*
to affect one emotionally

HEART *to search one's heart*
to have misgivings

HEART *to steal someone's heart*
to cause a person to fall in love with one

HEART *to steel one's heart against something*
to determine that, notwithstanding one's natural compassion, something shall not happen

HEART *to take heart from something*
to be encouraged by something

HEART *to take something to heart*
to learn to appreciate the significance of something or to be much saddened by something

HEART *to warm the cockles of someone's heart*
to delight a person

HEART *to wear one's heart on one's sleeve*
to lack the reserve expected of one

HEART *warm-hearted*
affectionate or generous

HEART *with a heavy heart*
in sorrow

HEART *with a sinking heart*
with growing despondency

HEART *you can eat your heart out*
you are entitled to feel sad or jealous

HEARTACHE *heartache*
sadness

HEARTBREAK *heartbreak*
despair

HEARTBURN *heartburn*
regret at some non-achievement

HEAT *if one can't stand the heat one should stay out of the kitchen*
a person should not put himself in a position involving pressures with which he cannot cope (words attributed to Harry S. Truman)

HEAT *to take the heat off someone*
to divert attention away from a person

HEAT *to turn the heat on something*
to intensify the investigation of some matter

HEAT *to turn up the heat on someone*
to increase the pressure on a person

HEAVE *to heave a sigh a relief*
to express satisfaction at the achievement of a solution to a difficult problem

HEAVEN *heaven help you!*
you are in trouble

HEAVEN *heaven only knows*
it is not known

HEAVEN *manna from heaven*
unexpected benefits (Exodus 16:15)

HEAVEN *to be in seventh heaven*
to be very happy

HEAVEN *to move heaven and earth*
to do everything possible

HEAVEN *to reek to high heaven*
to be patently unethical

HEAVY *to make heavy weather of something*
to struggle excessively with a relatively simple task

HEAVY *to run into heavy weather*
to encounter difficulties

HEAVY *with a heavy hand*
in an oppressive fashion

HEAVY *with a heavy heart*
in sorrow

HEAVYWEIGHT *a heavyweight*
a person of importance or influence

HEDGE *to be hedged around*
(of a statement) to be surrounded by qualifications

HEDGE *to hedge one's bets*
to take action involving a cost but which is designed to reduce the possible adverse consequences of some activity

HEEL *head over heels*
topsy-turvy

HEEL *to be hot on the heels of something*
to closely follow something

HEEL *to be someone's Achilles' heel*
to represent a weakness in an otherwise strong position (refers to the Greek warrior who was the hero of Homer's ILIAD)

HEEL *to bring someone to heel*
to make a person conform

HEEL *to cool one's heels*
to be kept waiting

HEEL *to dig one's heels in*
to become even more stubborn than at first

HEEL *to drag one's heels*
to perform unduly slowly

HEEL *to fall head over heels in love*
to fall very much in love

HEEL *to kick one's heels*
to be kept waiting

HEEL *to snap at someone's heels*
to be a minor irritation to a person

HEEL *well-heeled*
rich

HELL *all hell broke loose*
great confusion erupted

HELL *come hell or high water*
regardless of the consequences

HELL *on a cold day in hell*
never

HELL *to be hell bent on something*
to be very determined to achieve something, regardless of the adverse consequences

HELL *to frighten hell out of someone*
to alarm a person

HELL *to give someone hell*
to make life difficult for a person

HELL *to have a snowflake's chance in hell*
to have no hope or possibility at all

HELL *to raise merry hell*
to prominently involve others in a matter in the expectation of significant results from this action

HELM *to be at the helm*
to be in charge

HELP *to cry for help*
a subconscious or indirect indication that a person is in need of psychological counselling

HELP *heaven help you!*
you are in trouble

HELP *not to lift a finger to help someone*
to refuse to assist

HEM *to be hemmed in*
to be limited in the choice of actions available

HEMORRHAGE *to stem the hemorrhage*
to put a stop to the financial losses of a project

HEN *a mother hen*
an overly protective person

HEN *hen-pecked*
subject to domination by one's wife

HERCULEAN *a Herculean cleaning of the stables*
a thorough revision of operating procedure (refers to Hercules, a mythical Greek hero who cleaned the stables of Augeas)

HERCULEAN *to be a Herculean task*
to be laborious

HERD *to follow the herd*
to do what most other people are doing

HERE *the buck stops here*
I accept full responsibility (sign on the desk of Harry S. Truman when president of the United States)

HERE *to be neither here nor there*
to be irrelevant or unimportant

HERESY *heresy*
views different from those held by the majority

HERO *to make a hero of oneself*
to curry favors

HERRING *neither fish, flesh nor good red herring*
unclassifiable by virtue of being neither one thing nor another (from Cervantes'' DON QUIXOTE)

HERRING *to be a red herring*
to be something designed to divert attention away from the main question

HIDE *to cover one's hide*
to provide excuses or take other evasive action in an attempt to avoid the adverse consequences of one's actions

HIDE *to have a thick hide*
to be impervious to criticism

HIDE *to have the hide of a rhinoceros*
to be totally unaffected by and unresponsive to valid criticism

HIDE *to hide one's light under a bushel*
to keep others in ignorance of one's skills and experience

HIDE *to hide under someone's skirts*
to let someone else take the consequences of one's actions

HIDE *to want someone's hide*
to be keen to penalize a person

HIDEBOUND *hidebound*
narrow-minded

HIGH *come hell or high water*
regardless of the consequences

HIGH *high water mark*
triumph

HIGH *to be for the high jump*
to be threatened with a reprimand and punishment

HIGH *to be on one's high horse*
to be excessively pompous

HIGH *to fly high*
to be ambitious

HIGH *to have the high ground*
to have an advantage in moral terms

HIGH *to hold one's head high*
to stay unruffled and to maintain one's dignity despite attempts by others to embarrass

HIGH *to leave someone high and dry*
to withdraw all support from a person or to isolate a person from a desired involvement

HIGH *to ride high*
to be successful but vulnerable

HIGH *with a high hand*
arrogantly (Exodus 14:8)

HIGH-HANDED *high-handed*
overbearing

HIGHBROW *highbrow*
intellectual or cultural

HIGHFLYER *a highflyer*
an ambitious and/or successful person

HIGHLIGHT *a highlight*
a particularly important item

HIGHLIGHT *to highlight something*
to draw particular attention to a matter

HIGHWAY *highway robbery*
the charging of grossly excessive prices

HIJACK *to hijack a debate*
to involve oneself in the public discussion of some matter and turn that discussion to one's advantage

HILL *light on the hill*
distant goal acting as an inspiration

HILL *to be over the hill*
to be old

HILL *to be pushing uphill*
to face difficulties

HILL *to fight an uphill battle*
to face difficulties or to have formidable opposition

HILL *to go downhill*
to deteriorate

HILL *to head for the hills*
to seek to escape one's commitments

HILL *to push water uphill*
to foolishly attempt the impossible

HILT *to the hilt*
to the maximum extent

HIMALAYAN *of Himalayan proportions*
huge

HIND *to stand up on one's hind legs*
to exert one's authority

HIND *to talk the hind leg off a donkey*
to talk excessively

HINDSIGHT *with 20/20 hindsight*
with the benefit of knowing what happened

HIP *the hip pocket nerve*
the assessment of issues by their financial effects on one

HIP *to shoot from the hip*
to speak frankly and openly

HIRE *to be a gun for hire*
to be a person willing to undertake assignments for a fee

HIT *it hits one*
one comes to realize something

HIT *to hit one's stride*
to settle down to some task

HIT *to hit someone below the belt*
to act unfairly toward another person

HIT *to hit someone for six*
to damage a person's cause

HIT *to hit someone hard*
to greatly affect a person emotionally or to cost a person a lot of money

HIT *to hit someone right between the eyes*
to be brutally frank

HIT *to hit the bull's eye*
to make the correct decision

HIT *to hit the hay*
to go to sleep

HIT *to hit the jackpot*
to be very lucky

HIT *to hit the mark*
to achieve one's object or to make the correct decision (refers to archery)

HIT *to hit the nail right on the head*
to astutely come to the correct conclusion

HIT *to hit the roof*
to be very angry

HIT *to hit the straps*
to really get going

HOBBY *to be off on one's hobby horse*
to throw into conversation aspects of a subject in which one has a passionate interest

HOBSON *Hobson's choice*
no right at all to select (refers to Thomas Hobson, a horsekeeper in Cambridge, England, who offered customers seeking a change of horses a single beast on a "take it or leave it" basis)

HOE *to have a hard row to hoe*
to be a difficult assignment

HOG *a road hog*
an inconsiderate motorist

HOG *to go the whole hog*
to do something very thoroughly (refers to the close shearing of lambs)

HOG *to make a hog of oneself*
to demonstrate greed

HOGWASH *hogwash*
nonsense

HOIST *to be hoist with one's own petard*
to have one's own case used against one (refers to being blown up by one's own bomb)

HOLD *an argument holding water*
a debating point of substance

HOLD *hold your horses!*
just wait a little!

HOLD *no holds barred*
without any limitation

HOLD *not fit to hold a candle to someone*
greatly inferior to another person

HOLD *not to hold one's breath for something*
to give up all expectation

HOLD *to be left holding the baby*
to be tricked into accepting responsibility for someone else's problems

HOLD *to hold a winning hand*
to be in an unbeatable position to defeat others

HOLD *to hold all the aces*
to be in an unbeatable position to defeat others

HOLD *to hold all the cards*
to be assured of victory

HOLD *to hold fire*
to defer criticizing

HOLD *to hold one's head high*
to stay unruffled and to maintain one's dignity despite attempts by others to embarrass

HOLD *to hold one's tongue*
to keep quiet

HOLD *to hold out an olive branch*
to make peace overtures (Genesis 8:11)

HOLD *to hold someone at bay*
to successfully resist an attacker

HOLD *to hold someone's hand*
to give detailed on-the-job training and supervision

HOLD *to hold the floor*
to dominate a conversation

HOLD *to hold the fort*
to be in charge during the temporary absence of a superior

HOLD *to hold the purse strings*
to have control of expenditure

HOLD *to hold the trump card*
to be in an unbeatable position to defeat others

HOLD *to hold the wrong end of the stick*
to be completely mistaken about something

HOLD *to just hold one's head above water*
to cope with problems but with little margin to spare or to stay solvent

HOLD *to put something on ''hold''*
to put something aside for the time being with a view to resuming activity later on (refers to the telephone)

HOLE *a black hole*
an intermediate range of values producing anomalous results or a particularly obnoxious prison cell

HOLE *a dry hole*
an exercise which after much effort proves fruitless

HOLE *a fox hole*
space which is really too small for a person's needs or comfort

HOLE *a loop-hole*
means of getting around the intention of some regulation

HOLE *a square peg in a round hole*
a person much more suitable for a position rather different from the one held

HOLE *to be in a hole*
to experience some difficulties

HOLE *to expose holes*
to expose weaknesses in an argument

HOLE *to have money burning a hole in one's pocket*
to be impatient to spend or invest available funds

HOLE *to need something like a hole in the head*
to be landed with a completely undesired problem

HOLE *to pigeon-hole*
to put aside for further consideration in the distant future

HOLE *to stop up one hole in a sieve*
to do something quite useless

HOLE *watch the doughnut—not the hole*
look for the positive aspects

HOLE *watering hole*
a bar or place to get a drink

HOLLOW *that has a hollow ring to it*
that statement is insincere

HOLLOW *to hold the power to do something in the hollow of one's hand*
to have the right to make crucial decisions

HOLY *a holier-than-thou attitude*
excessive righteousness

HOLY *an unholy alliance*
a working relationship for a nefarious purpose between unlikely partners

HOLY *search for the Holy Grail*
work toward a difficult goal (refers to a vessel supposedly used by Christ at the last supper and featuring in the Arthurian legends)

HOME *charity begins at home*
a person's first responsibility should be to his family

HOME *nothing to write home about*
unimpressive

HOME *the chickens are coming home to roost*
the consequences of past actions are becoming obvious

HOME *to argue till the cows come home*
to argue forever

HOME *to be home and hosed*
to have won

HOME *to be home on the sheep's back*
to be doing well

HOME *to be too close to home*
to be too near the truth to be welcome

HOME *to bring a fact home to someone*
despite his inclination to the contrary to make a person realize a fact

HOME *to bring home the bacon*
to be successful

HOME *to drive the lesson home*
to take certain action which is unpleasant but which has the effect of registering a message

HOME *to eat someone out of house and home*
to ruin a person by eating all he has

HOME *to enter the home stretch*
to commence the last stage

HOME *to keep the home fires burning*
to maintain normal domestic activity during the temporary absence of the breadwinner

HOME *to take one's bat and ball home*
as a gesture of spite to remove an essential ingredient which one has contributed to a joint enterprise

HOMEWORK *to do one's homework*
to thoroughly analyze an issue

HONEY *a land of milk and honey*
a country in which everything is in abundant supply

HONEYMOON *a honeymoon*
a short period enjoyed by a newcomer to some activity before his performance is criticized

HOOK *by hook or by crook*
by fair means or foul

HOOK *hook line and sinker*
wholly

HOOK *to be hooked on something*
to be addicted to something

HOOK *to get someone off the hook*
to rescue a person from an embarrassing predicament

HOOK *to let someone off the hook*
to allow a person to escape the adverse consequences of his own actions

HOOP *to jump through hoops*
to undergo some ordeal

HOOT *not to care a hoot*
not to show the slightest concern or enthusiasm

HOP *something is but a hop, skip and jump away*
something is nearby

HOP *to be on the hop*
to be always bustling about

HOP *to catch someone on the hop*
to take a person by surprise

HOP *to hop onto the bandwagon*
to join the majority (the antonym of "bandwagon effect" is "underdog effect")

HORIZON *the one bright spot on the horizon*
the only hopeful aspect

HORIZON *there are black clouds on the horizon*
bad news is expected

HORIZON *to loom on the horizon*
to be expected but not immediately

HORN *the horns of a dilemma*
the unpalatable alternatives between which a choice must be made

HORN *to lock horns with someone*
to have an argument with another person

HORN *to pull one's horns in*
to retreat from previously stated views

HORN *to take the bull by the horns*
to come to grips with the realities of a difficult problem

HORNET *to stir up a hornet's nest*
to take action which results in unpleasant side-effects

HORSE *I could eat a horse*
I am very hungry

HORSE *a Trojan horse*
a trick (refers to a large gift horse full of soldiers used to bring about the fall of Troy, as described in Homer's ILIAD)

HORSE *a dark horse*
a person with unsuspected talents

HORSE *a nod is the same as a wink to a blind horse*
fine distinctions are not appropriate here

HORSE *a stalking horse*
an ostensible reason

HORSE *a two-horse race*
a contest between only two serious contestants

HORSE *a warhorse*
an old soldier who likes to relive past wartime experiences

HORSE *a willing horse*
a cheerful worker

HORSE *hold your horses!*
just wait a little!

HORSE *horse sense*
natural shrewdness

HORSE *horsetrading*
tough negotiations

HORSE *it is horses for courses*
some combinations work particularly well

HORSE *that is a horse of a very different color*
that is a much more acceptable proposition

HORSE *the horse and buggy days*
long ago

HORSE *to back the wrong horse*
to have faith in, give support to and/or invest in a project which proves to be unsuccessful

HORSE *to be off on one's hobby horse*
to throw into conversation aspects of a subject in which one has a passionate interest

HORSE *to be on one's high horse*
to be excessively pompous

HORSE *to drive a coach and horses through something*
to demonstrate major errors in something

HORSE *to flog a dead horse*
to misguidedly do something patently useless

HORSE *to frighten the horses*
to scare people off by one's ill-considered tactics

HORSE *to learn something from the horse's mouth*
to get information from someone qualified to impart it

HORSE *to look a gift horse in the mouth*
to be suspicious about a benefit which has been volunteered

HORSE *to put the cart before the horse*
to do things in the wrong order

HORSE *to shut the stable door after the horse has bolted*
to take preventive action only after the relevant event

HORSE *to swap horses in midstream*
to change direction during the course of a project

HORSE *wild horses would not cause me to do something*
I absolutely refuse to do something (refers to a form of torture)

HORSEPLAY *horseplay*
boisterous and undignified behavior

HOSED *to be home and hosed*
to have won

HOT *a hot potato*
an embarrassing issue

HOT *a hothead*
an impetuous person

HOT *hot-blooded*
very passionate

HOT *red-hot*
highly exciting and desirable

HOT *to be full of hot air*
to have an exaggerated opinion of one's own importance and to boast about it

HOT *to be hot off the press*
to be the latest news

HOT *to be hot on a subject*
to be knowledgeable and enthusiastic about a subject

HOT *to be hot on the heels of something*
to closely follow something

HOT *to be hot stuff*
to be skillful or very passionate

HOT *to be hot under the collar*
to be very agitated

HOT *to be in hot water*
to be very agitated

HOT *to be in hot water*
to be in trouble or to be in difficulty

HOT *to be in the hot seat*
to hold a position requiring one to answer criticism or accusations

HOT *to blow hot and cold*
to vacillate

HOT *to get hot*
to get close to the solution

HOT *to go hot foot*
to do something fast

HOT *to make some place too hot for someone*
to persecute a person and thus make conditions very unpleasant for him

HOT *to run hot*
(of equipment) to be subject to particularly high usage

HOT *to strike while the iron is hot*
to take advantage of a situation which cannot last

HOTBED *a hotbed of crime*
a place where crime flourishes

HOUND *to run with the hare and hunt with the hounds*
to keep in with two opposing sides

HOUND *to set the hounds baying*
to excite the gossips by providing material which they can use

HOUR *at the eleventh hour*
at the last moment (actually "at the twenty-fourth hour" would be more logical) (Matthew 20:9)

HOUSE *a half-way house*
an intermediate position

HOUSE *a house of cards*
an organization which gives a misleading impression of solidity

HOUSE *a madhouse*
an organization in great turmoil

HOUSE *a plague on both your houses!*
I am disgusted with both of you (from Shakespeare's ROMEO AND JULIET)

HOUSE *people in glass houses should not throw stones*
those who are less than perfect are foolish to criticize others

HOUSE *to be in the doghouse*
to be in disgrace

HOUSE *to be on the house*
to be free of cost

HOUSE *to bring the house down*
to greatly amuse an audience

HOUSE *to eat someone out of house and home*
to ruin a person by eating all he has

HOUSE *to put one's house in order*
to fix up the deficiencies in one's affairs

HOUSEHOLD *a household name*
a very familiar name

HOYLE *according to Hoyle*
with authority

HUMBLE *to eat humble pie*
to apologize

HUNT *a witchhunt*
an exercise seeking to find someone who can be blamed

HUNT *to run with the hare and hunt with the hounds*
to keep in with two opposing sides

HURDLE *to jump a hurdle*
to overcome a problem or difficulty

HURDLE *to jump that hurdle when one comes to it*
to deal with a particular problem only when it becomes necessary to do so

HURL *to hurl something in someone's face*
to reproach a person in regard to something

HURT *someone can't hurt a fly*
someone is very gentle and kindhearted

HYDE *to do a Jekyll and Hyde*
to have a split personality (refers to THE STRANGE CASE OF DR. JEKYLL AND MR. HYDE by Robert Louis Stevenson)

HYDRA *a hydra-headed monster*
an evil which is not readily destroyable

HYMNAL *to all sing from the same hymnal*
to act consistently with each other

I

I *to dot the i's and cross the t's*
to be meticulous in completing the documentation for a transaction

ICE *to break the ice*
to take the initiative in starting discussions

ICE *to cut no ice with someone*
to have little effect on a person

ICE *to put something on ice*
to put something aside for the time being

ICE *to skate on thin ice*
to act in disregard of obvious danger

ICEBERG *to be the tip of the iceberg*
to be only a very small portion of a much larger but less obvious whole

ICING *to be icing on top of the cake*
to be an additional benefit in an already satisfactory scenario

IMAGE *to tarnish one's image*
to become less highly regarded

IMPETUS *to have impetus*
to move along forcefully

IMPRIMATUR *imprimatur*
confirmation that something is in order (Latin, "'let it be printed"; refers to the formal ruling given by a Roman Catholic bishop authorizing the publication of a book on religion or morals)

INCH *give him an inch and he will take a mile*
make him a small concession and he will abuse it by taking much more

INCH *not to give an inch*
not to budge or concede to the slightest degree despite pressure to do so

INCH *to inch forward*
to make slow but steady progress

INCH *to resist something every inch of the way*
to utterly resist something

INDIAN *more chiefs than Indians*
a disproportionately large number of supervisors

INFLAME *to inflame a situation*
to aggravate a situation

INK *the ink is hardly dry*
something intended to last a long time is to be changed shortly after its establishment

INN *no room at the inn*
no room

INNER *a warm inner glow*
satisfaction at some achievement

INNINGS *to have had a good innings*
to have had a successful life

INSIDE *to know something inside out*
to know something very thoroughly

INSIDE *to turn something inside out*
to examine something thoroughly

INSTRUCTION *riding instructions*
directions as to how to do something

INTEREST *to pay something back with interest*
to return a small favor with a bigger favor or to extract retribution of greater value than the circumstances warrant

INTRODUCE *to introduce new blood*
to recruit new members to some organization

IRON *the iron curtain*
the border between the communist nations and the rest of the world (from a speech by Sir Winston Churchill in 1946)

IRON *to give a cast-iron guarantee*
to give a very secure undertaking to do something

IRON *to have a cast-iron case*
to be absolutely assured of victory in legal proceedings

IRON *to have other irons in the fire*
to have the opportunity to do something else as an alternative

IRON *to have something in an iron grip*
to hold something very securely

IRON *to iron out something*
to sort out a difficult problem

IRON *to rule with a rod of iron*
to keep strict discipline

IRON *to rule with an iron fist*
to keep strict discipline

IRON *to rule with an iron hand*
to keep strict discipline

IRON *to strike while the iron is hot*
to take advantage of a situation which cannot last

IRON *with an iron hand in a velvet glove*
with a hard attitude made to seem soft

ISSUE *to be a black and white issue*
to involve very clear distinctions

ITCH *to be itching to go*
to be highly enthusiastic and keen to start

ITCHY *itchy feet*
a desire to travel

ITCHY *to have itchy fingers*
to be impatient

IVORY *to be in an ivory tower*
to be immersed in theoretical considerations and ignorant of the practical realities (Song of Solomon 7:4)

J

JACK *a Jack of all trades*
an amateur who can turn his hand to anything

JACKAL *to keep the jackals at bay*
to pay one's creditors just sufficient to avoid repercussions

JACKET *to keep someone in a straitjacket*
to deny a person any discretionary powers at all

JACKPOT *to hit the jackpot*
to be very lucky

JAM *money for jam*
remuneration easily earned

JAM *to be in a jam*
to be in difficulties

JAM *to just pick the plums out of the jam*
to take only the very best items

JAM *to put jam on someone's bread*
to make a good situation even better

JAUNDICED *jaundiced*
affected by jealousy

JAW *someone's jaw dropped*
someone registered obvious disappointment, incredulity or shock

JEKYLL *to do a Jekyll and Hyde*
to have a split personality (refers to THE STRANGE CASE OF DR. JEKYLL AND MR. HYDE by Robert Louis Stevenson)

JELLY *to be set like a jelly*
to be very well established

JEREMIAH *Jeremiah*
a person who looks on the gloomy side of everything (refers to the prophet Jeremiah in the Old Testament)

JERICHO *walls of Jericho*
something seemingly solid but actually destructible (Joshua 6:20)

JERK *a knee-jerk reaction*
a response made instantaneously and without any proper consideration

JETSAM *flotsam and jetsam*
derelict persons, without a fixed abode or stable life

JETTISON *to jettison some proposal*
to abandon some proposal as worthless or impracticable

JEWEL *a jewel*
a valued assistant

JEWEL *the jewel in someone's crown*
the most significant component

JIB *the cut of someone's jib*
someone's personal appearance

JOB *something would try the patience of Job*
something is very vexatious (James 5:11)

JOB *to have a job in front of one*
to face difficulties

JOIN *join the club!*
you are only one of many people with similar problems

JOIN *to join forces*
to cooperate with one another in order to achieve a common objective

JOIN *to join hands with someone*
to cooperate with a person

JOINT *to put someone's nose out of joint*
to upset another person

JOT *not a jot*
not even a small amount (refers to the Greek letter iota or i)

JOWL *cheek by jowl*
close to each other

JOY *to jump for joy*
to express great satisfaction

JUAN *to be a Don Juan*
to be a libertine

JUDAS *to play Judas*
to betray a person (Matthew 26)

JUDGE *to judge a book by its cover*
foolishly to go only by superficial appearances

JUGULAR *to go for the jugular*
to attempt to destroy something completely

JUICE *to stew in one's juice*
to suffer the adverse consequences of one's acts or omissions

JUMP *something is but a hop, skip and jump away*
something is nearby

JUMP *to be for the high jump*
to be threatened with a reprimand and punishment

JUMP *to get the jump on someone*
to get an advantage over a person

JUMP *to jump a hurdle*
to overcome a problem or difficulty

JUMP *to jump at the opportunity*
to enthusiastically take immediate advantage of a good chance

JUMP *to jump down someone's throat*
to react angrily to the remarks of the other party to a conversation

JUMP *to jump for joy*
to express great satisfaction

JUMP *to jump in feet first*
to take a calculated risk

JUMP *to jump into bed with someone*
to enter into a joint enterprise with another person

JUMP *to jump into the ring*
to join in enthusiastically

JUMP *to jump on the bus*
to join an activity already well under way

JUMP *to jump straight in at the deep end*
to do something without a proper lead-in

JUMP *to jump that hurdle when one comes to it*
to deal with a particular problem only when it becomes necessary to do so

JUMP *to jump the gun*
to start before one is meant to

JUMP *to jump through hoops*
to undergo some ordeal

JUMP *to jump to a conclusion*
to infer something without proper consideration

JUMP *to jump to attention*
to show respect

JUMP *to jump up and down*
to show excitement or anger or frustration

JUMP *to nearly jump out of one's skin*
to receive a fright

JUMP *to see which way the cat jumps*
to await developments

JUMP *to want to jump all one's fences at once*
to be unrealistic

JUMP *you can jump in the lake*
I intend to take no notice whatsoever of you or your views

JUNGLE *a jungle*
a place where everyone makes his own rules

JUNGLE *the law of the jungle*
the principle that those having power will use it at the expense of all others

JURY *the jury is still out*
no decision has yet been made or the public has not yet given an indication of its views

K

KEEL *to keep something on an even keel*
to ensure that something is not harmed

KEELHAUL *to keelhaul someone*
to penalize a person

KEEP *to be unable to keep people away with a big stick*
to be faced with a large crowd or much demand

KEEP *to keep a civil tongue in one's head*
to be polite, especially under provocation

KEEP *to keep a level head*
to stay calm and rational in a crisis

KEEP *to keep a tally*
to keep a record (refers to a piece of wood with notches made on it to indicate a count)

KEEP *to keep a weather eye out for something*
to look out with particular care

KEEP *to keep body and soul together*
to keep alive

KEEP *to keep one's chin up*
to maintain one's morale

KEEP *to keep one's cotton-picking fingers off something*
not to interfere in something

KEEP *to keep one's distance*
to avoid familiarity

KEEP *to keep one's ears open*
to be on the lookout for useful information

KEEP *to keep one's eye on someone*
to supervise a person or to monitor a person's activities and behavior

KEEP *to keep one's eye on something*
to monitor a situation

KEEP *to keep one's eyes open*
to be on the lookout for useful information

KEEP *to keep one's eyes open for something*
to be on the lookout for an opportunity to do something

KEEP *to keep one's eyes peeled for something*
to be on the constant lookout for something

KEEP *to keep one's fingers crossed*
to hope for a good outcome

KEEP *to keep one's hair on*
to remain calm in a crisis

KEEP *to keep one's hands in*
to engage in activities which reinforce skills which one has previously acquired

KEEP *to keep one's head*
to remain calm in a crisis or to unexpectedly retain an elected or appointed position

KEEP *to keep one's head down*
to work very diligently

KEEP *to keep one's mouth shut*
not to discuss some matter

KEEP *to keep one's nose out of something*
not to meddle in something

KEEP *to keep one's nose to the grindstone*
to work with particular diligence

KEEP *to keep one's pecker up*
to stay cheerful

KEEP *to keep one's powder dry*
to retain key arguments or resources in reserve for use later

KEEP *to keep out of someone's hair*
to let another person get on with his work in his own way

KEEP *to keep someone in a straitjacket*
to deny a person any discretionary powers at all

KEEP *to keep someone in the dark*
to deliberately keep a person uninformed

KEEP *to keep someone on his toes*
to induce a person to be efficient

KEEP *to keep someone's seat warm*
to hold a position temporarily with a view to another person taking it over permanently in the near future

KEEP *to keep something dark*
to keep something secret

KEEP *to keep something on an even keel*
to ensure that something is not harmed

KEEP *to keep something under one's hat*
to maintain a confidence

KEEP *to keep something up one's sleeve*
to secretly retain something in reserve for use in the future or at a later stage of negotiations

KEEP *to keep tabs on something*
to monitor something

KEEP *to keep the ball rolling*
to take advantage of the existing momentum or to participate actively

KEEP *to keep the homes fires burning*
to maintain normal domestic activity during the temporary absence of the breadwinner

KEEP *to keep the jackals at bay*
to pay one's creditors just sufficient to avoid repercussions

KEEP *to keep the lid on something*
to keep a matter under control

KEEP *to keep the pot boiling*
to ensure that an issue stays current

KEEP *to keep the wolf from the door*
to avoid imminent trouble

KEEP *to keep track of something*
to be completely aware of where something is and how it is functioning

KEEP *to keep under wraps*
to keep confidential

KEEP *to keep up with the ball*
to stay on top of the situation

KEEP *why keep a dog and bark oneself?*
it is silly to pay for assistance and then do things personally

KEEPER *keepers of the flame*
persons keen to maintain old traditions

KEEPER *to let something go to the keeper*
to deliberately ignore a particular incident

KETTLE *the pot calling the kettle black*
a person criticizing another person without realizing his own even greater shortcomings

KETTLE *to be a different kettle of fish*
to be something very dissimilar

KETTLE *to be a fine kettle of fish*
to be a terrible muddle

KEY *to strike the right key*
to find the appropriate solution

KEYNOTE *keynote address*
opening address, designed to set the theme of a conference

KICK *I could kick myself*
I regret that I acted thus

KICK *a kick in the pants*
an admonition

KICK *to be alive and kicking*
to be in good form

KICK *to kick a man when he is down*
to take unfair advantage of a person already in difficulty

KICK *to kick heads in*
to demonstrate annoyance at or dislike of certain persons

KICK *to kick in*
to contribute financially

KICK *to kick off*
to start some action

KICK *to kick one's heels*
to be kept waiting

KICK *to kick over one's traces*
to become insubordinate

KICK *to kick some proposal around*
to examine a proposal from all angles

KICK *to kick someone around*
to abuse a person

KICK *to kick someone in the guts*
to take action needlessly hurtful to another person

KICK *to kick someone in the teeth*
to take action which demonstrates annoyance at or dislike of a person

KICK *to kick someone out*
to expel a person

KICK *to kick someone upstairs*
to promote a person to a purely ceremonial position

KICK *to kick the bucket*
to die

KICK *to kick the cat*
to take out one's anger on some innocent party

KICK *to kick up a fuss*
to create a fuss

KID *to treat someone with kid gloves*
to handle a person with great discretion

KILL *to be dressed to kill*
to be more finely dressed than the occasion warrants

KILL *to be in at the kill*
to be present at the climactic finish to something

KILL *to be killed in the rush*
to be the supplier of something extremely popular

KILL *to kill oneself laughing*
to be greatly amused

KILL *to kill some proposal stone dead*
to abandon some proposal completely

KILL *to kill the fatted calf*
to demonstrate welcome and forgiveness on a person's return (Luke 15:23)

KILL *to kill the goose that lays the golden eggs*
through excessive greed to destroy a very profitable enterprise

KILL *to kill two birds with one stone*
to achieve a second objective in the course of achieving the first objective

KILL *to make a killing*
to be in a very successful business venture

KINDRED *kindred spirit*
person with similar interests and eccentricities

KING *a cat may look at a king*
don't give yourself airs!

KING *to pay a king's ransom*
to pay a very large sum

KINGMAKER *kingmaker*
person engaging in behind-the-scenes activities to promote another person to a particular leadership position

KISS *to be the kiss of death*
to be something intended to be helpful but resulting in total destruction

KISS *to kiss and make up*
to reconcile one's differences

KISS *to kiss something good-bye*
to give something up as permanently lost

KISS *to kiss the ground*
to suffer a loss

KISS *to kiss the rod*
to accept punishment meekly

KIT *to have a field marshal's baton in one's kit*
to be ambitious

KITCHEN *everything but the kitchen sink*
a lot of things

KITCHEN *if one can't stand the heat one should stay out of the kitchen*
a person should not put himself in a position involving pressures with which he cannot cope (words attributed to Harry S. Truman)

KITCHEN *to get the rounds of the kitchen*
(of a husband) to be subject to personal abuse by his wife

KITE *to fly a kite*
to issue uncovered checks in the hope that they will be covered before clearance or to test public reaction to legislation in contemplation by leaking broad details of it to the media

KITTEN *to have kittens*
to be in a state of great dismay (refers to a superstition that certain acts would cause women to bear kittens instead of children)

KNEE *a knee-jerk reaction*
a response made instantaneously and without any proper consideration

KNEE *since he was knee high to a grasshopper*
since he was a very young child

KNEE *to be cut off at the knees*
to have a pet project aborted

KNEE *to beg on bended knees*
to request in great earnestness

KNEE *to force someone onto his knees*
to inflict a humiliating defeat on a person

KNEE *to go down on one's hand and knees to someone*
with great humility to ask a favor of a person

KNEE *weak-kneed*
unassertive or irresolute

KNELL *to sound the death knell of something*
to indicate the impending end of something

KNICKERS *to get one's knickers in a knot*
to get unduly excited

KNIFE *before one can say "knife"*
very quickly

KNIFE *one could have cut the atmosphere with a knife*
those present were very tense

KNIFE *the knives are out*
there is an active campaign against someone

KNIFE *to be on a knife edge*
to be in danger

KNIFE *to hold a knife at someone's throat*
to exert undue pressure on another person in an endeavor to achieve a result which would otherwise not be forthcoming

KNIFE *to sharpen the knives*
to get ready for a concerted attack on some principle

KNIFE *to stick a knife into someone*
to act vindictively toward a person

KNIGHT *a knight in shining armor*
a very helpful person

KNIGHT *a white knight*
a party voluntarily coming to the assistance of another party at considerable cost to itself

KNIT *to knit one's brows*
to indicate one's displeasure

KNOCK *on the deathknock*
at the last possible moment

KNOCK *to knock an idea on the head*
to utterly reject a proposal

KNOCK *to knock on doors*
to seek out opportunities to do business

KNOCK *to knock someone off his perch*
to displace a person from his leadership position in some competitive situation

KNOCK *to knock something into a cocked hat*
to twist something so that its original form is hardly recognizable

KNOCK *to knock the stuffing out of someone*
to completely demoralize a person

KNOCK *to knock two heads together*
to make two persons come to their senses and deal with each other

KNOT *at a rate of knots*
very fast

KNOT *to cut the Gordian knot*
to solve, especially by force, a virtually insoluble problem (refers to a complicated knot tied by Gordius and eventually cut by Alexander the Great)

KNOT *to get into a knot*
to get into a state of confusion

KNOT *to get one's knickers in a knot*
to get unduly excited

KNOT *to tie the knot*
to marry

KNOW *I don't know whether I'm Arthur or Martha*
I haven't time to think

KNOW *by their fruits ye shall know them*
their reputation will be based on their results (Matthew 7:20)

KNOW *father knows best*
as an expert I know better than you do just what is most suitable for you

KNOW *not to know someone from Adam*
to be unable to recognize a person

KNOW *the devil one knows is better than the devil one does not know*
the status quo is more comfortable than change

KNOW *the left hand does not know what the right hand is doing*
one section of a large bureaucracy does not realize that another section is simultaneously doing something inconsistent

KNOW *to know a thing or two about something*
to have acquired a lifetime of cunning about a subject

KNOW *to know how many beans make five*
to have common sense

KNOW *to know one's mind*
to form and adhere to an opinion

KNOW *to know the ropes*
to know how to do one's job

KNOW *to know where one stands*
to know what one supports or how one is affected

KNOW *to know which way to turn*
to know which strategy to adopt or where to seek assistance

KNUCKLE *to rap someone over the knuckles*
to admonish a person

KOSHER *to be kosher*
to fulfill all requirements (refers to food complying with all aspects of Jewish religious law)

L

LABEL *to give something a label*
to classify something

LABOR *to labor mightily and bring forth a mouse*
to be quite ineffective

LACE *strait-laced*
puritanical

LADDER *a game of snakes and ladders*
a series of ups and downs

LADDER *rungs up a ladder*
gradual steps to an ultimate goal

LADDER *to be at the bottom of the ladder*
to be in the most junior position in some hierarchy

LADY *it's not over till the fat lady sings*
it is not finished yet

LAKE *you can jump in the lake*
I intend to take no notice whatsoever of you or your views

LAMB *a lamb led to slaughter*
a naive person allowing himself to be exploited

LAMB *one might as well be hanged for a sheep as for a lamb*
further action will not increase the adverse consequences already in train (refers to the stealing of both sheep and lambs being capital crimes under old English law)

LAMB *sacrificial lamb*
somebody unfairly made to suffer for the mistakes of others

LAMB *to be mutton dressed up as lamb*
to foolishly pretend to be younger

LAMB *to wait two shakes of a lamb's tail*
to wait just a few moments

LAME *a lame dog*
a person under some disadvantage needing attention and assistance

LAME *a lame duck*
a person unable to fend for himself (a lame duck president—a president still in office but without influence because the commencement of his successor's term is imminent)

LAND *to ascertain the lay of the land*
to establish the pertinent facts and opinions

LAND *to be in cloud cuckoo land*
to be mad or to have unrealistic expectations

LAND *to be in the land of the living*
to be alive

LAND *to land something*
to achieve something

LANDMARK *a landmark ruling*
a decision marking a turning point in the way a matter is approached

LANDSCAPE *to be part of the landscape*
to be present and fully accepted without question

LANDSLIDE *a landslide*
an electoral result involving victory or defeat by an unexpectedly large margin

LANE *life in the fast lane*
existence full of exciting but worthless activity

LANE *to go down memory lane*
to reminisce

LANGUAGE *to speak the same language*
to have a good understanding and similar ideas

LAP *to be in the lap of the gods*
to be a matter of pure chance (refers to wax tablets inscribed with requests and placed on the knees of statues of Greek gods)

LAP *to drop into one's lap*
to turn up fortuitously

LAP *to dump something in someone's lap*
to impose some responsibility on another person

LAP *to lap it up*
to enjoy the attention

LARGE *larger than life*
in person and full of enthusiasm

LARGE *to be a small cog in a large wheel*
to be a relatively unimportant person in a large organization

LARK *to rise with the lark*
to get up early

LAST *a cobbler should stick to his last*
every person should confine himself to activities for which he has been trained

LAST *the final straw*
the latest step, which, when added to a large number of seemingly harmless previous steps, sets off a disaster resulting from the cumulative effect

LAST *the last bastion*
the only remaining defensive measure

LAST *the last of the Mohicans*
to be the last of a group (refers to a near extinct tribe of American Indians) (title of a novel by James Fenimore Cooper)

LAST *to be on one's last legs*
to be nearly worn out

LAST *to have come down in the last shower*
to be naive

LAST *to make a last-ditch stand*
to make a brave effort to stave off final defeat

LAST *to play the last card in the pack*
to lower one's standards in a final desperate effort

LAST *to squeeze the last drop out of something*
to get the maximum advantage out of some favorable situation

LATE *late in the day*
only when a project is well advanced

LATHER *to get a lather up*
to get unduly excited

LATHER *to whip oneself into a lather*
to become unduly excited

LAUGH *to laugh all the way to the bank*
to appreciate one's good fortune

LAUGH *to laugh one's head off*
to greatly enjoy something

LAUGH *to laugh something out of court*
to ridicule a proposition as having no basis whatsoever

LAUGH *you will laugh on the other side of your face*
you will regret this

LAUREL *to look to one's laurels*
to be careful not to lose one's reputation for some skill

LAUREL *to rest on one's laurels*
to use a reputation for success earned in earlier times as a substitute for current endeavor

LAW *Murphy's law*
the principle that everything which can go wrong will go wrong

LAW *Parkinson's law*
the principle that work expands to match the work capacity available (title of a book by Prof. C. Northcote Parkinson)

LAW *the law of the jungle*
the principle that those having power will use it at the expense of all others

LAW *to lay down the law*
to be officious

LAY *not to lay a finger on someone*
to refrain from hurting a person

LAY *to be a laid-down misere*
to be very easily accomplished and/or to be certain of outcome (refers to the declaration in certain card games undertaking to win no tricks)

LAY *to be able to lay one's hands on something*
to be able to locate something

LAY *to kill the goose that lays the golden eggs*
through excessive greed to destroy a very profitable enterprise

LAY *to lay a proposal on the table*
to make a proposal available for discussion or to adjourn discussion on a proposal for an indefinite period

LAY *to lay down the law*
to be officious

LAY *to lay it on the line*
to make clear what the accepted rules of behavior are

LAY *to lay it on with a trowel*
to flatter

LAY *to lay one's cards on the table*
to be utterly frank and open or to honestly disclose one's position

LAY *to lay one's hands on something*
to acquire something

LAY *to lay some theory to rest*
to abandon some theory as being no longer appropriate

LEAD *a lamb led to slaughter*
a naive person allowing himself to be exploited

LEAD *all roads lead to Rome*
all alternatives will have the same outcome

LEAD *the blind leading the blind*
persons without the necessary skills for a task purporting to impart those skills to others

LEAD *to go down like a lead balloon*
to receive a very cool reception

LEAD *to lead a dog's life*
to be ill-treated

LEAD *to lead someone a merry dance*
to mislead a person

LEAD *to lead someone by the nose*
to induce another person to comply with one's wishes

LEAD *to lead someone up the garden path*
to mislead a person by deliberately fallacious arguments

LEAD *to lead with one's chin*
by one's brash behavior to virtually invite one's opponents to take action against one

LEAD *to swing the lead*
to cheat an employer by not working while being paid to do so

LEADING *a leading question*
a very pertinent question (the misuse of a legal term, which actually means a question so framed as to suggest the answer)

LEADING *to be the leading light*
to be the most important person in a venture

LEADING *to have a leading edge*
to have an advantage

LEAF *to take a leaf out of someone's book*
to model oneself on another person

LEAF *to turn over a new leaf*
to reform

LEAGUE *to be in the same league*
to have comparable skills

LEAN *a shoulder to lean on*
sympathy

LEAN *to lean on someone*
to utilize the support of another person or to pressure another person to do something against his inclination

LEAP *a leap into the dark*
a rash move

LEAP *a quantum leap*
a gigantic step forward

LEAP *by leaps and bounds*
with surprisingly fast progress

LEAP *to leap at an idea*
to accept a suggestion enthusiastically

LEAP *to leapfrog something*
to overtake something, with the likelihood of in turn being overtaken (refers to a game in which participants jump over each other in turn)

LEAP *to leap in*
to commence an activity without considering the wisdom of doing so or the best way to proceed

LEARN *to learn a lesson*
to benefit from one's experience

LEARN *to learn something from the horse's mouth*
to get information from someone qualified to impart it

LEARN *to learn the ropes*
to be taught the elementary features

LEASE *a new lease on life*
the prospect of a worry-free existence from now on

LEASH *to hold someone on a short leash*
to give a person very little authority

LEAST *to take the line of least resistance*
to succumb to outside pressure

LEAVE *a case of rats leaving a sinking ship*
the desertion of an enterprise in anticipation of imminent failure

LEAVE *to be left holding the baby*
to be tricked into accepting responsibility for someone else's problems

LEAVE *to leave no stone unturned*
to be very thorough

LEAVE *to leave one's mark on something*
to be responsible for permanently altering the way something is operated

LEAVE *to leave oneself wide open*
to act in such a way that one's opponents will find much which can be easily criticized

LEAVE *to leave others for dead*
to be vastly superior

LEAVE *to leave someone cold*
to fail to impress a person

LEAVE *to leave someone high and dry*
to withdraw all support from a person or to isolate a person from a desired involvement

LEAVE *to leave someone in the lurch*
to desert a person who is in difficulties (refers to the score in certain games)

LEAVE *to leave someone out in the cold*
to deny a desired objective to a person

LEAVE *to leave something up in the air*
to continue with an unresolved problem

LEAVE *to leave the door open*
to issue a standing invitation for the resumption of some negotiations

LEAVE *without leaving any footprints*
without making any impression

LEECH *leech*
person taking undue advantage of others

LEEWAY *to make up leeway*
to get back to a normal position or to get to the position held by one's competitors

LEFT *a left-handed compliment*
a thinly-disguised insult

LEFT *the left hand does not know what the right hand is doing*
one section of a large bureaucracy does not realize that another section is simultaneously doing something inconsistent

LEFT *to have two left feet*
to be clumsy

LEG *not to have a leg to stand on*
to have one's arguments completely demolished or to be without acceptable excuse or explanation

LEG *to be on one's last legs*
to be nearly worn out

LEG *to cost an arm and a leg*
to be excessively expensive

LEG *to do the leg work*
to carry out the tedious part of a project

LEG *to give someone a leg up*
to give a person some assistance

LEG *to have a leg in*
to have an opportunity which has the potential to lead to bigger things

LEG *to have one's tail between one's legs*
to show great humility in the light of a backdown

LEG *to pull someone's leg*
to tell a false but plausible story as an act of humor

LEG *to shake a leg*
to hurry up

LEG *to stand up on one's hind legs*
to exert one's authority

LEG *to talk the hind leg off a donkey*
to talk excessively

LEG *with his tail between his legs*
contritely

LEG ROPE *to put a leg rope on someone*
to give a person very little authority

LEMON *the answer is a lemon*
the outcome is inconclusive

LEMON *to sell someone a lemon*
to sell a person a grossly defective product on the basis that it represents quality

LEMON *to suck the lemon dry*
to get the maximum advantage out of some favorable situation

LEND *to lend a hand*
to assist

LEND *to lend one's name to something*
to endorse something

LEND *to lend someone an ear*
to pay attention to a person

LEND *to lend weight to something*
to use one's influence in support of some cause

LENGTH *at arm's length*
between parties who are strangers bearing no special duty to each other and who have no financial or other relationship with each other (a legal term)

LENGTH *to go to great lengths*
to take much trouble

LEOPARD *a leopard cannot change his spots*
each person is born with certain unalterable characteristics

LESSON *to drive the lesson home*
to take certain action which is unpleasant but which has the effect of registering a message

LESSON *to learn a lesson*
to benefit from one's experience

LESSON *to teach someone a lesson*
to inflict something unpleasant on a person in the hope that it will lead to a change in his behavior.

LET *bloodletting*
planned reductions

LET *to let blood*
to allow some harm as the price for achieving some greater benefit

LET *to let someone off the hook*
to allow a person to escape the adverse consequences of his own actions

LETTER *a dead letter*
a rule still in existence but no longer observed in practice

LETTER *a red-letter day*
an important occasion (refers to the color used to print saints' days on some calendars)

LEVEL *a level playing field*
competition on equal terms

LEVEL *to be on the level*
to be honest

LEVEL *to keep a level head*
to stay calm and rational in a crisis

LEVEL *water will find its own level*
people will reach an appropriate position relative to others

LEVEL-HEADED *level-headed*
rational

LIBERTY *liberty hall*
a place where one is free to do as one wishes

LICENSE *a license to print money*
a lucrative government-conferred monopoly or privilege

LICK *to lick one's chops*
to look forward to something with pleasurable anticipation

LICK *to lick one's wounds*
to adjust oneself to defeat

LICK *to lick someone's boots*
to show humility

LICK *to lick something into shape*
to make something presentable and effective

LID *to blow the lid off something*
to expose something no matter how embarrassing this might be

LID *to keep the lid on something*
to keep a matter under control

LIE *one has made one's bed and one will now have to lie on it*
one has to bear the consequences of one's actions

LAY *to ascertain the lay of the land*
to establish the pertinent facts and opinions

LIE *to let sleeping dogs lie*
to refrain from raising an issue which is not obviously requiring attention

LIE *to lie low*
to stay inconspicuous

LIE *to take something lying down*
to accept a disadvantage without protest

LIE *uneasy lies the head that wears a crown*
responsibility involves some risks and some burdens (from Shakespeare's HENRY IV)

LIFE *I cannot for the life of me*
I just cannot

LIFE *a new lease on life*
the prospect of a worry-free existence from now on

LIFE *larger than life*
in person and full of enthusiasm

LIFE *life in the fast lane*
existence full of exciting but worthless activity

LIFE *life raft*
financial assistance sufficient to avert insolvency

LIFE *not on your life*
definitely not

LIFE *to be the life and soul of the party*
to be the prime enthusiast for a cause

LIFE *to breathe life into a corpse*
to revive something moribund

LIFE *to lead a dog's life*
to be ill-treated

LIFE *to save someone's life*
to be of great help to a person

LIFE *you can bet your life on something*
something is certain to happen

LIFEBLOOD *the lifeblood*
the main or essential ingredient; or the person or factor instilling enthusiasm

LIFT *not to lift a finger to help someone*
to refuse to assist

LIFT *to lift one's game*
to raise the standard of one's performance

LIGHT *a chink of light*
a small hope of a solution or breakthrough

LIGHT *a highlight*
a particularly important item

LIGHT *a light in the sky*
a sign of great hope

LIGHT *guiding light*
yardstick for ethical behavior

LIGHT *in the cold light of day*
in an unemotional atmosphere at a later stage

LIGHT *light dawns*
the point is grasped

LIGHT *light on the hill*
distant goal acting as an inspiration

LIGHT *light-fingered*
good at stealing

LIGHT *shining light*
eminent or scholarly person

LIGHT *to be in the limelight*
to be exposed to public attention

LIGHT *to be the leading light*
to be the most important person in a venture

LIGHT *to bring something to light*
to draw to public attention

LIGHT *to get the red light*
to be forbidden to do something

LIGHT *to give the green light*
to grant permission

LIGHT *to hide one's light under a bushel*
to keep others in ignorance of one's skills and experience

LIGHT *to highlight something*
to draw particular attention to a matter

LIGHT *to light a fuse*
to cause serious reactions

LIGHT *to see red lights flashing*
to be conscious of the danger

LIGHT *to see someone in a good light*
to regard a person favorably

LIGHT *to see the light*
to understand the real situation

LIGHT *to see the light at the end of the tunnel*
to be close to finalizing a long exercise

LIGHT *to see the light of day*
to be made public

LIGHT *to shed light on something*
to give explanations

LIGHT *to steal the spotlight*
to set out to be the center of attention

LIGHT *to turn the spotlight on something*
to draw public attention to something

LIGHTLY *to tread lightly*
to be careful

LIGHTNING *a lightning rod*
a person who attracts trouble to himself

LIGHTWEIGHT *lightweight*
uninfluential

LILLIPUTIAN *Lilliputian*
small (refers to a place in Swift's GULLIVER'S TRAVELS)

LILY *lily-livered*
cowardly

LILY *lily-white*
honest and incorruptible

LILY *to gild the lily*
(actually: to gild refined gold, to paint the lily) to do something patently unnecessary

LIMB *to go out on a limb*
to put oneself at risk through foolish action

LIMBO *to be in limbo*
to have one's ultimate fate yet to be determined

LIMBO *to consign something to limbo*
to consider something as permanently disposed of

LIMELIGHT *to be in the limelight*
to be exposed to public attention

LIMIT *the sky is the limit*
the cost is no obstacle

LINCHPIN *linchpin*
essential feature central to a project

LINE *hook, line and sinker*
wholly

LINE *someone's job is on the line*
a person's career path is under consideration and/or his present position is at risk

LINE *the Plimsoll line*
the standard

LINE *the bottom line*
the conclusion which matters or the net effect of a series of developments

LINE *to be further down the line*
to have a low priority

LINE *to be in the firing line*
to be among the first to be under attack

LINE *to be line ball*
to be equal

LINE *to be out of line*
to adopt a stance not held by others

LINE *to draw the line at that*
to refuse to go any further

LINE *to fall into line*
to conform with others

LINE *to lay it on the line*
to make clear what the accepted rules of behavior are

LINE *to line one's pockets*
to make, improperly and secretly, a profit out of some transaction

LINE *to make a beeline for something*
to go straight to something with great enthusiasm or to head for some goal by the most direct route

LINE *to put one's reputation on the line*
to take a public stance in the realization that there is a risk that one's reputation will suffer if one is proved wrong

LINE *to read between the lines*
to appreciate the true significance of something not put into words

LINE *to sign on the dotted line*
to confirm one's agreement

LINE *to sit on the sidelines*
not to take part in the main action

LINE *to step out of line*
to infringe accepted rules of behavior

LINE *to swallow the line*
to accept as truth the story being proffered

LINE *to take a hard line*
to be uncompromising

LINE *to take the line of least resistance*
to succumb to outside pressure

LINE *to toe the line*
to conform

LINE *to tread the thin line*
cautiously to take action in circumstances where either too much or too little will cause difficulties

LINEN *to wash one's dirty linen in public*
to expose one's domestic differences to the world at large

LINGER *the melody lingers on*
the benefit of past actions remains

LINING *every cloud has a silver lining*
there are benefits even in seemingly adverse situations

LINK *the weakest link in the chain*
the least efficient component in a project the overall efficiency of which is governed by the efficiency of the least efficient component

LION *the lion's share*
the biggest portion

LION *to beard the lion in his dean*
to visit someone important at his headquarters

LION *to put one's head into the lion's mouth*
to recklessly expose oneself to great danger

LION *to throw someone to the lions*
to abandon a person

LIP *a stiff upper lip*
obstinate courage in the face of pain or adversity

LIP *to be tight-lipped*
to keep confidences or to be uncommunicative

LIP *to bite one's lip*
to control one's anger

LIP *to pay lip service to some rules*
to disregard some rules in practice while acknowledging them in words

LIP *to seal one's lips*
to keep a confidence

LIST *a shopping list*
a catalogue of demands

LISTEN *a listening post*
a place where information of strategic value can be collected

LITMUS *a litmus test*
an event which allows the outcome of future events to be predicted more accurately

LITTLE *a little bird told me*
I heard from an unnameable informant (Ecclesiastes 10:20)

LITTLE *a little tin god*
a petty tyrant

LITTLE *little pitchers have long ears*
children have a tendency to overhear things

LITTLE *tall oaks from little acorns grow*
even major enterprises have to have small beginnings (from "'Lines written for a School Declamation'" by David Everett)

LITTLE *to be a big fish in a little pond*
to be a person holding an important office but in an unimportant organization

LITTLE *to twist someone around one's little finger*
by charm to get one's way

LIVE *not to live in each other's pockets*
to each follow his own lifestyle

LIVE *to be a live wire*
to be an enthusiast

LIVE *to live from hand to mouth*
being in poor financial circumstances, to survive with little by way of safety margin

LIVE *to live in a fool's paradise*
to delude oneself

LIVER *lily-livered*
cowardly

LIZARD *flat out like a lizard*
to be hard at work (a play on words, not a simile)

LLOYD *to be A1 at Lloyd's*
to be in perfect order (refers to the classification of ships in Lloyd's register in London)

LOAD *that has taken a load off my mind*
I am relieved

LOAD *to be the throw of a loaded die*
to be an act of deceit

LOCK *lock, stock and barrel*
entirely

LOCK *to lock horns with someone*
to have an argument with another person

LOCK *to lock someone into some arrangement*
to create an agreement which cannot be broken by one of the parties

LOCK *to lock something up in the old oak chest*
to put in a safe place and out of mind

LOGGERHEAD *to be at loggerheads*
to constantly fight one another

LOGJAM *a logjam*
a stoppage of activity caused by input in greater volume than allowed for

LOIN *to gird up one's loins*
to get ready for action

LONDON *it is London to a brick*
it is virtually certain

LONE *a lone wolf*
a person who prefers to act without involving others

LONE *to be a lone voice in the wilderness*
to be the only person stating unpopular views

LONG *for the long haul*
as a long-term proposition

LONG *he must have a long spoon that sups with the devil*
great care is needed when negotiating deals with disreputable parties

LONG *it is a long time between drinks*
activity is occurring only very spasmodically

LONG *it is as broad as it is long*
it does not really matter

LONG *little pitchers have long ears*
children have a tendency to overhear things

LONG *take a long walk on a short pier*
go away, I want no dealings with you

LONG *that is a long shot*
there is only a remote possibility

LONG *the long and the short of it*
all that needs to be said about this

LONG *to be long in the tooth*
to be old

LONG *to draw a long bow*
to state a conclusion which while possible is unlikely on the known facts

LONG *to enter a long road*
to commence a task which will take a long time

LONG *to have a long arm*
to have far-reaching power

LONG *to have a long face*
to look miserable

LONG *to throw a long shadow*
to have wide-spread ramifications

LONG *to win by a long chalk*
to win very conclusively

LOOK *a cat may look at a king*
don't give yourself airs!

LOOK *distant fields look greener*
activities of which one has no experience seem much easier than is really the case

LOOK *one looks for elephants in elephant country*
one needs to search in the right place

LOOK *someone looks as if butter would not melt in his mouth*
a person looks sweet and innocent

LOOK *things look black*
there is little hope of success or prosperity or a favorable outcome

LOOK *to give someone a black look*
to indicate one's displeasure with a person

LOOK *to look a gift horse in the mouth*
to be suspicious about a benefit which has been volunteered

LOOK *to look after number one*
to act selfishly

LOOK *to look at someone sideways*
to silently and politely indicate one's disapproval

LOOK *to look daggers at someone*
to look at a person in a way which indicates great animosity

LOOK *to look down the barrel of a gun*
to be given little choice in a matter

LOOK *to look down the nose at something*
to treat a matter with obvious contempt

LOOK *to look for a needle in a haystack*
to attempt something with a very small chance of success

LOOK *to look on the dark side*
to be pessimistic

LOOK *to look to one's laurels*
to be careful not to lose one's reputation for some skill

LOOK *to need to look over one's shoulder*
to be subject to attack which is not obvious

LOOM *to loom on the horizon*
to be expected but not immediately

LOOP *a loop-hole*
a means of getting around the intention of some regulation

LOOSE *a loose cannon on the deck*
a mistake likely to cause trouble

LOOSE *to have a loose tongue*
to speak foolishly or indiscreetly

LOOSE *to have a screw loose*
to be mentally unbalanced

LOOSE *to play fast and loose*
to disregard one's obligations

LOOSE *to tie up the loose ends*
to complete the minor outstanding items of some substantially finished project

LOSE *get lost!*
just go away!

LOSE *heads I win—tails you lose*
whichever way this matter goes I will benefit at your expense

LOSE *not to lose any sleep over something*
not to worry about some matter

LOSE *to be on the losing end of the stick*
to be worse off while the other party to a transaction becomes correspondingly better off

LOSE *to lose face*
to endure embarrassment by virtue of being defeated or having one's errors found out

LOSE *to lose heart*
to cease being enthusiastic

LOSE *to lose money hand over fist*
to lose money very fast and convincingly

LOSE *to lose one's head*
to become confused

LOSE *to lose one's marbles*
to become senile

LOSE *to lose one's nerve*
to abandon, out of fear, a decision to do something

LOSE *to lose one's right arm*
to lose some highly-valued assistance

LOSE *to lose one's touch*
to cease to be familiar with something

LOSE *to lose steam*
to slow down

LOSE *what one loses on the swings one gains on the roundabouts*
there are advantages and disadvantages which offset each other

LOSE *you can get lost*
I intend to take no notice whatsoever of you or your views

LOUD *to come through loud and clear*
to be well understood

LOVE *love me—love my dog*
if you accept me then you must also accept my associates

LOVE *not for love or money*
definitely not

LOVELY *everything in the garden is lovely*
everything is fine

LOW *low-down*
confidential information relevant to something

LOW *the lowest common denominator*
the highest level of taste found among all the members of some target audience

LOW *to lie low*
to stay inconspicuous

LOWER *to lower one's rights*
to reduce one's ambition

LOWER *to lower the boom*
to terminate an activity

LUCK *the very best of British luck*
you will have a hard time of it, but you carry my best wishes

LUCK *to be the luck of the draw*
to be a chance result

LUCK *to push one's luck*
having already done well in something, to then take risks which can prejudice everything

LUCK *to take pot luck*
to take whatever happens by chance to be available

LUCKY *one can thank one's lucky stars*
one was extremely fortunate

LUKEWARM *lukewarm*
unenthusiastic though not hostile

LUMP *to have a lump in one's throat*
to feel emotional

LURCH *to leave someone in the lurch*
to desert a person who is in difficulties (refers to the score in certain games)

LURK *to lurk in the shadows*
to have a low profile at the moment, but with the possibility of becoming much more conspicuous at any time

LYNX *lynx-eyed*
having acute vision

M

MACABRE *danse macabre*
gruesome final step (French, "ghastly dance")

MACHINE *a sausage machine*
the turning out of large volumes without particular thought

MACHINE *when the wash comes through the machine*
in due course

MACHINERY *to be a well-oiled piece of machinery*
to be functioning very satisfactorily

MACKEREL *to throw a sprat to catch a mackerel*
to risk a little in the hope of gaining much

MAD *a madhouse*
an organization in great turmoil

MAGIC *a magic bullet*
a guaranteed remedy

MAGIC *the magic moment*
the perfect time

MAGIC *there is no magic in that*
that is quite ordinary

MAGIC *to get a magic carpet ride to something*
to be very fortunate in achieving some objective

MAGIC *to wave a magic wand*
to direct affairs without the restraints of the real world

MAGNET *to be a magnet*
to be a factor drawing a crowd of people

MAHOMET *if the mountain will not come to Mahomet then Mahomet will go to the mountain*
on recognizing that one has insufficient power to effect one's most desired solution, one decides to make do with the next best alternative

MAIDEN *the answer to a maiden's prayer*
an unexpected but very welcome happening

MAIN *to splice the main brace*
to serve an extra ration of rum

MAINSTREAM *mainstream*
orthodox

MAKE *matchmaker*
intermediary facilitating or instigating some merger

MAKE *not to be made of money*
not to be wealthy

MAKE *ready-made*
easily fabricated or available without difficulty

MAKE *to kiss and make up*
to reconcile one's differences

MAKE *to make or break someone*
to be a factor leading either to a person's success or to his failure, with no intermediate position

MAN *a poor man's something*
a second-best version

MAN *every man and his dog*
everybody

MAN *he is your man*
he conforms to an ideal

MAN *one man's meat is another man's poison*
people's tastes differ

MAN *one's right-hand man*
one's chief aide

MAN *the man in the street*
the average citizen

MAN *to be a man of straw*
to have no assets while giving a contrary appearance

MAN *to be one's own man*
to approach every issue in a totally objective manner

MAN *to kick a man when he is down*
to take unfair advantage of a person already in difficulty

MAN *to separate the men from the boys*
to distinguish between those with and without certain skills

MAN *two men and a dog*
very few people

MANAGE *to stage-manage something*
to arrange how something happens

MANGER *to be a dog in the manger*
to spitefully deny something to others, notwithstanding its uselessness to oneself

MANNA *manna from heaven*
unexpected benefits (Exodus 16:15)

MANSIZE *a mansize job*
a large task worth doing well

MANTLE *to assume someone's mantle*
to take over another person's role

MAP *to put some organization on the map*
to make the organization a force to be reckoned with

MARATHON *marathon*
requiring great endurance (refers to the run to get aid during the battle of Marathon in 490 BC)

MARBLE *to be carved in marble*
to be virtually unalterable

MARBLE *to lose one's marbles*
to become senile

MARCH *in the course of a day's march*
while carrying out one's normal activities

MARCH *to get one's marching orders*
to be told to leave

MARCH *to march to a different drum*
to show an independent approach

MARCH *to steal a march on someone*
to anticipate another person's actions and get in ahead

MARE *a mare's nest*
a discovery with illusory benefits

MARGIN *safety margin*
allowance for miscalculations

MARINE *tell it to the marines*
such nonsense is not believable

MARINER *to be an albatross around someone's neck*
to be a great burden (popularized by Coleridge's ANCIENT MARINER)

MARK *a hallmark*
a standard (refers to the official assay mark on gold and silver, originally put on at the Goldsmiths' Hall)

MARK *a landmark ruling*
a decision marking a turning point in the way a matter is approached

MARK *high water mark*
triumph

MARK *mark my words*
you will find out that I am right

MARK *the mark of Cain*
disgrace (Genesis 4:15)

MARK *the river found its mark*
equilibrium between two pressures has been achieved

MARK *to be first off the mark*
to start ahead of all others

MARK *to be slow off the mark*
to be slow to start something

MARK *to be up to the mark*
to be of the right standard

MARK *to be wide off the mark*
to have a belief which is far removed from the true position

MARK *to get full marks for something*
to deserve praise for something

MARK *to have a black mark against one's name*
to have a tarnished reputation

MARK *to hit the mark*
to achieve one's object or to make the correct decision (refers to archery)

MARK *to leave one's mark on something*
to be responsible for permanently altering the way something is operated

MARK *to make one's mark*
to make an impression on people (refers to the cross made as the signature of illiterate persons)

MARK *to make something one's trademark*
to earn a reputation for maintaining some stance

MARK *to mark time*
to do nothing while awaiting developments

MARK *to overstep the mark*
to fail to observe the proprieties

MARKET *to be a drug on the market*
to be in overplentiful supply

MARSHAL *to have a field marshal's baton in one's kit*
to be ambitious

MARTHA *I don't know whether I'm Arthur or Martha*
I haven't time to think

MASK *to unmask someone*
to discover a person's true identity

MAST *to nail one's colors to the mast*
to publicly declare one's position and to maintain it in the face of criticism

MASTER *a chessmaster*
a clever strategist

MASTER *a master stroke*
particularly brilliant action

MASTER *a past master*
an expert with long experience

MATCH *game, set and match*
completion

MATCH *the whole shooting match*
the whole lot

MATCH *to put a match to gasoline*
to make a bad situation worse

MATCHMAKER *matchmaker*
intermediary facilitating or instigating some merger

MATTER *it is mind over matter*
one's resolve to overcome suffering will succeed

MATTER *not to matter a row of beans*
to be utterly unimportant

MAVERICK *maverick*
a person who likes to do things differently from other persons (refers to unbranded livestock)

MCCOY *to be the real McCoy*
the genuine article (refers to an American boxer who became world welterweight champion in 1890)

MEALY *mealy-mouthed*
not at all forceful in debate

MEASURE *to take someone's measure*
to sum up a person's character or skills

MEAT *one man's meat is another man's poison*
people's tastes differ

MEAT *to be easy meat*
to be an opponent who is readily outwitted

MEAT *to be meat and drink*
to be very pleasurable

MEAT *to be the ham in the sandwich*
to be caught in the middle of a dispute between other parties

MEAT *to contain much meat*
to contain much material worthy of consideration

MEAT *to make mincemeat of something*
to devastate something

MECCA *a Mecca for something*
a place at which supporters of something congregate

MEDICINE *strong medicine*
a tough remedy

MEDICINE *to get a taste of one's own medicine*
to suffer from an initiative intended to affect only other persons

MEDICINE *to take one's medicine*
to submit to something unpleasant but necessary

MEET *to make ends meet*
to live within one's income

MEET *to meet one's Waterloo*
to receive a decisive defeat (refers to Napoleon's fate at the Battle of Waterloo)

MELODY *the melody lingers on*
the benefit of past actions remains

MELT *someone looks as if butter would not melt in his mouth*
a person looks sweet and innocent

MELT *to go back into the melting pot*
to be up for reconsideration ab initio

MELTING *a melting pot*
a country where people with different ethnic backgrounds over time merge into one nation

MEND *to mend fences*
to achieve a reconciliation

MERRY *the more the merrier*
everyone is welcome

MERRY *to be on a merry-go-round*
to be sent from one bureaucrat to another

MERRY *to lead someone a merry dance*
to mislead a person

MERRY *to raise merry hell*
to prominently involve others in a matter in the expectation of significant results from this action

MESS *to clean up a mess*
to sort out mistakes or neglect

MESS *to sell one's birthright for a mess of pottage*
through foolishness to exchange something of substance for something of little value (Genesis 25)

MESSAGE *to get the message*
to understand the real import of what is being said

METEORIC *meteoric*
rapid

MEXICAN *a Mexican standoff*
a situation where neither of two parties is making a move

MICROSCOPE *to be under the microscope*
to be the subject of close examination

MID *to swap horses in midstream*
to change direction during the course of a project

MIDAS *the Midas touch*
attributes which cause a person's ventures to be extremely profitable (refers to King Midas of Phrygia, who had the power to turn everything he touched into gold)

MIDDLE *a middle-of-the-road solution*
a solution near the middle of a range of possibilities

MIDNIGHT *to burn the midnight oil*
to work late into the night

MILCH *a milch cow*
an easy and plentiful source of some desired benefit

MILE *a milestone*
an achievement

MILE *someone would run a mile*
a person would do anything to escape his responsibilities

MILE *to be able to spot trouble a mile away*
to be able to spot trouble before it actually happens

MILE *to be miles apart*
to have great philosophical differences

MILE *to be miles away*
to have one's mind on other matters

MILE *to go the extra mile*
to work beyond the call of duty

MILE *to miss something by a mile*
to be nowhere near one's target

MILE *to stick out a mile*
to be very apparent

MILE *give him an inch and he will take a mile*
make him a small concession and he will abuse it by taking much more

MILEAGE *to get some mileage out of something*
to benefit from something

MILK *a land of milk and honey*
a country in which everything is in abundant supply

MILK *it is no use crying over spilt milk*
lamenting over a disaster achieves nothing

MILK *to be cream on top of the milk*
to be an additional benefit in an already satisfactory scenario

MILL *it is all grist to the mill*
this is useful but unexciting additional material

MILL *run of the mill*
normal or average

MILL *the mills of God grind slowly*
retribution may be delayed but is inevitable

MILL *to put someone through the mill*
to give a person practical experience

MILLSTONE *a millstone round someone's neck*
a great burden

MINCE *not to mince words*
to speak bluntly

MINCE *to make mincemeat of something*
to devastate something

MIND *a thought in the back of one's mind*
an undeveloped idea

MIND *in one's mind's eye*
using a vivid imagination

MIND *it is mind over matter*
one's resolve to overcome suffering will succeed

MIND *that has taken a load off my mind*
I am relieved

MIND *the mind boggles*
this is astonishing

MIND *to be a weight off one's mind*
to be a great relief

MIND *to be of two minds*
to be undecided between two alternatives

MIND *to be of one mind*
(of several people) to be agreed

MIND *to be out of one's cotton-picking mind*
to act irrationally

MIND *to broaden someone's mind*
to expose a person to a greater variety of experiences and interests than he had previously

MIND *to change one's mind*
to alter the views which one had previously formed

MIND *to cloud one's mind*
to allow irrelevant or extraneous factors to affect one's impartiality or judgment

MIND *to cross one's mind*
to occur to one

MIND *to drive someone out of his mind*
to cause great worry to a person

MIND *to give someone a piece of one's mind*
to abuse another person

MIND *to have a mind of one's own*
not to be easily influenced

MIND *to have a one-track mind*
to keep coming back to one narrow topic of conversation

MIND *to have an open mind*
to be willing to assess evidence on its merits and without prejudging it

MIND *to have half a mind to do something*
to be tempted or mildly inclined to do something

MIND *to know one's mind*
to form and adhere to an opinion

MIND *to make up one's mind*
to reach a conclusion after contemplating a matter

MIND *to prey on one's mind*
(of a problem) to keep worrying one

MIND *to put someone's mind at rest*
to reassure a person

MIND *to slip one's mind*
to be overlooked or forgotten

MIND *to speak one's mind*
to express one's views frankly and forcefully

MIND *to spring to mind*
to suddenly occur to a person

MINE *a goldmine*
a source of much wealth or of many facts

MINE *a minefield*
a source of great hidden danger or of difficulties not obvious on a first encounter

MINNOW *to miss the sharks while netting the minnows*
to succeed in minor aspects but fail in the ones that really matter

MINT *to charge a mint*
to impose very high prices

MIRAGE *mirage*
illusory benefit

MIRE *to sink deeper into the mire*
to get into further difficulties

MISERE *to be a laid-down misere*
to be very easily accomplished and/or to be certain of outcome (refers to the declaration in certain card games undertaking to win no tricks)

MISS *not to miss a beat*
to carry on without the slightest interruption

MISS *to miss something by a mile*
to be nowhere near ones target

MISS *to miss the boat*
to fail to exploit an opportunity

MISS *to miss the bus*
to fail to exploit an opportunity

MISS *to miss the sharks while netting the minnows*
to succeed in minor aspects but fail in the ones that really matter

MISS *to miss the train*
to fail to exploit an opportunity

MITE *not a mite*
not at all (refers to a Flemish coin of small value)

MIX *a mixed bag*
some advantages and some disadvantages

MIX *to be a mixed blessing*
to be an outcome with some desirable and some undesirable features

MOHICAN *the last of the Mohicans*
to be the last of a group (refers to a near extinct tribe of American Indians) (title of a novel by James Fenimore Cooper)

MOLD *to be cast in someone's mold*
to take after another person

MOLE *to make mountains out of molehills*
to treat a minor problem as though it were a major disaster

MOMENT *at the psychological moment*
at the most appropriate instant of time (a phrase which actually confuses the German word for "motive" with the term for an instant of time)

MOMENT *the magic moment*
the perfect time

MOMENTUM *to have momentum*
to move along forcefully

MONEY *a license to print money*
a lucrative government-conferred monopoly or privilege

MONEY *money for jam*
remuneration easily earned

MONEY *not for love or money*
definitely not

MONEY *not to be made of money*
not to be wealthy

MONEY *pin money*
an allowance to a wife for her personal use

MONEY *that is money down the drain*
money has been wastefully lost on a failed project

MONEY *the money is rolling in*
the scheme is very profitable

MONEY *to have a run for one's money*
to at least get some enjoyment out of an otherwise abortive exercise

MONEY *to have money burning a hole in one's pocket*
to be impatient to spend or invest available funds

MONEY *to have money flowing out of one's ears*
to be very rich

MONEY *to lose money hand over fist*
to lose money very fast and convincingly

MONEY *to put money on the table*
to back one's judgment in a tangible way or to demonstrate one's sincerity

MONEY *to put one's money where one's mouth is*
to back one's judgment by putting assets at risk

MONEY *to see the color of someone's money*
to get evidence of the sincerity of a person's proposal

MONEY *to throw good money after bad*
to waste further money in a vain attempt to recover money already lost

MONKEY *monkey business*
mischievous or underhand activity

MONKEY *to play monkey tricks on someone*
to engage in discreditable behavior affecting a person

MONSTER *a hydra-headed monster*
an evil which is not readily destroyable

MONSTER *to create a Frankenstein*
to create something wicked and out of control (a reference to the fictional creator of a monster, in mistake for a reference to the monster itself)

MONTH *to be the flavor of the month*
to be a commodity temporarily popular without a logical reason

MOON *once in a blue moon*
very rarely (refers to the volcanic eruption at Krakatoa in 1883 when volcanic dust caused the moon to appear blue)

MOON *to be over the moon*
to be very excited

MOONLIGHT *a moonlight flit*
an escape from creditors

MOONSHINE *moonshine*
unrealistic ideas

MORTEM *to conduct a postmortem on something*
to review past actions with a view to learning lessons for the future (Latin, "after the death")

MORTGAGE *to have a mortgage on something*
to have a moral claim in regard to a matter

MORTGAGE *to mortgage the future*
to get benefits now but at a cost in due course

MOSAIC *a mosaic*
something with a large number of different aspects to it

MOTE *a mote in someone's eye*
a fault in another person which is trifling in comparison to an unrecognized major fault in oneself (Matthew 7:3)

MOTH *moth-eaten*
(of ideas, etc.) antiquated

MOTHBALL *to mothball equipment*
to put equipment on a "care and maintenance" basis

MOTHER *a mother hen*
an overly protective person

MOTHERHOOD *a motherhood statement*
a statement so obvious and uncontroversial as not to be worth making (such as "motherhood is a good thing")

MOTION *to set the wheels in motion*
to institute appropriate action

MOUNTAIN *if the mountain will not come to Mahomet then Mahomet will go to the mountain*
on recognizing that one has insufficient power to effect one's most desired solution one decides to make do with the next best alternative

MOUNTAIN *to make mountains out of molehills*
to treat a minor problem as though it were a major disaster

MOUSE *a game of cat and mouse*
negotiations between two parties of unequal bargaining power during which the stronger makes some temporary concessions to the weaker without, however, affecting the latter's eventual total default

MOUSE *mice have been here*
intruders have entered this place

MOUSE *to labor mightily and bring forth a mouse*
to be quite ineffective

MOUSE *when the cat is away the mice will play*
in the absence of supervision discipline will be lax

MOUTH *hard-mouthed*
uncontrollable

MOUTH *mealy-mouthed*
not at all forceful in debate

MOUTH *out of the mouths of babes*
(as indiscreetly revealed) the truth

MOUTH *someone looks as if butter would not melt in his mouth*
a person looks sweet and innocent

MOUTH *to be a big mouth*
to lack discretion in one's conversation

MOUTH *to be born with a silver spoon in one's mouth*
to be brought up by wealthy parents

MOUTH *to be down in the mouth*
to be depressed

MOUTH *to be left with a nasty taste in one's mouth*
to be appalled or very disappointed at another person's unethical behavior to one

MOUTH *to foam at the mouth*
to show anger

MOUTH *to have one's heart in one's mouth*
to be startled

MOUTH *to keep one's mouth shut*
not to discuss some matter

MOUTH *to learn something from the horse's mouth*
to get information from someone qualified to impart it

MOUTH *to live from hand to mouth*
being in poor financial circumstances to survive with little by way of safety margin

MOUTH *to look a gift horse in the mouth*
to be suspicious about a benefit which has been volunteered

MOUTH *to make one's mouth water*
to excite desire

MOUTH *to put one's foot in one's mouth*
to say something foolish

MOUTH *to put one's head into the lion's mouth*
to recklessly expose oneself to great danger

MOUTH *to put one's money where one's mouth is*
to back one's judgment by putting assets at risk

MOUTH *to put words into someone's mouth*
to attempt to get someone to say something in the particular terms drafted by another person

MOUTH *to shoot one's mouth off*
to speak without thinking

MOUTH *to take food out of the mouths of children*
cruelly to deprive the needy

MOUTH *you took the words right out of my mouth*
you have just said what I was about to say

MOVE *a moving target*
an objective subject to constant revision

MOVE *move over and let the greyhound see the rabbit*
move over

MOVE *to move down a notch*
to accept a lower position

MOVE *to move heaven and earth*
to do everything possible

MOVE *your move!*
the next step is up to you

MOVER *prime mover*
person initiating and promoting a cause

MUCKRAKER *a muckraker*
a person who sets out to publicize misconduct of prominent persons or institutions

MUD *a stick-in-the-mud*
an unenterprising person

MUD *his name is mud*
he completely lacks credibility (a play on the name of one Dr. Samuel Mudd)

MUD *some mud will stick*
reputations will be hurt even after accusations are proved false

MUD *to muddy the waters*
to deliberately confuse an issue by creating a diversion

MUD *to sink deeper into the mud*
to get into even greater difficulty

MUD *to sling mud*
to make unfair imputations

MUDRAKER *a mudraker*
a person who sets out to publicize features harming another person's reputation

MUG *a mug's game*
activity which wise persons would eschew

MUMBO *mumbo jumbo*
blatant nonsense (refers to a deity worshipped by primitive tribes)

MURDER *to be sheer murder*
to be extremely unpleasant or difficult; or to be an inglorious defeat

MURDER *to get away with murder*
to do something outrageous without penalty

MURPHY *Murphy's law*
the principle that everything which can go wrong will go wrong

MUSCLE *to flex one's muscles*
to exert one's personality or powers

MUSEUM *a museum piece*
an old article the use of which is no longer efficient

MUSHROOM *to mushroom*
to expand rapidly

MUSIC *to be music to one's ears*
to be comments which one is very pleased to hear

MUSIC *to face the music*
to accept responsibility when confronted by one's critics

MUSIC *when the music stops*
suddenly and soon (refers to an imminent crisis leading to some resolution of a matter as in a game of musical chairs)

MUSICAL *to play musical chairs*
to be a part of a general reshuffling of duties or functions which is not necessarily to everyone's liking

MUTTON *to be mutton dressed up as lamb*
to foolishly pretend to be younger

MYOPIA *myopia*
the inability to appreciate an argument (lit., short-sightedness)

N

N *to the nth degree*
with great precision

NAIL *a thumbnail sketch*
brief but pertinent details

NAIL *on the nail*
immediately

NAIL *to be another nail in someone's coffin*
to represent a further step toward someone's downfall

NAIL *to bite one's fingernails*
to anxiously await a decision

NAIL *to fight tooth and nail*
to strive very hard to win

NAIL *to hang on by one's fingernails*
to have only a slender hold

NAIL *to hit the nail right on the head*
to astutely come to the correct conclusion

NAIL *to nail a lie*
to expose an untruth

NAIL *to nail one's colors to the mast*
to publicly declare one's position and to maintain it in the face of criticism

NAIL *to nail someone*
to put the blame on a person

NAIL *to nail someone to the wall*
to outmaneuver another person

NAIL *to nail something down*
to tie up the loose ends of an arrangement

NAME *a rose by any other name would smell as sweet*
the form does not affect the substance (from Shakespeare's ROMEO AND JULIET)

NAME *his name is mud*
he completely lacks credibility (a play on the name of one Dr. Samuel Mudd)

NAME *no names—no packdrill*
the identities of the parties will be kept confidential in order to protect them

NAME *so-and-so is the name of the game*
so-and-so is the essential element of the exercise

NAME *to drop names*
to slip names of celebrities allegedly known to the speaker into a conversation in an attempt to impress

NAME *to give a dog a bad name*
to malign a person

NAME *to have a black mark against one's name*
to have a tarnished reputation

NAME *to lend one's name to something*
to endorse something

NAME *to make a name for oneself*
to earn a good reputation by virtue of some skill

NARROW *to be on the straight and narrow*
to be completely honest

NASTY *a nasty piece of work*
an unpleasant person

NASTY *to be left with a nasty taste in one's mouth*
to be appalled or very disappointed at another person's unethical behavior to one

NATURAL *to die a natural death*
by virtue of changed circumstances or the effluxion of time to be no longer relevant

NATURE *the nature of the beast*
the reality of the situation

NATURE *to be second nature to someone*
to be something which a person does intuitively

NAVEL *to contemplate one's navel*
to be introspective

NECK *a bottleneck*
a factor obstructing an even flow

NECK *a millstone round someone's neck*
a great burden

NECK *at a break-neck pace*
very fast

NECK *it is neck or nothing*
a desperate effort is called for

NECK *neck and neck*
(of contestants) with little between them

NECK *neck of the woods*
localized area

NECK *to be a pain in the neck*
to be an unpleasant person or to be a nuisance

NECK *to be an albatross around someone's neck*
to be a great burden (popularized by Coleridge's ANCIENT MARINER)

NECK *to be up to one's neck in something*
to be very deeply involved in something

NECK *to break one's neck to do something*
to be particularly keen

NECK *to breathe down someone's neck*
to cause annoyance to another person by remaining in his vicinity or by supervising him too closely; or to be narrowly behind another person in some competitive situation

NECK *to cop it in the neck*
to suffer a severe disaster

NECK *to save someone's neck*
to come to the rescue of a person

NECK *to send a chill down someone's neck*
to be worrying news

NECK *to stick one's neck out*
to have the courage of one's convictions or to take a calculated risk

NEED *to need something like a hole in the head*
to be landed with a completely undesired problem

NEEDLE *to be on pins and needles*
to be very agitated

NEEDLE *to find a needle in a haystack*
to find something when the probability of finding it is very small

NEEDLE *to look for a needle in a haystack*
to attempt something with a very small chance of success

NELLY *nervous Nellies*
persons unwilling to take any risks

NEMESIS *nemesis*
downfall serving as retribution (refers to a goddess in Greek mythology)

NERVE *the hip pocket nerve*
the assessment of issues by their financial effects on one

NERVE *to get on someone's nerves*
by one's behavior to cause annoyance to a person

NERVE *to have a nerve*
to be impudent

NERVE *to have nerves of steel*
not to be easily frightened

NERVE *to lose one's nerve*
to abandon, out of fear, a decision to do something

NERVE *to touch a nerve*
to mention something which another person would rather pretend did not exist

NERVOUS *nervous Nellies*
persons unwilling to take any risks

NEST *a mare's nest*
a discovery with illusory benefits

NEST *a nest egg*
life savings

NEST *to be a cuckoo in the nest*
to purport to be a member of a group of people although having no such right

NEST *to feather one's own nest*
to improperly arrange a transaction on behalf of others to one's own financial advantage

NEST *to foul one's own nest*
to disparage one's home or workplace

NEST *to stir up a hornet's nest*
to take action which results in unpleasant side-effects

NET *a safety net scheme*
a scheme for dealing with the exceptional cases not covered by normal arrangements

NET *to catch someone in the net*
to unexpectedly involve a particular person in the course of activity designed to involve many others

NET *to draw the nets closer*
to intensify one's efforts

NET *to miss the sharks while netting the minnows*
to succeed in minor aspects but fail in the ones that really matter

NET *to slip through the net*
to happen as an isolated case despite steps taken to prevent such events

NET *to spread the net more widely*
to become more comprehensive

NETTLE *to grasp the nettle*
to deal with a neglected difficulty

NEW *a new broom*
a changed regime which is likely to alter the status quo

NEW *a new lease on life*
the prospect of a worry-free existence from now on

NEW *new guard*
changed regime

NEW *one cannot teach an old dog new tricks*
people get irreversibly set in their ways

NEW *to be a new ball game*
to be subject to completely revised rules or very different conditions

NEW *to be the dawn of a new day*
to be the start of a different regime

NEW *to break new ground*
to do something for which there is no precedent

NEW *to introduce new blood*
to recruit new members to some organization

NEW *to plow new ground*
to laboriously engage in an untried activity

NEW *to put a new face on something*
to alter the way something should be regarded

NEW *to turn over a new leaf*
to reform

NEWCASTLE *to carry coals to Newcastle*
to do something ridiculously unnecessary

NICHE *to carve out a niche for oneself*
to deliberately create an opportunity to use one's talents effectively

NICHE *to find one's niche*
to find the opportunity to use one's talents

NIGGER *the nigger in the woodpile*
the factor spoiling an otherwise satisfactory arrangement

NIGHT *a fly-by-night operator*
a confidence trickster

NIGHT *ships that pass in the night*
persons who fail to meet up

NIGHT *the night is young*
the project is only at a very early stage

NIGHT *to be a night owl*
to habitually go to bed late

NIGHT *to spend a sleepless night*
to worry about something

NIGHTMARE *a nightmare*
an unpleasant experience

NIMBLE *nimble-footed*
quick to change the direction of one's activities when circumstances warrant

NINE *a nine-day wonder*
an exciting event, but one which will cease to arouse interest when the novelty has worn off

NINE *a stitch in time saves nine*
preventive maintenance saves money in the long run

NINE *to be dressed up to the nines*
to be attired in excessively elaborate garments

NINE *to be on cloud nine*
to be very happy

NINETEEN *to talk nineteen to the dozen*
to engage in much idle chatter

NIP *to nip something in the bud*
to stop some activity in its early stages when stopping it is still relatively easy

NIT *to nitpick*
to criticize a person in respect to very minor matters

NOBODY *to be a nobody*
to be unimportant

NOD *a nod and a wink*
a sign that understanding has been reached in a matter which in the interests of discretion has not been discussed aloud

NOD *a nod is the same as a wink to a blind horse*
fine distinctions are not appropriate here

NOD *to get the nod*
to receive approval

NOIRE *to be someone's bete noire*
to be a person whose ideas and actions cause upset and loathing in another person (French, ''black beast'')

NOISE *to make a noise about something*
to complain or express dissatisfaction about something

NOOK *in every nook and cranny*
everywhere

NOOSE *to put one's head in the noose*
to recklessly and unnecessarily expose oneself to great danger

NOOSE *to tighten the noose*
to get closer to inflicting defeat

NOSE *hard-nosed*
tough in negotiations

NOSE *to be no skin off someone's nose*
not to matter to a person

NOSE *to be on the nose*
to be accurate (of a proposal or scheme)

NOSE *to bite someone's nose off*
to speak to a person aggressively

NOSE *to cut one's nose off to spite one's face*
to act in pique in a way which harms only oneself

NOSE *to escape by the skin of one's nose*
to only just avoid some disaster

NOSE *to follow one's nose*
to act intuitively

NOSE *to get a bloody nose*
to suffer an undignified rebuff

NOSE *to get up someone's nose*
to irritate a person

NOSE *to have a good nose for business*
to be able to identify profitable business situations

NOSE *to keep one's nose clean*
to act with circumspection and honesty despite temptation to do otherwise

NOSE *to keep one's nose out of something*
not to meddle in something

NOSE *to keep one's nose to the grindstone*
to work with particular diligence

NOSE *to lead someone by the nose*
to induce another person to comply with one's wishes

NOSE *to look down the nose at something*
to treat a matter with obvious contempt

NOSE *to pay through the nose*
to pay an excessive price

NOSE *to poke one's nose into something*
to interfere

NOSE *to poke one's nose outside*
to venture outside

NOSE *to put someone's nose out of joint*
to upset another person

NOSE *to rub someone's nose in it*
to humiliate a person by highlighting something embarrassing to him

NOSE *to take a nosedive*
to suddenly and unexpectedly fall steeply

NOSE *to take something on the nose*
to meekly accept a rebuff

NOSE *to thumb one's nose at someone*
to show one's contempt for someone in authority and to ostentatiously disregard his orders

NOSE *to turn up one's nose at something*
to express one's disdain

NOSE *under someone's nose*
in a person's immediate area of responsibility or in circumstances where he should have known something

NOTCH *to move down a notch*
to accept a lower position

NOTE *to compare notes*
to exchange information about some subject of mutual interest

NOTE *to hit a sour note*
to discover an unexpected flaw in an otherwise satisfactory piece of work

NOTE *to strike the right note*
to make a good impression

NUDGE *to give something a nudge forward*
to give modest encouragement to something

NUMBER *one's days are numbered*
one is about to be abolished

NUMBER *one's opposite number*
a person with similar responsibilities in another organization

NUMBER *someone's number is up*
a person's period of activity or influence is about to expire

NUMBER *to look after number one*
to act selfishly

NURSE *to nurse one's bruises*
to face up to the consequences of defeat

NUT *nuts and bolts*
basic ingredients

NUT *someone is a hard nut to crack*
it is very difficult to persuade a person to do something

NUT *to be nuts*
to be crazy

NUT *to be nuts about someone*
to be infatuated with a person

NUT *to use a sledgehammer to crack a nut*
to devote vastly more resources to a project than is warranted by all the circumstances

NUTSHELL *in a nutshell*
by way of summary

O

OAK *tall oaks from little acorns grow*
even major enterprises have to have small beginnings (from ''Lines written for a School Declamation'' by David Everett)

OAK *to have a heart of oak*
to be brave

OAK *to lock something up in the old oak chest*
to put in a safe place and out of mind

OAR *to stick one's oar in*
to intervene without invitation in a dispute to which one is not a party

OATS *to feel one's oats*
to display self-importance

OATS *to sow wild oats*
to indulge in foolish behavior while a young adult

OCEAN *an ocean full of fish*
plenty of opportunity

OCEAN *to be only a drop in the ocean*
to be quite insignificant in the total scene

ODDS *that is over the odds*
that is unacceptable

ODDS *to be at odds with someone*
to disagree with a person

ODDS *to beat the odds*
to do better than could reasonably have been expected

ODDS *to have the odds stacked against one*
to be faced with many difficulties frustrating a project

ODDS *to pay over the odds*
to pay too much

OIL *not to be an oil painting*
to be ugly

OIL *to be a well-oiled piece of machinery*
to be functioning very satisfactorily

OIL *to burn the midnight oil*
to work late into the night

OIL *to get the good oil*
to receive useful, reliable and timely information

OIL *to oil the wheels*
to make things go smoothly

OIL *to pour oil on troubled waters*
to calm down a situation

OIL *to run something on the smell of an oil rag*
to run something very economically and efficiently

OINTMENT *a fly in the ointment*
a flaw (refers to dead flies turning perfumes rancid) (Ecclesiastes 10:1)

OLD *an old flame*
a former lover

OLD *an old head on young shoulders*
experience, knowledge and maturity in a young person

OLD *it is on for young and old*
the excitement has started

OLD *one cannot teach an old dog new tricks*
people get irreversibly set in their ways

OLD *to be old hat*
to be a very widely known fact

OLD *to lock something up in the old oak chest*
to put in a safe place and out of mind

OLD *to rekindle an old flame*
to inspire the reinstatement of a former loving relationship

OLIVE *to hold out an olive branch*
to make peace overtures (Genesis 8:11)

OMEGA *from alpha to omega*
from start to finish (refers to the first and last letters of the Greek alphabet)

OMELETTE *one cannot make an omelette without breaking eggs*
the desired end dictates the means even if they cause harm to others

OMELETTE *to unscramble the omelette*
to undo something which cannot be undone

ONE *a one-way street*
a flow of activity in only one direction

ONE *a one-man band*
a person performing many different roles single-handedly

ONE *on the one hand*
putting one side of the proposition

ONE *one for the road*
a final drink before leaving

ONE *one-eyed*
biased

ONE *to be one in the eye for someone*
to represent an unexpected and unwelcome defeat

ONE *to be one out of the box*
to be unexpectedly superb

ONE *to be only round one*
to be only the first of many stages

ONE *to go back to square one*
to start all over again

ONE *to have a one-track mind*
to keep coming back to one narrow topic of conversation

ONE *to look after number one*
to act selfishly

ONION *to know one's onions*
to be well informed in some area (refers to Dr. C. T. Onions, editor of the SHORTER OXFORD ENGLISH DICTIONARY)

OPEN *an open sesame*
access to something normally inaccessible

OPEN *one's door is always open*
people can take their problems to one at any time

OPEN *open slather*
freedom for people to do what they want

OPEN *open-hearted*
cordial

OPEN *to be an eye opener*
to be a surprise

OPEN *to be an open and shut case*
to be an unarguable proposition (a phrase popular in detective novels and probably a play on the two meanings of the word '''case''')

OPEN *to be out in the open*
(of information) to be publicly available

OPEN *to come out into the open*
to start being frank

OPEN *to have an open mind*
to be willing to assess evidence on its merits and without prejudging it

OPEN *to keep one's ears open*
to be on the lookout for useful information

OPEN *to keep one's eyes open*
to be on the lookout for useful information

OPEN *to keep one's eyes open for something*
to be on the lookout for an opportunity to do something

OPEN *to leave oneself wide open*
to act in such a way that one's opponents will find much which can be easily criticized

OPEN *to leave the door open*
to issue a standing invitation for the resumption of some negotiations

OPEN *to open someone's eyes to something*
to alert another person to the truth of something

OPEN *to open the batting*
to be the first in a series of persons speaking or doing something

OPEN *to open up a Pandora's box*
to do something which produces all sorts of undesired and unexpected side-effects (refers to the woman in Greek mythology who brought misery to mankind; the box contained human ills)

OPEN *to open up an old wound*
to take action which revives a long-standing grievance

OPEN *to open up doors*
to create opportunities

OPEN *to open up the floodgates*
to take action which will have massive consequences

OPEN *with an open hand*
generously

OPEN *with one's eyes wide open*
fully conscious of the ramifications

OPEN *with open arms*
enthusiastically

OPENING *an opening wide enough to drive a coach and four through*
an excellent opportunity

OPENING *opening gambit*
the first in a series of strategic moves (a tautological expression which also involves a misunderstanding of a technical chess term)

OPENING *opening shot*
first step in an activity expected to last a long time

OPERA *a soap opera*
a radio or television serial, often based on exaggerated domestic situations of no great importance (refers to sponsorship by soap manufacturers)

OPPOSITE *one's opposite number*
a person with similar responsibilities in another organization

ORANGE *to add apples to oranges*
to quite illogically lump unconnected things together

ORCHESTRATE *to orchestrate something*
to arrange for something to happen

ORDER *in apple pie order*
in perfect order and condition

ORDER *just what the doctor ordered*
exactly right

ORDER *the order of the day*
the customary behavior

ORDER *to be a tall order*
to be an unreasonable expectation

ORDER *to get one's marching orders*
to be told to leave

ORDER *to put one's house in order*
to fix up the deficiencies in one's affairs

OSTRICH *to be an ostrich*
to refuse to face up to an unpleasant truth (refers to the reputed habit of ostriches in danger)

OTHER *to be on the other side of the fence*
to have an opposing point of view or position

OUNCE *not to have an ounce of sense*
to be stupid

OUNCE *to drain every ounce out of something*
to get the maximum use or pleasure out of something

OUTGUN *to outgun someone*
to outmaneuver a person

OVER *to be all over bar the shouting*
to be virtually finished

OVERBOARD *to go overboard*
to act foolishly and in an excessive way

OVERKILL *overkill*
more action than really required for the purpose

OVERSHADOW *to overshadow someone*
to reduce the influence of a person by outshining him

OVERSTEP *to overstep the mark*
to fail to observe the proprieties

OVERTIME *to work overtime at something*
to spend a lot of time and effort at doing something

OVERTONE *overtones*
implied threats

OVERTURE *to make overtures to someone*
to make suggestions to a person, inviting further negotiations

OWL *to be a night owl*
to habitually go to bed late

OYSTER *the world is one's oyster*
one has enormous scope for activity

P

P *to watch one's p's and q's*
to be very careful (may refer to pints and quarts of beer on a hotel slate or to easily-confused printer's type)

PACE *to put someone through his paces*
to test a person

PACE *to set the pace*
to give a lead in regard to a rate of progression

PACK *to be at the head of the pack*
to be the best of many or the de facto leader

PACK *to bring someone back to the pack*
to make a person conform

PACK *to pack one's bags*
to signal one's intention to depart

PACK *to play every card in the pack*
to try very hard and use every conceivable argument

PACK *to play the last card in the pack*
to lower one's standards in a final desperate effort

PACK *to send someone packing*
to dismiss a person ignominiously

PACKDRILL *no names—no packdrill*
the identities of the parties will be kept confidential in order to protect them

PAD *to keep off someone's pad*
not to interfere with or compete against another person in his customary area of activity

PADDLE *to paddle one's canoe*
to do something unaided and in one's own way

PADDOCK *to have a spell in the paddock*
to have leave of absence

PAIN *growing pains*
problems encountered by virtue of expansion

PAIN *to be a pain in the neck*
to be an unpleasant person or to be a nuisance

PAINT *to paint a black picture*
to state a set of unfavorable factors

PAINT *to paint oneself into a corner*
to foolishly put oneself into a position from which escape is impossible

PAINT *to paint someone black*
to ruin a person's reputation

PAINT *to paint the town red*
to go on an exciting social outing

PAINTER *to cut the painter*
to become separated

PAINTING *not to be an oil painting*
to be ugly

PAIR *a pigeon pair*
one son and one daughter as the sole offspring

PAJAMAS *to be the cat's pajamas*
to have an exaggerated idea of one's importance

PALACE *a palace revolt*
the overthrow of those in authority by their subordinates

PALE *to be beyond the pale*
to be socially unacceptable, especially for unacceptable standards or behavior

PALE *to be only a pale shadow of something*
to be a weak imitation

PALM *to grease someone's palms*
to bribe a person

PALPABLE *palpable*
readily understandable

PAN *a flash in the pan*
something which begins promisingly but does not last (refers to the priming of old guns)

PAN *out of the frying pan into the fire*
from one bad situation to an even worse one

PAN *to pan out*
to succeed

PANCAKE *every Pancake Tuesday*
only on rare occasions (refers to Shrove Tuesday, when pancakes are traditionally eaten)

PANDORA *to open up a Pandora's box*
to do something which produces all sorts of undesired and unexpected side-effects (refers to the woman in Greek mythology who brought misery to mankind; the box contained human ills)

PANIC *to hit the panic button*
to act hastily and irrationally

PANTS *a kick in the pants*
an admonition

PANTS *to bore the pants off someone*
to weary a person by dull and uninteresting conversation

PANTS *to catch someone with his pants down*
to act when another person least expects it

PANTS *to charm the pants off someone*
to delight a person

PANTS *to fly by the seat of one's pants*
to act unprofessionally

PANTS *to scare the pants off someone*
to greatly frighten a person

PANTS *to wear the trousers*
to be the dominant party

PAPER *only a cigarette paper between them*
virtually equal or close together

PAPER *a paper tiger*
an empty threat

PAPER *paper warfare*
an excessive amount of correspondence or red tape

PAPER *to have shares in a paper company*
to institute unnecessary clerical procedures

PAPER *to paper over the cracks*
to institute extremely superficial and basically ineffective remedies

PAPER *to start with a blank sheet of paper*
to commence an exercise without being bound by any established practices

PAR *to be below par*
to be less than the desired standard

PAR *to be par for the course*
to be normal

PARACHUTE *golden parachute*
generous provisions in a remuneration package which come into play in certain circumstances

PARADISE *to live in a fool's paradise*
to delude oneself

PARALLEL *parallel*
similar or corresponding

PARALYZE *to paralyze something*
to bring something to a standstill

PARCEL *to be part and parcel*
to be the essential ingredients

PARE *cheese paring*
stingy

PARIAH *pariah*
social outcast (refers to members of a low caste in India)

PARISH *parish pump issues*
issues of trivial importance

PARK *to be in the right ballpark*
to be approximately correct

PARKINSON *Parkinson's law*
the principle that work expands to match the work capacity available (title of a book by Prof. C. Northcote Parkinson)

PAROCHIAL *parochial*
narrow minded

PARRY *to parry some argument*
to deflect some argument (refers to fencing)

PART *to be part and parcel*
to be the essential ingredients

PART *to be part of the furniture*
to be so familiar that one's presence goes completely unnoticed

PART *to be part of the landscape*
to be present and fully accepted without question

PART *to fire a parting shot*
to make a defiant gesture on leaving

PART *to play one's part*
to cooperate or carry out one's obligations under some arrangement

PARTHIAN *a Parthian shaft*
a cutting remark made at the moment of departure (refers to missiles shot backward by flying Parthian horsemen)

PARTY *the party is over*
the previous pleasant arrangements have been discontinued

PARTY *to be the life and soul of the party*
to be the prime enthusiast for a cause

PARTY *to come to the party*
to agree to someone's terms

PAS *faux pas*
something indiscreet or offending social conventions (French, "false step")

PASS *ships that pass in the night*
persons who fail to meet up

PASS *to pass the buck*
in an uncooperative spirit to decline responsibility for a matter on the grounds that someone else more properly has responsibility for it

PASS *to pass with flying colors*
to be very successful

PASSPORT *to be a passport to success*
to be a means of achieving success

PASSWORD *the password is so-and-so*
the main attraction is so-and-so

PAST *a past master*
an expert with long experience

PASTOR *pastor*
religious official in charge of a congregation

PASTURE *to move on to greener pastures*
to commence a new, better career

PAT *to pat oneself on the back*
immodestly to congratulate oneself

PAT *to pat someone on the back*
to congratulation a person or to reassure a person

PATCH *a sticky patch*
a period fraught with difficulties

PATCH *not to be a patch on someone*
not to be comparable to a person

PATCH *to be on someone's cabbage patch*
to engage in a competitive activity in a territory regarded by someone already there as rightfully belonging exclusively to him

PATCH *to patch up some quarrel*
to reconcile one's differences

PATCHWORK *a patchwork quilt*
a result arising from many uncoordinated inputs

PATH *path*
means of achieving an objective

PATH *slippery path*
dangerous course of action

PATH *to be on a path strewn with roses*
to lead a very pleasant life

PATH *to be on the warpath*
to be on the lookout for faults which can be criticized

PATH *to beat a path to someone's door*
to seek a person out in great numbers

PATH *to block someone's path*
to interfere with a person's opportunity to advance himself

PATH *to cross someone's path*
to meet another person by chance

PATH *to lead someone up the garden path*
to mislead a person by deliberately fallacious arguments

PATH *to smooth the path for someone*
to use one's influence to make arrangements so that a person's task will be easier or more readily accomplished

PATH *to tread a particular path*
to take certain initiatives

PATIENCE *something would try the patience of Job*
something is very vexatious (James 5:11)

PATIENCE *to have the patience of a saint*
to endure annoyances with particular calm

PAUL *to rob Peter in order to pay Paul*
to fix up one grievance by causing another

PAVE *to pave the way*
to prepare for something

PAW *to be a cat's paw*
to be a person who is being used as a tool by others

PAWN *a pawn*
a person of small importance who is manipulated by others

PAY *he who pays the piper calls the tune*
a person contributing money or resources to a project is entitled to a say in its control

PAY *that has put paid to it*
the project can no longer proceed

PAY *to pay a king's ransom*
to pay a very large sum

PAY *to pay lip service to some rules*
to disregard some rules in practice while acknowledging them in words

PAY *to pay off*
to be successful

PAY *to pay someone back in his own coin*
to retaliate in kind

PAY *to pay something back with interest*
to return a small favor with a bigger favor or to extract retribution of greater value than the circumstances warrant

PAY *to pay the price*
to suffer the adverse consequences of one's acts or omissions

PAY *to rob Peter in order to pay Paul*
to fix up one grievance by causing another

PAY *to strike pay dirt*
to become successful

PEA *a pea and thimble trick*
a clever fraud committed in the presence of its victim without this being obvious at the time

PEANUT *to earn peanuts*
to get a reward which is far too small in relation to the value of the services rendered

PEARL *a pearl*
a thing of great excellence

PEARL *to cast pearls before swine*
to confer valuable benefits on someone who neither recognizes nor appreciates them

PEBBLE *not to be the only pebble on the beach*
not to be the only available person

PEBBLE *to throw a pebble against the window*
to gently draw attention to oneself

PECK *hen-pecked*
subject to domination by one's wife

PECK *pecking order*
order of seniority

PECKER *to keep one's pecker up*
to stay cheerful

PEDAL *to backpedal*
to reverse to some extent previously applied policies

PEDAL *to softpedal*
to restrain oneself

PEDESTAL *to put someone on a pedestal*
to admire a person and regard him as more marvelous than is warranted

PEDESTRIAN *pedestrian*
uninspired

PEEL *to keep one's eyes peeled for something*
to be on the constant lookout for something

PEG *a peg to hang a hat on*
something which provides a convenient or plausible excuse for some particular action

PEG *a square peg in a round hole*
a person much more suitable for a position rather different from the one held

PEG *off the peg*
(of clothes) ready-made

PEG *to be level pegging*
(of contestants) to have little between them

PEG *to peg out*
to die (refers to the final stroke in a game of croquet)

PEG *to take someone down a peg or two*
to point out to a person that he is not as good as he thinks he is

PEN *to put pen to paper*
to set out one's ideas in written form

PEN *with a stroke of the pen*
by edict

PENCIL *to need to sharpen one's pencil*
to be required to improve one's performance

PENDULUM *the swing of the pendulum*
the alternation of voter acceptance between opposing political parties

PENETRATE *to penetrate someone's thick skull*
to make a person understand something difficult or acknowledge something unwelcome

PENNY *a twopenny halfpenny outfit*
a quite insignificant operation

PENNY *in for a penny—in for a pound*
once something is commenced it ought to be finished; or if one is willing to take a small risk then one might as well take a bigger one

PENNY *penny-pinching*
excessively frugal

PENNY *the penny dropped*
a person has just realized a fact which should have been obvious (refers to old-fashioned pay toilets)

PENNY *to be only ten pence in the shilling*
to be slightly stupid

PENNY *to throw in one's six pennies' worth*
to modestly supply one's own facts or views

PENNY *to turn an honest penny*
to earn money out of odd jobs

PEOPLE *people in glass houses should not throw stones*
those who are less than perfect are foolish to criticize others

PEOPLE *to be unable to keep people away with a big stick*
to be faced with a large crowd or much demand

PERCH *to knock someone off his perch*
to displace a person from his leadership position in some competitive situation

PERSPECTIVE *to put something into perspective*
to explain the background of something so that its significance in relation to other things can be better appreciated

PETARD *to be hoist with one's own petard*
to have one's own case used against one (refers to being blown up by one's own bomb)

PETER *to rob Peter in order to pay Paul*
to fix up one grievance by causing another

PETER *to tickle the Peter*
to rob one's employer

PETREL *to be a stormy petrel*
a person who disturbs a pleasant state of affairs by agitating for change

PETRIFY *to be petrified*
to be badly scared

PETTICOAT *petticoat government*
rule by women

PHOENIX *to rise from the ashes like a Phoenix*
to be the replacement for something destroyed in some disaster (refers to a mythical bird which was supposed to rise from the ashes in its funeral pyre with renewed youth)

PHOTO *a photo finish*
a close result in a contest

PICK *not to just pick something out of a hat*
to choose carefully, after weighing all the considerations

PICK *to handpick someone*
to carefully choose a person for his individual attributes

PICK *to have a bone to pick*
to have a grievance which requires discussion

PICK *to just pick the plums out of the jam*
to take only the best items

PICK *to keep one's cotton-picking fingers off something*
not to interfere in something

PICK *to nitpick*
to criticize a person in respect to very minor matters

PICK *to pick someone's brain*
to get the benefit of another person's knowledge and experience

PICK *to pick up the pieces*
to resume previous activities to the maximum extent possible after some setback

PICKLE *to be in a pickle*
to be in difficulties

PICNIC *to be no picnic*
to be unpleasant

PICTURE *to balance the picture*
to put the other side of the story or to quote facts in contradiction

PICTURE *to change the whole picture*
to alter the major assumptions on which some assessment was based

PICTURE *to conjure up a picture*
to use words to convey a vivid impression

PICTURE *to have a clear picture of something*
to have a good understanding of something

PICTURE *to paint a black picture*
to state a set of unfavorable factors

PICTURE *to present a rosy picture*
to state a set of favorable factors

PICTURE *to put someone in the picture*
to fill a person in with the background of a situation

PICTURE *to see the big picture*
to have the vision and imagination enabling a project to be developed as part of a bigger whole

PIE *in apple pie order*
in perfect order and condition

PIE *pie in the sky*
a hoped for result unlikely to be achieved

PIE *to eat humble pie*
to apologize

PIE *to have a finger in the pie*
to have an interest in a project

PIE *to have one's fingers in many different pies*
to be engaged in a variety of separate activities

PIECE *a museum piece*
an old article the use of which is no longer efficient

PIECE *a nasty piece of work*
an unpleasant person

PIECE *early in the piece*
at an early stage of some activity

PIECE *to be a piece of cake*
to be very easy or greatly to one's liking

PIECE *to be a well-oiled piece of machinery*
to be functioning very satisfactorily

PIECE *to be cut to pieces*
to be very upset

PIECE *to be shot to pieces*
to have one's case seriously damaged

PIECE *to be thrilled to pieces*
to be greatly thrilled

PIECE *to fall to pieces*
(of a plan) to collapse

PIECE *to give someone a piece of one's mind*
to abuse another person

PIECE *to have a piece of someone*
to vent one's frustration on a person

PIECE *to have a piece of the action*
to be one of several parties to a project

PIECE *to pick up the pieces*
to resume previous activities to the maximum extent possible after some setback

PIER *take a long walk on a short pier*
go away, I want no dealings with you

PIG *a guinea pig*
a person on whom some new practice is tried out

PIG *to buy a pig in a poke*
to buy goods of unknown quality

PIGEON *a pigeon pair*
one son and one daughter as the sole offspring

PIGEON *to be one's pigeon*
to be one's area of responsibility

PIGEON *to pigeon-hole*
to put aside for further consideration in the distant future

PIGEON *to throw a cat among the pigeons*
to cause consternation by revealing an unpleasant and unexpected fact

PIGHEADED *pigheaded*
unduly obstinate

PILL *to be a bitter pill to swallow*
to be great humiliation and disappointment which have to be endured

PILL *to sugar the pill*
to cause something to be more acceptable

PILLAR *a pillar of some organization*
a significant supporter of some organization

PILLAR *to drive someone from pillar to post*
to send a person to a series of places in a vain attempt to achieve something

PILLORY *to put someone in the pillory*
to hold a person up to ridicule for his beliefs

PIN *for two pins I would do so-and-so*
my tolerance is almost exhausted and I am very tempted to do so-and-so

PIN *not to care a pin for something*
not to have the slightest interest in something

PIN *pin money*
an allowance to a wife for her personal use

PIN *to be on pins and needles*
to be very agitated

PIN *to pin someone down*
to find a person willing to accept blame or responsibility or to force a person to announce a decision or concede a point

PIN *with one's ears pinned back*
chastened

PINCH *penny-pinching*
excessively frugal

PINCH *to feel the pinch*
to be adversely affected by financial stringency

PINEAPPLE *to have hold of the wrong end of the pineapple*
to be utterly mistaken

PINK *to be tickled pink*
to be very pleased

PINK *to look in the pink*
to look well

PINPOINT *to pinpoint*
to identify very precisely

PINPRICK *a pinprick*
a trifling irritation

PINT *one can't get a quart into a pint pot*
one cannot do the impossible

PINTSIZE *pintsize*
small

PIP *to pip someone at the post*
to achieve something only just ahead of a rival

PIPE *put that in your pipe and smoke it*
contemplate that fact

PIPE *to pipe someone on board*
to welcome a person

PIPEDREAM *a pipedream*
a fanciful notion, wished for but unlikely

PIPELINE *a pipeline to someone*
an intermediary used as a means of communicating ideas to a person

PIPELINE *to be in the pipeline*
to be being dealt with

PIPER *he who pays the piper calls the tune*
a person contributing money or resources to a project is entitled to a say in its control

PIRATE *pirate*
(of radio) unlicensed; (of recordings or computer software) published in breach of copyright law

PISTOL *to hold a pistol at someone's head*
to put pressure on a person to make a particular decision regardless of his desires in the matter

PIT *a pit of disaster*
great and unexpected misfortune

PITCH *to be at fever pitch*
to be in a state of excited activity

PITCH *to be up to concert pitch*
to be ready

PITCH *to cruel someone's pitch*
to spoil a person's chances

PITCH *to queer the pitch for someone*
to spoil the opportunity a person has to do something

PITCHER *little pitchers have long ears*
children have a tendency to overhear things

PITFALL *pitfall*
unsuspected danger

PLACE *a place in the sun*
a favorable situation

PLACE *to be between a rock and a hard place*
to be faced with two equally difficult and uncomfortable choices

PLACE *to have one's heart in the right place*
to have a well-developed social conscience

PLACE *to put someone back in his place*
to make it clear to a person that he should not continue to act as though he had greater seniority than he really has

PLAGUE *a plague on both your houses!*
I am disgusted with both of you (from Shakespeare's ROMEO AND JULIET)

PLAGUE *to be of plague proportions*
to be great in number

PLAIN *to be plain sailing*
to be quite straightforward and very easy

PLANET *to be off the planet*
to be extremely naive or uninformed

PLANK *to walk the plank*
to face certain doom

PLATE *to bring a plate*
to take food to a party

PLATE *to have too much on one's plate*
to be unable to cope with one's workload

PLATE *to serve something up to someone on a plate*
to make something especially easy for a particular person

PLATTER *to hand over something on a silver platter*
to provide a valuable benefit for virtually nothing

PLAY *a level playing field*
competition on equal terms

PLAY *don't play games with me!*
do not insult my intelligence by that line of conduct

PLAY *foul play*
treachery or murder

PLAY *horseplay*
boisterous and undignified behavior

PLAY *to be child's play*
to be easy or to require only elementary skills and knowledge

PLAY *to be in full play*
to be fully operational

PLAY *to find out the state of play*
to ascertain the current position of some project

PLAY *to play Judas*
to betray a person (Matthew 26)

PLAY *to play Russian roulette*
to take stupid risks

PLAY *to play a deep game*
to show cunning

PLAY *to play ball*
to cooperate

PLAY *to play by Marquis of Queensberry rules*
to act ethically

PLAY *to play by the book*
to apply the rules strictly

PLAY *to play down something*
to seek to have less emphasis or attention given to something

PLAY *to play ducks and drakes*
not to treat the matter seriously

PLAY *to play every card in the pack*
to try very hard and use every conceivable argument

PLAY *to play fast and loose*
to disregard one's obligations

PLAY *to play gooseberry*
to act as an unwelcome chaperon

PLAY *to play it by ear*
to develop one's strategy to always fit in with circumstances as they change from time to time

PLAY *to play it cool*
to take a low-key and rational approach

PLAY *to play it safe*
to take no risks

PLAY *to play monkey tricks on someone*
to engage in discreditable behavior affecting a person

PLAY *to play musical chairs*
to be a part of a general reshuffling of duties or functions which is not necessarily to everyone's liking

PLAY *to play one's cards right*
to approach a matter sensibly

PLAY *to play one's part*
to cooperate or carry out one's obligations under some arrangement

PLAY *to play possum*
to pretend that one is not present

PLAY *to play right into someone's hands*
to act so as to give a person an unintended advantage

PLAY *to play second fiddle*
to fulfill a subordinate role

PLAY *to play the cards as they fall*
to deal with problems as they arise

PLAY *to play the game*
to observe the letter and the spirit of the rules or to act honorably

PLAY *to play the giddy goat*
to act the fool

PLAY *to play the last card in the pack*
to lower one's standards in a final desperate effort

PLAY *to play the trump card*
to make a final move, thereby defeating one's opponents

PLAY *to play the gallery*
to do something which appeals to the general public rather than something which is right

PLAY *to play with dynamite*
to invite trouble by virtue of one's risky conduct

PLAY *to play with fire*
to invite trouble through one's foolish conduct

PLAY *to underplay some situation*
to hold something in reserve

PLAY *two can play at that game*
it is possible to retaliate

PLAY *when the cat is away the mice will play*
in the absence of supervision, discipline will be lax

PLAY *without any cards to play*
without the means to achieve something

PLAYERS *a trap for young players*
a good opportunity for the inexperienced or naive to make mistakes

PLEAD *to plead the Fifth Amendment*
to refuse to answer an unwelcome question (refers to the Fifth Amendment of the United States Constitution, which provides protection against self-incrimination)

PLIMSOLL *the Plimsoll line*
the standard

PLOT *to plot a safe course through troubled waters*
to make a plan which overcomes certain difficulties

PLOW *speed the plow!*
let us get on with this as fast as possible!

PLOW *to plow new ground*
to laboriously engage in an untried activity

PLOW *to plow on*
to methodically and painstakingly continue with an activity

PLOW *to plow profits back*
to retain profits in a business

PLOW *to put one's hand to the plow*
voluntarily to undertake some task (Luke 9:62)

PLUCK *to pluck figures out of the air*
to just make figures up arbitrarily

PLUG *to have the plug pulled out from under one*
to have a successful activity destroyed by the actions of someone else

PLUM *the plum*
the best item in a collection

PLUM *to just pick the plums out of the jam*
to take only the best items

PLUNGE *to take the plunge*
to expose oneself to certain risks

POACH *to poach on someone's preserves*
to encroach uninvited on another person's territory

POCKET *not to live in each other's pockets*
to each follow his own lifestyle

POCKET *the hip pocket nerve*
the assessment of issues by their financial effects on one

POCKET *to be in someone's pocket*
to be subject to undue influence by another person

POCKET *to be out of pocket*
to have been forced to spend money which cannot be recovered from others

POCKET *to have deep pockets*
to have large financial resources

POCKET *to have money burning a hole in one's pocket*
to be impatient to spend or invest available funds

POCKET *to line one's pockets*
to make, improperly and secretly, a profit out of some transaction

POCKET *to put one's hands in one's pockets*
to spend

POINT *it is pointing in the right direction*
success looks likely

POINT *not to put too fine a point on it*
speaking bluntly

POINT *to get brownie points*
to do a person a favor with the likely result that the recipient will do a favor in return in due course

POINT *to pinpoint*
to identify very precisely

POINT *to point the bone at someone*
to accuse a person (actually, an Australian Aboriginal method of applying a curse)

POINT *to point the finger at someone*
to accuse a person or allege some indiscretion on his part

POINT *to reach boiling point*
to reach a climax

POINT *to refuse point blank*
to refuse outright

POINT *to score a point*
to make a clever contribution in the course of debate

POINT *to score points*
to make a good impression

POINT *to score top points*
to outwit other persons

POINT *to take the point*
to understand the proposition being advanced without necessarily accepting it

POISON *one man's meat is another man's poison*
people's tastes differ

POKE *to be better than a poke in the eye with a burnt stick*
to be particularly welcome

POKE *to be more than one can poke a stick at*
to be more than can reasonably be handled

POKE *to buy a pig in a poke*
to buy goods of unknown quality

POKE *to poke one's nose into something*
to interfere

POKE *to poke one's nose outside*
to venture outside

POKER *a game of poker*
negotiations in which the parties try to bluff each other

POKER *a poker face*
a facial expression which does not reveal one's thoughts during negotiations

POLARIZE *to polarize*
to cause people to identify themselves as belonging to groups holding opposing views

POLE *not to touch something with a ten-foot pole*
to go out of one's way to avoid something

POLE *to be at the bottom of the totem pole*
to be in the most junior position in some hierarchy

POLE *to be poles apart*
to have ideas which are very different

POND *to be a big fish in a little pond*
to be a person holding an important office but in an unimportant organization

PONTIFICATE *to pontificate*
to speak as if with great authority and with an assumed air of infallibility

PONY *a show pony*
a pompous person

POOR *a poor man's something*
a second best version

POOR *poor devil*
person to be pitied

POP *someone's eyes popped*
a person expressed great surprise

POPPY *a tall poppy*
a person with great power or responsibility and/or in receipt of high remuneration

POPPY *to cut tall poppies down to size*
to humiliate haughty persons

PORK *to pork barrel*
to spend taxpayers' money in one area in order to attract political support

PORT *any port in a storm*
anything which helps to avoid difficulties is welcome

PORT *port of call*
one of a series of places being visited

POSSUM *to play possum*
to pretend that one is not present

POSSUM *to stir the possum*
to set out to raise controversial issues

POST *a listening post*
a place where information of strategic value can be collected

POST *a staging post*
a place where action is initiated

POST *to conduct a postmortem on something*
to review past actions with a view to learning lessons for the future (Latin, "after the death")

POST *to drive someone from pillar to post*
to send a person to a series of places in a vain attempt to achieve something

POST *to go post haste*
to go very fast

POST *to keep someone posted*
to keep a person informed

POST *to pip someone at the post*
to achieve something only just ahead of a rival

POST *to signpost something*
to give an indication of the alternatives available

POSTAGE *only a postage stamp between them*
virtually equal or close together

POT *a melting pot*
a country where people with different ethnic backgrounds over time merge into one nation

POT *a pot of gold*
wealth

POT *fleshpots*
sumptuous living (Exodus 16:3)

POT *one can't get a quart into a pint pot*
one cannot do the impossible

POT *the pot calling the kettle black*
a person criticizing another person without realizing his own even greater shortcomings

POT *to go back into the melting pot*
to be up for reconsideration ab initio

POT *to keep the pot boiling*
to ensure that an issue stays current

POT *to seek the pot of gold at the end of the rainbow*
to have naive expectations

POT *to stir the pot*
to set out to raise controversial issues

POT *to sweeten the pot*
to provide a few additional inducements

POT *to take pot luck*
to take whatever happens by chance to be available

POTATO *a hot potato*
an embarrassing issue

POTATO *to be small potatoes*
to be quite unimportant

POTSHOT *to take a potshot at someone*
to make disparaging remarks about a person

POTTAGE *to sell one's birthright for a mess of pottage*
through foolishness to exchange something of substance for something of little value (Genesis 25)

POUND *in for a penny—in for a pound*
once something is commenced it ought to be finished; or if one is willing to take a small risk then one might as well take a bigger one

POUND *one's pound of flesh*
that which is due to one (from Shakespeare's MERCHANT OF VENICE)

POUR *it never rains but it pours*
crises often occur together

POUR *to pour cold water on some idea*
to be unenthusiastic about some proposal or scornful of its apparent weaknesses

POUR *to pour oil on troubled waters*
to calm down a situation

POUR *to pour one's heart out to someone*
to inflict one's woes on another person

POUR *to pour gasoline on the flames*
to make a bad situation worse

POUR *to pour vitriol on something*
to sharply criticize something

POWDER *to keep one's powder dry*
to retain key arguments or resources in reserve for use later

POWER *more power to your elbow*
may your praiseworthy efforts lead to success

POWER *the power behind the throne*
a person exercising the real authority but without having the official right to do so (the antonym of "titular head")

POWER *under one's own power*
without external help

PRAYER *on a wing and a prayer*
without proper resources

PRAYER *the answer to a maiden's prayer*
an unexpected but very welcome happening

PRE-EMPT *to pre-empt some issue*
to deliberately do something which has the effect of limiting the range of alternative approaches to a matter

PREACH *to preach to the converted*
to say something to those who already believe in it

PREPARE *to prepare one's ground*
to get ready for a confrontation

PRESENT *to present a rosy picture*
to state a set of favorable factors

PRESERVES *to poach on someone's preserves*
to encroach uninvited on another person's territory

PRESS *to be hot off the press*
to be the latest news

PRESS *to press a button*
to make something happen

PRESSURE *to apply pressure on someone*
to induce a person to do something which he would otherwise not do by implying adverse consequences if he does not cooperate

PRETTY *to sit pretty*
to be comfortably off

PREY *to prey on one's mind*
(of a problem) to keep worrying one

PRICE *that has nothing to do with the price of fish*
that is quite irrelevant

PRICE *to pay the price*
to suffer the adverse consequences of one's acts or omissions

PRICK *a pinprick*
a trifling irritation

PRICK *to prick up one's ears*
to suddenly start paying attention to a conversation in progress as a result of a half-heard phrase

PRIEST *the high priest of something*
the leading advocate of something

PRIMA *a prima donna*
a person with an exaggerated opinion of his own importance which makes relations with others needlessly difficult (Italian, "first lady")

PRIME *prime mover*
person initiating and promoting a cause

PRIME *to engage in pump priming*
to spend public money with the aim of attracting parochial electoral support

PRINT *a license to print money*
a lucrative government-conferred monopoly or privilege

PRINT *to fill in the fine print*
to provide the precise details in respect of something presently existing in broad outline only

PRIZE *not to be here to win prizes*
to be altruistic

PRIZE *to win the booby prize*
to do worse than all others

PRIZE *to win the prize in a canter*
to win very easily

PROBLEM *a problem child*
a source of unnecessary difficulty

PRODUCE *to produce something out of thin air*
to get hold of something in circumstances where this seemed impossible

PROFILE *profile*
description

PROMISE *to promise the earth*
to give extravagant assurances

PROOF *the proof of the pudding is in the eating*
the success of a venture will be measured by its results

PROPORTION *to be of plague proportions*
to be great in number

PRUNE *to prune*
to remove the superfluous

PSYCHOLOGY *at the psychological moment*
at the most appropriate instant of time (a phrase which actually confuses the German word for "motive" with the term for an instant of time)

PUBLIC *to wash one's dirty linen in public*
to expose one's domestic differences to the world at large

PUDDING *the proof of the pudding is in the eating*
the success of a venture will be measured by its results

PULL *not to pull any punches*
to be brutally frank

PULL *pull your head in!*
do not interfere in this!

PULL *to have pull*
to have influence

PULL *to have the plug pulled out from under one*
to have a successful activity destroyed by the actions of someone else

PULL *to pull a fast one*
to engage in a dirty trick

PULL *to pull a rabbit out of the hat*
to produce an unexpected and seemingly miraculous but highly desirable solution

PULL *to pull at one's heart strings*
to affect one emotionally

PULL *to pull one's fingers out*
to get on with a job with alacrity

PULL *to pull one's head in*
to retreat from a previously held stance

PULL *to pull one's horns in*
to retreat from previously stated views

PULL *to pull one's socks up*
to set out to improve or correct one's inadequate behavior or performance

PULL *to pull one's weight*
to do one's proper share of the work requiring to be done

PULL *to pull oneself together*
to cease acting without purpose or enthusiasm

PULL *to pull oneself up by one's bootstraps*
to make a praiseworthy effort to better oneself unaided

PULL *to pull oneself up by one's own shoelaces*
to make a superhuman effort

PULL *to pull out all stops*
to make maximum effort

PULL *to pull someone's chestnuts out of the fire*
to retrieve a situation

PULL *to pull someone's leg*
to tell a false but plausible story as an act of humor

PULL *to pull something off*
to achieve success in some enterprise

PULL *to pull something out of the fire*
to salvage something in a seemingly hopeless situation

PULL *to pull strings*
to use one's special influence with those in a position to make favorable decisions which might otherwise not be forthcoming

PULL *to pull the rug out from under someone*
to unexpectedly withdraw support and in the process cause embarrassment

PULL *to pull the wool over someone's eyes*
to deceive or deliberately mislead another person

PULL *to pull together*
to work in harmony

PULL *to pull up the drawbridge*
to refuse to cooperate

PULSE *to have one's fingers on the pulse*
to know what is going on

PUMP *all hands to the pumps*
everybody is requested to help out

PUMP *parish pump issues*
issues of trivial importance

PUMP *to engage in pump priming*
to spend public money with the aim of attracting parochial electoral support

PUNCH *not to pull any punches*
to be brutally frank

PUNCH *to be punch drunk*
to be stupefied by some news

PUNCH *to beat someone to the punch*
to get to some objective ahead of some keen rival

PUNCH *to telegraph one's punches*
by one's actions to give advance warning of one's future plans

PUNCTUATE *to punctuate something*
to interrupt something

PUNISHMENT *to be a glutton for punishment*
to act irresponsibly in the face of inevitable retribution

PUNT *to take a punt*
to take a calculated risk

PUP *to sell someone a pup*
to cheat a person in a transaction, especially by misrepresentation as to the true value of something

PURPLE *to be purple with rage*
to be very angry

PURPOSE *the devil can cite scripture for his purpose*
a person can quote a respectable or hostile authority while advocating a disreputable cause of his own (from Shakespeare's MERCHANT OF VENICE)

PURR *to positively purr*
(of a person) to be very pleased; (of an engine) to run very smoothly

PURSE *one can't make a silk purse out of a sow's ear*
it is impossible to manufacture something of a high standard without appropriate raw materials

PURSE *to button up one's purse*
to refuse to spend money

PURSE *to hold the purse strings*
to have control of expenditure

PURSE *to tighten the purse strings*
to reduce outlays

PUSH *to be pushing uphill*
to face difficulties

PUSH *to push a barrow*
to promote a particular cause

PUSH *to push one's luck*
having already done well in something, to then take risks which can prejudice everything

PUSH *to push someone around*
to exercise, in an obnoxious manner, one's superiority over another person

PUSH *to push someone over the brink*
by a small action to cause the absolute ruin (financially or emotionally) of someone already in peril

PUSH *to push water uphill*
to foolishly attempt the impossible

PUSSY *to pussyfoot around*
to take ineffectual steps

PUTTY *to be putty in someone's hands*
to be far too easily influenced by another person

PUZZLE *a Chinese puzzle*
a perplexing enigma

PYRRHIC *a Pyrrhic victory*
a win which costs more than if there had been a loss (refers to the battle at which King Pyrrhus of Epirus defeated the Romans at Asculum)

Q

Q *to watch one's p's and q's*
to be very careful (may refer to pints and quarts of beer on a hotel slate or to easily-confused printer's type)

QUAGMIRE *to be in a quagmire*
to be in great difficulty

QUAKE *to quake in one's boots*
to be afraid

QUANTUM *a quantum leap*
a gigantic step forward

QUART *one can't get a quart into a pint pot*
one cannot do the impossible

QUEENSBERRY *to play by Marquis of Queensberry rules*
to act ethically

QUEER *a queer fish*
an unusual type of person

QUEER *to be in Queer Street*
to be in debt

QUEER *to queer the pitch for someone*
to spoil the opportunity a person has to do something

QUESTION *a leading question*
a very pertinent question (the misuse of a legal term, which actually means a question so framed as to suggest the answer)

QUESTION *burning question*
a much-discussed question

QUESTION *there is a big question mark hanging over someone's head*
there are considerable doubts about a person's competence, integrity or suitability

QUICK *to be quick on one's feet*
to cleverly take advantage of a situation

QUICK *to be quick on the draw*
to act precipitately

QUIET *on the quiet*
surreptitiously

QUIET *to shed a quiet tear for something*
to lament the passing of something

QUIETLY *to quietly fold up one's tent*
to surreptitiously abandon a previously-cherished stance

QUILT *a patchwork quilt*
a result arising from many uncoordinated inputs

QUIT *to quit the scene*
to depart

QUIVER *another arrow in one's quiver*
an additional reason

QUOTE *to quote chapter and verse*
to authenticate the information

R

RABBIT *move over and let the greyhound see the rabbit*
move over

RABBIT *to pull a rabbit out of the hat*
to produce an unexpected and seemingly miraculous but highly desirable solution

RACE *a two-horse race*
a contest between only two serious contestants

RACE *not to be in the race*
to lack the required standard

RACE *rat race*
pressures of modern living

RACE *your race is run*
you have had your opportunity

RACK *to go to rack and ruin*
to face downfall or destruction

RAFT *life raft*
financial assistance sufficient to avert insolvency

RAG *rags to riches*
the transition from poverty to wealth

RAG *to be a red rag to a bull*
to be something which makes a person very angry and very excited (refers to the erroneous belief that the color red, rather than the motion of waving, excites a bull)

RAG *to run something on the smell of an oil rag*
to run something very economically and efficiently

RAGE *to be purple with rage*
to be very angry

RAIL *to run off the rails*
to significantly depart from the intended course of action

RAILROAD *to railroad something through*
to rush people into accepting a proposal

RAILWAY *what a way to run a railway!*
the way things are done is disgraceful (refers to a cartoon)

RAIN *it never rains but it pours*
crises often occur together

RAIN *to rain cats and dogs*
to rain heavily

RAINBOW *to chase rainbows*
to be quite unrealistic

RAINBOW *to seek the pot of gold at the end of the rainbow*
to have naive expectations

RAINY *to keep something for a rainy day*
to keep something in reserve

RAISE *curtain raiser*
introduction

RAISE *hair-raising*
scary

RAISE *to raise Cain*
to create a disturbance (Genesis 4:5)

RAISE *to raise merry hell*
to prominently involve others in a matter in the expectation of significant results from this action

RAISE *to raise one's eyebrows*
to express one's utter astonishment

RAISE *to raise one's voice for some cause*
to publicly advocate some cause

RAISE *to raise someone's hackles*
to make a person angry

RAISE *to raise something to a fine art form*
to become very clever at doing something

RAISE *to raise the stake*
to increase the amount of potential gain or loss in a project

RAKE *a muckraker*
a person who sets out to publicize misconduct of prominent persons or institutions

RAKE *a mudraker*
a person who sets out to publicize features harming another person's reputation

RALLY *to rally to the flag*
to show support for a cause

RAM *to ram something down someone's throat*
to pressure another person into accepting an idea with which he does not agree

RANK *to be the first cab off the rank*
to start ahead of all others

RANK *to break ranks*
to identify oneself as having separate interests or views from the rest of a group

RANK *to close ranks*
to sink minor differences in order to present a unified front to a common enemy

RANSOM *to pay a king's ransom*
to pay a very large sum

RAP *to rap someone over the knuckles*
to admonish a person

RARE *to be a rare bird*
to be an unusual type of individual

RAREFY *in a rarefied atmosphere*
in ignorance of the real world

RAT *a case of rats leaving a sinking ship*
the desertion of an enterprise in anticipation of imminent failure

RAT *rat race*
pressures of modern living

RAT *to smell a rat*
to become suspicious

RATE *at a rate of knots*
very fast

RATTLE *saber rattling*
hints of retribution if certain conduct does not cease

RAW *a raw deal*
unfair treatment

RAZOO *not to have a brass razoo*
to be very poor

RAZOR *to be on the razor's edge*
to be in great danger

READ *to need to have one's head examined*
to be foolish

READ *to read between the lines*
to appreciate the true significance of something not put into words

READ *to read the Riot Act*
to reprimand persons who are excessively noisy (refers to the police reading out to a rowdy crowd extracts from a law requiring its dispersement)

READ *you want your head examined*
you should reconsider this matter

READ *you wouldn't read about it!*
that is unbelievable

READY *ready-made*
easily fabricated or available without difficulty

REAL *to be a real trooper*
to be a person willing to try anything

REAP *to reap as one has sown*
to experience the consequences of one's own actions

REAP *to reap the whirlwind*
to suffer the adverse consequences of a bad act

REAP *to sow the wind and reap the whirlwind*
to make bad mistakes and to suffer the even worse consequences

REAR *to rear its ugly head*
to make an unwelcome appearance

REARRANGE *to rearrange the deckchairs on the Titanic*
to take some initiative which is quite useless because it does not take much greater change into account

REASON *without rhyme or reason*
quite unaccountably

RECEIVE *to receive the coup de grace*
to be finished off by an opponent (French, "mercy stroke")

RECHARGE *to recharge one's batteries*
to have a recuperative break

RECIPE *a recipe for disaster*
a certain way of achieving disaster

RECORD *track record*
proven performance

RED *a red-letter day*
an important occasion (refers to the color used to print saints' days on some calendars)

RED *neither fish, flesh nor good red herring*
unclassifiable by virtue of being neither one thing nor another (from Cervantes' DON QUIXOTE)

RED *red-hot*
highly exciting and desirable

RED *red tape*
excessively bureaucratic procedures

RED *the red-carpet treatment*
courtesies extended to a person to make him feel important and welcome

RED *to be a red herring*
to be something designed to divert attention away from the main question

RED *to be a red rag to a bull*
to be something which makes a person very angry and very excited (refers to the erroneous belief that the color red, rather than the motion of waving, excites a bull)

RED *to be in the red*
to owe money

RED *to be left red-faced*
to be embarrassed

RED *to catch someone red-handed*
to apprehend a person in the course of committing a crime

RED *to get the red light*
to be forbidden to do something

RED *to paint the town red*
to go on an exciting social outing

RED *to see red*
to become very angry

RED *to see red lights flashing*
to be conscious of the danger

REED *to be a broken reed*
to be a weak and unreliable person

REEK *to reek to high heaven*
to be patently unethical

REEL *to leave someone reeling*
to leave a person in a state of shock

REHEARSAL *dress rehearsal*
preliminary skirmish

REIN *a tight rein*
strong controls

REIN *to give rein to one's fancy*
to let one's imagination have free scope

REIN *to give someone free rein*
to confer complete discretion on another person

REIN *to rein in something*
to keep better control over something

REIN *to take over the reins*
to assume control

REINVENT *to reinvent the wheel*
to waste resources doing something already accomplished

REKINDLE *to rekindle an old flame*
to inspire the reinstatement of a former loving relationship

RELIGIOUSLY *religiously*
conscientiously

REPEL *to repel boarders*
to keep out unwanted persons

REPUBLIC *a banana republic*
a country with a poor economy

RESISTANCE *to take the line of least resistance*
to succumb to outside pressure

RESPONSIVE *to strike a responsive chord*
to get a favorable reaction to a proposal

REST *to be head and shoulders above the rest*
to be significantly more capable than others

REST *to lay some theory to rest*
to abandon some theory as being no longer appropriate

REST *to put someone's mind at rest*
to reassure a person

REST *to rest on one's laurels*
to use a reputation for success earned in earlier times as a substitute for current endeavor

RETREAT *to beat a retreat*
to abandon some project

RETREAT *to retreat into one's shell*
to become shy and introversive

RETURN *to return the compliment*
to reciprocate or to extract revenge

RHINOCEROS *to have the hide of a rhinoceros*
to be totally unaffected by and unresponsive to valid criticism

RHYME *without rhyme or reason*
quite unaccountably

RIBBON *blue ribbon*
of superb quality (refers to the insignia of the Order of the Garter)

RIBBON *to be shot to ribbons*
(of an argument) to be utterly discredited

RIBBON *to tear something to ribbons*
to damage something severely

RICH *that is a bit rich*
that is very cheeky

RICHES *rags to riches*
the transition from poverty to wealth

RID *to get rid of the dead wood*
to terminate the services of unsatisfactory personnel

RIDE *a roller coaster ride*
a series of successes followed by failures

RIDE *riding instructions*
directions as to how to do something

RIDE *to be riding for a fall*
to act in a reckless manner

RIDE *to get a magic carpet ride to something*
to be very fortunate in achieving some objective

RIDE *to get an armchair ride*
to be given a particularly easy time

RIDE *to go along for the ride*
to seek to benefit from a project in which others contribute the effort

RIDE *to ride high*
to be successful but vulnerable

RIDE *to ride on the back of someone*
without effort to benefit from the prior efforts of others

RIDE *to ride on the sheep's back*
to benefit from the production of wool

RIDE *to ride out the storm*
to come safely through some dangerous situation

RIDE *to ride roughshod over someone*
to disregard the feelings and wishes of a person

RIDE *to ride the wave*
to be successful for the time being

RIDE *to take someone for a ride*
to deceive a person

RIGHT *I would give my right arm for something*
I am very keen to acquire something

RIGHT *a step in the right direction*
the first in a series of measures designed to correct some problem

RIGHT *one's right-hand man*
one's chief aide

RIGHT *the left hand does not know what the right hand is doing*
one section of a large bureaucracy does not realize that another section is simultaneously doing something inconsistent

RIGHT *to be in the right ballpark*
to be approximately correct

RIGHT *to get on someone's right side*
to make a good impression on a person

RIGHT *to have one's heart in the right place*
to have a well-developed social conscience

RIGHT *to lose one's right arm*
to lose some highly-valued assistance

RIGHT *to play one's cards right*
to approach a matter sensibly

RIGHT *to sell one's birthright for a mess of pottage*
through foolishness to exchange something of substance for something of little value (Genesis 25)

RIGHT *to set someone on the right road*
to show a person how to go about doing something

RIGHT *to start off on the right foot*
to commence an operation with great care to do it correctly

RIGHT *to strike the right chord*
to appeal successfully to someone's emotions

RIGHT *to strike the right key*
to find the appropriate solution

RIGHT *to strike the right note*
to make a good impression

RING *that has a hollow ring to it*
that statement is insincere

RING *that has a nice ring to it*
that sounds attractive

RING *the alarm bells are ringing*
it is unwise to proceed

RING *to jump into the ring*
to join in enthusiastically

RING *to ring a bell*
to sound familiar or recall something to mind

RING *to ring down the curtain on something*
to treat something as concluded

RING *to ring the changes*
to exhaust the number of different ways of doing something (refers to the permutations used for ringing peals of church bells)

RING *to run rings around someone*
to easily outwit another person

RING *to step into the ring*
to enter a competitive environment

RING *to throw one's hat into the ring*
to publicly announce one's interest in some position

RIOT *to read the Riot Act*
to reprimand persons who are excessively noisy (refers to the police reading out to a rowdy crowd extracts from a law requiring its dispersement)

RIOT *to run riot*
to act impetuously and without restraint

RIP *to be a Rip van Winkle*
to be a person out of touch with current conditions (title of and character in a book by Washington Irving)

RIP *to rip someone off*
to exploit a person

RIP *to rip something to shreds*
to damage something severely

RIPPLE *to make ripples*
to disturb the status quo

RISE *rising star*
person making good progress in his career

RISE *the curtain rises on something*
something is about to start

RISE *to rise from the ashes like a Phoenix*
to be the replacement for something destroyed in some disaster (refers to a mythical bird which was supposed to rise from the ashes of its funeral pyre with renewed youth)

RISE *to rise with the lark*
to get up early

RIVER *the river found its mark*
equilibrium between two pressures has been achieved

RIVER *to be a river of gold*
to be a source of ongoing great profitability

RIVER *to sell someone down the river*
to betray a person who has placed his trust in one

RIVET *to be riveted to one's seat*
to find the activity being watched very exciting and worthy of full attention

ROAD *a middle-of-the-road solution*
a solution near the middle of a range of possibilities

ROAD *all roads lead to Rome*
all alternatives will have the same outcome

ROAD *fork in the road*
turning point for decisions

ROAD *one for the road*
a final drink before leaving

ROAD *roadblocks*
difficulties

ROAD *the royal road to success*
the way of attaining success without effort

ROAD *this is the end of the road for someone*
a person will have no further opportunity to do something

ROAD *to be at the crossroads*
to need to choose between several mutually exclusive alternatives

ROAD *to be on the road to Damascus*
to see the error of one's ways (Acts 9:3)

ROAD *to enter a long road*
to commence a task which will take a long time

ROAD *to face a rocky road ahead*
to be likely to encounter difficulties

ROAD *to get the show on the road*
to commence a planned activity

ROAD *to go down a particular road*
to adopt a particular strategy

ROAD *to happen down the road*
to happen later

ROAD *to road test something*
to try something out under real conditions

ROAD *to set someone on the right road*
to show a person how to go about doing something

ROAR *to be within a bull's roar of something*
to be very close to something

ROAST *a roasting*
a scolding

ROB *to rob Peter in order to pay Paul*
to fix up one grievance by causing another

ROBBERY *daylight robbery*
the charging of grossly excessive prices

ROBBERY *highway robbery*
the charging of grossly excessive prices

ROBIN *a round robin*
(1) series of checks from A to B, from B to C, from C to A, and so on, leaving all of them in the same net position as before

ROBIN *a round robin*
(2) a document signed by members of an organization which has the same effect as a resolution of a meeting

ROBINSON *before one can say "Jack Robinson"*
very quickly

ROCK *bedrock price*
lowest possible price

ROCK *rock bottom*
very low

ROCK *someone's marriage is on the rocks*
someone's marriage has broken down

ROCK *to be between a rock and a hard place*
to be faced with two equally difficult and uncomfortable choices

ROCK *to be on the rocks*
to be bankrupt

ROCK *to have rocks in the head*
to be mentally unbalanced

ROCK *to rock the boat*
to disturb the comfortable status quo

ROCKET *to give someone a rocket*
to severely reprimand a person

ROCKET *to put a rocket under someone*
to induce a person to take some action

ROCKET *to skyrocket*
(of a price or value) to increase greatly in a short time

ROCKY *to face a rocky road ahead*
to be likely to encounter difficulties

ROD *to kiss the rod*
to accept punishment meekly

ROD *to make a rod for one's own back*
to act in disregard of likely disadvantages for oneself

ROD *to rule with a rod of iron*
to keep strict discipline

ROGUE *a rogue elephant*
a person of vicious temper who acts in an undisciplined way

ROLL *heads will roll*
trangressors will be punished

ROLL *the caravan will roll on*
the activity will continue

ROLL *the money is rolling in*
the scheme is very profitable

ROLL *to get rolled*
to be outvoted

ROLL *to have an audience rolling in the aisles*
to amuse an audience

ROLL *to keep the ball rolling*
to take advantage of the existing momentum or to participate actively

ROLL *to roll off the tongue*
to be said very easily

ROLL *to roll up one's sleeves*
to get on with a job energetically

ROLL *to start the ball rolling*
to commence and enthusiastically advance an activity involving people

ROLLER *a roller coaster ride*
a series of successes followed by failures

ROME *all roads lead to Rome*
all alternatives will have the same outcome

ROME *to fiddle while Rome burns*
to neglect important considerations while concentrating on trivial side-issues

ROME *when in Rome do as the Romans do*
it is best to conform to the local customs

ROOF *the roof has fallen in*
an enterprise has collapsed

ROOF *to go through the roof*
(of a person) to be very upset or (of prices) to escalate greatly

ROOF *to hit the roof*
to be very angry

ROOF *to scream something from the rooftops*
to communicate a message to a wide audience

ROOF *under one roof*
under the same management

ROOM *no room at the inn*
no room

ROOM *there is no room to swing a cat*
this place is very small (actually refers to a cat-o'-nine-tails)

ROOST *the chickens are coming home to roost*
the consequences of past actions are becoming obvious

ROOST *to rule the roost*
to dominate

ROOT *deep-rooted*
strongly felt

ROOT *grass roots*
at the lowest level

ROOT *to put one's roots down*
to settle in

ROOT *to strike at the roots of something*
to work toward the destruction of something

ROPE *to be on the ropes*
to be facing defeat

ROPE *to give someone enough rope to hang himself*
to give a person the opportunity to do something which is likely to get him into severe trouble

ROPE *to give someone too much rope*
to give a person too much latitude

ROPE *to know the ropes*
to know how to do one's job

ROPE *to learn the ropes*
to be taught the elementary features

ROPE *to put a leg rope on someone*
to give a person very little authority

ROPE *to show someone the ropes*
to teach a beginner how to do something

ROSE *a rose between two thorns*
something beautiful in the midst of ugliness

ROSE *a rose by any other name would smell as sweet*
the form does not affect the substance (from Shakespeare's ROMEO AND JULIET)

ROSE *to be no bed of roses*
to be difficult or uncomfortable

ROSE *to be on a path strewn with roses*
to lead a very pleasant life

ROSE *to come up smelling like a rose*
not to have a stain on one's character

ROSE *to see something through rose-colored spectacles*
to appreciate only the advantages and to completely disregard the disadvantages

ROSY *to present a rosy picture*
to state a set of favorable factors

ROT *the rot set in*
conditions started to deteriorate

ROTTEN *a rotten apple*
an isolated dishonest person in an otherwise honest group

ROTTEN *rotten to the core*
completely corrupt

ROTTEN *something is rotten in the state of Denmark*
the situation is not correct (from Shakespeare's HAMLET)

ROUGH *to be a rough diamond*
to have many attributes but a gruff manner

ROUGH *to feel the rough side of someone's tongue*
to be verbally abused by a person

ROUGH *to take the rough with the smooth*
to accept the hardships of life along with its pleasant features

ROUGHSHOD *to ride roughshod over someone*
to disregard the feelings and wishes of a person

ROULETTE *to play Russian roulette*
to take stupid risks

ROUND *a round robin*
(1) a series of checks from A to B, from B to C, from C to A, and so on, leaving all of them in the same net position as before

ROUND *a round robin*
(2) a document signed by members of an organization which has the same effect as a resolution of a meeting

ROUND *a square peg in a round hole*
a person much more suitable for a position rather different from the one held

ROUND *going the rounds*
(of a rumor) being spread

ROUND *to be only round one*
to be only the first of many stages

ROUND *to be round the bend*
to be crazy

ROUND *to get the rounds of the kitchen*
(of a husband) to be subject to personal abuse by his wife

ROUND *to make the wheels go round*
to cause something to happen

ROUND *to turn round*
to reverse one's policy

ROUND *to win some rounds*
to be partly successful

ROUNDABOUT *what one loses on the swings one gains on the roundabouts*
there are advantages and disadvantages which offset each other

ROW *not to matter a row of beans*
to be utterly unimportant

ROW *to be on skid row*
to have no means

ROW *to have a hard row to hoe*
to be a difficult assignment

ROYAL *a battle royal*
a fight or argument with many simultaneous participants

ROYAL *the royal road to success*
the way of attaining success without effort

RUB *here's the rub*
this is where a difficulty arises (a term used in lawn bowling)

RUB *not to have the wherewithal to rub two sticks together*
to be very poor

RUB *to rub it in*
to humiliate another person by emphasizing his defeat

RUB *to rub off on someone*
to benefit a person through an association which increases his skills

RUB *to rub one's chin*
to muse

RUB *to rub one's eyes*
to express astonishment

RUB *to rub one's hands with glee*
to express great satisfaction

RUB *to rub salt into someone's wound*
to deliberately make damage even worse

RUB *to rub shoulders with someone*
to mingle with a person

RUB *to rub someone up the wrong way*
to annoy someone with actions failing to recognize his current mood

RUB *to rub someone's nose in it*
to humiliate a person by highlighting something embarrassing to him

RUBBER *to rubber-stamp something*
to endorse without considering the merits

RUBBISH *a load of rubbish*
blatant nonsense

RUBICON *to cross the Rubicon*
to make an irreversible decision in regard to some commitment

RUDDER *to be a rudderless ship*
to be a project not managed properly

RUFFLE *to ruffle someone's feathers*
to engage in behavior which irritates another person

RUG *to pull the rug out from under someone*
to unexpectedly withdraw support and in the process cause embarrassment

RUG *to sweep something under the carpet*
to pretend that some blemish does not exist

RUIN *to go to rack and ruin*
to face downfall or destruction

RULE *ground rules*
basic principles

RULE *to bend the rules*
to overlook minor infractions of the rules

RULE *to let one's heart rule one's head*
to act on emotion rather than on reason

RULE *to play by Marquis of Queensberry rules*
to act ethically

RULE *to rule the roost*
to dominate

RUMINATE *to ruminate*
to ponder over a matter (lit., to chew the cud)

RUN *a dry run*
a trial exercise

RUN *run of the mill*
normal or average

RUN *someone would run a mile*
a person would do anything to escape his responsibilities

RUN *the sands are running out*
the time available for some action is nearly at an end

RUN *the tide is running in favor of some proposition*
public opinion supports some proposition

RUN *to be up and running*
to be operative

RUN *to duck for cover*
to seek to avoid blame

RUN *to have a dream run*
to encounter no difficulties

RUN *to have a run for one's money*
to at least get some enjoyment out of an otherwise abortive exercise

RUN *to have the runs on the board*
to have a demonstrable record of achievement

RUN *to run a tight ship*
to manage an efficient organization

RUN *to run around in circles*
to engage in excited but useless activity

RUN *to run hot*
(of equipment) to be subject to particularly high usage

RUN *to run into a dead end*
to get nowhere in an investigation

RUN *to run into heavy weather*
to encounter difficulties

RUN *to run its course*
to come to a natural end

RUN *to run off the rails*
to significantly depart from the intended course of action

RUN *to run one's own ship*
to do things and organize subordinates in one's own way

RUN *to run out of steam*
to lose one's energy and enthusiasm

RUN *to run rings around someone*
to easily outwit another person

RUN *to run riot*
to act impetuously and without restraint

RUN *to run someone off his feet*
to keep a person very busy on some physical task

RUN *to run someone to earth*
to locate a person

RUN *to run someone to the ground*
to discover the whereabouts of a person

RUN *to run the gauntlet*
to be subjected to criticism (from the Spanish word for ''passage,'' in reference to punishment inflicted on delinquents made to run between two files of soldiers)

RUN *to run to seed*
to become shabby

RUN *to run with something*
to take advantage of some current development

RUN *to run with the ball*
to make the most of the opportunity

RUN *to run with the hare and hunt with the hounds*
to keep in with two opposing sides

RUN *to set a hare running*
in order to achieve some desired effect to initiate some related activity

RUN *your race is run*
you have had your opportunity

RUNG *rungs up a ladder*
gradual steps to an ultimate goal

RUNNER *front-runner*
person expected to win

RUSH *fools rush in where angels fear to tread*
unsophisticated persons take unwise risks in circumstances where more knowledgeable persons would exercise caution

RUSH *to be killed in the rush*
to be the supplier of something extremely popular

RUSH *to rush one's fences*
to act precipitately

RUSSIAN *to play Russian roulette*
to take stupid risks

RUT *to be in a rut*
to lead a dull life, with no change from long-established habits

S

SABER *saber rattling*
hints of retribution if certain conduct does not cease

SACK *to get the sack*
to be dismissed (refers to the bag of tradesmen's tools)

SACKCLOTH *to wear sackcloth and ashes*
humbly to demonstrate repentance

SACRED *a sacred cow*
an institution so well established that it is virtually unalterable

SACRED *a sacred trust*
a moral obligation

SACRED *nothing is sacred*
nothing is safe from interference

SACRIFICIAL *sacrificial lamb*
somebody unfairly made to suffer for the mistakes of others

SADDLE *to be in the saddle*
to be in command

SAFE *to play it safe*
to take no risks

SAFE *to plot a safe course through troubled waters*
to make a plan which overcomes certain difficulties

SAFETY *a safety net scheme*
a scheme for dealing with the exceptional cases not covered by normal arrangements

SAFETY *safety margin*
allowance for miscalculations

SAFETY *to act as a safety valve*
to be a procedure which allows persons with grievances to ventilate them in an orderly fashion

SAIL *to be plain sailing*
to be quite straightforward and very easy

SAIL *to sail against the wind*
to oppose the views currently being held by others

SAIL *to sail close to the wind*
to act in a very dangerous manner

SAIL *to sail under false colors*
to pretend that one's real character or beliefs are different from what they really are

SAIL *to set sail*
to commence a voyage

SAIL *to take the wind out of someone's sails*
to upset a person by anticipating his actions or using arguments which he was proposing to use

SAIL *to trim one's sails*
to institute austerity

SAINT *a saint*
a good person

SAINT *to have the patience of a saint*
to endure annoyances with particular calm

SALE *fire sale*
a forced sale, realizing bargain prices

SALLY *an Aunt Sally*
a person who can readily be singled out and criticized as the proxy for a group

SALT *below the salt*
in a subordinate position (refers to the seating order at ancient Roman dining tables)

SALT *not to be worth one's salt*
not to be pulling one's weight (refers to Roman soldiers being paid in salt—a practice giving rise to the modern word "salary")

SALT *to be the salt of the earth*
to be a person whose ordinary efforts benefit the community (Matthew 5:13)

SALT *to rub salt into someone's wound*
to deliberately make damage even worse

SALT *to take something with a grain of salt*
to regard the facts in a statement with considerable skepticism

SALVAGE *to salvage something out of the wreck*
to achieve some minor benefits out of a disastrous situation

SALVO *to fire a salvo at someone*
to present a series of criticisms to a person

SAMARITAN *a good Samaritan*
a person going out of his way to do a kindness to others (Luke 10:33)

SAME *to all sing from the same hymnal*
to act consistently with each other

SAME *to be in the same boat*
to share a common set of difficulties

SAME *to be in the same league*
to have comparable skills

SAND *shifting sands*
arguments which are constantly being changed

SAND *the sands are running out*
the time available for some action is nearly at an end

SAND *to bury one's head in the sand*
to refuse to face up to an unpleasant truth (refers to the reputed habit of ostriches in danger)

SANDWICH *to be the ham in the sandwich*
to be caught in the middle of a dispute between other parties

SAUCE *what is sauce for the goose is sauce for the gander*
arguments which apply in one case also apply in another

SAUSAGE *a sausage machine*
the turning out of large volumes without particular thought

SAVE *saved by the bell*
rescued before disaster strikes

SAVE *to save face*
to be allowed to keep one's dignity despite having suffered a defeat or made an error

SAVE *to save one's bacon*
to escape harm

SAVE *to save one's skin*
to get off safely

SAVE *to save someone's life*
to be of great help to a person

SAVE *to save someone's neck*
to come to the rescue of a person

SAY *before one can say "Jack Robinson"*
very quickly

SCALES *to tip the scales*
to be a factor which in combination with other factors results in a particular decision which would otherwise not have been reached

SCALP *to be after someone's scalp*
to be keen to penalize a person

SCAPEGOAT *a scapegoat*
a person unfairly blamed for something not his fault

SCAR *to scar someone*
to leave a person permanently grieving

SCARCE *to make oneself scarce*
to take oneself out of view

SCARE *to scare the pants off someone*
to greatly frighten a person

SCATTER *a scattergun approach*
an effort going here, there and everywhere, instead of being properly targeted

SCATTER *to scatter something to the four winds*
to permanently get rid of something

SCENARIO *scenario*
details of arrangements

SCENE *behind the scenes*
out of public view or awareness

SCENE *to make a scene*
to create a fuss

SCENE *to quit the scene*
to depart

SCENE *to set the scene for something*
to get things ready for something

SCENT *to throw someone off the scent*
to deceive a person by giving out misleading indications

SCHOOL *to tell tales out of school*
to deliberately leak a secret

SCHOOLBOY *as every schoolboy knows*
as is recognized by everyone

SCORE *to even the score*
to get one's own back for some past action

SCORE *to score a goal*
to achieve an objective

SCORE *to score a hat trick*
to have three successive favorable outcomes

SCORE *to score a point*
to make a clever contribution in the course of debate

SCORE *to score an own goal*
to blow oneself up

SCORE *to score points*
to make a good impression

SCORE *to score top points*
to outwit other persons

SCORE *to see the score*
to appreciate the reality of a situation

SCORE *to underscore something*
to emphasize something

SCOT *to get off scot free*
to go unpunished (refers to an exemption from tax)

SCRAPE *to really scrape the bottom of the barrel*
to lower one's standards because one is short of important or relevant issues

SCRAP-HEAP *to be destined for the scrap-heap*
to face a future in which one will have no meaningful role

SCRATCH *to be back to scratch*
to have to start all over again

SCRATCH *to be up to scratch*
to be of the required standard

SCRATCH *to only scratch the surface*
to deal with only a small portion of a much larger whole

SCRATCH *to scratch one another's backs*
to help each other

SCRATCH *to scratch one's head*
to be amazed or puzzled

SCRATCH *to scratch something together*
to improvise

SCRATCH *to start from behind scratch*
to be faced with a handicap

SCRATCH *to start from scratch*
to commence something without the benefit of any past activity

SCREAM *to scream and yell*
to protest violently

SCREAM *to scream blue murder*
to make serious allegations

SCREAM *to scream something from the rooftops*
to communicate a message to a wide audience

SCREEN *to set up a smokescreen*
to deliberately confuse an issue by disguising its salient features

SCREW *to have a screw loose*
to be mentally unbalanced

SCREW *to have one's head screwed on straight*
to be shrewd

SCREW *to put the screws on someone*
to exert pressure on a person

SCREW *to tighten the screw*
to increase the moral and psychological pressure

SCRIPTURE *the devil can cite scripture for his purpose*
a person can quote a respectable or hostile authority while advocating a disreputable cause of his own (from Shakespeare's MERCHANT OF VENICE)

SCROOGE *to be a real Scrooge*
to be miserly and unmoved (refers to a character in Charles Dickens' A CHRISTMAS CAROL)

SCYLLA *to be between Scylla and Charybdis*
to be faced with two equally unpalatable alternatives which cannot both be avoided (refers to the voyage of Ulysses)

SEA *a South Sea bubble*
an unrealistic financial venture which is bound to result in total loss

SEA *between the devil and the deep blue sea*
to be faced with two equally unpalatable alternatives which cannot both be avoided

SEA *to be all at sea*
to be confused as to what is going on and what to do next

SEAL *a seal of approval*
confirmation that something is satisfactory

SEAL *to seal one's lips*
to keep a confidence

SEAL *to seal someone's fate*
to cause a certain outcome adversely affecting a person

SEAL *to set the seal on something*
to confirm absolutely that something is agreed

SEAM *to be bursting at the seams*
to be very crowded

SEAM *to come apart at the seams*
(of an arrangement) to break down

SEARCH *a soul-searching exercise*
an examination of the advantages and disadvantages of a proposal

SEARCH *search for the Holy Grail*
work toward a difficult goal (refers to a vessel supposedly used by Christ at the last supper and featuring in the Arthurian legends)

SEARCH *to search one's heart*
to have misgivings

SEASON *the silly season*
the holiday period, when hard news is scarce and journalistic standards are lowered

SEAT *a backseat driver*
a person seeking to exercise control

SEAT *to be in the box seat*
to be in a very powerful position to control activity

SEAT *to be in the driver's seat*
to be in charge

SEAT *to be in the hot seat*
to hold a position requiring one to answer criticism or accusations

SEAT *to be on the edge of one's seat*
to be very excited at what is currently happening

SEAT *to be riveted to one's seat*
to find the activity being watched very exciting and worthy of full attention

SEAT *to fly by the seat of one's pants*
to act unprofessionally

SEAT *to keep someone's seat warm*
to hold a position temporarily with a view to another person taking it over permanently in the near future

SEAT *to take a backseat*
not to actively involve oneself

SECOND *a second-class citizen*
a person not treated as an equal

SECOND *second childhood*
dotage

SECOND *the second eleven*
persons performing an important function but one which is less important than that performed by others (refers to cricket)

SECOND *to be second nature to someone*
to be something which a person does intuitively

SECOND *to have a second string to one's bow*
to have an additional qualification appropriate to the task

SECOND *to play second fiddle*
to fulfill a subordinate role

SEE *blind Freddy could see that something is such-and-such*
it is very obvious that something is such-and-such

SEE *not to see the wood for the trees*
to overlook the general picture because of undue concentration on the details

SEE *suck it and see*
discover experimentally how something works

SEE *to see blood*
to be very angry

SEE *to see daylight*
to get the right answer

SEE *to see eye to eye with someone*
to agree

SEE *to see red*
to become very angry

SEE *to see red lights flashing*
to be conscious of the danger

SEE *to see someone in a good light*
to regard a person favorably

SEE *to see something with half an eye*
to sum up a matter instantly

SEE *to see the back of someone*
to know that a person is no longer involved in something

SEE *to see the big picture*
to have the vision and imagination enabling a project to be developed as part of a bigger whole

SEE *to see the color of someone's eyes*
to see how a person matches expectations or requirements

SEE *to see the color of someone's money*
to get evidence of the sincerity of a person's proposal

SEE *to see the light*
to understand the real situation

SEE *to see the light at the end of the tunnel*
to be close to finalizing a long exercise

SEE *to see the light of day*
to be made public

SEE *to see the score*
to appreciate the reality of a situation

SEE *to see the writing on the wall*
to appreciate the inevitability of some event (Daniel 5)

SEE *to see which way the cat jumps*
to await developments

SEED *to run to seed*
to become shabby

SEED *to sow seeds*
to propagate ideas in the hope that they will be adopted

SEEK *to seek the pot of gold at the end of the rainbow*
to have naive expectations

SELL *to be sold on something*
to be utterly dedicated to a proposal

SELL *to sell off the family silver*
to sell off one's prized possessions

SELL *to sell one's birthright for a mess of pottage*
through foolishness to exchange something of substance for something of little value (Genesis 25)

SELL *to sell someone a lemon*
to sell a person a grossly defective product on the basis that it represents quality

SELL *to sell someone a pup*
to cheat a person in a transaction, especially by misrepresentation as to the true value of something

SELL *to sell someone down the river*
to betray a person who has placed his trust in one

SEND *to send a chill down someone's neck*
to be worrying news

SEND *to send a cold shiver down someone's spine*
to horrify a person

SEND *to send a smoke signal*
to give an indication

SEND *to send someone away with a flea in his ear*
to give a person frank but unwelcome facts (refers to fleas trapped in the armor of ancient knights)

SEND *to send someone packing*
to dismiss a person ignominiously

SEND *to send someone to Coventry*
to ostentatiously and collectively ignore a person by way of punishment

SENSE *a sixth sense*
intuition (refers to the five senses—sight, hearing, smell, taste and touch)

SENSE *horse sense*
natural shrewdness

SENTENCE *to be sentenced to some fate*
to be condemned by circumstances to endure some fate

SEPARATE *to separate the men from the boys*
to distinguish between those with and without certain skills

SEPARATE *to separate the sheep from the goats*
to distinguish between those with and without certain attributes (Matthew 25:32)

SEPARATE *to separate the wheat from the chaff*
to distinguish between important and unimportant ingredients

SERVE *to serve something up to someone on a plate*
to make something especially easy for a particular person

SERVICE *to pay lip service to some rules*
to disregard some rules in practice wile acknowledging them in words

SESAME *an open sesame*
access to something normally inaccessible

SET *game, set and match*
completion

SET *the rot set in*
conditions started to deteriorate

SET *the stage is set*
something is about to happen

SET *the sun has set on something*
something has concluded

SET *to be set like a jelly*
to be very well established

SET *to have one's heart set on something*
to be very keen to achieve something

SET *to set a hare running*
in order to achieve some desired effect, to initiate some related activity

SET *to set one's cap at someone*
(of females) to try to attract a person as a marriage partner

SET *to set one's sights on something*
to aim to achieve something

SET *to set sail*
to commence a voyage

SET *to set someone on the right road*
to show a person how to go about doing something

SET *to set someone's teeth on edge*
to cause a person to feel unhappy at a situation

SET *to set something in concrete*
to make something virtually unalterable

SET *to set the Thames on fire*
to do something noteworthy

SET *to set the hounds baying*
to excite the gossips by providing material which they can use

SET *to set the pace*
to give a lead in regard to a rate of progression

SET *to set the scene for something*
to get things ready for something

SET *to set the seal on something*
to confirm absolutely that something is agreed

SET *to set the wheels in motion*
to institute appropriate action

SET *to set the world on fire*
to do something particularly brilliant

SET *to set tongues wagging*
to behave in a way which encourages scandal mongers

SET *to set up a smokescreen*
to deliberately confuse an issue by disguising its salient features

SETTLE *when the dust settles*
when sufficient time has passed

SEVEN *to be at sixes and sevens*
to be confused, concerned and undecided

SEVEN *to be in seventh heaven*
to be very happy

SEVERE *to be a severe blow*
to be a great disappointment

SEW *to sew something up*
to negotiate a deal

SHACKLE *golden shackles*
financial arrangements designed to discourage employees changing employers

SHADE *to throw someone in the shade*
to surpass a person

SHADOW *to be in someone's shadow*
to be unable to exert one's personality because of association with a more important person

SHADOW *to be only a pale shadow of something*
to be a weak imitation

SHADOW *to cast a shadow over something*
to introduce a note of warning or sadness in regard to some matter

SHADOW *to lurk in the shadows*
to have a low profile at the moment, but with the possibility of becoming much more conspicuous at any time

SHADOW *to overshadow someone*
to reduce the influence of a person by outshining him

SHADOW *to shadow box*
to go through the motions without achieving or intending to achieve anything

SHADOW *to throw a long shadow*
to have widespread ramifications

SHAFT *a Parthian shaft*
a cutting remark made at the moment of departure (refers to missiles shot backward by flying Parthian horsemen)

SHAGGY *a shaggy-dog story*
an amusing anecdote with an unexpected ending, often involving talking animals given certain human skills

SHAKE *a golden handshake*
a large payment in connection with or as an inducement to retirement

SHAKE *in two shakes of a duck's tail*
in an instant

SHAKE *to shake a leg*
to hurry up

SHAKE *to shake a tree*
to do something in order to see what will result

SHAKE *to shake down*
to sleep on an improvised bed

SHAKE *to shake one's head*
to indicate disbelief or wonder or disapproval

SHAKE *to wait two shakes of a lamb's tail*
to wait just a few moments

SHAKY *to be on shaky ground*
not to have strong arguments

SHAMBLES *to throw something into a shambles*
to make something messy and useless

SHAPE *not to do something in any shape or form*
not to do something

SHAPE *shipshape*
in excellent condition

SHAPE *to lick something into shape*
to make something presentable and effective

SHARE *a share of the cake*
a portion of the total available for distribution

SHARE *the lion's share*
the biggest portion

SHARE *to have shares in a paper company*
to institute unnecessary clerical procedures

SHARK *to miss the sharks while netting the minnows*
to succeed in minor aspects but fail in the ones that really matter

SHARP *sharp dealer*
person engaging in barely honest or mildly unethical practices

SHARP *to have a sharp tongue*
to speak one's mind in forceful language

SHARPEN *to need to sharpen one's pencil*
to be required to improve one's performance

SHARPEN *to sharpen one's ax*
to get ready for a difficult task

SHARPEN *to sharpen the knives*
to get ready for a concerted attack on some principle

SHATTER *earth-shattering*
very significant

SHAVE *to be a close shave*
to be a narrow escape

SHED *to shed a quiet tear for something*
to lament the passing of something

SHED *to shed crocodile tears*
to be a hypocrite

SHED *to shed light on something*
to give explanations

SHEEP *a black sheep*
a disreputable member of an otherwise reputable group

SHEEP *one might as well be hanged for a sheep as for a lamb*
further action will not increase the adverse consequences already in train (refers to the stealing of both sheep and lambs being capital crimes under old English law)

SHEEP *to be a wolf in sheep's clothing*
to be a hypocrite or to be dangerous although masquerading as something harmless (Matthew 7:15)

SHEEP *to be home on the sheep's back*
to be doing well

SHEEP *to cast sheep's eyes at someone*
to look at a person amorously

SHEEP *to ride on the sheep's back*
to benefit from the production of wool

SHEEP *to separate the sheep from the goats*
to distinguish between those with and without certain attributes (Matthew 25:32)

SHEEP *to spoil the ship for a ha' p' orth of tar*
to engage in a false economy (the current word "ship" is actually a mistake for the original word "sheep" and the tar refers to the treatment of wounds)

SHEEPISH *sheepish*
embarrassed, as though guilty

SHEER *to be sheer murder*
to be extremely unpleasant or difficult; or to be an inglorious defeat

SHEET *the sheet anchor*
the source of one's confidence

SHEET *to start with a blank sheet of paper*
to commence an exercise without being bound by any established practices

SHELF *to be on the shelf*
to be available for marriage

SHELL *to be shell-shocked*
to be stunned by unexpected bad news

SHELL *to retreat into one's shell*
to become shy and introversive

SHELVE *to shelve some proposal*
to abandon some proposal

SHEPHERD *to shepherd some group*
to marshall the members of some group

SHIBBOLETH *a shibboleth*
a doctrine once held as essential but now abandoned as having outlived its usefulness (a word used as a test to determine to which tribe an Israelite belonged) (Judges 12:6)

SHIFT *shifting sands*
arguments which are constantly being changed

SHILLING *to be only ten pence in the shilling*
to be slightly stupid

SHILLING *to cut someone off with a shilling*
to exclude a person as a beneficiary under one's will (refers to the mistaken belief that a will cannot be upset in favor of a person actually named in a will and clearly not overlooked)

SHINE *a knight in shining armor*
a very helpful person

SHINE *shining light*
eminent or scholarly person

SHINE *to make hay while the sun shines*
to utilize an opportunity before it disappears

SHINE *to take a shine to someone*
to be keen on a person

SHINE *to take the shine off something*
to spoil the performance of something

SHINE *to take the shine out of something*
to demonstrably surpass

SHINGLE *to hang up one's shingle*
to go into business offering expert personal services

SHIP *a case of rats leaving a sinking ship*
the desertion of an enterprise in anticipation of imminent failure

SHIP *enough to sink a battleship*
more than sufficient

SHIP *shipshape*
in excellent condition

SHIP *ships that pass in the night*
persons who fail to meet up

SHIP *to abandon ship*
to abrogate one's responsibilities or to abandon a project

SHIP *to be a rudderless ship*
to be a project not managed properly

SHIP *to run a tight ship*
to manage an efficient organization

SHIP *to run one's own ship*
to do things and organize subordinates in one's own way

SHIP *to spoil the ship for a ha'p'orth of tar*
to engage in false economy (the current word "ship" is actually a mistake for the original word "sheep" and the tar refers to the treatment of wounds)

SHIP *when one's ship comes in*
when one's business venture is successfully completed or when luck arrives

SHIRT *keep your shirt on!*
relax!

SHIRT *so-and-so would give one the shirt off his back*
so-and-so is very generous

SHIRT *to lose one's shirt*
to suffer heavy financial losses

SHIRT *to put one's shirt on something*
to invest heavily in some speculative venture

SHIRT *to wear a hair shirt*
to practice self-discipline

SHIVER *to send a cold shiver down someone's spine*
to horrify a person

SHOAL *to founder on the shoals of something*
to come to grief because of unexpected dangers

SHOCK *to be shell-shocked*
to be stunned by unexpected bad news

SHOE *to be in someone's shoes*
to have another person's responsibility

SHOE *to fill someone's shoes*
to be a good successor

SHOE *to wait for the other shoe to drop*
to await the seemingly imminent and inevitable (refers to a man undressing, disturbing a neighbor by dropping one shoe, then frustrating his expectation by putting the other shoe down gently)

SHOELACE *to pull oneself up by one's own shoelaces*
to make a superhuman effort

SHOESTRING *to do something on a shoestring*
to do something with great economy

SHOOT *a straight shooter*
a person who is frank and outspoken

SHOOT *a troubleshooter*
a person good at finding and then rectifying faults

SHOOT *shoot!*
go on, speak!

SHOOT *the whole shooting match*
the whole lot

SHOOT *to be on a slippery shoot*
to court disaster

SHOOT *to be shot to pieces*
to have one's case seriously damaged

SHOOT *to be shot to ribbons*
(of an argument) to be utterly discredited

SHOOT *to shoot from the hip*
to speak frankly and openly

SHOOT *to shoot one's bolt*
to lose one's temper

SHOOT *to shoot one's mouth off*
to speak without thinking

SHOOT *to shoot oneself in the foot*
to act in a foolish way and thus harm one's own cause

SHOOT *to shoot someone down in flames*
to utterly destroy another person's arguments

SHOOT *to shoot something out of the water*
to frustrate something

SHOP *a bull in a china shop*
a careless person likely to cause great damage

SHOP *a shopping list*
a catalogue of demands

SHOP *to shop around*
to explore alternatives

SHOP *to shut up shop*
to cease an established activity

SHOP *to talk shop*
to discuss business or professional matters on a social occasion

SHORT *take a long walk on a short pier*
go away, I want no dealings with you

SHORT *the long and the short of it*
all that needs to be said about this

SHORT *to be short and sweet*
to be very brief and to the point

SHORT *to be shortchanged*
to be given less than is due to one

SHORT *to draw the short straw*
to be the one appointed to do something

SHORT *to get someone by the short and curly hairs*
to have domination over a person

SHORT *to give someone short shift*
to be impatient with a person (refers to the confession to a priest just before an execution)

SHORT *to have a short fuse*
to lose one's temper very readily

SHORT *to hold someone on a short leash*
to give a person very little authority

SHORT *to short-circuit something*
to do something, eliminating various intermediate steps

SHORT *to take shortcuts*
to do something by a faster but less thorough method

SHORTHAND *to be a shorthand way of saying something*
to be a way of saying something in summarized form

SHORTSIGHTED *to be shortsighted*
not to recognize the likely consequences

SHOT *a bit shot*
an important person

SHOT *a shot in the arm*
something to revive a person's enthusiasm

SHOT *a shot in the dark*
an intelligent or lucky guess

SHOT *a sitting shot*
an initial move which is designed to establish facts for use in a later action

SHOT *opening shot*
first step in an activity expected to last a long time

SHOT *shots across the bow*
warnings

SHOT *that is a long shot*
there is only a remote possibility

SHOT *to be a sitting shot*
to be a person whose actions make him very vulnerable to criticism

SHOT *to beat by a long shot*
to defeat very convincingly

SHOT *to call the shots*
to have the direction over a project

SHOT *to fire a parting shot*
to make a defiant gesture on leaving

SHOT *to give one's best shot*
to make the best attempt possible

SHOT *to have a shot at someone*
to use subtly chosen words implying friendly criticism but designed to embarrass another person

SHOT *to have a shot at something*
to attempt to achieve something

SHOT *to take a potshot at someone*
to make disparaging remarks about a person

SHOTGUN *a shotgun wedding*
a wedding held to ensure that an impending birth will be legitimate (refers to threats by the bride's father to kill the bridegroom)

SHOULDER *a shoulder to cry on*
sympathy

SHOULDER *a shoulder to lean on*
sympathy

SHOULDER *an old head on young shoulders*
experience, knowledge and maturity in a young person

SHOULDER *shoulder to shoulder*
in close proximity

SHOULDER *straight from the shoulder*
bluntly

SHOULDER *to be head and shoulders above the rest*
to be significantly more capable than others

SHOULDER *to carry the world on one's shoulders*
to resent being left to perform a huge task single-handedly (refers to Atlas, who was condemned to bear the heavens on his shoulders for leading the Titans against the gods)

SHOULDER *to give someone the cold shoulder*
to ostentatiously ignore a person

SHOULDER *to have a chip on one's shoulder*
to unreasonably resent something

SHOULDER *to have broad shoulders*
to be able to cope well with responsibility

SHOULDER *to need to look over one's shoulder*
to be subject to attack which is not obvious

SHOULDER *to put a burden on someone's shoulders*
to impose responsibilities on a person

SHOULDER *to put one's shoulder to the wheel*
to make a strong effort

SHOULDER *to rub shoulders with someone*
to mingle with a person

SHOULDER *to shoulder the blame*
to accept the blame

SHOULDER *to shrug one's shoulders*
to indicate that one does not know or care or that one is unable or unwilling to assist

SHOULDER *to stand on someone's shoulders*
to build upon another person's ideas

SHOULDER *to take a weight off someone's shoulder*
to assist a person by relieving him of some responsibility

SHOULDER *to work shoulder to shoulder*
to work with united effort

SHOUT *to be all over bar the shouting*
to be virtually finished

SHOW *a show pony*
a pompous person

SHOW *a sideshow*
an unimportant adjunct

SHOW *the show must go on*
despite difficulties the action in contemplation has to proceed

SHOW *to bare one's teeth*
to imply threats

SHOW *to get the show on the road*
to commence a planned activity

SHOW *to give the show away*
to indiscreetly reveal sensitive information

SHOW *to show dividends*
to be successful

SHOW *to show one's face*
to put in an appearance

SHOW *to show one's true colors*
to disclose one's real character or beliefs

SHOW *to show someone the door*
to ask a person to leave

SHOW *to show someone the ropes*
to teach a beginner how to do something

SHOW *to show the flag*
to visit a place in order to boost morale there

SHOW *to show the white feather*
to indicate cowardice (refers to crossbred birds, not regarded as useful in cock fighting)

SHOW *to steal the show*
to have the maximum appeal to those watching

SHOWCASE *showcase*
magnificent

SHOWDOWN *showdown*
disclosure of certain pertinent facts

SHOWER *to have come down in the last shower*
to be naive

SHRED *to rip something to shreds*
to damage something severely

SHRIFT *to give someone short shrift*
to be impatient with a person (refers to the confession to a priest just before an execution)

SHRINK *a shrinking violet*
a shy person

SHRUG *to shrug one's shoulders*
to indicate that one does not know or care or that one is unable or unwilling to assist

SHRUG *to shrug something off*
to indicate that one is unable or unwilling to do something

SHUDDER *one shudders to think what the outcome might be*
there is great concern as to the outcome

SHUT *to be an open and shut case*
to be an unarguable proposition (a phrase popular in detective novels and probably a play on the two meanings of the word ''case'')

SHUT *to keep one's mouth shut*
not to discuss some matter

SHUT *to shut one's eyes to something*
to deliberately take no notice of something, especially in dereliction of one's duty

SHUT *to shut the door on someone*
to deny another person a desired opportunity

SHUT *to shut the stable door after the horse has bolted*
to take preventive action only after the relevant event

SHUT *to shut up shop*
to cease an established activity

SHUTTER *to put up the shutters*
to cease an established activity

SHYLOCK *a Shylock*
a hard-hearted creditor who insists on his legal due (from Shakespeare's MERCHANT OF VENICE)

SIDE *a broadside*
a short verbal attack

SIDE *on our side of the fence*
in the group representing our vested interest

SIDE *the bright side*
the favorable aspects

SIDE *the other side of the coin*
the arguments for the opposite point of view

SIDE *to be a thorn in someone's flesh*
to be a person whose persistent presence and righteous views annoy

SIDE *to be born on the wrong side of the blanket*
to be illegitimate

SIDE *to be on the other side of the fence*
to have an opposing point of view or position

SIDE *to be on the side of the angels*
to be on the side of righteousness (from a speech by Benjamin Disraeli)

SIDE *to feel the rough side of someone's tongue*
to be verbally abused by a person

SIDE *to get on someone's right side*
to make a good impression on a person

SIDE *to get out of bed on the wrong side*
to be grumpy

SIDE *to know on which side one's bread is buttered*
to be aware of the important considerations

SIDE *to look on the dark side*
to be pessimistic

SIDE *to split one's side*
to be convulsed with laughter

SIDE *you will laugh on the other side of your face*
you will regret this

SIDELIGHT *sidelight*
incidential happening

SIDELINE *to sit on the sidelines*
not to take part in the main action

SIDESHOW *a sideshow*
an unimportant adjunct

SIDEWAYS *to look at someone sideways*
to silently and politely indicate one's disapproval

SIEVE *to stop up one hole in a sieve*
to do something quite useless

SIFT *to sift*
to closely examine the evidence or a set of facts with a view to attaching different significance as appropriate to each of the various components

SIGH *to heave a sigh of relief*
to express satisfaction at the achievement of a solution to a difficult problem

SIGHT *to be a sight for sore eyes*
to be something welcome

SIGHT *to be shortsighted*
not to recognize the likely consequences

SIGHT *to lower one's sights*
to reduce one's ambition

SIGHT *to set one's sights on something*
to aim to achieve something

SIGHT *with 20/20 hindsight*
with the benefit of knowing what happened

SIGN *to sign on the dotted line*
to confirm one's agreement

SIGN *to sign one's own death warrant*
to foolishly do something which is inevitably bound to lead to utter disaster

SIGNAL *to send a smoke signal*
to give an indication

SIGNPOST *to signpost something*
to give an indication of the alternatives available

SILENCE *deafening silence*
great apathy and lack of enthusiasm

SILENCE *silence is golden*
it is better not to incriminate anyone

SILK *one can't make a silk purse out of a sow's ear*
it is impossible to manufacture something of a high standard without appropriate raw materials

SILLY *the silly season*
the holiday period, when hard news is scarce and journalistic standards are lowered

SILVER *every cloud has a silver lining*
there are benefits even in seemingly adverse situations

SILVER *to be born with a silver spoon in one's mouth*
to be brought up by wealthy parents

SILVER *to hand over something on a silver platter*
to provide a valuable benefit for virtually nothing

SILVER *to have a silver tongue*
to be eloquent

SILVER *to sell off the family silver*
to sell off one's prized possessions

SIMON *a simple Simon*
a foolish, gullible or half-witted person

SIMPLE *a simple Simon*
a foolish, gullible or half-witted person

SIN *for one's sins*
by way of punishment, as it were

SING *it's not over till the fat lady sings*
it is not finished yet

SING *to all sing from the same hymnal*
to act consistently with each other

SING *to sing a particular song*
to state particular views

SING *to sing for one's supper*
to carry out a task in order to receive a favor in return

SING *to sing someone's praises*
to commend a person exuberantly

SINGLE *single-handedly*
without help from other persons

SINK *a case of rats leaving a sinking ship*
the desertion of an enterprise in anticipation of imminent failure

SINK *enough to sink a battleship*
more than sufficient

SINK *everything but the kitchen sink*
a lot of things

SINK *it is a case of sink or swim*
the attempt is worthwhile, despite the risk of failure

SINK *one's heart sank*
one realized the extent of some disaster

SINK *to sink deeper into the mire*
to get into further difficulties

SINK *to sink deeper into the mud*
to get into even greater difficulty

SINK *to sink slowly in the west*
to fail gradually

SINK *to sink without a trace*
to disappear completely

SINK *with a sinking heart*
with growing despondency

SINKER *hook, line and sinker*
wholly

SIT *to be a sitting duck*
to be readily exploited

SIT *to be a sitting shot*
to be a person whose actions make him very vulnerable to criticism

SIT *to sit on one's hands*
deliberately to do nothing

SIT *to sit on someone*
to repress a person

SIT *to sit on the fence*
to refuse to choose between two alternatives

SIT *to sit on the sidelines*
not to take part in the main action

SIT *to sit pretty*
to be comfortably off

SIT *to sit tight*
obstinately to do nothing

SITE *a siting shot*
an initial move which is designed to establish facts for use in a later action

SIX *it is six of one and half a dozen of the other*
it does not matter

SIX *to be at sixes and sevens*
to be confused, concerned and undecided

SIX *to be six feet under*
to be dead

SIX *to hit someone for six*
to damage a person's cause

SIX *to throw in one's six pennies' worth*
to modestly supply one's own facts or views

SIXTH *a sixth sense*
intuition (refers to the five senses—sight, hearing, smell, taste and touch)

SIXTY-FOUR *a sixty-four thousand dollar question*
a pertinent but very difficult question (refers to a TV quiz show in which an initial prize doubles with the successful answering of progressively more difficult questions)

SIZE *to cut tall poppies down to size*
to humiliate haughty persons

SIZE *to try something on for size*
to cheekily do something

SKATE *to get one's skates on*
to hurry up

SKATE *to skate around some subject*
by diversionary tactics to avoid discussing some subject

SKATE *to skate on thin ice*
to act in disregard of obvious danger

SKELETON *a skeleton in the cupboard*
an unpleasant truth the knowledge of which has been deliberately suppressed

SKELETON *to flesh out the skeleton*
to supply the missing pertinent details

SKETCH *a thumbnail sketch*
brief but pertinent details

SKID *to be on skid row*
to have no means

SKID *to put the skids under someone*
to ruin a person

SKIN *a cleanskin*
a person without a criminal record

SKIN *there is more than one way to skin a cat*
this can achieved in a variety of acceptable ways

SKIN *to be no skin off someone's nose*
not to matter to a person

SKIN *to escape by the skin of one's nose*
to only just avoid some disaster

SKIN *to escape by the skin of one's teeth*
to only just avoid some disaster

SKIN *to get under someone's skin*
to annoy another person through stupidity

SKIN *to hang on by the skin of one's teeth*
to only just survive

SKIN *to have a thick skin*
to be impervious to criticism

SKIN *to nearly jump out of one's skin*
to receive a fright

SKIN *to save one's skin*
to get off safely

SKIP *something is but a hop, skip and jump away*
something is nearby

SKIRT *to hide under someone's skirts*
to let someone else take the consequences of one's actions

SKIRT *to skirt around the difficulties*
to act as though the difficulties did not exist

SKITTLES *not to be all beer and skittles*
not to be all pleasant and easy

SKULL *to penetrate someone's thick skull*
to make a person understand something difficult or acknowledge something unwelcome

SKY *a light in the sky*
a sign of great hope

SKY *blue sky*
supremely optimistic

SKY *pie in the sky*
a hoped for result unlikely to be achieved

SKY *the sky fell in*
a very serious problem arose

SKY *the sky is the limit*
the cost is no obstacle

SKYROCKET *to skyrocket*
(of a price or value) to increase greatly in a short time

SLACK *to take up the slack*
to take advantage of surplus capacity

SLAM *to slam the door in someone's face*
ostentatiously to refuse to have any dealings with a person

SLAP *a slap in the face*
a calculated insult or action amounting to a rebuke

SLAP *a slap on the wrist*
a mild rebuke

SLATE *to wipe the slate clean*
to forgive past indiscretions

SLATHER *open slather*
freedom for people to do what they want

SLAUGHTER *a lamb led to slaughter*
a naive person allowing himself to be exploited

SLEDGEHAMMER *to use a sledgehammer to crack a nut*
to devote vastly more resources to a project than is warranted by all the circumstances

SLEEP *not to lose any sleep over something*
not to worry about some matter

SLEEP *to go to sleep*
to become inactive

SLEEP *to let sleeping dogs lie*
to refrain from raising an issue which is not obviously requiring attention

SLEEP *to sleep on one's rights*
to fail to exercise some entitlement within a reasonable period

SLEEP *to spend a sleepless night*
to worry about something

SLEEVE *to have a card up one's sleeve*
to secretly have information relevant to a transaction

SLEEVE *to have an ace up one's sleeve*
to hold an impressive counter-argument in reserve

SLEEVE *to keep something up one's sleeve*
to secretly retain something in reserve for use in the future or at a later stage of negotiations

SLEEVE *to laugh up one's sleeve*
to laugh surreptitiously

SLEEVE *to roll up one's sleeves*
to get on with a job energetically

SLEEVE *to wear one's heart on one's sleeve*
to lack the reserve expected of one

SLEIGHT *sleight of hand*
deceit by trickery

SLENDER *to hang by a slender thread*
to only just survive

SLICE *to claim that something is the best thing since sliced bread*
to have an exaggerated opinion of the importance or novelty of an invention or practice

SLICE *to have a piece of the action*
to be one of several parties to a project

SLIDE *to be on a slippery shoot*
to court disaster

SLING *to sling mud*
to make unfair imputations

SLIP *a slip of the tongue*
incorrect words uttered accidentally

SLIP *to be slipping*
to be losing one's cunning or expertise

SLIP *to let something slip through one's fingers*
to allow something to escape from one's ownership or control

SLIP *to slip one's mind*
to be overlooked or forgotten

SLIP *to slip through the net*
to happen as an isolated case despite steps taken to prevent such events

SLIP *to slip under one's guard*
to cause a mistake to be made despite care being taken to prevent this

SLIPPERY *a slippery customer*
a shifty person

SLIPPERY *slippery path*
dangerous course of action

SLIPPERY *to be on a slippery shoot*
to court disaster

SLOUGH *a slough of despond*
a feeling of hopelessness

SLOW *to be slow off the mark*
to be slow to start something

SLOWLY *to slowly bleed to death*
to be heading in gradual steps toward total ruin

SLUG *to slug it out*
to engage in a minor skirmish

SLY *a sly dog*
a person who is discreet about his weaknesses

SMACK *a smack in the eye*
a rebuff

SMALL *it's a small world*
it is surprising to meet people one knows in unexpected places

SMALL *to be a small cog in a large wheel*
to be a relatively unimportant person in a large organization

SMALL *to be small beer*
to be quite unimportant

SMALL *to be small potatoes*
to be quite unimportant

SMART *to be a smart Alec*
to give witty but cheeky responses to one's superiors or customers

SMELL *a rose by any other name would smell as sweet*
the form does not affect the substance (from Shakespeare's ROMEO AND JULIET)

SMELL *something smells*
something is suspicious

SMELL *to come up smelling like a rose*
not to have a stain on one's character

SMELL *to run something on the smell of an oil rag*
to run something very economically and efficiently

SMELL *to smell a rat*
to become suspicious

SMELL *to smell blood*
to divine imminent victory

SMELL *to smell out something*
to discover something by careful investigation

SMELL *to smell trouble*
to perceive difficulties

SMILE *to wipe the smile off someone's face*
to destroy a person's complacency

SMILE *wipe that smile off your face!*
treat this matter more seriously!

SMOKE *put that in your pipe and smoke it*
contemplate that fact

SMOKE *the big smoke*
the big city

SMOKE *to go up in smoke*
to come to nothing

SMOKE *to send a smoke signal*
to give an indication

SMOKE *to set up a smokescreen*
to deliberately confuse an issue by disguising its salient features

SMOKE *when the smoke clears*
when sufficient time has passed

SMOKE *where there is smoke there is fire*
if there is a hint of trouble, then it is highly likely that there really is trouble

SMOOTH *to be in smooth water*
to have no troubles

SMOOTH *to smooth the path for someone*
to use one's influence to make arrangements so that a person's task will be easier or more readily accomplished

SMOOTH *to take the rough with the smooth*
to accept the hardships of life along with its pleasant features

SMORGASBORD *smorgasbord*
a series of different items from which a number can be chosen (from the Swedish words for "butter," "goose" and "table")

SNAG *to strike a snag*
to encounter a difficulty

SNAIL *at a snail's pace*
very slowly

SNAKE *a game of snakes and ladders*
a series of ups and downs

SNAKE *a snake in the grass*
a person of low character

SNAP *to snap at someone's heels*
to be a minor irritation to a person

SNAP *to snap someone's head off*
to speak to a person aggressively

SNEEZE *that is not to be sneezed at*
that is so significant that it should not be rejected

SNOW *to snow someone under*
to overload a person with work

SNOWBALL *to snowball*
to grow rapidly in size or influence

SNOWFLAKE *to have a snowflake's chance in hell*
to have no hope or possibility at all

SOAP *a soap opera*
a radio or television serial, often based on exaggerated domestic situations of no great importance (refers to sponsorship by soap manufacturers)

SOAP *to be on one's soap box*
to hold forth on an issue about which one feels keenly

SOAP *to soft-soap someone*
to flatter a person

SOCK *to chop someone off at the socks*
to stop someone's proposals prematurely

SOCK *to pull one's socks up*
to set out to improve or correct one's inadequate behavior or performance

SODOM *a Sodom and Gomorrah*
a place of vice (Genesis 18:20)

SOFT *to have a soft spot for someone*
to be very fond of a person

SOFT *to have a soft underbelly*
to have a weakness which can be exploited

SOFT *to soft-pedal*
to restrain oneself

SOFT *to soft-soap someone*
to flatter a person

SOFTEN *to soften someone up*
to make a person more favorably disposed to one's wishes

SOFTEN *to soften the blow*
to take action to reduce the trauma of bad news

SOFTLY *speak softly and carry a big stick*
be polite to your potential enemies but maintain an active and visible defense capability (from a speech by Theodore Roosevelt in 1901)

SOLDIER *to be a brave soldier*
to be brave

SOLDIER *to soldier on*
to carry on despite difficulties

SOLOMON *to need the wisdom of Solomon*
to be faced with the need to make a difficult decision (1 Kings 3:16-28)

SOMERSAULT *to turn a complete somersault*
to reverse one's established policy

SON *favorite son*
person preferred by many people for some office

SONG *nothing to make a song or dance about*
unexciting or unimportant

SONG *swan song*
last appearance before retirement

SONG *to buy something for a song*
to buy something very cheaply

SONG *to make a song and dance about something*
to create a fuss

SONG *to sing a particular song*
to state particular views

SOOTHE *soothing syrup*
insincere expressions of sympathy or flattery

SORE *eyesore*
extremely ugly object

SORE *to be a sight for sore eyes*
to be something welcome

SORE *to open up a festering sore*
to upset a person by drawing attention to a long-standing grievance

SORROW *to drown one's sorrows*
to drink by way of solace and in an attempt to forget some misfortune

SOUL *a soul brother*
a person of similar ideals

SOUL *a soul-searching exercise*
an examination of the advantages and disadvantages of a proposal

SOUL *heart and soul*
with great energy

SOUL *soul-destroying*
extremely boring and demotivating

SOUL *to bare one's soul*
talkatively to give a revealing insight into oneself

SOUL *to be the life and soul of the party*
to be the prime enthusiast for a cause

SOUL *to keep body and soul together*
to keep alive

SOUND *to sound alarm bells*
to give warning

SOUND *to sound the death knell of something*
to indicate the impending end of something

SOUNDING *to act as a sounding board*
to give, on request, constructive criticisms of ideas tentatively held

SOUNDING *to take a sounding*
to ascertain people's views

SOUP *to be in the soup*
to be in great difficulties

SOUR *that is just sour grapes*
those are disparaging remarks made only because he is peeved and resentful at someone else's better fortune

SOUR *to hit a sour note*
to discover an unexpected flaw in an otherwise satisfactory piece of work

SOUR *to turn sour*
to become impracticable or unprofitable

SOUTH *a South Sea bubble*
an unrealistic financial venture which is bound to result in total loss

SOW *one can't make a silk purse out of a sow's ear*
it is impossible to manufacture something of a high standard without appropriate raw materials

SOW *to get the wrong sow by the ear*
to reach an incorrect conclusion

SOW *to reap as one has sown*
to experience the consequences of one's own actions

SOW *to sow seeds*
to propagate ideas in the hope that they will be adopted

SOW *to sow the wind and reap the whirlwind*
to make bad mistakes and to suffer the even worse consequences

SOW *to sow wild oats*
to indulge in foolish behavior while a young adult

SPACE *to get some breathing space*
to get more time in which to accomplish something

SPADE *to call a spade a spade*
not to mince words

SPADE *to do the spadework*
to prepare

SPAIN *a castle in Spain*
an impracticable proposition

SPANNER *to throw a spanner into the works*
to cause an unexpected complication

SPARE *to carry a spare tire*
to be fat

SPARK *to make sparks fly*
to cause rapid activity to take place

SPARK *to spark on all cylinders*
to work extremely well

SPARTAN *Spartan*
tough and efficient, with a complete absence of the finer things of life

SPEAK *speak softly and carry a big stick*
be polite to your potential enemies but maintain an active and visible defense capability (from a speech by Theodore Roosevelt in 1901)

SPEAK *speak of the devil*
here is the person we were just discussing

SPEAK *to speak one's mind*
to express one's views frankly and forcefully

SPEAK *to speak the same language*
to have a good understanding and similar ideas

SPEAK *to speak volumes for something*
to place something in a favorable light

SPEARHEAD *to spearhead something*
to lead a movement

SPECTACLES *to see something through rose-colored spectacles*
to appreciate only the advantages and to completely disregard the disadvantages

SPECTER *to raise the specter of something*
to draw attention to a worrying expectation of something

SPECTRUM *spectrum*
wide range of different opinions or backgrounds

SPEED *speed the plow!*
let us get on with this as fast as possible!

SPELL *to break the spell*
to spoil the effect

SPELL *to have a spell in the paddock*
to have leave of absence

SPELL *to spell something out*
to explain something in detail

SPELLBINDING *spellbinding*
fascinating to an audience

SPEND *to spend a sleepless night*
to worry about something

SPIDER *to be the center of the spider's web*
to control an operation which involves numerous and/or complex ingredients

SPIKE *to spike someone's guns*
to cause something to become useless

SPILL *it is no use crying over spilt milk*
lamenting over a disaster achieves nothing

SPILL *to spill the beans*
to indiscreetly reveal sensitive information

SPIN *tailspin*
very fast fall

SPIN *to be a money spinner*
to produce large profits easily and quickly

SPIN *to be in a flat spin*
to be in a state of high excitement

SPIN *to spin a yarn*
to tell an amusing or unlikely story

SPIN *to spin something out*
to prolong some matter

SPINE *to send a cold shiver down someone's spine*
to horrify a person

SPIRIT *kindred spirit*
persons with similar interests and eccentricities

SPIRIT *the spirit is willing but the flesh is weak*
the body is not up to the demands made on it

SPIT *spit it out!*
unburden yourself!

SPITE *to cut one's nose off to spite one's face*
to act in pique in a way which harms only oneself

SPLASH *to make a splash*
to create a sensation

SPLEEN *to vent one's spleen on someone*
to demonstrate one's ill temper to a person

SPLICE *to splice the main brace*
to serve an extra ration of rum

SPLIT *to split hairs*
to draw absurdly fine distinctions

SPLIT *to split one's side*
to be convulsed with laughter

SPOIL *to spoil the ship for a ha'p'orth of tar*
to engage in a false economy (the current word ''ship'' is actually a mistake for the original word ''sheep'' and the tar refers to the treatment of wounds)

SPOIL *too many cooks spoil the broth*
one leader is all that is required

SPOKE *to put a spoke in someone's wheel*
to interfere with another person's activity, so preventing its continuance

SPONGE *to throw up the sponge*
to concede defeat

SPOON *he must have a long spoon that sups with the devil*
great care is needed when negotiating deals with disreputable parties

SPOON *to be born with a silver spoon in one's mouth*
to be brought up by wealthy parents

SPOON *to get the wooden spoon*
to come in gloriously last

SPOT *a leopard cannot change his spots*
each person is born with certain unalterable characteristics

SPOT *the one bright spot on the horizon*
the only hopeful aspect

SPOT *to be a tender spot*
to be a subject on which a person is touchy

SPOT *to have a blind spot about something*
to fail to recognize the adverse aspects of something

SPOT *to have a soft spot for someone*
to be very fond of a person

SPOT *to put someone on the spot*
to embarrass a person

SPOTLIGHT *to steal the spotlight*
to set out to be the center of attention

SPOTLIGHT *to turn the spotlight on something*
to draw public attention to something

SPRAT *to throw a sprat to catch a mackerel*
to risk a little in the hope of gaining much

SPREAD *to spread one's wings*
to assert authority which has not yet been conferred by one's superiors and for which one may not be ready

SPREAD *to spread oneself thin*
to attempt to do more than is feasible in the available time

SPREAD *to spread the net more widely*
to become more comprehensive

SPRING *a spring cleaning*
a thorough review occurring a long time after the previous one

SPRING *to spring to mind*
to suddenly occur to a person

SPRINGBOARD *a springboard*
a situation from which one intends to make a rapid advance

SPUR *to spur someone on*
to agitate a person into doing something

SPUR *to win one's spurs*
to gain recognition after a period of effort (refers to the earning of a knighthood in battle)

SQUARE *a square peg in a round hole*
a person much more suitable for a position rather different from the one held

SQUARE *four square*
honest and reliable

SQUARE *to go back to square one*
to start all over again

SQUARE *to try to square the circle*
to attempt the impossible (refers to a classical problem in geometry, namely, to construct with a compass a square of the same area as a given circle)

SQUEAKY *the squeaky wheel gets the most attention*
those complaining the most loudly will get their problems sorted out first

SQUEEZE *to squeeze someone out*
to force a person to leave

SQUEEZE *to squeeze the last drop out of something*
to get the maximum advantage out of some favorable situation

SQUIB *a damp squib*
disappointingly ineffective action (refers to fireworks which fail to go off)

STAB *a stab in the dark*
a sheer guess

STAB *to stab someone in the back*
to deliberately and surreptitiously harm a person who regarded one as a friend

STABLE *a Herculean cleaning of the stables*
a thorough revision of operating procedure (refers to Hercules, a mythical Greek hero who cleaned the stables of Augeas)

STABLE *to shut the stable door after the horse has bolted*
to take preventive action only after the relevant event

STACK *to have the cards stacked against one*
to be faced with many difficulties frustrating a project

STACK *to have the odds stacked against one*
to be faced with many difficulties frustrating a project

STAGE *the stage is set*
something is about to happen

STAGE *to be center stage*
to have everyone's attention

STAGE *to be on a world stage*
to be prominent in international affairs

STAGE *to stage-manage something*
to arrange how something happens

STAGE *to upstage someone*
to deprive another person of the glory which he would otherwise have enjoyed

STAGING *a staging post*
a place where action is initiated

STAKE *to raise the stake*
to increase the amount of potential gain or loss in a project

STAKE *to stake a claim*
to indicate one's desire to obtain something

STALEMATE *stalemate*
a final result in which neither party to a dispute is victorious

STALK *a stalking horse*
an ostensible reason

STAMP *only a postage stamp between them*
virtually equal or close together

STAMP *to put one's own stamp on something*
to affect something with one's own characteristic style

STAMP *to rubber-stamp something*
to endorse without considering the merits

STAMPEDE *to stampede someone into something*
to pressure a person into taking some action

STAND *if one can't stand the heat one should stay out of the kitchen*
a person should not put himself in a position involving pressures with which he cannot cope (words attributed to Harry S. Truman)

STAND *not to have a leg to stand on*
to have one's arguments completely demolished or to be without acceptable excuse or explanation

STAND *to be able to do something standing on one's head*
to be able to do something very easily

STAND *to know where one stands*
to know what one supports or how one is affected

STAND *to make a last-ditch stand*
to make a brave effort to stave off final defeat

STAND *to make someone's hair stand on end*
to give a person shocking news

STAND *to stand in someone's way*
to prevent a person achieving his goal

STAND *to stand in the breach*
to bear the brunt of criticisms

STAND *to stand on one's own two feet*
not to require the help of others

STAND *to stand on someone's shoulders*
to build upon another person's ideas

STAND *to stand one's ground*
to maintain a stance in the face of opposition

STAND *to stand out from the crowd*
to be noticeably better than one's competitors

STAND *to stand over someone with a big stick*
to intimidate a person in order to get him to act in a particular way

STAND *to stand up and be counted*
to publicly announce one's position on some issue

STAND *to stand up on one's hind legs*
to exert one's authority

STANDARD *a standard bearer*
a highly visible activist for a cause

STANDOFF *a Mexican standoff*
a situation where neither of two parties is making a move

STANDSTILL *a standstill*
an inability to proceed

STAR *one can thank one's lucky stars*
one was extremely fortunate

STAR *rising star*
person making good progress in his career

STAR *to have stars in one's eyes*
(for emotional rather than rational reasons) to be ecstatic

STAR *to shoot for the stars*
to be unrealistic

STARE *to stare someone in the face*
(of a solution, etc.) to become obvious

START *to have a head start*
to have an advantage over others

START *to start from behind scratch*
to be faced with a handicap

START *to start from scratch*
to commence something without the benefit of any past activity

START *to start the ball rolling*
to commence and enthusiastically advance an activity involving people

START *to start with a blank sheet of paper*
to commence an exercise without being bound by any established practices

STATE *to be in a state of flux*
to be subject to continuous change

STATE *to find out the state of play*
to ascertain the current position of some project

STAY *if one can't stand the heat one should stay out of the kitchen*
a person should not put himself in a position involving pressure with which he cannot cope (words attributed to Harry S. Truman)

STAY *to stay tuned*
to keep in touch for further information as it becomes available

STEAL *to steal a march on someone*
to anticipate another person's actions and get in ahead

STEAL *to steal someone's clothes*
to plagiarize another person's ideas

STEAL *to steal someone's heart*
to cause a person to fall in love with one

STEAL *to steal someone's thunder*
to take credit for another person's good work (refers to a dispute over the copying of a machine invented by a 17th-century dramatist to reproduce the sound of thunder during a play)

STEAL *to steal the show*
to have the maximum appeal to those watching

STEAL *to steal the spotlight*
to set out to be the center of attention

STEAM *full steam ahead!*
get going as fast as possible!

STEAM *to develop a head of steam*
to gain momentum

STEAM *to let off steam*
to engage in noisy or robust activity as a form of relaxation

STEAM *to lose steam*
to slow down

STEAM *to run out of steam*
to lose one's energy and enthusiasm

STEAM *under one's own steam*
without external help

STEAMROLL *to steamroll something through*
to use enormous force to achieve an objective

STEEL *to be a man of steel*
to be a person with moral courage

STEEL *to have nerves of steel*
not to be easily frightened

STEEL *to steel one's heart against something*
to determine that, notwithstanding one's natural compassion, something shall not happen

STEM *to stem the hemorrhage*
to put a stop to the financial losses of a project

STEM *to stem the tide*
to make progress against something

STEP *a step in the right direction*
the first in a series of measures designed to correct some problem

STEP *a stepping stone*
a means to an end

STEP *by small steps*
gradually

STEP *step by step*
gradually

STEP *to follow in someone's footsteps*
to do as another person did

STEP *to get in step with someone*
to do as another person does

STEP *to overstep the mark*
to fail to observe the proprieties

STEP *to step down*
to retire from some position

STEP *to step into the ring*
to enter a competitive environment

STEP *to step out of line*
to infringe accepted rules of behavior

STEP *to take a giant step forward*
to make a significant advance

STEP *to take a step backward*
to move farther away from one's goal

STEP *to step on someone's corns*
to upset another person by interfering in his area of responsibility

STEP *to step on someone's toes*
to upset another person by interfering in his area of responsibility

STEP *to watch one's step*
to be on the lookout for danger or to set out to improve one's behavior

STEW *to be in a stew*
to be in difficulties

STEW *to stew in one's juice*
to suffer the adverse consequences of one's acts or omissions

STICK *a cobbler should stick to his last*
every person should confine himself to activities for which he has been trained

STICK *a stick-in-the-mud*
an unenterprising person

STICK *any stick to beat a dog*
any excuse will do if it serves one's purpose

STICK *it sticks in my throat*
I find it galling

STICK *not to have the wherewithal to rub two sticks together*
to be very poor

STICK *some mud will stick*
reputations will be hurt even after accusations are proved false

STICK *speak softly and carry a big stick*
be polite to your potential enemies but maintain an active and visible defense capability (from a speech by Theodore Roosevelt in 1901)

STICK *sticks and carrots*
disincentives and incentives in combination (refers to the handling of donkeys)

STICK *the words stuck in my throat*
I just could not get myself to say the intended words

STICK *to be a good old stick*
to be a kind and thoughtful person

STICK *to be better than a poke in the eye with a burnt stick*
to be particularly welcome

STICK *to be in a cleft stick*
to be in a dilemma

STICK *to be more than one can poke a stick at*
to be more than can reasonably be handled

STICK *to be on the losing end of the stick*
to be worse off while the other party to a transaction becomes correspondingly better off

STICK *to be unable to keep people away with a big stick*
to be faced with a large crowd or much demand

STICK *to get stuck into some problem*
to attempt to solve a problem with great vigor

STICK *to get stuck into someone*
to castigate a person

STICK *to give someone a bit of stick*
to mildly criticize a person

STICK *to hold the wrong end of the stick*
to be completely mistaken about something

STICK *to stand over someone with a big stick*
to intimidate a person in order to get him to act in a particular way

STICK *to stick a knife into someone*
to act vindictively toward a person

STICK *to stick one's neck out*
to have the courage of one's convictions or to take a calculated risk

STICK *to stick out a mile*
to be very apparent

STICK *to stick to one's game*
to confine oneself to activities in areas in which one has knowledge and expertise

STICK *to stick to one's guns*
to continue to hold certain beliefs notwithstanding opposition by others

STICK *to wield a big stick*
to exert power

STICKY *a sticky patch*
a period fraught with difficulties

STICKY *to be a sticky beak*
to show excessive curiosity into matters not of one's concern

STICKY *to be on a sticky wicket*
to face some difficulties

STICKY *to come to a sticky end*
to endure an unpleasant fate

STICKY *to have sticky fingers*
to be dishonest

STIFF *a stiff upper lip*
obstinate courage in the face of pain or adversity

STIFF *stiff cheese!*
circumstances which may be unwelcome but which will not be altered and in respect of which no great sympathy is felt

STILL *still waters run deep*
a person with a quiet manner may have a surprisingly great knowledge of a subject

STING *to be the sting in the tail*
to be the unexpected unpleasant conclusion

STIR *to stir a finger*
to make some minimum effort

STIR *to stir a hand*
to volunteer assistance

STIR *to stir the possum*
to set out to raise controversial issues

STIR *to stir the pot*
to set out to raise controversial issues

STIR *to stir up a hornet's nest*
to take action which results in unpleasant side-effects

STITCH *a stitch in time saves nine*
preventive maintenance saves money in the long run

STITCH *to have someone in stitches*
to greatly amuse a person

STITCH *to stitch up a deal*
to successfully conclude a deal

STOCK *lock, stock and barrel*
entirely

STOCK *to be a blue-chip stock*
to be of excellent quality

STOCK *to take stock*
to contemplate the alternatives

STOKE *to stoke the fires*
to provoke a violent reaction

STOMACH *someone's eyes are bigger than his stomach*
a person is unrealistic

STOMACH *to have butterflies in one's stomach*
a feeling of anxiety

STOMACH *to have no stomach for something*
to have no taste or fortitude for something

STONE *a milestone*
an achievement

STONE *a stepping stone*
a means to an end

STONE *cornerstone*
key ingredient

STONE *people in glass houses should not throw stones*
those who are less than perfect are foolish to criticize others

STONE *the touchstone*
the standard

STONE *to draw blood from a stone*
to do the impossible

STONE *to have a heart of stone*
to be unfeeling

STONE *to kill some proposal stone dead*
to abandon some proposal completely

STONE *to kill two birds with one stone*
to achieve a second objective in the course of achieving the first objective

STONE *to leave no stone unturned*
to be very thorough

STONE *within a stone's throw*
very close

STONEWALLING *stonewalling*
deliberate obstruction or delaying tactics

STOOL *to fall between two stools*
not to fit neatly into either of two available alternatives and waver between them

STOP *a whistlestop tour*
a hurried (especially ceremonial) visit to many places

STOP *heart-stopping*
exciting

STOP *the buck stops here*
I accept full responsibility (sign on the desk of Harry S. Truman when president of the United States)

STOP *to be stopped in one's tracks*
suddenly and unexpectedly to be prevented from carrying on with a project

STOP *to come to a full stop*
to completely cease activity

STOP *to pull out all stops*
to make maximum effort

STOP *to stop up one hole in a sieve*
to do something quite useless

STOP *when the music stops*
suddenly and soon (refers to an imminent crisis leading to some resolution of a matter, as in a game of musical chairs)

STORAGE *to put something into cold storage*
to put something aside for dealing with at some indeterminate future time

STORE *to take over the store*
to assume the management

STORM *any port in a storm*
anything which helps to avoid difficulties is welcome

STORM *the calm before the storm*
the quiet period before an expected or inevitable crisis

STORM *there are black clouds on the horizon*
bad news is expected

STORM *to barnstorm*
to visit accompanied by a show of force

STORM *to be in the eye of the storm*
to be at the center of a controversy

STORM *to brainstorm*
to pool thoughts in the course of a session designed to generate fresh ideas and especially to build upon the ideas of others

STORM *to create a storm*
to kick up a fuss

STORM *to ride out the storm*
to come safely through some dangerous situation

STORM *to run into a firestorm*
to be faced with many protests

STORM *to take someone by storm*
to captivate an audience

STORM *to weather the storm*
to come safely through a crisis

STORMY *to be a stormy petrel*
a person who disturbs a pleasant state of affairs by agitating for change

STORY *a cock and bull story*
an explanation which is completely unbelievable and unacceptable

STORY *a tall story*
an interesting but untrue and unbelievable tale

STRAIGHT *a straight face*
a facial expression which does not reveal one's thoughts in a humorous situation

STRAIGHT *a straight shooter*
a person who is frank and outspoken

STRAIGHT *straight from the shoulder*
bluntly

STRAIGHT *to be on the straight and narrow*
to be completely honest

STRAIGHT *to jump straight in at the deep end*
to do something without a proper lead in

STRAIGHT *to maintain a straight bat*
to be efficient

STRAIN *to strain at a gnat*
to be scrupulous about trifles

STRAIT *in dire straits*
in great need

STRAIT *strait-laced*
puritanical

STRAIT *to keep someone in a straitjacket*
to deny a person any discretionary powers at all

STRANGLE *to strangle some discussion*
to cut off some unfinished discussion

STRANGLEHOLD *a stranglehold*
a firm grip on a commercial situation, effectively freezing out a competitor

STRAP *to hit the straps*
to really get going

STRAW *one can't make bricks without straw*
one cannot achieve results in the absence of adequate resources

STRAW *straws in the wind*
unofficial preliminary indications of something likely to be formally revealed soon

STRAW *the final straw*
the latest step, which, when added to a large number of seemingly harmless previous steps, sets off a disaster resulting from the cumulative effect

STRAW *the straw which broke the camel's back*
the latest step, which, when added to a large number of seemingly harmless previous steps, sets off a disaster resulting from the cumulative effect

STRAW *to be a man of straw*
to have no assets while giving a contrary appearance

STRAW *to buy straw hats in winter*
to buy in a depressed market when most other people are sellers

STRAW *to clasp at straws*
to have a hopeless case but show unjustified optimism on noting minor positive features

STRAW *to draw the short straw*
to be the one appointed to do something

STREAM *mainstream*
orthodox

STREAM *to get on stream*
to now operate successfully following the end of a settling-in period

STREAM *to swap horses in midstream*
to change direction during the course of a project

STREET *a one-way street*
a flow of activity in only one direction

STREET *not to be in the same street as someone*
not to be of comparable quality

STREET *the man in the street*
the average citizen

STREET *there is blood in the streets*
much damage has been done to a cause

STREET *to be in Queer Street*
to be in debt

STREET *to be streets ahead*
to outperform one's competitors by a wide margin

STREET *to be up one's alley*
to be right within a person's expertise or area of interest

STREET *to walk in off the street*
to come without prior arrangement or notification

STRENGTH *to be a tower of strength*
to be a person who supports and comforts another

STRENGTHEN *to strengthen someone's hand*
to give a person additional authority or greater moral support or more facts to support his case

STRETCH *to enter the home stretch*
to commence the last stage

STREW *to be on a path strewn with roses*
to lead a very pleasant life

STRICTLY *that is strictly for the birds*
that is blatant and naive nonsense

STRIDE *to hit one's stride*
to settle down to some task

STRIDE *to take something in one's stride*
to cope with something easily

STRIKE *it strikes me*
it occurs to me

STRIKE *to be thunderstruck*
to be amazed

STRIKE *to be within striking distance*
to be fairly close

STRIKE *to strike a blow*
to resume work

STRIKE *to strike a blow for some principle*
to work toward the attainment of some principle

STRIKE *to strike a chord*
to sound familiar or recall something to mind

STRIKE *to strike a responsive chord*
to get a favorable reaction to a proposal

STRIKE *to strike a snag*
to encounter a difficulty

STRIKE *to strike at the roots of something*
to work toward the destruction of something

STRIKE *to strike gold*
to have one's efforts suddenly rewarded by great success

STRIKE *to strike pay dirt*
to become successful

STRIKE *to strike the right chord*
to appeal successfully to someone's emotions

STRIKE *to strike the right key*
to find the appropriate solution

STRIKE *to strike the right note*
to make a good impression

STRIKE *to strike while the iron is hot*
to take advantage of a situation which cannot last

STRING *to be tied to someone's apron strings*
to be excessively influenced by a female

STRING *to have a second string to one's bow*
to have an additional qualification appropriate to the task

STRING *to have strings attached*
to be subject to conditions

STRING *to hold the purse strings*
to have control of expenditures

STRING *to pull at one's heart strings*
to affect one emotionally

STRING *to pull strings*
to use one's special influence with those in a position to make favorable decisions which might otherwise not be forthcoming

STRING *to tighten the purse strings*
to reduce outlays

STRIPE *to earn one's stripes*
to deserve promotion

STROKE *a master stroke*
particularly brilliant action

STROKE *with a stroke of the pen*
by edict

STUFF *to be hot stuff*
to be skillful or very passionate

STUFFING *to knock the stuffing out of someone*
to completely demoralize a person

STUMBLE *stumbling block*
an impediment or difficulty preventing the easy completion of some project or a dilemma involving a moral issue

STUMPS *until stumps are drawn*
until the project ends (refers to cricket)

SUCK *suck it and see*
discover experimentally how something works

SUCK *to suck someone in*
to embroil an innocent party in an unethical enterprise

SUCK *to suck the lemon dry*
to get the maximum advantage out of some favorable situation

SUCK *to teach one's grandmother how to suck eggs*
to try to tell a much more experienced person something very obvious to him

SUDDEN *sudden death*
instantaneously or without phasing in

SUGAR *to sugar the pill*
to cause something to be more acceptable

SUIT *one's long suit*
one's main skills

SUIT *to follow suit*
to do the same as others

SUMMER *one swallow does not make a summer*
much further evidence is desirable before any action taken

SUN *a place in the sun*
a favorable situation

SUN *everything under the sun*
everything

SUN *the sun has set on something*
something has concluded

SUN *to make hay while the sun shines*
to utilize an opportunity before it disappears

SUP *he must have a long spoon that sups with the devil*
great care is needed when negotiating deals with disreputable parties

SUPPER *to sing for one's supper*
to carry out a task in order to receive a favor in return

SURE *sure-fire*
guaranteed

SURFACE *on the surface*
on the basis of a superficial first impression

SURFACE *to only scratch the surface*
to deal with only a small portion of a much larger whole

SWALLOW *one swallow does not make a summer*
much further evidence is desirable before any action taken

SWALLOW *someone has swallowed a dictionary*
a person uses excessively long words

SWALLOW *to be a bitter pill to swallow*
to be a great humiliation and disappointment which have to be endured

SWALLOW *to be hard to swallow*
not to be readily acceptable

SWALLOW *to swallow one's pride*
to take action despite the humiliating nature of this course

SWALLOW *to swallow the bait*
to succumb to a temptation deliberately put in one's way

SWALLOW *to swallow the line*
to accept as truth the story being proffered

SWAMP *to swamp someone*
to overload a person

SWAN *swan song*
last appearance before retirement

SWAP *to swap horses in midstream*
to change direction during the course of a project

SWARM *to swarm out*
to gather in large numbers

SWEAT *blood, sweat and tears*
hard work and much effort

SWEAT *no sweat*
this presents no difficulty

SWEAT *to be in a cold sweat*
to be afraid

SWEAT *to sweat it out*
to await one's fate calmly

SWEEP *a clean sweep*
the complete removal in an election of all sitting members

SWEEP *to sweep someone off her feet*
to cause a person to lose all discernment

SWEEP *to sweep something under the carpet*
to pretend that some blemish does not exist

SWEET *a rose by any other name would smell as sweet*
the form does not affect the substance (from Shakespeare's ROMEO AND JULIET)

SWEET *to be short and sweet*
to be very brief and to the point

SWEETEN *to sweeten a deal*
to offer some concessions or incentives

SWEETEN *to sweeten the pot*
to provide a few additional inducements

SWEETHEART *a sweetheart deal*
an agreement negotiated in private without full regard to the interests of those affected

SWELL *a swelled head*
an exaggerated idea of one's abilities or status

SWIM *it is a case of sink or swim*
the attempt is worthwhile, despite the risk of failure

SWIM *to be in the swim*
to be a member of a group knowing what is going on

SWIM *to swim against the tide*
to take up a minority position

SWINE *to cast pearls before swine*
to confer valuable benefits on someone who neither recognizes nor appreciates them

SWING *the swing of the pendulum*
the alternation of voter acceptance between opposing political parties

SWING *there is no room to swing a cat*
this place is very small (actually refers to a cat-o'-nine-tails)

SWING *to be in full swing*
to be very active

SWING *to swing the lead*
to cheat an employer by not working while being paid to do so

SWING *what one loses on the swings one gains on the roundabouts*
there are advantages and disadvantages which offset each other

SWIPE *to take a swipe at someone*
to attempt to embarrass a person for something that person has done

SWOOP *in one fell swoop*
all at the same time

SWORD *to be a two-edged sword*
to involve both advantages and disadvantages of similar significance

SWORD *to cross swords with someone*
to have a disagreement with another person

SWORD *to have a sword of Damocles hanging over one*
to be in imminent danger despite normal activity going on all around one

SWORD *to hold a sword at someone's throat*
to exert undue pressure on another person in an endeavor to achieve a result which would otherwise not be forthcoming

SYRUP *soothing syrup*
insincere expressions of sympathy or flattery

SYSTEM *to be all systems "'go'"*
to go ahead as fast as possible

T

T *to a t*
exactly

T *to dot the i's and cross the t's*
to be meticulous in completing the documentation for a transaction

TAB *to keep tabs on something*
to monitor something

TABLE *to lay a proposal on the table*
to make a proposal available for discussion or to adjourn discussion on a proposal for an indefinite period

TABLE *to lay one's cards on the table*
to be utterly frank and open or to honestly disclose one's position

TABLE *to put money on the table*
to back one's judgment in a tangible way or to demonstrate one's sincerity

TABLE *to turn the tables on someone*
to cause the relative positions of oneself and another person to be reversed

TACK *to be on the wrong tack*
to be using an incorrect procedure or policy

TACK *to change tack*
to alter one's direction

TACK *to get down to brass tacks*
to discuss the aspects which really matter

TACKLE *to tackle someone head-on*
to confront a person

TAIL *bright-eyed and bushy-tailed*
naive but enthusiastic

TAIL *heads I win—tails you lose*
whichever way this matter goes I will benefit at your expense

TAIL *in two shakes of a duck's tail*
in an instant

TAIL *the tail end of something*
the very end of something

TAIL *the tail wagging the dog*
a minor aspect with disproportionate effect on a major aspect

TAIL *to be the sting in the tail*
to be the unexpected unpleasant conclusion

TAIL *to be unable to make head or tail of something*
to be unable to understand how something functions or what something means

TAIL *to get off one's tail*
to stir oneself from one's inertia

TAIL *to grab the devil by the tail*
to face up to difficulties

TAIL *to hang onto someone's coat-tails*
to excessively rely on another person's initiatives

TAIL *to have a tiger by the tail*
to be involved in an activity which is much more dangerous than one had realized

TAIL *to have one's tail between one's legs*
to show great humility in the light of a backing down

TAIL *to trail one's coat-tails*
to invite a quarrel

TAIL *to wait two shakes of a lamb's tail*
to wait just a few moments

TAIL *with his tail between his legs*
contritely

TAILEND *tailend Charlie*
a person who habitually comes last

TAILOR *to tailor something*
to do something in a way which has regard to the specific needs or preferences of a particular person

TAILSPIN *tailspin*
very fast fall

TALE *a telltale sign*
a visible indication revealing true facts despite efforts at concealment

TALE *an old wives' tale*
a traditionally-held theory without any scientific backing

TALE *to tell tales out of school*
to deliberately leak a secret

TALK *talk of the devil*
here is the person we were just discussing

TALK *to talk shop*
to discuss business or professional matters on a social occasion

TALK *to talk turkey*
to talk realistically

TALL *a tall poppy*
a person with great power or responsibility and/or in receipt of high remuneration

TALL *a tall story*
an interesting but untrue and unbelievable tale

TALL *tall oaks from little acorns grow*
even major enterprises have to have small beginnings (from "Lines written for a School Declamation" by David Everett)

TALL *to be a tall order*
to be an unreasonable expectation

TALL *to cut tall poppies down to size*
to humiliate haughty persons

TALLY *to keep a tally*
to keep a record (refers to a piece of wood with notches made on it to indicate a count)

TANGENT *to go off at a tangent*
to depart from the main matter under consideration and follow instead some other matter only marginally related to it

TANGLE *a tangled web*
a series of lies, especially with inconsistencies leading to exposure (from Sir Walter Scott's MARMION)

TANGO *it takes two to tango*
some activities cannot be carried out single-handedly

TAP *to be on tap*
to be readily available on request

TAP *to turn off the tap*
to deny further access to supplies or information

TAPE *red tape*
excessively bureaucratic procedures

TAR *to be tarred with the same brush*
to be damned merely because of one's association with another person

TAR *to have a touch of the tarbrush*
to be not quite a full-blood Caucasian

TAR *to spoil the ship for a ha'p'orth of tar*
to engage in a false economy (the current word "ship" is actually a mistake for the original word "sheep" and the tar refers to the treatment of wounds)

TARGET *a moving target*
an objective subject to constant revision

TARGET *target*
objective

TARGET *to zero in on a target*
to move directly toward one's objective

TARNISH *to tarnish one's image*
to become less highly regarded

TASTE *to be left with a nasty taste in one's mouth*
to be appalled or very disappointed at another person's unethical behavior to one

TASTE *to get a taste of one's own medicine*
to suffer from an initiative intended to affect only other persons

TAT *tit for tat*
reprisals

TATTER *in tatters*
utterly destroyed

TEA *I would not do so-and-so for all the tea in China*
I will never do so-and-so

TEA *not to be someone's cup of tea*
to be outside a person's expertise or area of interest

TEACH *one cannot teach an old dog new tricks*
people get irreversibly set in their ways

TEACH *to teach one's grandmother how to suck eggs*
to try to tell a much more experienced person something very obvious to him

TEACH *to teach someone a lesson*
to inflict something unpleasant on a person in the hope that it will lead to a change in his behavior

TEACUP *a tempest in a teacup*
a controversy about a minor matter but one which looms large in the minds of the parties

TEAM *a cricket team*
eleven people

TEAR *blood, sweat and tears*
hard work and much effort

TEAR *that's torn it*
that has foiled the proposal

TEAR *to almost drive someone to tears*
to present information designed to make another person express sympathy not warranted by the facts

TEAR *to bore someone to tears*
to greatly weary a person by dull and uninteresting conversation or by lack of action

TEAR *to shed a quiet tear for something*
to lament the passing of something

TEAR *to shed crocodile tears*
to be a hypocrite

TEAR *to tear one's hair out*
to be agitated

TEAR *to tear oneself away*
to leave despite a great desire to stay

TEAR *to tear someone apart*
to ruthlessly destroy another person's case

TEAR *to tear something to ribbons*
to damage something severely

TELEGRAPH *to telegraph one's punches*
by one's actions to give advance warning of one's future plans

TELL *a telltale sign*
a visible indication revealing true facts despite efforts at concealment

TELL *if I've told you once I've told you a thousand times*
I express resentment at the need to constantly repeat some statement

TELL *tell it to the marines*
such nonsense is not believable

TELL *to tell tales out of school*
to deliberately leak a secret

TEMPEST *a tempest in a teacup*
a controversy about a minor matter but one which looms large in the minds of the parties

TEN *to be only ten pence in the shilling*
to be slightly stupid

TEN *not to touch something with a ten-foot pole*
to go out of one's way to avoid something

TENDER *to be a tender spot*
to be a subject on which a person is touchy

TENT *to quietly fold up one's tent*
to surreptitiously abandon a previously-cherished stance

TENTACLE *tentacles*
strong and unpleasant influence extending a long way from its base and in many directions

TENTERHOOK *to be on tenterhooks*
to anxiously await some result

TERRIBLE *an enfant terrible*
a person who raises pertinent but unpalatable issues (French, "little terror")

TEST *a litmus test*
an event which allows the outcome of future events to be predicted more accurately

TEST *to be the acid test*
to establish something beyond doubt

TEST *to road test something*
to try something out under real conditions

TEST *to test the water*
to try out an idea in a small way

TETHER *to be at the end of one's tether*
to be frustrated by a lack of knowledge, authority or patience

THAMES *to set the Thames on fire*
to do something noteworthy

THANK *one can thank one's lucky stars*
one was extremely fortunate

THEME *variations on a theme*
alternative approaches in similar vein

THERE *to be neither here nor there*
to be irrelevant or unimportant

THICK *through thick and thin*
regardless of any obstacles

THICK *to be in the thick of things*
to get involved at the center of some activity

THICK *to come in thick and fast*
to arrive quickly and in great volume

THICK *to have a thick skin*
to be impervious to criticism

THICK *to have the hide of a rhinoceros*
to be totally unaffected by and unresponsive to valid criticism

THICK *to penetrate someone's thick skull*
to make a person understand something difficult or acknowledge something unwelcome

THIMBLE *a pea and thimble trick*
a clever fraud committed in the presence of its victim without this being obvious at the time

THIN *that argument is wearing a bit thin*
that is a very weak case

THIN *through thick and thin*
regardless of any obstacles

THIN *to be the thin edge of the wedge*
by conceding a small point to create an undesirable precedent for much larger issues

THIN *to be thin on the ground*
to be scarce

THIN *to produce something out of thin air*
to get hold of something in circumstances where this seemed impossible

THIN *to skate on thin ice*
to act in disregard of obvious danger

THIN *to spread oneself thin*
to attempt to do more than is feasible in the available time

THIN *to tread the thin line*
cautiously to take action in circumstances where either too much or too little will cause difficulties

THIN *to vanish into thin air*
unexpectedly to disappear

THING *to be in the thick of things*
to get involved at the center of some activity

THINK *one shudders to think what the outcome might be*
there is great concern as to the outcome

THINK *to put one's thinking cap on*
to concentrate on finding a solution to a difficult problem

THINK *to think twice before doing something*
to consider with particular care

THINLY *thinly-veiled*
barely concealed

THIRD *to give someone the third degree*
to apply pressure while questioning closely a person under suspicion

THIRST *to thirst for blood*
to be eager for revenge

THOMAS *a doubting Thomas*
a person who refuses to believe claims in the absence of proof (John 20:25)

THORN *a rose between two thorns*
something beautiful in the midst of ugliness

THORN *to be a thorn in someone's flesh*
to be a person whose persistent presence and righteous views annoy

THORN *to wear one's crown of thorns*
to have one's own difficulties (John 19:5)

THOUSAND *a sixty-four thousand dollar question*
a pertinent but very difficult question (refers to a TV quiz show in which an initial prize doubles with the successful answering of progressively more difficult questions)

THOUSAND *a thousand and one*
many

THOUSAND *if I've told you once I've told you a thousand times*
I express resentment at the need to constantly repeat some statement

THREAD *the thread*
the connecting link of a set of arguments

THREAD *to hang by a slender thread*
to only just survive

THREE *a three-card trick*
a ruse used by a dishonest person in order to induce his victims to hand over some of their assets

THREE *yes sir—yes sir—three bags full!*
(in servile response to some request) yes, very willingly!

THROAT *cut-throat*
highly competitive

THROAT *it sticks in my throat*
I find it galling

THROAT *the words stuck in my throat*
I just could not get myself to say the intended words

THROAT *to be at each other's throats*
to be always fighting

THROAT *to cut one's own throat*
to act in a way which damages one's own interests

THROAT *to have a lump in one's throat*
to feel emotional

THROAT *to have someone by the throat*
to claim victory over an opponent

THROAT *to hold a knife at someone's throat*
to exert undue pressure on another person in an endeavor to achieve a result which would otherwise not be forthcoming

THROAT *to hold a sword at someone's throat*
to exert undue pressure on another person in an endeavor to achieve a result which would otherwise not be forthcoming

THROAT *to jump down someone's throat*
to react angrily to the remarks of the other party to a conversation

THROAT *to ram something down someone's throat*
to pressure another person into accepting an idea with which he does not agree

THRONE *the power behind the throne*
a person exercising the real authority but without having the official right to do so (the antonym of "titular head")

THROUGH *a breakthrough*
success in overcoming resistance to a proposal

THROUGH *to fall through*
not to eventuate as expected

THROW *people in glass houses should not throw stones*
those who are less than perfect are foolish to criticize others

THROW *to be the throw of a loaded die*
to be an act of deceit

THROW *to throw a blanket over a proposal*
to refuse to proceed with a proposal

THROW *to throw a cat among the pigeons*
to cause consternation by revealing an unpleasant and unexpected fact

THROW *to throw a long shadow*
to have wide-spread ramifications

THROW *to throw a pebble against the window*
to gently draw attention to oneself

THROW *to throw a spanner into the works*
to cause an unexpected complication

THROW *to throw a sprat to catch a mackerel*
to risk a little in the hope of gaining much

THROW *to throw brickbats at someone*
to express displeasure with a person

THROW *to throw down the gauntlet*
to issue a challenge (refers to the glove worn by a knight)

THROW *to throw dust into someone's eyes*
to deceive a person by presenting inaccurate or misleading information

THROW *to throw good money after bad*
to waste further money in a vain attempt to recover money already lost

THROW *to throw in one's hand*
to give in or to give up

THROW *to throw in the towel*
to concede defeat

THROW *to throw one's cap into the air*
to celebrate some achievement

THROW *to throw one's hat into the air*
to express joy

THROW *to throw one's weight about*
to use one's real or imagined status in order to achieve certain results

THROW *to throw out the baby with the bathwater*
to discard a major benefit in the course of obtaining a comparatively minor advantage

THROW *to throw someone a bone*
to fob a person off with a symbolic but unimportant gesture

THROW *to throw someone a few crumbs*
to fob a person off with a few symbolic but unimportant concessions

THROW *to throw someone in the shade*
to surpass a person

THROW *to throw someone off the scent*
to deceive a person by giving out misleading indications

THROW *to throw someone to the lions*
to abandon a person

THROW *to throw someone to the wolves*
to expose a person to exploitation by more sophisticated persons

THROW *to throw something into a shambles*
to make something messy and useless

THROW *to throw something out of the window*
to completely reject an idea or proposal

THROW *to throw something to the dogs*
to sacrifice something

THROW *to throw the book at someone*
to prosecute a person with all the vigor allowed by law

THROW *to throw up one's hands*
to express disgust

THROW *to throw up the sponge*
to concede defeat

THROW *within a stone's throw*
very close

THUD *to come down with a thud*
to be suddenly disillusioned

THUMB *a rule of thumb*
a simple yet useful approximation

THUMB *a thumbnail sketch*
brief but pertinent details

THUMB *someone's fingers are all thumbs*
a person is clumsy with his hands

THUMB *to be under someone's thumb*
to be dominated by a person

THUMB *to give a thumbs up*
to approve or grant permission (refers to sign given by Roman emperor sparing a life)

THUMB *to thumb one's nose at someone*
to show one's contempt for someone in authority and to ostentatiously disregard his orders

THUMB *to twiddle one's thumbs*
not to be involved in any worthwhile activity

THUMP *a tub thumper*
a preacher who rants and raves

THUNDER *to be thunderstruck*
to be amazed

THUNDER *to steal someone's thunder*
to take credit for another person's good work (refers to a dispute over the copying of a machine invented by a 17th-century dramatist to reproduce the sound of thunder during a play)

THUNDERBOLT *a thunderbolt*
a surprise

TICK *what makes someone tick*
what causes a person to act as he does

TICKET *just the ticket*
just what is needed

TICKET *that's the ticket!*
that is the proper thing to do

TICKET *to write one's own ticket*
to set one's own terms and conditions

TICKLE *to be tickled pink*
to be very pleased

TICKLE *to tickle the Peter*
to rob one's employer

TICKLISH *ticklish*
awkward, requiring delicate handling

TIDE *the tide has turned*
conditions have changed

TIDE *the tide is running in favor of some proposition*
public opinion supports some proposition

TIDE *to be caught by the tide*
to be dealt with by something inevitable

TIDE *to stem the tide*
to make progress against something

TIDE *to swim against the tide*
to take up a minority position

TIDE *to turn the tide*
to reverse the direction of something

TIE *to be tied down*
to have responsibilities precluding alternative activities

TIE *to be tied to someone's apron strings*
to be excessively influenced by a female

TIE *to be tied up*
to be engaged

TIE *to tie in with something*
to be consistent with something

TIE *to tie someone's hands*
to prevent a person from acting as he sees fit

TIE *to tie someone's hands behind his back*
to make it impossible for a person to act at all

TIE *to tie something up*
to finalize the arrangements for something

TIE *to tie the knot*
to marry

TIE *to tie up the loose ends*
to complete the minor outstanding items of some substantially finished project

TIGER *a paper tiger*
an empty threat

TIGER *a toothless tiger*
an authority which has been given totally inadequate powers for its task

TIGER *to have a tiger by the tail*
to be involved in an activity which is much more dangerous than one had realized

TIGHT *a tight rein*
strong controls

TIGHT *a watertight contract*
a contract without loopholes or escape clauses

TIGHT *tight-fisted*
stingy

TIGHT *to be in a tight corner*
to experience a crisis

TIGHT *to be tight-lipped*
to keep confidences or to be uncommunicative

TIGHT *to run a tight ship*
to manage an efficient organization

TIGHT *to sit tight*
obstinately to do nothing

TIGHTEN *to tighten one's belt*
to lower one's rate of spending

TIGHTEN *to tighten the noose*
to get closer to inflicting defeat

TIGHTEN *to tighten the purse strings*
to reduce outlays

TIGHTEN *to tighten the screw*
to increase the moral and psychological pressure

TIGHTROPE *to walk a tightrope*
to do something very dangerous

TILL *to have one's fingers in the till*
to steal from one's employer

TILT *to tilt at windmills*
to attack an imagined but nonexistent enemy (from Cervantes' DON QUIXOTE)

TIME *a stitch in time saves nine*
preventive maintenance saves money in the long run

TIME *a time bomb*
a source of serious problems which are certain to surface later on

TIME *he would not give one the time of day*
he is unwilling to help anybody

TIME *if I've told you once I've told you a thousand times*
I express resentment at the need to constantly repeat some statement

TIME *to live on borrowed time*
to live longer than expected

TIME *to mark time*
to do nothing while awaiting developments

TIN *a little tin god*
a petty tyrant

TINKER *not worth a tinker's curse*
worthless

TINKER *to tinker at the edges*
to make minor or cosmetic changes without affecting the substance

TIP *it is on the tip of my tongue*
the right word has momentarily escaped me

TIP *to be the tip of the iceberg*
to be only a very small portion of a much larger but less obvious whole

TIP *to cling on by one's fingertips*
to have only a slender hold

TIP *to have some subject at one's fingertips*
to be very familiar with a subject

TIP *to tip a bucket on someone*
to point out in a humiliating way another person's faults

TIP *to tip one's hand*
to disclose details of one's position

TIP *to tip someone over the edge*
to cause a person to become mentally ill

TIP *to tip the balance*
to provide further information or argument which results in an issue, which could have been decided either way, being determined in a particular way

TIP *to tip the scales*
to be a factor which in combination with other factors results in a particular decision which would otherwise not have been reached

TIP *to tiptoe around the difficulties*
to act as though the difficulties did not exist

TIRE *to carry a spare tire*
to be fat

TISSUE *only a tissue between them*
virtually equal or close together

TIT *tit for tat*
reprisals

TITANIC *to rearrange the deckchairs on the Titanic*
to take some initiative which is quite useless because it does not take much greater change into account

TOAST *to have someone on toast*
to be victorious over a person

TOE *a toehold*
an opportunity small in itself but with the potential to lead to bigger things

TOE *to dig one's toes in*
to become even more stubborn than at first

TOE *to dip one's toe in the water*
to gently explore an opportunity

TOE *to keep someone on his toes*
to induce a person to be efficient

TOE *to tiptoe around the difficulties*
to act as though the difficulties did not exist

TOE *to toe the line*
to conform

TOE *to tread on someone's toes*
to upset another person by interfering in his area of responsibility

TOKEN *by the same token*
by way of corroboration

TOM *every Tom, Dick and Harry*
just about everybody

TONE *overtones*
implied threats

TONGS *to go hammer and tongs*
to do something with great energy

TONGUE *I could have bitten my tongue off*
I wish that I had not made such a hurtful remark

TONGUE *a slip of the tongue*
incorrect words uttered accidently

TONGUE *it is on the tip of my tongue*
the right word has momentarily escaped me

TONGUE *to feel the rough side of someone's tongue*
to be verbally abused by a person

TONGUE *to find one's tongue*
to overcome one's shyness and speak

TONGUE *to have a loose tongue*
to speak foolishly or indiscreetly

TONGUE *to have a sharp tongue*
to speak one's mind in forceful language

TONGUE *to have a silver tongue*
to be eloquent

TONGUE *to hold one's tongue*
to keep quiet

TONGUE *to keep a civil tongue in one's head*
to be polite, especially under provocation

TONGUE *to roll off the tongue*
to be said very easily

TONGUE *to set tongues wagging*
to behave in a way which encourages scandal mongers

TONGUE *to speak with forked tongues*
to utter half-truths with the intention of misleading the listener

TONGUE *tongue in cheek*
full of irony

TONIC *to be a tonic*
to cheer someone up

TOOL *tools*
the means to do something

TOOTH *a tooth for a tooth*
retaliation (Exodus 21:24)

TOOTH *one would give one's eye teeth for something*
a person would very much like to achieve some objective

TOOTH *teething trouble*
problems in the early stages of a project

TOOTH *to bare one's teeth*
to imply threats

TOOTH *to be armed to the teeth*
to carry many weapons

TOOTH *to be fed up to the back teeth*
to be disgusted

TOOTH *to be long in the tooth*
to be old

TOOTH *to believe in the tooth fairy*
to be particularly gullible

TOOTH *to cut one's teeth on something*
to get one's first experience by doing something

TOOTH *to escape by the skin of one's teeth*
to only just avoid some disaster

TOOTH *to fight tooth and nail*
to strive very hard to win

TOOTH *to get one's teeth into something*
to tackle a task with enthusiasm

TOOTH *to gnash one's teeth*
to express frustration

TOOTH *to go through something with a fine-tooth comb*
to conduct an extremely thorough investigation

TOOTH *to grit one's teeth*
to get ready to suffer pain

TOOTH *to hang on by the skin of one's teeth*
to only just survive

TOOTH *to have a sweet tooth*
to be particularly fond of cakes and confectionery

TOOTH *to have teeth*
to be effective

TOOTH *to kick someone in the teeth*
to take action which demonstrates annoyance at or dislike of a person

TOOTH *to lie through one's teeth*
to tell blatant untruths

TOOTH *to set someone's teeth on edge*
to cause a person to feel unhappy at a situation

TOOTH *to take the bit between one's teeth*
to face up to a problem

TOOTHLESS *a toothless tiger*
an authority which has been given totally inadequate powers for its task

TOP *off the top of one's head*
based on experience but without detailed consideration

TOP *the top dog*
the person in the most powerful position

TOP *to be at the top of the tree*
to be a leading member of one's profession

TOP *to be icing on top of the cake*
to be an additional benefit in an already satisfactory scenario

TOP *to be in top gear*
to be making excellent progress

TOP *to be on top of the world*
to be very happy

TOP *to be over the top*
to be quite outrageous

TOP *to blow one's top*
to show anger (refers to a volcano)

TOP *to score top points*
to outwit other persons

TOP *top drawer*
first class

TORCH *to carry a torch for someone*
to act as an enthusiastic advocate of another person's cause

TORCH *to hand on the torch*
to pass on accumulated knowledge

TORPEDO *to torpedo something*
to make something ineffective

TORRENT *a torrent of words*
a rapid and uninterrupted outpouring of words

TOSS *it is a toss-up*
either alternative is equally acceptable

TOSS *to argue the toss*
to dispute a decision

TOSS *to toss up*
to decide on a fairly arbitrary basis

TOTEM *to be at the bottom of the totem pole*
to be in the most junior position in some hierarchy

TOUCH *it was touch and go*
there were considerable risks—the objective was achieved, but only just

TOUCH *not to touch a hair on someone's head*
not to harm a person

TOUCH *not to touch something with a ten-foot pole*
to go out of one's way to avoid something

TOUCH *the Midas touch*
attributes which cause a person's ventures to be extremely profitable (refers to King Midas of Phrygia, who had the power to turn everything he touched into gold)

TOUCH *the touchstone*
the standard

TOUCH *to have a touch of the tarbrush*
to be not quite a full-blood Caucasian

TOUCH *to lose one's touch*
to cease to be familiar with something

TOUCH *to touch a nerve*
to mention something which another person would rather pretend did not exist

TOUCH *to touch wood*
it is to be hoped that our good luck will not go away

TOUCHE *touche*
well said (French, "touched")

TOUR *a Cook's tour*
a guided tour of inspection (refers to Thomas Cook, the travel company)

TOUR *a whistlestop tour*
a hurried (especially ceremonial) visit to many places

TOUR *tour de force*
feat of skill or strength (French, "feat of strength")

TOWEL *to throw in the towel*
to concede defeat

TOWER *a tower of Babel*
a noisy and confused assembly (Genesis 11)

TOWER *to be a tower of strength*
to be a person who supports and comforts another

TOWER *to be in an ivory tower*
to be immersed in theoretical considerations and ignorant of the practical realities (Song of Solomon 7:4)

TOWN *the only game in town*
the only event worthy of attention

TOWN *to go to town*
to spend lavishly

TOWN *to paint the town red*
to go on an exciting social outing

TRACE *to kick over one's traces*
to become insubordinate

TRACK *to be down the track*
to be making progress

TRACK *to be off the beaten track*
to do unconventional things

TRACK *to be off the track*
to be irrelevant

TRACK *to be on the wrong track*
to be heading toward an incorrect solution

TRACK *to be on track*
to be making the scheduled progress

TRACK *to be stopped in one's tracks*
suddenly and unexpectedly to be prevented from carrying on with a project

TRACK *to cover one's tracks*
to hide the evidence of one's involvement

TRACK *to go down a particular track*
to make decisions aimed at a particular goal

TRACK *to have a one-track mind*
to keep coming back to one narrow topic of conversation

TRACK *to keep track of something*
to be completely aware of where something is and how it is functioning

TRACK *to make tracks*
to leave

TRACK *track record*
proven performance

TRADE *a Jack of all trades*
an amateur who can turn his hand to anything

TRADE *horsetrading*
tough negotiations

TRADE *to make something one's trademark*
to earn a reputation for maintaining some stance

TRAIL *to blaze a trail*
to be the first person to do something

TRAIL *to trail one's coat-tails*
to invite a quarrel

TRAIN *to get on a gravy train*
to take steps to become a recipient of benefits which are available but undeserved

TRAIN *to miss the train*
to fail to exploit an opportunity

TRAM *to be on the wrong tram*
to be completely mistaken as to the basic facts

TRAMPLE *to trample someone underfoot*
by virtue of one's great power to treat a person's rights with contempt and not to give them proper consideration

TRANSFUSION *to give something a blood transfusion*
to give something new enthusiasm

TRANSPARENT *transparent*
(of behavior, etc.) to be easily seen as not genuine

TRAP *a trap for young players*
a good opportunity for the inexperienced or naive to make mistakes

TRAP *to walk into a trap*
to be tricked into doing something

TREACHEROUS *to enter treacherous waters*
to engage in an enterprise with risks which are not obvious

TREAD *fools rush in where angels fear to tread*
unsophisticated persons take unwise risks in circumstances where more knowledgeable persons would exercise caution

TREAD *to tread a particular path*
to take certain initiatives

TREAD *to tread lightly*
to be careful

TREAD *to tread on someone's corns*
to upset another person by interfering in his area of responsibility

TREAD *to tread on someone's toes*
to upset another person by interfering in his area of responsibility

TREAD *to tread someone under foot*
to oppress a person

TREAD *to tread the thin line*
cautiously to take action in circumstances where either too much or too little will cause difficulties

TREADMILL *to be on a treadmill*
to be involved in some unpleasant ongoing activity which cannot readily be stopped

TREASURE *a treasure trove*
a valuable discovery

TREAT *to treat someone with kid gloves*
to handle a person with great discretion

TREATMENT *the red-carpet treatment*
courtesies extended to a person to make him feel important and welcome

TREE *not to see the wood for the trees*
to overlook the general picture because of undue concentration on the details

TREE *to bark up the wrong tree*
to reach an incorrect conclusion

TREE *to be at the top of the tree*
to be a leading member of one's profession

TREE *to be up a gum tree*
to be in difficulty or at the end of one's resources

TREE *to be up a tree*
to be perplexed or cornered

TREE *to shake a tree*
to do something in order to see what will result

TREMBLE *in fear and trembling*
in a state of apprehension

TRENCH *to be back in the trenches*
to be made to carry out menial tasks

TRICK *a pea and thimble trick*
a clever fraud committed in the presence of its victim without this being obvious at the time

TRICK *a three-card trick*
a ruse used by a dishonest person in order to induce his victims to hand over some of their assets

TRICK *a whole bag of tricks*
a series of articles or a series of artificial devices

TRICK *one cannot teach an old dog new tricks*
people get irreversibly set in their ways

TRICK *something has done the trick*
something has achieved the desired purpose

TRICK *to be unable to take a trick*
to be unable to achieve success in anything

TRICK *to play monkey tricks on someone*
to engage in discreditable behavior affecting a person

TRICK *to score a hat trick*
to have three successive favorable outcomes

TRICK *to use every trick in the book*
to try very hard and use every conceivable argument

TRICKLE *a trickle*
a small amount, in gradual stages

TRIGGER *to be trigger-happy*
to be impetuous

TRIGGER *trigger*
factor responsible for certain events occurring at that particular time

TRIM *to trim one's sails*
to institute austerity

TRIM *to trim the fat*
to increase efficiency by reducing outlays

TROJAN *a Trojan horse*
a trick (refers to a large gift horse full of soldiers used to bring about the fall of Troy, as described in Homer's ILIAD)

TROOPER *to be a real trooper*
to be a person willing to try anything

TROUBLE *a troubleshooter*
a person good at finding and then rectifying faults

TROUBLE *teething trouble*
problems in the early stages of a project

TROUBLE *to fish in troubled waters*
to profit from a disturbed situation

TROUBLE *to plot a safe course through troubled waters*
to make a plan which overcomes certain difficulties

TROUBLE *to pour oil on troubled waters*
to calm down a situation

TROUBLE *to smell trouble*
to perceive difficulties

TROUSERS *to catch someone with his trousers down*
to act when another person least expects it

TROUSERS *to wear the trousers*
to be the dominant party

TROVE *a treasure trove*
a valuable discovery

TROWEL *to lay it on with a trowel*
to flatter

TRUCK *it fell off the back of a truck*
(of goods) they were stolen; (of a politically sensitive document) it was leaked to me

TRUCK *to have no truck with someone*
to refuse to deal with a person

TRUE *to show one's true colors*
to disclose one's real character or beliefs

TRUE *true blue*
superbly loyal

TRUMP *to hold the trump card*
to be in an unbeatable position to defeat others

TRUMP *to play the trump card*
to make a final move, thereby defeating one's opponents

TRUMP *to trump someone*
to defeat a person

TRUMP *to turn up trumps*
to finish up better than expected or to experience unexpected good luck

TRUMPET *to blow one's own trumpet*
to immodestly publicize one's own attributes

TRUMPET *with a flourish of trumpets*
triumphantly

TRUST *a sacred trust*
a moral obligation

TRY *something would try the patience of Job*
something is very vexatious (James 5:11)

TRY *to try something on for size*
to cheekily do something

TUB *a tub thumper*
a preacher who rants and raves

TUBE *to go down the tube*
to fail

TUCK *to tuck something away in a drawer*
to put something aside for the time being

TUESDAY *every Pancake Tuesday*
only on rare occasions (refers to Shrove Tuesday, when pancakes are traditionally eaten)

TUG *a tug of war*
a dispute in which each protagonist desires a different course of action

TUNE *he who pays the piper calls the tune*
a person contributing money or resources to a project is entitled to a say in its control

TUNE *to be in tune with someone*
to think on the same lines as another person

TUNE *to change one's tune*
to alter one's publicly-expressed views

TUNE *to fine-tune something*
to adjust something in order to bring it to perfection or to make it fit the circumstances in a much more appropriate fashion

TUNE *to stay tuned*
to keep in touch for further information as it becomes available

TUNE *to tune in*
to pay attention

TUNNEL *to see the light at the end of the tunnel*
to be close to finalizing a long exercise

TUNNEL *tunnel vision*
an extremely narrow and inflexible way of considering issues

TURF *to be on one's own turf*
to engage in one's own customary area of activity

TURK *young Turks*
members of an organization who hold ideas regarded as too revolutionary

TURKEY *cold turkey*
the sudden cessation of drugs to an addict

TURKEY *to talk turkey*
to talk realistically

TURN *as soon as someone's back was turned*
at the moment it became possible to do something without a person's knowledge

TURN *he would turn in his grave*
he would have been very surprised or displeased if he had known while still alive

TURN *not to turn a hair*
to remain composed

TURN *the tide has turned*
conditions have changed

TURN *the wheel has turned*
circumstances have changed

TURN *the wheel has turned the complete circle*
things are now back to where they were before

TURN *the worm has turned*
a previously compliant person is now exerting his personality

TURN *to be a turn up for the books*
to be a surprising development

TURN *to do a U-turn*
to reverse one's thinking

TURN *to know which way to turn*
to know which strategy to adopt or where to seek assistance

TURN *to leave no stone unturned*
to be very thorough

TURN *to turn a blind eye to something*
to pretend something obvious does not exist (refers to action by Nelson when disregarding Admiralty signals)

TURN *to turn a complete somersault*
to reverse one's established policy

TURN *to turn an honest penny*
to earn money out of odd jobs

TURN *to turn around 180 degrees*
to completely reverse a stance

TURN *to turn back the clock*
to have another opportunity to do something which should have been done already or to undo something which cannot be undone

TURN *to turn green*
to become very envious

TURN *to turn handstands*
to express great joy

TURN *to turn off the tap*
to deny further access to supplies or information

TURN *to turn one's back on someone*
to decline to further assist or deal with a person

TURN *to turn one's chips in*
to convert one's assets or entitlements into cash

TURN *to turn one's guns on someone*
to criticize a person

TURN *to turn one's hand to something*
to tackle some project

TURN *to turn over a new leaf*
to reform

TURN *to turn round*
to reverse one's policy

TURN *to turn someone on*
to excite a person

TURN *to turn something inside out*
to examine something thoroughly

TURN *to turn something on its ear*
to reverse something

TURN *to turn something on its head*
to reverse something

TURN *to turn something upside down*
to greatly revolutionize something

TURN *to turn sour*
to become impractical or unprofitable

TURN *to turn the corner*
to commence being successful after initial failures

TURN *to turn the heat on something*
to intensify the investigation of some matter

TURN *to turn the other cheek*
to show that one has not been intimidated (Matthew 5:39)

TURN *to turn the spotlight on something*
to draw public attention to something

TURN *to turn the tables on someone*
to cause the relative positions of oneself and another person to be reversed

TURN *to turn the tide*
to reverse the direction of something

TURN *to turn turtle*
to capsize

TURN *to turn up one's nose at something*
to express one's disdain

TURN *to turn up the heat on someone*
to increase the pressure on a person

TURN *to turn up trumps*
to finish up better than expected or to experience unexpected good luck

TURN *to turn white*
to express shock at unexpected news

TURNCOAT *a turncoat*
a person changing sides (refers to the practice of mercenary soldiers switching to the winning side and displaying that side's colors by turning their coats inside out)

TURTLE *to turn turtle*
to capsize

TWENTY *with 20/20 hindsight*
with the benefit of knowing what happened

TWICE *to think twice before doing something*
to consider with particular care

TWIDDLE *to twiddle one's thumbs*
not to be involved in any worthwhile activity

TWILIGHT *twilight zone*
state of imperfect understanding

TWIST *to twist someone around one's little finger*
by charm to get one's way

TWIST *to twist someone's arms*
to coerce another person to do something against his will or better judgment

TWO *a two-horse race*
a contest between only two serious contestants

TWO *for two pins I would do so-and-so*
my tolerance is almost exhausted and I am very tempted to do so-and-so

TWO *in two shakes of a duck's tail*
in an instant

TWO *it takes two to tango*
some activities cannot be carried out single-handedly

TWO *not to have the wherewithal to rub two sticks together*
to be very poor

TWO *to be a two-edged sword*
to involve both advantages and disadvantages of similar significance

TWO *to be of two minds*
to be undecided between two alternatives

TWO *to have two bob each way*
to equivocate

TWO *to have two left feet*
to be clumsy

TWO *to kill two birds with one stone*
to achieve a second objective in the course of achieving the first objective

TWO *to knock two heads together*
to make two persons come to their senses and deal with each other

TWO *to put two and two together*
to reach a conclusion by combining isolated pieces of information

TWO *to take someone down a peg or two*
to point out to a person that he is not as good as he thinks he is

TWO *to throw in one's two cents' worth*
to modestly supply one's own facts or views

TWO *to wait two shakes of a lamb's tail*
to wait just a few moments

TWO *two can play at that game*
it is possible to retaliate

TWO *two men and a dog*
very few people

TWO *two-faced*
insincere

TWOPENNY *a twopenny halfpenny outfit*
a quite insignificant operation

U

U-TURN *to do a U-turn*
to reverse one's thinking

UGLY *an ugly duckling*
a person initially thought unintelligent who develops and becomes brilliant (refers to a cygnet in a brood of ducks in a children's story of that name by Hans Christian Andersen)

UGLY *to rear its ugly head*
to make an unwelcome appearance

UMBRELLA *an umbrella*
protection; or something all-embracing

UMBRELLA *under the umbrella of some organization*
under the auspices of some organization

UNCHARTED *to be in uncharted waters*
to be the first to experience something

UNCLE *Bob's your uncle*
that solves the problem

UNDER *to have the plug pulled out from under one*
to have a successful activity destroyed by the actions of someone else

UNDERBELLY *to have a soft underbelly*
to have a weakness which can be exploited

UNDERCURRENT *an undercurrent*
a barely noticeable feeling of dissent in the community which is not being vocalized

UNDERDOG *underdog*
object of sympathy (the antonym of "underdog effect" is "bandwagon effect")

UNDERFOOT *to trample someone underfoot*
by virtue of one's great power to treat a person's rights with contempt and not to give them proper consideration

UNDERMINE *to undermine someone's position*
to injure another person's reputation and influence by unfair and secret tactics

UNDERMINE *to undermine something*
to sabotage something

UNDERPLAY *to underplay some situation*
to hold something in reserve

UNDERSCORE *to underscore something*
to emphasize something

UNEARTH *to unearth something*
to discover something after research

UNEASY *uneasy lies the head that wears a crown*
responsibility involves some risks and some burdens (from Shakespeare's HENRY IV)

UNHOLY *an unholy alliance*
a working relationship for a nefarious purpose between unlikely partners

UNMASK *to unmask someone*
to discover a person's true identity

UNSCRAMBLE *to unscramble the omelette*
to undo something which cannot be undone

UNSTUCK *he came unstuck*
his plans did not work out

UNVEIL *to unveil something*
to give details not previously available

UP *to be up and running*
to be operative

UPHILL *to be pushing uphill*
to face difficulties

UPHILL *to fight an uphill battle*
to face difficulties or to have formidable opposition

UPHILL *to push water uphill*
to foolishly attempt the impossible

UPPER *to gain the upper hand*
to attain, after some effort, an advantage over another person

UPSET *to upset the applecart*
to engage in conduct disturbing a peaceful state of affairs and thereby cause discomfort

UPSIDE *the upside*
the advantage

UPSIDE *to turn something upside down*
to greatly revolutionize something

UPSTAGE *to upstage someone*
to deprive another person of the glory which he would otherwise have enjoyed

UPSTAIRS *to kick someone upstairs*
to promote a person to a purely ceremonial position

USE *to use every trick in the book*
to try very hard and use every conceivable argument

UTOPIAN *Utopian*
ideally perfect (refers to the mythical island in Sir Thomas More's UTOPIA)

V

VACUUM *to fill a vacuum*
to take advantage of an opportunity not acted on by others

VALUE *to take something at face value*
(of alleged facts) to accept something without question or challenge

VALVE *to act as a safety valve*
to be a procedure which allows persons with grievances to ventilate them in an orderly fashion

VANGUARD *to be at the vanguard of something*
to be among the first to do something

VANISH *to vanish into thin air*
unexpectedly to disappear

VAPOR *to have a fit of the vapors*
to be horrified

VARIATION *variations on a theme*
alternative approaches in similar vein

VEGETABLE *to become a vegetable*
to lose one's mental and physical faculties

VEIL *thinly-veiled*
barely concealed

VEIL *to draw a veil over something*
pointedly to avoid discussing something

VEIL *to unveil something*
to give details not previously available

VEIL *under the veil of something*
on the pretext of something

VEIN *in another vein*
as an alternative way of looking at things

VELVET *with an iron hand in a velvet glove*
with a hard attitude made to seem soft

VENGEANCE *to attack with a vengeance*
to attack strongly

VENGEANCE *to rebound with a vengeance*
to return to an issue with great enthusiasm

VENOM *venom*
deep-rooted ill will

VENT *to vent one's spleen on someone*
to demonstrate one's ill temper to a person

VERSE *to quote chapter and verse*
to authenticate the information

VICTORY *a Pyrrhic victory*
a win which costs more than if there had been a loss (refers to the battle at which King Pyrrhus of Epirus defeated the Romans at Asculum)

VIEW *a bird's-eye view*
a general overview or summary of a subject, emphasizing the major features

VIEW *to take a dim view of something*
not to regard something favorably

VINE *to hear on the grapevine*
to learn unofficially

VINE *to wither on the vine*
by virtue of changed circumstances or the effluxion of time to be no longer relevant

VIOLET *a shrinking violet*
a shy person

VISION *tunnel vision*
an extremely narrow and inflexible way of considering issues

VITRIOL *to pour vitriol on something*
to sharply criticize something

VOICE *to be a lone voice in the wilderness*
to be the only person stating unpopular views

VOICE *to raise one's voice for some cause*
to publicly advocate some cause

VOLCANO *to be sitting on a volcano*
to be safe for the time being but exposed to the risk of a sudden great disaster

VOLLEY *to fire a volley at someone*
to send a series of angry messages to someone

VOLTE *volte face*
a reversal of previously-held beliefs (French, "a turning around")

VOLUME *to speak volumes for something*
to place something in a favorable light

VOTE *to vote with one's feet*
to show one's displeasure by terminating an association

VULTURE *vulture*
person benefiting from another's misfortune

W

WAG *the tail wagging the dog*
a minor aspect with disproportionate effect on a major aspect

WAG *to set tongues wagging*
to behave in a way which encourages scandal mongers

WAGON *to be on the water wagon*
to be teetotal

WAIT *to wait for the other shoe to drop*
to await the seemingly imminent and inevitable (refers to a man undressing, disturbing a neighbor by dropping one shoe, then frustrating his expectation by putting the other shoe down gently)

WAIT *to wait hand and foot on someone*
to accommodate a person's every real or imagined whim

WAIT *to wait in the wings*
to be prepared to stay unobtrusive till the appropriate time for action arrives

WAIT *to wait with bated breath*
to be excited in anticipation of some event

WAKE *in the wake of someone*
following a person's example

WAKE *to make noise enough to wake the dead*
to be excessively noisy

WAKE *to wake up to something*
to realize a fact or its significance

WALK *take a long walk on a short pier*
go away, I want no dealings with you

WALK *to walk a tightrope*
to do something very dangerous

WALK *to walk all over someone*
to act in a way which completely disregards another person's sensibility

WALK *to walk away from something*
to abrogate one's responsibilities in regard to some matter

WALK *to walk away with a profit*
to achieve a profit on concluding a project

WALK *to walk in off the street*
to come without prior arrangement or notification

WALK *to walk into a trap*
to be tricked into doing something

WALK *to walk on air*
to be joyful

WALK *to walk the plank*
to face certain doom

WALKOVER *a walkover*
an easy victory

WALL *Chinese walls*
a system to ensure that different parts of some organization do not gain access to each other's confidential information

WALL *I would love to be a fly on the wall*
I would love to hear what goes on

WALL *a chink in the wall*
an opportunity to do something which otherwise could not be done

WALL *to bang one's head up against a brick wall*
to fight an unwinnable case

WALL *to be a crack in the wall*
to represent a small unintended opportunity which can be exploited

WALL *to be up against a brick wall*
to be unable to achieve anything because of intractable opposition or apathy

WALL *to drive someone to the wall*
to ruin a person

WALL *to drive someone up the wall*
to annoy another person by one's actions

WALL *to go to the wall*
to become bankrupt

WALL *to have one's back to the wall*
to be hard-pressed by creditors or opponents

WALL *to nail someone to the wall*
to outmaneuver another person

WALL *to put a wall around someone*
to stop a person associating with others

WALL *to see the writing on the wall*
to appreciate the inevitability of some event (Daniel 5)

WALL *walls have ears*
someone may be overhearing (words on wartime posters, reminding people of the existence of spies; may also refer to certain rooms in the Louvre, constructed so that conversations could be heard in other rooms)

WALL *walls of Jericho*
something seemingly solid but actually destructible (Joshua 6:20)

WAND *to wave a magic wand*
to direct affairs without the restraints of the real world

WANT *to want something both ways*
to desire two mutually exclusive objectives

WANT *to want the best of both worlds*
to unreasonably desire to get some advantage without incurring a corresponding disadvantage

WANT *you want your head read*
you should reconsider this matter

WAR *a tug of war*
a dispute in which each protagonist desires a different course of action

WAR *the cold war*
the unfriendly relations between the communist nations and the rest of the world

WAR *to be on the warpath*
to be on the lookout for faults which can be criticized

WARFARE *paper warfare*
an excessive amount of correspondence or red tape

WARHORSE *a warhorse*
an old soldier who likes to relive past wartime experiences

WARM *a warm inner glow*
satisfaction at some achievement

WARM *to keep someone's seat warm*
to hold a position temporarily with a view to another person taking it over permanently in the near future

WARM *to warm the cockles of someone's heart*
to delight a person

WARM *to warm up*
to get ready

WARM *warm-hearted*
affectionate or generous

WARRANT *to sign one's own death warrant*
to foolishly do something which is inevitably bound to lead to utter disaster

WART *warts and all*
with the unfavorable features as well as the favorable ones (Oliver Cromwell's direction to an artist painting his portrait)

WASH *backwash*
consequence

WASH *hogwash*
nonsense

WASH *in the wash-up*
when everything is finalized

WASH *it will all come out in the wash*
the facts will emerge as work proceeds

WASH *it won't wash*
this explanation is not acceptable

WASH *someone's brain needs washing*
a person is very silly

WASH *that washes with me*
I agree

WASH *to be all washed out*
to feel feeble

WASH *to be eye wash*
to be nonsense

WASH *to wash one's dirty linen in public*
to expose one's domestic difference to the world at large

WASH *to wash one's hands of something*
to emphatically decline future responsibility

WASH *when the wash comes through the machine*
in due course

WASTE *to waste one's breath*
to talk or request something without achieving anything

WATCH *a watchdog*
a person or organization monitoring behavior

WATCH *to need to watch one's back*
to find it necessary to take care in case others act against one's interest

WATCH *to watch one's p's and q's*
to be very careful (may refer to pints and quarts of beer on a hotel slate or to easily-confused printer's type)

WATCH *to watch one's step*
to be on the lookout for danger or to set out to improve one's behavior

WATCH *watch the doughnut—not the hole*
look for the positive aspects

WATER *a backwater*
a place of little activity

WATER *a lot of water has flowed under the bridge since then*
much has happened since then

WATER *an argument holding water*
a debating point of substance

WATER *come hell or high water*
regardless of the consequences

WATER *high water mark*
triumph

WATER *still waters run deep*
a person with a quiet manner may have a surprisingly great knowledge of a subject

WATER *there is blood in the water*
something is likely to cause a person to go into a frenzy

WATER *to be a fish out of water*
to be in difficulty by virtue of being in a strange environment

WATER *to be above water*
(of securities) to have a market value in excess of the cost price

WATER *to be in deep water*
to be in great difficulty

WATER *to be in hot water*
to be in trouble or to be in difficulty

WATER *to be in smooth water*
to have no troubles

WATER *to be in uncharted waters*
to be the first to experience something

WATER *to be like water off a duck's back*
(of advice or criticism) to be completely rejected

WATER *to be on the water wagon*
to be teetotal

WATER *to be water under the bridge*
to matter no longer

WATER *to blow something out of the water*
to destroy something

WATER *to brave the water*
to enter a venture with courage and determination

WATER *to cast one's bread upon the waters*
not to expect gratitude or recognition for one's good works (Ecclesiastes 11:1)

WATER *to dip one's toe in the water*
to gently explore an opportunity

WATER *to enter treacherous waters*
to engage in an enterprise with risks which are not obvious

WATER *to fish in troubled waters*
to profit from a disturbed situation

WATER *to go through fire and water*
to undertake all attendant risks

WATER *to go to water*
to succumb to pressure

WATER *to just hold one's head above water*
to cope with problems but with little margin to spare or to stay solvent

WATER *to make one's mouth water*
to excite desire

WATER *to muddy the waters*
to deliberately confuse an issue by creating a diversion

WATER *to plot a safe course through troubled waters*
to make a plan which overcomes certain difficulties

WATER *to pour cold water on some idea*
to be unenthusiastic about some proposal or scornful of its apparent weakness

WATER *to pour oil on troubled waters*
to calm down a situation

WATER *to push water uphill*
to foolishly attempt the impossible

WATER *to shoot something out of the water*
to frustrate something

WATER *to test the water*
to try out an idea in a small way

WATER *to water down something*
to reduce the severe impact of something

WATER *water will find its own level*
people will reach an appropriate position relative to others

WATER *watering hole*
hotel

WATERLOO *to meet one's Waterloo*
to receive a decisive defeat (refers to Napoleon's fate at the Battle of Waterloo)

WATERSHED *a watershed*
an occasion dividing two distinct phases of activity

WATERTIGHT *a watertight contract*
a contract without loopholes or escape clauses

WAVE *a brainwave*
a suddenly occurring bright idea

WAVE *to be on the crest of a wave*
to enjoy success which may not last

WAVE *to cause waves*
to disturb the status quo

WAVE *to ride the wave*
to be successful for the time being

WAVE *to wave a finger at someone*
to indicate mild displeasure at another person's actions

WAVE *to wave a flag for someone*
to promote a person's cause

WAVE *to wave a magic wand*
to direct affairs without the restraints of the real world

WAVELENGTH *to be on the same wavelength*
to think on similar lines

WAVELENGTH *to be on the wrong wavelength*
to be incorrect in one's thinking

WAY *a half-way house*
an intermediate position

WAY *a one-way street*
a flow of activity in only one direction

WAY *no way!*
definitely not!

WAY *that is the way the chips fall*
that is the actual situation

WAY *there is more than one way to skin a cat*
this can be achieved in a variety of acceptable ways

WAY *to cut both ways*
to involve both advantages and disadvantages of similar significance

WAY *to go the way of all flesh*
to die

WAY *to have fifty cents each way*
to equivocate

WAY *to have two bob each way*
to equivocate

WAY *to know which way to turn*
to know which strategy to adopt or where to seek assistance

WAY *to laugh all the way to the bank*
to appreciate one's good fortune

WAY *to make headway*
to make progress

WAY *to pave the way*
to prepare for something

WAY *to resist something every inch of the way*
to utterly resist something

WAY *to rub someone up the wrong way*
to annoy someone with actions failing to recognize his current mood

WAY *to see which way the cat jumps*
to await developments

WAY *to see which way the wind is blowing*
to establish the factors relevant to a situation

WAY *to stand in someone's way*
to prevent a person achieving his goal

WAY *to want something both ways*
to desire two mutually exclusive objectives

WAY *to worm one's way in*
to subtly insinuate oneself into a person's trust

WAYSIDE *to fall by the wayside*
to abandon and not complete what one set out to do

WEAK *the spirit is willing but the flesh is weak*
the body is not up to the demands made on it

WEAK *the weakest link in the chain*
the least efficient component in a project the overall efficiency of which is governed by the efficiency of the least efficient component

WEAK *weak-kneed*
unassertive or irresolute

WEALTH *a wealth of something*
a great quantity of something

WEAPON *to use all the weapons at one's disposal*
to utilize all available advantages

WEAR *if the cap fits then wear it*
if your circumstances correspond with those described then you must endure the consequences

WEAR *that argument is wearing a bit thin*
that is a very weak case

WEAR *to have to wear something*
to have to put up with something

WEAR *to wear a hair shirt*
to practice self-discipline

WEAR *to wear one's crown of thorns*
to have one's own difficulties (John 19:5)

WEAR *to wear sackcloth and ashes*
humbly to demonstrate repentance

WEAR *to wear the trousers*
to be the dominant party

WEAR *uneasy lies the head that wears a crown*
responsibility involves some risks and some burdens (from Shakespeare's HENRY IV)

WEATHER *a fair-weather friend*
a person purporting to be a friend who offers no support in difficult times

WEATHER *to be under the weather*
to be drunk or (less often) sick

WEATHER *to keep a weather eye out for something*
to look out with particular care

WEATHER *to make heavy weather of something*
to struggle excessively with a relatively simple task

WEATHER *to run into heavy weather*
to encounter difficulties

WEATHER *to weather the storm*
to come safely through a crisis

WEB *a tangled web*
a series of lies, especially with inconsistencies leading to exposure (from Sir Walter Scott's MARMION)

WEB *to be the center of the spider's web*
to control an operation which involves numerous and/or complex ingredients

WED *to be wed to something*
to be utterly dedicated to a proposal

WEDDING *a shotgun wedding*
a wedding held to ensure that an impending birth will be legitimate (refers to threats by the bride's father to kill the bridegroom)

WEDDING *wedding*
amalgamation

WEDGE *to be the thin end of the wedge*
by conceding a small point, to create an undesirable precedent for much larger issues

WEDGE *to drive a wedge between two persons*
to set out to cause two persons to confront each other

WEED *to weed some group out*
to get rid of some elements not meeting a desired standard

WEIGH *to weigh anchor*
to move to another address

WEIGH *to weigh in with a particular argument*
to produce a strong argument

WEIGH *to weigh in with something*
to bring something along

WEIGH *to weigh two alternative propositions in the balance*
to assess the relative significance of two alternative propositions

WEIGHT *a heavyweight*
a person of importance or influence

WEIGHT *lightweight*
uninfluential

WEIGHT *to be a weight off one's mind*
to be a great relief

WEIGHT *to be worth one's weight in gold*
to be very desirable

WEIGHT *to carry weight*
to be influential

WEIGHT *to lend weight to something*
to use one's influence in support of some cause

WEIGHT *to pull one's weight*
to do one's proper share of the work requiring to be done

WEIGHT *to take a weight off someone's shoulder*
to assist a person by relieving him of some responsibility

WEIGHT *to throw one's weight about*
to use one's real or imagined status in order to achieve certain results

WELL *to go back to the well*
to go to the original source

WEST *to sink slowly in the west*
to fail gradually

WET *to be a wet blanket*
to be a spoilsport

WET *to be wet behind the ears*
to be excessively naive and inexperienced

WET *to get one's feet wet*
to do the necessary but unpleasant or menial parts of a task

WETHER *bell-wether*
first indication

WHEAT *to separate the wheat from the chaff*
to distinguish between important and unimportant ingredients

WHEEL *a big wheel*
an important person

WHEEL *fortune's wheel*
the vicissitudes of life

WHEEL *the squeaky wheel gets the most attention*
those complaining the most loudly will get their problems sorted out first

WHEEL *the wheel has turned*
circumstances have changed

WHEEL *the wheel has turned the complete circle*
things are now back to where they were before

WHEEL *the wheels are back under the bus*
normal activity has been resumed

WHEEL *the wheels fell off*
the plan failed

WHEEL *to be a fifth wheel*
to be superfluous

WHEEL *to be a small cog in a large wheel*
to be a relatively unimportant person in a large organization

WHEEL *to make the wheels go round*
to cause something to happen

WHEEL *to oil the wheels*
to make things go smoothly

WHEEL *to put a spoke in someone's wheel*
to interfere with another person's activity, so preventing its continuance

WHEEL *to put one's shoulder to the wheel*
to make a strong effort

WHEEL *to reinvent the wheel*
to waste resources doing something already accomplished

WHEEL *to set the wheels in motion*
to institute appropriate action

WHEEL *to wheel and deal*
to energetically enter into commercial transactions of dubious propriety

WHEEL *to wheel someone in*
to bring a person along for a confrontation

WHEEL *wheels within wheels*
secret machinations

WHET *to whet one's appetite*
to arouse one's curiosity or interest

WHIP *a whipping boy*
a person made to suffer for the faults of others

WHIP *to be a fair crack of the whip*
to be just

WHIP *to crack the whip*
to exert one's authority

WHIP *to have the whip hand*
to be in control of a situation

WHIP *to whip oneself into a lather*
to become unduly excited

WHIRL *to reap the whirlwind*
to suffer the adverse consequences of a bad act

WHIRLWIND *to sow the wind and reap the whirlwind*
to make bad mistakes and to suffer the even worse consequences

WHISKER *by a whisker*
only just

WHISPER *to hear a whisper*
to learn a rumored hypothesis

WHISTLE *a whistlestop tour*
a hurried (especially ceremonial) visit to many places

WHISTLE *bells and whistles*
imaginative variations

WHISTLE *to blow the whistle on someone*
to report a person's improper behavior to the authorities or to publicize it

WHISTLE *to whistle in the dark*
to feign greater confidence than one really has

WHISTLE *you can whistle for it*
you wish in vain

WHITE *a white elephant*
an expensive and useless luxury (refers to gifts of sacred elephants by the King of Siam to persons then ruined by the expense of their upkeep)

WHITE *a white knight*
a party voluntarily coming to the assistance of another party at considerable cost to itself

WHITE *a white lie*
a false statement uttered in a good cause

WHITE *in black and white*
in writing, spelling out all the details

WHITE *lily-white*
honest and incorruptible

WHITE *to be a black and white issue*
to involve very clear distinctions

WHITE *to show the white feather*
to indicate cowardice (refers to crossbred birds, not regarded as useful in cock fighting)

WHITE *to turn white*
to express shock at unexpected news

WHITE *to white ant someone*
to surreptitiously seek to destroy a person

WHITEWASH *to whitewash*
to exonerate when this is not warranted by the facts

WHOA *from go to whoa*
from start to finish (refers to the command given to horses)

WHOLE *a whole bag of tricks*
a series of articles or a series of artificial devices

WHOLE *the whole box and dice*
all relevant components

WHOLE *to go the whole hog*
to do something very thoroughly (refers to the close shearing of lambs)

WICKET *to be on a sticky wicket*
to face some difficulties

WIDE *to be wide off the mark*
to have a belief which is far removed from the true position

WIDE *to give something a wide berth*
to go out of one's way to avoid contact with a person

WIELD *to wield a big stick*
to exert power

WIFE *an old wives' tale*
a traditionally-held theory without any scientific backing

WILD *a wild card*
an unexpected development

WILD *a wild goose chase*
a foolish search for something which does not exist

WILD *to be successful beyond one's wildest dreams*
to be far more successful than one could have expected

WILD *to sow wild oats*
to indulge in foolish behavior while a young adult

WILD *wildcat*
(of a strike) unofficial; (of an oil well) drilled as a pure prospect; (of a financial scheme) very hazardous

WILD *wild horses would not cause me to do something*
I absolutely refuse to do something (refers to a form of torture)

WILDERNESS *to be a lone voice in the wilderness*
to be the only person stating unpopular views

WILDERNESS *to be in the wilderness*
to be out of office against one's will

WILLING *a willing horse*
a cheerful worker

WILLING *the spirit is willing but the flesh is weak*
the body is not up to the demands made on it

WIN *a breadwinner*
a person earning by personal exertion the income of a household

WIN *heads I win—tails you lose*
whichever way this matter goes I will benefit at your expense

WIN *to hold a winning hand*
to be in an unbeatable position to defeat others

WIN *to win by a long chalk*
to win very conclusively

WIN *to win hands down*
to win very convincingly

WIN *to win one's spurs*
to gain recognition after a period of effort (refers to the earning of a knighthood in battle)

WIN *to win some rounds*
to be partly successful

WIN *to win the booby prize*
to do worse than all others

WIN *to win the prize in a canter*
to win very easily

WIND *something in the wind*
something is going on secretly (this phrase uses the actual word ''something'')

WIND *straws in the wind*
unofficial preliminary indications of something likely to be formally revealed soon

WIND *the cold wind of change*
the unpleasant realities of new circumstances

WIND *to cast prudence to the winds*
to cease being prudent

WIND *to get wind of something*
to hear rumors giving advance information

WIND *to put the wind up someone*
to alarm a person

WIND *to reap the whirlwind*
to suffer the adverse consequences of a bad act

WIND *to sail against the wind*
to oppose the views currently being held by others

WIND *to sail close to the wind*
to act in a very dangerous manner

WIND *to scatter something to the four winds*
to permanently get rid of something

WIND *to see which way the wind is blowing*
to establish the factors relevant to a situation

WIND *to sow the wind and reap the whirlwind*
to make bad mistakes and to suffer the even worse consequences

WIND *to take the wind out of someone's sails*
to upset a person by anticipating his actions or using arguments which he was proposing to use

WINDFALL *windfall*
unexpected good fortune

WINDMILL *to tilt at windmills*
to attack an imagined but nonexistent enemy (from Cervantes' DON QUIXOTE)

WINDOW *a window of opportunity*
an opportunity temporarily available

WINDOW *to engage in window dressing*
to present figures in an artificially favorable light

WINDOW *to fly out the window*
to be lost

WINDOW *to throw a pebble against the window*
to gently draw attention to oneself

WINDOW *to throw something out of the window*
to completely reject an idea or proposal

WING *on a wing and a prayer*
without proper resources

WING *to clip someone's wings*
to reduce another person's freedom to act as he thinks fit

WING *to spread one's wings*
to assert authority which has not yet been conferred by one's superiors and for which one may not be ready

WING *to take someone under one's wing*
to protect a person

WING *to wait in the wings*
to be prepared to stay unobtrusive till the appropriate time for action arrives

WINK *a nod and a wink*
a sign that understanding has been reached in a matter which in the interest of discretion has not been discussed aloud

WINK *a nod is the same as a wink to a blind horse*
fine distinctions are not appropriate here

WINK *not to get a wink of sleep*
not to sleep at all

WINKLE *to be a Rip van Winkle*
to be a person out of touch with current conditions (title of and character in a book by Washington Irving)

WINNER *to be on a winner*
to have faith in, give support to and/or invest in a project which proves to be successful

WINTER *to buy straw hats in winter*
to buy in a depressed market when most other people are sellers

WIPE *to wash one's hands of something*
to emphatically decline future responsibility

WIPE *to wipe the floor with someone*
to inflict a humiliating defeat on a person

WIPE *to wipe the slate clean*
to forgive past indiscretions

WIPE *to wipe the smile off someone's face*
to destroy a person's complacency

WIPE *wipe that smile off your face!*
treat this matter more seriously!

WIRE *to be a live wire*
to be an enthusiast

WIRE *to go haywire*
to refuse to function properly

WIRE *to have one's wires crossed*
to be mistaken about key facts

WISH *a death wish*
the contemplation of action so foolish that it is likely to lead to utter disaster

WITCH *a witchhunt*
an exercise seeking to find someone who can be blamed

WITH *to be with it*
to think on the same lines as the current generation or to be fully informed

WITHER *to wither on the vine*
by virtue of changed circumstances or the effluxion of time to be no longer relevant

WOLF *a lone wolf*
person who prefers to act without involving others

WOLF *to be a wolf in sheep's clothing*
to be a hypocrite or to be dangerous although masquerading as something harmless (Matthew 7:15)

WOLF *to cry "wolf"*
to repeatedly raise an unjustified concern with the result that one will be ignored when the circumstances change

WOLF *to keep the wolf from the door*
to avoid imminent trouble

WOLF *to throw someone to the wolves*
to expose a person to exploitation by more sophisticated persons

WONDER *a nine-day wonder*
an exciting event, but one which will cease to arouse interest when the novelty has worn off

WONDER *gutless wonder*
coward

WOOD *neck of the woods*
localized area

WOOD *not to see the wood for the trees*
to overlook the general picture because of undue concentration on the details

WOOD *to be babes in the wood*
to be excessively naive and inexperienced and thus ripe for exploitation

WOOD *to be out of the woods*
the previous difficulties have been overcome

WOOD *to get rid of the dead wood*
to terminate the services of unsatisfactory personnel

WOOD *to touch wood*
it is to be hoped that our good luck will not go away

WOODEN *to get the wooden spoon*
to come ingloriously last

WOODPILE *the nigger in the woodpile*
the factor spoiling an otherwise satisfactory arrangement

WOODWORK *to crawl out of the woodwork*
to turn up unexpectedly and in large numbers

WOOL *dyed in the wool*
very loyal and partisan

WOOL *to pull the wool over someone's eyes*
to deceive or deliberately mislead another person

WOOL *to wrap someone in cotton wool*
to be overprotective toward a person

WOOL *woolly-headed*
slightly muddled

WORD *a torrent of words*
a rapid and uninterrupted outpouring of words

WORD *a word in someone's ear*
a confidential discussion

WORD *from the word "go"*
from the beginning

WORD *mark my words*
you will find out that I am right

WORD *not to mince words*
to speak bluntly

WORD *the password is so-and-so*
the main attraction is so-and-so

WORD *the word is out*
it is now known

WORD *the words stuck in my throat*
I just could not get myself to say the intended words

WORD *to eat one's words*
to retract

WORD *to echo someone's words*
to repeat another person's views as though they were one's own

WORD *to get words in edgeways*
to manage to interrupt a conversation in order to put in a separate point of view

WORD *to put words into someone's mouth*
to attempt to get someone to say something in the particular terms drafted by another person

WORD *you took the words right out of my mouth*
you have just said what I was about to say

WORK *a nasty piece of work*
an unpleasant person

WORK *donkey work*
necessary but uninspiring routine work

WORK *to do someone's dirty work*
to do something unethical on behalf of another person

WORK *to do the leg work*
to carry out the tedious part of a project

WORK *to do the spadework*
to prepare

WORK *to have one's work cut out to do something*
it will be difficult to achieve something

WORK *to work hand in glove with someone*
to work in close cooperation with a person or to be in collusion with a person to the detriment of others

WORKS *to be in the works*
to be being dealt with

WORKS *to get the works*
to get the full treatment

WORKS *to gum up the works*
to cause an activity to be halted

WORKS *to throw a spanner into the works*
to cause an unexpected complication

WORLD *it's a small world*
it is surprising to meet people one knows in unexpected places

WORLD *to be on top of the world*
to be very happy

WORLD *to be out of this world*
to be superb

WORLD *to carry, the world on one's shoulders*
to resent being left to perform a huge task single-handedly (refers to Atlas, who was condemned to bear the heavens on his shoulders for leading the Titans against the gods)

WORLD *to get the worst of all worlds*
to get a series of disadvantages without achieving any corresponding advantages

WORLD *to make a world of difference*
to make a great deal of difference

WORLD *to se the world on fire*
to do something particularly brilliant

WORLD *to want the best of both worlds*
to unreasonably desire to get some advantage without incurring a corresponding disadvantage

WORLD *why in the world?*
why?

WORM *a bookworm*
a person who likes reading and study

WORM *a can of worms*
a heterogeneous collection of unexpected problems

WORM *the early bird gets the worm*
a person who acts ahead of others gets an advantage over them

WORM *the worm has turned*
a previously compliant person is now exerting his personality

WORM *to worm one's way in*
to subtly insinuate oneself into a person's trust

WORSE *someone's bark is worse than his bite*
the harsh words belie the reality of mild action

WORST *to get the worst of all worlds*
to get a series of disadvantages without achieving any corresponding advantages

WORTH *not to be worth one's salt*
not to be pulling one's weight (refers to Roman soldiers being paid in salt—a practice giving rise to the modern word "salary")

WORTH *not worth a tinker's curse*
worthless

WORTH *to be worth one's weight in gold*
to be very desirable

WORTH *to throw in one's six pennies' worth*
to modestly supply one's own facts or views

WORTH *to throw in one's two-cents' worth*
to modestly supply one's own facts or views

WOUND *to charge like a wounded bull*
to impose excessive prices (a play on words; not a simile)

WOUND *to heal wounds*
to affect a reconciliation

WOUND *to lick one's wounds*
to adjust oneself to defeat

WOUND *to open up an old wound*
to take action which revives a long-standing grievance

WOUND *to rub salt into someone's wound*
to deliberately make damage even worse

WRAP *that wraps it up*
that is the end

WRAP *to be wrapped in something*
to enjoy something

WRAP *to keep under wraps*
to keep confidential

WRAP *to wrap someone in cotton wool*
to be overprotective toward a person

WRAP *to wrap up a deal*
to bring a deal to a successful conclusion

WRECK *to salvage something out of the wreck*
to achieve some minor benefits out of a disastrous situation

WRING *to wring one's hands*
to express despair

WRIST *a slap on the wrist*
a mild rebuke

WRITE *nothing to write home about*
unimpressive

WRITE *to see the writing on the wall*
to appreciate the inevitability of some event (Daniel 5)

WRITE *to write one's own ticket*
to set one's own terms and conditions

WRONG *not to put a foot wrong*
to behave impeccably

WRONG *to back the wrong horse*
to have faith in, give support to and/or invest in a project which proves to be unsuccessful

WRONG *to bark up the wrong tree*
to reach an incorrect conclusion

WRONG *to be born on the wrong side of the blanket*
to be illegitimate

WRONG *to be on the wrong tack*
to be using an incorrect procedure or policy

WRONG *to be on the wrong track*
to be heading toward an incorrect solution

WRONG *to be on the wrong tram*
to be completely mistaken as to the basic facts

WRONG *to be on the wrong wavelength*
to be incorrect in one's thinking

WRONG *to get off on the wrong foot with someone*
to make an unfavorable initial impression on a person

WRONG *to get out of bed on the wrong side*
to be grumpy

WRONG *to get the wrong sow by the ear*
to reach an incorrect conclusion

WRONG *to have hold of the wrong end of the pineapple*
to be utterly mistaken

WRONG *to hold the wrong end of the stick*
to be completely mistaken about something

WRONG *to rub someone up the wrong way*
to annoy someone with actions failing to recognize his current mood

Y

YARD *in one's own backyard*
in one's own domain

YARDSTICK *a yardstick*
a standard by which something is measured

YARN *to spin a yarn*
to tell an amusing or unlikely story

YEAR *for donkey's years*
for a long time

YEAR *from the year dot*
from time immemorial

YELL *to scream and yell*
to protest violently

YEOMAN *yeoman service*
valuable assistance over a long time

YESTERDAY *not to have been born yesterday*
not to be naive

YOUNG *a trap for young players*
a good opportunity for the inexperienced or naive to make mistakes

YOUNG *an old head on young shoulders*
experience, knowledge, and maturity in a young person

YOUNG *it is on for young and old*
the excitement has started

YOUNG *the night is young*
the project is only at a very early stage

YOUNG *young Turks*
members of an organization who hold ideas regarded as too revolutionary

Z

Z *from a to z*
from start to finish

ZERO *to zero in on a target*
to move directly toward one's objective

180 *to turn around 180 degrees*
to completely reverse a stance

9

THEMATIC SECTION

ANIMALS

ALBATROSS *to be an albatross around someone's neck*
to be a great burden (popularized by Coleridge's ANCIENT MARINER)

ANIMAL *there is no such animal*
that does not exist

ANIMAL *to be a political animal*
to want to be in politics

ANT *to white ant someone*
to surreptitiously seek to destroy a person

ASS *to make an ass of oneself*
to act stupidly in public

BAIT *to swallow the bait*
to succumb to a temptation deliberately put in one's way

BARK *someone's bark is worse than his bite*
the harsh words belie the reality of mild action

BARK *to bark up the wrong tree*
to reach an incorrect conclusion

BAT *to have bats in the belfry*
to be mad

BAY *to hold someone at bay*
to successfully resist an attacker

BEAK *to be a sticky beak*
to show excessive curiosity into matters not of one's concern

BEAST *the nature of the beast*
the reality of the situation

BEAVER *an eager beaver*
a person with great drive and enthusiasm even if this causes annoyance to others

BEAVER *to beaver away*
to work diligently at some task

BEE *to be a busy bee*
to work with great diligence

BEE *to have a bee in one's bonnet*
to have an obsession

BEELINE *to make a beeline for something*
to go straight to something with great enthusiasm or to head for some goal by the most direct route

BETE *to be someone's bete noire*
to be a person whose ideas and actions cause upset and loathing in another person (French ''black heart'')

BIRD *a bird in the hand is worth two in the bush*
a benefit currently available is more valuable than a seemingly much larger benefit which may or may not be achieved in the future

BIRD *a bird's-eye view*
a general overview or summary of a subject, emphasizing the major features

BIRD *a little bird told me*
I heard from an unnamable informant (Ecclesiastes 10:20)

BIRD *birds of a feather flock together*
persons of like interests gather in the same place

BIRD *that is strictly for the birds*
that is blatant and naive nonsense

BIRD *the bird has flown*
the person sought is no longer about

BIRD *the early bird gets the worm*
a person who acts ahead of others gets an advantage over them

BIRD *to be a rare bird*
to be an unusual type of individual

BIRD *to have a bird brain*
to be stupid

BIRD *to kill two birds with one stone*
to achieve a second objective in the course of achieving the first objective

BIT *to champ at the bit*
to be impatient

BLOOD *to smell blood*
to divine imminent victory

BONE *a bone of contention*
the subject matter of violent disagreement

BONE *the bare bones*
(of a story) nothing but the essential elements

BONE *to have a bone to pick*
the have a grievance which requires discussion

BONE *to throw someone a bone*
to fob a person off with a symbolic but unimportant gesture

BULL *a bull in a china shop*
a careless person likely to cause great damage

BULL *a cock and bull story*
an explanation which is completely unbelievable and unacceptable

BULL *to be a red rag to a bull*
to be something which makes a person very angry and very excited (refers to the erroneous belief that the color red, rather than the motion of waving, excites a bull)

BULL *to be within a bull's roar of something*
to be very close to something

BULL *to charge like a wounded bull*
to impose excessive prices (a play on words; not a simile)

BULL *to hit the bull's eye*
to make the correct decision

BULL *to take the bull by the horns*
to come to grips with the realities of a difficult problem

BUTT *to butt in*
uninvited to involve oneself in someone else's conversation

BUTTERFLY *to have a butterfly mind*
not to concentrate on the matter on hand

BUTTERFLY *to have butterflies in one's stomach*
a feeling of anxiety

BUZZ *to buzz off*
to go away

CALF *to kill the fatted calf*
to demonstrate welcome and forgiveness on a person's return (Luke 15:23)

CAMEL *the straw which broke the camel's back*
the latest step, which, when added to a large number of seemingly harmless previous steps, sets off a disaster resulting from the cumulative effect

CAT *a cat and dog existence*
a life full of frequent squabbles

CAT *a cat may look at a king*
don't give yourself airs!

CAT *a copycat*
a person who imitates another person's ideas

CAT *a game of cat and mouse*
negotiations between two parties of unequal bargaining power during which the stronger makes some temporary concessions to the weaker without, however, affecting the latter's eventual total defeat

CAT *there is more than one way to skin a cat*
this can be achieved in a variety of acceptable ways

CAT *there is no room to swing a cat*
this place is very small (actually refers to a cat-o'-nine-tails)

CAT *to be a cat's paw*
to be a person who is being used as a tool by others

CAT *to be the cat's pajamas*
to have an exaggerated idea of one's own importance

CAT *to bell the cat*
to do some dangerous but highly useful mission (refers to a fable in which none of the mice was willing to put a warning bell on a cat)

CAT *to kick the cat*
to take out one's anger on some innocent party

CAT *to let the cat out of the bag*
to reveal an embarrassing secret (refers to the exposure of cheats at fairs, attempting to pass a cat wrapped in a sack off as a piglet)

CAT *to rain cats and dogs*
to rain heavily

CAT *to see which way the cat jumps*
to await developments

CAT *to throw a cat among the pigeons*
to cause consternation by revealing an unpleasant and unexpected fact

CAT *when the cat is away the mice will play*
in the absence of supervision discipline will be lax

CAT *wildcat*
(of a strike) unofficial; (of an oil well) drilled as a pure prospect; (of a financial scheme) very hazardous

CHAMELEON *a chameleon*
a person without character who changes his stance all the time to reflect the current circumstances

CHICKEN *chicken and egg*
two factors each of which results in the other

CHICKEN *chicken-hearted*
showing little courage

CHICKEN *the chickens are coming home to roost*
the consequences of past actions are becoming obvious

CHICKEN *to be chicken feed*
to be small and unimportant

CHICKEN *to count one's chickens before they are hatched*
to treat as fact the expected results of a future proposal

CHOP *to lick one's chops*
to look forward to something with pleasurable anticipation

COBWEB *to blow the cobwebs away*
to revive an old issue

COCK *a cock and bull story*
an explanation which is completely unbelievable and unacceptable

COCK *cock-eyed*
stupid

COCOON *in a cocoon*
in a safe and isolated environment

COW *a cash cow*
a source of ready money

COW *a milch cow*
an easy and plentiful source of some desired benefit

COW *a sacred cow*
an institution so well established that it is virtually unalterable

COW *to argue till the cows come home*
to argue forever

CRAWL *to crawl out of the woodwork*
to turn up unexpectedly and in large numbers

CRESTFALLEN *crestfallen*
dejected

CROCODILE *to shed crocodile tears*
to be a hypocrite

CROW *as the crow flies*
by the shortest distance

CROW *to eat crow*
to accept a humiliating defeat

CUCKOO *to be a cuckoo in the nest*
to purport to be a member of a group of people although having no such right

CUCKOO *to be in cloud cuckoo land*
to be mad or to have unrealistic expectations

CUD *to chew the cud*
to reflect on something

DINOSAUR *a dinosaur*
a person with incredibly outmoded idea

DOG *a cat and dog existence*
a life full of frequent squabbles

DOG *a dogfight*
a small side-skirmish, especially between airplanes

DOG *a lame dog*
a person under some disadvantage needing attention and assistance

DOG *a shaggy dog story*
an amusing anecdote with an unexpected ending, often involving talking animals given certain human skills

DOG *a sly dog*
a person who is discreet about his weaknesses

DOG *a watchdog*
a person or organization monitoring behavior

DOG *all the dogs are barking*
this news is being widely disseminated

DOG *any stick to beat a dog*
any excuse will do if it serves one's purpose

DOG *dog-eared*
(of pages) well-thumbed

DOG *dog-tired*
tired out

DOG *every dog has his day*
good luck comes sooner or later

DOG *every man and his dog*
everybody

DOG *love me—love my dog*
if you accept me then you must also accept my associates

DOG *not a dog's chance*
no hope at all

DOG *one cannot teach an old dog new tricks*
people get irreversibly set in their ways

DOG *the tail wagging the dog*
a minor aspect with disproportionate effect on a major aspect

DOG *the top dog*
the person in the most powerful position

DOG *to be a dog in the manger*
to spitefully deny something to others, notwithstanding its uselessness to oneself

DOG *to be a dog's breakfast*
to be a very messy arrangement

DOG *to be a gay dog*
to lead an idle life while flaunting the symbols of wealth

DOG *to be in the doghouse*
to be in disgrace

DOG *to call off the dogs*
to abandon an audit or other inquiry

DOG *to give a dog a bad name*
to malign a person

DOG *to go to the dogs*
to be ruined

DOG *to have a hair of the dog that bit one*
to drink more in an attempt to overcome the effects of alcohol already consumed

DOG *to lead a dog's life*
to be ill-treated

DOG *to let sleeping dogs lie*
to refrain from raising an issue which is not obviously requiring attention

DOG *to rain cats and dogs*
to rain heavily

DOG *to throw something to the dogs*
to sacrifice something

DOG *two men and a dog*
very few people

DOG *underdog*
object of sympathy (the antonym of ''underdog effect'' is ''bandwagon effect'')

DOG *why keep a dog and bark oneself?*
it is silly to pay for assistance and then do things personally

DONKEY *donkey work*
necessary but uninspiring routine work

DONKEY *for donkey's years*
for a long time

DONKEY *to talk the hind leg off a donkey*
to talk excessively

DRAKE *to play ducks and drakes*
not to treat the matter seriously

DRONE *a drone*
an idle person

DROVE *people stayed away in droves*
few people came

DUCK *a lame duck*
a person unable to fend for himself (a lame duck president - a president still in office but without influence because the commencement of his successor's term is imminent)

DUCK *in two shakes of a duck's tail*
in an instant

DUCK *to be a dead duck*
to have failed

DUCK *to be a sitting duck*
to be readily exploited

DUCK *to be like water off a duck's back*
(of advice or criticism) to be completely rejected

DUCK *to play ducks and drakes*
not to treat the matter seriously

DUCKLING *an ugly duckling*
a person initially thought unintelligent who develops and becomes brilliant (refers to a cygnet in a brood of ducks in a children's story of that name by Hans Christian Andersen)

EAGLE *to have an eagle eye*
to be able to notice small mistakes very readily

EAR *to turn something on its ear*
to reverse something

EARMARK *to earmark*
to allocate to a specific purpose

EGG *to be a bad egg*
to engage in dishonest behavior

ELEPHANT *a rogue elephant*
a person of vicious temper who acts in an undisciplined way

ELEPHANT *a white elephant*
an expensive and useless luxury (refers to gifts of sacred elephants by the King of Siam to persons then ruined by the expense of their upkeep)

ELEPHANT *one looks for elephants in elephant country*
one needs to search in the right place

EYE *bright-eyed and bushy-tailed*
naive but enthusiastic

FEATHER *to make feathers fly*
to cause trouble to those misbehaving

FEATHER *to ruffle someone's feathers*
to engage in behavior which irritates another person

FEATHER *to show the white feather*
to indicate cowardice (refers to cross-bred birds, not regarded as useful in cock fighting)

FEATHER *to thrash with a feather*
to award only a minor punishment for a very serious offense

FERRET *to ferret something out*
by diligent research to discover some secret

FETTER *to fetter someone*
to stop a person acting on his own initiative

FISH *a queer fish*
an unusual type of person

FISH *an ocean full of fish*
plenty of opportunity

FISH *neither fish, flesh nor good red herring*
unclassifiable by virtue of being neither one thing nor another (from Cervantes' DON QUIXOTE)

FISH *that has nothing to do with the price of fish*
that is quite irrelevant

FISH *to be a big fish in a little pond*
to be a person holding an important office but in an unimportant organization

FISH *to be a cold fish*
to be an unemotional person

FISH *to be a different kettle of fish*
to be something very dissimilar

FISH *to be a fine kettle of fish*
to be a terrible muddle

FISH *to be a fish out of water*
to be in difficulty by virtue of being in a strange environment

FISH *to fish in troubled waters*
to profit from a disturbed situation

FISHY *to be fishy*
to be suspicious

FLEA *to send someone away with a flea in his ear*
to give a person frank but unwelcome facts (refers to fleas trapped in the armor of ancient knights)

FLOCK *flock*
congregation in the charge of a religious official

FLY *I would love to be a fly on the wall*
I would love to hear what goes on

FLY *a fly in the ointment*
a flaw (refers to dead flies turning perfumes rancid) (Ecclesiastes 10:1)

FLY *a fly-by-night operator*
a confidence trickster

FLY *someone can't hurt a fly*
someone is very gentle and kindhearted

FLY *there are no flies on someone*
a person is alert

FLY *to fly the coop*
to grow up and become independent

FOLD *the fold*
the body of believers (refers to an enclosure for sheep)

FOOT *to put something back on its feet*
to repair something

FOUR *an opening wide enough to drive a coach and four through*
an excellent opportunity

FOX *a fox hole*
space which is really too small for a person's needs or comfort

FROG *to have a frog in one's throat*
to be hoarse

FROG *to leap frog something*
to overtake something, with the likelihood of in turn being overtaken (refers to a game in which participants jump over each other in turn)

FUR *to make the fur fly*
to create a disturbance

GAME *to be fair game*
to be someone who can legitimately be attacked

GANDER *what is sauce for the goose is sauce for the gander*
arguments which apply in one case also apply in another

GNAT *to strain at a gnat*
to be scrupulous about trifles

GO *from the word "go"*
from the beginning

GOAT *a scapegoat*
a person unfairly blamed for something not his fault

GOAT *to play the giddy goat*
to act the fool

GOAT *to separate the sheep from the goats*
to distinguish between those with and without certain attributes (Matthew 25:32)

GOLDFISH *to be in a goldfish bowl*
to be very open to view

GOLDFISH *what is this—a bunch of grapes or a bowl of goldfish?*
surely you know what this is!

GOOSE *a wild goose chase*
a foolish search for something which does not exist

GOOSE *to be too frightened to say "boo" to a goose*
to be excessively shy

GOOSE *to cook one's goose*
to do something which backfires on one

GOOSE *to kill the goose that lays the golden eggs*
through excessive greed to destroy a very profitable enterprise

GOOSE *what is sauce for the goose is sauce for the gander*
arguments which apply in one case also apply in another

GRASSHOPPER *since he was knee high to a grasshopper*
since he was a very young child

HACKLE *to raise someone's hackles*
to make a person angry

HALCYON *in Halcyon days*
in past happier times (refers to the 14 days about the winter solstice when winds were calm and to the mythical bird said to breed in a floating nest at that time)

HAMSTRUNG *to be hamstrung*
to have limited freedom to act as one would wish

HARE *first catch your hare*
do things in logical order and after proper preparation (advice on how to cook a hare in Mrs. Beeton's celebrated COOK BOOK)

HARE *hare-brained*
wildly stupid

HARE *to chase every hare*
to be easily sidetracked

HARE *to run with the hare and hunt with the hounds*
to keep in with two opposing sides

HARE *to set a hare running*
in order to achieve some desired effect to initiate some related activity

HARNESS *in harness*
before retirement

HEAD *to rear its ugly head*
to make an unwelcome appearance

HEN *a mother hen*
an overly protective person

HEN *hen-pecked*
subject to domination by one's wife

HERD *to follow the herd*
to do what most other people are doing

HERRING *to be a red herring*
to be something designed to divert attention away from the main question

HIDE *to cover one's hide*
to provide excuses or take other evasive action in an attempt to avoid the adverse consequences of one's actions

HIDEBOUND *hidebound*
narrow-minded

HOG *a road hog*
an inconsiderate motorist

HOG *to go the whole hog*
to do something very thoroughly (refers to the close shearing of lambs)

HOG *to make a hog of oneself*
to demonstrate greed

HOGWASH *hogwash*
nonsense

HOOT *not to care a hoot*
not to show the slightest concern or enthusiasm

HORN *the horns of a dilemma*
the unpalatable alternatives between which a choice must be made

HORN *to lock horns with someone*
to have an argument with another person

HORN *to pull one's horns in*
to retreat from previously stated views

HORSE *I could eat a horse*
I am very hungry

HORSE *a Trojan horse*
a trick (refers to a large gift horse full of soldiers used to bring about the fall of Troy, as described in Homer's ILIAD)

HORSE *a dark horse*
a person with unsuspected talents

HORSE *a nod is the same as a wink to a blind horse*
fine distinctions are not appropriate here

HORSE *a stalking horse*
an ostensible reason

HORSE *a two-horse race*
a contest between only two serious contestants

HORSE *a warhorse*
an old soldier who likes to relive past wartime experiences

HORSE *a willing horse*
a cheerful worker

HORSE *hold your horses!*
just wait a little!

HORSE *horse sense*
natural shrewdness

HORSE *horsetrading*
tough negotiations

HORSE *it is horses for courses*
some combinations work particularly well

HORSE *that is a horse of a very different color*
that is a much more acceptable proposition

HORSE *the horse and buggy days*
long ago

HORSE *to back the wrong horse*
to have faith in, give support to and/or invest in a project which proves to be unsuccessful

HORSE *to be off on one's hobby horse*
to throw into conversation aspects of a subject in which one has a passionate interest

HORSE *to be on one's high horse*
to be excessively pompous

HORSE *to drive a coach and horses through something*
to demonstrate major errors in something

HORSE *to flog a dead horse*
to misguidedly do something patently useless

HORSE *to frighten the horses*
to scare people off by one's ill-considered tactics

HORSE *to learn something from the horse's mouth*
to get information from someone qualified to impart it

HORSE *to look a gift horse in the mouth*
to be suspicious about a benefit which has been volunteered

HORSE *to put the cart before the horse*
to do things in the wrong order

HORSE *to shut the stable door after the horse has bolted*
to take preventive action only after the relevant event

HORSE *to swap horses in midstream*
to change direction during the course of a project

HORSE *wild horses would not cause me to do something*
I absolutely refuse to do something (refers to a form of torture)

HORSEPLAY *horseplay*
boisterous and undignified behavior

HOUND *to run with the hare and hunt with the hounds*
to keep in with two opposing sides

HOUND *to set the hounds baying*
to excite the gossips by providing material which they can use

JACKAL *to keep the jackals at bay*
to pay one's creditors just sufficient to avoid repercussions

KID *to treat someone with kid gloves*
to handle a person with great discretion

KITTEN *to have kittens*
to be in a state of great dismay (refers to a superstition that certain acts would cause women to bear kittens instead of children)

LAMB *a lamb led to slaughter*
a naive person allowing himself to be exploited

LAMB *one might as well be hanged for a sheep as for a lamb*
further action will not increase the adverse consequences already in train (refers to the stealing of both sheep and lambs being capital crimes under old English law)

LAMB *sacrificial lamb*
somebody unfairly made to suffer for the mistakes of others

LAMB *to be mutton dressed up as lamb*
to foolishly pretend to be younger

LAMB *to wait two shakes of a lamb's tail*
to wait just a few moments

LAP *to lap it up*
to enjoy the attention

LARK *to rise with the lark*
to get up early

LEASH *to hold someone on a short leash*
to give a person very little authority

LEECH *leech*
person taking undue advantage of others

LEOPARD *a leopard cannot change his spots*
each person is born with certain unalterable characteristics

LION *the lion's share*
the biggest portion

LION *to beard the lion in his den*
to visit someone important at his headquarters

LION *to put one's head into the lion's mouth*
to recklessly expose oneself to great danger

LION *to throw someone to the lions*
to abandon a person

LIZARD *flat out like a lizard*
to be hard at work (a play on words, not a simile)

LYNX *lynx-eyed*
having acute vision

MACKEREL *to throw a sprat to catch a mackerel*
to risk a little in the hope of gaining much

MARE *a mare's nest*
a discovery with illusory benefits

MAVERICK *maverick*
a person who likes to do things differently from other persons (refers to unbranded livestock)

MINNOW *to miss the sharks while netting the minnows*
to succeed in minor aspects but fail in the ones that really matter

MOLE *to make mountains out of molehills*
to treat a minor problem as though it were a major disaster

MONKEY *monkey business*
mischievous or underhand activity

MONKEY *to play monkey tricks on someone*
to engage in discreditable behavior affecting a person

MOTH *moth-eaten*
(of ideas, etc.) antiquated

MOTHBALL *to mothball equipment*
to put equipment on a "care and maintenance" basis

MOUSE *a game of cat and mouse*
negotiations between two parties of unequal bargaining power during which the stronger makes some temporary concessions to the weaker without, however, affecting the latter's eventual total defeat

MOUSE *mice have been here*
intruders have entered this place

MOUSE *to labor mightily and bring forth a mouse*
to be quite ineffective

MOUSE *when the cat is away the mice will play*
in the absence of supervision discipline will be lax

NEST *a nest egg*
life savings

NEST *to feather one's own nest*
to improperly arrange a transaction on behalf of others to one's own financial advantage

NEST *to foul one's own nest*
to disparage one's home or workplace

NIT *to nitpick*
to criticize a person in respect of very minor matters

OSTRICH *to be an ostrich*
to refuse to face up to an unpleasant truth (refers to the reputed habit of ostriches in danger)

OWL *to be a night owl*
to habitually go to bed late

OYSTER *the world is one's oyster*
one has enormous scope for activity

PACK *to be at the head of the pack*
to be the best of many or the de facto leader

PACK *to bring someone back to the pack*
to make a person conform

PEARL *a pearl*
a thing of great excellence

PECK *pecking order*
order of seniority

PECKER *to keep one's pecker up*
to stay cheerful

PERCH *to knock someone off his perch*
to displace a person from his leadership position in some competitive situation

PETREL *to be a stormy petrel*
a person who disturbs a pleasant state of affairs by agitating for change

PIG *a guinea pig*
a person on whom some new practice is tried out

PIG *to buy a pig in a poke*
to buy goods of unknown quality

PIGEON *a pigeon pair*
one son and one daughter as the sole offspring

PIGEON *to be one's pigeon*
to be one's area of responsibility

PIGEON *to pigeon-hole*
to put aside for further consideration in the distant future

PIGEON *to throw a cat among the pigeons*
to cause consternation by revealing an unpleasant and unexpected fact

PIGHEADED *pigheaded*
unduly obstinate

PITFALL *pitfall*
unsuspected danger

PLAGUE *to be of plague proportions*
to be great in number

PONY *a show pony*
a pompous person

POSSUM *to play possum*
to pretend that one is not present

POSSUM *to stir the possum*
to set out to raise controversial issues

PUP *to sell someone a pup*
to cheat a person in a transaction, especially by misrepresentation as to the true value of something

PURR *to positively purr*
(of a person) to be very pleased; (of an engine) to run very smoothly

PUSSY *to pussyfoot around*
to take ineffectual steps

RABBIT *move over and let the greyhound see the rabbit*
move over

RABBIT *to pull a rabbit out of the hat*
to produce an unexpected and seemingly miraculous but highly desirable solution

RAT *a case of rats leaving a sinking ship*
the desertion of an enterprise in anticipation of imminent failure

RAT *rat race*
pressures of modern living

RAT *to smell a rat*
to become suspicious

REIN *a tight rein*
strong controls

REIN *to give rein to one's fancy*
to let one's imagination have free scope

REIN *to rein in something*
to keep better control over something

RHINOCEROS *to have the hide of a rhinoceros*
to be totally unaffected by and unresponsive to valid criticism

ROBIN *a round robin*
(1) a series of checks from A to B, from B to C, from C to A, and so on, leaving all of them in the same net position as before

ROBIN *a round robin*
(2) a document signed by members of an organization which has the same effect as a resolution of a meeting

ROOST *to rule the roost*
to dominate

RUMINATE *to ruminate*
to ponder over a matter (lit., to chew the cud)

SHARK *to miss the sharks while netting the minnows*
to succeed in minor aspects but fail in the ones that really matter

SHEEP *a black sheep*
a disreputable member of an otherwise reputable group

SHEEP *one might as well be hanged for a sheep as for a lamb*
further action will not increase the adverse consequences already in train (refers to the stealing of both sheep and lambs being capital crimes under old English law)

SHEEP *to be a wolf in sheep's clothing*
to be a hypocrite or to be dangerous although masquerading as something harmless (Matthew 7:15)

SHEEP *to be home on the sheep's back*
to be doing well

SHEEP *to cast sheep's eyes at someone*
to look at a person amorously

SHEEP *to ride on the sheep's back*
to benefit from the production of wool

SHEEP *to separate the sheep from the goats*
to distinguish between those with and without certain attributes (Matthew 25:32)

SHEEP *to spoil the ship for a ha'p'orth of tar*
to engage in a false economy (the current word "ship" is actually a mistake for the original word "sheep" and the tar refers to the treatment of wounds)

SHEEPISH *sheepish*
embarrassed, as though guilty

SHELL *to retreat into one's shell*
to become shy and introversive

SKIN *a cleanskin*
a person without a criminal record

SNAIL *at a snail's pace*
very slowly

SNAKE *a game of snakes and ladders*
a series of ups and downs

SNAKE *a snake in the grass*
a person of low character

SNAP *to snap at someone's heels*
to be a minor irritation to a person

SOW *one can't make a silk purse out of a sow's ear*
it is impossible to manufacture something of a high standard without appropriate raw materials

SOW *to get the wrong sow by the ear*
to reach an incorrect conclusion

SPIDER *to be the center of the spider's web*
to control an operation which involves numerous and/or complex ingredients

SPRAT *to throw a sprat to catch a mackerel*
to risk a little in the hope of gaining much

SPUR *to spur someone on*
to agitate a person into doing something

SQUIB *a damp squib*
disappointingly ineffective action (refers to fireworks which fail to go off)

STAMPEDE *to stampede someone into something*
to pressure a person into taking some action

STICK *sticks and carrots*
disincentives and incentives in combination (refers to the handling of donkeys)

STING *to be the sting in the tail*
to be the unexpected unpleasant conclusion

STIR *to stir up a hornet's nest*
to take action which results in unpleasant side-effects

SWALLOW *one swallow does not make a summer*
much further evidence is desirable before any action taken

SWARM *to swarm out*
to gather in large numbers

SWINE *to cast pearls before swine*
to confer valuable benefits on someone who neither recognizes nor appreciates them

TAIL *bright-eyed and bushy-tailed*
naive but enthusiastic

TAIL *the tail end of something*
the very end of something

TAIL *to be the sting in the tail*
to be the unexpected unpleasant conclusion

TAIL *to get off one's tail*
to stir oneself from one's inertia

TAIL *to have one's tail between one's legs*
to show great humility in the light of a back down

TAIL *with his tail between his legs*
contritely

TENTACLE *tentacles*
strong and unpleasant influence extending a long way from its base and in many directions

TIGER *a paper tiger*
an empty threat

TIGER *a toothless tiger*
an authority which has been given totally inadequate powers for its task

TIGER *to have a tiger by the tail*
to be involved in an activity which is much more dangerous than one had realized

TOOTH *to bare one's teeth*
to imply threats

TOOTH *to take the bit between one's teeth*
to face up to a problem

TRACE *to kick over one's traces*
to become insubordinate

TRAMPLE *to trample someone underfoot*
by virtue of one's great power to treat a person's rights with contempt and not to give them proper consideration

TURKEY *cold turkey*
the sudden cessation of drugs to an addict

TURKEY *to talk turkey*
to talk realistically

TURTLE *to turn turtle*
to capsize

UNDERBELLY *to have a soft underbelly*
to have a weakness which can be exploited

VENOM *venom*
deep-rooted ill will

VULTURE *vulture*
person benefiting from another's misfortune

WEB *a tangled web*
a series of lies, especially with inconsistencies leading to exposure (from Sir Walter Scott's MARMION)

WETHER *bell-wether*
first indication

WHISKER *by a whisker*
only just

WHOA *from go to whoa*
from start to finish (refers to the command given to horses)

WING *to clip someone's wings*
to reduce another person's freedom to act as he thinks fit

WING *to spread one's wings*
to assert authority which has not yet been conferred by one's superiors and for which one may not be ready

WING *to take someone under one's wing*
to protect a person

WOLF *a lone wolf*
a person who prefers to act without involving others

WOLF *to be a wolf in sheep's clothing*
to be a hypocrite or to be dangerous although masquerading as something harmless (Matthew 7:15)

WOLF *to cry "wolf"*
to repeatedly raise an unjustified concern with the result that one will be ignored when the circumstances change

WOLF *to keep the wolf from the door*
to avoid imminent trouble

WOLF *to throw someone to the wolves*
to expose a person to exploitation by more sophisticated persons

WOOL *dyed in the wool*
very loyal and partisan

WORM *a bookworm*
a person who likes reading and study

WORM *a can of worms*
a heterogeneous collection of unexpected problems

WORM *the early bird gets the worm*
a person who acts ahead of others gets an advantage over them

WORM *the worm has turned*
a previously compliant person is now exerting his personality

WORM *to worm one's way in*
to subtly insinuate oneself into a person's trust

ART

ART *to raise something to a fine art form*
to become very clever at doing something

CANVAS *to have a blank canvas*
to be bereft of ideas

EXHIBITION *to make an exhibition of oneself*
to behave in a way which invites ridicule

MOSAIC *a mosaic*
something with a large number of different aspects to it

PAINT *to paint a black picture*
to state a set of unfavorable factors

PAINTING *not to be an oil painting*
to be ugly

PEDESTAL *to put someone on a pedestal*
to admire a person and regard him as more marvelous than is warranted

PERSPECTIVE *to put something into perspective*
to explain the background of something so that its significance in relation to other things can be better appreciated

PICTURE *to balance the picture*
to put the other side of the story or to quote facts in contradiction

PICTURE *to change the whole picture*
to alter the major assumptions on which some assessment was based

PICTURE *to conjure up a picture*
to use words to convey a vivid impression

PICTURE *to have a clear picture of something*
to have a good understanding of something

PICTURE *to put someone in the picture*
to fill a person in with the background of a situation

PICTURE *to see the big picture*
to have the vision and imagination enabling a project to be developed as part of a bigger whole

SKETCH *a thumbnail sketch*
brief but pertinent details

AVIATION

BAIL *to bail out of something*
to abandon an enterprise in anticipation of disaster

BALLOON *to go down like a lead balloon*
to receive a very cool reception

BALLOON *when the balloon goes up*
when the adverse facts come to light

EDGE *to have a leading edge*
to have an advantage

FLY *a highflyer*
an ambitious and/or successful person

FLY *time flies*
time passes very quickly, but if wasted can never be recovered (from Virgil's GEORGICS)

FLY *to fly by the seat of one's pants*
to act unprofessionally

FLY *to fly high*
to be ambitious

FLY *to have to fly*
to need to leave in order to reach the next destination quickly

FLY *to let fly at someone*
to attack a person with strong words

FLYING *to achieve a flying start*
to get operational very quickly

GROUND *to get something off the ground*
to take a project beyond its initial stages and make it operational

LAND *to land something*
to achieve something

PARACHUTE *golden parachute*
generous provisions in a remuneration package which come into play in certain circumstances

TAILSPIN *tailspin*
very fast fall

WING *on a wing and a prayer*
without proper resources

ZERO *to zero in on a target*
to move directly toward one's objective

BUILDINGS

ARCHITECT *to be the architect of something*
to be the person devising something innovative

BACKYARD *in one's own backyard*
in one's own domain

BELFRY *to have bats in the belfry*
to be mad

BENCHMARK *a benchmark*
a standard by which something is measured

BLOWTORCH *to apply the blowtorch to something*
to totally destroy something

BLUEPRINT *blueprint*
a master plan for some activity or a model which others can copy

BOLT *nuts and bolts*
basic ingredients

BRICK *it is London to a brick*
it is virtually certain

BRICK *one can't make bricks without straw*
one cannot achieve results in the absence of adequate resources

BRICK *to be up against a brick wall*
to be unable to achieve anything because of intractable opposition or apathy

BRICK *to drop a brick*
to make a sudden shattering and unexpected announcement

BRICKBATS *to throw brickbats at someone*
to express displeasure with a person

BRIDGE *a lot of water has flowed under the bridge since then*
much has happened since then

BRIDGE *to be water under the bridge*
to matter no longer

BRIDGE *to bridge a gap*
to fill a need or make up a shortfall

BRIDGE *to bridge a gulf*
to overcome a wide divergence in views

BRIDGE *to build bridges*
to work at improving relationships

BRIDGE *to burn one's bridges*
to do something irreversible

BRIDGE *to cross a bridge only when one comes to it*
to await the crystallization of a situation before sorting it out

BRUSH *a broad brush approach*
rough justice

BRUSH *to be tarred with the same brush*
to be damned merely because of one's association with another person

CARPET *to be on the carpet*
to be lectured in regard to one's alleged misdeeds

CASTLE *a castle in Spain*
an impracticable proposition

CASTLE *a castle in the air*
an impracticable proposition

CEILING *ceiling*
upper permitted limit

CEMENT *to cement a relationship*
to do something in an endeavor to make a relationship permanent

CHISEL *to chisel away at something*
to reduce the size of something in a series of small stages

CLOSET *to come out of the closet*
to publicly admit one's homosexuality

CORNER *to be around the corner*
to be imminent

CORNER *to be in a tight corner*
to experience a crisis

CORNER *to cut corners*
to lower one's standards in order to complete something more quickly

DOOR *a foot in the door*
the opportunity to do business

DOOR *never darken my door again*
do not ever return

DOOR *not to break someone's door down*
to be quite unenthusiastic about someone's goods or services

DOOR *one's door is always open*
people can take their problems to one at any time

DOOR *through the back door*
unofficially or surreptitiously

DOOR *to be out the door*
to have one's position terminated

DOOR *to beat a path to someone's door*
to seek a person out in great numbers

DOOR *to leave the door open*
to issue a standing invitation for the resumption of some negotiations

DOOR *to open up doors*
to create opportunities

DOOR *to put something at someone's door*
to blame a person

DOOR *to show someone the door*
to ask a person to leave

DOOR *to shut the door on someone*
to deny another person a desired opportunity

DOOR *to slam the door in someone's face*
ostentatiously to refuse to have any dealings with a person

DOORSTEP *on one's own doorstep*
in one's own domain

DRAIN *that is money down the drain*
money has been wastefully lost on a failed project

DRAW *back to the drawing board*
the details need to be reconsidered

DRAW *to be on the drawing board*
to be being planned in detail

DRAWBRIDGE *to pull up the drawbridge*
to refuse to cooperate

DUST *when the dust settles*
when sufficient time has passed

EAVESDROP *to eavesdrop*
to deliberately listen to conversations to which one is not a party

FENCE *on our side of the fence*
in the group representing our vested interest

FENCE *to be on the other side of the fence*
to have an opposing point of view or position

FENCE *to be over the fence*
to be unreasonable

FENCE *to mend fences*
to achieve a reconciliation

FENCE *to sit on the fence*
to refuse to choose between two alternatives

FENCE *to want to jump all one's fences at once*
to be unrealistic

FLOOR *to get in on the ground floor*
to invest on very favorable terms

FLOOR *to hold the floor*
to dominate a conversation

FLOOR *to wipe the floor with someone*
to inflict a humiliating defeat on a person

FRAMEWORK *framework*
outline of a proposal, on which further details can be developed

FUSE *to have a short fuse*
to lose one's temper very readily

GARDEN *everything in the garden is lovely*
everything is fine

GATE *to close the gate*
to deny an opportunity which was previously available

GATE *to gatecrash a gathering*
to attend a gathering without any right to be there

GATEPOST *between you and me and the gatepost*
confidentially

GATEWAY *gateway to something*
method of achieving something

HALL *liberty hall*
a place where one is free to do as one wishes

HAMMER *to go hammer and tongs*
to do something with great energy

HOLE *a square peg in a round hole*
a person much more suitable for a position rather different from the one held

HOME *charity begins at home*
a person's first responsibility should be to his family

HOME *to be too close to home*
to be too near the truth to be welcome

HOME *to keep the home fires burning*
to maintain normal domestic activity during the temporary absence of the breadwinner

HOUSE *a half-way house*
an intermediate position

HOUSE *people in glass houses should not throw stones*
those who are less than perfect are foolish to criticize others

HOUSE *to be on the house*
to be free of cost

HOUSE *to bring the house down*
to greatly amuse an audience

HOUSE *to eat someone out of house and home*
to ruin a person by eating all he has

HOUSE *to put one's house in order*
to fix up the deficiencies in one's affairs

HOUSEHOLD *a household name*
a very familiar name

INN *no room at the inn*
no room

KITCHEN *to get the rounds of the kitchen*
(of a husband) to be subject to personal abuse by his wife

LADDER *a game of snakes and ladders*
a series of ups and downs

LADDER *rungs up a ladder*
gradual steps to an ultimate goal

LADDER *to be at the bottom of the ladder*
to be in the most junior position in some hierarchy

LEAD *to swing the lead*
to cheat an employer by not working while being paid to do so

LOCK *to lock someone into some arrangement*
to create an agreement which cannot be broken by one of the parties

MARBLE *to be carved in marble*
to be virtually unalterable

NAIL *on the nail*
immediately

NAIL *to hit the nail right on the head*
to astutely come to the correct conclusion

NAIL *to nail someone*
to put the blame on a person

NAIL *to nail something down*
to tie up the loose ends of an arrangement

NICHE *to carve out a niche for oneself*
to deliberately create an opportunity to use one's talents effectively

NICHE *to find one's niche*
to find the opportunity to use one's talents

NOOK *in every nook and cranny*
everywhere

NUT *nuts and bolts*
basic ingredients

PAINT *to paint oneself into a corner*
to foolishly put oneself into a position from which escape is impossible

PAPER *to paper over the cracks*
to institute extremely superficial and basically ineffective remedies

PATH *path*
means of achieving an objective

PATH *slippery path*
dangerous course of action

PATH *to be on a path strewn with roses*
to lead a very pleasant life

PATH *to beat a path to someone's door*
to seek a person out in great numbers

PATH *to block someone's path*
to interfere with a person's opportunity to advance himself

PATH *to cross someone's path*
to meet another person by chance

PATH *to lead someone up the garden path*
to mislead a person by deliberately fallacious arguments

PATH *to smooth the path for someone*
to use one's influence to make arrangements so that a person's task will be easier or more readily accomplished

PATH *to tread a particular path*
to take certain initiatives

PEG *a square peg in a round hole*
a person much more suitable for a position rather different from the one held

PENNY *the penny dropped*
a person has just realized a fact which should have been obvious (refers to old-fashioned pay toilets)

PILLAR *a pillar of some organization*
a significant supporter of some organization

PLUG *to have the plug pulled out from under one*
to have a successful activity destroyed by the actions of someone else

PUTTY *to be putty in someone's hands*
to be far too easily influenced by another person

RIVET *to be riveted to one's seat*
to find the activity being watched very exciting and worthy of full attention

ROCK *bedrock price*
lowest possible price

ROOF *the roof has fallen in*
an enterprise has collapsed

ROOF *to go through the roof*
(of a person) to be very upset or (of prices) to escalate greatly

ROOF *to hit the roof*
to be very angry

ROOF *to scream something from the rooftops*
to communicate a message to a wide audience

ROOF *under one roof*
under the same management

ROOM *there is no room to swing a cat*
this place is very small (actually refers to a cat-o'-nine-tails)

SCREW *to have a screw loose*
to be mentally unbalanced

SCREW *to tighten the screw*
to increase the moral and psychological pressure

SHINGLE *to hang up one's shingle*
to go into business offering expert personal services

SINK *everything but the kitchen sink*
a lot of things

SLEDGEHAMMER *to use a sledgehammer to crack a nut*
to devote vastly more resources to a project than is warranted by all the circumstances

STABLE *a Herculean cleaning of the stables*
a thorough revision of operating procedure (refers to Hercules, a mythical Greek hero who cleaned the stables of Augeas)

STEAMROLL *to steamroll something through*
to use enormous force to achieve an objective

STONE *cornerstone*
key ingredient

STONE *the touchstone*
the standard

TACK *to get down to brass tacks*
to discuss the aspects which really matter

TAR *to have a touch of the tarbrush*
to be not quite a full-blood Caucasian

TONGS *to go hammer and tongs*
to do something with great energy

TOOLS *tools*
the means to do something

TOWER *a tower of Babel*
a noisy and confused assembly (Genesis 11)

TOWER *to be a tower of strength*
to be a person who supports and comforts another

TROWEL *to lay it on with a trowel*
to flatter

TUNNEL *tunnel vision*
an extremely narrow and inflexible way of considering issues

WALL *Chinese walls*
a system to ensure that different parts of some organization do not gain access to each other's confidential information

WALL *I would love to be a fly on the wall*
I would love to hear what goes on

WALL *a chink in the wall*
an opportunity to do something which otherwise could not be done

WALL *to be a crack in the wall*
to represent a small unintended opportunity which can be exploited

WALL *to drive someone to the wall*
to ruin a person

WALL *to drive someone up the wall*
to annoy another person by one's actions

WALL *to go to the wall*
to become bankrupt

WALL *to have one's back to the wall*
to be hard-pressed by creditors or opponents

WALL *to nail someone to the wall*
to outmaneuver another person

WALL *to put a wall around someone*
to stop a person associating with others

WALL *to see the writing on the wall*
to appreciate the inevitability of some event (Daniel 5)

WALL *walls have ears*
someone may be overhearing (words on wartime posters, reminding people of the existence of spies; may also refer to certain rooms in the Louvre, constructed so that conversations could be heard in other rooms)

WALL *walls of Jericho*
something seemingly solid but actually destructible (Joshua 6:20)

WAY *to pave the way*
to prepare for something

WEDGE *to be the thin end of the wedge*
by conceding a small point to create an undesirable precedent for much larger issues

WHITEWASH *to whitewash*
to exonerate when this is not warranted by the facts

WINDMILL *to tilt at windmills*
to attack an imagined but non-existent enemy (from Cervantes' DON QUIXOTE)

WINDOW *a window of opportunity*
an opportunity temporarily available

WINDOW *to engage in window dressing*
to present figures in an artificially favorable light

WINDOW *to fly out the window*
to be lost

WINDOW *to throw a pebble against the window*
to gently draw attention to oneself

WINDOW *to throw something out of the window*
to completely reject an idea or proposal

YARDSTICK *a yardstick*
a standard by which something is measured

CARDS

ACE *to be within an ace of something*
to be extremely close to something

ACE *to have an ace up one's sleeve*
to hold an impressive counter-argument in reserve

ACE *to hold all the aces*
to be in an unbeatable position to defeat others

BUCK *the buck stops here*
I accept full responsibility (sign on the desk of Harry S. Truman when President of the United States)

BUCK *to pass the buck*
in an uncooperative spirit to decline responsibility for a matter on the grounds that someone else more properly has responsibility for it

CARD *a house of cards*
an organization which gives a misleading impression of solidity

CARD *a three-card trick*
a ruse used by a dishonest person in order to induce his victims to hand over some of their assets

CARD *a wild card*
an unexpected development

CARD *let the cards fall where they may*
irrespective of what happens

CARD *to have the cards stacked against one*
to be faced with many difficulties frustrating a project

CARD *to hold all the cards*
to be assured of victory

CARD *to hold one's cards close to one's chest*
to keep one's plans and strategies secret

CARD *to lay one's cards on the table*
to be utterly frank and open or to honestly disclose one's position

CARD *to play every card in the pack*
to try very hard and use every conceivable argument

CARD *to play one's cards right*
to approach a matter sensibly

CARD *to play the cards as they fall*
to deal with problems as they arise

CARD *to play the last card in the pack*
to lower one's standards in a final desperate effort

CARD *without any cards to play*
without the means to achieve something

DEALER *sharp dealer*
person engaging in barely honest or mildly unethical practices

HAND *to deal the final hand*
to take steps which conclude a matter

HAND *to disclose one's hand*
to give away information regarding one's intention

HAND *to force someone's hand*
to take action causing another person to react

HAND *to hold a winning hand*
to be in an unbeatable position to defeat others

HAND *to throw in one's hand*
to give in or to give up

HAND *to tip one's hand*
to disclose details of one's position

HANDS *to win hands down*
to win very convincingly

MISERE *to be a laid-down misere*
to be very easily accomplished and/or to be certain of outcome (refers to the declaration in certain card games undertaking to win no tricks)

ODDS *to have the odds stacked against one*
to be faced with many difficulties frustrating a project

PACK *to play the last card in the pack*
to lower one's standards in a final desperate effort

PEG *to be level pegging*
(of contestants) to have little between them

POKER *a game of poker*
negotiations in which the parties try to bluff each other

POKER *a poker face*
a facial expression which does not reveal one's thoughts during negotiations

SHOWDOWN *showdown*
disclosure of certain pertinent facts

SUIT *one's long suit*
one's main skills

SUIT *to follow suit*
to do the same as others

TRICK *to be unable to take a trick*
to be unable to achieve success in anything

TRUMP *to hold the trump card*
to be in an unbeatable position to defeat others

TRUMP *to play the trump card*
to make a final move, thereby defeating one's opponents

TRUMP *to trump someone*
to defeat a person

TRUMP *to turn up trumps*
to finish up better than expected or to experience unexpected good luck

UNDERPLAY *to underplay some situation*
to hold something in reserve

CHESS

CHECKMATE *checkmate*
defeat

CHESS *to be a chess game*
to be a complex exercise, requiring great skill

CHESSMASTER *a chessmaster*
a clever strategist

GAMBIT *a gambit*
an opening move in a competitive situation which involves short term losses in the expectation of long term gains

GAMBIT *opening gambit*
the first in a series of strategic moves (a tautological expression which also involves a misunderstanding of a technical chess term)

KNIGHT *a white knight*
a party voluntarily coming to the assistance of another party at considerable cost to itself

MOVE *your move!*
the next step is up to you

PAWN *a pawn*
a person of small importance who is manipulated by others

STALEMATE *stalemate*
a final result in which neither party to a dispute is victorious

CIRCUSES

AUNT *an Aunt Sally*
a person who can readily be singled out and criticized as the proxy for a group

BALL *to have too many balls in the air*
to attempt to do more than can be coped with

CARD *to be on the cards*
to be likely

CARD *to have a card up one's sleeve*
to secretly have information relevant to a transaction

CIRCUS *to be a real circus*
to be a highly disorganized affair

CONJURE *to conjure up a picture*
to use words to convey a vivid impression

CONJURE *to conjure up something*
to produce something in circumstances where this seemed impossible

HOOP *to jump through hoops*
to undergo some ordeal

LINE *to tread the thin line*
cautiously to take action in circumstances where either too much or too little will cause difficulties

MAGIC *the magic moment*
the perfect time

MAGIC *there is no magic in that*
that is quite ordinary

MERRY *to be on a merry-go-round*
to be sent from one bureaucrat to another

NET *a safety net scheme*
a scheme for dealing with the exceptional cases not covered by normal arrangements

PULL *to pull a rabbit out of the hat*
to produce an unexpected and seemingly miraculous but highly desirable solution

ROLLER *a roller coaster ride*
a series of successes followed by failures

SLEIGHT *sleight of hand*
deceit by trickery

SPOTLIGHT *to turn the spotlight on something*
to draw public attention to something

SWING *what one loses on the swings one gains on the roundabouts*
there are advantages and disadvantages which offset each other

TIGHTROPE *to walk a tightrope*
to do something very dangerous

TRICK *one cannot teach an old dog new tricks*
people get irreversibly set in their ways

TRICK *something has done the trick*
something has achieved the desired purpose

TRICK *to score a hat trick*
to have three successive favorable outcomes

TRICK *to use every trick in the book*
to try very hard and use every conceivable argument

WAND *to wave a magic wand*
to direct affairs without the restraints of the real world

CLOTHES

APRON *to be tied to someone's apron strings*
to be excessively influenced by a female

BELT *to get something under one's belt*
to achieve something

BELT *to hit someone below the belt*
to act unfairly toward another person

BELT *to tighten one's belt*
to lower one's rate of spending

BONNET *to have a bee in one's bonnet*
to have an obsession

BOOT *to be too big for one's boots*
to have an unwarranted belief as to one's capabilities or status

BOOT *to give someone the boot*
to terminate a person's appointment

BOOT *to go in boots and all*
to do something very roughly

BOOT *to hang up one's boots*
to retire

BOOT *to have one's heart in one's boots*
to be terrified

BOOT *to lick someone's boots*
to show humility

BOOT *to put the boot in*
to reprimand a person

BOOT *to quake in one's boots*
to be afraid

BOOTSTRAP *to be British to one's bootstraps*
to be very demonstrative about one's Britishness

BOOTSTRAP *to pull oneself up by one's bootstraps*
to make a praiseworthy effort to better oneself unaided

BREECHES *to be too big for one's breeches*
to have an exaggerated idea of one's own importance

CAP *a feather in one's cap*
a meritorious personal achievement

CAP *cap*
upper permitted limit

CAP *if the cap fits then wear it*
if your circumstances correspond with those described then you must endure the consequences

CAP *to cap a story*
to tell an even funnier story than the one just told

CAP *to earn a dunce's cap*
to do something stupid

CAP *to go cap in hand*
to show humility while soliciting a favor

CAP *to put one's thinking cap on*
to concentrate on finding a solution to a difficult problem

CAP *to set one's cap at someone*
(of females) to try to attract a person as a marriage partner

CAP *to throw one's cap into the air*
to celebrate some achievement

CLOAK *cloak and dagger activity*
secret activity

CLOAK *to cloak something*
to disguise the true nature of something

CLOTHES *to steal someone's clothes*
to plagiarise another person's ideas

CLOTHING *to be a wolf in sheep's clothing*
to be a hypocrite or to be dangerous although masquerading as something harmless (Matthew 7:15)

COAT *to cut one's coat according to the cloth*
to accommodate oneself to limitations beyond one's control and to do the best in the circumstances

COAT *to hang onto someone's coat-tails*
to excessively rely on another person's initiatives

COAT *to trail one's coattails*
to invite a quarrel

COLLAR *to be hot under the collar*
to be very agitated

CUFF *off the cuff*
impromptu

DRESS *first in best dressed*
persons acting early will do better than latecomers

DRESS *to dress someone down*
to scold a person

GARTER *I will have his guts for garters*
I am extremely angry and dissatisfied with him

GAUNTLET *to throw down the gauntlet*
to issue a challenge (refers to the glove worn by a knight)

GLOVE *the gloves are off*
the challenge has been accepted

GLOVE *to treat someone with kid gloves*
to handle a person with great discretion

GLOVE *to work hand in glove with someone*
to work in close cooperation with a person or to be in collusion with a person to the detriment of others

GLOVE *with an iron hand in a velvet glove*
with a hard attitude made to seem soft

HAT *I'll eat my hat if so-and-so happens*
I do not believe that so-and-so will happen

HAT *a peg to hang a hat on*
something which provides a convenient or plausible excuse for some particular action

HAT *at the drop of a hat*
very readily

HAT *not to just pick something out of a hat*
to choose carefully, after weighing all the considerations

HAT *to be old hat*
to be a very widely-known fact

HAT *to keep something under one's hat*
to maintain a confidence

HAT *to knock something into a cocked hat*
to twist something so that its original form is hardly recognizable

HAT *to pull a rabbit out of the hat*
to produce an unexpected and seemingly miraculous but highly desirable solution

HAT *to score a hat trick*
to have three successive favorable outcomes

HAT *to take one's hat off to someone*
to be full of admiration for a person

HAT *to talk through one's hat*
to say things which demonstrate the speaker's ignorance of the subject

HAT *to throw one's hat into the air*
to express joy

HAT *to wear a particular hat*
to act in a particular capacity or for a particular vested interest

IRON *to iron out something*
to sort out a difficult problem

JACKET *to keep someone in a strait-jacket*
to deny a person any discretionary powers at all

KNICKERS *to get one's knickers in a knot*
to get unduly excited

LACE *strait-laced*
puritanical

LINEN *to wash one's dirty linen in public*
to expose one's domestic differences to the world at large

MANTLE *to assume someone's mantle*
to take over another person's role

MASK *to unmask someone*
to discover a person's true identity

PAJAMAS *to be the cat's pajamas*
to have an exaggerated idea of one's importance

PANTS *a kick in the pants*
an admonition

PANTS *to bore the pants off someone*
to weary a person by dull and uninteresting conversation

PANTS *to catch someone with his pants down*
to act when another person least expects it

PANTS *to charm the pants off someone*
to delight a person

PANTS *to fly by the seat of one's pants*
to act unprofessionally

PANTS *to scare the pants off someone*
to greatly frighten a person

PETTICOAT *petticoat government*
rule by women

PIN *for two pins I would do so-and-so*
my tolerance is almost exhausted and I am very tempted to do so-and-so

PIN *not to care a pin for something*
not to have the slightest interest in something

PIN *pin money*
an allowance to a wife for her personal use

PIN *to be on pins and needles*
to be very agitated

PINPOINT *to pinpoint*
to identify very precisely

POCKET *not to live in each other's pockets*
to each follow his own lifestyle

POCKET *the hip pocket nerve*
the assessment of issues by their financial effects on one

POCKET *to be in someone's pocket*
to be subject to undue influence by another person

POCKET *to be out of pocket*
to have been forced to spend money which cannot be recovered from others

POCKET *to have deep pockets*
to have large financial resources

POCKET *to have money burning a hole in one's pocket*
to be impatient to spend or invest available funds

POCKET *to line one's pockets*
to make, improperly and secretly, a profit out of some transaction

POCKET *to put one's hands in one's pockets*
to spend

PURSE *one can't make a silk purse out of a sow's ear*
it is impossible to manufacture something of a high standard without appropriate raw materials

PURSE *to button up one's purse*
to refuse to spend money

PURSE *to hold the purse strings*
to have control of expenditure

PURSE *to tighten the purse strings*
to reduce outlays

SACKCLOTH *to wear sackcloth and ashes*
humbly to demonstrate repentance

SEAM *to be bursting at the seams*
to be very crowded

SEAM *to come apart at the seams*
(of an arrangement) to break down

SEW *to sew something up*
to negotiate a deal

SHIRT *keep your shirt on!*
relax!

SHIRT *so-and-so would give one the shirt off his back*
so-and-so is very generous

SHIRT *to lose one's shirt*
to make heavy financial losses

SHIRT *to put one's shirt on something*
to invest heavily in some speculative venture

SHIRT *to wear a hair shirt*
to practice self-discipline

SHOE *to be in someone's shoes*
to have another person's responsibility

SHOE *to fill someone's shoes*
to be a good successor

SHOE *to wait for the other shoe to drop*
to await the seemingly imminent and inevitable (refers to a man undressing, disturbing a neighbor by dropping one shoe, then frustrating his expectation by putting the other shoe down gently)

SHOELACE *to pull oneself up by one's own shoelaces*
to make a superhuman effort

SHOESTRING *to do something on a shoestring*
to do something with great economy

SKIRT *to hide under someone's skirts*
to let someone else take the consequences of one's actions

SLEEVE *to have an ace up one's sleeve*
to hold an impressive counter-argument in reserve

SLEEVE *to keep something up one's sleeve*
to secretly retain something in reserve for use in the future or at a later stage of negotiations

SLEEVE *to laugh up one's sleeve*
to laugh surreptitiously

SLEEVE *to roll up one's sleeves*
to get on with a job energetically

SLEEVE *to wear one's heart on one's sleeve*
to lack the reserve expected of one

SOCK *to chop someone off at the socks*
to stop someone's proposals prematurely

SOCK *to pull one's socks up*
to set out to improve or correct one's inadequate behavior or performance

STITCH *a stitch in time saves nine*
preventive maintenance saves money in the long run

STITCH *to stitch up a deal*
to successfully conclude a deal

THREAD *to hang by a slender thread*
to only just survive

TROUSERS *to catch someone with his trousers down*
to act when another person least expects it

TROUSERS *to wear the trousers*
to be the dominant party

TRY *to try something on for size*
to cheekily do something

UMBRELLA *an umbrella*
protection; or something all embracing

UMBRELLA *under the umbrella of some organization*
under the auspices of some organization

UNVEIL *to unveil something*
to give details not previously available

VEIL *thinly-veiled*
barely concealed

VEIL *to draw a veil over something*
pointedly to avoid discussing something

VEIL *under the veil of something*
on the pretext of something

WASH *it will all come out in the wash*
the facts will emerge as work proceeds

WASH *it won't wash*
this explanation is not acceptable

WASH *when the wash comes through the machine*
in due course

WEAR *that argument is wearing a bit thin*
that is a very weak case

WEAR *to have to wear something*
to have to put up with something

COLORS

BLACK *a black hole*
an intermediate range of values producing anomalous results or a particularly obnoxious prison cell

BLACK *a black sheep*
a disreputable member of an otherwise reputable group

BLACK *in black and white*
in writing, spelling out all the details

BLACK *the pot calling the kettle black*
a person criticizing another person without realizing his own even greater shortcomings

BLACK *there are black clouds on the horizon*
bad news is expected

BLACK *things look black*
there is little hope of success or prosperity or a favorable outcome

BLACK *to be a black and white issue*
to involve very clear distinctions

BLACK *to be in someone's black books*
to be out of favor with a person

BLACK *to be in the black*
to have money

BLACK *to blackball someone*
to reject a person as unsuitable

BLACK *to give someone a black look*
to indicate one's displeasure with a person

BLACK *to have a black mark against one's name*
to have a tarnished reputation

BLACK *to paint a black picture*
to state a set of unfavorable factors

BLACK *to paint someone black*
to ruin a person's reputation

BLUE *a blueblood*
a person of high birth (refers to the appearance of veins on the skin of members of some royal families)

BLUE *between the devil and the deep blue sea*
to be faced with two equally unpalatable alternatives which cannot both be avoided

BLUE *blue ribbon*
of superb quality (refers to the insignia of the Order of the Garter)

BLUE *blue sky*
supremely optimistic

BLUE *blue-eyed boy*
person shown unjustified favoritism

BLUE *once in a blue moon*
very rarely (refers to the volcanic eruption at Krakatoa in 1883 when volcanic dust caused the moon to appear blue)

BLUE *to be a blue-chip stock*
to be of excellent quality

BLUE *to be a bolt from the blue*
to be a totally unexpected event

BLUE *to be in a blue funk*
to be terrified

BLUE *to come out of the blue*
to be totally unexpected

BLUE *to feel blue*
to feel depressed

BLUE *to go on till one is blue in the face*
to argue for a long time

BLUE *to have a blue fit*
to be very agitated

BLUE *to scream blue murder*
to make serious allegations

BLUE *true blue*
superbly loyal

BROWN *to be browned off*
to be fed-up

COLOR *that takes on added color*
there are now further facts which alter the appearance of a matter

COLOR *to see the color of someone's money*
to get evidence of the sincerity of a person's proposal

GILD *to gild the lily*
(actually: to gild refined gold, to paint the lily) to do something patently unnecessary

GILT *gilt-edged*
very safe

GOLD *a golden opportunity*
an unparalleled opportunity

GOLD *silence is golden*
it is better not to incriminate anyone

GRAY *to be a gray area*
to be in an undefined position straddling two or more possibilities

GREEN *a green chum*
an inexperienced person

GREEN *distant fields look greener*
activities of which one has no experience seem much easier than is really the case

GREEN *to be green*
to be naive

GREEN *to give the green light*
to grant permission

GREEN *to have green fingers*
to be good at gardening

GREEN *to move on to greener pastures*
to commence a new, better career

GREEN *to turn green*
to become very envious

PINK *to be tickled pink*
to be very pleased

PINK *to look in the pink*
to look well

PURPLE *to be purple with rage*
to be very angry

RED *a red-letter day*
an important occasion (refers to the color used to print saints' days on some calendars)

RED *neither fish, flesh nor good red herring*
unclassifiable by virtue of being neither one thing nor another (from Cervantes' DON QUIXOTE)

RED *red-hot*
highly exciting and desirable

RED *red tape*
excessively bureaucratic procedures

RED *the red-carpet treatment*
courtesies extended to a person to make him feel important and welcome

RED *to be a red herring*
to be something designed to divert attention away from the main question

RED *to be a red rag to a bull*
to be something which makes a person very angry and very excited (refers to the erroneous belief that the color red, rather than the motion of waving, excites a bull)

RED *to be in the red*
to owe money

RED *to be left red-faced*
to be embarrassed

RED *to catch someone red-handed*
to apprehend a person in the course of committing a crime

RED *to get the red light*
to be forbidden to do something

RED *to paint the town red*
to go on an exciting social outing

RED *to see red*
to become very angry

RED *to see red lights flashing*
to be conscious of the danger

ROSY *to present a rosy picture*
to state a set of favorable factors

SILVER *every cloud has a silver lining*
there are benefits even in seemingly adverse situations

WHITE *a white elephant*
an expensive and useless luxury (refers to gifts of sacred elephants by the King of Siam to persons then ruined by the expense of their upkeep)

WHITE *a white knight*
a party voluntarily coming to the assistance of another party at considerable cost to itself

WHITE *a white lie*
a false statement uttered in a good cause

WHITE *in black and white*
in writing, spelling out all the details

WHITE *lily-white*
honest and incorruptible

WHITE *to be a black and white issue*
to involve very clear distinctions

WHITE *to show the white feather*
to indicate cowardice (refers to cross-bred birds, not regarded as useful in cock fighting)

WHITE *to turn white*
to express shock at unexpected news

WHITE *to white ant someone*
to surreptitiously seek to destroy a person

COMMERCE

ADD *it adds up*
it makes sense

BANK *to laugh all the way to the bank*
to appreciate one's good fortune

BANKRUPT *to be bankrupt of ideas*
to be bereft of ideas

BARGAIN *to be more than one bargained for*
to be more than one expected

BASKET *to put something into the "too hard" basket*
to defer consideration of a difficult issue

BLANK *to give someone a blank check*
to give another person unlimited delegated authority

BOOK *to balance the books*
to get one's own back

BUY *I buy that*
I accept that idea

BUY *to buy into some argument*
to seek to participate in some discussion

BUY *to buy straw hats in winter*
to buy in a depressed market when most other people are sellers

CENT *to throw in one's two cents' worth*
to modestly supply one's own facts or views

CHANGE *to be shortchanged*
to be given less than is due to one

COAL *to carry coals to Newcastle*
to do something ridiculously unnecessary

COIN *the other side of the coin*
the arguments for the opposite point of view

COIN *to pay someone back in his own coin*
to retaliate in kind

CUSTOMER *a slippery customer*
a shifty person

DIVIDENDS *to show dividends*
to be successful

HEDGE *to be hedged around*
(of a statement) to be surrounded by qualifications

I *to dot the i's and cross the t's*
to be meticulous in completing the documentation for a transaction

INK *the ink is hardly dry*
something intended to last a long time is to be changed shortly after its establishment

IRON *to give a cast-iron guarantee*
to give a very secure undertaking to do something

LINE *the bottom line*
the conclusion which matters or the net effect of a series of developments

LINE *to sign on the dotted line*
to confirm one's agreement

LIST *a shopping list*
a catalogue of demands

MARK *to make something one's trademark*
to earn a reputation for maintaining some stance

MESSAGE *to get the message*
to understand the real import of what is being said

MITE *not a mite*
not at all (refers to a Flemish coin of small value)

MONEY *not for love or money*
definitely not

MONEY *not to be made of money*
not to be wealthy

MONEY *to put one's money where one's mouth is*
to back one's judgment by putting assets at risk

MONEY *to see the color of someone's money*
to get evidence of the sincerity of a person's proposal

PAPER *to start with a blank sheet of paper*
to commence an exercise without being bound by any established practices

PAR *to be below par*
to be less than the desired standard

PAY *that has put paid to it*
the project can no longer proceed

PAY *to pay off*
to be successful

PAY *to pay something back with interest*
to return a small favor with a bigger favor or to extract retribution of greater value than the circumstances warrant

PENNY *a twopenny halfpenny outfit*
a quite insignificant operation

PENNY *in for a penny—in for a pound*
once something is commenced it ought to be finished; or if one is willing to take a small risk then one might as well take a bigger one

PENNY *to throw in one's six pennies' worth*
to modestly supply one's own facts or views

PENNY *to turn an honest penny*
to earn money out of odd jobs

PITCH *to queer the pitch for someone*
to spoil the opportunity a person has to do something

POUND *in for a penny—in for a pound*
once something is commenced it ought to be finished; or if one is willing to take a small risk then one might as well take a bigger one

PRE-EMPT *to pre-empt some issue*
to deliberately do something which has the effect of limiting the range of alternative approaches to a matter

PRICE *to pay the price*
to suffer the adverse consequences of one's acts or omissions

RAZOO *not to have a brass razoo*
to be very poor

SALE *fire sale*
a forced sale, realizing bargain prices

SELL *to be sold on something*
to be utterly dedicated to a proposal

SELL *to sell one's birthright for a mess of pottage*
through foolishness to exchange something of substance for something of little value (Genesis 25)

SELL *to sell someone down the river*
to betray a person who has placed his trust in one

SHAKE *a golden handshake*
a large payment in connection with or as an inducement to retirement

SHARE *to have shares in a paper company*
to institute unnecessary clerical procedures

SHILLING *to be only ten pence in the shilling*
to be slightly stupid

SHILLING *to cut someone off with a shilling*
to exclude a person as a beneficiary under one's will (refers to the mistaken belief that a will cannot be upset in favor of a person actually named in a will and clearly not overlooked)

SHOP *to shop around*
to explore alternatives

SHOP *to shut up shop*
to cease an established activity

SHOP *to talk shop*
to discuss business or professional matters on a social occasion

SHOWCASE *showcase*
magnificent

SHUTTER *to put up the shutters*
to cease an established activity

SLATE *to wipe the slate clean*
to forgive past indiscretions

STAMP *to rubber-stamp something*
to endorse without considering the merits

STOCK *to take stock*
to contemplate the alternatives

STORE *to take over the store*
to assume the management

TRADE *a Jack of all trades*
an amateur who can turn his hand to anything

TRUCK *to have no truck with someone*
to refuse to deal with a person

VALUE *to take something at face value*
(of alleged facts) to accept something without question or challenge

WEALTH *a wealth of something*
a great quantity of something

CRIME

FELONY *to compound the felony*
having already acted improperly to make matters worse (the misuse of a legal term: compounding a felony is the crime of agreeing for money not to prosecute a person for felony; in reality it is therefore an offense by a different person—not a second and worse offense by the original culprit)

HIJACK *to hijack a debate*
to involve oneself in the public discussion of some matter and turn that discussion to one's advantage

MURDER *to be sheer murder*
to be extremely unpleasant or difficult; or to be an inglorious defeat

MURDER *to get away with murder*
to do something outrageous without penalty

MURDER *to scream blue murder*
to make serious allegations

PINCH *penny-pinching*
excessively mean

ROB *to rob Peter in order to pay Paul*
to fix up one grievance by causing another

ROBBERY *daylight robbery*
the charging of grossly excessive prices

ROBBERY *highway robbery*
the charging of grossly excessive prices

SHOTGUN *a shotgun wedding*
a wedding held to ensure that an impending birth will be legitimate (refers to threats by the bride's father to kill the bridegroom)

THROAT *cut-throat*
highly competitive

DEATH

BLOCK *someone's head is on the block*
a person is in danger of having his appointment terminated

BLOW *death blow*
incident which results in the destruction of something

BODY *over my dead body*
never

COFFIN *to be another nail in someone's coffin*
to represent a further step toward someone's downfall

CORPSE *to breathe life into a corpse*
to revive something moribund

CORPSE *to chase a corpse*
to harp on something long ago resolved or a lost cause

DEAD *I wouldn't be caught dead without some object*
I regard some object as very important

DEAD *a dead letter*
a rule still in existence but no longer observed in practice

DEAD *dead and buried*
(of some issue) definitely concluded, especially so long ago as to be nearly forgotten

DEAD *drop dead!*
go away, I want no dealings with you

DEAD *to be a dead duck*
to have failed

DEAD *to cut someone dead*
to snub a person

DEAD *to leave others for dead*
to be vastly superior

DEAD *to make noise enough to wake the dead*
to be excessively noisy

DEAD *to run into a dead end*
to get nowhere in an investigation

DEATH *a death wish*
the contemplation of action so foolish that it is likely to lead to utter disaster

DEATH *sudden death*
instantaneously or without phasing in

DEATH *to be in at the death*
to be present at the conclusion of something

DEATH *to be on one's death bed*
(of an organization or a piece of equipment) to be about to cease functioning

DEATH *to be the kiss of death*
to be something intended to be helpful but resulting in total destruction

DEATH *to bore someone to death*
to greatly weary a person by dull and uninteresting conversation or by lack of action

DEATH *to die a natural death*
by virtue of changed circumstances or the effluxion of time to be no longer relevant

DEATH *to sign one's own death warrant*
to foolishly do something which is inevitably bound to lead to utter disaster

DEATH *to slowly bleed to death*
to be heading in gradual steps toward total ruin

DEATH *to sound the death knell of something*
to indicate the impending end of something

DEATHKNOCK *on the deathknock*
at the last possible moment

DIE *to be dying to do something*
to be extremely keen to do something

DIE *to die hard*
not to give up easily

FATAL *to be fatal*
to be sufficient to destroy some proposal

FUNERAL *that is your funeral!*
that is the fate which you will have to suffer

GRAVE *he would turn in his grave*
he would have been very surprised or displeased if he had known while still alive

GRAVE *to dig one's own grave*
to take action which results in an unintended disaster for oneself

GRAVE *to have one foot in the grave*
to be dying

HANG *one might as well be hanged for a sheep as for a lamb*
further action will not increase the adverse consequences already in train (refers to the stealing of both sheep and lambs being capital crimes under old English law)

KILL *to be dressed to kill*
to be more finely dressed than the occasion warrants

KILL *to be in at the kill*
to be present at the climatic finish to something

KILL *to be killed in the rush*
to be the supplier of something extremely popular

KILL *to kill oneself laughing*
to be greatly amused

KILL *to kill some proposal stone dead*
to abandon some proposal completely

KILL *to kill the fatted calf*
to demonstrate welcome and forgiveness on a person's return (Luke 15:23)

KILL *to kill the goose that lays the golden eggs*
through excessive greed to destroy a very profitable enterprise

MORTEM *to conduct a postmortem on something*
to review past actions with a view to learning lessons for the future (Latin, "after the death")

NOOSE *to put one's head in the noose*
to recklessly and unnecessarily expose oneself to great danger

NOOSE *to tighten the noose*
to get closer to inflicting defeat

SLAUGHTER *a lamb led to slaughter*
a naive person allowing himself to be exploited

EDUCATION

BOOK *to take a leaf out of someone's book*
to model oneself on another person

CANE *to take a caning*
to suffer the adverse consequences of one's acts or omissions

COPYBOOK *to blot one's copybook*
to spoil one's previously good reputation or record

DICTIONARY *someone has swallowed a dictionary*
a person uses excessively long words

DUNCE *to earn a dunce's cap*
to do something stupid

HOMEWORK *to do one's homework*
to thoroughly analyze an issue

LESSON *to drive the lesson home*
to take certain action which is unpleasant but which has the effect of registering a message

LESSON *to learn a lesson*
to benefit from one's experience

LESSON *to teach someone a lesson*
to inflict something unpleasant on a person in the hope that it will lead to a change in his behavior

SCHOOL *to tell tales out of school*
to deliberately leak a secret

SCHOOLBOY *as every schoolboy knows*
as is recognized by everyone

SPELL *to spell something out*
to explain something in detail

FARMING

AX *the ax has fallen*
it is now too late

AX *to ax*
to cancel

AX *to have an ax to grind*
to have a vested interest

AX *to sharpen one's ax*
to get ready for a difficult task

AX *where the ax falls*
who gets terminated

BAG *it is in the bag*
the enterprise has succeeded

BARN *to barnstorm*
to visit accompanied by a show of force

BELL *bell-wether*
first indication

BLOCK *to be a chip off the old block*
to resemble one's father

BUCKET *to kick the bucket*
to die

BULLDOZE *to bulldoze some proposal through*
to ensure the passage of some measure in complete disregard of criticism or opposition

CHIP *that is the way the chips fall*
that is the actual situation

CHIP *when the chips are down*
when all facts are known and taken into consideration

COTTON *to be out of one's cotton-picking mind*
to act irrationally

COTTON *to keep one's cotton-picking fingers off something*
not to interfere in something

EARTH *a down-to-earth solution*
a realistic solution

FIELD *distant fields look greener*
activities of which one has no experience seem much easier than is really the case

FLEECE *to fleece someone*
to cheat a person out of some asset

GROUND *to clear the ground*
to dispose of the preliminaries

HARVEST *harvest*
end result of labor

HAY *to hit the hay*
to go to sleep

HAYSTACK *to find a needle in a haystack*
to find something when the probability of finding it is very small

HOOK *to get someone off the hook*
to rescue a person from an embarrassing predicament

HOOK *to let someone off the hook*
to allow a person to escape the adverse consequences of his own actions

MILL *it is all grist to the mill*
this is useful but unexciting additional material

MILL *run of the mill*
normal or average

MILL *the mills of God grind slowly*
retribution may be delayed but is inevitable

MILL *to put someone through the mill*
to give a person practical experience

MOVER *prime mover*
person initiating and promoting a cause

OATS *to sow wild oats*
to indulge in foolish behavior while a young adult

PADDOCK *to have a spell in the paddock*
to have leave of absence

PASTOR *pastor*
religious official in charge of a congregation

PASTURE *to move on to greener pastures*
to commence a new, better career

PLOW *speed the plow!*
let us get on with this as fast as possible!

PLOW *to plow new ground*
to laboriously engage in an untried activity

PLOW *to plow on*
to methodically and painstakingly continue with an activity

PLOW *to plow profits back*
to retain profits in a business

PLOW *to put one's hand to the plow*
voluntarily to undertake some task (Luke 9:62)

PUMP *to engage in pump priming*
to spend public money with the aim of attracting parochial electoral support

REAP *to reap as one has sown*
to experience the consequences of one's own actions

REAP *to sow the wind and reap the whirlwind*
to make bad mistakes and to suffer the even worse consequences

REIN *to give someone free rein*
to confer complete discretion on another person

ROOST *the chickens are coming home to roost*
the consequences of past actions are becoming obvious

ROW *to have a hard row to hoe*
to be a difficult assignment

SHEPHERD *to shepherd some group*
to marshall the members of some group

SOW *to sow the wind and reap the whirlwind*
to make bad mistakes and to suffer the even worse consequences

SPADE *to call a spade a spade*
not to mince words

SPADE *to do the spadework*
to prepare

TALLY *to keep a tally*
to keep a record (refers to a piece of wood with notches made on it to indicate a count)

TETHER *to be at the end of one's tether*
to be frustrated by a lack of knowledge, authority or patience

TRAP *to walk into a trap*
to be tricked into doing something

WHIP *to be a fair crack of the whip*
to be just

WHIP *to crack the whip*
to exert one's authority

WOOL *woolly-headed*
slightly muddled

FOOD AND DRINK

APPLE *a rotten apple*
an isolated dishonest person in an otherwise honest group

APPLECART *to upset the applecart*
to engage in conduct disturbing a peaceful state of affairs and thereby cause discomfort

BACON *to bring home the bacon*
to be successful

BACON *to save one's bacon*
to escape harm

BAKE *half-baked*
not well thought out

BANANA *a banana republic*
a country with a poor economy

BARREL *to really scrape the bottom of the barrel*
to lower one's standards because one is short of important or relevant issues

BEAN *to be full of beans*
to be very cheerful

BEAN *to spill the beans*
to indiscreetly reveal sensitive information

BEER *not to be all beer and skittles*
not to be all pleasant and easy

BEER *to be small beer*
to be quite unimportant

BEER *to cry in one's beer*
to show remorse

BOIL *it boils down to this*
the essential features are as follows

BOTTLE *a bottleneck*
a factor obstructing an even flow

BOTTLE *to be a full bottle on something*
to be very knowledgeable

BREAD *a bread and butter issue*
a basic issue which is of importance to many people

BREAD *a breadwinner*
a person earning by personal exertion the income of a household

BREAD *to be someone's bread and butter*
to be a person's livelihood or to be a person's everyday experience

BREAD *to cast one's bread upon the waters*
not to expect gratitude or recognition for one's good works (Ecclesiastes 11:1)

BREAD *to know on which side one's bread is buttered*
to be aware of the important considerations

BREAD *to put jam on someone's bread*
to make a good situation even better

BREAKFAST *to be able to eat someone for breakfast*
to be able to outwit a person very easily

BROTH *too many cooks spoil the broth*
one leader is all that is required

BUN *a bunfight*
a minor and relatively friendly skirmish

BUTTER *a bread and butter issue*
a basic issue which is of importance to many people

BUTTER *a butter fingers*
a person unable to catch and/or hold on to an object

BUTTER *someone looks as if butter would not melt in his mouth*
a person looks sweet and innocent

BUTTER *to be someone's bread and butter*
to be a person's livelihood or to be a person's everyday experience

CAKE *a share of the cake*
a portion of the total available for distribution

CAKE *that takes the cake*
that is quite absurd or outrageous or excessively cheeky

CAKE *to be a piece of cake*
to be very easy or greatly to one's liking

CAKE *to be icing on top of the cake*
to be an additional benefit in an already satisfactory scenario

CAKE *to want to have one's cake and eat it too*
to want two mutually exclusive alternatives

CAN *to carry the can for someone*
to accept the blame for another person's actions or inactions

CHEESE *cheese paring*
stingy

CHEESE *stiff cheese!*
circumstances which may be unwelcome but which will not be altered and in respect of which no great sympathy is felt

CHEESE *to be cheesed off*
to be disgusted

CHESTNUT *to pull someone's chestnuts out of the fire*
to retrieve a situation

CHEW *to bite off more than one can chew*
to be overly ambitious and thus unrealistic as to one's capabilities

CHEW *to have something to chew on*
to have firm facts on which to base a decision

CHIP *to have had one's chips*
to have received all that is going to be forthcoming

COOK *to be cooking with gas*
to be fully operational

COOK *to cook the books*
fraudulently to maintain false records of financial transactions

COOKIE *that is the way the cookie crumbles*
that is the actual situation

CREAM *to be cream on top of the milk*
to be an additional benefit in an already satisfactory scenario

CREME *creme de la creme*
something quite superlative (French, "the cream of the cream")

CRUMB *to throw someone a few crumbs*
to fob a person off with a few symbolic but unimportant concessions

DINNER *to be done like a dinner*
to be defeated and humiliated

DOUGHNUT *watch the doughnut—not the hole*
look for the positive aspects

DRINK *it is a long time between drinks*
activity is occurring only very spasmodically

DRINK *to be meat and drink*
to be very pleasurable

DROP *to squeeze the last drop out of something*
to get the maximum advantage out of some favorable situation

DRUG *to be a drug on the market*
to be in overplentiful supply

EAT *I'll eat my hat if so-and-so happens*
I do not believe that so-and-so will happen

EAT *to eat crow*
to accept a humiliating defeat

EAT *to eat one's words*
to retract

EAT *to eat out of someone's hands*
to be unduly compliant

EAT *you can eat your heart out*
you are entitled to feel sad or jealous

EGG *a nest egg*
life savings

EGG *as sure as eggs are eggs*
with great certainty

EGG *chicken and egg*
two factors each of which results in the other

EGG *not to put all one's eggs in one basket*
to spread one's risks

EGG *there are many ways to cook eggs*
there are many ways to achieve an objective

EGG *to be a curate's egg*
to be good only in parts (refers to an 1895 cartoon in PUNCH)

EGG *to have egg on one's face*
to be embarrassed by the results of one's own stupidity

EGG *to kill the goose that lays the golden eggs*
through excessive greed to destroy a very profitable enterprise

EGG *to teach one's grandmother how to suck eggs*
to try to tell a much more experienced person something very obvious to him

FAT *the fat is in the fire*
action with certain unstoppable consequences has now been initiated

FAT *to chew fat*
to eat and talk together

FAT *to trim the fat*
to increase efficiency by reducing outlays

FATTEN *to kill the fatted calf*
to demonstrate welcome and forgiveness on a person's return (Luke 15:23)

FEAST *a movable feast*
an event not customarily held on a set date

FEAST *to be either feast or famine*
to go from one extreme to the other

FISH *to have more important fish to fry*
to have more important things to do

FLAVOR *to be the flavor of the month*
to be a commodity temporarily popular without a logical reason

FLESH *one's pound of flesh*
that which is due to one (from Shakespeare's MERCHANT OF VENICE)

FLESHPOT *fleshpots*
sumptuous living (Exodus 16:3)

FOOD *food for thought*
material for examination in one's mind

FOOD *to take food out of the mouths of children*
cruelly to deprive the needy

FRY *out of the frying pan into the fire*
from one bad situation to an even worse one

GEL *to gel*
to make sense

GRAVY *to get on a gravy train*
to take steps to become a recipient of benefits which are available but undeserved

HARD-BOILED *hard-boiled*
toughened by experience

HONEY *a land of milk and honey*
a country in which everything is in abundant supply

ICE *to put something on ice*
to put something aside for the time being

ICING *to be icing on top of the cake*
to be an additional benefit in an already satisfactory scenario

JAM *money for jam*
remuneration easily earned

JAM *to be in a jam*
to be in difficulties

JAM *to just pick the plums out of the jam*
to take only the very best items

JAM *to put jam on someone's bread*
to make a good situation even better

JELLY *to be set like a jelly*
to be very well established

KITCHEN *if one can't stand the heat one should stay out of the kitchen*
a person should not put himself in a position involving pressures with which he cannot cope (words attributed to Harry S. Truman)

KNIFE *before one can say "knife"*
very quickly

KNIFE *one could have cut the atmosphere with a knife*
those present were very tense

KNIFE *the knives are out*
there is an active campaign against someone

KNIFE *to be on a knife edge*
to be in danger

KNIFE *to hold a knife at someone's throat*
to exert undue pressure on another person in an endeavor to achieve a result which would otherwise not be forthcoming

KNIFE *to sharpen the knives*
to get ready for a concerted attack on some principle

KNIFE *to stick a knife into someone*
to act vindictively toward a person

KOSHER *to be kosher*
to fulfill all requirements (refers to food complying with all aspects of Jewish religious law)

MANNA *manna from heaven*
unexpected benefits (Exodus 16:15)

MEAT *to be easy meat*
to be an opponent who is readily outwitted

MEAT *to be meat and drink*
to be very pleasurable

MEAT *to contain much meat*
to contain much material worthy of consideration

MILK *a land of milk and honey*
a country in which everything is in abundant supply

MILK *it is no use crying over spilt milk*
lamenting over a disaster achieves nothing

MILK *to be cream on top of the milk*
to be an additional benefit in an already satisfactory scenario

MINCE *not to mince words*
to speak bluntly

MINCE *to make mincemeat of something*
to devastate something

MUG *a mug's game*
activity which wise persons would eschew

MUTTON *to be mutton dressed up as lamb*
to foolishly pretend to be younger

NUT *someone is a hard nut to crack*
it is very difficult to persuade a person to do something

NUT *to use a sledgehammer to crack a nut*
to devote vastly more resources to a project than is warranted by all the circumstances

OMELETTE *one cannot make an omelette without breaking eggs*
the desired end dictates the means even if they cause harm to others

OMELETTE *to unscramble the omelette*
to undo something which cannot be undone

P *to watch one's p's and q's*
to be very careful (may refer to pints and quarts of beer on a hotel slate or to easily-confused printer's type)

PANCAKE *every Pancake Tuesday*
only on rare occasions (refers to Shrove Tuesday, when pancakes are traditionally eaten)

PAPER *only a cigarette paper between them*
virtually equal or close together

PARTY *to come to the party*
to agree to someone's terms

PEANUT *to earn peanuts*
to get a reward which is far too small in relation to the value of the services rendered

PICKLE *to be in a pickle*
to be in difficulties

PICNIC *to be no picnic*
to be unpleasant

PIE *in apple pie order*
in perfect order and condition

PIE *pie in the sky*
a hoped for result unlikely to be achieved

PIE *to eat humble pie*
to apologize

PIE *to have a finger in the pie*
to have an interest in a project

PIE *to have one's fingers in many different pies*
to be engaged in a variety of separate activities

PLATE *to bring a plate*
to take food to a party

PLATE *to have too much on one's plate*
to be unable to cope with one's workload

PLATE *to serve something up to someone on a plate*
to make something especially easy for a particular person

PLATTER *to hand over something on a silver platter*
to provide a valuable benefit for virtually nothing

PLUM *to just pick the plums out of the jam*
to take only the best items

PORK *to pork barrel*
to spend taxpayers' money in one area in order to attract political support

POT *one can't get a quart into a pint pot*
one cannot do the impossible

POT *the pot calling the kettle black*
a person criticizing another person without realizing his own even greater shortcomings

POT *to keep the pot boiling*
to ensure that an issue stays current

POT *to stir the pot*
to set out to raise controversial issues

POT *to sweeten the pot*
to provide a few additional inducements

POT *to take pot luck*
to take whatever happens by chance to be available

POTTAGE *to sell one's birthright for a mess of pottage*
through foolishness to exchange something of substance for something of little value (Genesis 25)

PUDDING *the proof of the pudding is in the eating*
the success of a venture will be measured by its results

RECIPE *a recipe for disaster*
a certain way of achieving disaster

ROAST *a roasting*
a scolding

SALT *below the salt*
in a subordinate position (refers to the seating order at ancient Roman dining tables)

SALT *not to be worth one's salt*
not to be pulling one's weight (refers to Roman soldiers being paid in salt—a practice giving rise to the modern word "salary")

SALT *to be the salt of the earth*
to be a person whose ordinary efforts benefit the community (Matthew 5:13)

SALT *to rub salt into someone's wound*
to deliberately make damage even worse

SALT *to take something with a grain of salt*
to regard the facts in a statement with considerable skepticism

SAND *the sands are running out*
the time available for some action is nearly at an end

SANDWICH *to be the ham in the sandwich*
to be caught in the middle of a dispute between other parties

SAUCE *what is sauce for the goose is sauce for the gander*
arguments which apply in one case also apply in another

SAUSAGE *a sausage machine*
the turning out of large volumes without particular thought

SILVER *to sell off the family silver*
to sell off one's prized possessions

SMORGASBORD *smorgasbord*
a series of different items from which a number can be chosen (from the Swedish words for ''butter,'' ''goose'' and ''table'')

SOUP *to be in the soup*
to be in great difficulties

SOUR *to turn sour*
to become impracticable or unprofitable

SPOON *to be born with a silver spoon in one's mouth*
to be brought up by wealthy parents

SPOON *to get the wooden spoon*
to come ingloriously last

STEW *to be in a stew*
to be in difficulties

STEW *to stew in one's juice*
to suffer the adverse consequences of one's acts or omissions

STORAGE *to put something into cold storage*
to put something aside for dealing with at some indeterminate future time

SUCK *suck it and see*
discover experimentally how something works

SUCK *to suck the lemon dry*
to get the maximum advantage out of some favorable situation

SUP *he must have a long spoon that sups with the devil*
great care is needed when negotiating deals with disreputable parties

SUPPER *to sing for one's supper*
to carry out a task in order to receive a favor in return

SWEET *to be short and sweet*
to be very brief and to the point

SWEETEN *to sweeten a deal*
to offer some concessions or incentives

SYRUP *soothing syrup*
insincere expressions of sympathy or flattery

TEA *I would not do so-and-so for all the tea in China*
I will never do so-and-so

TEA *not to be someone's cup of tea*
to be outside a person's expertise or area of interest

TEACUP *a storm in a teacup*
a controversy about a minor matter but one which looms large in the minds of the parties

TOAST *to have someone on toast*
to be victorious over a person

FURNITURE

BED *a hotbed of crime*
a place where crime flourishes

BED *one has made one's bed and one will now have to lie on it*
one has to bear the consequences of one's actions

BED *to be on one's death bed*
(of an organization or a piece of equipment) to be about to cease functioning

BED *to bed something down*
to find a taker for something

BED *to get out of bed on the wrong side*
to be grumpy

BED *to jump into bed with someone*
to enter into a joint enterprise with another person

BED *to put something to bed*
to finally dispose of

BEDDING *feather bedding*
(in industrial relations) creating unnecessary jobs solely to increase employment; (in economics) assisting an inefficient industry by government grants or excessive tariff protection

BLANKET *to be a wet blanket*
to be a spoilsport

BLANKET *to be born on the wrong side of the blanket*
to be illegitimate

BLANKET *to throw a blanket over a proposal*
to refuse to proceed with a proposal

BOWL *to be in a goldfish bowl*
to be very open to view

CARPET *the red-carpet treatment*
courtesies extended to a person to make him feel important and welcome

CARPET *to get a magic carpet ride to something*
to be very fortunate in achieving some objective

CARPET *to sweep something under the carpet*
to pretend that some blemish does not exist

CENTERPIECE *the centerpiece*
(of a proposal) the highlight or the main ingredient

CHAIR *to play musical chairs*
to be a part of a general reshuffling of duties or functions which is not necessarily to everyone's liking

CHEST *to lock something up in the old oak chest*
to put in a safe place and out of mind

CLOCK *to turn back the clock*
to have another opportunity to do something which should have been done already or to undo something which cannot be undone

CUPBOARD *a skeleton in the cupboard*
an unpleasant truth the knowledge of which has been deliberately suppressed

CUPBOARD *the cupboard is bare*
the wished-for resources are just not available

CURTAIN *the iron curtain*
the border between the communist nations and the rest of the world (from a speech by Sir Winston Churchill in 1946)

DECKCHAIR *to rearrange the deckchairs on the Titanic*
to take some initiative which is quite useless because it does not take much greater change into account

DOOR *to knock on doors*
to seek out opportunities to do business

DRAWER *to tuck something away in a drawer*
to put something aside for the time being

DRAWER *top drawer*
first class

FURNITURE *to be part of the furniture*
to be so familiar that one's presence goes completely unnoticed

PAD *to keep off someone's pad*
not to interfere with or compete against another person in his customary area of activity

PEG *a peg to hang a hat on*
something which provides a convenient or plausible excuse for some particular action

PEG *off the peg*
(of clothes) ready-made

PEG *to take someone down a peg or two*
to point out to a person that he is not as good as he thinks he is

PICTURE *to paint a black picture*
to state a set of unfavorable factors

PICTURE *to present a rosy picture*
to state a set of favorable factors

QUILT *a patchwork quilt*
a result arising from many uncoordinated inputs

RUG *to pull the rug out from under someone*
to unexpectedly withdraw support and in the process cause embarrassment

SEAT *to be in the hot seat*
to hold a position requiring one to answer criticism or accusations

SEAT *to keep someone's seat warm*
to hold a position temporarily with a view to another person taking it over permanently in the near future

SHELF *to be on the shelf*
to be available for marriage

SHELVE *to shelve some proposal*
to abandon some proposal

SPRING *a spring cleaning*
a thorough review occurring a long time after the previous one

STOOL *to fall between two stools*
not to fit neatly into either of two available alternatives and waver between them

TABLE *to lay a proposal on the table*
to make a proposal available for discussion or to adjourn discussion on a proposal for an indefinite period

TABLE *to lay one's cards on the table*
to be utterly frank and open or to honestly disclose one's position

TABLE *to put money on the table*
to back one's judgment in a tangible way or to demonstrate one's sincerity

TABLE *to turn the tables on someone*
to cause the relative positions of oneself and another person to be reversed

GAMBLING

BET *a good bet*
a good proposition

BET *to hedge one's bets*
to take action involving a cost but which is designed to reduce the possible adverse consequences of some activity

BET *you bet!*
definitely!

BET *you can bet your life on something*
something is certain to happen

BLANK *to draw a blank*
to be unsuccessful

BOB *to have two bob each way*
to equivocate

BOOK *to be a turn up for the books*
to be a surprising development

CENT *to have fifty cents each way*
to equivocate

CHIP *bargaining chips*
benefits which can be conceded in negotiations in order to obtain some advantage

CHIP *to turn one's chips in*
to convert one's assets or entitlements into cash

DIE *no dice*
the proposal is totally unacceptable

DIE *the die is cast*
the course of action in train is irreversible

DIE *the whole box and dice*
all relevant components

DIE *to be the throw of a loaded die*
to be an act of deceit

DRAW *to be the luck of the draw*
to be a chance result

HEAD *heads I win—tails you lose*
whichever way this matter goes I will benefit at your expense

HEAD *to be unable to make head or tail of something*
to be unable to understand how something functions or what something means

JACKPOT *to hit the jackpot*
to be very lucky

LONDON *it is London to a brick*
it is virtually certain

LUCK *to push one's luck*
having already done well in something to then take risks which can prejudice everything

ODDS *that is over the odds*
that is unacceptable

ODDS *to be at odds with someone*
to disagree with a person

ODDS *to beat the odds*
to do better than could reasonably have been expected

ODDS *to pay over the odds*
to pay too much

PUNT *to take a punt*
to take a calculated risk

ROULETTE *to play Russian roulette*
to take stupid risks

SIX *to be at sixes and sevens*
to be confused, concerned and undecided

STAKE *to raise the stake*
to increase the amount of potential gain or loss in a project

TAIL *heads I win—tails you lose*
whichever way this matter goes I will benefit at your expense

TAIL *to be unable to make head or tail of something*
to be unable to understand how something functions or what something means

TOSS *it is a toss-up*
either alternative is equally acceptable

TOSS *to argue the toss*
to dispute a decision

TOSS *to toss up*
to decide on a fairly arbitrary basis

WHEEL *fortune's wheel*
the vicissitudes of life

GEOGRAPHY

ABYSS *to be close to the abyss*
to face imminent total destruction

AVALANCHE *avalanche*
a great volume manifesting itself in a short time

BEACH *not to be the only pebble on the beach*
not to be the only available person

BRINK *to push someone over the brink*
by a small action to cause the absolute ruin (financially or emotionally) of someone already in peril

CAVE *to cave in*
to yield to pressure

CHINA *I would not do so-and-so for all the tea in China*
I will never do so-and-so

CHINESE *a Chinese puzzle*
a perplexing enigma

CHINESE *Chinese walls*
a system to ensure that different parts of some organization do not gain access to each other's confidential information

CLIFF *to be a cliff-hanger*
to be very exciting

COAST *the coast is clear*
there are no observers to one's activity around

CORNER *from the four corners of the globe*
from everywhere

COUNTRY *one looks for elephants in elephant country*
one needs to search in the right place

COURSE *to runs its course*
to come to a natural end

CURRENT *an undercurrent*
a barely noticeable feeling of dissent in the community which is not being vocalized

DAM *the dam burst*
the cumulative effect of many things caused a disaster

DAMASCUS *to be on the road to Damascus*
to see the error of one's ways (Acts 9:3)

DISTANCE *to keep one's distance*
to avoid familiarity

DOWNHILL *to go downhill*
to deteriorate

DRY *to dry up*
to cease

EARTH *earth-shattering*
very significant

EARTH *how on earth?*
just how?

EARTH *to bring someone down to earth*
to disillusion a person

EARTH *to charge the earth*
to impose very high prices

EARTH *to move heaven and earth*
to do everything possible

EARTH *to promise the earth*
to give extravagant assurances

EARTH *to run someone to earth*
to locate a person

ECHO *to echo someone's words*
to repeat another person's views as though they were one's own

FOUNTAINHEAD *fountainhead*
source of all wisdom

GREEK *I fear the Greeks even when they bear gifts*
I am suspicious of generous behavior from traditional opponents (from Virgil's AENEID, in reference to the Trojan horse)

GREEK *something is all Greek to someone*
something is incomprehensible to a person

GROUND *to be on shaky ground*
not to have strong arguments

GROUND *to fall to the ground*
to fail

GROUND *to give ground*
to make some concessions or to retreat or to concede some arguments

GROUND *to go to ground*
to become unavailable to those seeking a person

GROUND *to have the high ground*
to have an advantage in moral terms

GROUND *to run someone to the ground*
to discover the whereabouts of a person

GULF *to bridge a gulf*
to overcome a wide divergence in views

HERE *to be neither here nor there*
to be irrelevant or unimportant

HILL *light on the hill*
distant goal acting as an inspiration

HILL *to be over the hill*
to be old

HILL *to head for the hills*
to seek to escape one's commitments

HIMALAYAN *of Himalayan proportions*
huge

HORIZON *there are black clouds on the horizon*
bad news is expected

JUNGLE *a jungle*
a place where everyone makes his own rules

LAKE *you can jump in the lake*
I intend to take no notice whatsoever of you or your views

LAND *to be in cloud cuckoo land*
to be mad or to have unrealistic expectations

LAND *to be in the land of the living*
to be alive

LANDMARK *a landmark ruling*
a decision marking a turning-point in the way a matter is approached

LANDSCAPE *to be part of the landscape*
to be present and fully accepted without question

LANDSLIDE *a landslide*
an electoral result involving victory or defeat by an unexpectedly large margin

LANE *to go down memory lane*
to reminisce

LANGUAGE *to speak the same language*
to have a good understanding and similar ideas

LEVEL *to be on the level*
to be honest

LOSE *you can get lost*
I intend to take no notice whatsoever of you or your views

MAINSTREAM *mainstream*
orthodox

MAP *to put some organization on the map*
to make the organization a force to be reckoned with

MARATHON *marathon*
requiring great endurance (refers to the run to get aid during the battle of Marathon in 490 BC)

MECCA *a Mecca for something*
a place at which supporters of something congregate

MEXICAN *a Mexican standoff*
a situation where neither of two parties is making a move

MILE *a milestone*
an achievement

MILE *to be miles apart*
to have great philosophical differences

MILE *to be miles away*
to have one's mind on other matters

MILE *to go the extra mile*
to work beyond the call of duty

MILE *to miss something by a mile*
to be nowhere near one's target

MILE *to stick out a mile*
to be very apparent

MIRAGE *mirage*
illusory benefit

MIRE *to sink deeper into the mire*
to get into further difficulties

MOUNTAIN *if the mountain will not come to Mahomet then Mahomet will go to the mountain*
on recognizing that one has insufficient power to effect one's most desired solution, one decides to make do with the next best alternative

MUD *to sink deeper into the mud*
to get into even greater difficulty

PATCH *a sticky patch*
a period fraught with difficulties

PLACE *a place in the sun*
a favorable situation

POND *to be a big fish in a little pond*
to be a person holding an important office but in an unimportant organization

QUAGMIRE *to be in a quagmire*
to be in great difficulty

RIVER *the river found its mark*
equilibrium between two pressures has been achieved

RIVER *to be a river of gold*
to be a source of ongoing great profitability

RIVER *to sell someone down the river*
to betray a person who has placed his trust in one

ROME *all roads lead to Rome*
all alternatives will have the same outcome

ROME *when in Rome do as the Romans do*
it is best to conform to the local customs

SAMARITAN *a good Samaritan*
a person going out of his way to do a kindness to others (Luke 10:33)

SAND *shifting sands*
arguments which are constantly being changed

SLOUGH *a slough of despond*
a feeling of hopelessness

SODOM *a Sodom and Gomorrah*
a place of vice (Genesis 18:20)

SPAIN *a castle in Spain*
an impracticable proposition

STONE *a stepping stone*
a means to an end

STRAIT *in dire straits*
in great need

STREAM *to swap horses in midstream*
to change direction during the course of a project

STREET *to be in Queer Street*
to be in debt

SWAMP *to swamp someone*
to overload a person

THAMES *to set the Thames on fire*
to do something noteworthy

TOP *to blow one's top*
to show anger (refers to a volcano)

TOWN *to go to town*
to spend lavishly

TOWN *to paint the town red*
to go on an exciting social outing

TRACK *to be down the track*
to be making progress

TRACK *to be off the beaten track*
to do unconventional things

TRACK *to be off the track*
to be irrelevant

TRACK *to be on the wrong track*
to be heading toward an incorrect solution

TRACK *to be on track*
to be making the scheduled progress

TRACK *to be stopped in one's tracks*
suddenly and unexpectedly to be prevented from carrying on with a project

TRACK *to cover one's tracks*
to hide the evidence of one's involvement

TRACK *to go down a particular track*
to make decisions aimed at a particular goal

TRACK *to have a one-track mind*
to keep coming back to one narrow topic of conversation

TRACK *to keep track of something*
to be completely aware of where something is and how it is functioning

TRACK *to make tracks*
to leave

TRICKLE *a trickle*
a small amount, in gradual stages

TURK *young Turks*
members of an organization who hold ideas regarded as too revolutionary

UPHILL *to be pushing uphill*
to face difficulties

UTOPIAN *Utopian*
ideally perfect (refers to the mythical island in Sir Thomas More's UTOPIA)

VOLCANO *to be sitting on a volcano*
to be safe for the time being but exposed to the risk of a sudden great disaster

WATER *a backwater*
a place of little activity

WATER *come hell or high water*
regardless of the consequences

WATER *high water mark*
triumph

WATER *still waters run deep*
a person with a quiet manner may have a surprisingly great knowledge of a subject

WATER *to be above water*
(of securities) to have a market value in excess of the cost price

WATER *to be in deep water*
to be in great difficulty

WATER *to be in smooth water*
to have no troubles

WATER *to blow something out of the water*
to destroy something

WATER *to brave the water*
to enter a venture with courage and determination

WATER *to cast one's bread upon the waters*
not to expect gratitude or recognition for one's good works (Ecclesiastes 11:1)

WATER *to dip one's toe in the water*
to gently explore an opportunity

WATER *to enter treacherous waters*
to engage in an enterprise with risks which are not obvious

WATER *to fish in troubled waters*
to profit from a disturbed situation

WATER *to go through fire and water*
to undertake all attendant risks

WATER *to go to water*
to succumb to pressure

WATER *to muddy the waters*
to deliberately confuse an issue by creating a diversion

WATER *to plot a safe course through troubled waters*
to make a plan which overcomes certain difficulties

WATER *to pour cold water on some idea*
to be unenthusiastic about some proposal or scornful of its apparent weaknesses

WATER *to pour oil on troubled waters*
to calm down a situation

WATER *to push water uphill*
to foolishly attempt the impossible

WATER *to shoot something out of the water*
to frustrate something

WATER *to test the water*
to try out an idea in a small way

WATER *water will find its own level*
people will reach an appropriate position relative to others

WATERLOO *to meet one's Waterloo*
to receive a decisive defeat (refers to Napoleon's fate at the Battle of Waterloo)

WATERSHED *a watershed*
an occasion dividing two distinct phases of activity

WATERTIGHT *a watertight contract*
a contract without loop-holes or escape clauses

WAVE *to ride the wave*
to be successful for the time being

WAY *no way!*
definitely not!

WAY *to cut both ways*
to involve both advantages and disadvantages of similar significance

WAY *to know which way to turn*
to know which strategy to adopt or where to seek assistance

WAY *to want something both ways*
to desire two mutually exclusive objectives

WAYSIDE *to fall by the wayside*
to abandon and not complete what one set out to do

WILDERNESS *to be a lone voice in the wilderness*
to be the only person stating unpopular views

WILDERNESS *to be in the wilderness*
to be out of office against one's will

WIND *to get wind of something*
to hear rumors giving advance information

WOOD *neck of the woods*
localized area

WOOD *to be babes in the wood*
to be excessively naive and inexperienced and thus ripe for exploitation

WOOD *to be out of the woods*
the previous difficulties have been overcome

WORLD *it's a small world*
it is surprising to meet people one knows in unexpected places

WORLD *to be on top of the world*
to be very happy

WORLD *to be out of this world*
to be superb

WORLD *to carry the world on one's shoulders*
to resent being left to perform a huge task single-handedly (refers to Atlas, who was condemned to bear the heavens on his shoulders for leading the Titans against the gods)

WORLD *to get the worst of all worlds*
to get a series of disadvantages without achieving any corresponding advantages

WORLD *to make a world of difference*
to make a great deal of difference

WORLD *to set the world on fire*
to do something particularly brilliant

WORLD *to want the best of both worlds*
to unreasonably desire to get some advantage without incurring a corresponding disadvantage

WORLD *why in the world?*
why?

GOVERNMENT

AMENDMENT *to plead the Fifth Amendment*
to refuse to answer an unwelcome question (refers to the Fifth Amendment of the United States Constitution, which provides protection against self-incrimination)

BAILIWICK *to be in someone's bailiwick*
to be some other person's responsibility

COURT *to have a friend at court*
a person with influence who is willing to use it on one's behalf

CROWN *the crowning point*
the height of a person's achievement

CROWN *the jewel in someone's crown*
the most significant component

CROWN *uneasy lies the head that wears a crown*
responsibility involves some risks and some burdens (from Shakespeare's HENRY IV)

DENMARK *something is rotten in the state of Denmark*
the situation is not correct (from Shakespeare's HAMLET)

EMPIRE *to engage in empire building*
to set out to expand the size of the business or bureaucratic unit for which one is responsible, especially as a means of increasing one's own importance

ESTATE *the fourth estate*
the press

FLAG *to rally to the flag*
to show support for a cause

HALL *one can't beat City Hall*
the ordinary citizen is powerless against bureaucracy

HARD *to put something into the "too hard" basket*
to defer consideration of a difficult issue

KING *a cat may look at a king*
don't give yourself airs!

KING *to pay a king's ransom*
to pay a very large sum

KINGMAKER *kingmaker*
person engaging in behind-the-scenes activities to promote another person to a particular leadership position

LICENSE *a license to print money*
a lucrative government-conferred monopoly or privilege

MINT *to charge a mint*
to impose very high prices

PALACE *a palace revolt*
the overthrow of those in authority by their subordinates

ROYAL *the royal road to success*
the way of attaining success without effort

SCOT *to get off scot free*
to go unpunished (refers to an exemption from tax)

STONEWALLING *stonewalling*
deliberate obstruction or delaying tactics

THRONE *the power behind the throne*
a person exercising the real authority but without having the official right to do so (the antonym of "titular head")

HERALDRY

ESCUTCHEON *to be a blot on someone's escutcheon*
to be a blemish on a person's character

LEFT *a left-handed compliment*
a thinly-disguised insult

RIBBON *blue ribbon*
of superb quality (refers to the insignia of the Order of the Garter)

STANDARD *a standard bearer*
a highly visible activist for a cause

HISTORY

ALL *warts and all*
with the unfavorable features as well as the favorable ones (Oliver Cromwell's direction to an artist painting his portrait)

BARREL *to have someone over a barrel*
to take advantage of someone's weakened position in relation to oneself

BEDLAM *bedlam*
a scene of uproar (refers to the Hospital of St. Mary of Bethlehem, which was used as a lunatic asylum from 1547 onwards)

BELOW *below the salt*
in a subordinate position (refers to the seating order at ancient Roman dining tables)

BOY *a whipping boy*
a person made to suffer for the faults of others

BURN *to burn the midnight oil*
to work late into the night

CANDLE *not fit to hold a candle to someone*
greatly inferior to another person

CANDLE *not to be worth the candle*
to be too expensive in relation to the true value

CANDLE *to burn the candle at both ends*
to work excessively long hours

CONTINENTAL *not to be worth a continental*
to have no value (refers to currency notes)

CROSS *to be a cross which one has to bear*
to be a difficulty which one has to endure

CRUSADE *a crusade*
an aggressive campaign to achieve some political or social objective

FEATHER *a feather in one's cap*
a meritorious personal achievement

HOBSON *Hobson's choice*
no right at all to select (refers to Thomas Hobson, a horsekeeper in Cambridge, England, who offered customers seeking a change of horses a single beast on a ''take it or leave it'' basis)

INDIAN *more chiefs than Indians*
a disproportionately large number of supervisors

KNIGHT *a knight in shining armor*
a very helpful person

MEET *to meet one's Waterloo*
to receive a decisive defeat (refers to Napoleon's fate at the Battle of Waterloo)

NAME *his name is mud*
he completely lacks credibility (a play on the name of Dr. Samuel Mudd)

PALE *to be beyond the pale*
to be socially unacceptable, especially for unacceptable standards or behavior

PARTHIAN *a Parthian shaft*
a cutting remark made at the moment of departure (refers to missiles shot backward by flying Parthian horsemen)

PILLORY *to put someone in the pillory*
to hold a person up to ridicule for his beliefs

PYRRHIC *a Pyrrhic victory*
a win which costs more than if there had been a loss (refers to the battle at which King Pyrrhus of Epirus defeated the Romans at Asculum)

REARRANGE *to rearrange the deckchairs on the Titanic*
to take some initiative which is quite useless because it does not take much greater change into account

RIOT *to read the Riot Act*
to reprimand persons who are excessively noisy (refers to the police reading out to a rowdy crowd extracts from a law requiring its dispersement)

RUBICON *to cross the Rubicon*
to make an irreversible decision in regard to some commitment

SPARTAN *Spartan*
tough and efficient, with a complete absence of the finer things of life

TREADMILL *to be on a treadmill*
to be involved in some unpleasant ongoing activity which cannot readily be stopped

TURNCOAT *a turncoat*
a person changing sides (refers to the practice of mercenary soldiers switching to the winning side and displaying that side's colors by turning their coats inside out)

WITCH *a witchhunt*
an exercise seeking to find someone who can be blamed

HUMAN BODY

APPETITE *to whet one's appetite*
to arouse one's curiosity or interest

ARM *I would give my right arm for something*
I am very keen to acquire something

ARM *a shot in the arm*
something to revive a person's enthusiasm

ARM *at arm's length*
between parties who are strangers bearing no special duty to each other and who have no financial or other relationship with each other (a legal term)

ARM *to chance one's arm*
to take a great risk (refers to the stripes on the uniforms of non-commissioned officers)

ARM *to cost an arm and a leg*
to be excessively expensive

ARM *to have a long arm*
to have far-reaching power

ARM *to lose one's right arm*
to lose some highly-valued assistance

ARM *to twist someone's arms*
to coerce another person to do something against his will or better judgment

ARM *with open arms*
enthusiastically

ARMPIT *to be in something up to one's armpits*
to be very deeply involved in something

BABE *to be babes in the wood*
to be excessively naive and inexperienced and thus ripe for exploitation

BABY *to be left holding the baby*
to be tricked into accepting responsibility for someone else's problems

BABY *to be one's baby*
to be one's area of responsibility

BABY *to throw out the baby with the bathwater*
to discard a major benefit in the course of obtaining a comparatively minor advantage

BACK *as soon as someone's back was turned*
at the moment it became possible to do something without a person's knowledge

BACK *back-breaking*
overburdening

BACK *behind someone's back*
in a way which deliberately conceals an activity from a person

BACK *put your back into it!*
work energetically!

BACK *so-and-so would give one the shirt off his back*
so-and-so is very generous

BACK *to be able to do something with one hand behind one's back*
to be able to do something very easily

BACK *to cover one's back*
to take precautions

BACK *to engage in back biting*
to criticize in an unfriendly manner

BACK *to get off someone's back*
to leave a person alone to carry on without constant criticism

BACK *to get one's own back on someone*
to extract revenge

BACK *to get someone's back up*
to annoy or antagonize a person

BACK *to have one's back to the wall*
to be hard-pressed by creditors or opponents

BACK *to make a rod for one's own back*
to act in disregard of likely disadvantages for oneself

BACK *to need to watch one's back*
to find it necessary to take care in case others act against one's interests

BACK *to pat oneself on the back*
immodestly to congratulate oneself

BACK *to pat someone on the back*
to congratulate a person or to reassure a person

BACK *to put one's back into something*
to work hard at achieving some goal

BACK *to ride on the back of someone*
without effort to benefit from the prior efforts of others

BACK *to scratch one another's backs*
to help each other

BACK *to see the back of someone*
to know that a person is no longer involved in something

BACK *to stab someone in the back*
to deliberately and surreptitiously harm a person who regarded one as a friend

BACK *to tie someone's hands behind his back*
to make it impossible for a person to act at all

BACK *to turn one's back on someone*
to decline to further assist or deal with a person

BACKBONE *backbone*
chief strength or character

BAREFACED *barefaced*
shameless

BELLY *I've had a belly full*
I have had enough of this

BELLY *a fire in someone's belly*
great enthusiasm

BEND *to bend over backward to do something*
to go to great trouble to accommodate another person's wishes

BITE *hard-bitten*
toughened by experience

BITE *to be bitten*
to be swindled

BITE *to be bitten with something*
to become very enthusiastic over something

BITE *to bite*
to respond predictively to a remark designed to provoke

BITE *to bite someone's head off*
to rudely express displeasure at some person

BITE *to bite the bullet*
to face up to the difficulties of a situation

BITE *to bite the dust*
to die

BITE *to get only one bite at the cherry*
to receive no further opportunity

BITE *to start to bite*
to start to be effective

BLIND *the blind leading the blind*
persons without the necessary skills for a task purporting to impart those skills to others

BLIND *to be blind to something*
to be unaware of some matter and its significance

BLINDLY *to follow someone blindly*
to follow a person unquestioningly

BLINKER *to take one's blinkers off*
to face reality

BLOOD *a blueblood*
a person of high birth (refers to the appearance of veins on the skin of members of some royal families)

BLOOD *bad blood*
animosity

BLOOD *blood, sweat and tears*
hard work and much effort

BLOOD *bloodshed*
retribution

BLOOD *fresh blood*
newly joined members of some organization

BLOOD *full-blooded*
vigorous

BLOOD *hot-blooded*
very passionate

BLOOD *one's own flesh and blood*
one's offspring

BLOOD *there is blood in the streets*
much damage has been done to a cause

BLOOD *there is blood in the water*
something is likely to cause a person to go into a frenzy

BLOOD *there is blood on the floor*
this has caused great anguish

BLOOD *to be after someone's blood*
to be keen to make a person the victim of an angry confrontation

BLOOD *to be in someone's blood*
to be something about which a person is very knowledgeable or keen

BLOOD *to curdle one's blood*
to be horrific

BLOOD *to do something in cold blood*
to be cruel without feeling any emotion about it

BLOOD *to draw first blood*
to get an advantage

BLOOD *to give something a blood transfusion*
to give something new enthusiasm

BLOOD *to have blood on one's hands*
to be the person responsible for someone else's predicament

BLOOD *to introduce new blood*
to recruit new members to some organization

BLOOD *to let blood*
to allow some harm as the price for achieving some greater benefit

BLOOD *to make bad blood between two parties*
to cause ill feeling between two parties

BLOOD *to make someone's blood boil*
to make a person very angry

BLOOD *to see blood*
to be very angry

BLOOD *to thirst for blood*
to be eager for revenge

BLOODBATH *a bloodbath*
catastrophic losses

BLOODLETTING *bloodletting*
planned reductions

BLUSH *at first blush*
prima facie

BODY *a body blow*
a very damaging event

BODY *to keep body and soul together*
to keep alive

BONE *to cut costs to the bone*
to economize

BONE *to feel something in one's bones*
to suspect something without having any real evidence for it

BONE *to get close to the bone*
to cause discomfort by being accurate

BONE *to make no bones about it*
to be brutally frank

BONE *to point the bone at someone*
to accuse a person (actually, an Australian Aboriginal method of applying a curse)

BONE *to put flesh and bone on something*
to supply details of a proposal previously revealed only in outline

BONE *to work one's fingers to the bone*
to work very hard

BONEHEADED *boneheaded*
stupid

BOUNCE *to bounce back*
to resume a cheerful existence after some setback

BOW *to bow down*
to succumb to pressure

BRAIN *anyone with even half a brain*
everyone

BRAIN *someone's brain needs washing*
a person is very silly

BRAIN *to have something on one's brain*
to be obsessed with some notion

BRAIN *to pick someone's brain*
to get the benefit of another person's knowledge and experience

BRAINCHILD *brainchild*
inspired original idea

BRAINSTORM *to brainstorm*
to pool thoughts in the course of a session designed to generate fresh ideas and especially to build upon the ideas of others

BRAINWAVE *a brainwave*
a suddenly occurring bright idea

BREAST *to beat one's breast*
to express sorrow

BREAST *to make a clean breast of something*
to confess

BREATH *not to hold one's breath for something*
to give up all expectation

BREATH *to be a breath of fresh air*
to be a pleasant change from the past

BREATH *to draw a deep breath*
to get ready for exertion or for emotional news

BREATH *to take one's breath away*
to greatly surprise or astonish

BREATH *to wait with bated breath*
to be excited in anticipation of some event

BREATH *to waste one's breath*
to talk or request something without achieving anything

BREATHE *to breathe easy*
(following some crisis) to relax

BREATHE *to get some breathing space*
to get more time in which to accomplish something

BROW *highbrow*
intellectual or cultural

BROW *to knit one's brows*
to indicate one's displeasure

BRUISE *to nurse one's bruises*
to face up to the consequences of defeat

BUMP *to bump into someone*
to meet a person accidentally

BUTT *to get up off one's butt*
to cease being apathetic

CHEEK *cheek by jowl*
close to each other

CHEEK *to turn the other cheek*
to show that one has not been intimidated (Matthew 5:39)

CHEEK *tongue in cheek*
full of irony

CHEER *the cheering could be heard a block away*
there was great rejoicing

CHEST *to get something off one's chest*
to confess

CHEST *to hold one's cards close to one's chest*
to keep one's plans and strategies secret

CHILD *a problem child*
a source of unnecessary difficulty

CHIN *to keep one's chin up*
to maintain one's morale

CHIN *to lead with one's chin*
by one's brash behavior to virtually invite one's opponents to take action against one

CHIN *to rub one's chin*
to muse

CHIN *to take it on the chin*
to cheerfully accept a misfortune

COLD *to leave someone cold*
to fail to impress a person

CORD *to cut the cord*
to sever a connection (refers to the umbilical cord)

CORN *to tread on someone's corns*
to upset another person by interfering in his area of responsibility

CRADLE *to be the cradle of something*
to be the place where some idea was first nurtured

CRUCIFY *to crucify someone*
to unfairly do severe damage to a person's reputation or credibility

CRUSOE *not to be Robinson Crusoe*
to be one of a large number of people with a common problem (from Daniel Defoe's ROBINSON CRUSOE)

CRUTCH *a crutch*
an artificial non-permanent support

CRY *a cry for help*
a subconscious or indirect indication that a person is in need of psychological counselling

DADDY *the daddy of them all*
the progenitor

DREAM *a pipedream*
a fanciful notion, wished for but unlikely

DREAM *to be successful beyond one's wildest dreams*
to be far more successful than one could have expected

DREAM *to dream up some story*
to concoct a false story naively or maliciously

DREAM *to have a dream run*
to encounter no difficulties

EAR *a word in someone's ear*
a confidential discussion

EAR *little pitchers have long ears*
children have a tendency to overhear things

EAR *to be all ears*
to be very attentive

EAR *to be music to one's ears*
to be comments which one is very pleased to hear

EAR *to be out on one's ear*
to have one's services abruptly terminated

EAR *to be up to one's ears in something*
to be very deeply involved in something

EAR *to be wet behind the ears*
to be excessively naive and inexperienced

EAR *to chew someone's ears*
to force one's conversation on an unwilling listener

EAR *to come out of one's ears*
to be plentiful

EAR *to come to someone's ears*
to come to someone's attention

EAR *to drag someone by the head and ears*
to force a person to reveal the true facts

EAR *to fall around one's ears*
to collapse utterly

EAR *to fall on deaf ears*
to be totally disregarded

EAR *to go in one ear and out the other*
to leave no impression

EAR *to have money flowing out of one's ears*
to be very rich

EAR *to have someone's ear*
to have a person's attention

EAR *to keep an ear to the ground*
to be well informed as to current developments

EAR *to keep one's ears open*
to be on the lookout for useful information

EAR *to lend someone an ear*
to pay attention to a person

EAR *to play it by ear*
to develop one's strategy to always fit in with circumstances as they change from time to time

EAR *to prick up one's ears*
to suddenly start paying attention to a conversation in progress as a result of a half-heard phrase

EAR *to send someone away with a flea in his ear*
to give a person frank but unwelcome facts (refers to fleas trapped in the armor of ancient knights)

EAR *walls have ears*
someone may be overhearing (words on wartime posters, reminding people of the existence of spies; may also refer to certain rooms in the Louvre, constructed so that conversations could be heard in other rooms)

EAR *were your ears burning?*
we were discussing you

EAR *with one's ears pinned back*
chastened

ELBOW *elbow grease*
hard manual work

ELBOW *more power to your elbow*
may your praiseworthy efforts lead to success

ELBOW *to be up to one's elbow in something*
to be deeply involved in something

ELBOW *to elbow someone out*
to force a person out of some office and oneself into it

ENFANT *an enfant terrible*
a person who raises pertinent but unpalatable issues (French, "terrible child")

EYE *a mote in someone's eye*
a fault in another person which is trifling in comparison to an unrecognized major fault in oneself (Matthew 7:3)

EYE *a smack in the eye*
a rebuff

EYE *all eyes are on something*
everyone's attention is focused on something

EYE *an eye for an eye*
retaliation (Exodus 21:24)

EYE *beauty is in the eye of the beholder*
some things are matters for subjective judgments

EYE *blue-eyed boy*
person shown unjustified favoritism

EYE *in someone's eyes*
in a person's judgment

EYE *one-eyed*
biased

EYE *someone's eyes are bigger than his stomach*
a person is unrealistic

EYE *someone's eyes popped*
a person expressed great surprise

EYE *to be a sight for sore eyes*
to be something welcome

EYE *to be all eyes*
to observe very closely

EYE *to be an eye opener*
to be a surprise

EYE *to be better than a poke in the eye with a burnt stick*
to be particularly welcome

EYE *to be easy on the eye*
to be visually attractive

EYE *to be eye wash*
to be nonsense

EYE *to be in the public eye*
to have one's every action subject to scrutiny by the community

EYE *to be one in the eye for someone*
to represent an unexpected and unwelcome defeat

EYE *to be only a gleam in someone's eyes*
to be a long way from final achievement

EYE *to be the apple of someone's eye*
to be a person of whom another person is proud

EYE *to cast an eye over something*
to look at something critically

EYE *to catch someone's eye*
to attract the attention of another person or to seek permission to address that person

EYE *to clap eyes on something*
to catch sight of something

EYE *to cock one's eye at someone*
to glance knowingly at a person

EYE *to cry one's eyes out*
to express great sadness at a situation

EYE *to do someone in the eye*
to cheat a person

EYE *to have an eye for something*
to appreciate the appearance of something

EYE *to have eyes at the back of one's head*
to know more of what is going on than is generally realized

EYE *to have one's beady eyes on something*
to await the chance to acquire something to which one is not properly entitled

EYE *to have one's eyes glued to something*
to concentrate on looking at something to the exclusion of other competing calls for attention

EYE *to have stars in one's eyes*
(for emotional rather than rational reasons) to be ecstatic

EYE *to hit someone right between the eyes*
to be brutally frank

EYE *to keep a weather eye out for something*
to look out with particular care

EYE *to keep an eye on the ball*
to monitor a fast-changing situation

EYE *to keep one's eye on someone*
to supervise a person or to monitor a person's activities and behavior

EYE *to keep one's eye on something*
to monitor a situation

EYE *to keep one's eyes open*
to be on the lookout for useful information

EYE *to keep one's eyes open for something*
to be on the lookout for an opportunity to do something

EYE *to keep one's eyes peeled for something*
to be on the constant lookout for something

EYE *to make eyes at someone*
to look at a person amorously

EYE *to open someone's eyes to something*
to alert another person to the truth of something

EYE *to pick the eyes out of something*
to choose the most valuable items from among a large number

EYE *to pull the wool over someone's eyes*
to deceive or deliberately mislead another person

EYE *to rub one's eyes*
to express astonishment

EYE *to see eye to eye with someone*
to agree

EYE *to see something with half an eye*
to sum up a matter instantly

EYE *to see the color of someone's eyes*
to see how a person matches expectations or requirements

EYE *to shut one's eyes to something*
to deliberately take no notice of something, especially in dereliction of one's duty

EYE *to throw dust into someone's eyes*
to deceive a person by presenting inaccurate or misleading information

EYE *to turn a blind eye to something*
to pretend something obvious does not exist (refers to action by Nelson when disregarding Admiralty signals)

EYE *with an eye toward doing something*
with the intention that something particular be done

EYE *with one's eyes wide open*
fully conscious of the ramifications

EYEBALL *eyeball to eyeball*
confronting each other and taking account of each other's reactions

EYEBALL *to be up to the eyeballs in something*
to be very deeply involved in something

EYEBROW *to raise one's eyebrows*
to express one's utter astonishment

EYEFUL *to get an eyeful of something*
to see something impressive

EYELASH *not to bat an eyelash*
to fail to express any surprise

EYELID *to hang on by the eyelids*
to have only a slender hold

EYESORE *eyesore*
extremely ugly object

FACE *a poker face*
a facial expression which does not reveal one's thoughts during negotiations

FACE *a slap in the face*
a calculated insult or action amounting to a rebuke

FACE *a straight face*
a facial expression which does not reveal one's thoughts in a humorous situation

FACE *someone's face fell*
someone registered obvious disappointment

FACE *to be left red-faced*
to be embarrassed

FACE *to blow up in someone's face*
to rebound on a person

FACE *to cut one's nose off to spite one's face*
to act in pique in a way which harms only oneself

FACE *to do an about-face*
to reverse a previously enunciated policy

FACE *to fall flat on one's face*
to make a bad error of judgment

FACE *to go on till one is blue in the face*
to argue for a long time

FACE *to have a long face*
to look miserable

FACE *to have egg on one's face*
to be embarrassed by the results of one's own stupidity

FACE *to hurl something in someone's face*
to reproach a person in regard to something

FACE *to lose face*
to endure embarrassment by virtue of being defeated or having one's errors found out

FACE *to present a happy face to the world*
bravely to gloss over one's problems

FACE *to put a brave face on it*
to face adversity cheerfully

FACE *to put a new face on something*
to alter the way something should be regarded

FACE *to put one's best face on something*
to focus on the positive features surrounding a basically disastrous situation

FACE *to save face*
to be allowed to keep one's dignity despite having suffered a defeat or made an error

FACE *to set one's face against something*
to oppose some matter

FACE *to show one's face*
to put in an appearance

FACE *to slam the door in someone's face*
ostentatiously to refuse to have any dealings with a person

FACE *stare someone in the face*
(of a solution, etc) to become obvious

FACE *to wipe the smile off someone's face*
to destroy a person's complacency

FACE *two-faced*
insincere

FACE *wipe that smile off your face!*
treat this matter more seriously!

FACE *you will laugh on the other side of your face*
you will regret this

FALL *they fell over themselves to do something*
they showed great keenness while doing something

FINGER *light-fingered*
good at stealing

FINGER *not to lay a finger on someone*
to refrain from hurting person

FINGER *not to lift finger to help someone*
to refuse to assist

FINGER *someone's fingers are all thumbs*
a person is clumsy with his hands

FINGER *to burn one's fingers*
to lose money through foolishness

FINGER *to gnaw one's fingers to the bone*
to fret

FINGER *to have a finger in something*
to be involved in something

FINGER *to have a finger in the pie*
to have an interest in a project

FINGER *to have green fingers*
to be good at gardening

FINGER *to have itchy fingers*
to be impatient

FINGER *to have one's fingers in many different pies*
to be engaged in a variety of separate activities

FINGER *to have one's finger in the till*
to steal from one's employer

FINGER *to have one's fingers on the pulse*
to know what is going on

FINGER *to have sticky fingers*
to be dishonest

FINGER *to keep one's cotton-picking finger off something*
not to interfere in something

FINGER *to keep one's fingers crossed*
to hope for a good outcome

FINGER *to let something slip through one's fingers*
to allow something to escape from one's ownership or control

FINGER *to point the finger at someone*
to accuse a person or allege some indiscretion on his part

FINGER *to pull one's fingers out*
to get on with a job with alacrity

FINGER *to put one's finger on something*
to identify the essential features of something

FINGER *to stir a finger*
to make some minimum effort

FINGER *to twist someone around one's little finger*
by charm to get one's way

FINGER *to wave a finger at someone*
to indicate mild displeasure at another person's actions

FINGER *to work one's fingers to the bone*
to work very hard

FINGERNAIL *to hang on by one's fingernails*
to have only a slender hold

FINGERTIP *to cling on by ones fingertips*
to have only a slender hold

FINGERTIP *to have some subject at one's fingertips*
to be very familiar with a subject

FIST *ham-fisted*
undiplomatic and clumsy

FIST *hand over fist*
rapidly overtaking each other during progress toward a common goal

FIST *hard-fisted*
stingy

FIST *tight-fisted*
stingy

FIST *to lose money hand over fist*
to lose money very fast and convincingly

FIST *to make a good fist of something*
to be successful in a difficult task

FIST *to rule with an iron fist*
to keep strict discipline

FISTFUL *to hold out a fistful of dollars*
to offer money by way of inducement

FIT *not to get along with someone in a fit*
not to get along with a person

FIT *to have a blue fit*
to be very agitated

FIT *to have a fit*
to be in a state of great agitation

FIT *to have a fit of the vapors*
to be horrified

FLANK *to expose one's flank*
to allow others to take advantage of one

FLESH *one's own flesh and blood*
one's offspring

FLESH *the spirit is willing but the flesh is weak*
the body is not up to the demands made on it

FLESH *to be a thorn in someone's flesh*
to be a person whose persistent presence and righteous views annoy

FLESH *to be more than flesh can stand*
to be more than a person can reasonably be expected to endure

FLESH *to flesh out the skeleton*
to supply the missing pertinent details

FLESH *to go the way of all flesh*
to die

FLESH *to make someone's flesh creep*
to frighten a person with something horrific

FLESH *to put flesh and bone on something*
to supply details of a proposal previously revealed only in outline

FLESH *to see someone in the flesh*
to see someone in person

FOOT *a foot in the door*
the opportunity to do business

FOOT *itchy feet*
a desire to travel

FOOT *nimble-footed*
quick to change the direction of one's activities when circumstances warrant

FOOT *not to let grass grow under one's feet*
not to let inertia or delay spoil something

FOOT *not to put a foot wrong*
to behave impeccably

FOOT *the boot is on the other foot*
the real facts are the other way round

FOOT *to be at one's feet*
to be in the immediate vicinity

FOOT *to be quick on one's feet*
to cleverly take advantage of a situation

FOOT *to be rushed off one's feet*
to be rushed

FOOT *to bind someone hand and foot*
to completely limit a person's freedom to act

FOOT *to catch someone flat-footed*
to embarrass a person in the course of his making mistakes or being unprepared

FOOT *to cut the ground from under someone's feet*
to unexpectedly withdraw support and in the process cause embarrassment or to demolish a person's case

FOOT *to drag one's feet*
to perform unduly slowly

FOOT *to fall on one's feet*
surprisingly to succeed despite difficulties

FOOT *to fall over one's own feet*
to be very clumsy

FOOT *to find one's feet*
to develop one's skills

FOOT *to get back on one's feet*
to recover from an illness or some other setback

FOOT *to get cold feet*
to become scared

FOOT *to get off on the wrong foot with someone*
to make an unfavorable initial impression on a person

FOOT *to get one's feet wet*
to do the necessary but unpleasant or menial parts of a task

FOOT *to go hot foot*
to do something fast

FOOT *to have feet of clay*
to be vulnerable (Daniel 2:33)

FOOT *to have one foot in the grave*
to be dying

FOOT *to have one's feet firmly on the ground*
to know what one is doing

FOOT *to have one's feet in both camps*
to have good relations with two opponents

FOOT *to have one's foot on something*
to be about to acquire something or to be able to acquire something

FOOT *to have the ball at one's feet*
to have unlimited opportunity

FOOT *to have two left feet*
to be clumsy

FOOT *to jump in feet first*
to take a calculated risk

FOOT *to put one's best foot forward*
to make a special effort

FOOT *to put one's feet up*
to relax

FOOT *to put one's foot down*
to exert one's authority and insist on something

FOOT *to put one's foot in it*
to make a foolish mistake

FOOT *to put one's foot in one's mouth*
to say something foolish

FOOT *to put someone on the back foot*
to cause a person to adopt a lower profile

FOOT *to run someone off his feet*
to keep a person very busy on some physical task

FOOT *to shoot oneself in the foot*
to act in a foolish way and thus harm one's own cause

FOOT *to stand on one's own two feet*
not to require the help of others

FOOT *to start off on the right foot*
to commence an operation with great care to do it correctly

FOOT *to sweep someone off her feet*
to cause a person to lose all discernment

FOOT *to tread someone under foot*
to oppress a person

FOOT *to vote with one's feet*
to show one's displeasure by terminating an association

FOOT *to wait hand and foot on someone*
to accommodate a person's every real or imagined whim

FOOTHOLD *to gain a foothold*
to achieve a position from which further advances can readily be made

FOOTLOOSE *footloose and fancyfree*
unmarried and without any romantic attachments

FOOTPRINT *without leaving any footprints*
without making any impression

FOOTSTEP *to follow in someone's footsteps*
to do as another person did

FROWN *to frown on something*
to disapprove of some matter

GALL *gall*
impudence

GIANT *a giant*
a person whose ability and achievements exceed that of most other people

GRIN *to grin and bear it*
to suffer adversity cheerfully

GRIP *to come to grips with some problem*
to be on the way to solving a problem

GUT *a gut feeling*
a belief based purely on intuition and unsupported by facts or evidence

GUT *gutless wonder*
coward

GUT *something has no guts in it*
something has no real value to it

GUTFUL *to have had a gutful*
to be disgusted

GUTS *I will have his guts for garters*
I am extremely angry and dissatisfied with him

GUTS *to kick someone in the guts*
to take action needlessly hurtful to another person

HAIR *hair-raising*
scary

HAIR *not to touch a hair on someone's head*
not to harm a person

HAIR *not to turn a hair*
to remain composed

HAIR *to a hair*
exactly

HAIR *to be within a hair's breadth of something*
to be extremely close to something

HAIR *to get someone by the short and curly hairs*
to have domination over a person

HAIR *to keep one's hair on*
to remain calm in a crisis

HAIR *to keep out of someone's hair*
to let another person get on with his work in his own way

HAIR *to let one's hair down*
to relax

HAIR *to make someone's hair curl*
(of news) to give someone a shock

HAIR *to make someone's hair stand on end*
to give a person shocking news

HAIR *to split hairs*
to draw absurdly fine distinctions

HAIR *to tear one's hair out*
to be agitated

HAND *a backhanded compliment*
a polite expression seemingly of praise but really intended as an insult

HAND *a bird in the hand is worth two in the bush*
a benefit currently available is more valuable than a seemingly much larger benefit which may or may not be achieved in the future

HAND *a left-handed compliment*
a thinly-disguised insult

HAND *at first hand*
personally

HAND *hand over fist*
rapidly overtaking each other during progress toward a common goal

HAND *high-handed*
overbearing

HAND *on the one hand*
putting one side of the proposition

HAND *one's right-hand man*
one's chief aide

HAND *single-handedly*
without help from other persons

HAND *sleight of hand*
deceit by trickery

HAND *the hand of fate*
chance

HAND *the left hand does not know what the right hand is doing*
one section of a large bureaucracy does not realize that another section is simultaneously doing something inconsistent

HAND *to accept something with both hands*
to accept something eagerly

HAND *to be able to do something with one hand behind one's back*
to be able to do something very easily

HAND *to be able to lay one's hands on something*
to be able to locate something

HAND *to be at hand*
to be in the vicinity, ready to help

HAND *to be in hand*
to be under control

HAND *to be in someone's hands*
to be being dealt with by someone with the necessary authority

HAND *to be out of someone's hands*
to be up for decision by a different person

HAND *to be putty in someone's hand*
to be far too easily influenced by another person

HAND *to bind someone hand and foot*
to completely limit a person's freedom to act

HAND *to bite the hand that feeds one*
to show ingratitude

HAND *to catch someone red-handed*
to apprehend a person in the course of committing a crime

HAND *to eat out of someone's hands*
to be unduly compliant

HAND *to gain the upper hand*
to attain, after some effort, an advantage over another person

HAND *to get one's hands dirty*
to do the necessary but unpleasant or menial parts of a task

HAND *to get out of hand*
to get out of control

HAND *to give someone a free hand*
to authorize a person to act as he sees fit

HAND *to give someone a hand*
to assist a person

HAND *to go cap in hand*
to show humility while soliciting a favor

HAND *to go down on one's hands and knees to someone*
with great humility to ask a favor of a person

HAND *to grab some opportunity with both hands*
to seize some opportunity with great enthusiasm

HAND *to handpick someone*
to carefully choose a person for his individual attributes

HAND *to have a fight on one's hands*
to encounter resistance or opposition to a proposal

HAND *to have a hand in something*
to be one of the participants in some project

HAND *to have blood on one's hands*
to be the person responsible for someone else's predicament

HAND *to have clean hands*
to be innocent or to act ethically

HAND *to have one's hands full*
to be fully occupied

HAND *to have the whip hand*
to be in control of a situation

HAND *to hold someone's hand*
to give detailed on-the-job training and supervision

HAND *to hold the power to do something in the hollow of one's hand*
to have the right to make crucial decisions

HAND *to join hands with someone*
to cooperate with a person

HAND *to keep one's hands in*
to engage in activities which reinforce skills which one has previously acquired

HAND *to lay one's hands on something*
to acquire something

HAND *to lend a hand*
to assist

HAND *to live from hand to mouth*
being in poor financial circumstances, to survive with little by way of safety margin

HAND *to lose money hand over fist*
to lose money very fast and convincingly

HAND *to play right into someone's hands*
to act so as to give a person an unintended advantage

HAND *to put one's hand to the plow*
voluntarily to undertake some task (Luke 9:62)

HAND *to put one's hand up*
to identify oneself

HAND *to put one's hands in one's pockets*
to spend

HAND *to rub one's hands with glee*
to express great satisfaction

HAND *to rule with an iron hand*
to keep strict discipline

HAND *to sit on one's hands*
deliberately to do nothing

HAND *to stir a hand*
to volunteer assistance

HAND *to strengthen someone's hand*
to give a person additional authority or greater moral support or more facts to support his case

HAND *to take something in hand*
to assume control over something

HAND *to throw up one's hands*
to express disgust

HAND *to tie someone's hands*
to prevent a person from acting as he sees fit

HAND *to tie someone's hands behind his back*
to make it impossible for a person to act at all

HAND *to try one's hand at something*
to attempt a new activity, especially by way of experiment

HAND *to turn one's hand to something*
to tackle something

HAND *to wait hand and foot on someone*
to accommodate a person's every real or imagined whim

HAND *to wash one's hands of something*
to emphatically decline future responsibility

HAND *to work hand in glove with someone*
to work in close cooperation with a person or to be in collusion with a person to the detriment of others

HAND *to wring one's hands*
to express despair

HAND *with a heavy hand*
in an oppressive fashion

HAND *with a high hand*
arrogantly (Exodus 14:8)

HAND *with an iron hand in a velvet glove*
with a hard attitude made to seem soft

HAND *with an open hand*
generously

HANDFUL *a handful*
a small number

HANDFUL *to be a handful*
to be difficult to manage

HANDSHAKE *a golden handshake*
a large payment in connection with or as an inducement to retirement

HANDSTAND *to turn handstands*
to express great joy

HANG *to give someone enough rope to hang himself*
to give a person the opportunity to do something which is likely to get him into severe trouble

HEAD *a hothead*
an impetuous person

HEAD *a swelled head*
an exaggerated idea of one's abilities or status

HEAD *an old head on young shoulders*
experience, knowledge and maturity in a young person

HEAD *hard-headed*
realistic

HEAD *head first*
precipitately

HEAD *head over heels*
topsy-turvy

HEAD *heads will roll*
transgressors will be punished

HEAD *level-headed*
rational

HEAD *not to touch a hair on someone's head*
not to harm a person

HEAD *off the top of one's head*
based on experience but without detailed consideration

HEAD *pull your head in!*
do not interfere in this!

HEAD *someone's head is on the block*
a person is in danger of having his appointment terminated

HEAD *that is on your head*
you will have to accept responsibility for that

HEAD *there is a big question mark hanging over someone's head*
there are considerable doubts about a persons' competence, integrity or suitability

HEAD *to bang one's head up against a brick wall*
to fight an unwinnable case

HEAD *to be able to do something standing on one's head*
to be able to do something very easily

HEAD *to be head and shoulders above the rest*
to be significantly more capable than others

HEAD *to be off one's head*
to be crazy

HEAD *to be over someone's head*
to be beyond a person's ability to understand

HEAD *to beat each other over the head*
to be always fighting

HEAD *to belt someone over the head*
to override someone's views or arguments

HEAD *to bite someone's head off*
to rudely express displeasure at some person

HEAD *to bury one's head in the sand*
to refuse to face up to an unpleasant truth (refers to the reputed habit of ostriches in danger)

HEAD *to come to a head*
to reach culmination

HEAD *to confront someone head-on*
to confront a person

HEAD *to drag someone by the head and ears*
to force a person to reveal the true facts

HEAD *to eat one's head off*
to eat excessively

HEAD *to fall head over heels in love*
to fall very much in love

HEAD *to get one's head blown off*
to be very soundly abused

HEAD *to give someone his head*
to let a person do as he wants to

HEAD *to go off one's head*
to lose one's temper

HEAD *to go over someone's head*
to bypass lower levels of authority and approach someone more senior instead

HEAD *to go to someone's head*
to cause a person to get an exaggerated idea of his abilities or status

HEAD *to hang one's head*
to be ashamed of oneself

HEAD *to have a cloud hanging over one's head*
there is doubt as to one's future

HEAD *to have a head start*
to have an advantage over others

HEAD *to have a threat hanging over one's head*
to fear some intimated unpleasant action

HEAD *to have eyes at the back of one's head*
to know more of what is going on than is generally realized

HEAD *to have one's head in the clouds*
to be unrealistic

HEAD *to have one's head screwed on straight*
to be shrewd

HEAD *to have rocks in the head*
to be mentally unbalanced

HEAD *to hold a gun at someone's head*
to put pressure on a person to make a particular decision regardless of his desires in the matter

HEAD *to hold one's head high*
to stay unruffled and to maintain one's dignity despite attempts by others to embarrass

HEAD *to just hold one's head above water*
to cope with problems but with little margin to spare or to stay solvent

HEAD *to keep a civil tongue in one's head*
to be polite, especially under provocation

HEAD *to keep a cool head*
to stay calm and rational in a crisis

HEAD *to keep a level head*
to stay calm and rational in a crisis

HEAD *to keep one's head*
to remain calm in a crisis or to unexpectedly retain an elected or appointed position

HEAD *to keep one's head down*
to work very diligently

HEAD *to kick heads in*
to demonstrate annoyance at or dislike of certain persons

HEAD *to knock an idea on the head*
to utterly reject a proposal

HEAD *to knock two heads together*
to make two persons come to their senses and deal with each other

HEAD *to laugh one's head off*
to greatly enjoy something

HEAD *to let one's head go*
to do as one wants to

HEAD *to let one's heart rule one's head*
to act on emotion rather than on reason

HEAD *to lose one's head*
to become confused

HEAD *to need something like a hole in the head*
to be landed with a completely undesired problem

HEAD *to need to have one's head read*
to be foolish

HEAD *to promote someone over the heads of others*
to promote a person to a position more senior than that held by some persons previously outranking him

HEAD *to pull one's head in*
to retreat from a previously held stance

HEAD *to put one's head in the noose*
to recklessly and unnecessarily expose oneself to great danger

HEAD *to put one's head into the lion's mouth*
to recklessly expose oneself to great danger

HEAD *to put one's head on the block*
to have the courage of one's convictions

HEAD *to put one's head together*
to confer and pool ideas

HEAD *to scratch one's head*
to be amazed or puzzled

HEAD *to scream one's head off*
to scream very loudly

HEAD *to shake one's head*
to indicate disbelief or wonder or disapproval

HEAD *to snap someone's head off*
to speak to a person aggressively

HEAD *to tackle someone head-on*
to confront a person

HEAD *to turn someone's head*
to cause a person to get an exaggerated idea of his abilities or status

HEAD *uneasy lies the head that wears a crown*
responsibility involves some risk and some burdens (from Shakespeare's HENRY IV)

HEAD *woolly-headed*
slightly muddled

HEAD *you want your head read*
you should reconsider this matter

HEADACHE *a headache*
a cause for worry

HEADWAY *to make headway*
to make progress

HEALTH *to get a clean bill of health*
after proper investigation to be found not wanting

HEAR *to hear a whisper*
to learn a rumored hypothesis

HEART *cold-hearted*
cruel or mean or unmoved

HEART *from the bottom of one's heart*
very sincerely

HEART *half-hearted*
unenthusiastic

HEART *hard-hearted*
unsympathetic

HEART *heart and soul*
with great energy

HEART *heart failure*
a shock

HEART *heart-stopping*
exciting

HEART *one's heart bleeds for someone*
one feels truly sad for a person's fate

HEART *one's heart is not in some cause*
one has little enthusiasm for some cause

HEART *one's heart sank*
one realized the extent of some disaster

HEART *open-hearted*
cordial

HEART *this does my heart good*
I rejoice at this

HEART *to be close to one's heart*
to be a project on which one is very keen

HEART *to be in good heart*
to be brave in adversity

HEART *to be of good heart*
to be brave in adversity

HEART *to be someone after one's own heart*
to be a person who shares one's beliefs

HEART *to break someone's heart*
to act in a way causing great upset to another person

HEART *to eat one's heart out*
to suffer bitterly

HEART *to give someone heart*
to cause a person to cheer up

HEART *to have a change of heart*
to form a new view in place of a strongly-held previous view

HEART *to have a heart*
to have compassion

HEART *to have a heart of gold*
to have a generous disposition

HEART *to have a heart of oak*
to be brave

HEART *to have a heart of stone*
to be unfeeling

HEART *to have a heart-to-heart talk*
to have a confidential discussion on a highly personal matter

HEART *to have one's heart in one's boots*
to be terrified

HEART *to have one's heart in one's mouth*
to be startled

HEART *to have one's heart in something*
to be enthusiastic about and committed to a cause

HEART *to have one's heart in the right place*
to have a well-developed social conscience

HEART *to have one's heart set on something*
to be very keen to achieve something

HEART *to know something in one's heart of hearts*
to know something while reluctant to admit it, even to oneself

HEART *to let one's heart rule one's head*
to act on emotion rather than on reason

HEART *to lose heart*
to cease being enthusiastic

HEART *to pour one's heart out to someone*
to inflict one's woes on another person

HEART *to pull at one's heart strings*
to affect one emotionally

HEART *to search one's heart*
to have misgivings

HEART *to steal someone's heart*
to cause a person to fall in love with one

HEART *to steel one's heart against something*
to determine that, notwithstanding one's natural compassion, something shall not happen

HEART *to take heart from something*
to be encouraged by something

HEART *to take something to heart*
to learn to appreciate the significance of something or to be much saddened by something

HEART *to warm the cockles of someone's heart*
to delight a person

HEART *to wear one's heart on one's sleeve*
to lack the reserve expected of one

HEART *warm-hearted*
affectionate or generous

HEART *with a heavy heart*
in sorrow

HEART *with a sinking heart*
with growing despondency

HEART *you can eat your heart out*
you are entitled to feel sad or jealous

HEARTACHE *heartache*
sadness

HEARTBREAK *heartbreak*
despair

HEARTBURN *heartburn*
regret at some non-achievement

HEEL *head over heels*
topsy-turvy

HEEL *to be hot on the heels of something*
to closely follow something

HEEL *to be someone's Achilles' heel*
to represent a weakness in an otherwise strong position (refers to the Greek warrior who was the hero of Homer's ILIAD)

HEEL *to bring someone to heel*
to make a person conform

HEEL *to cool one's heels*
to be kept waiting

HEEL *to dig one's heels in*
to become even more stubborn than at first

HEEL *to drag one's heels*
to perform unduly slowly

HEEL *to fall head over heels in love*
to fall very much in love

HEEL *to kick one's heels*
to be kept waiting

HEEL *to snap at someone's heels*
to be a minor irritation to a person

HEEL *well-heeled*
rich

HEMORRHAGE *to stem the hemorrhage*
to put a stop to the financial losses of a project

HIDE *to want someone's hide*
to be keen to penalize a person

HINDSIGHT *with 20/20 hindsight*
with the benefit of knowing what happened

HIP *to shoot from the hip*
to speak frankly and openly

HIT *to hit someone hard*
to greatly affect a person emotionally or to cost a person a lot of money

HOP *to catch someone on the hop*
to take a person by surprise

ITCH *to be itching to go*
to be highly enthusiastic and keen to start

JAUNDICED *jaundiced*
affected by jealousy

JAW *someone's jaw dropped*
someone registered obvious disappointment, incredulity or shock

JOWL *cheek by jowl*
close to each other

JUGULAR *to go for the jugular*
to attempt to destroy something completely

JUMP *to be for the high jump*
to be threatened with a reprimand and punishment

JUMP *to get the jump on someone*
to get an advantage over a person

JUMP *to jump at the opportunity*
to enthusiastically take immediate advantage of a good chance

JUMP *to jump for joy*
to express great satisfaction

JUMP *to jump to a conclusion*
to infer something without proper consideration

JUMP *to jump to attention*
to show respect

JUMP *to jump up and down*
to show excitement or anger or frustration

JUMP *to want to jump all one's fences at once*
to be unrealistic

KICK *I could kick myself*
I regret that I acted thus

KICK *a kick in the pants*
an admonition

KICK *to be alive and kicking*
to be in good form

KICK *to kick a man when he is down*
to take unfair advantage of a person already in difficulty

KICK *to kick in*
to contribute financially

KICK *to kick some proposal around*
to examine a proposal from all angles

KICK *to kick someone around*
to abuse a person

KICK *to kick someone out*
to expel a person

KICK *to kick someone upstairs*
to promote a person to a purely ceremonial position

KNEE *a knee-jerk reaction*
a response made instantaneously and without any proper consideration

KNEE *since he was knee high to a grasshopper*
since he was a very young child

KNEE *to be cut off at the knees*
to have a pet project aborted

KNEE *to beg on bended knees*
to request in great earnestness

KNEE *to force someone onto his knees*
to inflict a humiliating defeat on a person

KNEE *to go down on one's hands and knees to someone*
with great humility to ask a favor of a person

KNEE *weak-kneed*
unassertive or irresolute

KNUCKLE *to rap someone over the knuckles*
to admonish a person

LAP *to drop into one's lap*
to turn up fortuitously

LAP *to dump something in someone's lap*
to impose some responsibility on another person

LATHER *to get a lather up*
to get unduly excited

LEAN *to lean on someone*
to utilize the support of another person or to pressure another person to do something against his inclination

LEAP *by leaps and bounds*
with surprisingly fast progress

LEAP *to leap at an idea*
to accept a suggestion enthusiastically

LEAP *to leap in*
to commence an activity without considering the wisdom of doing so or the best way to proceed

LEG *not to have a leg to stand on*
to have one's arguments completely demolished or to be without acceptable excuse or explanation

LEG *to be on one's last legs*
to be nearly worn out

LEG *to cost an arm and a leg*
to be excessively expensive

LEG *to do the leg work*
to carry out the tedious part of a project

LEG *to give someone a leg up*
to give a person some assistance

LEG *to have a leg in*
to have an opportunity which has the potential to lead to bigger things

LEG *to pull someone's leg*
to tell a false but plausible story as an act of humor

LEG *to shake a leg*
to hurry up

LEG *to stand up on one's hind legs*
to exert one's authority

LICK *to lick one's chops*
to look forward to something with pleasurable anticipation

LICK *to lick someone's boots*
to show humility

LICK *to lick something into shape*
to make something presentable and effective

LIE *to lie low*
to stay inconspicuous

LIE *to take something lying down*
to accept a disadvantage without protest

LIFE *I cannot for the life of me*
I just cannot

LIFE *not on your life*
definitely not

LIFE *to be the life and soul of the party*
to be the prime enthusiast for a cause

LIFE *to save someone's life*
to be of great help to a person

LIFEBLOOD *the lifeblood*
the main or essential ingredient; or the person or factor instilling enthusiasm

LIP *a stiff upper lip*
obstinate courage in the face of pain or adversity

LIP *to be tight-lipped*
to keep confidences or to be uncommunicative

LIP *to bite one's lip*
to control one's anger

LIP *to pay lip service to some rules*
to disregard some rules in practice while acknowledging them in words

LIP *to seal one's lips*
to keep a confidence

LISTEN *a listening post*
a place where information of strategic value can be collected

LIVER *lily-livered*
cowardly

LOIN *to gird up one's loins*
to get ready for action

LOOK *to look at someone sideways*
to silently and politely indicate one's disapproval

MAN *every man and his dog*
everybody

MAN *he is your man*
he conforms to an ideal

MAN *one man's meat is another man's poison*
people's taste differ

MAN *to be one's own man*
to approach every issue in a totally objective manner

MAN *to separate the men from the boys*
to distinguish between those with and without certain skills

MAN *two men and a dog*
very few people

MIND *a thought in the back of one's mind*
an undeveloped idea

MIND *in one's mind's eye*
using a vivid imagination

MIND *it is mind over matter*
one's resolve to overcome suffering will succeed

MIND *that has taken a load off my mind*
I am relieved

MIND *the mind boggles*
this is astonishing

MIND *to be a weight off one's mind*
to be a great relief

MIND *to be of two minds*
to be undecided between two alternatives

MIND *to be of one mind*
(of several people) to be agreed

MIND *to be out of one's cotton-picking mind*
to act irrationally

MIND *to broaden someone's mind*
to expose a person to a greater variety of experiences and interests than he had previously

MIND *to change one's mind*
to alter the views which one had previously formed

MIND *to cross one's mind*
to occur to one

MIND *to drive someone out of his mind*
to cause great worry to a person

MIND *to give someone a piece of one's mind*
to abuse another person

MIND *to have a mind of one's own*
not to be easily influenced

MIND *to have a one-track mind*
to keep coming back to one narrow topic of conversation

MIND *to have an open mind*
to be willing to assess evidence on its merits and without prejudging it

MIND *to have half a mind to do something*
to be tempted or mildly inclined to do something

MIND *to know one's mind*
to form and adhere to an opinion

MIND *to make up one's mind*
to reach a conclusion after contemplating a matter

MIND *to prey on one's mind*
(of a problem) to keep worrying one

MIND *to put someone's mind at rest*
to reassure a person

MIND *to slip one's mind*
to be overlooked or forgotten

MIND *to speak one's mind*
to express one's views frankly and forcefully

MIND *to spring to mind*
to suddenly occur to a person

MOHICAN *the last of the Mohicans*
to be the last of a group (refers to a near extinct tribe of American Indian) (title of a novel by James Fenimore Cooper)

MOTHERHOOD *a motherhood statement*
a statement so obvious and uncontroversial as not to be worth making (such as ''motherhood is a good thing'')

MOUTH *hard-mouthed*
uncontrollable

MOUTH *mealy-mouthed*
not at all forceful in debate

MOUTH *out of the mouths of babes*
(as indiscreetly revealed) the truth

MOUTH *someone looks as if butter would not melt in his mouth*
a person looks sweet and innocent

MOUTH *to be a big mouth*
to lack discretion in one's conversation

MOUTH *to be born with a silver spoon in one's mouth*
to be brought up by wealthy parents

MOUTH *to be down in the mouth*
to be depressed

MOUTH *to be left with a nasty taste in one's mouth*
to be appalled or very disappointed at another person's unethical behavior to one

MOUTH *to foam at the mouth*
to show anger

MOUTH *to have one's heart in one's mouth*
to be startled

MOUTH *to keep one's mouth shut*
not to discuss some matter

MOUTH *to live from hand to mouth*
being in poor financial circumstances, to survive with little by way of safety margin

MOUTH *to make one's mouth water*
to excite desire

MOUTH *to put one's foot in one's mouth*
to say something foolish

MOUTH *to put one's money where one's mouth is*
to back one's judgment by putting assets at risk

MOUTH *to put words into someone's mouth*
to attempt to get someone to say something in the particular terms drafted by another person

MOUTH *to shoot one's mouth off*
to speak without thinking

MOUTH *to take food out of the mouths of children*
cruelly to deprive the needy

MOUTH *you took the words right out of my mouth*
you have just said what I was about to say

MUSCLE *to flex one's muscles*
to exert one's personality or powers

MYOPIA *myopia*
the inability to appreciate an argument (lit., short-sightedness)

NAIL *to bite one's fingernails*
to anxiously await a decision

NAIL *to fight tooth and nail*
to strive very hard to win

NAIL *to hang on by one's nails*
to have only a slender hold

NAVEL *to contemplate one's navel*
to be introspective

NECK *a millstone round someone's neck*
a great burden

NECK *at a break-neck pace*
very fast

NECK *it is neck or nothing*
a desperate effort is called for

NECK *neck and neck*
(of contestants) with little between them

NECK *to be a pain in the neck*
to be an unpleasant person or to be a nuisance

NECK *to be an albatross around someone's neck*
to be a great burden (popularized by Coleridge's ANCIENT MARINER)

NECK *to be up to one's neck in something*
to be very deeply involved in something

NECK *to break one's neck to do something*
to be particularly keen

NECK *to breathe down someone's neck*
to cause annoyance to another person by remaining in his vicinity or by supervising him too closely; or to be narrowly behind another person in some competitive situation

NECK *to cop it in the neck*
to suffer a severe disaster

NECK *to save someone's neck*
to come to the rescue of a person

NECK *to send a chill down someone's neck*
to be worrying news

NECK *to stick one's neck out*
to have the courage of one's convictions or to take a calculated risk

NERVE *the hip pocket nerve*
the assessment of issues by their financial effects on one

NERVE *to get on someone's nerves*
by one's behavior to cause annoyance to a person

NERVE *to have a nerve*
to be impudent

NERVE *to have nerves of steel*
not to be easily frightened

NERVE *to lose one's nerve*
to abandon, out of fear, a decision to do something

NERVE *to touch a nerve*
to mention something which another person would rather pretend did not exist

NIGGER *the nigger in the woodpile*
the factor spoiling an otherwise satisfactory arrangement

NIGHTMARE *a nightmare*
an unpleasant experience

NOD *a nod and a wink*
a sign that understanding has been reached in a matter which in the interests of discretion has not been discussed aloud

NOD *to get the nod*
to receive approval

NOSE *hard-nosed*
tough in negotiations

NOSE *to be no skin off someone's nose*
not to matter to a person

NOSE *to be on the nose*
(of a proposal or scheme) to be accurate

NOSE *to bite someone's nose off*
to speak to a person aggressively

NOSE *to cut one's nose off to spite one's face*
to act in pique in a way which harms only oneself

NOSE *to escape by the skin of one's nose*
to only just avoid some disaster

NOSE *to follow one's nose*
to act intuitively

NOSE *to get a bloody nose*
to suffer an undignified rebuff

NOSE *to get up someone's nose*
to irritate a person

NOSE *to have a good nose for business*
to be able to identify profitable business situations

NOSE *to keep one's nose clean*
to act with circumspection and honesty despite temptation to do otherwise

NOSE *to keep one's nose out of something*
not to meddle in something

NOSE *to keep one's nose to the grindstone*
to work with particular diligence

NOSE *to lead someone by the nose*
to induce another person to comply with one's wishes

NOSE *to look down the nose at something*
to treat a matter with obvious contempt

NOSE *to pay through the nose*
to pay an excessive price

NOSE *to poke one's nose into something*
to interfere

NOSE *to poke one's nose outside*
to venture outside

NOSE *to put someone's nose out of joint*
to upset another person

NOSE *to rub someone's nose in it*
to humiliate a person by highlighting something embarrassing to him

NOSE *to take a nosedive*
to suddenly and unexpectedly fall steeply

NOSE *to take something on the nose*
to meekly accept a rebuff

NOSE *to thumb one's nose at someone*
to show one's contempt for someone in authority and to ostentatiously disregard his orders

NOSE *to turn up one's nose at something*
to express one's disdain

NOSE *under someone's nose*
in a person's immediate area of responsibility or in circumstances where he should have known something

NUDGE *to give something a nudge forward*
to give modest encouragement to something

OLD *it is on for young and old*
the excitement has started

PALM *to grease someone's palms*
to bribe a person

PALPABLE *palpable*
readily understandable

PARALYZE *to paralyze something*
to bring something to a standstill

PAS *faux pas*
something indiscreet or offending social conventions (French, "false step")

PEOPLE *to be unable to keep people away with a big stick*
to be faced with a large crowd or much demand

PIECE *to have a piece of someone*
to vent one's frustration on a person

PROFILE *profile*
description

PULL *to pull oneself together*
to cease acting without purpose or enthusiasm

PULSE *to have one's fingers on the pulse*
to know what is going on

PUNCH *not to pull any punches*
to be brutally frank

PUSH *to push someone around*
to exercise, in an obnoxious manner, one's superiority over another person

REEL *to leave someone reeling*
to leave a person in a state of shock

RUB *to rub someone up the wrong way*
to annoy someone with actions failing to recognize his current mood

RUN *to run around in circles*
to engage in excited but useless activity

RUN *to run with something*
to take advantage of some current development

SCALP *to be after someone's scalp*
to be keen to penalize a person

SCAR *to scar someone*
to leave a person permanently grieving

SCENT *to throw someone off the scent*
to deceive a person by giving out misleading indications

SCREAM *to scream and yell*
to protest violently

SENSE *a sixth sense*
intuition (refers to the five senses—sight, hearing, smell, taste and touch)

SHADOW *to be in someone's shadow*
to be unable to exert one's personality because of association with a more important person

SHAVE *to be a close shave*
to be a narrow escape

SHORTSIGHTED *to be shortsighted*
not to recognize the likely consequences

SHOULDER *a shoulder to cry on*
sympathy

SHOULDER *a shoulder to lean on*
sympathy

SHOULDER *an old head on young shoulders*
experience, knowledge and maturity in a young person

SHOULDER *shoulder to shoulder*
in close proximity

SHOULDER *straight from the shoulder*
bluntly

SHOULDER *to be head and shoulders above the rest*
to be significantly more capable than others

SHOULDER *to carry the world on one's shoulders*
to resent being left to perform a huge task single-handedly (refers to Atlas, who was condemned to bear the heavens on his shoulders for leading the Titans against the gods)

SHOULDER *to give someone the cold shoulder*
to ostentatiously ignore a person

SHOULDER *to have a chip on one's shoulder*
to unreasonably resent something

SHOULDER *to have broad shoulders*
to be able to cope well with responsibility

SHOULDER *to need to look over one's shoulder*
to be subject to attack which is not obvious

SHOULDER *to put a burden on someone's shoulders*
to impose responsibilities on a person

SHOULDER *to put one's shoulder to the wheel*
to make a strong effort

SHOULDER *to rub shoulders with someone*
to mingle with a person

SHOULDER *to shoulder the blame*
to accept the blame

SHOULDER *to shrug one's shoulders*
to indicate that one does not know or care or that one is unable or unwilling to assist

SHOULDER *to stand on someone's shoulders*
to build upon another person's ideas

SHOULDER *to take a weight off someone's shoulder*
to assist a person by relieving him of some responsibility

SHOULDER *to work shoulder to shoulder*
to work with united effort

SHOUT *to be all over bar the shouting*
to be virtually finished

SHRUG *to shrug something off*
to indicate that one is unable or unwilling to do something

SHUDDER *one shudders to think what the outcome might be*
there is great concern as to the outcome

SIDE *to get on someone's right side*
to make a good impression on a person

SIDE *to split one's side*
to be convulsed with laughter

SIGH *to heave a sigh a relief*
to express satisfaction at the achievement of a solution to a difficult problem

SIT *to sit on someone*
to repress a person

SIT *to sit pretty*
to be comfortably off

SIT *to sit tight*
obstinately to do nothing

SKELETON *a skeleton in the cupboard*
an unpleasant truth the knowledge of which has been deliberately suppressed

SKELETON *to flesh out the skeleton*
to supply the missing pertinent details

SKIN *to be no skin off someone's nose*
not to matter to a person

SKIN *to get under someone's skin*
to annoy another person through stupidity

SKIN *to have a thick skin*
to be impervious to criticism

SKIN *to nearly jump out of one's skin*
to receive a fright

SKIN *to save one's skin*
to get off safely

SKULL *to penetrate someone's thick skull*
to make a person understand something difficult or acknowledge something unwelcome

SLEEP *not to lose any sleep over something*
not to worry about some matter

SLEEP *to go to sleep*
to become inactive

SLEEP *to sleep on one's rights*
to fail to exercise some entitlement within a reasonable period

SLEEP *to spend a sleepless night*
to worry about something

SMELL *something smells*
something is suspicious

SMELL *to run something on the smell of an oil rag*
to run something very economically and efficiently

SMELL *to smell out something*
to discover something by careful investigation

SMELL *to smell trouble*
to perceive difficulties

SNEEZE *that is not to be sneezed at*
that is so significant that it should not be rejected

SORE *to open up a festering sore*
to upset a person by drawing attention to a long-standing grievance

SPINE *to send a cold shiver down someone's spine*
to horrify a person

SPIT *spit it out!*
unburden yourself!

SPLEEN *to vent one's spleen on someone*
to demonstrate one's ill temper to a person

SPOT *to be a tender spot*
to be a subject on which a person is touchy

SPOT *to have a blind spot about something*
to fail to recognize the adverse aspects of something

SPOT *to have a soft spot for someone*
to be very fond of a person

SPREAD *to spread oneself thin*
to attempt to do more than is feasible in the available time

STAND *to know where one stands*
to know what one supports or how one is affected

STAND *to stand out from the crowd*
to be noticeably better than one's competitors

STAND *to stand up and be counted*
to publicly announce one's position on some issue

STEP *a step in the right direction*
the first in a series of measures designed to correct some problem

STEP *by small steps*
gradually

STEP *step by step*
gradually

STEP *to get in step with someone*
to do as another person does

STEP *to take a giant step forward*
to make a significant advance

STEP *to take a step backward*
to move farther away from one's goal

STEP *to watch one's step*
to be on the lookout for danger or to set out to improve one's behavior

STICK *to give someone a bit of stick*
to mildly criticize a person

STITCH *to have someone in stitches*
to greatly amuse a person

STOMACH *someone's eyes are bigger than his stomach*
a person is unrealistic

STOMACH *to have butterflies in one's stomach*
a feeling of anxiety

STOMACH *to have no stomach for something*
to have no taste or fortitude for something

STRANGLEHOLD *a stranglehold*
a firm grip on a commercial situation, effectively freezing out a competitor

STRIDE *to hit one's stride*
to settle down to some task

STRIDE *to take something in one's stride*
to cope with something easily

SUCK *to suck someone in*
to embroil an innocent party in an unethical enterprise

SUCK *to teach one's grandmother how to suck eggs*
to try to tell a much more experienced person something very obvious to him

SWALLOW *someone has swallowed a dictionary*
a person uses excessively long words

SWALLOW *to be a bitter pill to swallow*
to be a great humiliation and disappointment which have to be endured

SWALLOW *to be hard to swallow*
not to be readily acceptable

SWALLOW *to swallow one's pride*
to take action despite the humiliating nature of this course

SWALLOW *to swallow the line*
to accept as truth the story being proffered

SWEAT *blood, sweat and tears*
hard work and much effort

SWEAT *no sweat*
this presents no difficulty

SWEAT *to be in a cold sweat*
to be afraid

SWEAT *to sweat it out*
to await one's fate calmly

TASTE *to get a taste of one's own medicine*
to suffer from an initiative intended to affect only other persons

TEAR *blood, sweat and tears*
hard work and much effort

TEAR *to almost drive someone to tears*
to present information designed to make another person express sympathy not warranted by the facts

TEAR *to bore someone to tears*
to greatly weary a person by dull and uninteresting conversation or by lack of action

TEAR *to shed a quiet tear for something*
to lament the passing of something

TEAR *to tear someone apart*
to ruthlessly destroy another person's case

THINK *to think twice before doing something*
to consider with particular care

THROAT *it sticks in my throat*
I find it galling

THROAT *the words stuck in my throat*
I just could not get myself to say the intended words

THROAT *to be at each other's throats*
to be always fighting

THROAT *to cut one's own throat*
to act in a way which damages one's own interests

THROAT *to have a lump in one's throat*
to feel emotional

THROAT *to have someone by the throat*
to claim victory over an opponent

THROAT *to hold a knife at someone's throat*
to exert undue pressure on another person in an endeavor to achieve a result which would otherwise not be forthcoming

THROAT *to hold a sword at someone's throat*
to exert undue pressure on another person in an endeavor to achieve a result which would otherwise not be forthcoming

THROAT *to jump down someone's throat*
to react angrily to the remarks of the other party to a conversation

THROAT *to ram something down someone's throat*
to pressure another person into accepting an idea with which he does not agree

THUMB *a rule of thumb*
a simple yet useful approximation

THUMB *a thumbnail sketch*
brief but pertinent details

THUMB *someone's fingers are all thumbs*
a person is clumsy with his hands

THUMB *to be under someone's thumb*
to be dominated by a person

THUMB *to give a thumbs up*
to approve or grant permission (refers to sign given by Roman emperor sparing a life)

THUMB *to twiddle one's thumbs*
not to be involved in any worthwhile activity

TICKLE *to be tickled pink*
to be very pleased

TICKLE *to tickle the Peter*
to rob one's employer

TICKLISH *ticklish*
awkward, requiring delicate handling

TOE *a toehold*
an opportunity small in itself but with the potential to lead to bigger things

TOE *to dig one's toes in*
to become even more stubborn than at first

TOE *to dip one's toes in the water*
to gently explore an opportunity

TOE *to keep someone on his toes*
to induce a person to be efficient

TOE *to tiptoe around the difficulties*
to act though the difficulties did not exist

TOE *to toe the line*
to conform

TOE *to tread on someone's toes*
to upset another person by interfering in his area of responsibility

TONGUE *I could have bitten my tongue off*
I wish that I had not made such a hurtful remark

TONGUE *a slip of the tongue*
incorrect words uttered accidentally

TONGUE *it is on the tip of my tongue*
the right word has momentarily escaped me

TONGUE *to feel the rough side of someone's tongue*
to be verbally abused by a person

TONGUE *to find one's tongue*
to overcome one's shyness and speak

TONGUE *to have a loose tongue*
to speak foolishly or indiscreetly

TONGUE *to have a sharp tongue*
to speak one's mind in forceful language

TONGUE *to have a silver tongue*
to be eloquent

TONGUE *to hold one's tongue*
to keep quiet

TONGUE *to keep a civil tongue in one's head*
to be polite, especially under provocation

TONGUE *to roll off the tongue*
to be said very easily

TONGUE *to set tongues wagging*
to behave in a way which encourages scandal mongers

TONGUE *to speak with forked tongues*
to utter half-truths with the intention of misleading the listener

TONGUE *tongue in cheek*
full of irony

TOOTH *a tooth for a tooth*
retaliation (Exodus 21:24)

TOOTH *one would give one's eye teeth for something*
a person would very much like to achieve some objective

TOOTH *teething trouble*
problems in the early stages of a project

TOOTH *to be armed to the teeth*
to carry many weapons

TOOTH *to be fed up to the back teeth*
to be disgusted

TOOTH *to be long in the tooth*
to be old

TOOTH *to cut one's teeth on something*
to get one's first experience by doing something

TOOTH *to escape by the skin of one's teeth*
to only just avoid some disaster

TOOTH *to fight tooth and nail*
to strive very hard to win

TOOTH *to get one's teeth into something*
to tackle a task with enthusiasm

TOOTH *to gnash one's teeth*
to express frustration

TOOTH *to grit one's teeth*
to get ready to suffer pain

TOOTH *to hang on by the skin of one's teeth*
to only just survive

TOOTH *to have a sweet tooth*
to be particularly fond of cakes and confectionery

TOOTH *to have teeth*
to be effective

TOOTH *to kick someone in the teeth*
to take action which demonstrates annoyance at or dislike of a person

TOOTH *to lie through one's teeth*
to tell blatant untruths

TOOTH *to set someone's teeth on edge*
to cause a person to feel unhappy at a situation

TOUCH *the touchstone*
the standard

TOUCH *to lose one's touch*
to cease to be familiar with something

TOUCHE *touche*
well said (French, "touched")

TREAD *to tread lightly*
to be careful

TURN *to turn around 180 degrees*
to completely reverse a stance

TURN *to turn round*
to reverse one's policy

VEIN *in another vein*
as an alternative way of looking at things

VISION *tunnel vision*
an extremely narrow and inflexible way of considering issues

VOICE *to be a lone voice in the wilderness*
to be the only person stating unpopular views

VOICE *to raise one's voice for some cause*
to publicly advocate some cause

WAKE *to wake up to something*
to realize a fact or its significance

WALK *to take a long walk on a short pier*
go away, I want no dealings with you

WALK *to walk away with a profit*
to achieve a profit on concluding a project

WALK *to walk on air*
to be joyful

WART *warts and all*
with the unfavorable features as well as the favorable ones (Oliver Cromwell's direction to an artist painting his portrait)

WEIGHT *to pull one's weight*
to do one's proper share of the work requiring to be done

WEIGHT *to throw one's weight about*
to use one's real or imagined status in order to achieve certain results

WINK *a nod and a wink*
a sign that understanding has been reached in a matter which in the interests of discretion has not been discussed aloud

WINK *not to get a wink of sleep*
not to sleep at all

WOUND *to heal wounds*
to affect a reconciliation

WOUND *to lick one's wounds*
to adjust oneself to defeat

WOUND *to open up an old wound*
to take action which revives a long-standing grievance

WOUND *to rub salt into someone's wound*
to deliberately make damage even worse

WRIST *a slap on the wrist*
a mild rebuke

YOUNG *it is on for young and old*
the excitement has started

LAW

ACT *to read the Riot Act*
to reprimand persons who are excessively noisy (refers to the police reading out to a rowdy crowd extracts from a law requiring its dispersement)

BAIL *to bail someone out*
to render assistance to someone unable to help himself

CASE *to make a Federal case out of something*
to attach far too much significance to a trivial issue

COMPOUND *to compound the felony*
having already acted improperly to make matters worse (the misuse of a legal term: compounding a felony is the crime of agreeing for money not to prosecute a person for felony; in reality it is therefore an offense by a different person—not a second and worse offense by the original culprit)

COURT *to laugh something out of court*
to ridicule a proposition as having no basis whatsoever

COURT *to put oneself out of court*
to disqualify oneself from being considered for something

DOCK *to be in the dock*
to need to defend one's stance

HANG *not to be a hanging matter*
to be only a minor mistake

JURY *the jury is still out*
no decision has yet been made or the public has not yet given an indication of its views

LAW *to lay down the law*
to be officious

LEADING *a leading question*
a very pertinent question (the misuse of a legal term, which actually means a question so framed as to suggest the answer)

MORTGAGE *to have a mortgage on something*
to have a moral claim in regard to a matter

MORTGAGE *to mortgage the future*
to get benefits now but at a cost in due course

SENTENCE *to be sentenced to some fate*
to be condemned by circumstances to endure some fate

T *to dot the i's and cross the t's*
to be meticulous in completing the documentation for a transaction

MANUFACTURE

BALANCE *to tip the balance*
to provide further information or argument which results in an issue, which could have been decided either way, being determined in a particular way

BOILER *not to bust one's boiler*
not to exert oneself unduly

BRONZE *to be cast in bronze*
to be virtually unalterable

BUTTON *to hit the panic button*
to act hastily and irrationally

BUTTON *to press a button*
to make something happen

CHAIN *the weakest link in the chain*
the least efficient component in a project the overall efficiency of which is governed by the efficiency of the least efficient component

CHAIN *to drag the chain*
to perform unduly slowly

COBBLER *a cobbler should stick to his last*
every person should confine himself to activities for which he has been trained

COG *to be a small cog in a large wheel*
to be a relatively unimportant person in a large organization

COMB *to go through something with a fine-tooth comb*
to conduct an extremely thorough investigation

CUT *to be at the cutting edge of something*
to be in a position where important decisions need to be made

CUT *to be cut and dried*
to be well settled or long established

CUT *to cut one's coat according to the cloth*
to accommodate oneself to limitations beyond one's control and to do the best in the circumstances

FIRE *to add fuel to the fire*
to make a bad situation worse

GOODS *to deliver the goods*
to achieve the objective

GRINDSTONE *to keep one's nose to the grindstone*
to work with particular diligence

HALLMARK *a hallmark*
a standard (refers to the official assay mark on gold and silver, originally put on at the Goldsmith's Hall)

IRON *to have a cast-iron case*
to be absolutely assured of victory in legal proceedings

IRON *to have other irons in the fire*
to have the opportunity to do something else as an alternative

IRON *to strike while the iron is hot*
to take advantage of a situation which cannot last

LINCHPIN *linchpin*
essential feature central to a project

LOGJAM *a logjam*
a stoppage of activity caused by input in greater volume than allowed for

MACHINERY *to be a well-oiled piece of machinery*
to be functioning very satisfactorily

MAKE *ready-made*
easily fabricated or available without difficulty

MOLD *to be cast in someone's mold*
to take after another person

PIPELINE *a pipeline to someone*
an intermediary used as a means of communicating ideas to a person

PIPELINE *to be in the pipeline*
to be being dealt with

POT *a melting pot*
a country where people with different ethnic backgrounds over time merge into one nation

POT *to go back into the melting pot*
to be up for reconsideration ab initio

PRESS *to be hot off the press*
to be the latest news

PRESSURE *to apply pressure on someone*
to induce a person to do something which he would otherwise not do by implying adverse consequences if he does not cooperate

PRINT *to fill in the fine print*
to provide the precise details in respect of something presently existing in broad outline only

P *to watch one's p's and q's*
to be very careful (may refer to pints and quarts of beer on a hotel slate or to easily-confused printer's type)

SACK *to get the sack*
to be dismissed (refers to the bag of tradesmen's tools)

SAFETY *safety margin*
allowance for miscalculations

SEAL *a seal of approval*
confirmation that something is satisfactory

SIFT *to sift*
to closely examine the evidence or a set of facts with a view to attaching different significance as appropriate to each of the various components

SKIN *there is more than one way to skin a cat*
this can be achieved in a variety of acceptable ways

SPARK *to make sparks fly*
to cause rapid activity to take place

SPIN *to be a money spinner*
to produce large profits easily and quickly

SPIN *to spin something out*
to prolong some matter

STEEL *to be a man of steel*
to be a person with moral courage

STEEL *to have nerves of steel*
not to be easily frightened

SYSTEM *to be all systems "go"*
to go ahead as fast as possible

TAILOR *to tailor something*
to do something in a way which has regard to the specific needs or preferences of a particular person

TENTERHOOK *to be on tenterhooks*
to anxiously await some result

THREAD *the thread*
the connecting link of a set of arguments

TINKER *not worth a tinker's curse*
worthless

TUNE *to fine-tune something*
to adjust something in order to bring it to perfection or to make it fit the circumstances in a much more appropriate fashion

VALVE *to act as a safety valve*
to be a procedure which allows persons with grievances to ventilate them in an orderly fashion

WHEEL *a big wheel*
an important person

WHEEL *to be a small cog in a large wheel*
to be a relatively unimportant person in a large organization

WHEEL *to oil the wheels*
to make things go smoothly

WHEEL *to set the wheels in motion*
to institute appropriate action

WHEEL *wheels within wheels*
secret machinations

WIRE *to be a live wire*
to be an enthusiast

WIRE *to go haywire*
to refuse to function properly

WOOL *to pull the wool over someone's eyes*
to deceive or deliberately mislead another person

WORKS *to be in the works*
to be being dealt with

WORKS *to get the works*
to get the full treatment

WORKS *to gum up the works*
to cause an activity to be halted

WORKS *to throw a spanner into the works*
to cause an unexpected complication

YARN *to spin a yarn*
to tell an amusing or unlikely story

METEOROLOGY

AIR *a feeling in the air*
a premonition held by many people

AIR *to be a breath of fresh air*
to be a pleasant change from the past

AIR *to clear the air*
to remove any possible misunderstandings

AIR *to leave something up in the air*
to continue with an unresolved problem

AIR *to pluck figures out of the air*
to continue with an unresolved problem

AIR *to produce something out of thin air*
to get hold of something in circumstances where this seemed impossible

AIR *to vanish into thin air*
unexpectedly to disappear

ATMOSPHERE *atmosphere*
psychological environment

ATMOSPHERE *in a rarefied atmosphere*
in ignorance of the real world

BOLT *to be a bolt from the blue*
to be a totally unexpected event

BREEZE *it's a breeze*
it is easy

CLIMATE *climate*
commercial environment

CLOUD *every cloud has a silver lining*
there are benefits even in seemingly adverse situation

CLOUD *there are black clouds on the horizon*
bad news is expected

CLOUD *to be in cloud cuckoo land*
to be mad or to have unrealistic expectations

CLOUD *to be on cloud nine*
to be very happy

CLOUD *to be under a cloud*
to be under suspicion or to be out of favor

CLOUD *to cast a cloud over something*
to spoil the pleasure of an occasion

CLOUD *to cloud one's mind*
to allow irrelevant or extraneous factors to affect one's impartiality or judgment

CLOUD *to have a cloud hanging over one's head*
there is doubt as to one's future

CLOUD *to have one's head in the clouds*
to be unrealistic

COLD *a cold day in hell*
never

COLD *to come in out of the cold*
to be welcomed into a group

COLD *to leave someone out in the cold*
to deny a desired objective to a person

DARK *to be in the dark*
to be uninformed

DAWN *a false dawn*
an incident giving rise to unjustified hope

DAWN *to be the dawn of a new day*
to be the start of a different regime

DRAFT *to feel the draft*
to experience unfavorable conditions

DROUGHT *to break a drought*
to resume supplies after an interval

EVE *to be on the eve of something*
to occur just before some event

FLASH *in a flash*
in an instant

FLOODGATE *to open up the floodgates*
to take action which will have massive consequences

FOG *to be in a fog*
to be in a state of confusion

FOGGY *not to have the foggiest notion*
to know nothing at all about the subject

ICE *to break the ice*
to take the initiative in starting discussions

ICE *to cut no ice with someone*
to have little effect on a person

ICE *to skate on thin ice*
to act in disregard of obvious danger

LIGHTNING *a lightning rod*
a person who attracts trouble to himself

MOON *once in a blue moon*
very rarely (refers to the volcanic eruption at Krakatoa in 1883 when volcanic dust caused the moon to appear blue)

MOON *to be over the moon*
to be very excited

MOONLIGHT *a moonlight flit*
an escape from creditors

MOONSHINE *moonshine*
unrealistic ideas

RAIN *it never rains but it pours*
crises often occur together

RAINBOW *to chase rainbows*
to be quite unrealistic

RAINBOW *to seek the pot of gold at the end of the rainbow*
to have naive expectations

RAINY *to keep something for a rainy day*
to keep something in reserve

SEASON *the silly season*
the holiday period, when hard news is scarce and journalistic standards are lowered

SHOWER *to have come down in the last shower*
to be naive

SKY *a light in the sky*
a sign of great hope

SKY *blue sky*
supremely optimistic

SKY *pie in the sky*
a hoped for result unlikely to be achieved

SKY *the sky fell in*
a very serious problem arose

SKY *the sky is the limit*
the cost is no obstacle

SNOW *to snow someone under*
to overload a person with work

STORM *any port in a storm*
anything which helps to avoid difficulties is welcome.

STORM *to be in the eye of the storm*
to be at the center of a controversy

STORM *to create a storm*
to kick up a fuss

STORM *to ride out the storm*
to come safely through some dangerous situation

STORM *to run into a firestorm*
to be faced with many protests

STORM *to take someone by storm*
to captivate an audience

STORM *to weather the storm*
to come safely through a crisis

SUMMER *one swallow does not make a summer*
much further evidence is desirable before any action taken

TEMPEST *a tempest in a teacup*
a controversy about a minor matter but one which looms large in the minds of the parties

THUNDER *to be thunderstruck*
to be amazed

THUNDER *to steal someone's thunder*
to take credit for another person's good work (refers to a dispute over the copying of a machine invented by a 17th-century dramatist to reproduce the sound of thunder during a play)

THUNDERBOLT *a thunderbolt*
a surprise

TORRENT *a torrent of words*
a rapid and uninterrupted outpouring of words

WEATHER *a fair-weather friend*
a person purporting to be a friend who offers no support in difficult times

WEATHER *to be under the weather*
to be drunk or (less often) sick

WEATHER *to keep a weather eye out for something*
to look out with particular care

WEATHER *to make heavy weather of something*
to struggle excessively with a relatively simple task

WEATHER *to run into heavy weather*
to encounter difficulties

WHIRLWIND *to sow the wind and reap the whirlwind*
to make bad mistakes and to suffer the even worse consequences

WIND *something is in the wind*
something is going on secretly (this phrase uses the actual word "something")

WIND *straws in the wind*
unofficial preliminary indications of something likely to be formally revealed soon

WIND *the cold wind of change*
the unpleasant realities of new circumstances

WIND *to cast prudence to the winds*
to cease being prudent

WIND *to put the wind up someone*
to alarm a person

WIND *to reap the whirlwind*
to suffer the adverse consequences of a bad act

WIND *to sail against the wind*
to oppose the views currently being held by others

WIND *to sail close to the wind*
to act in a very dangerous manner

WIND *to scatter something to the four winds*
to permanently get rid of something

WIND *to see which way the wind is blowing*
to establish the factors relevant to a situation

WIND *to sow the wind and reap the whirlwind*
to make bad mistakes and to suffer the even worse consequences

WIND *to take the wind out of someone's sails*
to upset a person by anticipating his actions or using arguments which he was proposing to use

WINDFALL *windfall*
unexpected good fortune

MINING and OIL

CLAIM *to stake a claim*
to indicate one's desire to obtain something

COAL *to be at the coal face*
to be in the place where the real work is done

COAL *to haul someone over the coals*
to reprimand a person

DIAMOND *to be a rough diamond*
to have many attributes but a gruff manner

DIRT *to strike pay dirt*
to become successful

DRY *a dry hole*
an exercise which after much effort proves fruitless

FUSE *to light a fuse*
to cause serious reactions

GOLD *a golden handshake*
a large payment in connection with or as an inducement to retirement

GOLD *a pot of gold*
wealth

GOLD *all that glitters is not gold*
things are not always what they seem

GOLD *golden parachute*
generous provisions in a remuneration package which come into play in certain circumstances

GOLD *golden shackles*
financial arrangements designed to discourage employees changing employers

GOLD *to be a river of gold*
to be a source of ongoing great profitability

GOLD *to be worth one's weight in gold*
to be very desirable

GOLD *to have a heart of gold*
to have a generous disposition

GOLD *to kill the goose that lays the golden eggs*
through excessive greed to destroy a very profitable enterprise

GOLD *to seek the pot of gold at the end of the rainbow*
to have naive expectations

GOLD *to strike gold*
to have one's efforts suddenly rewarded by great success

GOLDMINE *a goldmine*
a source of much wealth or of many facts

IRON *to rule with a rod of iron*
to keep strict discipline

JEWEL *a jewel*
a valued assistant

OIL *get the good oil*
to receive useful, reliable and timely information

PAN *a flash in the pan*
something which begins promisingly but does not last (refers to the priming of old guns)

PAN *to pan out*
to succeed

PETRIFY *to be petrified*
to be badly scared

ROCK *rock bottom*
very low

ROCK *someone's marriage is on the rocks*
someone's marriage has broken down

ROCK *to be between a rock and a hard place*
to be faced with two equally difficult and uncomfortable choices

ROCK *to be on the rocks*
to be bankrupt

ROCK *to have rocks in the head*
to be mentally unbalanced

SILVER *to be born with a silver spoon in one's mouth*
to be brought up by wealthy parents

SILVER *to have a silver tongue*
to be eloquent

STONE *to draw blood from a stone*
to do the impossible

STONE *to have a heart of stone*
to be unfeeling

STONE *to kill two birds with one stone*
to achieve a second objective in the course of achieving the first objective

STONE *to leave no stone unturned*
to be very thorough

TIN *a little tin god*
a petty tyrant

TREASURE *a treasure trove*
a valuable discovery

UNDERMINE *to undermine someone's position*
to injure another person's reputation and influence by unfair and secret tactics

UNDERMINE *to undermine something*
to sabotage something

MUSIC

BAND *a one-man band*
a person performing many different roles single-handedly

BANDWAGON *to hop onto the bandwagon*
to join the majority (the antonym of ''bandwagon effect'' is ''underdog effect'')

BEAT *not to miss a beat*
to carry on without the slightest interruption

BEAT *to beat a retreat*
to abandon some project

BOARD *to act as a sounding board*
to give, on request, constructive criticisms of ideas tentatively held

BOW *to have a second string to one's bow*
to have an additional qualification appropriate to the task

CHORD *to strike a chord*
to sound familiar or recall something to mind

CHORD *to strike a responsive chord*
to get a favorable reaction to a proposal

CHORD *to strike the right chord*
to appeal successfully to someone's emotions

DONNA *a prima donna*
a person with an exaggerated opinion of his own importance which makes relations with others needlessly difficult (Italian, "first lady")

DRUM *to beat a drum for someone*
to propagate another person's cause

DRUM *to beat one's drum*
to immodestly publicize one's own attributes

DRUM *to drum up support*
to actively seek out support

DRUM *to march to a different drum*
to show an independent approach

FANFARE *with much fanfare*
with great enthusiasm and public acclaim

FIDDLE *to fiddle while Rome burns*
to neglect important considerations while concentrating on trivial side-issues

FIDDLE *to play second fiddle*
to fulfill a subordinate role

GAMUT *the whole gamut*
the whole range of some activity

HARMONIZE *to harmonize several things*
to make several things conform with each other

HARMONY *to be in harmony with someone*
to act in the same way as another person

KEY *to strike the right key*
to find the appropriate solution

KEYNOTE *keynote address*
opening address, designed to set the theme of a conference

MELODY *the melody lingers on*
the benefit of past actions remains

MUSIC *to be music to one's ears*
to be comments which one is very pleased to hear

MUSIC *to face the music*
to accept responsibility when confronted by one's critics

MUSIC *when the music stops*
suddenly and soon (refers to an imminent crisis leading to some resolution of a matter, as in a game of musical chairs)

MUSICAL *to play musical chairs*
to be a part of a general reshuffling of duties or functions which is not necessarily to everyone's liking

NOTE *to hit a sour note*
to discover an unexpected flaw in an otherwise satisfactory piece of work

NOTE *to strike the right note*
to make a good impression

OPERA *a soap opera*
a radio or television serial, often based on exaggerated domestic situations of no great importance (refers to sponsorship by soap manufacturers)

ORCHESTRATE *to orchestrate something*
to arrange for something to happen

OVERTONE *overtones*
implied threats

OVERTURE *to make overtures to someone*
to make suggestions to a person, inviting further negotiations

PEDAL *to softpedal*
to restrain oneself

PIPE *to pipe someone on board*
to welcome a person

PIPER *he who pays the piper calls the tune*
a person contributing money or resources to a project is entitled to a say in its control

PITCH *to be up to concert pitch*
to be ready

PLAY *to play it by ear*
to develop one's strategy to always fit in with circumstances as they change from time to time

SING *it's not over till the fat lady sings*
it is not finished yet

SING *to all sing from the same hymnal*
to act consistently with each other

SING *to sing for one's supper*
to carry out a task in order to receive a favor in return

SING *to sing someone's praises*
to commend a person exuberantly

SONG *nothing to make a song or dance about*
unexciting or unimportant

SONG *to buy something for a song*
to buy something very cheaply

SONG *to make a song and dance about something*
to create a fuss

SONG *to sing a particular song*
to state particular views

SWAN *swan song*
last appearance before retirement

TANGO *it takes two to tango*
some activities cannot be carried out single-handedly

THEME *variations on a theme*
alternative approaches in similar vein

TIME *to mark time*
to do nothing while awaiting developments

TRUMPET *to blow one's own trumpet*
to immodestly publicize one's own attributes

TRUMPET *with a flourish of trumpets*
triumphantly

TUNE *he who pays the piper calls the tune*
a person contributing money or resources to a project is entitled to a say in its control

TUNE *to be in tune with someone*
to think on the same lines as another person

TUNE *to change one's tune*
to alter one's publicly-expressed views

WHISTLE *you can whistle for it*
you wish in vain

MYTHOLOGY

ACHILLES *to be someone's Achilles' heel*
to represent a weakness in an otherwise strong position (refers to the Greek warrior who was the hero of Homer's ILIAD)

ALADDIN *an Aladdin's cave*
a place full of unexpected treasure

CARRY *to carry the world on one's shoulders*
to resent being left to perform a huge task single-handedly (refers to Atlas, who was condemned to bear the heavens on his shoulders for leading the Titans against the gods)

CRYSTAL *a crystal ball*
accurate knowledge of the future

DAMOCLES *to have a sword of Damocles hanging over one*
to be in imminent danger despite normal activity going on all around one

DAY *in Halcyon days*
in past happier times (refers to the 14 days about the winter solstice when winds were calm and to the mythical bird said to breed in a floating nest at that time)

DELPHIC *Delphic*
deliberately obscure (refers to the oracle at Delphi)

FAIRY *a fairy godmother*
a person showing great kindness

FAIRY *to believe in the tooth fairy*
to be particularly gullible

GENIE *to let the genie out of the bottle*
to cause something irreversible to take place

GENIE *to put the genie back in the bottle*
to undo something which cannot be undone

GHOST *not the ghost of a chance*
no hope at all

GHOST *to give up the ghost*
to die

GIFT *I fear the Greeks even when they bear gifts*
I am suspicious of generous behavior from traditional opponents (from Virgil's AENEID, in reference to the Trojan horse)

GOD *to be in the lap of the gods*
to be a matter of pure chance (refers to wax tablets inscribed with requests and placed on the knees of statues of Greek gods)

GORDIAN *to cut the Gordian knot*
to solve, especially by force, a virtually insoluble problem (refers to a complicated knot tied by Gordius and eventually cut by Alexander the Great)

HERCULEAN *a Herculean cleaning of the stables*
a thorough revision of operating procedure (refers to Hercules, a mythical Greek hero who cleaned the stables of Augeas)

HERCULEAN *to be a Herculean task*
to be laborious

HYDRA *a hydra-headed monster*
an evil which is not readily destroyable

MAGIC *a magic bullet*
a guaranteed remedy

MAGIC *to get a magic carpet ride to something*
to be very fortunate in achieving some objective

MARINER *to be an albatross around someone's neck*
to be a great burden (popularized by Coleridge's ANCIENT MARINER)

MIDAS *the Midas touch*
attributes which cause a person's ventures to be extremely profitable (refers to King Midas of Phrygia, who had the power to turn everything he touched into gold)

NEMESIS *nemesis*
downfall serving as retribution (refers to a goddess in Greek mythology)

PANDORA *to open up a Pandora's box*
to do something which produces all sorts of undesired and unexpected side-effects (refers to the woman in Greek mythology who was meant to bring misery to mankind; the box contained human ills)

PHOENIX *to rise from the ashes like a Phoenix*
to be the replacement for something destroyed in some disaster (refers to a mythical bird which was supposed to rise from the ashes of its funeral pyre with renewed youth)

SCYLLA *to be between Scylla and Charybdis*
to be faced with two equally unpalatable alternatives which cannot both be avoided (refers to the voyage of Ulysses)

SPELL *to break the spell*
to spoil the effect

SPIRIT *kindred spirit*
person with similar interests and eccentricities

TROJAN *a Trojan horse*
a trick (refers to a large gift horse full of soldiers used to bring about the fall of Troy, as described in Homer's ILIAD)

NAUTICAL

ADRIFT *to come adrift*
(of a plan) not to work out as intended

AFLOAT *to stay afloat*
to remain solvent

ANCHOR *the sheet anchor*
the source of one's confidence

ANCHOR *to anchor*
to fix firmly

ANCHOR *to weigh anchor*
to move to another address

BACKWASH *backwash*
consequence

BERTH *to give someone a wide berth*
to go out of one's way to avoid contact with a person

BOARD *to pipe someone on board*
to welcome a person

BOARD *to take something on board*
to offer to give further consideration to a matter

BOARDER *to repel boarders*
to keep out unwanted persons

BOAT *to be in the same boat*
to share a common set of difficulties

BOAT *to get off the boat*
to disassociate oneself from some project

BOAT *to miss the boat*
to fail to exploit an opportunity

BOAT *to rock the boat*
to disturb the comfortable status quo

BOW *shots across the bow*
warnings

BRACE *to splice the main brace*
to serve an extra ration of rum

CANOE *to paddle one's own canoe*
to do something unaided and in one's own way

COLOR *to pass with flying colors*
to be very successful

COLOR *to sail under false colors*
to pretend that one's real character or beliefs are different from what they really are

COLOR *to show one's true colors*
to disclose one's real character or beliefs

COURSE *to be on course*
to be progressing satisfactorily toward one's goal

DECK *a loose cannon on the deck*
a mistake likely to cause trouble

DECK *all hands on deck*
everybody is requested to help out

DECK *to be back on deck*
to have returned after an absence

DECK *to clear the decks*
to get ready for action

DOLDRUMS *to be in the doldrums*
to be depressed or to show no activity (refers to a region of little wind near the equator, becalming sailing ships)

EBB *ebb and flow*
fluctuations

EBB *to ebb away*
to decline gradually

FIGUREHEAD *a figurehead*
the ceremonial chief officer of some organization without any real power (refers to the carving at the front of a ship)

FISH *a fishing expedition*
an exercise designed to get information to which one is not strictly entitled

FLAGSHIP *flagship*
most important member of a group of related entities

FLOTSAM *flotsam and jetsam*
derelict persons, without a fixed abode or stable life (refers to goods found floating and to goods thrown overboard deliberately, respectively)

FLOW *ebb and flow*
fluctuations

HATCH *to batten down the hatches*
to get ready for expected difficulties

HELM *to be at the helm*
to be in charge

HIGH *to leave someone high and dry*
to withdraw all support from a person

ICEBERG *to be the tip of the iceberg*
to be only a very small portion of a much larger but less obvious whole

JETSAM *flotsam and jetsam*
derelict persons, without a fixed abode or stable life (see flotsam)

JETTISON *to jettison some proposal*
to abandon some proposal as worthless or impracticable

JIB *the cut of someone's jib*
someone's personal appearance

KEEL *to keep something on an even keel*
to ensure that something is not harmed

KEELHAUL *to keelhaul someone*
to penalize a person

KEEP *to keep a weather eye out for something*
to look out with particular care

KNOT *at a rate of knots*
very fast

LEEWAY *to make up leeway*
to get back to a normal position or to get to the position held by one's competitors

LLOYD *to be A1 at Lloyd's*
to be in perfect order (refers to the classification of ships in Lloyd's register in London)

MAST *to nail one's colors to the mast*
to publicly declare one's position and to maintain it in the face of criticism

NET *to catch someone in the net*
to unexpectedly involve a particular person in the course of activity designed to involve many others

NET *to draw the nets closer*
to intensify one's efforts

NET *to slip through the net*
to happen as an isolated case despite steps taken to prevent such events

NET *to spread the net more widely*
to become more comprehensive

OCEAN *an ocean full of fish*
plenty of opportunity

OCEAN *to be only a drop in the ocean*
to be quite insignificant in the total scene

OIL *to pour oil on troubled waters*
to calm down a situation

OVERBOARD *to go overboard*
to act foolishly and in an excessive way

PAINTER *to cut the painter*
to become separated

PEBBLE *not to be the only pebble on the beach*
not to be the only available person

PIER *take a long walk on a short pier*
go away, I want no dealings with you

PIRATE *pirate*
(of radio) unlicensed; (of recordings or computer software) published in breach of copyright law

PLANK *to walk the plank*
to face certain doom

PLIMSOLL *the Plimsoll line*
the standard

POLE *not to touch something with a ten-foot pole*
to go out of one's way to avoid something

PORT *any port in a storm*
anything which helps to avoid difficulties is welcome

PORT *port of call*
one of a series of places being visited

PUMP *all hands to the pumps*
everybody is requested to help out

RAFT *life raft*
financial assistance sufficient to avert insolvency

RIDE *to ride out the storm*
to come safely through some dangerous situation

RIPPLE *to make ripples*
to disturb the status quo

ROPE *to know the ropes*
to know how to do one's job

ROPE *to learn the ropes*
to be taught the elementary features

ROPE *to show someone the ropes*
to teach a beginner how to do something

SAIL *to be plain sailing*
to be quite straightforward and very easy

SAIL *to sail against the wind*
to oppose the views currently being help by others

SAIL *to sail close to the wind*
to act in a very dangerous manner

SAIL *to set sail*
to commence a voyage

SAIL *to take the wind out of someone's sails*
to upset a person by anticipating his actions or using arguments which he was proposing to use

SAIL *to trim one's sails*
to institute austerity

SEA *between the devil and deep blue sea*
to be faced with two equally unpalatable alternatives which cannot both be avoided

SEA *to be all at sea*
to be confused as to what is going on and what to do next

SHIP *a case of rats leaving a sinking ship*
the desertion of an enterprise in anticipation of imminent failure

SHIP *enough to sink a battleship*
more than sufficient

SHIP *ship shape*
in excellent condition

SHIP *ships that pass in the night*
persons who fail to meet up

SHIP *to abandon ship*
to abrogate one's responsibilities or to abandon a project

SHIP *to be a rudderless ship*
to be a project not managed properly

SHIP *to run a tight ship*
to manage an efficient organization

SHIP *to run one's own ship*
to do things and organize subordinates in one's own way

SHIP *to spoil the ship for ha'p'orth of tar*
to engage in a false economy (the current word ''ship'' is actually a mistake for the original word ''sheep'' and the tar refers to the treatment of wounds)

SHIP *when one's ship comes in*
when one's business venture is successfully completed or when luck arrives

SHOAL *to founder on the shoals of something*
to come to grief because of unexpected dangers

SIDE *a broadside*
a short verbal attack

SINK *it is a case of sink or swim*
the attempt is worthwhile, despite the risk of failure

SINK *to sink without a trace*
to disappear completely

SLACK *to take up the slack*
to take advantage of surplus capacity

SNAG *to strike a snag*
to encounter a difficulty

SOUNDING *to take a sounding*
to ascertain people's views

STORM *the calm before the storm*
the quiet period before an expected or inevitable crisis

TACK *to be on the wrong tack*
to be using an incorrect procedure or policy

TACK *to change tack*
to alter one's direction

TIDE *the tide has turned*
conditions have changed

TIDE *the tide is running in favor of some proposition*
public opinion supports some proposition

TIDE *to be caught by the tide*
to be dealt with by something inevitable

TIDE *to stem the tide*
to make progress against something

TIDE *to swim against the tide*
to take up a minority position

TIDE *to turn the tide*
to reverse the direction of something

TITANIC *to rearrange the deckchairs on the Titanic*
to take some initiative which is quite useless because it does not take much greater change into account

TOUCH *it was touch and go*
there were considerable risks—the objective was achieved, but only just

WAKE *in the wake of someone*
following a person's example

WATER *to be in uncharted waters*
to be the first to experience something

WAVE *to be on the crest of a wave*
to enjoy success which may not last

WAVE *to cause waves*
to disturb the status quo

WRECK *to salvage something out of the wreck*
to achieve some minor benefits out of a disastrous situation

PLANTS

ACORN *tall oaks from little acorns grow*
even major enterprises have to have small beginnings (from "Lines written for a School Declamation" by David Everett)

APPLE *to add apples to oranges*
to quite illogically lump unconnected things together

APPLE *to be the apple of someone's eye*
to be a person of whom another person is proud

BEAN *not to have a bean*
to have no money

BEAN *not to matter a row of beans*
to be utterly unimportant

BEAN *to know how many beans make five*
to have common sense

BLOSSOM *to blossom*
(of a person's attributes) to develop

BUD *to nip something in the bud*
to stop some activity in its early stages when stopping it is still relatively easy

BUSH *a bird in the hand is worth two in the bush*
a benefit currently available is more valuable than a seemingly much larger benefit which may or may not be achieved in the future

BUSH *to beat about the bush*
to hide the unpleasant truth

BUSHEL *to hide one's light under a bushel*
to keep others in ignorance of one's skills and experience

BUSHFIRE *to fight bushfires*
to deal with crises as they arise rather than take preventative action

CABBAGE *to be on someone's cabbage patch*
to engage in a competitive activity in a territory regarded by someone already there as rightfully belonging exclusively to him

CARROT *sticks and carrots*
disincentives and incentives in combination (refers to the handling of donkeys)

CHAFF *to separate the wheat from the chaff*
to distinguish between important and unimportant ingredients

CHERRY *to get only one bite at the cherry*
to receive no further opportunity

CLOVER *to be in clover*
to enjoy a life of ease and luxury

CORE *rotten to the core*
completely corrupt

CORE *to be the hard core*
to be the central and most difficult problem

DEFLOWER *to deflower*
to deprive of virginity

DISSEMINATE *to disseminate ideas*
to spread ideas to a wide audience (lit., "to scatter seeds in various places")

FALL *windfall*
unexpected good fortune

FIG *one would not give a fig for something*
one regards something as worthless

FRUIT *by their fruits ye shall know them*
their reputation will be based on their results (Matthew 7:20)

FRUIT *forbidden fruit*
something particularly desired just because it is not allowed (Genesis 2:17)

FRUIT *to bear fruit*
to result in success

FRUITLESS *fruitless*
yielding no benefit

GOOSEBERRY *to play gooseberry*
to act as an unwelcome chaperon

GRAIN *something goes against the grain*
something is completely and frustratingly against a person's inclination

GRAPE *that is just sour grapes*
those are disparaging remarks made only because he is peeved and resentful at someone else's better fortune

GRAPE *to hear on the grapevine*
to learn unofficially

GRAPE *what is this — a bunch of grapes or a bowl of goldfish?*
surely you know what this is!

GRASS *a snake in the grass*
a person of low character

GRASS *grass roots*
at the lowest level

GRASS *not to let grass grow under one's feet*
not to let inertia or delay spoil something

HAY *to look for a needle in a haystack*
to attempt something with a very small chance of success

HAY *to make hay while the sun shines*
to utilize an opportunity before it disappears

JUNGLE *the law of the jungle*
the principle that those having power will use it at the expense of all others

LEMON *the answer is a lemon*
the outcome is inconclusive

LEMON *to sell someone a lemon*
to sell a person a grossly defective product on the basis that it represents quality

LEMON *to suck the lemon dry*
to get the maximum advantage out of some favorable situation

LILY *lily-livered*
cowardly

LILY *lily-white*
honest and incorruptible

LILY *to gild the lily*
(actually: to gild refined gold, to paint the lily) to do something patently unnecessary

LIMB *to go out on a limb*
to put oneself at risk through foolish action

MUSHROOM *to mushroom*
to expand rapidly

NETTLE *to grasp the nettle*
to deal with a neglected difficulty

NUT *to be nuts*
to be crazy

NUT *to be nuts about someone*
to be infatuated with a person

NUTSHELL *in a nutshell*
by way of summary

OAK *tall oaks from little acorns grow*
even major enterprises have to have small beginnings (from "Lines written for a School Declamation" by David Everett)

OAK *to have a heart of oak*
to be brave

OATS *to feel one's oats*
to display self-importance

OLIVE *to hold out an olive branch*
to make peace overtures (Genesis 8:11)

ONION *to know one's onions*
to be well informed in some area (refers to Dr. C.T. Onions, editor of the SHORTER OXFORD ENGLISH DICTIONARY)

ORANGE *to add apples to oranges*
to quite illogically lump unconnected things together

PEA *a pea and thimble trick*
a clever fraud committed in the presence of its victim without this being obvious at the time

PINEAPPLE *to have hold of the wrong end of the pineapple*
to be utterly mistaken

PLUM *the plum*
the best item in a collection

POPPY *a tall poppy*
a person with great power or responsibility and/or in receipt of high remuneration

POPPY *to cut tall poppies down to size*
to humiliate haughty persons

POTATO *a hot potato*
an embarrassing issue

POTATO *to be small potatoes*
to be quite unimportant

PRUNE *to prune*
to remove the superfluous

REED *to be a broken reed*
to be a weak and unreliable person

ROOT *deep-rooted*
strongly felt

ROOT *to put one's roots down*
to settle in

ROOT *to strike at the roots of something*
to work toward the destruction of something

ROSE *a rose between two thorns*
something beautiful in the midst of ugliness

ROSE *a rose by any other name would smell as sweet*
the form does not affect the substance (from Shakespeare's ROMEO AND JULIET)

ROSE *to be no bed of roses*
to be difficult or uncomfortable

ROSE *to be on a path strewn with roses*
to lead a very pleasant life

ROSE *to come up smelling like a rose*
not to have a stain on one's character

SEED *to run to seed*
to become shabby

SEED *to sow seeds*
to propagate ideas in the hope that they will be adopted

STRAW *straws in the wind*
unofficial preliminary indications of something likely to be formally revealed soon

STRAW *the final straw*
the latest step, which, when added to a large number of seemingly harmless previous steps, sets off a disaster resulting from cumulative effect

STRAW *to be a man of straw*
to have no assets while giving a contrary appearance

STRAW *to clasp at straws*
to have a hopeless case but show unjustified optimism on noting minor positive features

STRAW *to draw the short straw*
to be the one appointed to do something

THORN *to be a thorn in someone's flesh*
to be a person whose persistent presence and righteous views annoy

THORN *to wear one's crown of thorns*
to have one's own difficulties (John 19:5)

TREE *to bark up the wrong tree*
to reach an incorrect conclusion

TREE *to be at the top of the tree*
to be a leading member of one's profession

TREE *to be up a gum tree*
to be in difficulty or at the end of one's resources

TREE *to be up a tree*
to be perplexed or cornered

TREE *to shake a tree*
to do something in order to see what will result

VEGETABLE *to become a vegetable*
to lose one's mental and physical faculties

VINE *to wither on the vine*
by virtue of changed circumstances of the effluxion of time to be no longer relevant

VIOLET *a shrinking violet*
a shy person

WEED *to weed some group out*
to get rid of some elements not meeting a desired standard

WHEAT *to separate the wheat from the chaff*
to distinguish between important and unimportant ingredients

WOOD *not to see the wood for the trees*
to overlook the general picture because of undue concentration on the details

WOOD *to get rid of the dead wood*
to terminate the services of unsatisfactory personnel

RELIGION AND BIBLICAL

ADAM *not to know someone from Adam*
to be unable to recognize a person

ADAM *since Adam was a boy*
for a very long time

ALTAR *to sacrifice something on the altar of some belief*
to give up some benefit as a matter of principle

ANGEL *a fallen angel*
a previously trusted person who has transgressed

ANGEL *fools rush in where angels fear to tread*
unsophisticated persons take unwise risks in circumstances where more knowledgeable persons would exercise caution

ANGEL *someone's guardian angel*
someone's friend, watching over him and advancing his interests

ANGEL *to be an angel*
to be very helpful

ANGEL *to be no angel*
to have a great many serious faults

ANGEL *to be on the side of the angels*
to be on the side of righteousness (from a speech by Benjamin Disraeli)

ANOINT *the anointed one*
the desired successor

ANTEDILUVIAN *antediluvian*
very outmoded

APOCRYPHAL *apocryphal*
fictitious but resembling truth and illustrating a point

BABEL *a tower of Babel*
a noisy and confused assembly (Genesis 11)

BAPTISM *a baptism of fire*
the commencement of an operation which presented great difficulty

BE *to be kosher*
to fulfill all requirements (refers to food complying with all aspects of Jewish religious law)

BEADLEDOM *beadledom*
stupid officiousness

BIBLE *a bible basher*
a person who makes unwelcome attempts to force his religious beliefs on others

BIBLE *to be the bible*
to be the authority

BLESSING *a blessing in disguise*
an unwelcome but salutary experience

BLESSING *to be a mixed blessing*
to be an outcome with some desirable and some undesirable features

BLESSING *to give one's blessing to something*
to indicate one's approval of something

BRANCH *to hold out an olive branch*
to make peace overtures (Genesis 8:11)

CAST *to cast one's bread upon the waters*
not to expect gratitude or recognition for one's good works (Ecclesiastes 11:1)

CHANGE *to ring the changes*
to exhaust the number of different ways of doing something (refers to the permutations used for ringing peals of church bells)

CHRISTMAS *all his Christmases came at once*
he was overjoyed

COMMANDMENT *eleventh commandment*
unwritten rule

CURATE *to be curate's egg*
to be good only in parts (refers to an 1895 cartoon in PUNCH)

DAY *a red-letter day*
an important occasion (refers to the color used to print saints' days on some calendars)

DEVIL *a devil-may-care attitude*
a reckless attitude

DEVIL *be a devil!*
take a chance!

DEVIL *between the devil and the deep blue sea*
to be faced with two equally unpalatable alternatives which cannot both be avoided

DEVIL *he must have a long spoon that sups with the devil*
great care is needed when negotiating deals with disreputable parties

DEVIL *poor devil*
person to be pitied

DEVIL *talk of the devil*
here is the person we were just discussing

DEVIL *the devil can cite scripture for his purpose*
a person can quote a respectable or hostile authority while advocating a disreputable cause of his own (from Shakespeare's MERCHANT OF VENICE)

DEVIL *the devil one knows is better than the devil one does not know*
the status quo is more comfortable than change

DEVIL *to act as a devil's advocate*
to put a point of view which one does not hold in order to draw out the best arguments regarding a proposition (refers to a church official vetting a candidate for sainthood)

DEVIL *to give the devil his due*
to be fair (a phrase used in parenthesis, and only in the infinitive)

DEVIL *to grab the devil by the tail*
to face up to difficulties

ENSHRINE *to enshrine*
to incorporate as an important part of something

FAITH *an article of faith*
a fundamental belief on which certain behavior is based

FAITHFUL *the old faithful*
a greatly loved article

FOR *a tooth for a tooth*
retaliation (Exodus 21:24)

GOD *a little tin god*
a petty tyrant

GOD *the mills of God grind slowly*
retribution may be delayed but is inevitable

GODFORSAKEN *godforsaken*
dismal and without any redeeming feature

GOLIATH *a Goliath*
a giant or a person whose ability and achievements exceed those of most other people (1 Samuel 17)

GOSPEL *to take something as gospel*
to believe that something is true

HEAVEN *heaven help you!*
you are in trouble

HEAVEN *heaven only knows*
it is not known

HEAVEN *manna from heaven*
unexpected benefits (Exodus 16:15)

HEAVEN *to be in seventh heaven*
to be very happy

HEAVEN *to move heaven and earth*
to do everything possible

HEAVEN *to reek to high heaven*
to be patently unethical

HELL *all hell broke loose*
great confusion erupted

HELL *come hell or high water*
regardless of the consequences

HELL *on a cold day in hell*
never

HELL *to be hell bent on something*
to be very determined to achieve something, regardless of the adverse consequences

HELL *to frighten hell out of someone*
to alarm a person

HELL *to give someone hell*
to make life difficult for a person

HELL *to have a snowflake's chance in hell*
to have no hope or possibility at all

HELL *to raise merry hell*
to prominently involve others in a matter in the expectation of significant results from this action

HERESY *heresy*
views different from those held by the majority

HOLY *a holier-than-thou attitude*
excessive righteousness

HOLY *search for the Holy Grail*
work toward a difficult goal (refers to a vessel supposedly used by Christ at the last supper and featuring in the Arthurian legends)

HYMNAL *to all sing from the same hymnal*
to act consistently with each other

IMPRIMATUR *imprimatur*
confirmation that something is in order (Latin, "let it be printed"; refers to the formal ruling given by a Roman Catholic bishop authorizing the publication of a book on religion or morals)

JEREMIAH *Jeremiah*
a person who looks on the gloomy side of everything (refers to the prophet Jeremiah in the Old Testament)

JERICHO *walls of Jericho*
something seemingly solid but actually destructible (Joshua 6:20)

JUDAS *to play Judas*
to betray a person (Matthew 26)

LIMBO *to be in limbo*
to have one's ultimate fate yet to be determined

LIMBO *to consign something to limbo*
to consider something as permanently disposed of

MAHOMET *if the mountain will not come to Mahomet then Mahomet will go to the mountain*
on recognizing that one has insufficient power to effect one's most desired solution, one decides to make do with the next best alternative

MOTE *a mote in someone's eye*
a fault in another person which is trifling in comparison to an unrecognized major fault in oneself (Matthew 7:3)

MUMBO *mumbo jumbo*
blatant nonsense (refers to a deity worshipped by primitive tribes)

PARADISE *to live in a fool's paradise*
to delude oneself

PARISH *parish pump issues*
issues of trivial importance

PAROCHIAL *parochial*
narrow minded

POINT *to point the bone at someone*
to accuse a person (actually, an Australian Aboriginal method of applying a curse)

PONTIFICATE *to pontificate*
to speak as if with great authority and with an assumed air of infallibility

PRAYER *on a wing and a prayer*
without proper resources

PRAYER *the answer to a maiden's prayer*
an unexpected but very welcome happening

PREACH *to preach to the converted*
to say something to those who already believe in it

PRIEST *the high priest of something*
the leading advocate of something

RELIGIOUSLY *religiously*
conscientiously

SACRED *a sacred cow*
an institution so well established that it is virtually unalterable

SACRED *a sacred trust*
a moral obligation

SACRED *nothing is sacred*
nothing is safe from interference

SACRIFICIAL *sacrificial lamb*
somebody unfairly made to suffer for the mistakes of others

SAINT *a saint*
a good person

SAINT *to have the patience of a saint*
to endure annoyances with particular calm

SCAPEGOAT *a scapegoat*
a person unfairly blamed for something not his fault

SCRIPTURE *the devil can cite scripture for his purpose*
a person can quote a respectable or hostile authority while advocating a disreputable cause of his own (from Shakespeare's MERCHANT OF VENICE)

SHIBBOLETH *a shibboleth*
a doctrine once held as essential but now abandoned as having outlived its usefulness (a word used as a test to determine to which tribe an Israelite belonged) (Judges 12:6)

SHRIFT *to give someone short shrift*
to be impatient with a person (refers to the confession to a priest just before an execution)

SIN *for one's sins*
by way of punishment, as it were

SOLOMON *to need the wisdom of Solomon*
to be faced with the need to make a difficult decision (1 Kings 3:16-28)

SOUL *a soul brother*
a person of similar ideals

SOUL *a soul-searching exercise*
an examination of the advantages and disadvantages of a proposal

SOUL *heart and soul*
with great energy

SOUL *soul-destroying*
extremely boring and demotivating

SOUL *to bare one's soul*
talkatively to give a revealing insight into oneself

SOUL *to be the life and soul of the party*
to be the prime enthusiast for a cause

SOUL *to keep body and soul together*
to keep alive

SPIRIT *the spirit is willing but the flesh is weak*
the body is not up to the demands made on it

TOTEM *to be at the bottom of the totem pole*
to be in the most junior position in some hierarchy

UNHOLY *an unholy alliance*
a working relationship for a nefarious purpose between unlikely partners

VERSE *to quote chapter and verse*
to authenticate the information

SCIENCE AND MEDICINE

ACID *to be the acid test*
to establish something beyond doubt

ACID *to put the acid on someone*
to make demands on a person

BALANCE *to weigh two alternative propositions in the balance*
to assess the relative significance to two alternative propositions

BLOW *to blow up*
(of a person) to express rage

BREAD *to claim that something is the best thing since sliced bread*
to have an exaggerated opinion of the importance or novelty of an invention or practice

BUBBLE *the bubble has burst*
the inevitable has occurred or the scheme has come to ruination

BURNER *something is on the back burner*
consideration is postponed pending further research

CATALYST *a catalyst*
a factor causing something to happen

CHEMISTRY *good chemistry*
a good ability to work closely together

CIRCLE *to try to square the circle*
to attempt the impossible (refers to a classical problem in geometry, namely, to construct with a compass a square of the same area as a given circle)

CIRCUIT *to short-circuit something*
to do something, eliminating various intermediate steps

CONCRETE *to set something in concrete*
to make something virtually unalterable

COUNT *the final countdown*
the last stages of something (refers to the launch of space vehicles)

CRYSTALLIZE *to crystallize*
to emerge in its final form

CURE *the cure is worse than the disease*
the remedy involves more disadvantages than if it were not applied

DEGREE *to the nth degree*
with great precision

DENOMINATOR *the lowest common denominator*
the highest level of taste found among all the members of some target audience

DOCTOR *just what the doctor ordered*
exactly right

ECLIPSE *to eclipse someone*
to outshine a person

ELEMENT *to be in one's element*
to very comfortable in familiar surroundings or in an environment in which one can cope very readily

EMOLLIENT *to be an emollient*
to be a measure designed to make people more favorably disposed to one's wishes

ENCAPSULATE *to encapsulate some idea*
to reduce the essential points of a complicated proposal to a small number of words

FEEDBACK *feedback*
response from a target audience to those seeking to influence it

FEVER *to be at fever pitch*
to be in a state of excited activity

FILTER *to filter through to someone*
(of information) to eventually reach a person

FIREWORKS *fireworks*
aggressive behavior because of anger

FLAME *an old flame*
a former lover

FLAME *keepers of the flame*
persons keen to maintain old traditions

FLAME *to fan the flames*
to increase unrest

FLAME *to pour gasoline on the flames*
to make a bad situation worse

FLAME *to rekindle an old flame*
to inspire the reinstatement of a former loving relationship

FLUX *to be in a state of flux*
to be subject to continuous change

FOCUS *to bring something into focus*
to put some matter into its proper context and explain its true significance

FOCUS *to focus on something*
to concentrate attention on something

FREEZE *to freeze someone out*
to deliberately exclude a person

GALVANIZE *to galvanize someone into action*
to enthuse a person into doing something

GRAVITY *the center of gravity*
the place most convenient to the greatest number

GRAVITY *to defy gravity*
to go up when the expectation is to go down

HOT *red hot*
highly exciting and desirable

HOYLE *according to Hoyle*
with authority

IMPETUS *to have impetus*
to move along forcefully

LINE *to take the line of least resistance*
to succumb to outside pressure

LITMUS *a litmus test*
an event which allows the outcome of future events to be predicted more accurately

LOUD *to come through loud and clear*
to be well understood

MAGNET *to be a magnet*
to be a factor drawing a crowd of people

MEDICINE *strong medicine*
a tough remedy

MEDICINE *to get a taste of one's own medicine*
to suffer from an initiative intended to affect only other persons

MEDICINE *to take one's medicine*
to submit to something unpleasant but necessary

METEORIC *meteoric*
rapid

MICROSCOPE *to be under the microscope*
to be the subject of close examination

MOMENTUM *to have momentum*
to move along forcefully

PENDULUM *the swing of the pendulum*
the alternation of voter acceptance between opposing political parties

PILL *to be a bitter pill to swallow*
to be a great humiliation and disappointment which have to be endured

PILL *to sugar the pill*
to cause something to be more acceptable

PLANET *to be off the planet*
to be extremely naive or uninformed

POLARIZE *to polarize*
to cause people to identify themselves as belonging to groups holding opposing views

PSYCHOLOGY *at the psychological moment*
at the most appropriate instant of time (a phrase which actually confuses the German word for "motive" with the term for an instant of time)

QUANTUM *a quantum leap*
a gigantic step forward

SCALES *to tip the scales*
to be a factor which in combination with other factors results in a particular decision which would otherwise not have been reached

SHOT *a shot in the arm*
something to revive a person's enthusiasm

SKYROCKET *to skyrocket*
(of a price of value) to increase greatly in a short time

SOFTEN *to soften someone up*
to make a person more favorably disposed to one's wishes

SPECTACLES *to see something through rose-colored spectacles*
to appreciate only the advantages and to completely disregard the disadvantages

SPECTRUM *spectrum*
wide range of different opinions or backgrounds

STAR *one can thank one's lucky stars*
one was extremely fortunate

STAR *rising star*
person making good progress in his career

STAR *to have stars in one's eyes*
(for emotional rather than rational reasons) to be ecstatic

STAR *to shoot for the stars*
to be unrealistic

TANGENT *to go off at a tangent*
to depart from the main matter under consideration and follow instead some other matter only marginally related to it

TONIC *to be a tonic*
to cheer someone up

TUNE *to stay tuned*
to keep in touch for further information as it becomes available

TUNE *to tune in*
to pay attention

VACUUM *to fill a vacuum*
to take advantage of an opportunity not acted on by others

VITRIOL *to pour vitriol on something*
to sharply criticize something

WATER *to water down something*
to reduce the severe impact of something

WAVELENGTH *to be on the same wavelength*
to think on similar lines

WAVELENGTH *to be on the wrong wavelength*
to be incorrect in one's thinking

WHEEL *to reinvent the wheel*
to waste resources doing something already accomplished

WIRE *to have one's wires crossed*
to be mistaken about key facts

SEX

BASTARD *a bastard*
an unpleasant person

BEAR *not to have been born yesterday*
not be naive

BEAR *to be born on the wrong side of the blanket*
to be illegitimate

BEAR *to be born with a silver spoon in one's mouth*
to be brought up by wealthy parents

BIRTH *to give birth to something*
to create or invent something

EMASCULATE *to emasculate something*
to delete the essential features of something

JUMP *to jump into bed with someone*
to enter into a joint enterprise with another person

PULL *to pull one's fingers out*
to get on with a job with alacrity

SPORT

AND *neck and neck*
(of contestants) with little between them

BACK *to back the wrong horse*
to have faith in, give support to and/or invest in a project which proves to be unsuccessful

BALL *to be a new ball game*
to be subject to completely revised rules or very different conditions

BALL *to be in the right ballpark*
to be approximately correct

BALL *to be on the ball*
to be fully informed

BALL *to be right behind the eight ball*
to be in a position of extreme disadvantage

BALL *to have the ball at one's feet*
to have unlimited opportunity

BALL *to keep an eye on the ball*
to monitor a fast-changing situation

BALL *to keep the ball rolling*
to take advantage of the existing momentum or to participate actively

BALL *to keep up with the ball*
to stay on top of the situation

BALL *to pass the ball along*
to cooperate with others

BALL *to play ball*
to cooperate

BALL *to run with the ball*
to make the most of the opportunity

BALL *to start the ball rolling*
to commence and enthusiastically advance an activity involving people

BALL *to take one's bat and ball home*
as a gesture of spite to remove an essential ingredient which one has contributed to a joint enterprise

BANDY *to bandy something about*
to discuss something in a light-hearted manner

BASE *to get to first base*
to succeed in getting others to start comprehending a problem

BAT *off one's own bat*
on a person's own initiative and without outside help

BAT *to go in to bat for someone*
to carry out a task on another person's behalf

BAT *to maintain a straight bat*
to be efficient

BAT *to open the batting*
to be the first in a series of persons speaking or doing something

BAT *to take one's bat and ball home*
as a gesture of spite to remove an essential ingredient which one has contributed to a joint enterprise

BELL *saved by the bell*
rescued before disaster strikes

BLOCK *stumbling block*
an impediment or difficulty preventing the easy completion fo some project or a dilemma involving a moral issue

BLOW *a blow-by-blow description*
a description overburdened by unimportant or irrelevant detail

BLOW *to soften the blow*
to take action to reduce the trauma of bad news

BORE *full bore ahead!*
proceed forward!

BOX *to shadow box*
to go through the motions without achieving or intending to achieve anything

CANTER *to win the prize in a canter*
to win very easily

CANVAS *to get off the canvas*
to recover after near defeat

CHALK *to win by a long chalk*
to win very conclusively

COMPETE *to compete on all fours with someone*
to strive on equal terms

COUP *to receive the coup de grace*
to be finished off by an opponent (French, "mercy stroke")

COURSE *it is horses for courses*
some combinations work particularly well

COURSE *to be par for the course*
to be normal

COURT *the ball is in someone's court*
it is some other person's responsibility

CRICKET *a cricket team*
eleven people

CRICKET *not to be cricket*
to be unfair

DRAW *to draw first blood*
to get an advantage

DUCK *to break one's duck*
to end a spell without results

ELEVEN *the second eleven*
persons performing an important function but one which is less important than that performed by others (refers to cricket)

END *to go off the deep end*
to lose one's temper

END *to jump straight in at the deep end*
to do something without a proper lead-in

FACE *volte face*
a reversal of previously-held beliefs (French, "a turning around")

FENCE *to rush one's fences*
to act precipitately

FIELD *a field day*
a very enjoyable and successful occasion

FIELD *a level playing field*
competition on equal terms

FIELD *to be ahead of the field*
to be better than one's competitors

FIELD *to cover the field*
to be comprehensive

FIELD *to exhaust the field*
to use up all the possibilities

FINISH *a photo finish*
a close result in a contest

FOOTBALL *a political football*
a political issue which is not being debated on its merits

GAME *I'll soon stop his little game*
his activities are not tolerated and I will ensure that they cease

GAME *a mug's game*
activity which wise persons would eschew

GAME *fun and games*
amusement derived in the course of a serious activity

GAME *game, set and match*
completion

GAME *it is just a game to someone*
it is an exercise which a person does not take seriously

GAME *the game is up*
escape is now impossible

GAME *the only game in town*
the only event worthy of attention

GAME *to beat someone at his own game*
to outwit a person in his own specialization

GAME *to give the game away*
to cease involvement with some activity

GAME *to lift one's game*
to raise the standard of one's performance

GAME *to play a deep game*
to show cunning

GAME *to play the game*
to observe the letter and the spirit of the rules or to act honorably

GAME *to stick to one's game*
to confine oneself to activities in areas in which one has knowledge and expertise

GAME *what is his game?*
what is the significance of his actions?

GLOVE *to take off the gloves*
to fight mercilessly or to debate with great ferocity

GOAL *to score a goal*
to achieve an objective

GOAL *to score an own goal*
to blow oneself up

GOLD *to go for the gold*
to aim for victory (refers to Olympic medals)

GRANDSTAND *to grandstand*
to bignote oneself

GREYHOUND *move over and let the greyhound see the rabbit*
move over

GROUND *to kiss the ground*
to suffer a loss

GROUND *to prepare one's ground*
to get ready for a confrontation

GUARD *to catch someone off guard*
to surprise a person (a fencing term)

GUARD *to slip under one's guard*
to cause a mistake to be made despite care being taken to prevent this

GUN *to jump the gun*
to start before one is meant to

HEAVYWEIGHT *a heavyweight*
a person of importance or influence

HIT *to hit someone below the belt*
to act unfairly toward another person

HIT *to hit someone for six*
to damage a person's cause (refers to cricket)

HOLD *no holds barred*
without any limitation

HOLD *to hold someone at bay*
to successfully resist an attacker

HOOK *hook, line and sinker*
wholly

HOP *something is but a hop, skip and jump away*
something is nearby

HURDLE *to jump a hurdle*
to overcome a problem or difficulty

HURDLE *to jump that hurdle when one comes to it*
to deal with a particular problem only when it becomes necessary to do so

INNINGS *to have had a good innings*
to have had a successful life (refers to cricket)

KEEPER *to let something go to the keeper*
to deliberately ignore a particular incident

KICK *to kick off*
to start some action

LAUREL *to look to one's laurels*
to be careful not to lose one's reputation for some skill

LAUREL *to rest on one's laurels*
to use a reputation for success earned in earlier times as a substitute for current endeavor

LEAGUE *to be in the same league*
to have comparable skills

LEAP *to leap frog something*
to overtake something, with the likelihood of in turn being overtaken (refers to a game in which participants jump over each other in turn)

LIGHTWEIGHT *lightweight*
uninfluential

LINE *someone's job is on the line*
a person's career path is under consideration and/or his present position is at risk

LINE *to be line ball*
to be equal

LOOK *to need to look over one's shoulder*
to be subject to attack which is not obvious

LURCH *to leave someone in the lurch*
to desert a person who is in difficulties (refers to the score in certain games)

MARK *to be first off the mark*
to start ahead of all others

MARK *to be slow off the mark*
to be slow to start something

MARK *to be up to the mark*
to be of the right standard

MARK *to be wide off the mark*
to have a belief which is far removed from the true position

MARK *to hit the mark*
to achieve one's object or to make the correct decision (refers to archery)

MARK *to overstep the mark*
to fail to observe the proprieties

MCCOY *to be the real McCoy*
the genuine article (refers to an American boxer who became world welterweight champion in 1890)

OAR *to stick one's oar in*
to intervene without invitation in a dispute to which one is not a party

PACE *to put someone through his paces*
to test a person

PACE *to set the pace*
to give a lead in regard to a rate of progression

PADDLE *to paddle one's canoe*
to do something unaided and in one's own way

PARRY *to parry some argument*
to deflect some argument (refers to fencing)

PEDAL *to backpedal*
to reverse to some extent previously applied policies

PEG *to peg out*
to die (refers to the final stroke in a game of croquet)

PIN *to pin someone down*
to find a person willing to accept blame or responsibility or to force a person to announce a decision or concede a point

PLAY *foul play*
treachery or murder

PLAY *to be in full play*
to be fully operational

PLAY *to find out the state of play*
to ascertain the current position of some project

PLAY *to play by Marquis of Queensberry rules*
to act ethically

PLAY *to play by the book*
to apply the rules strictly

PLAY *to play fast and loose*
to disregard one's obligations

PLAY *to play it safe*
to take no risks

PLAYERS *a trap for young players*
a good opportunity for the inexperienced or naive to make mistakes

PLUNGE *to take the plunge*
to expose oneself to certain risks

POINT *to score points*
to make a good impression

POINT *to score top points*
to outwit other persons

POST *to pip someone at the post*
to achieve something only just ahead of a rival

PRESERVES *to poach on someone's preserves*
to encroach uninvited on another person's territory

PRIZE *not to be here to win prizes*
to be altruistic

PRIZE *to win the booby prize*
to do worse than all others

PUNCH *to be punch drunk*
to be stupefied by some news

PUNCH *to beat someone to the punch*
to get to some objective ahead of some keen rival

PUNCH *to telegraph one's punches*
by one's actions to give advance warning of one's future plans

RACE *not to be in the race*
to lack the required standard

RACE *rat race*
pressures of modern living

RACE *your race is run*
you have had your opportunity

REIN *to take over the reins*
to assume control

RIDE *riding instructions*
directions as to how to do something

RIDE *to be riding for a fall*
to act in a reckless manner

RIDE *to ride high*
to be successful but vulnerable

RIDE *to ride roughshod over someone*
to disregard the feelings and wishes of a person

RING *to jump into the ring*
to join in enthusiastically

RING *to step into the ring*
to enter a competitive environment

RING *to throw one's hat into the ring*
to publicly announce one's interest in some position

ROPE *to be on the ropes*
to be facing defeat

ROUND *to be only round one*
to be only the first of many stages

ROUND *to win some rounds*
to be partly successful

RUB *here's the rub*
this is where a difficulty arises (a term used in bowling)

RUN *to be up and running*
to be operative

RUN *to have a run for one's money*
to at least get some enjoyment out of an otherwise abortive exercise

RUN *to have the runs on the board*
to have a demonstrable record of achievement

RUNNER *front-runner*
person expected to win

SADDLE *to be in the saddle*
to be in command

SCORE *to even the score*
to get one's own back for some past action

SCORE *to score a point*
to make a clever contribution in the course of debate

SCORE *to see the score*
to appreciate the reality of a situation

SCRATCH *to be back to scratch*
to have to start all over again

SCRATCH *to be up to scratch*
to be of the required standard

SCRATCH *to start from behind scratch*
to be faced with a handicap

SCRATCH *to start from scratch*
to commence something without the benefit of any past activity

SHOOT *to be on a slippery shoot*
to court disaster

SIDELINE *to sit on the sidelines*
not to take part in the main action

SIT *to be a sitting duck*
to be readily exploited

SKATE *to get one's skates on*
to hurry up

SKATE *to skate around some subject*
by diversionary tactics to avoid discussing some subject

SKITTLES *not to be all beer and skittles*
not to be all pleasant and easy

SOMERSAULT *to turn a complete somersault*
to reverse one's established policy

SPLASH *to make a splash*
to create a sensation

SPONGE *to throw up the sponge*
to concede defeat

SPRINGBOARD *a springboard*
a situation from which one intends to make a rapid advance

START *to have a head start*
to have an advantage over others

STRAP *to hit the straps*
to really get going

STRETCH *to enter the home stretch*
to commence the last stage

STROKE *a master stroke*
particularly brilliant action

STUMPS *until stumps are drawn*
until the project ends (refers to cricket)

SWIM *it is a case of sink or swim*
the attempt is worthwhile, despite the risk of failure

SWIM *to be in the swim*
to be a member of a group knowing what is going on

SWIM *to swim against the tide*
to take up a minority position

TOWEL *to throw in the towel*
to concede defeat

TRACK *track record*
proven performance

TUG *a tug of war*
a dispute in which each protagonist desires a different course of action

TURF *to be on one's own turf*
to engage in one's own customary area of activity

WALKOVER *a walkover*
an easy victory

WARM *to warm up*
to get ready

WICKET *to be on a sticky wicket*
to face some difficulties (refers to cricket)

WINNER *to be on a winner*
to have faith in, give support to and/or invest in a project which proves to be successful

WOODEN *to get the wooden spoon*
to come ingloriously last

THEATER

ACT *to be a hard act to follow*
to be an impressive performance, not easily matched by the next person

ACT *to clean up one's act*
to fix up the deficiencies in one's affairs

ACT *to get in on the act*
to participate in some activity started by others

ACT *to get one's act together*
to organize one's activities so as to make them efficient

AISLE *to have an audience rolling in the aisles*
to amuse an audience

BOW *to bow out*
to retire from some activity

BOW *to take a bow*
to receive recognition

CHARADE *to act out a charade*
ostentatiously to pretend to be doing something in an ethical fashion

CHOREOGRAPH *to choreograph something*
to organize the detail of who does what and when in a project

COMEDY *a comedy of errors*
a series of separate mistakes in relation to some matter (name of a Shakespeare play)

CURTAIN *curtain raiser*
introduction

CURTAIN *it's curtains!*
this is the end!

CURTAIN *the curtain rises on something*
something is about to start

CURTAIN *to ring down the curtain on something*
to treat something as concluded

DANCE *nothing to make a song or dance about*
unexciting or unimportant

DANCE *to lead someone a merry dance*
to mislead a person

DANCE *to make a song and dance about something*
to create a fuss

DANSE *danse macabre*
gruesome final step (French, "ghastly dance")

FRANKENSTEIN *to create a Frankenstein*
to create something wicked and out of control (a reference to the fictional creator of a monster, in mistake for a reference to the monster itself)

GALLERY *to play to the gallery*
to do something which appeals to the general public rather than something which is right

LIGHT *to be the leading light*
to be the most important person in a venture

LIMELIGHT *to be in the limelight*
to be exposed to public attention

PART *to play one's part*
to cooperate or carry out one's obligations under some arrangement

REHEARSAL *dress rehearsal*
preliminary skirmish

SCENARIO *scenario*
details of arrangements

SCENE *behind the scenes*
out of public view or awareness

SCENE *to make a scene*
to create a fuss

SCENE *to quit the scene*
to depart

SCENE *to set the scene for something*
to get things ready for something

SEAT *to be on the edge of one's seat*
to be very excited at what is currently happening

SHOW *the show must go on*
despite difficulties the action in contemplation has to proceed

SHOW *to get the show on the road*
to commence a planned activity

SHOW *to give the show away*
to indiscreetly reveal sensitive information

SHOW *to steal the show*
to have the maximum appeal to those watching

SIDESHOW *a sideshow*
an unimportant adjunct

SIXTY-FOUR *a sixty-four thousand dollar question*
a pertinent but very difficult question (refers to a TV show in which an initial prize doubles with the successful answering of progressively more difficult questions)

SPOTLIGHT *to steal the spotlight*
to set out to be the center of attention

STAGE *the stage is set*
something is about to happen

STAGE *to be center stage*
to have everyone's attention

STAGE *to be on a world stage*
to be prominent in international affairs

STAGE *to stage-manage something*
to arrange how something happens

STEAL *to steal someone's thunder*
to take credit for another person's good work (refers to a dispute over the copying of a machine invented by a 17th-century dramatist to reproduce the sound of thunder during a play)

STRING *to pull strings*
to use one's special influence with those in a position to make favorable decisions which might otherwise not be forthcoming

TRICK *a whole bag of tricks*
a series of articles or a series of artificial devices

UPSTAGE *to upstage someone*
to deprive another person of the glory which he would otherwise have enjoyed

WING *to wait in the wings*
to be prepared to stay unobtrusive till the appropriate time for action arrives

TRANSPORT

ALLEY *to be up one's alley*
to be right within a person's expertise of area of interest

ALLEY *to rush into a blind alley*
to make a precipitate move which does not lead one anywhere

AVENUE *avenue*
method of approach

BACKFIRE *to backfire*
to be counterproductive

BOX *to be in the box seat*
to be in a very powerful position to control activity

BRAKE *to put the brake on someone*
to stop a person

BUGGY *the horse and buggy days*
long ago

BUS *the wheels are back under the bus*
normal activity has been resumed

BUS *to jump on the bus*
to join an activity already well under way

BUS *to miss the bus*
to fail to exploit an opportunity

BUSMAN *a busman's holiday*
leisure time spent in a way not significantly different from one's normal business activities

CAB *to be the first cab off the rank*
to start ahead of all others

CARAVAN *the caravan will roll on*
the activity will continue

CARRY *to be carried away*
to be excited by something imaginative

CART *to put the cart before the horse*
to do things in the wrong order

CART *to upset the applecart*
to engage in conduct disturbing a peaceful state of affairs and thereby cause discomfort

CLASS *to be first class*
to be very satisfactory

COACH *an opening wide enough to drive a coach and four through*
an excellent opportunity

COACH *to drive a coach and horses through something*
to demonstrate major errors in something

COLLISION *to be on a collision course*
to be headed for a clash with an opponent

COOK *a Cook's tour*
a guided tour of inspection (refers to Thomas Cook, the travel company)

COVENTRY *to send someone to Coventry*
to ostentatiously and collectively ignore a person by way of punishment

CREEK *to be up the creek*
to be completely mistaken

CYLINDER *to spark on all cylinders*
to work extremely well

DERAIL *to derail some strategy*
to cause a strategy to fail

DRIFT *to drift apart*
to lose contact or to change feelings once held in common

DRIVE *to drive someone from pillar to post*
to send a person to a series of places in a vain attempt to achieve something

DRIVE *to drive someone up the wall*
to annoy another person by one's actions

DRIVER *a backseat driver*
a person seeking to exercise control

DRIVER *to be in the driver's seat*
to be in charge

GARAGE *garage sale*
sale of miscellaneous assets at cheap prices

GEAR *to be geared up to do something*
to have equipment, labor and know-how in place adequate for some task

GEAR *to be in top gear*
to be making excellent progress

GRADE *to be on the downgrade*
to be of deteriorating quality

HALT *to grind to a halt*
to cease some activity despite expectations that it would continue

HAUL *for the long haul*
as a long-term proposition

LANE *life in the fast lane*
existence full of exciting but worthless activity

MILEAGE *to get some mileage out of something*
to benefit from something

NOTCH *to move down a notch*
to accept a lower position

PASSPORT *to be a passport to success*
to be a means of achieving success

PEDESTRIAN *pedestrian*
uninspired

POLE *to be poles apart*
to have ideas which are very different

POST *a staging post*
a place where action is initiated

POST *to go post haste*
to go very fast

POWER *under one's own power*
without external help

RAIL *to run off the rails*
to significantly depart from the intended course of action

RAILROAD *to railroad something through*
to rush people into accepting a proposal

RAILWAY *what a way to run a railway!*
the way things are done is disgraceful (refers to a cartoon)

RIDE *to get a magic carpet ride to something*
to be very fortunate in achieving some objective

RIDE *to get an armchair ride*
to be given a particularly easy time

RIDE *to go along for the ride*
to seek to benefit from a project in which others contribute the effort

RIDE *to take someone for a ride*
to deceive a person

ROAD *a middle-of-the-road solution*
a solution near the middle of a range of possibilities

ROAD *all roads lead to Rome*
all alternatives will have the same outcome

ROAD *fork in the road*
turning point for decisions

ROAD *one for the road*
a final drink before leaving

ROAD *roadblocks*
difficulties

ROAD *the royal road to success*
the way of attaining success without effort

ROAD *this is the end of the road for someone*
a person will have no further opportunity to do something

ROAD *to be at the crossroads*
to need to choose between several mutually exclusive alternatives

ROAD *to enter a long road*
to commence a task which will take a long time

ROAD *to face a rocky road ahead*
to be likely to encounter difficulties

ROAD *to go down a particular road*
to adopt a particular strategy

ROAD *to happen down the road*
to happen later

ROAD *to road test something*
to try something out under real conditions

ROAD *to set someone on the right road*
to show a person how to go about doing something

SEAT *to take a backseat*
not to actively involve oneself

STEAM *full steam ahead!*
get going as fast as possible!

STEAM *to develop a head of steam*
to gain momentum

STEAM *to let off steam*
to engage in noisy or robust activity as a form of relaxation

STEAM *to lose steam*
to slow down

STEAM *to run out of steam*
to lose one's energy and enthusiasm

STEAM *under one's own steam*
without external help

STOP *to come to a full stop*
to completely cease activity

STOP *to pull out all stops*
to make maximum effort

STREAM *to get on stream*
to now operate successfully following the end of a settling-in period

STREET *a one-way street*
a flow of activity in only one direction

STREET *not to be in the same street as someone*
not to be of comparable quality

STREET *the man in the street*
the average citizen

STREET *to be streets ahead*
to outperform one's competitors by a wide margin

STREET *to walk in off the street*
to come without prior arrangement or notification

TIRE *to carry a spare tire*
to be fat

TRAIL *to blaze a trail*
to be the first person to do something

TRAIN *to get on a gravy train*
to take steps to become a recipient of benefits which are available but undeserved

TRAIN *to miss the train*
to fail to exploit an opportunity

TRAM *to be on the wrong tram*
to be completely mistaken as to the basic facts

TRUCK *it fell off the back of a truck*
it was leaked to me

TUNNEL *to see the light at the end of the tunnel*
to be close to finalizing a long exercise

U-TURN *to do a U-turn*
to reverse one's thinking

WAGON *to be on the water wagon*
to be teetotal

WAY *to stand in someone's way*
to prevent a person achieving his goal

WHEEL *the squeaky wheel gets the most attention*
those complaining the most loudly will get their problems sorted out first

WHEEL *the wheel has turned*
circumstances have changed

WHEEL *the wheel has turned the complete circle*
things are now back to where they were before

WHEEL *the wheels fell off*
the plan failed

WHEEL *to be a fifth wheel*
to be superfluous

WHEEL *to make the wheels go round*
to cause something to happen

WHEEL *to put a spoke in someone's wheel*
to interfere with another person's activity, so preventing its continuance

WHEEL *to wheel someone in*
to bring a person along for a confrontation

WAR AND MILITARY

AMMUNITION *ammunition*
arguments helpful to a case

ARM *to be armed to the teeth*
to carry many weapons

ARMOR *a chink in someone's armor*
an opportunity to do something which otherwise could not be done

ARMOR *a knight in shining armor*
a very helpful person

ARMS *to be up in arms against something*
to express violent opposition to a proposal

ARROW *another arrow in one's quiver*
an additional reason

AX *an old battle-ax*
a hostile woman

BARREL *with both barrels blazing*
with great intensity

BASTION *the last bastion*
the only remaining defensive measure

BATON *to have a field marshal's baton in one's kit*
to be ambitious

BATTLE *a battle royal*
a fight or argument with many simultaneous participants

BATTLE *to fight an uphill battle*
to face difficulties or to have formidable opposition

BATTLESHIP *enough to sink a battleship*
more than sufficient

BEARER *a standard bearer*
a highly visible activist for a cause

BOLT *to shoot one's bolt*
to lose one's temper

BOMB *a bombshell*
an unpleasant surprise

BOMB *a time bomb*
a source of serious problems which are certain to surface later on

BOMB *to be a bomb*
to be grossly defective

BOMB *to put a bomb under someone*
to induce a person to take some action

BOMBARD *to bombard someone with something*
to overwhelm a person with material or to persistently assail a person with words of argument or abuse

BOW *to draw a long bow*
to state a conclusion which while possible is unlikely on the known facts

BREACH *once more unto the breach*
let us get on with the task (from Shakespeare's HENRY V)

BREACH *to stand in the breach*
to bear the brunt of criticisms

BRIDGEHEAD *a bridgehead*
an advanced post set up to facilitate further access to some new market, etc.

BROADSIDE *a broadside*
a short verbal attack

BULLET *a gun with no bullets*
something incomplete and therefore useless for the desire purpose

BULLET *to bite the bullet*
to face up to the difficulties of a situation

BULLET *to have a bullet which can be fired*
to have available an effective response which can be used at will

BURN *to burn one's bridges*
to do something irreversible

CAMP *in our camp*
in the group representing our vested interest

CANNON *a loose cannon on the deck*
a mistake likely to cause trouble

CATAPULT *to catapult*
(of sales, etc.) to increase rapidly

CATAPULT *to catapult to fame*
to achieve fame unexpectedly quickly

CATCH *catch-22*
a situation made impossible because it requires as a prior fulfillment something which does not exist until that condition is satisfied (title of a novel by Joseph Heller)

COCK *to go off half-cocked*
to act without adequate thought or preparation (refers to a gun at the half-ready)

COLUMNIST *a fifth columnist*
a person using his position of trust to work for a rival cause

COMMAND *to be in a commanding position*
to have a strategic advantage

COMMAND *to be in command*
to be on top of a situation

CORPS *espirit de corps*
a feeling of camaraderie and concern for the good name of some organization of which one is a member (French, "vital breath of a body")

CUDGEL *to take up the cudgels for someone*
to defend a person

DAGGER *cloak and dagger activity*
secret activity

DAGGER *to look daggers at someone*
to look at a person in a way which indicates great animosity

DECIMATE *to decimate*
to greatly reduce in size (often used in the sense of "to reduce to one tenth," although the original meaning was "to reduce by one tenth")

DECIPHER *to decipher something*
to understand the significance of something

DEVASTATE *to be devastated*
to be extremely disappointed

DISASTER *a pit of disaster*
great and unexpected misfortune

DISPATCH *to be mentioned in dispatches*
to be favorably mentioned (refers to military recognition for bravery)

DITCH *to make a last-ditch stand*
to make a brave effort to stave off final defeat

DRAW *to be quick on the draw*
to act precipitately

DRUM *to drum someone out of some organization*
to terminate in ignominy a person's employment or membership (refers to the ceremonial cashiering in the army to the beating of parade drums)

DYNAMITE *to be dynamite*
to cause outrage

DYNAMITE *to play with dynamite*
to invite trouble by virtue of one's risky conduct

EXPLODE *to explode*
(of a person) to express rage

FIRE *sure-fire*
guaranteed

FIRE *to be in the firing line*
to be among the first to be under attack

FIRE *to draw fire*
to encounter criticism

FIRE *to hang fire*
to take no immediate action

FIRE *to hold fire*
to defer criticizing

FIRE *to hold one's fire*
to delay proposed action

FLAK *to attract flak*
to attract criticism

FORCE *to join forces*
to cooperate with one another in order to achieve a common objective

FORT *to hold the fort*
to be in charge during the temporary absence of a superior

GAUNTLET *to run the gauntlet*
to be subjected to criticism (from the Spanish word for "passage," in reference to punishment inflicted on delinquents made to run between two files of soldiers)

GROUND *to gain ground*
to advance one's position relative to others

GUARD *new guard*
changed regime

GUN *a gun with no bullets*
something incomplete and therefore useless for the desired purpose

GUN *a scattergun approach*
an effort going here, there and everywhere, instead of being properly targeted

GUN *to be a gun for hire*
to be a person willing to undertake assignments for a fee

GUN *to be going great guns*
to be making very successful progress

GUN *to be great guns at something*
to be very skilled at something

GUN *to bring out one's biggest guns*
to use the most impressive persons or arguments

GUN *to hold a gun at someone's head*
to put pressure on a person to make a particular decision regardless of his desires in the matter

GUN *to look down the barrel of a gun*
to be given little choice in a matter

GUN *to outgun someone*
to outmaneuver a person

GUN *to spike someone's guns*
to cause something to become useless

GUN *to stick to one's guns*
to continue to hold certain beliefs notwithstanding opposition by others

GUN *to turn one's guns on someone*
to criticize a person

HATCHET *to bury the hatchet*
to abandon hostilities

HERO *to make a hero of oneself*
to curry favors

HILT *to the hilt*
to the maximum extent

LAND *to ascertain the lay of the land*
to establish the pertinent facts and opinions

LINE *to be out of line*
to adopt a stance not held by others

LINE *to fall into line*
to conform with others

LINE *to put one's reputation on the line*
to take a public stance in the realization that there is a risk that one's reputation will suffer if one is proved wrong

LINE *to step out of line*
to infringe accepted rules of behavior

LOCK *lock, stock and barrel*
entirely

MARCH *in the course of a day's march*
while carrying out one's normal activities

MARINE *tell it to the marines*
such nonsense is not believable

MINE *a minefield*
a source of great hidden danger or of difficulties not obvious on a first encounter

ORDER *the order of the day*
the customary behavior

ORDER *to get one's marching orders*
to be told to leave

OVERKILL *overkill*
more action than really required for the purpose

PACKDRILL *no names—no packdrill*
the identities of the parties will be kept confidential in order to protect them

PASSWORD *the password is so-and-so*
the main attraction is so-and-so

PETARD *to be hoist with one's own petard*
to have one's own case used against one (refers to being blown up by one's own bomb)

POINT *to refuse point blank*
to refuse outright

POTSHOT *to take a potshot at someone*
to make disparaging remarks about a person

POWDER *to keep one's powder dry*
to retain key arguments or resources in reserve for use later

RANK *to break ranks*
to identify oneself as having separate interests or views from the rest of a group

RANK *to close ranks*
to sink minor differences in order to present a unified front to a common enemy

READ *to read between the lines*
to appreciate the true significance of something not put into words

RETREAT *to beat a retreat*
to abandon some project

ROCKET *to give someone a rocket*
to severely reprimand a person

ROCKET *to put a rocket under someone*
to induce a person to take some action

ROCKET *to skyrocket*
(of a price or value) to increase greatly in a short time

SABER *saber rattling*
hints of retribution if certain conduct does not cease

SALVO *to fire a salvo at someone*
to present a series of criticisms to a person

SHELL *to be shell-shocked*
to be stunned by unexpected bad news

SHOOT *a straight shooter*
a person who is frank and outspoken

SHOOT *a troubleshooter*
a person good at finding and then rectifying faults

SHOOT *shoot!*
go on, speak!

SHOOT *the whole shooting match*
the whole lot

SHOOT *to be shot to pieces*
to have one's case seriously damaged

SHOOT *to be shot to ribbons*
(of an argument) to be utterly discredited

SHOOT *to shoot from the hip*
to speak frankly and openly

SHOOT *to shoot one's mouth off*
to speak without thinking

SHOOT *to shoot someone down in flames*
to utterly destroy another person's arguments

SHOT *a big shot*
an important person

SHOT *a shot in the dark*
an intelligent or lucky guess

SHOT *a sitting shot*
an initial move which is designated to establish facts for use in a later action

SHOT *opening shot*
first step in an activity expected to last a long time

SHOT *shots across the bow*
warnings

SHOT *that is a long shot*
there is only a remote possibility

SHOT *to be a sitting shot*
to be a person whose actions make him very vulnerable to criticism

SHOT *to beat by a long shot*
to defeat very convincingly

SHOT *to call the shots*
to have the direction over a project

SHOT *to fire a parting shot*
to make a defiant gesture on leaving

SHOT *to give one's best shot*
to make the best attempt possible

SHOT *to have a shot at someone*
to use subtly chosen words implying friendly criticism but designed to embarrass another person

SHOT *to have a shot at something*
to attempt to achieve something

SIGHT *to lower one's sights*
to reduce one's ambition

SIGHT *to set one's sights on something*
to aim to achieve something

SIGNAL *to send a smoke signal*
to given an indication

SMOKE *to set up a smokescreen*
to deliberately confuse an issue by disguising its salient features

SMOKE *when the smoke clears*
when sufficient time has passed

SOLDIER *to be a brave soldier*
to be brave

SOLDIER *to soldier on*
to carry on despite difficulties

SPEARHEAD *to spearhead something*
to lead a movement

SPUR *to win one's spurs*
to gain recognition after a period of effort (refers to the earning of a knighthood in battle)

STANDOFF *a Mexican standoff*
a situation where neither of two parties is making a move

STORM *to barnstorm*
to visit accompanied by a show of force

STREET *there is blood in the streets*
much damage has been done to a cause

STRIKE *to be within striking distance*
to be fairly close

STRIPE *to earn one's stripes*
to deserve promotion

SWORD *to be a two-edged sword*
to involve both advantages and disadvantages of similar significance

SWORD *to cross swords with someone*
to have a disagreement with another person

SWORD *to have a sword of Damocles hanging over one*
to be in imminent danger despite normal activity going on all around one

SWORD *to hold a sword at someone's throat*
to exert undue pressure on another person in an endeavor to achieve a result which would otherwise not be forthcoming

TARGET *a moving target*
an objective subject to constant revision

TARGET *target*
objective

TORPEDO *to torpedo something*
to make something ineffective

TOWER *to be in an ivory tower*
to be emersed in theoretical considerations and ignorant of the practical realities (Song of Solomon 7:4)

TRENCH *to be back in the trenches*
to be made to carry out menial tasks

TRIGGER *to be trigger-happy*
to be impetuous

TRIGGER *trigger*
factor responsible for certain events occurring at that particular time

TROOPER *to be a real trooper*
to be a person willing to try anything

VANGUARD *to be at the vanguard of something*
to be among the first to do something

VICTORY *a Pyrrhic victory*
a win which costs more than if there had been a loss (refers to the battle at which King Pyrrhus of Epirus defeated the Romans at Asculum)

VOLLEY *to fire a volley at someone*
to send a series of angry messages to someone

WAR *the cold war*
the unfriendly relations between the communist nations and the rest of the world

WAR *to be on the warpath*
to be on the lookout for faults which can be criticized

WARFARE *paper warfare*
an excessive amount of correspondence or red tape

WEAPON *to use all the weapons at one's disposal*
to utilize all available advantages

10

THESAURUS

ABUSE

give him an inch and he will take a mile
make him a small concession and he will abuse it by taking much more

to feel the rough side of someone's tongue
to be verbally abused by a person

to get one's head blown off
to be very soundly abused

to get the rounds of the kitchen
(of a husband) to be subject to personal abuse by his wife

to give someone a piece of one's mind
to abuse another person

to kick someone around
to abuse a person

ACHIEVEMENT

a Goliath
a giant or a person whose ability and achievements exceed those of most other people (1 Samuel 17)

a bird in the hand is worth two in the bush
a benefit currently available is more valuable than a seemingly much larger benefit which may or may not be achieved in the future

a crusade
an aggressive campaign to achieve some political or social objective

a feather in one's cap
a meritorious personal achievement

a giant
a person whose ability and achievements exceed those of most other people

a milestone
an achievement

a recipe for disaster
a certain way of achieving disaster

a warm inner glow
satisfaction at some achievement

gateway to something
method of achieving something

heartburn
regret at some non-achievement

it is no use crying over spilt milk
lamenting over a disaster achieves nothing

it was touch and go
there were considerable risks—the objective was achieved, but only just

one can't make bricks without straw
one cannot achieve results in the absence of adequate resources

one would give one's eye teeth for something
a person would very much like to achieve some objective

path
means of achieving an objective

pie in the sky
a hoped-for result unlikely to be achieved

something has done the trick
something has achieved the desired purpose

the crowning point
the height of a person's achievement

the river found its mark
equilibrium between two pressures has been achieved

there are many ways to cook eggs
there are many ways to achieve an objective

there is more than one way to skin a cat
this can be achieved in a variety of acceptable ways

to achieve a flying start
to get operational very quickly

to be a passport to success
to be a means of achieving success

to be hell bent on something
to be very determined to achieve something, regardless of the adverse consequences

to be only a gleam in one's eyes
to be a long way from final achievement

to be unable to take a trick
to be unable to achieve success in anything

to be up against a brick wall
to be unable to achieve anything because of intractable opposition or apathy

to catapult to fame
to achieve fame unexpectedly quickly

to deliver the goods
to achieve the objective

to drive someone from pillar to post
to send a person to a series of places in a vain attempt to achieve something

to gain a foothold
to achieve a position from which further advances can readily be made

to get a magic carpet ride to something
to be very fortunate in achieving some objective

to get something under one's belt
to achieve something

to get the worst of all worlds
to get a series of disadvantages without achieving any corresponding advantages

to have a shot at something
to attempt to achieve something

to have one's heart set on something
to be very keen to achieve something

to have one's work cut out to do something
it will be difficult to achieve something

to have the runs on the board
to have a demonstrable record of achievement

to head someone in the right direction
to assist a person to achieve something

to heave a sigh of relief
to express satisfaction at the achievement of a solution to a difficult problem

to hit the mark
to achieve one's object or to make the correct decision (refers to archery)

to hold a knife at someone's throat
to exert undue pressure on another person in an endeavor to achieve a result which would otherwise not be forthcoming

to hold a sword at someone's throat
to exert undue pressure on another person in an endeavor to achieve a result which would otherwise not be forthcoming

to join forces
to cooperate with one another in order to achieve a common objective

to kill two birds with one stone
to achieve a second objective in the course of achieving the first objective

to land something
to achieve something

to let blood
to allow some harm as the price for achieving some greater benefit

to mend fences
to achieve a reconciliation

to pip someone at the post
to achieve something only just ahead of a rival

to pull something off
to achieve success in some enterprise

to put one's back into something
to work hard at achieving some goal

to salvage something out of the wreck
to achieve some minor benefits out of a disastrous situation

to score a goal
to achieve an objective

to set a hare running
in order to achieve some desired effect, to initiate some related activity

to set one's sights on something
to aim to achieve something

to shadow box
to go through the motions without achieving or intending to achieve anything

to stand in someone's way
to prevent a person achieving his goal

to steamroll something through
to use enormous force to achieve an objective

to throw one's cap into the air
to celebrate some achievement

to throw one's weight about
to use one's real or imagined status in order to achieve certain results

to walk away with a profit
to achieve a profit on concluding a project

to waste one's breath
to talk or request something without achieving anything

without any cards to play
without the means to achieve something

ACTIVITY

I'll soon stop his little game
his activities are not tolerated and I will ensure that they cease

a backwater
a place of little activity

a busman's holiday
leisure time spent in a way not significantly different from one's normal business activities

a cobbler should stick to his last
every person should confine himself to activities for which he has been trained

a honeymoon
a short period enjoyed by a newcomer to some activity before his performance is criticized

a logjam
a stoppage of activity caused by input in greater volume than allowed for

a mug's game
activity which wise persons would eschew

a one-way street
a flow of activity in only one direction

a standard bearer
a highly visible activist for a cause

a watershed
an occasion dividing two distinct phases of activity

across the board
over the whole range of activity

behind someone's back
in a way which deliberately conceals an activity from a person

blueprint
a master plan for some activity or a model which others can copy

cloak and dagger activity
secret activity

distant fields look greener
activities of which one has no experience seem much easier than is really the case

early in the piece
at an early stage of some activity

fun and games
amusement derived in the course of a serious activity

in the course of a day's march
while carrying out one's normal activities

it is a long time between drinks
activity is occurring only very spasmodically

it takes two to tango
some activities cannot be carried out single-handedly

kingmaker
person engaging in behind-the-scenes activities to promote another person to a particular leadership position

life in the fast lane
existence full of exciting but worthless activity

monkey business
mischievous or underhand activity

nimble-footed
quick to change the direction of one's activities when circumstances warrant

opening shot
first-step in an activity expected to last a long time

someone's number is up
a person's period of activity or influence is about to expire

the caravan will roll on
the activity will continue

the coast is clear
there are no observers to one's activity around

the wheels are back under the bus
normal activity has been resumed

the whole gamut
the whole range of some activity

the world is one's oyster
one has enormous scope for activity

to be at fever pitch
to be in a state of excited activity

to be in full swing
to be very active

to be in the box seat
to be in a very powerful position to control activity

to be in the doldrums
to be depressed or to show no activity (refers to a region of little wind near the equator, becalming sailing ships)

to be in the thick of things
to get involved at the center of some activity

to be on a treadmill
to be involved in some unpleasant ongoing activity which cannot readily be stopped

to be on one's own turf
to engage in one's own customary area of activity

to be on someone's cabbage patch
to engage in a competitive activity in a territory regarded by someone already there as rightfully belonging exclusively to him

to be riveted to one's seat
to find the activity being watched very exciting and worthy of full attention

to be tied down
to have responsibilities precluding alternative activities

to bow out
to retire from some activity

to call it a day
to cease involvement with some activity

to catch someone in the net
to unexpectedly involve a particular person in the course of activity designed to involve many others

to close the book on something
to terminate an activity

to come to a full stop
to completely cease activity

to do a hatchet job
to destroy some existing activity or to ruin a person's credibility

to get in on the act
to participate in some activity started by others

to get one's act together
to organize one's activities so as to make them efficient

to get the show on the road
to commence a planned activity

to give the game away
to cease involvement with some activity

to go to sleep
to become inactive

to grind to a halt
to cease some activity despite expectations that it would continue

to gum up the works
to cause an activity to be halted

to have a sword of Damocles hanging over one
to be in imminent danger despite normal activity going on all around one

to have a tiger by the tail
to be involved in an activity which is much more dangerous than one had realized

to have one's fingers in many different pies
to be engaged in a variety of separate activities

to have the plug pulled out from under one
to have a successful activity destroyed by the actions of someone else

to hedge one's bets
to take action involving a cost but which is designed to reduce the possible adverse consequences of some activity

to jump on the bus
to join an activity already well under way

to keep off someone's pad
not to interfere with or compete against another person in his customary area of activity

to keep one's eye on someone
to supervise a person or to monitor a person's activities and behavior

to keep one's hand in
to engage in activities which reinforce skills which one has previously acquired

to keep the ball rolling
to take advantage of the existing momentum or to participate actively

to keep the home fires burning
to maintain normal domestic activity during the temporary absence of the breadwinner

to leap in
to commence an activity without considering the wisdom of doing so or the best way to proceed

to let off steam
to engage in a noisy or robust activity as a form of relaxation

to lower the boom
to terminate an activity

to make sparks fly
to cause rapid activity to take place

to nip something in the bud
to stop some activity in its early stages when stopping it is still relatively easy

to pick up the pieces
to resume previous activities to the maximum extent possible after some setback

to plow new ground
to laboriously engage in an untried activity

to plow on
to methodically and painstakingly continue with an activity

to put a spoke in someone's wheel
to interfere with another person's activity, so preventing its continuance

to put something on "hold"
to put something aside for the time being with a view to resuming activity later on (refers to the telephone)

to put up the shutters
to cease an established activity

to run around in circles
to engage in excited but useless activity

to set a hare running
in order to achieve some desired effect, to initiate some related activity

to shut up shop
to cease an established activity

to start from scratch
to commence something without the benefit of any past activity

to start the ball rolling
to commence and enthusiastically advance an activity involving people

to stick to one's game
to confine oneself to activities in areas in which one has knowledge and expertise

to take a backseat
not to actively involve oneself

to try one's hand at something
to attempt a new activity, especially by way of experiment

to twiddle one's thumbs
not to be involved in any worthwhile activity

ADVANTAGE

a lame dog
a person under some disadvantage needing attention and assistance

a mixed bag
some advantages and some disadvantages

a soul-searching exercise
an examination of the advantages and disadvantages of a proposal

bargaining chips
benefits which can be conceded in negotiations in order to obtain some advantage

leech
person taking undue advantage of others

the cure is worse than the disease
the remedy involves more disadvantages than if it were not applied

the early bird gets the worm
a person who acts ahead of others gets an advantage over them

the upside
the advantage

to be a two-edged sword
to involve both advantages and disadvantages of similar significance

to be in a commanding position
to have a strategic advantage

to be quick on one's feet
to cleverly take advantage of a situation

to be right behind the eight ball
to be in a position of extreme disadvantage

to cut both ways
to involve both advantages and disadvantages of similar significance

to draw first blood
to get an advantage

to expose one's flank
to allow others to take advantage of one

to feather one's own next
to improperly arrange a transaction on behalf of others to one's own financial advantage

to fill a vacuum
to take advantage of an opportunity not acted on by others

to gain the upper hand
to attain, after some effort, an advantage over another person

to get the jump on someone
to get an advantage over a person

to get the worst of all worlds
to get a series of disadvantages without achieving any corresponding advantages

to give someone the edge
to give a person an advantage over others

to have a head start
to have an advantage over others

to have a leading edge
to have an advantage

to have someone over a barrel
to take advantage of someone's weakened position in relation to oneself

to have the high ground
to have an advantage in moral terms

to hijack a debate
to involve oneself in the public discussion of some matter and turn that discussion to one's advantage

to jump at the opportunity
to enthusiastically take immediate advantage of a good chance

to keep the ball rolling
to take advantage of the existing momentum or to participate actively

to kick a man when he is down
to take unfair advantage of a person already in difficulty

to make a rod for one's own back
to act in disregard of likely disadvantages for oneself

to play right into someone's hands
to act so as to give a person an unintended advantage

to run with something
to take advantage of some current development

to see something through rose-colored spectacles
to appreciate only the advantages and to completely disregard the disadvantages

to squeeze the last drop out of something
to get the maximum advantage out of some favorable situation

to strike while the iron is hot
to take advantage of a situation which cannot last

to suck the lemon dry
to get the maximum advantage out of some favorable situation

to take something lying down
to accept a disadvantage without protest

to take up the slack
to take advantage of surplus capacity

to throw out the baby with the bathwater
to discard a major benefit in the course of obtaining a comparatively minor advantage

to use all the weapons at one's disposal
to utilize all available advantages

to want the best of both worlds
to unreasonably desire to get some advantage without incurring a corresponding disadvantage

what one loses on the swings one gains on the roundabouts
there are advantages and disadvantages which offset each other

AGREEMENT

a bone of contention
the subject matter of violent disagreement

a sweetheart deal
an agreement negotiated in private without full regard to the interests of those affected

that washes with me
I agree

to be at odds with someone
to disagree with a person

to be of one mind
(of several people) to be agreed

to come to the party
to agree to someone's terms

to cross swords with someone
to have a disagreement with another person

to lock someone into some arrangement
to create an agreement which cannot be broken by one of the parties

to ram something down someone's throat
to pressure another person into accepting an idea with which he does not agree

to see eye to eye with someone
to agree

to set the seal on something
to confirm absolutely that something is agreed

to sign on the dotted line
to confirm one's agreement

AIM

a crusade
an aggressive campaign to achieve some political or social objective

a gun with no bullets
something incomplete and therefore useless for the desired purpose

a moving target
an objective subject to constant revision

an unholy alliance
a working relationship for a nefarious purpose between unlikely partners

any stick to beat a dog
any excuse will do if it serves one's purpose

it was touch and go
there were considerable risks—the objective was achieved, but only just

one would give one's eye teeth for something
a person would very much like to achieve some objective

overkill
more action than really required for the purpose

path
means of achieving an objective

something has done the trick
something has achieved the desired purpose

target
objective

the devil can cite scripture for his purpose
a person can quote a respectable or hostile authority while advocating a disreputable cause of his own (from Shakespeare's MERCHANT OF VENICE)

there are many ways to cook eggs
there are many ways to achieve an objective

to beat someone to the punch
to get to some objective ahead of some keen rival

to deliver the goods
to achieve the objective

to earmark
to allocate to a specific purpose

to engage in pump priming
to spend public money with the aim of attracting parochial electoral support

to get a magic carpet ride to something
to be very fortunate in achieving some objective

to go down a particular track
to make decisions aimed at a particular goal

to go for the gold
to aim for victory (refers to Olympic medals)

to hit the mark
to achieve one's object or to make the correct decision (refers to archery)

to join forces
to cooperate with one another in order to achieve a common objective

to kill two birds with one stone
to achieve a second objective in the course of achieving the first objective

to leave someone out in the cold
to deny a desired objective to a person

to pull oneself together
to cease acting without purpose or enthusiasm

to score a goal
to achieve an objective

to set one's sights on something
to aim to achieve something

to stake a claim
to indicate one's desire to obtain something

to steamroll something through
to use enormous force to achieve an objective

to want something both ways
to desire two mutually exclusive objectives

to zero in on a target
to move directly toward one's objective

ALTERNATIVE

all roads lead to Rome
all alternatives will have the same outcome

between the devil and the deep blue sea
to be faced with two equally unpalatable alternatives which cannot both be avoided

if the mountain will not come to Mahomet then Mahomet will go to the mountain
on recognizing that one has insufficient power to effect one's most desired solution, one decides to make do with the next best alternative

in another vein
as an alternative way of looking at things

it is a toss-up
either alternative is equally acceptable

the horns of a dilemma
the unpalatable alternatives between which a choice must be made

to be at the crossroads
to need to choose between several mutually exclusive alternatives

to be between Scylla and Charybdis
to be faced with two equally unpalatable alternatives which cannot both be avoided (refers to the voyage of Ulysses)

to be of two minds
to be undecided between two alternatives

to be tied down
to have responsibilities precluding alternative activities

to fall between two stools
not to fit neatly into either of two available alternatives and waver between them

to have other irons in the fire
to have the opportunity to do something else as an alternative

to pre-empt some issue
to deliberately do something which has the effect of limiting the range of alternative approaches to a matter

to shop around
to explore alternatives

to signpost something
to give an indication of the alternatives available

to sit on the fence
to refuse to choose between two alternatives

to take stock
to contemplate the alternatives

to want to have one's cake and eat it too
to want two mutually exclusive alternatives

to weigh two alternative propositions in the balance
to assess the relative significance of two alternative propositions

variations on a theme
alternative approaches in similar vein

ANGER

I will have his guts for garters
I am extremely angry and dissatisfied with him

fireworks
aggressive behavior because of anger

to be a red rag to a bull
to be something which makes a person very angry and very excited (refers to the erroneous belief that the color red, rather than the motion of waving, excites a bull)

to be after someone's blood
to be keen to make a person the victim of an angry confrontation

to be purple with rage
to be very angry

to bite one's lip
to control one's anger

to blow one's top
to show anger (refers to a volcano)

to blow up
(of a person) to express rage

to explode
(of a person) to express rage

to fire a volley at someone
to send a series of angry messages to someone

to fly off the handle
to show irrational anger

to foam at the mouth
to show anger

to hit the roof
to be very angry

to jump up and down
to show excitement or anger or frustration

to kick the cat
to take out one's anger on some innocent party

to make someone's blood boil
to make a person very angry

to raise someone's hackles
to make a person angry

to see blood
to be very angry

to see red
to become very angry

ANNOYANCE

an eager beaver
a person with great drive and enthusiasm even if this causes annoyance to others

to be a thorn in someone's flesh
to be a person whose persistent presence and righteous views annoy

to breathe down someone's neck
to cause annoyance to another person by remaining in his vicinity or by supervising him too closely; or to be narrowly behind another person in some competitive situation

to drive someone up the wall
to annoy another person by one's actions

to get on someone's nerves
by one's behavior to cause annoyance to a person

to get someone's back up
to annoy or antagonize a person

to get under someone's skin
to annoy another person through stupidity

to have the patience of a saint
to endure annoyances with particular calm

to kick heads in
to demonstrate annoyance at or dislike of certain persons

to kick someone in the teeth
to take action which demonstrates annoyance at or dislike of a person

to rub someone up the wrong way
to annoy someone with actions failing to recognize his current mood

APPROVAL

a seal of approval
confirmation that something is satisfactory

to frown on something
to disapprove of some matter

to get the nod
to receive approval

to give a thumbs up
to approve or grant permission (refers to sign given by Roman emperor sparing a life)

to give one's blessing to something
to indicate one's approval of something

to look at someone sideways
to silently and politely indicate one's disapproval

to shake one's head
to indicate disbelief or wonder or disapproval

ARGUMENT

a battle royal
a fight or argument with many simultaneous participants

a political football
a political issue which is not being debated on its merits

ammunition
arguments helpful to a case

an argument holding water
a debating point of substance

eyeball to eyeball
confronting each other and taking account of each other's reactions

mealy-mouthed
not at all forceful in debate

myopia
the inability to appreciate an argument (lit., short-sightedness)

not to have a leg to stand on
to have one's arguments completely demolished or to be without acceptable excuse or explanation

shifting sands
arguments which are constantly being changed

that argument is wearing a bit thin
that is a very weak case

the other side of the coin
the arguments for the opposite point of view

the thread
the connecting link of a set of arguments

to act as a devil's advocate
to put a point of view which one does not hold in order to draw out the best arguments regarding a proposition (refers to a church official vetting a candidate for sainthood)

to argue the toss
to dispute a decision

to argue till the cows come home
to argue forever

to be after someone's blood
to be keen to make a person the victim of an angry confrontation

to be an open and shut case
to be an unarguable proposition (a phrase popular in detective novels and probably a play on the two meanings of the word "case")

to be on shaky ground
not to have strong arguments

to be shot to ribbons
(of an argument) to be utterly discredited

to belt someone over the head
to override someone's views or arguments

to bring out one's biggest guns
to use the most impressive persons or arguments

to buy into some argument
to seek to participate in some discussion

to confront someone head-on
to confront a person

to drive a wedge between two persons
to set out to cause two persons to confront each other

to expose holes
to expose weaknesses in an argument

to face the music
to accept responsibility when confronted by one's critics

to give ground
to make some concessions or to retreat or to concede some arguments

to go on till one is blue in the face
to argue for a long time

to have an ace up one's sleeve
to hold an impressive counter-argument in reserve

to hijack a debate
to involve oneself in the public discussion of some matter and turn that discussion to one's advantage

to keep one's powder dry
to retain key arguments or resources in reserve for use later

to lead someone up the garden path
to mislead a person by deliberately fallacious arguments

to lock horns with someone
to have an argument with another person

to parry some argument
to deflect some argument (refers to fencing)

to play every card in the pack
to try very hard and use every conceivable argument

to prepare one's ground
to get ready for a confrontation

to score a point
to make a clever contribution in the course of debate

to shoot someone down in flames
to utterly destroy another person's arguments

to tackle someone head-on
to confront a person

to take off the gloves
to fight mercilessly or to debate with great ferocity

to take the wind out of someone's sails
to upset a person by anticipating his actions or using arguments which he was proposing to use

to talk one's book
to present arguments which, while plausible, are really designed to foster one's vested interest

to tip the balance
to be further information or argument which results in an issue which could have been decided either way to be determined in a particular way

to use every trick in the book
to try very hard and use every conceivable argument

to weigh in with a particular argument
to produce a strong argument

to wheel someone in
to bring a person along for a confrontation

what is sauce for the goose is sauce for the gander
arguments which apply in one case also apply in another

BEHAVIOR

I fear the Greeks even when they bear gifts
I am suspicious of generous behavior from traditional opponents (from Virgil's AENEID, in reference to the Trojan horse)

a watchdog
a person or organization monitoring behavior

an article of faith
a fundamental belief on which certain behavior is based

fireworks
aggressive behavior because of anger

guiding light
yardstick for ethical behavior

horseplay
boisterous and undignified behavior

not to put a foot wrong
to behave impeccably

the order of the day
the customary behavior

to be a bad egg
to engage in dishonest behavior

to be beyond the pale
to be socially unacceptable, especially for unacceptable standards or behavior

to be left with a nasty taste in one's mouth
to be appalled or very disappointed at another person's unethical behavior to one

to blow the whistle on someone
to report a person's improper behavior to the authorities or to publicize it

to get on someone's nerves
by one's behavior to cause annoyance to a person

to keep one's eye on someone
to supervise a person or to monitor a person's activities and behavior

to lay it on the line
to make clear what the accepted rules of behavior are

to lead with one's chin
by one's brash behavior to virtually invite one's opponents to take action against one

to make an exhibition of oneself
to behave in a way which invites ridicule

to make feathers fly
to cause trouble to those misbehaving

to play monkey tricks on someone
to engage in discreditable behavior affecting a person

to pull one's socks up
to set out to improve or correct one's inadequate behavior or performance

to ruffle someone's feathers
to engage in behavior which irritates another person

to set tongues wagging
to behave in a way which encourages scandal mongers

to sow wild oats
to indulge in foolish behavior while a young adult

to step out of line
to infringe accepted rules of behavior

to teach someone a lesson
to inflict something unpleasant on a person in the hope that it will lead to a change in his behavior

to watch one's step
to be on the lookout for danger or to set out to improve one's behavior

transparent
(of behavior, etc.) to be easily seen as not genuine

BELIEF

I'll eat my hat if so-and-so happens
I do not believe that so-and-so will happen

a bible basher
a person who makes unwelcome attempts to force his religious beliefs on others

a doubting Thomas
a person who refuses to believe claims in absence of proof (John 20:25)

a gut feeling
a belief based purely on intuition and unsupported by facts or evidence

a soul brother
a person of similar ideals

an article of faith
a fundamental belief on which certain behavior is based

anyone could be forgiven for believing that
it is understandable that people would believe that

he is your man
he conforms to an ideal

the fold
the body of believers (refers to an enclosure for sheep)

to be someone after one's own heart
to be a person who shares one's beliefs

to be too big for one's boots
to have an unwarranted belief as to one's capabilities or status

to be wide off the mark
to have a belief which is far removed from the true position

to believe in the tooth fairy
to be particularly gullible

to go to the barricades for something
to very strongly believe in something

to preach to the converted
to say something to those who already believe in it

to put someone in the pillory
to hold a person up to ridicule for his beliefs

to sacrifice something on the altar of some belief
to give up some benefit as a matter of principle

to sail under false colors
to pretend that one's real character or beliefs are different from what they really are

to shake one's head
to indicate disbelief or wonder or disapproval

to show one's true colors
to disclose one's real character or beliefs

to stick to one's guns
to continue to hold certain beliefs notwithstanding opposition by others

to take something as gospel
to believe that something is true

Utopian
ideally perfect (refers to the mythical island in Sir Thomas More's UTOPIA)

volte face
a reversal of previously-held beliefs (French, ''a turning around'')

BENEFIT

a bird in the hand is worth two in the bush
a benefit currently available is more valuable than a seemingly much larger benefit which may or may not be achieved in the future

a mare's nest
a discovery with illusory benefits

a milch cow
an easy and plentiful source of some desired benefit

bargaining chips
benefits which can be conceded in negotiations in order to obtain some advantage

every cloud has a silver lining
there are benefits even in seemingly adverse situations

fruitless
yielding no benefit

heads I win—tails you lose
whichever way this matter goes I will benefit at your expense

manna from heaven
unexpected benefits (Exodus 16:15)

mirage
illusory benefit

that is just sour grapes
those are disparaging remarks made only because he is peeved and resentful at someone else's better fortune

the melody lingers on
the benefit of past actions remains

to be cream on top of the milk
to be an additional benefit in an already satisfactory scenario

to be icing on top of the cake
to be an additional benefit in an already satisfactory scenario

to be the salt of the earth
to be a person whose ordinary efforts benefit the community (Matthew 5:13)

to cast pearls before swine
to confer valuable benefits on someone who neither recognizes nor appreciates them

to get on a gravy train
to take steps to become a recipient of benefits which are available but undeserved

to get some mileage out of something
to benefit from something

to go along for the ride
to seek to benefit from a project in which others contribute the effort

to hand over something on a silver platter
to provide a valuable benefit for virtually nothing

to laugh all the way to the bank
to appreciate one's good fortune

to learn a lesson
to benefit from one's experience

to let blood
to allow some harm as the price for achieving some greater benefit

to look a gift horse in the mouth
to be suspicious about a benefit which has been volunteered

to mortgage the future
to get benefits now but at a cost in due course

to pick someone's brain
to get the benefit of another person's knowledge and experience

to ride on the back of someone
without effort to benefit from the prior efforts of others

to ride on the sheep's back
to benefit from the production of wool

to rub off on someone
to benefit a person through an association which increases his skills

to sacrifice something on the altar of some belief
to give up some benefit as a matter of principle

to salvage something out of the wreck
to achieve some minor benefits out of a disastrous situation

to start from scratch
to commerce something without the benefit of any past activity

to throw out the baby with the bathwater
to discard a major benefit in the course of obtaining a comparatively minor advantage

vulture
person benefiting from another's misfortune

windfall
unexpected good fortune

BIGNESS

a big bang
a sudden major change in the environment

a big shot
an important person

a big wheel
an important person

a bird in the hand is worth two in the bush
a benefit currently available is more valuable than a seemingly much larger benefit which may or may not be achieved in the future

a golden handshake
a large payment in connection with or as an inducement to retirement

a landslide
an electoral result involving victory or defeat by an unexpectedly large margin

a mansize job
a large task worth doing well

a mosaic
something with a large number of different aspects to it

a sausage machine
the turning out of large volumes without particular thought

a tempest in a teacup
a controversy about a minor matter but one which looms large in the minds of the parties

a toehold
an opportunity small in itself but with the potential to lead to bigger things

in for a penny—in for a pound
once something is commenced it ought to be finished; or if one is willing to take a small risk then one might as well take a bigger one

more chiefs than Indians
a disproportionately large number of supervisors

not to be Robinson Crusoe
to be one of a large number of people with a common problem (from Daniel Defoe's ROBINSON CRUSOE)

someone's eyes are bigger than his stomach
a person is unrealistic

speak softly and carry a big stick
be polite to your potential enemies but maintain an active and visible defense capability (from a speech by Theodore Roosevelt in 1901)

the big smoke
the big city

the lion's share
the biggest portion

to be a big fish in a little pond
to be a person holding an important office but in an unimportant organization

to be a money spinner
to produce large profits easily and quickly

to be a small cog in a large wheel
to be a relatively unimportant person in a large organization

to be the thin end of the wedge
by conceding a small point to create an undesirable precedent for much larger issues

to be the tip of the iceberg
to be only a very small portion of a much larger but less obvious whole

to be too big for one's boots
to have an unwarranted belief as to one's capabilities or status

to be too big for one's breeches
to have an exaggerated idea of one's own importance

to be unable to keep people away with a big stick
to be faced with a large crowd or much demand

to bring out one's biggest guns
to use the most impressive persons or arguments

to crawl out of the woodwork
to turn up unexpectedly and in large numbers

to have a leg in
to have an opportunity which has the potential to lead to bigger things

to have deep pockets
to have large financial resources

to only scratch the surface
to deal with only a small portion of a much larger whole

to pay a king's ransom
to pay a very large sum

to pay something back with interest
to return a small favor with a bigger favor or to extract retribution of greater value than the circumstances warrant

to pick the eyes out of something
to choose the most valuable items from among a large number

to stand over someone with a big stick
to intimidate a person in order to get him to act in a particular way

to steamroll something through
to use enormous force to achieve an objective

to swarm out
to gather in large numbers

to wield a big stick
to exert power

CARE

a bull in a china shop
a careless person likely to cause great damage

he must have a long spoon that sups with the devil
great care is needed when negotiating deals with disreputable parties

not to just pick something out of a hat
to choose carefully, after weighing all the considerations

to handpick someone
to carefully choose a person for his individual attributes

to keep a weather eye out for something
to look out with particular care

to look to one's laurels
to be careful not to lose one's reputation for some skill

to need to watch one's back
to find it necessary to take care in case others act against one's interests

to slip under one's guard
to cause a mistake to be made despite care being taken to prevent this

to smell out something
to discover something by careful investigation

to start off on the right foot
to commence an operation with great care to do it correctly

to think twice before doing something
to consider with particular care

to tread lightly
to be careful

to watch one's p's and q's
to be very careful (may refer to pints and quarts of beer on a hotel slate or to easily-confused printer's type)

CHANCE

be a devil!
take a chance!

the hand of fate
chance

to be in the lap of the gods
to be a matter of pure chance (refers to wax tablets inscribed with requests and placed on the knees of statues of Greek gods)

to be the luck of the draw
to be a chance result

to cross someone's path
to meet another person by chance

to cruel someone's pitch
to spoil a person's chances

to have one's beady eyes on something
to await the chance to acquire something to which one is not properly entitled

to jump at the opportunity
to enthusiastically take immediate advantage of a good chance

to look for a needle in a haystack
to attempt something with a very small chance of success

to take pot luck
to take whatever happens by chance to be available

CHANGE

a big bang
a sudden major change in the environment

a chameleon
a person without character who changes his stance all the time to reflect the current circumstances

a leopard cannot change his spots
each person is born with certain unalterable characteristics

a new broom
a changed regime which is likely to alter the status quo

a sacred cow
an institution so well established that it is virtually unalterable

new guard
changed regime

nimble-footed
quick to change the direction of one's activities when circumstances warrant

shifting sands
arguments which are constantly being changed

stiff cheese!
circumstances which may be unwelcome but which will not be altered and in respect of which no great sympathy is felt

that takes on added color
there are now further facts which alter the appearance of a matter

the cold wind of change
the unpleasant realities of new circumstances

the devil one knows is better than the devil one does not know
the status quo is more comfortable than change

the ink is hardly dry
something intended to last a long time is to be changed shortly after its establishment

the tide has turned
conditions have changed

the wheel has turned
circumstances have changed

to be a breath of fresh air
to be a pleasant change from the past

to be a stormy petrel
a person who disturbs a pleasant state of affairs by agitating for change

to be carved in marble
to be virtually unalterable

to be cast in bronze
to be virtually unalterable

to be in a rut
to lead a dull life, with no change from long-established habits

to be in a state of flux
to be subject to continuous change

to change one's mind
to alter the views which one had previously formed

to change one's tune
to alter one's publicly-expressed views

to change tack
to alter one's direction

to change the whole picture
to alter the major assumptions on which some assessment was based

to cry "wolf"
to repeatedly raise an unjustified concern with the result that one will be ignored when the circumstances change

to die a natural death
by virtue of changed circumstances or the effluxion of time, to be no longer relevant

to drift apart
to lose contact or to change feelings once held in common

to have a change of heart
to form a new view in place of a strongly-held previous view

to leave one's mark on something
to be responsible for permanently altering the way something is operated

to play it by ear
to develop one's strategy to always fit in with circumstances as they change from time to time

to put a new face on something
to alter the way something should be regarded

to rearrange the deckchairs on the Titanic
to take some initiative which is quite useless because it does not take much greater change into account

to set something in concrete
to make something virtually unalterable

to swap horses in midstream
to change direction during the course of a project

to teach someone a lesson
to inflict something unpleasant on a person in the hope that it will lead to a change in his behavior

to tinker at the edges
to make minor or cosmetic changes without affecting the substance

to wither on the vine
by virtue of changed circumstances or the effluxion of time, to be no longer relevant

CONFUSION

a tower of Babel
a noisy and confused assembly (Genesis 11)

all hell broke loose
great confusion erupted

to be all at sea
to be confused as to what is going on and what to do next

to be at sixes and sevens
to be confused, concerned and undecided

to be in a fog
to be in a state of confusion

to get into a knot
to get into state of confusion

to lose one's head
to become confused

to muddy the waters
to deliberately confuse an issue by creating a diversion

to set up a smokescreen
to deliberately confuse an issue by disguising its salient features

to watch one's p's and q's
to be very careful (may refer to pints and quarts of beer on a hotel slate or to easily-confused printer's type)

CORRECTNESS

a step in the right direction
the first in a series of measures designed to correct some problem

it is on the tip of my tongue
the right word has momentarily escaped me

it is pointing in the right direction
success looks likely

just what the doctor ordered
exactly right

mark my words
you will find out that I am right

one looks for elephants in elephant country
one needs to search in the right place

to be in the right ballpark
to be approximately correct

to be up to the mark
to be of the right standard

to have one's heart in the right place
to have a well-developed social conscience

to head someone in the right direction
to assist a person to achieve something

to hit the bull's eye
to make the correct decision

to hit the mark
to achieve one's object or to make the correct decision (refers to archery)

to hit the nail right on the head
to astutely come to the correct conclusion

to play one's cards right
to approach a matter sensibly

to play to the gallery
to do something which appeals to the general public rather than something which is right

to pull one's socks up
to set out to improve or correct one's inadequate behavior or performance

to see daylight
to get the right answer

to set someone on the right road
to show a person how to go about doing something

to start off on the right foot
to commence an operation with great care to do it correctly

to strike the right key
to find the appropriate solution

to strike the right note
to make a good impression

COURAGE

a stiff upper lip
obstinate courage in the face of pain or adversity

chicken-hearted
showing little courage

to be a brave soldier
to be brave

to be a man of steel
to be a person with moral courage

to be of good heart
to be brave in adversity

to brave the water
to enter a venture with courage and determination

to have a heart of oak
to be brave

to make a last-ditch stand
to make a brave effort to stave off final defeat

to present a happy face to the world
bravely to gloss over one's problems

to put a brave face on it
to face adversity cheerfully

to put one's head on the block
to have the courage of one's convictions

to stick one's neck out
to have the courage of one's convictions or to take a calculated risk

CRITICISM

a honeymoon
a short period enjoyed by a newcomer to some activity before his performance is criticized

an Aunt Sally
a person who can readily be singled out and criticized as the proxy for a group

people in glass houses should not throw stones
those who are less than perfect are foolish to criticize others

the pot calling the kettle black
a person criticizing another person without realizing his own even greater shortcomings

to act as a sounding board
to give, on request, constructive criticisms of ideas tentatively held

to attract flak
to attract criticism

to be a sitting shot
to be a person whose actions make him very vulnerable to criticism

to be in the hot seat
to hold a position requiring one to answer criticism or accusations

to be like water off a duck's back
(of advice or criticism) to be completely rejected

to be on the warpath
to be on the lookout for faults which can be criticized

to bulldoze some proposal through
to ensure the passage of some measure in complete disregard of criticism or opposition

to cover oneself
to create evidence so that if one is criticized or accused later on, one can clear one's name

to draw fire
to encounter criticism

to engage in back biting
to criticize in an unfriendly manner

to face the music
to accept responsibility when confronted by one's critics

to fire a salvo at someone
to present a series of criticisms to a person

to get off someone's back
to leave a person alone to carry on without constant criticism

to give someone a bit of stick
to mildly criticize a person

to have a shot at someone
to use subtly chosen words implying friendly criticism but designed to embarrass another person

to have a thick skin
to be impervious to criticism

to have the hide of a rhinoceros
to be totally unaffected by and unresponsive to valid criticism

to hold fire
to defer criticizing

to leave oneself wide open
to act in such a way that one's opponents will find much which can be easily criticized

to nail one's colors to the mast
to publicly declare one's position and to maintain it in the face of criticism

to nitpick
to criticize a person in respect to very minor matters

to pour vitriol on something
to sharply criticize something

to run the gauntlet
to be subjected to criticism (from the Spanish word for ''passage,'' in reference to punishment inflicted on delinquents made to run between two files of soldiers)

to stand in the breach
to bear the brunt of criticisms

to turn one's guns on someone
to criticize a person

DANGER

a minefield
a course of great hidden danger or of difficulties not obvious on a first encounter

pitfall
unsuspected danger

slippery path
dangerous course of action

someone's head is on the block
a person is in danger of having his appointment terminated

to be a wolf in sheep's clothing
to be a hypocrite or to be dangerous although masquerading as something harmless (Matthew 7:15)

to be on a knife edge
to be in danger

to be on the razor's edge
to be in great danger

to bell the cat
to do some dangerous but highly useful mission (refers to a fable in which none of the mice was willing to put a warning bell on a cat)

to fight fire with fire
to counter a dangerous situation by making an equally dangerous move

to founder on the shoals of something
to come to grief because of unexpected dangers

to have a sword of Damocles hanging over one
to be in imminent danger despite normal activity going on all around one

to have a tiger by the tail
to be involved in an activity which is much more dangerous than one had realized

to push someone over the brink
by a small action to cause the absolute ruin (financially or emotionally) of someone already in peril

to put one's head in the noose
to recklessly and unnecessarily expose oneself to great danger

to put one's head into the lion's mouth
to recklessly expose oneself to great danger

to ride out the storm
to come safely through some dangerous situation

to sail close to the wind
to act in a very dangerous manner

to see red lights flashing
to be conscious of the danger

to skate on thin ice
to act in disregard of obvious danger

to walk a tightrope
to do something very dangerous

to watch one's step
to be on the lookout for danger or to set out to improve one's behavior

DECISION

a landmark ruling
a decision marking a turning point in the way a matter is approached

fork in the road
turning point for decisions

if the mountain will not come to Mahomet then Mahomet will go to the mountain
on recognizing that one has insufficient power to effect one's most desired solution, one decides to make do with the next best alternative

the jury is still out
no decision has yet been made or the public has not yet given an indication of its views

to argue the toss
to dispute a decision

to be at sixes and sevens
to be confused, concerned and undecided

to be at the cutting edge of something
to be in a position where important decisions need to be made

to be in two minds
to be undecided between two alternatives

to be out of someone's hands
to be up for decision by a different person

to bite one's fingernails
to anxiously await a decision

to cross the Rubicon
to make an irreversible decision in regard to some commitment

to go down a particular track
to make decisions aimed at a particular goal

to have something to chew on
to have firm facts on which to base a decision

to hit the bull's eye
to make the correct decision

to hit the mark
to achieve one's object or to make the correct decision (refers to archery)

to hold a gun at someone's head
to put pressure on a person to make a particular decision regardless of his desires in the matter

to hold the power to do something in the hollow of one's hand
to have the right to make crucial decisions

to lose one's nerve
to abandon, out of fear, a decision to do something

to need the wisdom of Solomon
to be faced with the need to make a difficult decision (1 Kings 3:16-28)

to pin someone down
to find a person willing to accept blame or responsibility or to force a person to announce a decision or concede a point

to pull strings
to use one's special influence with those in a position to make favorable decisions which might otherwise not be forthcoming

to tip the balance
to provide further information or argument which results in an issue, which could have been decided either way, being determined in a particular way

to tip the scales
to be a factor which in combination with other factors results in a particular decision which would otherwise not have been reached

to toss up
to decide on a fairly arbitrary basis

when it comes to the crunch
when the matter comes up for decision

DEVELOPMENT

a thought in the back of one's mind
an undeveloped idea

a wild card
an unexpected development

an ugly duckling
a person initially thought unintelligent who develops and becomes brilliant (refers to a cygnet in a brood of ducks in a children's story of that name by Hans Christian Andersen)

framework
outline of a proposal, on which further details can be developed

that is a turn up for the books
that is a surprising favorable development

the bottom line
the conclusion which matters or the net effect of a series of developments

to be a turn up for the books
to be a surprising development

to blossom
(of a person's attributes) to develop

to develop a head of steam
to gain momentum

to find one's feet
to develop one's skills

to keep an ear to the ground
to be well informed as to current developments

to mark time
to do nothing while awaiting developments

to play it by ear
to develop one's strategy to always fit in with circumstances as they change from time to time

to run with something
to take advantage of some current development

to see the big picture
to have the vision and imagination enabling a project to be developed as part of a bigger whole

to see which way the cat jumps
to await developments

DIFFICULTY

a baptism of fire
the commencement of an operation which presented great difficulty

a fair-weather friend
a person purporting to be a friend who offers no support in difficult times

a minefield
a source of great hidden danger or of difficulties not obvious on a first encounter

a prima donna
a person with an exaggerated opinion of his own importance which makes relations with others needlessly difficult (Italian, "first lady")

a problem child
a source of unnecessary difficulty

a sixty-four thousand dollar question
a pertinent but very difficult question (refers to a TV quiz show in which an initial prize doubles with the successful answering of progressively more difficult questions)

a sticky patch
a period fraught with difficulties

any port in a storm
anything which helps to avoid difficulties is welcome

blood, sweat and tears
hard work and much effort

elbow grease
hard manual work

here's the rub
this is where a difficulty arises (a term used in lawn bowling)

no sweat
this presents no difficulty

ready-made
easily fabricated or available without difficulty

road blocks
difficulties

search for the Holy Grail
work toward a difficult goal (refers to a vessel supposedly used by Christ at the last supper and featuring in the Arthurian legends)

someone is a hard nut to crack
it is very difficult to persuade a person to do something

stumbling block
an impediment or difficulty preventing the easy completion of some project or a dilemma involving a moral issue

that is hard to take
it is difficult to face up to the reality of this

the show must go on
despite difficulties the action in contemplation has to proceed

the very best of British luck
you will have a hard time of it, but you carry my best wishes

to back someone into a corner
to drive a person into a position from which escape is difficult

to batten down the hatches
to get ready for expected difficulties

to be a cross which one has to bear
to be a difficulty which one has to endure

to be a fish out of water
to be in difficulty by virtue of being in a strange environment

to be a handful
to be difficult to manage

to be a hard act to follow
to be an impressive performance, not easily matched by the next person

to be between a rock and a hard place
to be faced with two equally difficult and uncomfortable choices

to be in a hole
to experience some difficulties

to be in a jam
to be in difficulties

to be in a pickle
to be in difficulties

to be in a quagmire
to be in great difficulty

to be in a stew
to be in difficulties

to be in deep water
to be in great difficulty

to be in hot water
to be in trouble or to be in difficulty

to be in the same boat
to share a common set of difficulties

to be in the soup
to be in great difficulties

to be no bed of roses
to be difficult or uncomfortable

to be no fun
to be difficult

to be on a sticky wicket
to face some difficulties (refers to cricket)

to be out of one's depth
to find that some issue is too complicated or too difficult

to be out of the woods
the previous difficulties have been overcome

to be pushing uphill
to face difficulties

to be sheer murder
to be extremely unpleasant or difficult; or to be an inglorious defeat

to be the hard core
to be the central and most difficult problem

to be up a gum tree
to be in difficulty or at the end of one's resources

to bite the bullet
to face up to the difficulties of a situation

to catch someone in a bind
to find a person in a difficulty from which he cannot readily extricate himself

to face a rocky road ahead
to be likely to encounter difficulties

to fall on one's feet
surprisingly to succeed despite difficulties

to fight an uphill battle
to face difficulties or to have formidable opposition

to get around some difficulty
to use an approach which overcomes some difficulty

to give someone hell
to make life difficult for a person

to grab the devil by the tail
to face up to difficulties

to grasp the nettle
to deal with a neglected difficulty

to have a dream run
to encounter no difficulties

to have a hard row to hoe
to be a difficult assignment

to have a job in front of one
to face difficulties

to have one's work cut out to do something
it will be difficult to achieve something

to have the cards stacked against one
to be faced with many difficulties frustrating a project

to have the odds stacked against one
to be faced with many difficulties frustrating a project

to heave a sigh of relief
to express satisfaction at the achievement of a solution to a difficult problem

to iron out something
to sort out a difficult problem

to jump a hurdle
to overcome a problem or difficulty

to kick a man when he is down
to take unfair advantage of a person already in difficulty

to leave someone in the lurch
to desert a person who is in difficulties (refers to the score in certain games)

to make a good fist of something
to be successful in a difficult task

to need the wisdom of Solomon
to be faced with the need to make a difficult decision (1 Kings 3:16-28)

to penetrate someone's thick skull
to make a person understand something difficult or acknowledge something unwelcome

to plot a safe course through troubled waters
to make a plan which overcomes certain difficulties

to put one's thinking cap on
to concentrate on finding a solution to a difficult problem

to put something into the "too hard" basket
to defer consideration of a difficult issue

to run into heavy weather
to encounter difficulties

to sharpen one's ax
to get ready for a difficult task

to sink deeper into the mire
to get into further difficulties

to sink deeper into the mud
to get into even greater difficulty

to skirt around the difficulties
to act as though the difficulties did not exist

to smell trouble
to perceive difficulties

to soldier on
to carry on despite difficulties

to strike a snag
to encounter a difficulty

to take the bull by the horns
to come to grips with the realities of a difficult problem

to take the rough with the smooth
to accept the hardships of life along with its pleasant features

to tiptoe around the difficulties
to act as though the difficulties did not exist

to tread a fine line
cautiously to take action in circumstances whether either too much or too little will cause difficulties

to tread the thin line
cautiously to take action in circumstances whether either too much or too little will cause difficulties

to wear one's crown of thorns
to have one's own difficulties (John 19:5)

DISAPPOINTMENT

a damp squib
disappointingly ineffective action (refers to fireworks which fail to go off)

someone's face fell
someone registered obvious disappointment

someone's jaw dropped
someone registered obvious disappointment, incredulity, or shock

to be a bitter pill to swallow
to be a great humiliation and disappointment which have to be endured

to be a severe blow
to be a great disappointment

to be devastated
to be extremely disappointed

to be left with a nasty taste in one's mouth
to be appalled or very disappointed at another person's unethical behavior to one

DISPLEASURE

I will have his guts for garters
I am extremely angry and dissatisfied with him

a damp squib
disappointingly ineffective action (refers to fireworks which fail to go off)

he would turn in his grave
he would have been very surprised or displeased if he had known while still alive

someone's face fell
someone registered obvious disappointment

someone's jaw dropped
someone registered obvious disappointment

to be a bitter pill to swallow
to be a great humiliation and disappointment which have to be endured

to be a severe blow
to be a great disappointment

to be at the end of one's tether
to be frustrated by a lack of knowledge, authority or patience

to be cut to pieces
to be very upset

to be devastated
to be extremely disappointed

to be left with a nasty taste in one's mouth
to be appalled or very disappointed at another person's unethical behavior to one

to be someone's bete noire
to be a person whose ideas and actions cause upset and loathing in another person (French, ''black beast'')

to bite someone's head off
to rudely express displeasure at some person

to break someone's heart
to act in a way causing great upset to another person

to give someone a black look
to indicate one's displeasure with a person

to go through the roof
(of a person) to be very upset or (of prices) to escalate greatly

to knit one's brows
to indicate one's displeasure

to make a noise about something
to complain or express dissatisfaction about something

to open up a festering sore
to upset a person by drawing attention to a long-standing grievance

to put someone's nose out of joint
to upset another person

to take the wind out of someone's sails
to upset a person by anticipating his actions or using arguments which he was proposing to use

to throw brickbats at someone
to express displeasure with a person

to tread on someone's corns
to upset another person by interfering in his area of responsibility

to tread on someone's toes
to upset another person by interfering in his area of responsibility

to upset the applecart
to engage in conduct disturbing a peaceful state of affairs and thereby cause discomfort

to vote with one's feet
to show one's displeasure by terminating an association

to wave a finger at someone
to indicate mild displeasure at another person's actions

EASE

a milch cow
an easy and plentiful source of some desired benefit

a walkover
an easy victory

distant fields look greener
activities of which one has no experience seem much easier than is really the case

it's a breeze
it is easy

money for jam
remuneration easily earned

not to be all beer and skittles
not to be all pleasant and easy

ready-made
easily fabricated or available without difficulty

stumbling block
an impediment or difficulty preventing the easy completion of some project or a dilemma involving a moral issue

to be laid-down misere
to be very easily accomplished and/or to be certain of outcome (refers to the declaration in certain card games undertaking to win no tricks)

to be a money spinner
to produce large profits easily and quickly

to be a piece of cake
to be very easy or greatly to one's liking

to be able to do something standing on one's head
to be able to do something very easily

to be able to do something with one hand behind one's back
to be able to do something very easily

to be able to eat someone for breakfast
to be able to outwit a person very easily

to be child's play
to be easy or to require only elementary skills and knowledge

to be in clover
to enjoy a life of ease and luxury

to be plain sailing
to be quite straightforward and very easy

to be putty in someone's hands
to be far too easily influenced by another person

to chase every hare
to be easily sidetracked

to die hard
not to give up easily

to get an armchair ride
to be given a particularly easy time

to have a mind of one's own
not to be easily influenced

to have nerves of steel
not to be easily frightened

to leave oneself wide open
to act in such a way that one's opponents will find much which can be easily criticized

to nip something in the bud
to stop some activity in its early stages when stopping it is still relatively easy

to roll off the tongue
to be said very easily

to run rings around someone
to easily outwit another person

to serve something up to someone on a plate
to make something especially easy for a particular person

to smooth the path for someone
to use one's influence to make arrangements so that a person's task will be easier or more readily accomplished

to take something in one's stride
to cope with something easily

to win the prize in a canter
to win very easily

transparent
(of behavior, etc.) to be easily seen as not genuine

EMPLOYMENT

a dead-end position
a job with no prospects of advancement

feather bedding
(industrial relations) creating unnecessary jobs solely to increase employment; (in economics) assisting an inefficient industry by government grants or excessive tariff protection

golden shackles
financial arrangements designed to discourage employees changing employers

rising star
person making good progress in his career

someone's job is on the line
a person's career path is under consideration and/or his present position is at risk

to drum someone out of some organization
to terminate in ignominy a person's employment or membership (refers to the ceremonial cashiering in the army to the beating of parade drums)

to have one's fingers in the till
to steal from one's employer

to hold someone's hand
to give detailed on-the-job training and supervision

to know the ropes
to know how to do one's job

to move on to greener pastures
to commence a new, better career

to swing the lead
to cheat an employer by not working while being paid to do so

to tickle the Peter
to rob one's employer

to turn an honest penny
to earn money out of odd jobs

END

a clean sweep
the complete removal in an election of all sitting members

a dead-end position
a job with no prospects of advancement

a logjam
a stoppage of activity caused by input in greater volume than allowed for

a photo finish
a close result in a contest

at the end of the day
in due course or at the conclusion of a project

cold turkey
the sudden cessation of drugs to an addict

cut it out!
stop doing that!

danse macabre
gruesome final step (French, ''ghastly dance'')

dead and buried
(of some issue) definitely concluded, especially so long ago as to be nearly forgotten

from a to z
from start to finish

from alpha to omega
from start to finish (refers to the first and last letters of the Greek alphabet)

from go to whoa
from start to finish (refers to the command given to horses)

I'll soon stop his little game
his activities are not tolerated and I will ensure that they cease

in for a penny—in for a pound
once something is commenced it ought to be finished; or if one is willing to take a small risk then one might as well take a bigger one

in the wash-up
when everything is finalized

it's not over till the fat lady sings
it is not finished yet

one for the road
a final drink before leaving

saber rattling
hints of retribution if certain conduct does not cease

someone's head is on the block
a person is in danger of having his appointment terminated

stalemate
a final result in which neither party to a dispute is victorious

that wraps it up
that is the end

the bottom line
the conclusion which matters or the net effect of a series of developments

the buck stops here
I accept full responsibility (sign on the desk of Harry S. Truman when president of the United States)

the final countdown
the last stages of something (refers to the launch of space vehicles)

the final straw
the latest step, which, when added to a large number of seemingly harmless previous steps, sets off a disaster resulting from the cumulative effect

the sands are running out
the time available for some action is nearly at an end

the sun has set on something
something has concluded

the tail end of something
the very end of something

this is the end of the road for someone
a person will have no further opportunity to do something

to abandon ship
to abrogate one's responsibilities or to abandon a project

to bale out of something
to abandon an enterprise in anticipation of disaster

to be all over bar the shouting
to be virtually finished

to be in at the death
to be present at the conclusion of something

to be in at the kill
to be present at the climatic finish to something

to be on a treadmill
to be involved in some unpleasant ongoing activity which cannot readily be stopped

to be on one's death bed
(of an organization or a piece of equipment) to be about to cease functioning

to be only a gleam in someone's eyes
to be a long way from final achievement

to be out on one's ear
to have one's services abruptly terminated

to be out the door
to have one's position terminated

to be stopped in one's tracks
suddenly and unexpectedly to be prevented from carrying on with a project

to be the sting in the tail
to be the unexpected unpleasant conclusion

to be up a gum tree
to be in difficulty or at the end of one's resources

to beat a retreat
to abandon some project

to break one's duck
to end a spell without results (refers to cricket)

to break the back of a task
to complete the bulk of the work

to bury the hatchet
to abandon hostilities

to call it a day
to cease involvement with some activity

to call off the dogs
to abandon an audit or other inquiry

to cast prudence to the winds
to cease being prudent

to chop someone off at the socks
to stop someone's proposals prematurely

to close the book on something
to terminate an activity

to come to a full stop
to completely cease activity

to come to a head
to reach culmination

to come to a sticky end
to endure an unpleasant fate

to crystalize
to emerge in its final form

to cut corners
to lower one's standards in order to complete something more quickly

to deal the final hand
to take steps which conclude a matter

to dot the i's and cross the t's
to be meticulous in completing the documentation for a transaction

to drum someone out of some organization
to terminate in ignominy a person's employment or membership (refers to the ceremonial cashiering in the army to the beating of parade drums)

to dry up
to cease

to fall by the wayside
to abandon and not complete what one set out to do

to fetter someone
to stop a person acting on his own initiative

to finish with a bang
to conclude something in grand style

to get on stream
to now operate successfully following the end of a settling-in period

to get rid of the dead wood
to terminate the services of unsatisfactory personnel

to get up off one's butt
to cease being apathetic

to give someone the boot
to terminate a person's appointment

to give the game away
to cease involvement with some activity

to grind to a halt
to cease some activity despite expectations that it would continue

to jettison some proposal
to abandon some proposal as worthless or impracticable

to kill some proposal stone dead
to abandon some proposal completely

to lay some theory to rest
to abandon some theory as being no longer appropriate

to lose heart
to cease being enthusiastic

to lose one's nerve
to abandon, out of fear, a decision to do something

to lose one's touch
to cease to be familiar with something

to lower the boom
to terminate an activity

to make a last-ditch stand
to make a brave effort to stave off final defeat

to nip something in the bud
to stop some activity in its early stages when stopping it is still relatively easy

to peg out
to die (refers to the final stroke in a game of croquet)

to play the last card in the pack
to lower one's standards in a final desperate effort

to play the trump card
to make a final move, thereby defeating one's opponents

to pull oneself together
to cease acting without purpose or enthusiasm

to put a wall around someone
to stop a person associating with others

to put something to bed
to finally dispose of

to put the brake on someone
to stop a person

to put up the shutters
to cease an established activity

to quietly fold up one's tent
to surreptitiously abandon a previously-cherished stance

to receive the coup de grace
to be finished off by an opponent (French, "mercy stroke")

to ring down the curtain on something
to treat something as concluded

to run into a dead end
to get nowhere in an investigation

to run its course
to come to a natural end

to see the light at the end of the tunnel
to be close to finalizing a long exercise

to shelve some proposal
to abandon some proposal

to shut up shop
to cease an established activity

to sound the death knell of something
to indicate the impending end of something

to stem the hemorrhage
to put a stop to the financial losses of a project

to stitch up a deal
to successfully conclude a deal

to strangle some discussion
to cut off some unfinished discussion

to throw someone to the lions
to abandon a person

to tie something up
to finalize the arrangement for something

to tie up the loose ends
to complete the minor outstanding items of some substantially finished project

to turn a complete somersault
to reverse one's established policy

to turn up trumps
to finish up better than expected or to experience unexpected good luck

to vote with one's feet
to show one's displeasure by terminating an association

to walk away with a profit
to achieve a profit on concluding a project

to wrap up a deal
to bring a deal to a successful conclusion

until stumps are drawn
until the project ends

when the crunch comes
when the inevitable conclusion is reached

when the music stops
suddenly and soon (refers to an imminent crisis leading to some resolution of a matter, as in a game of musical chairs)

where the ax falls
who gets terminated

ENTHUSIASM

I would give my right arm for something
I am very keen to acquire something

a fire in someone's belly
great enthusiasm

a shot in the arm
something to revive a person's enthusiasm

an eager beaver
a person with great drive and enthusiasm even if this causes annoyance to others

bright-eyed and bushy-tailed
naive but enthusiastic

deafening silence
great apathy and lack of enthusiasm

half-hearted
unenthusiastic

heart and soul
with great energy

keepers of the flame
persons keen to maintain old traditions

larger than life
in person and full of enthusiasm

lukewarm
unenthusiastic though not hostile

not to break someone's door down
to be quite unenthusiastic about someone's goods or services

not to care a hoot
not to show the slightest concern or enthusiasm

one's heart is not in some cause
one has little enthusiasm for some cause

the lifeblood
the main or essential ingredient; or the person or factor instilling enthusiasm

they fell over themselves to do something
they showed great keenness while doing something

to be a live wire
to be an enthusiast

to be a political animal
to want to be in politics

to be after someone's blood
to be keen to make a person the victim of an angry confrontation

to be after someone's scalp
to be keen to penalize a person

to be bitten with something
to become very enthusiastic over something

to be close to one's heart
to be a project on which one is very keen

to be dying to do something
to be extremely keen to do something

to be hot on a subject
to be knowledgeable and enthusiastic about a subject

to be in someone's blood
to be something about which a person is very knowledgeable or keen

to be itching to go
to be highly enthusiastic and keen to start

to be on one's soap box
to hold forth on an issue about which one feels keenly

to be the life and soul of the party
to be the prime enthusiast for a cause

to beat someone to the punch
to get to some objective ahead of some keen rival

to break one's neck to do something
to be particularly keen

to carry a torch for someone
to act as an enthusiastic advocate of another person's cause

to galvanize someone into action
to enthuse a person into doing something

to get one's teeth into something
to tackle a task with enthusiasm

to give something a blood transfusion
to give something new enthusiasm

to go hammer and tongs
to do something with great energy

to grab some opportunity with both hands
to seize some opportunity with great enthusiasm

to have one's heart in something
to be enthusiastic about and committed to a cause

to have one's heart set on something
to be very keen to achieve something

to jump at the opportunity
to enthusiastically take immediate advantage of a good chance

to jump into the ring
to join in enthusiastically

to leap at an idea
to accept a suggestion enthusiastically

to lose heart
to cease being enthusiastic

to make a beeline for something
to go straight to something with great enthusiasm or to head for some goal by the most direct route

to pour cold water on some idea
to be unenthusiastic about some proposal or scornful of its apparent weaknesses

to pull oneself together
to cease acting without purpose or enthusiasm

to rebound with a vengeance
to return to an issue with great enthusiasm

to run out of steam
to lose one's energy and enthusiasm

to start the ball rolling
to commence and enthusiastically advance an activity involving people

to take a shine to someone
to be keen on a person

to want someone's hide
to be keen to penalize a person

with much fanfare
with great enthusiasm and public acclaim

with open arms
enthusiastically

EQUALITY

a level playing field
competition on equal terms

a second-class citizen
a person not treated as an equal

between the devil and the deep blue sea
to be faced with two equally unpalatable alternatives which cannot both be avoided

it is a toss-up
either alternative is equally acceptable

only a cigarette paper between them
virtually equal or close together

only a postage stamp between them
virtually equal or close together

only a tissue between them
virtually equal or close together

the river found its mark
equilibrium between two pressures has been achieved

to be between Scylla and Charybdis
to be faced with two equally unpalatable alternatives which cannot both be avoided (refers to the voyage of Ulysses)

to be between a rock and a hard place
to be faced with two equally difficult and uncomfortable choices

to be line ball
to be equal

to compete on all fours with someone
to strive on equal terms

to fight fire with fire
to counter a dangerous situation by making an equally dangerous move

EXCESS

a holier-than-thou attitude
excessive righteousness

daylight robbery
the charging of grossly excessive prices

feather bedding
(in industrial relations) creating unnecessary jobs solely to increasing employment; (in economics) assisting an inefficient industry by government grants or excessive tariff protection

highway robbery
the charging of grossly excessive prices

paper warfare
an excessive amount of correspondence or red tape

penny-pinching
excessively mean

red tape
excessively bureaucratic procedures

someone has swallowed a dictionary
a person uses excessively long words

that takes the cake
that is quite absurd or outrageous or excessively cheeky

to be a sticky beak
to show excessive curiosity into matters not of one's concern

to be above water
(of securities) to have a market value in excess of the cost price

to be babes in the wood
to be excessively naive and inexperienced and thus ripe for exploitation

to be dressed up to the nines
to be attired in excessively elaborate garments

to be on one's high horse
to be excessively pompous

to be tied to someone's apron strings
to be excessively influenced by a female

to be too frightened to say "boo" to a goose
to be excessively shy

to be wet behind the ears
to be excessively naive and inexperienced

to burn the candle at both ends
to work excessively long hours

to charge like a wounded bull
to impose excessive prices (a play on words; not a simile)

to cost an arm and a leg
to be excessively expensive

to eat one's head off
to eat excessively

to go overboard
to act foolishly and in an excessive way

to hang onto someone's coattails
to excessively rely on another person's initiatives

to kill the goose that lays the golden eggs
through excessive greed to destroy a very profitable enterprise

to make heavy weather of something
to struggle excessively with a relatively simple task

to make noise enough to wake the dead
to be excessively noisy

to pay through the nose
to pay an excessive price

to read the Riot Act
to reprimand persons who are excessively noisy (refers to the police reading out to a rowdy crowd extracts from a law requiring its dispersement)

to talk the hind leg off a donkey
to talk excessively

EXPECTATION

a gambit
an opening move in a competitive situation which involves short-term losses in the expectation of long-term gains

drawcard
feature expected to attract a crowd

front-runner
person expected to win

not to hold one's breath for something
to give up all expectation

opening shot
first step in an activity expected to last a long time

the calm before the storm
the quiet period before an expected or inevitable crisis

there are black clouds on the horizon
bad news is expected

to batten down the hatches
to get ready for expected difficulties

to be a tall order
to be an unreasonable expectation

to be in cloud cuckoo land
to be mad or to have unrealistic expectations

to be more than flesh can stand
to be more than a person can reasonably be expected to endure

to be more than one bargained for
to be more than one expected

to be successful beyond one's wildest dreams
to be far more successful than one could have expected

to beat the odds
to do better than could reasonably have been expected

to cast one's bread upon the waters
not to expect gratitude or recognition for one's good works (Ecclesiastes 11:1)

to catch someone with his pants down
to act when another person least expects it

to catch someone with his trousers down
to act when another person least expects it

to count one's chickens before they are hatched
to treat as fact the expected results of a future proposal

to defy gravity
to go up when the expectation is to go down

to fall through
not to eventuate as expected

to grind to a halt
to cease some activity despite expectations that it would continue

to live on borrowed time
to live longer than expected

to loom on the horizon
to be expected but not immediately

to raise merry hell
to prominently involve others in a matter in the expectation of significant results from this action

to raise the specter of something
to draw attention to a worrying expectation of something

to see the color of someone's eyes
to see how a person matches expectations or requirements

to seek the pot of gold at the end of the rainbow
to have naive expectations

to turn up trumps
to finish up better than expected or to experience unexpected good luck

to wait for the other shoe to drop
to await the seemingly imminent and inevitable (refers to a man undressing, disturbing a neighbor by dropping one shoe, then frustrating his expectation by putting the other shoe down gently)

to wear one's heart on one's sleeve
to lack the reserve expected of one

EXPENSE

a Pyrrhic victory
a win which costs more than if there had been a loss (refers to the battle at which King Pyrrhus of Epirus defeated the Romans at Asculum)

a white elephant
an expensive and useless luxury (refers to gifts of sacred elephants by the King of Siam to persons then ruined by the expense of their upkeep)

a white knight
a party voluntarily coming to the assistance of another party at considerable cost to itself

garage sale
sale of miscellaneous assets at cheap prices

heads I win—tails you lose
whichever way this matter goes I will benefit at your expense

not to be worth the candle
to be too expensive in relation to the true value

the law of the jungle
the principle that those having power will use it at the expense of all others

the sky is the limit
the cost is no obstacle

to be above water
(of securities) to have a market value in excess of the cost price

to be on the house
to be free of cost

to buy something for a song
to buy something very cheaply

to cost an arm and a leg
to be excessively expensive

to cut costs to the bone
to economize

to hedge one's bets
to take action involving a cost but which is designed to reduce the possible adverse consequences of some activity

to hit someone hard
to greatly affect a person emotionally or to cost a person a lot of money

to hold the purse strings
to have control of expenditure

to mortgage the future
to get benefits now but at a cost in due course

EXPERIENCE

a blessing in disguise
an unwelcome but salutary experience

a green chum
an inexperienced person

a nightmare
an unpleasant experience

a past master
an expert with long experience

a trap for young players
a good opportunity for the inexperienced or naive to make mistakes

a warhorse
an old soldier who likes to relive past wartime experiences

an old head on young shoulders
experience, knowledge and maturity in a young person

distant fields look greener
activities of which one has no experience seem much easier than is really the case

hard-bitten
toughened by experience

hard-boiled
toughened by experience

off the top of one's head
based on experience but without detailed consideration

to be babes in the wood
to be excessively naive and inexperienced and thus ripe for exploitation

to be in a hole
to experience some difficulties

to be in a tight corner
to experience a crisis

to be in uncharted waters
to be the first to experience something

to be someone's bread and butter
to be a person's livelihood or to be a person's everyday experience

to bet wet behind the ears
to be excessively naive and inexperienced

to broaden someone's mind
to expose a person to a greater variety of experiences and interests than he had previously

to cut one's teeth on something
to get one's first experience by doing something

to feel the draft
to experience unfavorable conditions

to hide one's light under a bushel
to keep others in ignorance of one's skills and experience

to learn a lesson
to benefit from one's experience

to pick someone's brain
to get the benefit of another person's knowledge and experience

to put someone through the mill
to give a person practical experience

to reap as one has sown
to experience the consequences of one's own actions

to teach one's grandmother how to suck eggs
to try to tell a much more experienced person something very obvious to him

to turn up trumps
to finish up better than expected or to experience unexpected good luck

EXPERTISE

a backroom boy
an expert unable to communicate effectively with the lay public

a past master
an expert with long experience

father knows best
as an expert I know better than you do just what is most suitable for you

not to be someone's cup of tea
to be outside a person's expertise or area of interest

to be slipping
to be losing one's cunning or expertise

to be up one's alley
to be right within a person's expertise or area of interest

to hang up one's shingle
to go into business offering expert personal services

to stick to one's game
to confine oneself to activities in areas in which one has knowledge and expertise

FACT

a goldmine
a source of much wealth or of many facts

a gut feeling
a belief based purely on intuition and unsupported by facts or evidence

a sitting shot
an initial move which is designed to establish facts for use in a later action

a telltale sign
a visible indication revealing true facts despite efforts at concealment

it will all come out in the wash
the facts will emerge as work proceeds

put that in your pipe and smoke it
contemplate that fact

showdown
disclosure of certain pertinent facts

that takes on added color
there are now further facts which alter the appearance of a matter

the affair blew up
certain unwelcome facts have become publicly available

the boot is on the other foot
the real facts are the other way round

the penny dropped
a person has just realized a fact which should have been obvious (refers to old-fashioned pay toilets)

to almost drive someone to tears
to present information designed to make another person express sympathy not warranted by the facts

to ascertain the lay of the land
to establish the pertinent facts and opinions

to balance the picture
to put the other side of the story or to quote facts in contradiction

to be old hat
to be a very widely-known fact

to be on the wrong tram
to be completely mistaken as to the basic facts

to bring a fact home to someone
despite his inclination to the contrary, to make a person realize a fact

to count one's chickens before they are hatched
to treat as fact the expected results of a future proposal

to drag someone by the head and ears
to force a person to reveal the true facts

to draw a long bow
to state a conclusion which while possible is unlikely on the known facts

to flush out the facts
to ascertain, after some effort, the truth of some matter

to have one's wires crossed
to be mistaken about key facts

to have something to chew on
to have firm facts on which to base a decision

to send someone away with a flea in his ear
to give a person frank but unwelcome facts (refers to fleas trapped in the armor of ancient knights)

to sift
to closely examine the evidence or a set of facts with a view to attaching different significance as appropriate to each of the various components

to strengthen someone's hand
to give a person additional authority or greater moral support or more facts to support his case

to take something at face value
(of alleged facts) to accept something without question or challenge

to take something with a grain of salt
to regard the facts in a statement with considerable skepticism

to throw a cat among the pigeons
to cause consternation by revealing an unpleasant and unexpected fact

to throw in one's six pennies' worth
to modestly supply one's own facts or views

to throw in one's two cents' worth
to modestly supply one's own facts or views

to wake up to something
to realize a fact or its significance

to whitewash
to exonerate when this is not warranted by the facts

when the balloon goes up
when the adverse facts come to light

when the chips are down
when all facts are known and taken into consideration

FACTOR

a bottleneck
a factor obstructing an even flow

a catalyst
a factor causing something to happen

chicken and egg
two factors each of which results in the other

the lifeblood
the main or essential ingredient; or the person or factor instilling enthusiasm

the nigger in the woodpile
the factor spoiling an otherwise satisfactory arrangement

to be a magnet
to be a factor drawing a crowd of people

to cloud one's mind
to allow irrelevant or extraneous factors to affect one's impartiality or judgment

to make or break someone
to be a factor leading either to a person's success or to his failure, with no intermediate position

to paint a black picture
to state a set of unfavorable factors

to present a rosy picture
to state a set of favorable factors

to see which way the wind is blowing
to establish the factors relevant to a situation

to tip the scales
to be a factor which in combination with other factors results in a particular decision which would otherwise not have been reached

trigger
factor responsible for certain events occurring at that particular time

FAILURE

a bloodbath
catastrophic losses

a case of rats leaving a sinking ship
the desertion of an enterprise in anticipation of imminent failure

a damp squib
dissappointingly ineffective action (refers to fireworks which fail to go off)

a flash in the pan
something that begins promisingly but does not last (refers to the priming of old guns)

a gambit
an opening move in a competitive situation which involves short-term losses in the expectation of long-term gains

a game of cat and mouse
negotiations between two parties of unequal bargaining power during which the stronger makes some temporary concessions to the weaker without, however, affecting the latter's eventual total defeat

a landslide
an electoral result involving victory or defeat by an unexpectedly large margin

a Pyrrhic victory
a win which costs more than if there had been a loss (refers to the battle at which King Pyrrhus of Epirus defeated the Romans at Asculum)

a roller coaster ride
a series of successes followed by failures

a South Sea bubble
an unrealistic financial venture which is bound to result in total loss

checkmate
defeat

it is a case of sink or swim
the attempt is worthwhile, despite the risk of failure

stalemate
a final result in which neither party to a dispute is victorious

that is money down the drain
money has been wastefully lost on a failed project

the wheels fell off
the plan failed

to back the wrong horse
to have faith in, give support to and/or invest in a project which proves to be unsuccessful

to bang one's head up against a brick wall
to fight an unwinnable case

to be a dead duck
to have failed

to be done like a dinner
to be defeated and humiliated

to be on the ropes
to be facing defeat

to be one in the eye for someone
to represent an unexpected and unwelcome defeat

to be sheer murder
to be extremely unpleasant or difficult; or to be an inglorious defeat

to be slipping
to be losing one's cunning or expertise

to beat by a long shot
to defeat very convincingly

to become a vegetable
to lose one's mental and physical faculties

to burn one's fingers
to lose money through foolishness

to chase a corpse
to harp on something long ago resolved or a lost cause

to derail some strategy
to cause a strategy to fail

to draw a blank
to be unsuccessful

to eat crow
to accept a humiliating defeat

to eat someone alive
to soundly defeat a person

to fall to the ground
to fail

to fly out the window
to be lost

to force someone onto his knees
to inflict a humiliating defeat on a person

to get off the canvas
to recover after near defeat

to give someone a bath
to dramatically defeat a person

to go down the tube
to fail

to hold a winning hand
to be in an unbeatable position to defeat others

to hold all the aces
to be in an unbeatable position to defeat others

to hold the trump card
to be in an unbeatable position to defeat others

to kiss something good-bye
to give something up as permanently lost

to kiss the ground
to suffer a loss

to lick one's wounds
to adjust oneself to defeat

to lose face
to endure embarrassment by virtue of being defeated or having one's errors found out

to lose money hand over fist
to lose money very fast and convincingly

to lose one's shirt
to make heavy financial losses

to make a last ditch stand
to make a brave effort to stave off final defeat

to make or break someone
to be a factor leading either to a person's success or his failure, with no intermediate position

to meet one's Waterloo
to receive a decisive defeat (refers to Napoleon's fate at the Battle of Waterloo)

to miss the boat
to fail to exploit an opportunity

to miss the bus
to fail to exploit an opportunity

to miss the sharks while netting the minnows
to succeed in minor aspects but fail in the ones that really matter

to miss the train
to fail to exploit an opportunity

to nurse one's bruises
to face up to the consequences of defeat

to overstep the mark
to fail to observe the proprieties

to play the trump card
to make a final move, thereby defeating one's opponents

to raise the stake
to increase the amount of potential gain or loss in a project

to rub it in
to humiliate another person by emphasizing his defeat

to save face
to be allowed to keep one's dignity despite having suffered a defeat or made an error

to sink slowly in the West
to fail gradually

to stem the hemorrhage
to put a stop to the financial losses of a project

to throw good money after bad
to waste further money in a vain attempt to recover money already lost

to throw in the towel
to concede defeat

to throw up the sponge
to concede defeat

to tighten the noose
to get closer to inflicting defeat

to trump someone
to defeat a person

to turn the corner
to commence being successful after initial failures

to wipe the floor with someone
to inflict a humiliating defeat on a person

FALSITY

a false dawn
an incident giving rise to unjustified hope

a tall story
an interesting but untrue and unbelievable tale

a white lie
a false statement uttered in a good cause

some mud will stick
reputations will be hurt even after accusations are proved false

to cook the books
fraudulently to maintain false records of financial transactions

to dream up some story
to concoct a false story naively or maliciously

to lie through one's teeth
to tell blatant untruths

to nail a lie
to expose an untruth

to pull someone's leg
to tell a false but plausible story as an act of humor

to sail under false colors
to pretend that one's real character or beliefs are different from what they really are

to speak with forked tongues
to utter half-truths with the intention of misleading the listener

to swallow the line
to accept as truth the story being proffered

FRANKNESS

a straight shooter
a person who is frank and outspoken

not to pull any punches
to be brutally frank

to come out into the open
to start being frank

to hit someone right between the eyes
to be brutally frank

to lay one's cards on the table
to be utterly frank and open or to honestly disclose one's position

to make no bones about it
to be brutally frank

to send someone away with a flea in his ear
to give a person frank but unwelcome facts (refers to fleas trapped in the armor of ancient knights)

to shoot from the hip
to speak frankly and openly

to speak one's mind
to express one's views frankly and forcefully

FRIGHT

in fear and trembling
in a state of apprehension

to frighten hell out of someone
to alarm a person

to frighten the horses
to scare people off by one's ill-considered tactics

to have a threat hanging over one's head
to fear some intimated unpleasant action

to have nerves of steel
not to be easily frightened

to lose one's nerve
to abandon, out of fear, a decision to do something

to make someone's flesh creep
to frighten a person with something horrific

to nearly jump out of one's skin
to receive a fright

to scare the pants off someone
to greatly frighten a person

FUTURE

a bird in the hand is worth two in the bush
a benefit currently available is more valuable than a seemingly much larger benefit which may or may not be achieved in the future

a crystal ball
accurate knowledge of the future

a litmus test
an event which allows the outcome of future events to be predicted more accurately

to be destined for the scrap-heap
to face a future in which one will have no meaningful role

to conduct a postmortem on something
to review past actions with a view of learning lessons for the future (Latin, "after the death")

to count one's chickens before they are hatched
to treat as fact the expected results of a future proposal

to have a cloud hanging over one's head
there is doubt as to one's future

to keep someone's seat warm
to hold a position temporarily with a view to another person taking it over permanently in the near future

to keep something up one's sleeve
to secretly retain something in reserve for use in the future or at a later stage of negotiations

to mortgage the future
to get benefits now but at a cost in due course

to pigeon-hole
to put aside for further consideration in the distant future

to put something into cold storage
to put something aside for dealing with at some indeterminate future time

to telegraph one's punches
by one's actions to give advance warning of one's future plans

to wash one's hands of something
to emphatically decline future responsibility

HAPPINESS AND ENJOYMENT

a field day
a very enjoyable and successful occasion

all his Christmases came at once
he was overjoyed

in Halcyon days
in past happier times (refers to the 14 days about the winter solstice when winds were calm and to the mythical bird said to breed in a floating nest at that time)

to be in a seventh heaven
to be very happy

to be in clover
to enjoy a life of ease and luxury

to be on cloud nine
to be very happy

to be on the crest of a wave
to enjoy success which may not last

to be on top of the world
to be very happy

to be wrapped in something
to enjoy something

to have a ball
to have an enjoyable time

to have a run for one's money
to at least get some enjoyment out of an otherwise abortive exercise

to jump for joy
to express great satisfaction

to lap it up
to enjoy the attention

to laugh one's head off
to greatly enjoy something

to throw one's hat into the air
to express joy

to turn handstands
to express great joy

to walk on air
to be joyful

to warm the cockles of someone's heart
to delight a person

HARM

a muckraker
a person who sets out to publicize misconduct of prominent persons or institutions

a mudraker
a person who sets out to publicize features harming another person's reputation

not to touch a hair on someone's head
not to harm a person

one cannot make an omelette without breaking eggs
the desired end dictates the means even if they cause harm to others

the final straw
the latest step, which, when added to a large number of seemingly harmless previous steps, sets off a disaster resulting from the cumulative effect

the straw which broke the camel's back
the latest step, which, when added to a large number of seemingly harmless previous steps, sets off a disaster resulting from the cumulative effect

to be a wolf in sheep's clothing
to be a hypocrite or to be dangerous although masquerading as something harmless (Matthew 7:15)

to cut one's nose off to spite one's face
to act in pique in a way which harms only oneself

to keep something on an even keel
to ensure that something is not harmed

to let blood
to allow some harm as the price for achieving some greater benefit

to save one's bacon
to escape harm

to shoot oneself in the foot
to act in a foolish way and thus harm one's own cause

to stab someone in the back
to deliberately and surreptitiously harm a person who regarded one as a friend

HOPE

a chink of light
a small hope of a solution or breakthrough

a false dawn
an incident giving rise to unjustified hope

a fat chance
little hope

a light in the sky
a sign of great hope

a slough of despond
a feeling of hopelessness

not a dog's chance
no hope at all

not the ghost of a chance
no hope at all

pie in the sky
a hoped-for result unlikely to be achieved

the one bright spot on the horizon
the only hopeful aspect

things look black
there is little hope of success or prosperity or a favorable outcome

to clasp at straws
to have a hopeless case but show unjustified optimism on noting minor positive features

to fish for compliments
to drop hints in the hope that one will receive praise or recognition

to fly a kite
to issue uncovered checks in the hope that they will be covered before clearance or to test public reaction to legislation in contemplation by leaking broad details of it to the media

to have a snowflake's chance in hell
to have no hope or possibility at all

to keep one's fingers crossed
to hope for a good outcome

to pull something out of the fire
to salvage something in a seemingly hopeless situation

to sow seeds
to propagate ideas in the hope that they will be adopted

to teach someone a lesson
to inflict something unpleasant on a person in the hope that it will lead to a change in his behavior

to throw a sprat to catch a mackerel
to risk a little in the hope of gaining much

to touch wood
it is to be hoped that our good luck will not go away

IDEA

I buy that
I accept that idea

a brainwave
a suddenly occurring bright idea

a copycat
a person who imitates another person's ideas

a dinosaur
a person with incredibly outmoded ideas

a pipeline to someone
an intermediary used as a means of communicating ideas to a person

a swelled head
an exaggerated idea of one's abilities or status

a thought in the back of one's mind
an undeveloped idea

brainchild
inspired original idea

moonshine
unrealistic ideas

moth-eaten
(of ideas, etc.) antiquated

to act as a sounding board
to give, on request, constructive criticisms of ideas tentatively held

to be bankrupt of ideas
to be bereft of ideas

to be poles apart
to have ideas which are very different

to be someone's bete noire
to be a person whose ideas and actions cause upset and loathing in another person (French, "black beast")

to be the cat's pajamas
to have an exaggerated idea of one's own importance

to be the cradle of something
to be the place where some idea was first nurtured

to be too big for one's breeches
to have an exaggerated idea of one's own importance

to brainstorm
to pool thoughts in the course of a session designed to generate fresh ideas and especially to build upon the ideas of others

to disseminate ideas
to spread ideas to a wide audience (lit., "to scatter seeds in various places")

to dust some idea off
to revive some proposal

to encapsulate some idea
to reduce the essential points of a complicated proposal to a small number of words

to go to someone's head
to cause a person to get an exaggerated idea of his abilities or status

to have a blank canvas
to be bereft of ideas

to knock an idea on the head
to utterly reject a proposal

to leap at an idea
to accept a suggestion enthusiastically

to pour cold water on some idea
to be unenthusiastic about some proposal or scornful of its apparent weaknesses

to put one's heads together
to confer and pool ideas

to put pen to paper
to set out one's ideas in written form

to ram something down someone's throat
to pressure another person into accepting an idea with which he does not agree

to sow seeds
to propagate ideas in the hope that they will be adopted

to speak the same language
to have a good understanding and similar ideas

to stand on someone's shoulders
to build upon another person's ideas

to steal someone's clothes
to plagiarize another person's ideas

to test the water
to try out an idea in a small way

to throw something out of the window
to completely reject an idea or proposal

to turn someone's head
to cause a person to get an exaggerated idea of his abilities or status

young Turks
members of an organization who hold ideas regarded as too revolutionary

INFERENCE

the answer is a lemon
the outcome is inconclusive

to bark up the wrong tree
to reach an incorrect conclusion

to draw a long bow
to state a conclusion which while possible is unlikely on the known facts

to get the wrong sow by the ear
to reach an incorrect conclusion

to hit the nail right on the head
to astutely come to the correct conclusion

to jump to a conclusion
to infer something without proper consideration

to make up one's mind
to reach a conclusion after contemplating a matter

to put two and two together
to reach a conclusion by combining isolated pieces of information

INTEREST

a nine-day wonder
an exciting event, but one which will cease to arouse interest when the novelty has worn off

a sweetheart deal
an agreement negotiated in private without full regard to the interests of those affected

a tall story
an interesting but untrue and unbelievable tale

birds of a feather flock together
persons of like interests gather in the same place

in our camp
in the group representing our vested interest

kindred spirit
person with similar interests and eccentricities

not to be someone's cup of tea
to be outside a person's expertise or area of interest

not to care a pin for something
not to have the slightest interest in something

on our side of the fence
in the group representing our vested interest

someone's guardian angel
someone's friend, watching over him and advancing his interests

to be off on one's hobby horse
to throw into conversation aspects of a subject in which one has a passionate interest

to be up one's alley
to be right within a person's expertise or area of interest

to bore someone to death
to greatly weary a person by full and uninteresting conversation or by lack of action

to bore someone to tears
to greatly weary a person by full and uninteresting conversation or by lack of action

to bore the pants off someone
to weary a person by dull and uninteresting conversation

to break ranks
to identify oneself as having separate interests or views from the rest of a group

to broaden someone's mind
to expose a person to a greater variety of experiences and interests than he had previously

to compare notes
to exchange information about some subject of mutual interest

to have a finger in the pie
to have an interest in a project

to have an ax to grind
to have a vested interest

to need to watch one's back
to find it necessary to take care in case others act against one's interests

to talk one's book
to present arguments which, while plausible, are really designed to foster one's vested interest

to throw one's hat into the ring
to publicly announce one's interest in some position

to wear a particular hat
to act in a particular capacity or for a particular vested interest

to whet one's appetite
to arouse one's curiosity or interest

INTERFERENCE

a logjam
a stoppage of activity caused by input in greater volume than allowed for

a palace revolt
the overthrow of those in authority by their subordinates

a stitch in time saves nine
preventive maintenance saves money in the long run

nothing is sacred
nothing is safe from interference

pull your head in!
do not interfere in this!

stumbling block
an impediment or difficulty preventing the easy completion of some project or a dilemma involving some moral issue

to be stopped in one's tracks
suddenly and unexpectedly to be prevented from carrying on with a project

to block someone's path
to interfere with a person's opportunity to advance himself

to break down the barriers
to do away with the prejudice preventing something

to cloud one's mind
to allow irrelevant or extraneous factors to affect one's impartiality or judgement

to get the red light
to be forbidden to do something

to go over someone's head
to bypass lower levels of authority and approach someone more senior instead

to hold someone on a short leash
to give a person very little authority

to keep off someone's pad
not to interfere with or compete against another person in his customary area of activity

to keep one's cotton-picking fingers off something
not to interfere in something

to keep someone in a straitjacket
to deny a person any discretionary powers at all

to let blood
to allow some harm as the price for achieving some greater benefit

to poke one's nose into something
to interfere

to put a legrope on someone
to give a person very little authority

to put a spoke in someone's wheel
to interfere with another person's activity, so preventing its continuance

to put one's foot down
to exert one's authority and insist on something

to queer the pitch for someone
to spoil the opportunity a person has to do something

to spike someone's guns
to cause something to become useless

to stand in someone's way
to prevent a person achieving his goal

to strengthen someone's hand
to give a person additional authority or greater moral support or more facts to support his case

to throw a spanner in the works
to cause an unexpected complication

to tie someone's hands
to prevent a person from acting as he sees fit

to tie someone's hands behind his back
to make it impossible for a person to act at all

to tread on someone's corns
to upset another person by interfering in his area of responsibility

to tread on someone's toes
to upset another person by interfering in his area of responsibility

to wipe the slate clean
to forgive past indiscretions

INVOLVEMENT

a lone wolf
a person who prefers to act without involving others

a shaggy-dog story
an amusing anecdote with an unexpected ending, often involving talking animals given certain human skills

to be in something up to one's armpits
to be very deeply involved in something

to be in the thick of things
to get involved at the center of some activity

to be on a treadmill
to be involved in some unpleasant ongoing activity which cannot readily be stopped

to be the center of the spider's web
to control an operation which involves numerous and/or complex ingredients

to be up to one's ears in something
to be very deeply involved in something

to be up to one's elbow in something
to be deeply involved in something

to be up to one's neck in something
to be very deeply involved in something

to be up to the eyeballs in something
to be very deeply involved in something

to butt in
uninvited to involve oneself in someone else's conversation

to call it a day
to cease involvement with some activity

to catch someone in the net
to unexpectedly involve a particular person in the course of activity designed to involve many others

to cover one's tracks
to hide the evidence of one's involvement

to give the game away
to cease involvement with some activity

to have a finger in something
to be involved in something

to have a tiger by the tail
to be involved in an activity which is much more dangerous than one had realized

to hijack a debate
to involve oneself in the public discussion of some matter and turn that discussion to one's advantage

to leave someone high and dry
to isolate a person from a desired involvement

to raise merry hell
to prominently involve others in a matter in the expectation of significant results from this action

to see the back of someone
to know that a person is no longer involved in something

to start the ball rolling
to commence and enthusiastically advance an activity involving people

to take a backseat
not to actively involve oneself

to twiddle one's thumbs
not to be involved in any worthwhile activity

JUDGMENT

beauty is in the eye of the beholder
some things are matters for subjective judgments

in someone's eyes
in a person's judgment

to cloud one's mind
to allow irrelevant or extraneous factors to affect one's impartiality or judgment

to fall flat on one's face
to make a bad error of judgment

to have an open mind
to be willing to assess evidence on its merits and without prejudging it

to judge a book by its cover
foolishly to go only by superficial appearances

to put money on the table
to back one's judgment in a tangible way or to demonstrate one's sincerity

to put one's money where one's mouth is
to back one's judgment by putting assets at risk

to twist someone's arm
to coerce another person to do something against his will or better judgment

KNOWLEDGE

a crystal ball
accurate knowledge of the future

a down-to-earth solution
a realistic solution

a skeleton in the cupboard
an unpleasant truth the knowledge of which has been deliberately suppressed

an old head on young shoulders
experience, knowledge and maturity in a young person

as soon as someone's back was turned
at the moment it became possible to do something without a person's knowledge

father knows best
as an expert I know better than you do just what is most suitable for you

fools rush in where angels fear to tread
unsophisticated persons take unwise risks in circumstances where more knowledgeable persons would exercise caution

hard-headed
realistic

he would turn in his grave
he would have been very surprised or displeased if he had known while still alive

heaven only knows
it is not known

it hits one
one comes to realize something

it's a small world
it is surprising to meet people one knows in unexpected places

not to have the foggiest notion
to know nothing at all about the subject

still waters run deep
a person with a quiet manner may have a surprisingly great knowledge of a subject

the left hand does not know what the right hand is doing
one section of a large bureaucracy does not realize that another section is simultaneously doing something inconsistent

the penny dropped
a person has just realized a fact which should have been obvious (refers to old-fashioned pay toilets)

the pot calling the kettle black
a person criticizing another person without realizing his own even greater shortcomings

the word is out
it is now known

to be a full bottle on something
to be very knowledgeable

to be at the end of one's tether
to be frustrated by a lack of knowledge, authority or patience

to be child's play
to be easy or to require only elementary skills and knowledge

to be geared up to do something
to have equipment, labor and know-how in place adequate for some task

to be hot on a subject
to be knowledgeable and enthusiastic about a subject

to be in someone's blood
to be something about which a person is very knowledgeable or keen

to be in the swim
to be a member of a group knowing what is going on

to be old hat
to be a very widely-known fact

to bring a fact home to someone
despite his inclination to the contrary, to make a person realize a fact

to buy a pig in a poke
to buy goods of unknown quality

to cock one's eye at someone
to glance knowingly at a person

to draw a long bow
to state a conclusion which while possible is unlikely on the known facts

to drop names
to slip names of celebrities allegedly known to the speaker into a conversation in an attempt to impress

to hand on the torch
to pass on accumulated knowledge

to have a tiger by the tail
to be involved in an activity which is much more dangerous than one had realized

to have eyes at the back of one's head
to know more of what is going on than is generally realized

to have one's feet firmly on the ground
to know what one is doing

to have one's fingers on the pulse
to know what is going on

to know something in one's heart of hearts
to know something while reluctant to admit it, even to oneself

to know something inside out
to know something very thoroughly

to know the ropes
to know how to do one's job

to know where one stands
to know what one supports or how one is affected

to know which way to turn
to know which strategy to adopt or where to seek assistance

to pick someone's brain
to get the benefit of another person's knowledge and experience

to put one's reputation on the line
to take a public stance in the realization that there is a risk that one's reputation will suffer if one is proved wrong

to see the back of someone
to know that a person is no longer involved in something

to shrug one's shoulders
to indicate that one does not know or care or that one is unable or unwilling to assist

to stick to one's game
to confine oneself to activities in areas in which one has knowledge and expertise

to wake up to something
to realize a fact or its significance

under someone's nose
in a person's immediate area of responsibility or in circumstances where he should have known something

what is this—a bunch of grapes or a bowl of goldfish?
surely you know what this is!

when the chips are down
when all facts are known and taken into consideration

with 20/20 hindsight
with the benefit of knowing what happened

LEADERSHIP

kingmaker
person engaging in behind-the-scenes activities to promote another person to a particular leadership position

the blind leading the blind
persons without the necessary skills for a task purporting to impart those skills to others

the high priest of something
the leading advocate of something

to be at the head of the pack
to be the best of many or the de facto leader

to be at the top of the tree
to be a leading member of one's profession

to be the leading light
to be the most important person in a venture

to knock someone off his perch
to displace a person from his leadership position in some competitive situation

to set the pace
to give a lead in regard to a rate of progression

to spearhead something
to lead a movement

too many cooks spoil the broth
one leader is all that is required

LIKELIHOOD

a bull in a china shop
a careless person likely to cause great damage

a cancer
an evil which is likely to spread

a death wish
the contemplation of action so foolish that it is likely to lead to utter disaster

a loose cannon on the deck
a mistake likely to cause trouble

a new broom
a changed regime which is likely to alter the status quo

a pipedream
a fanciful notion, wished for but unlikely

an unholy alliance
a working relationship for a nefarious purpose between unlikely partners

it is pointing in the right direction
success looks likely

pie in the sky
a hoped-for result unlikely to be achieved

straws in the wind
unofficial preliminary indications of something likely to be formally revealed soon

there is blood in the water
something is likely to cause a person to go into a frenzy

to be on the cards
to be likely

to be shortsighted
not to recognize the likely consequences

to draw a long bow
to state a conclusion which while possible is unlikely on the known facts

to face a rocky road ahead
to be likely to encounter difficulties

to find a needle in a haystack
to find something when the probability of finding it is very small

to get brownie points
to do a person a favor with the likely result that the recipient will do a favor in return in due course

to give someone enough rope to hang himself
to give a person the opportunity to do something which is likely to get him into severe trouble

to leap frog something
to overtake something, with the likelihood of in turn being overtaken (refers to a game in which participants jump over each other in turn)

to make a rod for one's own back
to act in disregard of likely disadvantages for oneself

to spin a yarn
to tell an amusing or unlikely story

where there is smoke there is fire
if there is a hint of trouble, then it is highly likely that there really is trouble

MEMBERSHIP

a black sheep
a disreputable member of an otherwise reputable group

a blueblood
a person of high birth (refers to the appearance of veins on the skin of members of some royal families)

a clean sweep
the complete removal in an election of all sitting members

esprit de corps
a feeling of camaraderie and concern for the good name of some organization of which one is a member (French, ''vital breath of a body'')

flagship
most important member of a group of related entities

fresh blood
newly joined members of some organization

pariah
social outcast (refers to members of a low caste in India)

the lowest common denominator
the highest level of taste found among all the members of some target audience

to be a cuckoo in the nest
to purport to be a member of a group of people although having no such right

to be at the top of the tree
to be a leading member of one's profession

to be in the swim
to be a member of a group knowing what is going on

to drum someone out of some organization
to terminate in ignominy a person's employment or membership (refers to the ceremonial cashiering in the army to the beating of parade drums)

to introduce new blood
to recruit new members to some organization

to shepherd some group
to marshall the members of some group

young Turks
members of an organization who hold ideas regarded as too revolutionary

MISLEADING

a house of cards
an organization which gives a misleading impression of solidity

to lead someone a merry dance
to mislead a person

to lead someone up the garden path
to mislead a person by deliberately fallacious arguments

to pull the wool over someone's eyes
to deceive or deliberately mislead another person

to speak with forked tongues
to utter half-truths with the intention of misleading the listener

to throw dust into someone's eyes
to deceive a person by presenting inaccurate or misleading information

to throw someone off the scent
to deceive a person by giving out misleading indications

MISTAKE

a comedy of errors
a series of separate mistakes in relation to some matter (name of a Shakespeare play)

a loose cannon on the deck
a mistake likely to cause trouble

a slip of the tongue
incorrect words uttered accidentally

a trap for young players
a good opportunity for the inexperienced or naive to make mistakes

glaring error
patently obvious mistake

Murphy's law
the principle that everything which can go wrong will go wrong

not to be a hanging matter
to be only a minor mistake

sacrificial lamb
somebody unfairly made to suffer for the mistakes of others

something is rotten in the state of Denmark
the situation is not correct (from Shakespeare's HAMLET)

to bark up the wrong tree
to reach an incorrect conclusion

to be off beam
to be mistaken

to be on the road to Damascus
to see the error of one's ways (Acts 9:3)

to be on the wrong tack
to be using an incorrect procedure or policy

to be on the wrong track
to be heading toward an incorrect solution

to be on the wrong tram
to be completely mistaken as to the basic facts

to be on the wrong wavelength
to be incorrect in one's thinking

to be up the creek
to be completely mistaken

to be wide off the mark
to have a belief which is far removed from the true position

to catch someone flat-footed
to embarrass a person in the course of his making mistakes or being unprepared

to clean up a mess
to sort out mistakes or neglect

to drive a coach and horses through something
to demonstrate major errors in something

to fall flat on one's face
to make a bad error of judgment

to get the wrong sow by the ear
to reach an incorrect conclusion

to have an eagle eye
to be able to notice small mistakes very readily

to have hold of the wrong end of the pineapple
to be utterly mistaken

to have one's wires crossed
to be mistaken about key facts

to hold the wrong end of the stick
to be completely mistaken about something

to lose face
to endure embarrassment by virtue of being defeated or having one's errors found out

to put one's foot in it
to make a foolish mistake

to put one's reputation on the line
to take a public stance in the realization that there is a risk that one's reputation will suffer if one is proved wrong

to put the cart before the horse
to do things in the wrong order

to save face
to be allowed to keep one's dignity despite having suffered a defeat or made an error

to slip under one's guard
to cause a mistake to be made despite care being taken to prevent this

to sow the wind and reap the whirlwind
to make bad mistakes and to suffer the even worse consequences

MONEY

a cash cow
a source of ready money

a license to print money
a lucrative government-conferred monopoly or privilege

a stitch in time saves nine
preventive maintenance saves money in the long run

he who pays the piper calls the tune
a person contributing money or resources to a project is entitled to a say in its control

money for jam
remuneration easily earned

not for love or money
definitely not

not to be made of money
not to be wealthy

not to have a bean
to have no money

pin money
an allowance to a wife for her personal use

that is money down the drain
money has been wastefully lost on a failed project

the money is rolling in
the scheme is very profitable

to be a money spinner
to produce large profits easily and quickly

to be in the black
to have money

to be in the red
to owe money

to be out of pocket
to have been forced to spend money which cannot be recovered from others

to burn one's fingers
to lose money through foolishness

to button up one's purse
to refuse to spend money

to engage in pump priming
to spend public money with the aim of attracting parochial electoral support

to have a run for one's money
to at least get some enjoyment out of an otherwise abortive exercise

to have deep pockets
to have large financial resources

to have money burning a hole in one's pocket
to be impatient to spend or invest available funds

to have money flowing out of one's ears
to be very rich

to hit someone hard
to greatly affect a person emotionally or to cost a person a lot of money

to hold out a fistful of dollars
to offer money by way of inducement

to hold the purse strings
to have control of expenditure

to line one's pockets
to make, improperly and secretly, a profit out of some transaction

to lose money hand over fist
to lose money very fast and convincingly

to pork barrel
to spend taxpayers' money in one area in order to attract political support

to put money on the table
to back one's judgment in a tangible way or to demonstrate one's sincerity

to put one's hand in one's pockets
to spend

to put one's money where one's mouth is
to back one's judgment by putting assets at risk

to save a bundle
to save much money

to see the color of someone's money
to get evidence of the sincerity of a person's proposal

to throw good money after bad
to waste further money in a vain attempt to recover money already lost

to tighten the purse strings
to reduce outlays

to turn an honest penny
to earn money out of odd jobs

to turn one's chips in
to convert one's assets or entitlements into cash

MONITORING

a watchdog
a person or organization monitoring behavior

to keep an eye on the ball
to monitor a fast-changing situation

to keep one's eye on someone
to supervise a person or to monitor a person's activities and behavior

to keep one's eye on something
to monitor a situation

to keep tabs on something
to monitor something

NAIVETE

a lamb led to slaughter
a naive person allowing himself to be exploited

a trap for young players
a good opportunity for the inexperienced or naive to make mistakes

bright-eyed and bushy-tailed
naive but enthusiastic

not to have been born yesterday
not to be naive

that is strictly for the birds
that is blatant and naive nonsense

to be babes in the wood
to be excessively naive and inexperienced and thus ripe for exploitation

to be green
to be naive

to be off the planet
to be extremely naive or uninformed

to be wet behind the ears
to be excessively naive and inexperienced

to dream up some story
to concoct a false story naively or maliciously

to have come down in the last shower
to be naive

to seek the pot of gold at the end of the rainbow
to have naive expectations

NONSENSE

a load of rubbish
blatant nonsense

hogwash
nonsense

mumbo jumbo
blatant nonsense (refers to a deity worshipped by primitive tribes)

tell it to the marines
such nonsense is not believable

that is strictly for the birds
that is blatant and naive nonsense

to be eye wash
to be nonsense

OPINION

a prima donna
a person with an exaggerated opinion of his own importance which makes relations with others needlessly difficult (Italian, "first lady")

heresy
views different from those held by the majority

spectrum
wide range of different opinions or backgrounds

the jury is still out
no decision has yet been made or the public has not yet given an indication of its views

the other side of the coin
the arguments for the opposite point of view

the tide is running in favor of some proposition
public opinion supports some proposition

to act as a devil's advocate
to put a point of view which one does not hold in order to draw out the best arguments regarding a proposition (refers to a church official vetting a candidate for sainthood)

to ascertain the lay of the land
to establish the pertinent facts and opinions

to be a lone voice in the wilderness
to be the only person stating unpopular views

to be a thorn in someone's flesh
to be a person whose persistent presence and righteous views annoy

to be full of hot air
to have an exaggerated opinion of one's own importance and to boast about it

to be on the other side of the fence
to have an opposing point of view or position

to belt someone over the head
to override someone's views or arguments

to break ranks
to identify oneself as having separate interests or views from the rest of a group

to bridge a gulf
to overcome a wide divergence in views

to change one's mind
to alter the views which one had previously formed

to change one's tune
to alter one's publicly-expressed views

to claim that something is the best thing since sliced bread
to have an exaggerated opinion of the importance or novelty of an invention or practice

to echo someone's words
to repeat another person's views as though they were one's own

to get words in edgeways
to manage to interrupt a conversation in order to put a separate point of view

to have a change of heart
to form a new view in place of a strongly-held previous view

to know one's mind
to form and adhere to an opinion

to polarize
to cause people to identify themselves as belonging to groups holding opposing views

to pull one's horns in
to retreat from previously stated views

to put someone back in his box
to make it clear to a person that his views are not welcome

to sail against the wind
to oppose the views currently being held by others

to sing a particular song
to state particular views

to speak one's mind
to express one's views frankly and forcefully

to take a sounding
to ascertain people's views

to throw in one's six pennies' worth
to modestly supply one's own facts or views

to throw in one's two cents' worth
to modestly supply one's own facts or views

you can get lost
I intend to take no notice whatsoever of you or your views

you can jump in the lake
I intend to take no notice whatsoever of you or your views

OPPORTUNITY

a chink in someone's armor
an opportunity to do something which otherwise could not be done

a chink in the wall
an opportunity to do something which otherwise could not be done

a foot in the door
the opportunity to do business

a golden opportunity
an unparalleled opportunity

a toehold
an opportunity small in itself but with the potential to lead to bigger things

a trap for young players
a good opportunity for the inexperienced or naive to make mistakes

a window of opportunity
an opportunity temporarily available

an ocean full of fish
plenty of opportunity

an opening wide enough to drive a coach and four through
an excellent opportunity

this is the end of the road for someone
a person will have no further opportunity to do something

to be a crack in the wall
to represent a small unintended opportunity which can be exploited

to block someone's path
to interfere with a person's opportunity to advance himself

to blow something
unintentionally to destroy some opportunity

to carve out a niche for oneself
to deliberately create an opportunity to use one's talents effectively

to close the gate
to deny an opportunity which was previously available

to dip one's toe in the water
to gently explore an opportunity

to fill a vacuum
to take advantage of an opportunity not acted on by others

to find one's niche
to find the opportunity to use one's talents

to get only one bite at the cherry
to receive no further opportunity

to give someone enough rope to hang himself
to give a person the opportunity to do something which is likely to get him into severe trouble

to grab some opportunity with both hands
to seize some opportunity with great enthusiasm

to have a leg in
to have an opportunity which has the potential to lead to bigger things

to have other irons in the fire
to have the opportunity to do something else as an alternative

to have the ball at one's feet
to have unlimited opportunity

to keep one's eyes open for something
to be on the lookout for an opportunity to do something

to knock on doors
to seek out opportunities to do business

to miss the boat
to fail to exploit an opportunity

to miss the bus
to fail to exploit an opportunity

to miss the train
to fail to exploit an opportunity

to open up doors
to create opportunities

to put one's toe in the water
to gently explore an opportunity

to queer the pitch for someone
to spoil the opportunity a person has to do something

to run with the ball
to make the most of the opportunity

to shut the door on someone
to deny another person a desired opportunity

to turn back the clock
to have another opportunity to do something which should have been done already or to undo something which cannot be undone

your race is run
you have had your opportunity

PAST

a past master
an expert with long experience

a warhorse
an old soldier who likes to relive past wartime experiences

in Halcyon days
in past happier times (refers to the 14 days about the winter solstice when winds are calm and to the mythical bird said to breed in a floating nest at that time)

the chickens are coming home to roost
the consequences of past actions are becoming obvious

the melody lingers on
the benefit of past actions remains

to be a breath of fresh air
to be a pleasant change from the past

to conduct a postmortem on something
to review past actions with a view to learning lessons for the future (Latin, "after the death")

to even the score
to get one's own back for some past action

to start from scratch
to commence something without the benefit of any past activity

to wipe the slate clean
to forgive past indiscretions

PLEASURE

a willing horse
a cheerful worker

fun and games
amusement derived in the course of a serious activity

not to be all beer and skittles
not to be all pleasant and easy

the cheering could be heard a block away
there was great rejoicing

the party is over
the previous pleasant arrangements have been discontinued

to be a breath of fresh air
to be a pleasant change from the past

to be a stormy petrel
a person who disturbs a pleasant state of affairs by agitating for change

to be a tonic
to cheer someone up

to be full of beans
to be very cheerful

to be in good heart
to be cheerful, especially in adversity

to be meat and drink
to be very pleasurable

to be music to one's ears
to be comments which one is very pleased to hear

to be on a path strewn with roses
to lead a very pleasant life

to be tickled pink
to be very pleased

to bounce back
to resume a cheerful existence after some setback

to bring the house down
to greatly amuse an audience

to cast a cloud over something
to spoil the pleasure of an occasion

to drain every ounce out of something
to get the maximum use or pleasure out of something

to give someone heart
to cause a person to cheer up

to have an audience rolling in the aisles
to amuse an audience

to have someone in stitches
to greatly amuse a person

to kill oneself laughing
to be greatly amused

to lick one's chops
to look forward to something with pleasurable anticipation

to positively purr
(of a person) to be very pleased; (of an engine) to run very smoothly

to take the rough with the smooth
to accept the hardships of life along with its pleasant features

POSSIBILITY

a middle-of-the-road solution
a solution near the middle of a range of possibilities

as soon as someone's back was turned
at the moment it became possible to do something without a person's knowledge

bedrock price
lowest possible price

catch-22
a situation made impossible because it requires as a prior fulfillment something which does not exist until that condition is satisfied (title of a novel by Joseph Heller)

on the deathknock
at the last possible moment

one can't get a quart into a pint pot
one cannot do the impossible

one can't make a silk purse out of a sow's ear
it is impossible to manufacture something of a high standard without appropriate raw materials

that has put paid to it
the project can no longer proceed

that is a long shot
there is only a remote possibility

the game is up
escape is now impossible

there is more than one way to skin a cat
this can be achieved in a variety of acceptable ways

to be a crack in the wall
to represent a small unintended opportunity which can be exploited

to be a gray area
to be in an undefined position straddling two or more possibilities

to be able to do something standing on one's head
to be able to do something very easily

to be able to do something with one hand behind one's back
to be able to do something very easily

to be able to eat someone for breakfast
to be able to outwit a person very easily

to be able to lay one's hand on something
to be able to locate something

to be able to spot trouble a mile away
to be able to spot trouble before it actually happens

to conjure up something
to produce something in circumstances where this seemed impossible

to draw a long bow
to state a conclusion which while possible is unlikely on the known facts

to draw blood from a stone
to do the impossible

to exhaust the field
to use up all the possibilities

to have a good nose for business
to be able to identify profitable business situations

to have a snowflake's chance in hell
to have no hope or possibility at all

to have an eagle eye
to be able to notice small mistakes very readily

to have broad shoulders
to be able to cope well with responsibility

to have one's foot on something
to be about to acquire something or to be able to acquire something

to lurk in the shadows
to have a low profile at the moment, but with the possibility of becoming much more conspicuous at any time

to move heaven and earth
to do everything possible

to paint oneself into a corner
to foolishly put oneself into a position from which escape is impossible

to produce something out of thin air
to get hold of something in circumstances where this seemed impossible

to push water uphill
to foolishly attempt the impossible

to tie someone's hands behind his back
to make it impossible for a person to act at all

to try to square the circle
to attempt the impossible (refers to a classical problem in geometry, namely, to construct with a compass a square of the same area as a given circle)

two can play at that game
it is possible to retaliate

POWER

a figurehead
the ceremonial chief officer of some organization without any real power (refers to the carving at the front of a ship)

a game of cat and mouse
negotiations between two parties of unequal bargaining power during which the stronger makes some temporary concessions to the weaker without, however, affecting the latter's eventual total defeat

a tall poppy
a person with great power or responsibility and/or in receipt of high remuneration

a toothless tiger
an authority which has been given totally inadequate powers for its task

if the mountain will not come to Mahomet then Mahomet will go to the mountain
on recognizing that one has insufficient power to effect one's most desired solution, one decides to make do with the next best alternative

more power to your elbow
may your praiseworthy efforts lead to success

one can't beat City Hall
the ordinary citizen is powerless against bureaucracy

the law of the jungle
the principles that those having power will use it at the expense of all others

the power behind the throne
a person exercising the real authority but without having the official right to do so (the antonym of ''titular head'')

the top dog
the person in the most powerful position

to be in the box seat
to be in a very powerful position to control activity

to flex one's muscles
to exert one's personality or powers

to have a long arm
to have far-reaching power

to hold the power to do something in the hollow of one's hand
to have the right to make crucial decisions

to keep someone in a straitjacket
to deny a person any discretionary powers at all

to trample someone underfoot
by virtue of one's great power to treat a person's rights with contempt and not to give them proper consideration

to wield a big stick
to exert power

under one's own power
without external help

PRACTICABILITY

a castle in Spain
an impractical proposition

a castle in the air
an impractical proposition

to be in an ivory tower
to be immersed in theoretical considerations and ignorant of the practical realities (Song of Solomon 7:4)

to jettison some proposal
to abandon some proposal as worthless or impracticable

to pay lip service to some rules
to disregard some rules in practice while acknowledging them in words

to put someone through the mill
to give a person practical experience

to start with a blank sheet of paper
to commence an exercise without being bound by any established practices

to turn sour
to become impracticable or unprofitable

PRAISE

a backhanded compliment
a polite expression seemingly of praise but really intended as an insult

more power to your elbow
may your praiseworthy efforts lead to success

to fish for compliments
to drop hints in the hope that one will receive praise or recognition

to get full marks for something
to deserve praise for something

to pull oneself up by one's bootstraps
to make a praiseworthy effort to better oneself unaided

to sing someone's praises
to commend a person exuberantly

PRETENSE

to act out a charade
ostentatiously to pretend to be doing something in an ethical fashion

to be mutton dressed up as lamb
to foolishly pretend to be younger

to play possum
to pretend that one is not present

to sail under false colors
to pretend that one's real character or beliefs are different from what they really are

to sweep something under the carpet
to pretend that some blemish does not exist

to touch a nerve
to mention something which another person would rather pretend did not exist

to turn a blind eye to something
to pretend something obvious does not exist (refers to action by Nelson when disregarding Admiralty signals)

PREVENTION

I'll soon stop his little game
his activities are not tolerated and I will ensure that they cease

a bottleneck
a factor obstructing an even flow

a logjam
a stoppage of activity caused by input in greater volume than allowed for

a stitch in time saves nine
preventive maintenance saves money in the long run

cut it out!
stop doing that!

stonewalling
deliberate obstruction or delaying tactics

stumbling block
an impediment or difficulty preventing the easy completion of some project or a dilemma involving a moral issue

the fat is in the fire
action with certain unstoppable consequences has now been initiated

to be on a treadmill
to be involved in some unpleasant ongoing activity which cannot readily be stopped

to be stopped in one's tracks
suddenly and unexpectedly to be prevented from carrying on with a project

to break down the barriers
to do away with the prejudice preventing something

to chop someone off at the socks
to stop someone's proposals prematurely

to come to a full stop
to completely cease activity

to fetter someone
to stop a person acting on his own initiative

to fight bushfires
to deal with crises as they arise rather than take preventive action

to nip something in the bud
to stop some activity in its early stages when stopping it is still relatively easy

to put a spoke in someone's wheel
to interfere with another person's activity, so preventing its continuance

to put a wall around someone
to stop a person associating with others

to put the brake on someone
to stop a person

to shut the stable door after the horse has bolted
to take preventive action only after the relevant event

to slip through the net
to happen as an isolated case despite steps taken to prevent such events

to slip under one's guard
to cause a mistake to be made despite care being taken to prevent this

to stand in someone's way
to prevent a person achieving his goal

to stem the hemorrhage
to put a stop to the financial losses of a project

to tie someone's hands
to prevent a person from acting as he sees fit

PRICE AND VALUE

a bird in the hand is worth two in the bush
a benefit currently available is more valuable than a seemingly much larger benefit which may or may not be achieved in the future

a jewel
a valued assistant

a listening post
a place where information of strategic value can be collected

a treasure trove
a valuable discovery

bedrock price
lowest possible price

daylight robbery
the charging of grossly excessive prices

fire sale
a forced sale, realizing bargain prices

garage sale
sale of miscellaneous assets at cheap prices

highway robbery
the charging of grossly excessive prices

not a mite
not at all (refers to a Flemish coin of small value)

not to be worth a continental
to have no value (refers to currency notes)

not to be worth the candle
to be too expensive in relation to the true value

something has no guts in it
something has no real value to it

to be above water
(of securities) have a market value in excess of the cost price

to cast pearls before swine
to confer valuable benefits on someone who neither recognizes nor appreciates them

to charge a mint
to impose very high prices

to charge like a wounded bull
to impose excessive prices (a play on words; not a simile)

to charge the earth
to impose very high prices

to earn peanuts
to get a reward which is far too small in relation to the value of the services rendered

to go through the roof
(of a person) to be very upset or (of prices) to escalate greatly

to hand over something on a silver platter
to provide a valuable benefit for virtually nothing

to lose one's right arm
to lose some highly-valued assistance

to pay something back with interest
to return a small favor with a bigger favor or to extract retribution of greater value than the circumstances warrant

to pay through the nose
to pay an excessive price

to pick the eyes out of something
to choose the most valuable items from among a large number

to sell one's birthright for a mess of pottage
through foolishness to exchange something of substance for something of little value (Genesis 25)

to sell someone a pup
to cheat a person in a transaction, especially by misrepresentation as to the true value of something

to skyrocket
(of a price or value) to increase greatly in a short time

yeoman service
valuable assistance over a long time

PRIDE AND HUMILITY

barefaced
shameless

to be done like a dinner
to be defeated and humiliated

to be in the doghouse
to be in disgrace

to be the apple of someone's eye
to be a person of whom another person is proud

to cut tall poppies down to size
to humiliate haughty persons

to hang one's head
to be ashamed of oneself

to put on airs and graces
to act in an affected manner

to rub it in
to humiliate another person by emphasizing his defeat

to rub someone's nose in it
to humiliate a person by highlighting something embarrassing to him

to swallow one's pride
to take action despite the humiliating nature of this course

PROBLEM

Bob's your uncle
that solves the problem

a can of worms
a heterogeneous collection of unexpected problems

a step in the right direction
the first in a series of measures designed to correct some problem

a time bomb
a source of serious problems which are certain to surface later on

growing pains
problems encountered by virtue of expansion

join the club!
you are only one of many people with similar problems

not to be Robinson Crusoe
to be one of a large number of people with a common problem (from Daniel Defoe's ROBINSON CRUSOE)

one's door is always open
people can take their problems to one at any time

teething trouble
problems in the early stages of a project

the sky fell in
a very serious problem arose

the squeaky wheel gets the most attention
those complaining the most loudly will get their problems sorted out first

to be left holding the baby
to be tricked into accepting responsibility for someone else's problems

to be the hard core
to be the central and most difficult problem

to come to grips with some problem
to be on the way to solving a problem

to cut the Gordian knot
to solve, especially by force, a virtually insoluble problem (refers to a complicated knot tied by Gordius and eventually cut by Alexander the Great)

to fiddle at the edges
to do some relatively minor things which do not deal with the substance of a problem

to get stuck into some problem
to attempt to solve a problem with great vigor

to get to first base
to succeed in getting others to start comprehending a problem

to heave a sigh of relief
to express satisfaction at the achievement of a solution to a difficult problem

to iron out something
to sort out a difficult problem

to jump a hurdle
to overcome a problem or difficulty

to jump that hurdle when one comes to it
to deal with a particular problem only when it becomes necessary to do so

to just hold one's head above water
to cope with problems but with little margin to spare or to stay solvent

to leave something up in the air
to continue with an unresolved problem

to make mountains out of molehills
to treat a minor problem as though it were a major disaster

to need something like a hole in the head
to be landed with a completely undesired problem

to play the cards as they fall
to deal with problems as they arise

to present a happy face to the world
bravely to gloss over one's problems

to prey on one's mind
(of a problem) to keep worrying one

to put one's thinking cap on
to concentrate on finding a solution to a difficult problem

to take the bit between one's teeth
to face up a problem

to take the bull by the horns
to come to grip with the realities of a difficult problem

to try to square the circle
to attempt the impossible (refers to a classical problem in geometry, namely, to construct with a compass a square of the same area as a given circle)

PUNISHMENT

for one's sins
by way of punishment, as it were

heads will roll
transgressors will be punished

to be a glutton for punishment
to act irresponsibly in the face of inevitable retribution

to be for the high jump
to be threatened with a reprimand and punishment

to get off scot free
to go unpunished (refers to an exemption from tax)

to kiss the rod
to accept punishment meekly

to send someone to Coventry
to ostentatiously and collectively ignore a person by way of punishment

to thrash with a feather
to award only a minor punishment for a very serious offense

READINESS

a cash cow
a source of ready money

off the peg
(of clothes) ready-made

ready-made
easily fabricated or available without difficulty

to batten down the hatches
to get ready for expected difficulties

to be at hand
to be in the vicinity, ready to help

to be up to concert pitch
to be ready

to clear the decks
to get ready for action

to draw a deep breath
to get ready for exertion or for emotional news

to gird up one's loins
to get ready for action

to grit one's teeth
to get ready to suffer pain

to prepare one's ground
to get ready for a confrontation

to set the scene for something
to get things ready for something

to sharpen one's ax
to get ready for a difficult task

to sharpen the knives
to get ready for a concerted attack on some principle

to spread one's wings
to assert authority which has not yet been conferred by one's superiors and for which one may not be ready

to warm up
to get ready

REFUSAL AND REJECTION

a doubting Thomas
a person who refuses to believe claims in the absence of proof (John 20:25)

not to lift a finger to help someone
to refuse to assist

that is not to be sneezed at
that is so significant that it should not be rejected

to be a dog in the manger
to spitefully deny something to others, notwithstanding its uselessness to oneself

to be an ostrich
to refuse to face up to an unpleasant truth (refers to the reputed habit of ostriches in danger)

to be like water off a duck's back
(of advice or criticism) to be completely rejected

to blackball someone
to reject a person as unsuitable

to bury one's head in the sand
to refuse to face up to an unpleasant truth (refers to the reputed habit of ostriches in danger)

to button up one's purse
to refuse to spend money

to close the gate
to deny an opportunity which was previously available

to draw the line at that
to refuse to go any further

to gather dust
not to be acted upon without being formally rejected

to go haywire
to refuse to function properly

to have no truck with someone
to refuse to deal with a person

to keep someone in a straitjacket
to deny a person any discretionary powers at all

to knock an idea on the head
to utterly reject a proposal

to leave someone out in the cold
to deny a desired objective to a person

to pass the buck
in an uncooperative spirit to decline responsibility for a matter on the grounds that someone else more properly has responsibility for it

to plead the Fifth Amendment
to refuse to answer an unwelcome question (refers to the Fifth Amendment of the United States Constitution, which provides protection against self-incrimination)

to pull up the drawbridge
to refuse to cooperate

to refuse point blank
to refuse outright

to shut the door on someone
to deny another person a desired opportunity

to sit on the fence
to refuse to choose between two alternatives

to slam the door in someone's face
ostentatiously to refuse to have any dealings with a person

to throw a blanket over a proposal
to refuse to proceed with a proposal

to throw something out of the window
to completely reject an idea or proposal

to turn off the tap
to deny further access to supplies or information

to turn one's back on someone
to decline to further assist or deal with a person

to wash one's hands of something
to emphatically decline future responsibility

wild horses would not cause me to do something
I absolutely refuse to do something (refers to a form of torture)

REPUTATION

a black sheep
a disreputable member of an otherwise reputable group

a muckraker
a person who sets out to publicize misconduct of famous persons or institutions

a mudraker
a person who sets out to publicize features harming another person's reputation

by their fruits ye shall know them
their reputation will be based on their results (Matthew 7:20)

he must have a long spoon that sups with the devil
great care is needed when negotiating deals with disreputable parties

some mud will stick
reputations will be hurt even after accusations are proved false

to blot one's copybook
to spoil one's previously good reputation or record

to crucify someone
to unfairly do severe damage to a person's reputation or credibility

to have a black mark against one's name
to have a tarnished reputation

to look to one's laurels
to be careful not to lose one's reputation for some skill

to make a name for oneself
to earn a good reputation by virtue of some skill

to make something one's trademark
to earn a reputation for maintaining some stance

to paint someone black
to ruin a person's reputation

to put one's reputation on the line
to take a public stance in the realization that there is a risk that one's reputation will suffer if one is proved wrong

to rest on one's laurels
to use a reputation for success earned in earlier times as a substitute for current endeavor

to undermine someone's position
to injure another person's reputation and influence by unfair and secret tactics

RESPONSIBILITY

a tall poppy
a person with great power or responsibility and/or in receipt of high remuneration

charity begins at home
a person's first responsibility should be to his family

one's opposite number
a person with similar responsibilities in another organization

someone would run a mile
a person would do anything to escape his responsibilities

that is on your head
you will have to accept responsibility for that

the ball is in someone's court
it is some other person's responsibility

the buck stops here
I accept full responsibility (sign on the desk of Harry S. Truman when president of the United States)

to abandon ship
to abrogate one's responsibilities or to abandon a project

to be a glutton for punishment
to act irresponsibly in the face of inevitable retribution

to be in someone's bailiwick
to be some other person's responsibility

to be in someone's shoes
to have another person's responsibility

to be left holding the baby
to be tricked into accepting responsibility for someone else's problems

to be one's baby
to be one's area of responsibility

to be one's pigeon
to be one's area of responsibility

to be tied down
to have responsibilities precluding alternative activities

to dump something in someone's lap
to impose some responsibility on another person

to engage in empire building
to set out to expand the size of the business or bureaucratic unit for which one is responsible, especially as a means of increasing one's own importance

to face the music
to accept responsibility when confronted by one's critics

to have blood on one's hands
to be the person responsible for someone else's predicament

to have broad shoulders
to be able to cope well with responsibility

to pass the buck
is an uncooperative spirit to decline responsibility for a matter on the grounds that someone else more properly has responsibility for it

to pin someone down
to find a person willing to accept blame or responsibility or to force a person to announce a decision or concede a point

to put a burden on someone's shoulders
to impose responsibilities on a person

to take a weight off someone's shoulder
to assist a person by relieving him of some responsibility

to tread on someone's corns
to upset another person by interfering in his area of responsibility

to tread on someone's toes
to upset another person by interfering in his area of responsibility

to walk away from something
to abrogate one's responsibilities in regard to some matter

to wash one's hands of something
to emphatically decline future responsibility

under someone's nose
in a person's immediate area of responsibility or in circumstances where he should have known something

uneasy lies the head that wears a crown
responsibility involves some risks and some burdens (from Shakespeare's HENRY IV)

RESULT

a South Sea bubble
an unrealistic financial venture which is bound to result in total loss

a landslide
an electoral result involving victory or defeat by an unexpectedly large margin

a litmus test
an event which allows the outcome of future events to be predicted more accurately

a patchwork quilt
a result arising from many uncoordinated inputs

a photo finish
a close result in a contest

all roads lead to Rome
all alternatives will have the same outcome

backwash
consequence

by their fruits ye shall know them
their reputation will be based on their results (Matthew 7:20)

chicken and egg
two factors each of which results in the other

come hell or high water
regardless of the consequences

death blow
incident which results in the destruction of something

harvest
end result of labor

if the cap fits then wear it
if your circumstances correspond with those described then you must endure the consequences

one can't make bricks without straw
one cannot achieve results in the absence of adequate resources

one has made one's bed and one will now have to lie on it
one has to bear the consequences of one's actions

one might as well be hanged for a sheep as for a lamb
further action will not increase the adverse consequences already in train (refers to the stealing of both sheep and lambs being capital crimes under old English law)

one shudders to think what the outcome might be
there is great concern as to the outcome

pie in the sky
a hoped-for result unlikely to be achieved

stalemate
a final result in which neither party to a dispute is victorious

the answer is a lemon
the outcome is inconclusive

the chickens are coming home to roost
the consequences of past actions are becoming obvious

the fat is in the fire
action with certain unstoppable consequences has now been initiated

the final straw
the latest step, which, when added to a large number of seemingly harmless previous steps, sets off a disaster resulting from the cumulative effect

the proof of the pudding is in the eating
the success of a venture will be measured by its results

the straw which broke the camel's back
the latest step, which, when added to a large number of seemingly harmless previous steps, sets off a disaster resulting from the cumulative effect

things look black
there is little hope of success or prosperity or a favorable outcome

to apply pressure on someone
to induce a person to do something which he would otherwise not do by implying adverse consequences if he does not cooperate

to be a laid-down misere
to be very easily accomplished and/or to be certain of outcome (refers to the declaration in certain card game undertaking to win no tricks)

to be a mixed blessing
to be an outcome with some desirable and some undesirable features

to be hell bent on something
to be very determined to achieve something, regardless of the adverse consequences

to be on tenterhooks
to anxiously await some result

to be shortsighted
not to recognize the likely consequences

to be the kiss of death
to be something intended to be helpful but resulting in total destruction

to be the luck of the draw
to be a chance result

to bear fruit
to result in success

to break one's duck
to end a spell without results

to count one's chickens before they are hatched
to treat as fact the expected results of a future proposal

to cover one's hide
to provide excess or take other evasive action in an attempt to avoid the adverse consequences of one's actions

to cry "wolf"
to repeatedly raise an unjustified concern with the result that one will be ignored when the circumstances change

to dig one's own grave
to take action which results in an unintended disaster for oneself

to get brownie points
to do a person a favor with the likely result that the recipient will do a favor in return in due course

to have egg on one's face
to be embarrassed by the results of one's own stupidity

to hedge one's bets
to take action involving a cost but which is designed to reduce the possible adverse consequences of some activity

to hide under someone's skirts
to let someone else take the consequences of one's actions

to hold a knife at someone's throat
to exert undue pressure on another person in an endeavor to achieve a result which would otherwise not be forthcoming

to hold a sword at someone's throat
to exert undue pressure on another person in an endeavor to achieve a result which would otherwise not be forthcoming

to keep one's fingers crossed
to hope for a good outcome

to let someone off the hook
to allow a person to escape the adverse consequences of his own actions

to nurse one's bruises
to face up to the consequences of defeat

to open up the floodgates
to take action which will have massive consequences

to pay the price
to suffer the adverse consequences of one's acts or omissions

to prick up one's ears
to suddenly start paying attention to a conversation in progress as a result of a half-heard phrase

to raise merry hell
to prominently involve others in a matter in the expectation of significant results from this action

to reap as one has sown
to experience the consequences of one's own actions

to reap the whirlwind
to suffer the adverse consequences of a bad act

to score a hat trick
to have three successive favorable outcomes

to seal someone's fate
to cause a certain outcome adversely affecting a person

to shake a tree
to do something in order to see what will result

to sow the wind and reap the whirlwind
to make bad mistakes and to suffer the even worse consequences

to stew in one's juice
to suffer the adverse consequences of one's acts or omissions

to stir up a hornet's nest
to take action which results in unpleasant side-effects

to take a caning
to suffer the adverse consequences of one's acts or omissions

to throw one's weight about
to use one's real or imagined status in order to achieve certain results

to tip the balance
to provide further information or argument which results in an issue which could have been decided either way being determined in a particular way

to tip the scales
to be a factor which in combination with other factors results in a particular decision which would otherwise not have been reached

RETIREMENT

a golden handshake
a large payment in connection with or as an inducement to retirement

in harness
before retirement

swan song
last appearance before retirement

to bow out
to retire from some activity

to hang up one's boots
to retire

to step down
to retire from some position

REVENGE

to get one's own back on someone
to extract revenge

to pay someone back in his own coin
to retaliate in kind

to return the compliment
to reciprocate or to extract revenge

to thirst for blood
to be eager for revenge

two can play at that game
it is possible to retaliate

REVERSAL

one cannot teach an old dog new tricks
people get irreversibly set in their ways

the die is cast
the course of action in train is irreversible

to backpedal
to reverse to some extent previously applied policies

to burn one's bridges
to do something irreversible

to cross the Rubicon
to make an irreversible decision in regard to some commitment

to do a U-turn
to reverse one's thinking

to do an about-face
to reverse a previously enunciated policy

to let the genie out of the bottle
to cause something irreversible to take place

to turn a complete somersault
to reverse one's established policy

to turn around 180 degrees
to completely reverse a stance

to turn round
to reverse one's policy

to turn something on its ear
to reverse something

to turn something on its head
to reverse something

to turn the tables on someone
to cause the relative positions of oneself and another person to be reversed

to turn the tide
to reverse the direction of something

volte face
a reversal of previously-held beliefs (French, "a turning around")

RISK

fools rush in where angels fear to tread
unsophisticated persons take unwise risks in circumstances where more knowledgeable persons would exercise caution

in for a penny—in for a pound
once something is commenced it ought to be finished; or if one is willing to take a small risk then one might as well take a bigger one

it is a case of sink or swim
the attempt is worthwhile, despite the risk of failure

it was touch and go
there were considerable risks—the objective was achieved, but only just

nervous Nellies
persons unwilling to take any risks

not to put all one's eggs in one basket
to spread one's risks

someone's job is on the line
a person's career path is under consideration and/or his present position is at risk

to be sitting on a volcano
to be safe for the time being but exposed to the risk of a sudden great disaster

to chance one's arm
to take a great risk (refers to the stripes on the uniforms of non-commissioned officers)

to enter treacherous waters
to engage in an enterprise with risks which are not obvious

to go out on a limb
to put oneself at risk through foolish action

to go through fire and water
to undertake all attendant risks

to jump in feet first
to take a calculated risk

to play Russian roulette
to take stupid risks

to play it safe
to take no risks

to play with dynamite
to invite trouble by virtue of one's risky conduct

to push one's luck
having already done well in something, to then take risks which can prejudice everything

to put one's money where one's mouth is
to back one's judgment by putting assets at risk

to put one's reputation on the line
to take a public stance in the realization that there is a risk that one's reputation will suffer if one is proved wrong

to stick one's neck out
to have the courage of one's convictions or to take a calculated risk

to take a punt
to take a calculated risk

to take the plunge
to expose oneself to certain risks

to throw a sprat to catch a mackerel
to risk a little in the hope of gaining much

uneasy lies the head that wears a crown
responsibility involves some risks and some burdens (from Shakespeare's HENRY IV)

SADNESS

heartache
sadness

heartbreak
despair

one's heart bleeds for someone
one feels truly sad for a person's fate

there is blood on the floor
this has caused great anguish

to beat one's breast
to express sorrow

to cast a shadow over something
to introduce a note of warning or sadness in regard to some matter

to cry one's eyes out
to express great sadness at a situation

to drown one's sorrows
to drink by way of solace and in an attempt to forget some misfortune

to set someone's teeth on edge
to cause a person to feel unhappy at a situation

to take something to heart
to learn to appreciate the significance of something or to be much saddened by something

with a heavy heart
in sorrow

you can eat your heart out
you are entitled to feel sad or jealous

SAMENESS

a nod is the same as a wink to a blind horse
fine distinctions are not appropriate here

a round robin
a series of checks from A to B, from B to C, from C to A, and so on, leaving all of them in the same net position as before

all roads lead to Rome
all alternatives will have the same outcome

birds of a feather flock together
persons of like interests gather in the same place

Box and Cox
two persons who are never around at the same time (from the name of a play)

by the same token
by way of corroboration

in one fell swoop
all at the same time

not to be in the same street as someone
not to be of comparable quality

to all sing from the same hymnal
to act consistently with each other

to be in harmony with someone
to act in the same way as another person

to be in the same boat
to share a common set of difficulties

to be in the same league
to have comparable skills

to be in tune with someone
to think on the same lines as another person

to be on the same wavelength
to think on similar lines

to be tarred with the same brush
to be damned merely because of one's association with another person

to be with it
to think on the same lines as the current generation or to be fully informed

to follow suit
to do the same as others

to speak the same language
to have a good understanding and similar ideas

under one roof
under the same management

SATISFACTION

a seal of approval
confirmation that something is satisfactory

a warm inner glow
satisfaction at some achievement

I will have his guts for garters
I am extremely angry and dissatisfied with him

the nigger in the woodpile
the factor spoiling an otherwise satisfactory arrangement

to be a well-oiled piece of machinery
to be functioning very satisfactorily

to be cream on top of the milk
to be an additional benefit in an already satisfactory scenario

to be first class
to be very satisfactory

to be icing on top of the cake
to be an additional benefit in an already satisfactory scenario

to be on course
to be progressing satisfactorily toward one's goal

to get rid of the dead wood
to terminate the services of unsatisfactory personnel

to heave a sigh a relief
to express satisfaction at the achievement of a solution to a difficult problem

to hit a sour note
to discover an unexpected flaw in an otherwise satisfactory piece of work

to jump for joy
to express great satisfaction

to make a noise about something
to complain or express dissatisfaction about something

to rub one's hands with glee
to express great satisfaction

SECRECY

a word in someone's ear
a confidential discussion

between you and me and the gatepost
confidentially

Chinese walls
a system to ensure that different parts of some organization do not gain access to each other's confidential information

cloak and dagger activity
secret activity

low-down
confidential information relevant to something

no names—no packdrill
the identities of the parties will be kept confidential in order to protect them

something is in the wind
something is going on secretly (this phrase uses the actual word "something")

to be a closed book
to be a secret

to be tight-lipped
to keep confidences or to be uncommunicative

to ferret something out
by diligent research to discover some secret

to have a card up one's sleeve
to secretly have information relevant to a transaction

to have a heart-to-heart talk
to have a confidential discussion on a highly personal matter

to hold one's cards close to one's chest
to keep one's plans and strategies secret

to keep something dark
to keep something secret

to keep something under one's hat
to maintain a confidence

to keep something up one's sleeve
to secretly retain something in reserve for use in the future or at a later stage of negotiations

to keep under wraps
to keep confidential

to let the cat out of the bag
to reveal an embarrassing secret (refers to the exposure of cheats at fairs, attempting to pass a cat wrapped in a sack off as a piglet)

to line one's pockets
to make, improperly and secretly, a profit out of some transaction

to seal one's lips
to keep a confidence

to tell tales out of school
to deliberately leak a secret

to undermine someone's position
to injure another person's reputation and influence by unfair and secret tactics

wheels within wheels
secret machinations

SITUATION

a Mexican standoff
a situation where neither of two parties is making a move

a gambit
an opening move in a competitive situation which involves short-term losses in the expectation of long-term gains

a place in the sun
a favorable situation

a springboard
a situation from which one intends to make a rapid advance

a straight face
a facial expression which does not reveal one's thoughts in a humorous situation

a stranglehold
a firm grip on a commercial situation, effectively freezing out a competitor

catch-22
a situation made impossible because it requires as a prior fulfillment something which does not exist until that condition is satisfied (title of a novel by Joseph Heller)

every cloud has a silver lining
there are benefits even in seemingly adverse situations

out of the frying pan into the fire
from one bad situation to an even worse one

something is rotten in the state of Denmark
the situation is not correct (from Shakespeare's HAMLET)

that is the way the chips fall
that is the actual situation

that is the way the cookie crumbles
that is the actual situation

the nature of the beast
the reality of the situation

to add fuel to the fire
to make a bad situation worse

to be in command
to be on top of a situation

to be quick on one's feet
to cleverly take advantage of a situation

to bite the bullet
to face up to the difficulties of a situation

to breathe down someone's neck
to cause annoyance to another person by remaining in his vicinity or by supervising him too closely; or to be narrowly behind another person in some competitive situation

to cross a bridge only when one comes to it
to await the crystallization of a situation before sorting it out

to cry one's eyes out
to express great sadness at a situation

to feed the fire
to exacerbate a situation

to fight fire with fire
to counter a dangerous situation by making an equally dangerous move

to fish in troubled waters
to profit from a disturbed situation

to have a good nose for business
to be able to identify profitable business situations

to have the whip hand
to be in control of a situation

to inflame a situation
to aggravate a situation

to keep an eye on the ball
to monitor a fast-changing situation

to keep one's eye on something
to monitor a situation

to keep up with the ball
to stay on top of the situation

to knock someone off his perch
to displace a person from his leadership position in some competitive situation

to pour oil on troubled waters
to calm down a situation

to pour gasoline on the flames
to make a bad situation worse

to pull someone's chestnuts out of the fire
to retrieve a situation

to pull something out of the fire
to salvage something in a seemingly hopeless situation

to put a match to petrol
to make a bad situation worse

to put jam on someone's bread
to make a good situation even better

to put one's best face on something
to focus on the positive features surrounding a basically disastrous situation

to put someone in the picture
to fill a person in with the background of a situation

to ride out the storm
to come safely through some dangerous situation

to salvage something out of the wreck
to achieve some minor benefits out of a disastrous situation

to see the light
to understand the real situation

to see the score
to appreciate the reality of a situation

to see which way the wind is blowing
to establish the factors relevant to a situation

to set someone's teeth on edge
to cause a person to feel unhappy at a situation

to squeeze the last drop out of something
to get the maximum advantage out of some favorable situation

to strike while the iron is hot
to take advantage of a situation which cannot last

to suck the lemon dry
to get the maximum advantage out of some favorable situation

to underplay some situation
to hold something in reserve

SKILL

a chessmaster
a clever strategist

a dark horse
a person with unsuspected talents

a pea and thimble trick
a clever fraud committed in the presence of its victim without this being obvious at the time

a shaggy-dog story
an amusing anecdote with an unexpected ending, often involving talking animals given certain human skills

one's long suit
one's main skills

the blind leading the blind
persons without the necessary skills for a task purporting to impart those skills to others

to be a chess game
to be a complex exercise, requiring great skill

to be child's play
to be easy or to require only elementary skills and knowledge

to be great guns at something
to be very skilled at something

to be hot stuff
to be skillful or very passionate

to be in the same league
to have comparable skills

to be quick on one's feet
to cleverly take advantage of a situation

to carve out a niche for oneself
to deliberately create an opportunity to use one's talents effectively

to find one's feet
to develop one's skills

to find one's niche
to find the opportunity to use one's talents

to hide one's light under a bushel
to keep others in ignorance of one's skills and experience

to keep one's hands in
to engage in activities which reinforce skills which one has previously acquired

to look to one's laurels
to be careful not to lose one's reputation for some skill

to make a name for oneself
to earn a good reputation by virtue of some skill

to raise something to a fine art form
to become very clever at doing something

to rub off on someone
to benefit a person through an association which increases his skills

to score a point
to make a clever contribution in the course of debate

to separate the men from the boys
to distinguish between those with and without certain skills

to take someone's measure
to sum up a person's character or skills

tour de force
feat of skill or strength (French, "feat of strength")

SLOWNESS

at a snail's pace
very slowly

the mills of God grind slowly
retribution may be delayed but is inevitable

to be slow off the mark
to be slow to start something

to drag one's feet
to perform unduly slowly

to drag one's heels
to perform unduly slowly

to drag the chain
to perform unduly slowly

to inch forward
to make slow but steady progress

to lose steam
to slow down

to sink slowly in the West
to fail gradually

to slowly bleed to death
to be heading in gradual steps toward total ruin

SMALLNESS

a backwater
a place of little activity

a bunfight
a minor and relatively friendly skirmish

a chink of light
a small hope of a solution or break-through

a dogfight
a small side-skirmish, especially between airplanes

a fat chance
little hope

a fox hole
space which is really too small for a person's needs or comfort

a handful
a small number

a pawn
a person of small importance who is manipulated by others

a tempest in a teacup
a controversy about a minor matter but one which looms large in the minds of the parties

a toehold
an opportunity small in itself but with the potential to lead to bigger things

a trickle
a small amount, in gradual stages

give him an inch and he will take a mile
make him a small concession and he will abuse it by taking much more

in for a penny—in for a pound
once something is commenced it ought to be finished; or if one is willing to take a small risk then one might as well take a bigger one

Lilliputian
small (refers to a place in Swift's GULLIVER'S TRAVELS)

not a jot
not even a small amount (refers to the Greek letter iota or i)

not to be a hanging matter
to be only a minor mistake

one's heart is not in some cause
one has little enthusiasm for some cause

people stayed away in droves
few people came

pintsize
small

tall oaks from little acorns grow
even major enterprises have to have small beginnings (from "Lines written for a School Declamation" by David Everett)

the tail wagging the dog
a minor aspect with disproportionate effect on a major aspect

there is no room to swing a cat
this place is very small (actually refers to a cat-o'-nine-tails)

to be a big fish in a little pond
to be a person holding an important office but in an unimportant organization

to be a crack in the wall
to represent a small unintended opportunity which can be exploited

to be a small cog in a large wheel
to be a relatively unimportant person in a large organization

to be chicken feed
to be small and unimportant

to be the thin end of the wedge
by conceding a small point, to create an undesirable precedent for much larger issues

to be the tip of the iceberg
to be only a small portion of a much larger but less obvious whole

to bend the rules
to overlook minor infractions of the rules

to chisel away at something
to reduce the size of something in a series of small stages

to cut no ice with someone
to have little effect on a person

to decimate
to greatly reduce in size (often used in the sense of "to reduce to one tenth," although the original meaning was "to reduce by one tenth")

to earn peanuts
to get a reward which is far too small in relation to the value of the services rendered

to encapsulate some idea
to reduce the essential points of a complicated proposal to a small number of words

to fiddle at the edges
to do some relatively minor things which do not deal with the substance of a problem

to find a needle in a haystack
to find something when the probability of finding it is very small

to have an eagle eye
to be able to notice small mistakes very readily

to hold someone on a short leash
to give a person very little authority

to live from hand to mouth
being in poor financial circumstances, to survive with little by way of safety margin

to look down the barrel of a gun
to be given little choice in a matter

to look for a needle in a haystack
to attempt something with a very small chance of success

to make mountains out of molehills
to treat a minor problem as though it were a major disaster

to miss the sharks while netting the minnows
to succeed in minor aspects but fail in the ones that really matter

to nitpick
to criticize a person in respect to very minor matters

to only scratch the surface
to deal with only a small portion of a much larger whole

to pay something back with interest
to return a small favor with a bigger favor or to extract retribution of greater value than the circumstances warrant

to push someone over the brink
by a small action to cause the absolute ruin (financially or emotionally) of someone already in peril

to salvage something out of the wreck
to achieve some minor benefits out of a disastrous situation

to sell one's birthright for a mess of pottage
through foolishness to exchange something of substance for something of little value (Genesis 25)

to slug it out
to engage in a minor skirmish

to snap at someone's heels
to be a minor irritation to a person

to test the water
to try out an idea in a small way

to thrash with a feather
to award only a minor punishment for a very serious offense

to throw a sprat to catch a mackerel
to risk a little in the hope of gaining much

to throw out the baby with the bathwater
to discard a major benefit in the course of obtaining a comparatively minor advantage

to throw someone a few crumbs
to fob a person off with a few symbolic but unimportant concessions

to tinker at the edges
to make minor or cosmetic changes without affecting the substance

two men and a dog
very few people

SPEECH

a nod and a wink
a sign that understanding has been reached in a matter which in the interests of discretion has not been discussed aloud

a shaggy-dog story
an amusing anecdote with an unexpected ending, often involving talking animals given certain human skills

a word in someone's ear
a confidential discussion

burning question
a much discussed question

not to mince words
to speak bluntly

not to put too fine a point on it
speaking bluntly

shoot!
go on, speak!

speak softly and carry a big stick
be polite to your potential enemies but maintain an active and visible defense capability (from a speech by Theodore Roosevelt in 1901)

talk of the devil
here is the person we were just discussing

to bandy something about
to discuss something in a light-hearted manner

to bare one's soul
talkatively to give a revealing insight into oneself

to bite someone's nose off
to speak to a person aggressively

to break the ice
to take the initiative in starting discussions

to buy into some argument
to seek to participate in some discussion

to chew fat
to eat and talk together

to draw a veil over something
pointedly to avoid discussing something

to drop names
to slip names of celebrities allegedly known to the speaker into a conversation in an attempt to impress

to find one's tongue
to overcome one's shyness and speak

to get down to brass tacks
to discuss the aspects which really matter

to have a bone to pick
to have a grievance which requires discussion

to have a heart-to-heart talk
to have a confidential discussion on a highly personal matter

to have a loose tongue
to speak foolishly or indiscreetly

to have a sharp tongue
to speak one's mind in forceful language

to hijack a debate
to involve oneself in the public discussion of some matter and turn that discussion to one's advantage

to keep one's mouth shut
not to discuss some matter

to lay a proposal on the table
to make a proposal available for discussion or to adjourn discussion on a proposal for an indefinite period

to open the batting
to be the first in a series of persons speaking or doing something

to pontificate
to speak as if with great authority and with an assumed air of infallibility

to shoot from the hip
to speak frankly and openly

to shoot one's mouth off
to speak without thinking

to skate around some subject
by diversionary tactics to avoid discussing some subject

to snap someone's head off
to speak to a person aggressively

to speak one's mind
to express one's views frankly and forcefully

to speak the same language
to have a good understanding and similar ideas

to speak with forked tongues
to utter half-truths with the intention of misleading the listener

to strangle some discussion
to cut off some unfinished discussion

to talk nineteen to the dozen
to engage in much idle chatter

to talk one's book
to present arguments which, while plausible, are really designed to foster one's vested interest

to talk shop
to discuss business or professional matters on a social occasion

to talk the hind leg off a donkey
to talk excessively

to talk through one's hat
to say things which demonstrate the speaker's ignorance of the subject

to talk turkey
to talk realistically

to waste one's breath
to talk or request something without achieving anything

were your ears burning?
we were discussing you

SPEED

at a break-neck pace
very fast

at a rate of knots
very fast

before you can say ''Jack Robinson''
very quickly

before one can say ''knife''
very quickly

by leaps and bounds
with surprisingly fast progress

fast and furious
in an exciting way, in quick succession

full steam ahead!
get going as fast as possible!

nimble-footed
quick to change the direction of one's activities when circumstances warrant

speed the plow!
let us get on with this as fast as possible!

tailspin
very fast fall

to achieve a flying start
to get operational very quickly

to be a money spinner
to produce large profits easily and quickly

to be all systems ''go''
to go ahead as fast as possible

to be quick on one's feet
to cleverly take advantage of a situation

to be quick on the draw
to act precipitately

to catapult to fame
to achieve fame unexpectedly quickly

to come in thick and fast
to arrive quickly and in great volume

to cut corners
to lower one's standards in order to complete something more quickly

to go hot foot
to do something fast

to go post haste
to go very fast

to have to fly
to need to leave in order to reach the next destination quickly

to keep an eye on the ball
to monitor a fast-changing situation

to lose money hand over fist
to lose money very fast and convincingly

to take shortcuts
to do something by a faster but less thorough method

STANDARD

a benchmark
a standard by which something is measured

a hallmark
a standard (refers to the official assay mark on gold and silver, originally put on at the Goldsmiths' Hall)

a yardstick
a standard by which something is measured

guiding light
yardstick for ethical behavior

not to be in the race
to lack the required standard

one can't make a silk purse out of a sow's ear
it is impossible to manufacture something of a high standard without appropriate raw materials

the Plimsoll line
the standard

the silly season
the holiday period, when hard news is scarce and journalistic standards are lowered

the touchstone
the standard

to be below par
to be less than the desired standard

to be beyond the pale
to be socially unacceptable, especially for unacceptable standards or behavior

to be up to scratch
to be of the required standard

to be up to the mark
to be of the right standard

to cut corners
to lower one's standards in order to complete something more quickly

to lift one's game
to raise the standard of one's performance

to play the last card in the pack
to lower one's standards in a final desperate effort

to really scrape the bottom of the barrel
to lower one's standards because one is short of important or relevant issues

to weed some group out
to get rid of some elements not meeting a desired standard

START

a baptism of fire
the commencement of an operation which presented great difficulty

from a to z
from start to finish

from alpha to omega
from start to finish (refers to the first and last letters of the Greek alphabet)

from go to whoa
from start to finish (refers to the command given to horses)

from the word "go"
from the beginning

in for a penny—in for a pound
once something is commenced it ought to be finished; or if one is willing to take a small risk then one might as well take a bigger one

it is on for young and old
the excitement has started

tall oaks from little acorns grow
even major enterprises have to have small beginnings (from "Lines written for a School Declamation" by David Everett)

the curtain rises on something
something is about to start

the rot set in
conditions started to deteriorate

to achieve a flying start
to get operational very quickly

to be back to scratch
to have to start all over again

to be first off the mark
to start ahead of all others

to be itching to go
to be highly enthusiastic and keen to start

to be slow off the mark
to be slow to start something

to be the dawn of a new day
to be the start of a different regime

to be the first cab off the rank
to start ahead of all others

to break the ice
to take the initiative in starting discussions

to come out into the open
to start being frank

to enter a long road
to commence a task which will take a long time

to enter the home stretch
to commence the last stage

to get in on the act
to participate in some activity started by others

to get the show on the road
to commence a planned activity

to get to first base
to succeed in getting others to start comprehending a problem

to go back to square one
to start all over again

to jump the gun
to start before one is meant to

to kick off
to start some action

to leap in
to commence an activity without considering the wisdom of doing so or the best way to proceed

to move on to greener pastures
to commence a new, better career

to prick up one's ears
to suddenly start paying attention to a conversation in progress as a result of a half-heard phrase

to set sail
to commence a voyage

to show someone the ropes
to teach a beginner how to do something

to start from scratch
to commence something without the benefit of any past activity

to start off on the right foot
to commence an operation with great care to do it correctly

to start the ball rolling
to commence and enthusiastically advance an activity involving people

to start to bite
to start to be effective

to start with a blank sheet of paper
to commence an exercise without being bound by any established practices

to turn the corner
to commence being successful after initial failures

STRATEGY

a chessmaster
a clever strategist

a listening post
a place where information of strategic value can be collected

opening gambit
the first in a series of strategic moves (a tautological expression which also involves a misunderstanding of a technical chess term)

to be in a commanding position
to have a strategic advantage

to derail some strategy
to cause a strategy to fail

to go down a particular road
to adopt a particular strategy

to hold one's cards close to one's chest
to keep one's plans and strategies secret

to play it by ear
to develop one's strategy to always fit in with circumstances as they change from time to time

STUPIDITY

a death wish
the contemplation of action so foolish that it is likely to lead to utter disaster

a simple Simon
a foolish, gullible or half-witted person

a wild goose chase
a foolish search for something which does not exist

beadledom
stupid officiousness

boneheaded
stupid

cock-eyed
stupid

hare-brained
wildly stupid

not to have an ounce of sense
to be stupid

people in glass houses should not throw stones
those who are less than perfect are foolish to criticize others

someone's brain needs washing
a person is very silly

to be mutton dressed up as lamb
to foolishly pretend to be younger

to be only ten pence in the shilling
to be slightly stupid

to burn one's fingers
to lose money through foolishness

to earn a dunce's cap
to do something stupid

to get under someone's skin
to annoy another person through stupidity

to go out on a limb
to put oneself at risk though foolish action

to go overboard
to act foolishly and in an excessive way

to have a bird brain
to be stupid

to have a loose tongue
to speak foolishly or indiscreetly

to have egg on one's face
to be embarrassed by the results of one's own stupidity

to judge a book by its cover
foolishly to go only by superficial appearances

to make an ass of oneself
to act stupidly in public

to need to have one's head read
to be foolish

to paint oneself into a corner
to foolishly put oneself into a position from which escape is impossible

to play Russian roulette
to take stupid risks

to play with fire
to invite trouble through one's foolish conduct

to push water uphill
to foolishly attempt the impossible

to put one's foot in it
to make a foolish mistake

to put one's foot in one's mouth
to say something foolish

to sell one's birthright for a mess of pottage
through foolishness to exchange something of substance for something of little value (Genesis 25)

to shoot oneself in the foot
to act in a foolish way and thus harm one's own cause

to sign one's own death warrant
to foolishly do something which is inevitably bound to lead to utter disaster

to sow wild oats
to indulge in foolish behavior while a young adult

why keep a dog and bark oneself?
it is silly to pay for assistance and then do things personally

SUCCESS

a breakthrough
success in overcoming resistance to a proposal

a field day
a very enjoyable and successful occasion

a flash in the pan
something which begins promisingly but does not last (refers to the priming of old guns)

a gambit
an opening move in the competitive situation which involves short-term losses in the expectation of long-term gains

a highflyer
an ambitious and/or successful person

a landslide
an electoral result involving victory or defeat by an unexpectedly large margin

a Pyrrhic victory
a win which costs more than if there had been a loss (refers to the battle at which King Pyrrhus of Epirus defeated the Romans at Asculum)

a roller coaster ride
a series of successes followed by failures

a walkover
an easy victory

chalk it up!
the success was unexpected

front-runner
person expected to win

it is in the bag
the enterprise has succeeded

it is mind over matter
one's resolve to overcome suffering will succeed

it is pointing in the right direction
success looks likely

more power to your elbow
may your praiseworthy efforts lead to success

stalemate
a final result in which neither party to a dispute is victorious

the proof of the pudding is in the eating
the success of a venture will be measured by its results

the royal road to success
the way of attaining success without effort

things look black
there is little hope of success or prosperity or a favorable outcome

to be a passport to success
to be a means of achieving success

to be going great guns
to be making very successful progress

to be home and hosed
to have won

to be on a winner
to have faith in, give support to and/or invest in a project which proves to be successful

to be on the crest of a wave
to enjoy success which may not last

to be successful beyond one's wildest dreams
to be far more successful than one could have expected

to be unable to take a trick
to be unable to achieve success in anything

to bear fruit
to result in success

to bring home the bacon
to be successful

to fight tooth and nail
to strive very hard to win

to get on stream
to now operate successfully following the end of a settling-in period

to get to first base
to succeed in getting others to start comprehending a problem

to go for the gold
to aim for victory (refers to Olympic medals)

to have a cast-iron case
to be absolutely assured of victory in legal proceedings

to have had a good innings
to have had a successful life

to have someone by the throat
to claim victory over an opponent

to have someone on toast
to be victorious over a person

to have the plug pulled out from under one
to have a successful activity destroyed by the actions of someone else

to hold a winning hand
to be in an unbeatable position to defeat others

to hold all the aces
to be in an unbeatable position to defeat others

to hold all the cards
to be assured of victory

to hold someone at bay
to successfully resist an attacker

to hold the trump card
to be in an unbeatable position to defeat others

to look for a needle in a haystack
to attempt something with a very small chance of success

to make a good fist of something
to be successful in a difficult task

to make a killing
to be in a very successful business venture

to make or break someone
to be a factor leading either to a person's success or to his failure, with no intermediate position

to make the grade
to succeed

to miss the sharks while netting the minnows
to success in minor aspects but fail in the ones that really matter

to pan out
to succeed

to pass with flying colors
to be very successful

to pay off
to be successful

to play the trump card
to make a final move, thereby defeating one's opponents

to pull something off
to achieve success in some enterprise

to raise the stake
to increase the amount of potential gain or loss in a project

to rest on one's laurels
to use a reputation for success earned in earlier times as a substitute for current endeavor

to ride high
to be successful but vulnerable

to ride the wave
to be successful for the time being

to score a hat trick
to have three successive favorable outcomes

to show dividends
to be successful

to smell blood
to divine imminent victory

to stitch up a deal
to successfully conclude a deal

to strike gold
to have one's efforts suddenly rewarded by great success

to strike pay dirt
to become successful

to strike the right chord
to appeal successfully to someone's emotions

to throw a sprat to catch a mackerel
to risk a little in the hope of gaining much

to turn the corner
to commence being successful after initial failures

to win by a long chalk
to win very conclusively

to win hands down
to win very convincingly

to win some rounds
to be partly successful

to win the prize in a canter
to win very easily

to wrap up a deal
to bring a deal to a successful conclusion

when one's ship comes in
when one's business venture is successfully completed or when luck arrives

SURPRISE

a bombshell
an unpleasant surprise

a thunderbolt
a surprise

he would turn in his grave
he would have been very surprised or displeased if he had known while still alive

not to bat an eyelid
to fail to express any surprise

someone's eyes popped
a person expressed great surprise

the mind boggles
this is astonishing

to be an eye opener
to be a surprise

to catch someone off guard
to surprise a person (a fencing term)

to catch someone on the hop
to take a person by surprise

to raise one's eyebrows
to express one's utter astonishment

to rub one's eyes
to express astonishment

to take one's breath away
to greatly surprise or astonish

TRUTH

a skeleton in the cupboard
an unpleasant truth the knowledge of which has been deliberately suppressed

a tall story
an interesting but untrue and unbelievable table

a telltale sign
a visible indication revealing true facts despite efforts at concealment

apocryphal
fictitious but resembling truth and illustrating a point

out of the mouths of babes
(as indiscreetly revealed) the truth

to be an ostrich
to refuse to face up to an unpleasant truth (refers to the reputed habit of ostriches in danger)

to be too close to home
to be too near the truth to be welcome

to beat about the bush
to hide the unpleasant truth

to bring something into focus
to put some matter into its proper context and explain its true significance

to bury one's head in the sand
to refuse to face up to an unpleasant truth (refers to the reputed habit of ostriches in danger)

to cloak something
to disguise the true nature of something

to drag someone by the head and ears
to force a person to reveal the true facts

to flush out the facts
to ascertain, after some effort, the truth of some matter

to open someone's eyes to something
to alert another person to the truth of something

to read between the lines
to appreciate the true significance of something not put into words

to sell someone a pup
to cheat a person in a transaction, especially by misrepresentation as to the true value of something

to show one's true colors
to disclose one's real character or beliefs

to speak with forked tongues
to utter half-truths with the intention of misleading the listener

to swallow the line
to accept as truth the story being proffered

to take something as gospel
to believe that something is true

to unmask someone
to discover a person's true identity

UNEXPECTED HAPPENINGS

a can of worms
a heterogeneous collection of unexpected problems

a landslide
an electoral result involving victory or defeat by an unexpectedly large margin

a pit of disaster
great and unexpected misfortune

a shaggy-dog story
an amusing anecdote with an unexpected ending, often involving talking animals given certain human skills

a wild card
an unexpected development

an Aladdin's cave
a place full of unexpected treasure

chalk it up!
the success was unexpected

it's a small world
it is surprising to meet people one knows in unexpected places

manna from heaven
unexpected benefits (Exodus 16:15)

the answer to a maiden's prayer
an unexpected but very welcome happening

to be a bolt from the blue
to be a totally unexpected event

to be one in the eye for someone
to represent an unexpected and unwelcome defeat

to be one out of the box
to be unexpectedly superb

to be shell-shocked
to be stunned by unexpected bad news

to be stopped in one's tracks
suddenly and unexpectedly to be prevented from carrying on with a project

to be the sting in the tail
to be the unexpected unpleasant conclusion

to catapult to fame
to achieve fame unexpectedly quickly

to catch someone in the net
to unexpectedly involve a particular person in the course of activity designed to involve many others

to come out of the blue
to be totally unexpected

to crawl out of the woodwork
to turn up unexpectedly and in large numbers

to cut the ground from under someone's feet
to unexpectedly withdraw support and in the process cause embarrassment or to demolish a person's case

to drop a brick
to make a sudden shattering and unexpected announcement

to founder on the shoals of something
to come to grief because of unexpected dangers

to hit a sour note
to discover an unexpected flaw in an otherwise satisfactory piece of work

to keep one's head
to remain calm in a crisis or to unexpectedly retain an elected or appointed position

to open up a Pandora's box
to do something which produces all sorts of undesired and unexpected side-effects (refers to the woman in Greek mythology who brought misery to mankind; the box contained human ills)

to pull a rabbit out of the hat
to produce an unexpected and seemingly miraculous but highly desirable solution

to pull the rug out from under someone
to unexpectedly withdraw support and in the process cause embarrassment

to take a nosedive
to suddenly and unexpectedly fall steeply

to throw a cat among the pigeons
to cause consternation by revealing an unpleasant and unexpected fact

to throw a spanner into the works
to cause an unexpected complication

to turn up trumps
to finish up better than expected or to experience unexpected good luck

to turn white
to express shock at unexpected news

to vanish into thin air
unexpectedly to disappear

windfall
unexpected good fortune

UNREALISTIC IDEAS

a South Sea bubble
an unrealistic financial venture which is bound to result in total loss

moonshine
unrealistic ideas

someone's eyes are bigger than his stomach
a person is unrealistic

to be in cloud cuckoo land
to be mad or to have unrealistic expectations

to bite off more than one can chew
to be overly ambitious and thus unrealistic as to one's capabilities

to chase rainbows
to be quite unrealistic

to have one's head in the clouds
to be unrealistic

to shoot for the stars
to be unrealistic

to talk turkey
to talk realistically

to want to jump all one's fences at once
to be unrealistic

UNWELCOME

a bible basher
a person who makes unwelcome attempts to force his religious beliefs on others

a blessing in disguise
an unwelcome but salutary experience

stiff cheese!
circumstances which may be unwelcome but which will not be altered and in respect of which no great sympathy is felt

the affair blew up
certain unwelcome facts have become publicly available

to be one in the eye for someone
to represent an unexpected and unwelcome defeat

to be too close to home
to be too near the truth to be welcome

to penetrate someone's thick skull
to make a person understand something difficult or acknowledge something unwelcome

to play gooseberry
to act as an unwelcome chaperon

to plead the Fifth Amendment
to refuse to answer an unwelcome question (refers to the Fifth Amendment of the United States Constitution, which provides protection against self-incrimination)

to put someone back in his box
to make it clear to a person that his views are not welcome

to rear its ugly head
to make an unwelcome appearance

to send someone away with a flea in his ear
to give a person frank but unwelcome facts (refers to fleas trapped in the armor of ancient knights)

WAITING

hold your horses!
just wait a little!

to be on tenterhooks
to anxiously await some result

to bite one's fingernails
to anxiously await a decision

to cool one's heels
to be kept waiting

to cross a bridge only when one comes to it
to await the crystallization of a situation before sorting it out

to have one's beady eyes on something
to await the chance to acquire something to which one is not properly entitled

to kick one's heels
to be kept waiting

to mark time
to do nothing while awaiting developments

to see which way the cat jumps
to await developments

to sweat it out
to await one's fate calmly

to wait for the other shoe to drop
to await the seemingly imminent and inevitable (refers to a man undressing, disturbing a neighbor by dropping one shoe, then frustrating his expectation by putting the other shoe down gently)

to wait in the wings
to be prepared to stay unobtrusive till the appropriate time for action arrives

to wait two shakes of a lamb's tail
to wait just a few moments

to wait with bated breath
to be excited in anticipation of some event

WEALTH

a banana republic
a country with a poor economy

a goldmine
a source of much wealth or of many facts

a pot of gold
wealth

life raft
financial assistance sufficient to avert insolvency

not to be made of money
not to be wealthy

not to have a brass razoo
to be very poor

not to have the wherewithal to rub two sticks together
to be very poor

rags to riches
the transition from poverty to wealth

to be a gay dog
to lead an idle life while flaunting the symbols of wealth

to be born with a silver spoon in one's mouth
to be brought up by wealthy parents

to have money flowing out of one's ears
to be very rich

to just hold one's head above water
to cope with problems but with little margin to spare or to stay solvent

to live from hand to mouth
being in poor financial circumstances, to survive with little by way of safety margin

to stay afloat
to remain solvent

well-heeled
rich

WELCOME

any port in a storm
anything which helps to avoid difficulties is welcome

the answer to a maiden's prayer
an unexpected but very welcome happening

the more the merrier
everyone is welcome

the red-carpet treatment
courtesies extended to a person to make him feel important and welcome

to be a sight for sore eyes
to be something welcome

to be better than a poke in the eye with a burnt stick
to be particularly welcome

to come in out of the cold
to be welcomed into a group

to kill the fatted calf
to demonstrate welcome and forgiveness on a person's return (Luke 15:23)

to pipe someone on board
to welcome a person

WORK AND EFFORT

a dry hole
an exercise which after much effort proves fruitless

a fifth columnist
a person using his position of trust to work for a rival cause

a scattergun approach
an effort going here, there and everywhere, instead of being properly targeted

a willing horse
a cheerful worker

an unholy alliance
a working relationship for a nefarious purpose between unlikely partners

blood, sweat and tears
hard work and much effort

donkey work
necessary but uninspiring routine work

elbow grease
hard manual work

flat out like a lizard
to be hard at work (a play on words, not a simile)

good chemistry
a good ability to work closely together

harvest
end result of labor

it is neck or nothing
a desperate effort is called for

it will all come out in the wash
the facts will emerge as work proceeds

more power to your elbow
may your praiseworthy efforts lead to success

Parkinson's law
the principle that work expands to match the work capacity available (title of a book by Prof. C. Northcote Parkinson)

put your back into it!
work energetically!

search for the Holy Grail
work toward a difficult goal (refers to a vessel supposedly used by Christ at the last supper and featuring in the Arthurian legends)

the royal road to success
the way of attaining success without effort

to be a busy bee
to work with great diligence

to be at the coal face
to be in the place where the real work is done

to be geared up to do something
to have equipment, labor and know-how in place adequate for some task

to be the salt of the earth
to be a person whose ordinary efforts benefit the community (Matthew 5:13)

to beaver away
to work diligently at some task

to break the back of a task
to complete the bulk of the work

to burn the candle at both ends
to work excessively long hours

to burn the midnight oil
to work late into the night

to caste one's bread upon the waters
not to expect gratitude or recognition for one's good works (Ecclesiastes 11:1)

to compete on all fours with someone
to strive on equal terms

to do the leg work
to carry out the tedious part of a project

to draw the nets closer
to intensify one's efforts

to fight tooth and nail
to strive very hard to win

to gain the upper hand
to attain, after some effort, an advantage over another person

to go along for the ride
to seek to benefit from a project in which others contribute the effort

to go the extra mile
to work beyond the call of duty

to have too much on one's plate
to be unable to cope with one's workload

to hit a sour note
to discover an unexpected flaw in an otherwise satisfactory piece of work

to keep one's head down
to work very diligently

to keep one's nose to the grindstone
to work with particular diligence

to keep out of someone's hair
to let another person get on with his work in his own way

to play the last card in the pack
to lower one's standards in a final desperate effort

to pull one's fingers out
to get on with a job with alacrity

to pull one's weight
to do one's proper share of the work requiring to be done

to pull oneself up by one's bootstraps
to make a praiseworthy effort to better oneself unaided

to pull oneself up by one's own shoelaces
to make a superhuman effort

to pull out all stops
to make maximum effort

to pull together
to work in harmony

to put one's back into something
to work hard at achieving some goal

to put one's best foot forward
to make a special effort

to put one's shoulder to the wheel
to make a strong effort

to ride on the back of someone
without effort to benefit from the prior efforts of others

to roll up one's sleeves
to get on with a job energetically

to snow someone under
to overload a person with work

to spark on all cylinders
to work extremely well

to steal someone's thunder
to take credit for another person's good work (refers to a dispute over the copying of a machine invented by a 17th-century dramatist to reproduce the sound of thunder during a play)

to stir a finger
to make some minimum effort

to strike a blow
to resume work

to strike a blow for some principle
to work toward the attainment of some principle

to strike at the roots of something
to work toward the destruction of something

to strike gold
to have one's efforts suddenly rewarded by great success

to swing the lead
to cheat an employer by not working while being paid to do so

to take the rough with the smooth
to accept the hardships of life along with its pleasant features

to win one's spurs
to gain recognition after a period of effort (refers to the earning of a knighthood in battle)

to work hand in glove with someone
to work in close cooperation with a person or to be in collusion with a person to the detriment of others

to work one's fingers to the bone
to work very hard

to work overtime at something
to spend a lot of time and effort at doing something

to work shoulder to shoulder
to work with united effort

WORRY

a headache
a cause for worry

a new lease on life
the prospect of a worry-free existence from now on

not to lose any sleep over something
not to worry about some matter

to drive someone out of his mind
to cause great worry to a person

to prey on one's mind
(of a problem) to keep worrying one

to raise the specter of something
to draw attention to a worrying expectation of something

to send a chill down someone's neck
to be worrying news

to spend a sleepless night
to worry about something

Appendix 1

KEYWORDS OCCURRING MOST FREQUENTLY

Word	*Frequency*
head	83
hand	81
eye	62
back	51
heart	47
foot	45
keep	45
turn	42
play	40
water	36
face	33
dog	32
all	32
throw	31
run	31
fall	30
ear	29
fire	28
blood	27
horse	26
mind	26
cut	26
stick	26
pull	25
light	25
nose	25
finger	24
come	24

Word	*Frequency*
line	23
open	23
game	23
set	22
tooth	22
jump	22
hold	22
mouth	22
fly	21
hang	21
blow	20
ground	20
see	20
way	20

Appendix 2

STATISTICAL SUMMARY OF THE CATEGORIES

PART II: THEMATIC SECTION

	Items	*%*	*CATEGORY*
1	964	23	HUMAN BODY
2	381	9	ANIMALS
3	186	4	SPORT
4	173	4	FOOD AND DRINK
5	163	4	WAR AND MILITARY
6	160	4	BUILDINGS
7	155	4	GEOGRAPHY
8	127	3	CLOTHES
9	112	3	NAUTICAL
10	109	3	RELIGION AND BIBLICAL
11	99	2	TRANSPORT
12	94	2	PLANTS
13	86	2	METEOROLOGY
14	79	2	SCIENCE AND MEDICINE
15	72	2	COLORS
16	66	2	COMMERCE
17	63	1	MANUFACTURE
18	56	1	MUSIC
19	54	1	FARMING
20	46	1	THEATER
21	45	1	FURNITURE
22	45	1	DEATH
23	41	1	CARDS
24	40	1	MINING AND OIL
25	34	1	GAMBLING
26	30	1	HISTORY

	Items	%	*CATEGORY*
27	30	1	MYTHOLOGY
28	24	1	CIRCUSES
29	22	1	GOVERNMENT
30	17	0*	AVIATION
31	15	0*	ART
32	15	0*	LAW
33	12	0*	EDUCATION
34	11	0*	CRIME
35	9	0*	CHESS
36	8	0*	SEX
37	4	0*	HERALDRY
	3647	87	**CLASSIFIED**
	568	13	**UNCLASSIFIED**
	4215	100	**TOTAL**

*Less than 1%.

PART III: THESAURUS

	Subject Area	*Items*
1	END	110
2	DIFFICULTY	86
3	ACTIVITY	85
4	SUCCESS	72
5	FAILURE	68
6	WORK AND EFFORT	66
7	RESULT	65
8	ACHIEVEMENT	63
9	SMALLNESS	58
10	ENTHUSIASM	52
11	KNOWLEDGE	51
12	SITUATION	49
13	ARGUMENT	47
14	SPEECH	45
15	ADVANTAGE	42
16	START	39
17	CHANGE	38
18	BIGNESS	38
19	OPPORTUNITY	37
20	MONEY	37
21	IDEA	37
22	UNEXPECTED HAPPENINGS	35
23	POSSIBILITY	35
24	FACT	35

	Subject Area	Items
25	STUPIDITY	34
26	MISTAKE	34
27	BENEFIT	34
28	PROBLEM	33
29	OPINION	33
30	EASE	32
31	INTERFERENCE	31
32	EXPECTATION	31
33	AIM	31
34	RESPONSIBILITY	30
35	REFUSAL AND REJECTION	30
36	PRICE AND VALUE	29
37	EXCESS	29
38	CRITICISM	29
39	EXPERIENCE	27
40	DISPLEASURE	27
41	BEHAVIOR	27
42	SKILL	25
43	PREVENTION	25
44	PLEASURE	25
45	INTEREST	25
46	DECISION	25
47	SPEED	24
48	RISK	24
49	INVOLVEMENT	24
50	BELIEF	24
51	SECRECY	23
52	LIKELIHOOD	22
53	TRUTH	21
54	DANGER	21
55	CORRECTNESS	21
56	HOPE	20
57	ALTERNATIVE	20
58	SAMENESS	19
59	ANGER	19
60	STANDARD	18
61	POWER	18
62	HAPPINESS AND ENJOYMENT	18
63	EXPENSE	17
64	REVERSAL	16
65	READINESS	16
66	MEMBERSHIP	16
67	DEVELOPMENT	16
68	WEALTH	15

	Subject Area	*Items*
69	SATISFACTION	15
70	REPUTATION	15
71	WAITING	14
72	FUTURE	14
73	FACTOR	13
74	EQUALITY	13
75	EMPLOYMENT	13
76	CARE	13
77	UNWELCOME	12
78	SURPRISE	12
79	SADNESS	12
80	NAIVETE	12
81	HARM	12
82	FALSITY	12
83	COURAGE	12
84	AGREEMENT	12
85	ANNOYANCE	11
86	CHANCE	10
87	UNREALISTIC IDEAS	10
88	SLOWNESS	10
89	PRIDE AND HUMILITY	10
90	PAST	10
91	LEADERSHIP	10
92	CONFUSION	10
93	WELCOME	9
94	JUDGMENT	9
95	FRIGHT	9
96	FRANKNESS	9
97	WORRY	8
98	STRATEGY	8
99	PUNISHMENT	8
100	PRACTICABILITY	8
101	INFERENCE	8
102	EXPERTISE	8
103	PRETENSE	7
104	MISLEADING	7
105	DISAPPOINTMENT	7
106	APPROVAL	7
107	RETIREMENT	6
108	PRAISE	6
109	NONSENSE	6
110	ABUSE	6
111	REVENGE	5
112	MONITORING	5

Appendix 3

MATERIAL FOR PARTY GAMES

As mentioned in Chapter 2, the lists in this book can also be used as the raw material for various party games and similar pursuits. Twelve illustrations are set out below:

- A keyword—say, "horse" (or "ball," "head," "water," etc.)—is selected. The object of the game is to see how many different metaphors using this keyword (whether included in this book or not) each player can recall within a short time limit. (Example: "to swap horses in midstream.")
- A category—say, "music" (or "colors," "domestic pets," "numerals," etc.)—is selected. The object of the game is to see how many different metaphors using words from this category (whether included in this book or not) each player can recall within a short time limit. (Examples: "to face the music" or "when the music stops," music expressions used figuratively to convey non-music meanings.)
- A subject area—say, "defeat" (or "price," "knowledge," "responsibility," etc.)—is selected. The object of the game is to see how many different metaphors using this particular subject area (whether included in this book or not) each player can recall within a short time limit. (Examples: "checkmate" or "to be on the ropes," expressions which, while not being used literally, convey the meaning "defeat.")
- The initial words (for example. "To beard . . .") of some well-known metaphors are quoted. The object of the game is to provide the concluding words (" . . . the lion in his den").
- A general topic is selected. The object of the game is to evolve the best paragraph using a certain minimum number of metaphors (say, ten). This would need to have regard to factors such as humor, originality and plausibility. (For an example of such a piece, see the passage in the box at the front of this book.) If desired, the players of this game could be given access to the book while drafting their paragraphs.

- One or two pages of the current issue of a daily newspaper are designated. The object of the game is to see how many different metaphors occurring on these pages each player can recognize. An element of luck as well as skill can be introduced by giving different pages to different players (say, the corresponding pages of successive issues).
- A number of specific metaphors are selected. The object of the game is to best translate them into bureaucratic language. (Example: "To flog a dead horse" could become "To impose flagellation measures on an equine quadruped which is permanently devoid of its original capacities.")
- The above game can also be played in reverse, with the players being given the bureaucratic versions and required to work out, within a short time limit, what the corresponding customary "Plain English" expressions are.
- The names of well-known persons are designated. The object of the game is to evolve appropriate "last words" for each, based on metaphors. (Example: Einstein—"To an observer on earth, my clock will appear to have stopped.")
- A series of definitions is given—say, "to strive very hard to win," "to be quite ineffective," "to be terrified," "to be a member of a group knowing what is going on," "to fight an unwinnable case," and so on. The object of the game is to match each definition with a well-known metaphor. (Examples: "to fight tooth and nail," "to labor mightily and produce a mouse," "to have one's heart in one's boots," "to be in the swim," "to bang one's head up against a brick wall," and so on, respectively.)
- The above game is rather difficult. An easier version involves producing two lists of, say, 20 items each, both in random order—one of metaphors and the other of definitions. The object of the game is to match up the items in the two lists as quickly as possible.
- One or two pages of the current issue of a daily newspaper are designated. The object of the game is to produce within a specified time limit fresh headlines for as many articles on these pages as possible, using for this purpose the metaphors which best fit in with the articles concerned. Judging would need to take into account the suitability and effectiveness of the metaphors chosen.

Appendix 4

METAPHORS DERIVED FROM THE BIBLE

ACTS *to be on the road to Damascus*
to see the error of one's ways (Acts 9:3)

BABEL *a tower of Babel*
a noisy and confused assembly (Genesis 11)

BIRD *a little bird told me*
I heard from an unnameable informant (Ecclesiastes 10:20)

BIRTHRIGHT *to sell one's birthright for a mess of pottage*
through foolishness to exchange something of substance for something of little value (Genesis 25)

BREAD *to cast one's bread upon the waters*
not to expect gratitude or recognition for one's good works (Ecclesiastes 11:1)

CAIN *the mark of Cain*
disgrace (Genesis 4:15)

CAIN *to raise Cain*
to create a disturbance (Genesis 4:5)

CALF *to kill the fatted calf*
to demonstrate welcome and forgiveness on a person's return (Luke 15:23)

CAST *to cast one's bread upon the waters*
not to expect gratitude or recognition for one's good works (Ecclesiastes 11:1)

CHEEK *to turn the other cheek*
to show that one has not been intimidated (Matthew 5:39)

CLAY *to have feet of clay*
to be vulnerable (Daniel 2:33)

CLOTHING *to be a wolf in sheep's clothing*
to be a hypocrite or to be dangerous although masquerading as something harmless (Matthew 7:15)

CROWN *to wear one's crown of thorns*
to have one's own difficulties (John 19:5)

DAMASCUS *to be on the road to Damascus*
to see the error of one's ways (Acts 9:3)

DANIEL *to have feet of clay*
to be vulnerable (Daniel 2:33)

DANIEL *to see the writing on the wall*
to appreciate the inevitability of some event (Daniel 5)

DOUBT *a doubting Thomas*
a person who refuses to believe claims in the absence of proof (John 20:25)

EARTH *to be the salt of the earth*
to be a person whose ordinary efforts benefit the community (Matthew 5:13)

ECCLESIASTES *a fly in the ointment*
a flaw (refers to dead flies turning perfumes rancid) (Ecclesiastes 10:1)

ECCLESIASTES *a little bird told me*
I heard from an unnameable informant (Ecclesiastes 10:20)

ECCLESIASTES *to cast one's bread upon the waters*
not to expect gratitude or recognition for one's good works (Ecclesiastes 11:1)

ELEVEN *at the eleventh hour*
at the last moment (actually ''at the twenty-fourth hour'' would be more logical) (Matthew 20:9)

EXODUS *a tooth for a tooth*
retaliation (Exodus 21:24)

EXODUS *an eye for an eye*
retaliation (Exodus 21:24)

EXODUS *fleshpots*
sumptuous living (Exodus 16:3)

EXODUS *manna from heaven*
unexpected benefits (Exodus 16:15)

EXODUS *with a high hand*
arrogantly (Exodus 14:8)

EYE *a mote in someone's eye*
a fault in another person which is trifling in comparison to an unrecognized major fault in oneself (Matthew 7:3)

EYE *an eye for an eye*
retaliation (Exodus 21:24)

FLESHPOT *fleshpots*
sumptuous living (Exodus 16:3)

FLY *a fly in the ointment*
a flaw (refers to dead flies turning perfumes rancid) (Ecclesiastes 10:1)

FOOT *to have feet of clay*
to be vulnerable (Daniel 2:33)

FORBID *forbidden fruit*
something particularly desired just because it is not allowed (Genesis 2:17)

FRUIT *by their fruits ye shall know them*
their reputation will be based on their results (Matthew 7:20)

FRUIT *forbidden fruit*
something particularly desired just because it is not allowed (Genesis 2:17)

GENESIS *a Sodom and Gomorrah*
a place of vice (Genesis 18:20)

GENESIS *a tower of Babel*
a noisy and confused assembly (Genesis 11)

GENESIS *forbidden fruit*
something particularly desired just because it is not allowed (Genesis 2:17)

GENESIS *the mark of Cain*
disgrace (Genesis 4:15)

GENESIS *to hold out an olive branch*
to make peace overtures (Genesis 8:11)

GENESIS *to raise Cain*
to create a disturbance (Genesis 4:5)

GENESIS *to sell one's birthright for a mess of pottage*
through foolishness to exchange something of substance for something of little value (Genesis 25)

GOAT *to separate the sheep from the goats*
to distinguish between those with and without certain attributes (Matthew 25:32)

GOLIATH *a Goliath*
a giant or a person whose ability and achievements exceed that of most other people (1 Samuel 17)

GOMORRAH *a Sodom and Gomarrah*
a place of vice (Genesis 18:20)

HAND *to put one's hand to the plow*
voluntarily to undertake some task (Luke 9:62)

HAND *with a high hand*
arrogantly (Exodus 14:8)

HEAVEN *manna from heaven*
unexpected benefits (Exodus 16:15)

HIGH *with a high hand*
arrogantly (Exodus 14:8)

HOUR *at the eleventh hour*
at the last moment (actually ''at the twenty-fourth hour'' would be more logical) (Matthew 20:9)

IVORY *to be in an ivory tower*
to be immersed in theoretical considerations and ignorant of the practical realities (Song of Solomon 7:4)

JAMES *something would try the patience of Job*
something is very vexatious (James 5:11)

JERICHO *walls of Jericho*
something seemingly solid but actually destructible (Joshua 6:20)

JEREMIAH *Jeremiah*
a person who looks on the gloomy side of everything (refers to the prophet Jeremiah in the Old Testament)

JOB *something would try the patience of Job*
something is very vexatious (James 5:11)

JOHN *a doubting Thomas*
a person who refuses to believe claims in the absence of proof (John 20:25)

JOHN *to wear one's crown of thorns*
to have one's own difficulties (John 19:5)

JOSHUA *walls of Jericho*
something seemingly solid but actually destructible (Joshua 6:20)

JUDAS *to play Judas*
to betray a person (Matthew 26)

JUDGES *a shibboleth*
a doctrine once held as essential but now abandoned as having outlived its usefulness (a word used as a test to determine to which tribe an Israelite belonged) (Judges 12:6)

KILL *to kill the fatted calf*
to demonstrate welcome and forgiveness on a person's return (Luke 15:23)

KINGS *to need the wisdom of Solomon*
to be faced with the need to make a difficult decision (1 Kings 3:16-28)

KNOW *by their fruits ye shall know them*
their reputation will be based on their results (Matthew 7:20)

LITTLE *a little bird told me*
I heard from an unnameable informant (Ecclesiastes 10:20)

LUKE *a good Samaritan*
a person going out of his way to do a kindness to others (Luke 10:33)

LUKE *to kill the fatted calf*
to demonstrate welcome and forgiveness on a person's return (Luke 15:23)

LUKE *to put one's hand to the plow*
voluntarily to undertake some task (Luke 9:62)

MANNA *manna from heaven*
unexpected benefits (Exodus 16:15)

MARK *the mark of Cain*
disgrace (Genesis 4:15)

MATTHEW *a mote in someone's eye*
a fault in another person which is trifling in comparison to an unrecognized major fault in oneself (Matthew 7:3)

MATTHEW *at the eleventh hour*
at the last moment (actually "at the twenty-fourth hour" would be more logical) (Matthew 20:9)

MATTHEW *by their fruits ye shall know them*
their reputation will be based on their results (Matthew 7:20)

MATTHEW *to be a wolf in sheep's clothing*
to be a hypocrite or to be dangerous although masquerading as something harmless (Matthew 7:15)

MATTHEW *to be the salt of the earth*
to be a person whose ordinary efforts benefit the community (Matthew 5:13)

MATTHEW *to play Judas*
to betray a person (Matthew 26)

MATTHEW *to separate the sheep from the goats*
to distinguish between those with and without certain attributes (Matthew 25:32)

MATTHEW *to turn the other cheek*
to show that one has not been intimidated (Matthew 5:39)

MESS *to sell one's birthright for a mess of pottage*
through foolishness to exchange something of substance for something of little value (Genesis 25)

MOTE *a mote in someone's eye*
a fault in another person which is trifling in comparison to an unrecognized major fault in oneself (Matthew 7:3)

OINTMENT *a fly in the ointment*
a flaw (refers to dead flies turning perfumes rancid) (Ecclesiastes 10:1)

OLIVE *to hold out an olive branch*
to make peace overtures (Genesis 8:11)

PATIENCE *something would try the patience of Job*
something is very vexatious (James 5:11)

PLOW *to put one's hand to the plow*
voluntarily to undertake some task (Luke 9:62)

POT *fleshpots*
sumptuous living (Exodus 16:3)

POTTAGE *to sell one's birthright for a mess of pottage*
through foolishness to exchange something of substance for something of little value (Genesis 25)

RAISE *to raise Cain*
to create a disturbance (Genesis 4:5)

ROAD *to be on the road to Damascus*
to see the error of one's ways (Acts 9:3)

SALT *to be the salt of the earth*
to be a person whose ordinary efforts benefit the community (Matthew 5:13)

SAMARITAN *a good Samaritan*
a person going out of his way to do a kindness to others (Luke 10:33)

SAMUEL *a Goliath*
a giant or a person whose ability and achievements exceed that of most other people (1 Samuel 17)

SELL *to sell one's birthright for a mess of pottage*
through foolishness to exchange something of substance for something of little value (Genesis 25)

SEPARATE *to separate the sheep from the goats*
to distinguish between those with and without certain attributes (Matthew 25:32)

SHEEP *to be a wolf in sheep's clothing*
to be a hypocrite or to be dangerous although masquerading as something harmless (Matthew 7:15)

SHEEP *to separate the sheep from the goats*
to distinguish between those with and without certain attributes (Matthew 25:32)

SHIBBOLETH *a shibboleth*
a doctrine once held as essential but now abandoned as having outlived its usefulness (a word used as a test to determine to which tribe an Israelite belonged) (Judges 12:6)

SODOM *a Sodom and Gomorrah*
a place of vice (Genesis 18:20)

SOLOMON *to need the wisdom of Solomon*
to be faced with the need to make a difficult decision (Kings 3:16-28)

SONG *to be in an ivory tower*
to be immersed in theoretical considerations and ignorant of the practical realities (Song of Solomon 7:4)

THOMAS *a doubting Thomas*
a person who refuses to believe claims in the absence of proof (John 20:25)

THORN *to wear one's crown of thorns*
to have one's own difficulties (John 19:5)

TOOTH *a tooth for a tooth*
retaliation (Exodus 21:24)

TOWER *to be in an ivory tower*
to be immersed in theoretical considerations and ignorant of the practical realities (Song of Solomon 7:4)

TRY *something would try the patience of Job*
something is very vexatious (James 5:11)

TURN *to turn the other cheek*
to show that one has not been intimidated (Matthew 5:39)

WALL *to see the writing on the wall*
to appreciate the inevitability of some event (Daniel 5)

WALL *walls of Jericho*
something seemingly solid but actually destructible (Joshua 6:20)

WATER *to cast one's bread upon the waters*
not to expect gratitude or recognition for one's good works (Ecclesiastes 11:1)

WEAR *to wear one's crown of thorns*
to have one's own difficulties (John 19:5)

WISDOM *to need the wisdom of Solomon*
to be faced with the need to make a difficult decision (1 Kings 3:16-28)

WOLF *to be a wolf in sheep's clothing*
to be a hypocrite or to be dangerous although masquerading as something harmless (Matthew 7:15)

WRITE *to see the writing on the wall*
to appreciate the inevitability of some event (Daniel 5)

Appendix 5

"YES, PRIME MINISTER"

The following extract from the ''Conflict of Interest'' episode of ''Yes, Prime Minister,'' the popular BBC television series which uses scripts written by Jonathan Lynn and Antony Jay, is reproduced with the permission of BBC Enterprises Limited.

It features a discussion between Sir Desmond Glazebrook, a leading banker who is keen to become Governor of the Bank of England, and James Hacker, the British Prime Minister.

Glazebrook:

City's a funny place, Prime Minister. You know, if you spill the beans you open up a whole can of worms. I mean, how can you let sleeping dogs lie if you let the cat out of the bag? You bring in a new broom and if you're not very careful you find you've thrown the baby out with the bathwater. Change horses in the middle of the stream, next thing you know you're up the creek without a paddle.

Hacker:

And then what happens?

Glazebrook:

Well! Obviously the balloon goes up. They hit you for six. An own goal, in fact.